Objective General English

CDS, NDA, SSC Banking, HM, MCA, B Ed Entrances & Other Exams

Revised Edition

Objective General English

CDS, NDA, SSC Banking, HM, MCA, B Ed Entrances & Other Exams

SP Bakshi

ARIHANT PUBLICATIONS (INDIA) LIMITED

ARIHANT PUBLICATIONS (INDIA) LIMITED

卐 **Administrative & Production Offices**

Regd. Office

'Ramchhaya' 4577/15, Agarwal Road, Darya Ganj, New Delhi -110002
Tele: 011- 47630600, 43518550

卐 **Head Office**

Kalindi, TP Nagar, Meerut (UP) - 250002
Tel: 0121-7156203, 7156204

卐 **Sales & Support Offices**

Agra, Ahmedabad, Bengaluru, Bareilly, Chennai, Delhi, Guwahati, Hyderabad, Jaipur, Jhansi, Kolkata, Lucknow, Nagpur & Pune.

卐 **ISBN** 978-93-25791-71-8

卐 **PRICE** ₹375.00

PO No. : TXT-59-T071696-7-26

Published by Arihant Publications (India) Ltd.

For further information about the books published by Arihant, log on to www.arihantbooks.com or e-mail at info@arihantbooks.com

Follow us on   

PREFACE

We feel a sense of rare achievement in bringing out this book on English Grammar for the benefit of the aspirants planning to take various competitive exams. This book would not have seen the light of the day if the authors had not felt the vacuum of a comprehensive book on the subject. In fact, we have always felt that there is still a need for a compact and easy-to-understand volume of this kind.

The authors have no hesitation in asserting, though with all humility, that the subject-matter of the book has been approved by and tempered with practical experience. Its authenticity has been accepted by a wider circle of student community with sustained interest. In a nutshell, the book is a brain child of practical teaching skill that the authors themselves imbibed while teaching.

As such a unique approach has been adopted to provide exhaustive coverage to important topics of Writing Ability and Verbal Ability. It has been our endeavour to provide a large number of Practice and Revision Exercises. A reasonable care has been taken to ensure that all the latest patterns of questions on English language find room in the book. Latest Sentences, Words and Expressions put up in the recent different exams have been duly incorporated to keep the students abreast of the present trends of the questions a student is expected to answer.

The authors do not claim any originality about the subject-matter but the innovative, systematic and lucid style adopted in the presentation of the theme is exclusively original.

The authors would fervently like to express their profound gratitude to Sh YC Jain of M/s Arihant Publications for his unstinted co-operation and enthusiasm in making the publication of the book possible. We would be failing in our duty if we fail to appreciate the motivation provided by young Sh. Deepesh Jain in bringing out this book in this form. We wish him success in life.

The valuable suggestions from student brothers are welcome. They would be incorporated in the ensuing editions of this book and also in other books that are on the anvil.

Minerva Institute
Jan 1,2000

Authors

CONTENT

PART A

Unit I **(Foundation Module)**

The Function of Tenses

A tense may be defined as that form of a verb which indicates the time and the **state of an action or event**. In this manner, a verb may refer to

(A) Time of an Action (Tense)

For example

(i) He goes to school. *(Present time of an action)*

(ii) He went to school. *(Past time of an action)*

(iii) He will go to school. *(Future time of an action)*

From the above sentences, it will be clear to the students that there are three main tenses.

1. The Present tense 2. The Past tense 3. The Future tense

(B) State of an Action (Function of Tenses)

For example

(i) I write letters regularly. *(Present tense, Habitual function)*

(ii) I am writing a letter. *(Present Continuous tense, Progressive function)*

(iii) I have just written a letter. *(Present Perfect tense, Preceding function)*

(iv) I have been writing a letter for some time. *(Present Perfect Continuous tense, Time expression)*

(C) Time Frame of a Tense

We have three time frames and in order to get a complete structure of tenses, we should briefly know each one of them. These are as follows

(i) **Point of time** is that time which denotes a specific/proper time. *e.g.*, in 1947, on Monday, etc.

(ii) **Period of time** is that time which denotes a specific duration of time. *e.g.*, from 1930 to 1950, from Monday to Saturday, etc.

(iii) **Expression of time** denotes the combination of both a point and a period of time. *e.g.*, winter 1947, summer 1950, etc.

The Tenses and their Functions

The Present Indefinite Tense

—Habitual Action

(A) This tense is generally used to denote **'habit, custom, practice, repeated action, permanent activity, general truth'**, etc.

These ideas are expressed by the adverbs of frequency such as **'often, seldom, usually, never, occassionally, sometimes, normally, generally, always, frequently, rarely, daily'**, etc.

For example

(i) The old lady goes for a walk in the morning daily.
(ii) Pearl usually believes everybody.
(iii) Arnav often gets late for lunch.
(iv) Suhani always comes in time.
(v) Shaurya seldom gets up late.

(B) This tense is also used to make a statement in the present **showing permanent nature and activity of the subject and eternal** principles.

For example

(i) I know him well.
(ii) He teaches in St. Xavier College.
(iii) The cow gives milk.
(iv) Rivers freeze at high altitude.
(v) Water boils at 100°C.
(vi) Plants prepare their own food.

Additional Uses of Present Indefinite Tense

Historical Present

(i) Now, Netaji enters and addresses the Indian soldiers.
(ii) Now, Arjun shoots arrows at Bhishma.

Future Arrangement

(i) The Prime Minister arrives from New York tomorrow.
(ii) He leaves for his job next week.

Work Book Exercise A

Directions *Complete the sentences using **Present Indefinite** tense with suitable forms of verbs given in the brackets.*

1. Buses .... on this road every hour. *(run)*
2. Apples .... ripe in autumn. *(get)*
3. Meena .... on the stage. *(dance)*
4. The last bus normally .... at midnight. *(leave)*
5. He .... dinner at 8 p.m. *(not have)*

The Present Continuous Tense — *Progressive Action*

(A) This tense is normally used **for an action in progress**, that is temporary in nature (not for a permanent activity), in the present at the time of speaking.

For example

(i) She is not working. She is swimming in the river.

(ii) It is raining outside.

(B) It also expresses **future action or a definite arrangement in the near future.**

For example

(i) I am going to the cinema tomorrow.

(ii) She is coming next week.

Additional Uses of Present Continuous Tense

(C) Continuous tense with 'always' may express an idea which is not to the liking of the speaker.

For example

(i) She is always teaching her children.

(ii) He is always praising his friends.

(D) There are some of the verbs which sometime don't admit of progressive action. Such verbs are called Non-progressive verbs (Stative verbs).

These include

(i) **Verbs of Perception** : See, taste, smell, hear, prefer, please.

(ii) **Verbs of Thinking Process** : Think, know, mean, mind.

(iii) **Verbs Showing Possession** : Own, have, belong, comprise, possess, contain.

(iv) **Verbs Expressing Feelings or State of Mind** : Believe, like, love, want, wish, desire, hate.

(v) **Verbs in General** : Look, seem, appear, affect, resemble, cost, require, stand, face, become.

(a) ***Study these sentences carefully.***

	Incorrect	Correct
1.	He is owning a car.	He owns a car.
2.	We are hearing the bell.	We hear the bell.
3.	This house is belonging to me.	This house belongs to me.
4.	I am not hating him.	I don't hate him.
5.	Are you forgetting my name?	Have you forgetten my name?
6.	I am not meaning this.	I don't mean this.
7.	I am having no house to live in.	I have no house to live in.
8.	She stands in the shade of a tree.	She is standing in the shade of a tree.
9.	The temple is standing in the heart of the city.	The temple stands in the heart of the city.
10.	The book is containing good subject-matter.	The book contains good subject-matter.

(b) ***Mark the difference in the use of stative verb and progressive verbs.***

1. The rose smells sweet.	Stative verb
2. She is smelling a black rose.	Progressive verb
3. He lives in Chennai.	Stative verb
4. She is living in India at present.	Stative verb
5. She has a large house to live in.	Stative verb
6. She is having lunch now.	Progressive verb
7. It looks it may rain soon.	Stative verb
8. She is looking at the sky.	Stative verb
9. I am seeing him next morning.	Progressive verb
10. The nurse is feeling her forehead.	Progressive verb
11. I think she is a miser.	Stative verb
12. I am thinking of leaving Chandigarh.	Progressive verb
13. I love my sister.	Stative verb
14. She is loving her daughter.	Progressive verb

(E) '**While, still, at the moment, presently** (at present) and **now**' may help students to express progressive present.

Work Book Exercise B

Directions *Complete the sentences using* ***Present Continuous*** *tense/form with suitable verbs given in the brackets.*

1. She ...., she .... chess with her friends. *(not work, play)*

2. She .... for America next year. *(leave)*

3. What are you .... at present? I .... a poem. *(read, read)*

4. We .... lunch at 2.00 tomorrow as Ram .... a noon train. *(have, catch)*

5. Meena usually does the cooking but I .... it today as she isn't here. *(do)*

The Present Perfect Tense (Imperfect Past) —*Preceding Action*

(A) This tense is a mixture of present and past. At the time of speaking, the action is already complete in the past. It always implies a strong connection with the present, though action took place in the past. Generally, adverbs and conjunctions are used to express the **preceding action.** *For example*

'**Ever, just, recently, already, yet, till** (time), **so far, of late, lately, before,** (by) **by the time, after**', etc. *For example*

(i) She has lived here all her life. (ii) We have seen this movie already.

(iii) We haven't seen Reeta lately.

NOTE (i) 'Just' is used in the sense of 'already'. Other meanings of 'just' are 'now' and 'exactly'. *For example*

- I have **just** seen that film.
- I have **already** had my breakfast.

(ii) '**Ever**' means 'any time in the past' and 'always'.

(iii) '**So far, yet, till**' means 'upto now', upto this. *(negative implication)*

(iv) Of late, lately *(recently, used only in Present Perfect Tense)*

(B) Present Perfect + Point of time = Simple Past
It should be noted that point of time in the past indicates that action took place at a point in the past. The point of time in the past is expressed by '**Since, ever since, last, yesterday, the other day, ago, before, back**', '**formerly**' (any time in the past), etc. *For example*

(i) She has returned two days ago. *(omit 'has')*
(ii) She returned two days ago. *(Correct)*

(C) Present Indefinite + Time expression = Present Perfect
This tense can also be used with '**since, for, how long, whole, all, throughout, all along**', etc to express time expression.

For example

(i) He has known me for two years.
(ii) She has owned this parlour since 2002.

Work Book Exercise C

Directions *Complete the sentences using* ***Present Perfect*** *tense/forms using suitable verbs given in the brackets.*

1. In the movie, we just .... the most extraordinary scene. *(see)*
2. This is the best book I ever .... *(read)*
3. How long you .... him? *(know)*
4. There are no taxies available because the drivers .... on strike lately. *(go)*
5. Vinay .... the punctured tyre of his car yet. *(mend)*

Work Book Exercise D

Directions *Complete the sentences by using the* ***Present Perfect*** *or the* ***Simple Past Tense*** *as the case may be.* ***Remember that***

(a) Present Perfect = Preceding action, (Action in the past used in present)
(b) Present Perfect + Point of time = Simple Past
(c) Present Indefinite + Time Expression = Present Perfect

1. Have you taken lunch?
   (a) Yes, I .... *(b)* Yes, I .... it at 1 p.m.
2. Have you prepared your lesson?
   (a) Yes, I .... *(b)* Yes, I .... in the morning.
3. Have you seen such a nice movie?
   (a) No, I .... it. *(b)* Yes, I ....
   (c) Yes, I .... one last year.
4. Have you opened a bank account?
   Yes, I .... only yesterday.
5. How long have you known this man?
   (a) I .... him since I arrived here. *(b)* I .... him when I was at school.

The Past Indefinite Tense

—Habitual Action

(A) This tense is used for a past habit, indicated generally by **'Often, seldom, usually, normally, generally, occasionally, sometimes, never, always, frequently, rarely, daily, used to, would'**, etc. *For example*

(i) They never drank wine. *(ii)* He always carried an umbrella.
(iii) I used to go to Delhi by train. *(iv)* She would go there daily.

(B) This tense is also used for a single act completed in the past. Definite point of time is denoted by **'Since, ever since, earlier, ago, back, before, last, yesterday, the other day'**, (any point of time in the past), etc. *For example*

(i) I met your brother yesterday.
(ii) She bought a car two years ago.

It is wrong to say. *For example*

(i) I have met your brother yesterday. *(remove 'have')*
(ii) She has bought a car two years ago. *(remove 'has')*

NOTE Present Perfect + Point of time = Simple Past

'Point of time' denotes the time when the action takes place. (Present, Past, Future Tense). *For example*

(i) I come here every Sunday.
(ii) I went to Delhi yesterday.
(iii) I shall go there tomorrow.

Work Book Exercise E

Directions *Complete the sentences using **Past Indefinite** tense/forms using suitable verbs given in the brackets.*

1. We .... a terrifying news last night. *(hear)*
2. They .... their success two days ago. *(celebrate)*
3. The police .... the dacoits at 9.00 p.m. *(catch)*
4. Seema .... her lost book since last night. *(not find)*
5. The train .... by 8.00 at the station yesterday. *(not arrive)*

The Past Continuous Tense

—Progressive Action

(A) This tense is chiefly used for past action in progress. *For example*

(i) It was still raining when I reached there. *(Past action in progress)*
(ii) He was busy packing last evening. *(Past action in progress)*

(B) It is also used for a definite arrangement for future in the past. *For example*

(i) He was leaving that night. *(Definite arrangement for future in the past)*
(ii) I asked her what she was doing next Sunday.
(Definite arrangement for future in the past)

(C) As mentioned in the case of the Present Continuous tense, certain verbs don't admit of progressive action. **Refer to such verbs under Present Continuous tense section.**

(D) 'While, still, at that moment, then' may help the students to express progressive action in the past.

Work Book Exercise F

Directions *Complete the sentences using **Past Continuous** tense/forms using suitable verbs given in the brackets.*

1. My cousin wears sandals but when I last saw him he ...... boots. *(wear)*
2. On the beach many children ...... and many girls ...... in the sea. *(play, swim)*
3. Seema was alone in the house at that time because her father ...... in the garage. *(work)*
4. As she ...... the stairs, she slipped and fell. *(climb)*
5. The teacher went to see what the students ...... in the garden. *(do)*

The Past Perfect Tense —*Past Preceding*

(A) This tense is used when out of two actions it is necessary to emphasize that the preceding action was completely finished before the succeeding action started.
For example

(i) I had gone to Delhi last week before my father came. *(Correct)*
(ii) I had gone to Delhi last week.*(Incorrect, because preceding action is not implied here)*

(B) Sometimes, preceding action is implied and is indicated by the use of **'Ever, just, recently, already, yet, so far, till** (time), **by the time** (by), **before, after'**, etc. *For example*

(i) I had already taken breakfast.
(ii) I had finished the book before he came.
(iii) I had returned from college just then.
(iv) I finished the book after I had returned from college.

(C) This tense is also used as time expression with **'Since, for, how long, whole, all, throughout, all along'**, etc. *For example*

(i) She had known him for two years.
(ii) He had owned this plaza for five years.

(D) Past Perfect tense used with verbs such as **'Want, hope, expect, think, suppose, mean, intend'** indicate that the action mentioned did not take place. *For example*

(i) I had wanted to help my brother. *(but could not help)*
(ii) I had expected to pass. *(but did not pass)*
(iii) My sister had hoped that I would send her money. *(unfulfilled hope)*
(iv) Vishal had intended to set up his own business. *(but could not)*

Work Book Exercise G

Directions *Complete the sentences using* ***Past Perfect*** *tense/forms using suitable verbs given in the brackets.*

1. After the guests .... we did the washing. *(leave)*

2. She .... all the material by last evening. *(type)*

3. We .... shopping before it started raining. *(finish)*

4. The house .... to him since his birth. *(belong)*

5. She was not present because she ...... office when her boss called her. *(leave)*

The Future Indefinite Tense

—Future Action

(A) This tense expresses an action that is to take place in future. *For example* **'Soon, shortly, in a few moments, tomorrow, presently** (soon or at present), **next year/month/ week'**, etc. indicate future action. *For example*

(i) They will come here shortly.

(ii) Ritu will take examination next month.

(B) It should be noted that there are several ways to express future action in English as given below.

(a) Future action is expressed in the **Present Continuous tense**. But, it is more definite action than the action expressed in the future indefinite. *For example*

(i) They are coming tomorrow. *(certain to come)*

(ii) She is marrying soon. *(certain to marry)*

(b) Future action is also expressed in the **Present Indefinite tense**. *For example*

(i) She arrives from the U.S.A. next month. *(will arrive)*

(ii) The Prime Minister leaves for Lucknow tomorrow. *(will leave)*

NOTE Ordinarily, **'shall'** is used with first person of pronoun 'I' and 'we'. **'Will'** is used with second and third persons.

Besides, there are following uses of 'shall' and 'will'

1. You shall not move.	Order
2. They shall be rewarded.	Assurance/promise
3. I will help my brother.	Determination
4. You shall look after elders.	Duty
5. I will go to Delhi tomorrow.	Intention
6. I shall go to Delhi.	(may or may not go)
7. I shall be drowned	(may be drowned)
8. I will be drowned	(determined to be drowned)

Work Book Exercise H

Directions *Put the verbs in the brackets using either* ***the Simple Future or the Present Continuous.***

1. I .... my friend tomorrow. *(meet)*
2. You .... college next year. *(join)*
3. He .... shortly. *(come)*
4. I am sure he .... in time for the class. *(come)*
5. You .... English after another two months of hard work. *(speak)*

The Future Continuous Tense —*Future Progressive*

(A) This tense is used to express an action that will be in progress at a point of time in future.

For example

(i) She will be waiting for me when I reach her home.

(ii) What will he be doing when you visit him?

(iii) Get home at once. Your mother will be wondering where you are.

(iv) Probably, it will be raining when you reach Bhopal.

(v) Rahul will be watching movie on television now.

(B) This tense is also used to express definite future arrangement.

For example

(i) He will be going to Pune by car today.

(ii) She will be arriving tomorrow to meet her husband.

(C) As mentioned in the case of the Present Continuous tense certain verbs do not admit of progressive action. Refer to such verbs under the Present Continuous tense section.

Work Book Exercise I

Directions *Complete the sentences using* ***Future Continuous*** *tense/forms using suitable verbs given in the brackets.*

1. He .... for Mr. Kapoor next week as his own assistant is expected to be on leave. *(work)*
2. In a few years time, we all .... in multi-storeyed houses. *(live)*
3. We .... ourselves in school today as our principal's mood is very upset now-a-days. *(behave)*
4. My brother .... at the party tonight as mother is likely to be present there. *(not drink)*
5. He surely .... if you visit his room now. *(smoke)*

The Future Perfect Tense

—Future Preceding

(A) This tense is used when out of two actions it is necessary to emphasize that the preceding action will be completely finished before the succeeding action starts in future.

Sometimes, preceding action is implied and indicated by the use of '**Ever, just, already, recently, yet, so far, till** (time), **before** (by), **by the time after.**' *For example*

(i) She will have already prepared food when I reach home.

(ii) He will have rung up his wife before he arrives.

(iii) I think the news will not have been published so far.

(iv) My assistant will have typed five letters by lunch today.

(B) This tense is also used to express time expression.

'**Since, for, how long, whole, all, throughout, all long**' denote that action started sometime in the past and is continuing into the present. *For example*

(i) He will have known her for two years next month.

(ii) He will have suffered a lot by now since his birth.

Work Book Exercise J

Directions *Complete the sentences using **Future Perfect** tense/forms using suitable verbs given in the brackets.*

1. I ...... this essay by tomorrow morning. *(complete)*
2. At the rate he is studying, he ...... by next year. *(qualify)*
3. The ship ...... before we reach the harbour. *(leave)*
4. If he continues with his exercises, he ......10 kg by the end of this month. *(lose)*
5. She ...... me for five years next month. *(know)*

Perfect Continuous : Past, Present, Future

—Time Expression

(A) Perfect Continuous tense (Past, Present, Future) denotes an action continuing from the past into the present. It implies the duration of an action. (past to present) The time expression is normally indicated by

'**Since, for, how long, whole, all, throughout, all along.**'

NOTE '**For**' is used for a period of time from the past to present. '**Since**' is used for a particular point of time or some event in the past to present.

(B) Time expression can be used with both continuous and indefinite tenses as follows

(a) **Continuous tense + Time expression = Perfect Continuous**
(Past, Present, Future) *(Action is not yet complete)*

(b) **Indefinite tense + Time expression = Perfect** (Past, Present, Future)
(Action is complete)

NOTE Students should note the difference between **point of time** and **time expression**.

(i) She goes to temple every Monday. *(Point of time)*
(ii) She visited her uncle yesterday. *(Point of time)*
(iii) She has completed two letters since last night. *(Time expression)*
(iv) She has been suffering from fever for two days. *(Time expression)*
(v) She had been playing Chess the whole day yesterday. *(Time expression)*

Work Book Exercise K

Directions *Complete the sentences using **Perfect Continuous** or **Perfect** tense/forms (Past, Present, Future) using suitable verbs given in the brackets.*

Past

1. The whole day long he .... at home and .... a book yesterday. *(sit, read)*

2. His radio .... since 8 a.m. yesterday. The neighbours were getting disturbed. *(play)*

3. He .... this building for the last ten years when he sold it. *(own)*

4. Yesterday, she .... for her lost dog since morning. *(search)*

5. Last night, the dog .... for a long time. *(bark)*

Present

6. She .... me since 2004. *(know)*

7. For the last ten years he .... this factory. *(own)*

8. He .... in the same class for the last three years. *(study)*

9. Neena .... nutritious food since morning. *(not eat)*

10. It .... for two days now. *(rain)*

Future

11. How long Richa .... in this house when the new guests arrive tomorrow? *(stay)*

12. My aunt .... in England for five years when I go there. *(live)*

13. She .... for two hours when they reach there. *(sleep)*

14. She .... as the Principal of that school for five years next month. *(work)*

15. She .... me for ten years by next month. *(know)*

Revision Exercise

Directions (Q. Nos. 1-10) *Read each sentence to find out whether there is any grammatical or idiomatic error in it. The error, if any, will be in one part of the sentence. The alphabet corresponding to that part is your answer. If there is 'No error', the answer is (e). (Ignore errors of punctuation, if any).*

1. Why are (A)/Ramit not (B)/cooking (C)/food today? (D)/No error (E).
(a) A (b) B (c) C (d) D
(e) E

2. At present (A)/Kavya is not studying (B)/as she is (C)/playing in the garden (D)/No error (E).
(a) A (b) B (c) C (d) D
(e) E

3. Noni had (A)/brushes (B)/her teeth (C)/every night (D)/No error (E).
(a) A (b) B (c) C (d) D
(e) E

4. While they (A)/were having (B)/dinner lights (C)/went out (D)/No error (E).
(a) E (b) C (c) B (d) A
(e) D

5. I would (A)/completed my work (B)/in a week's (C)/time (D)/No error (E).
(a) E (b) C (c) B (d) A
(e) D

6. She did not (A)/opened the (B)/door because she (C)/was washing her hair. (D)/No error (E).
(a) B (b) A (c) D (d) C
(e) E

7. Naina found (A)/that her (B)/pocket had been (C)/picked. (D)/No error (E).
(a) B (b) A (c) E (d) C
(e) D

8. By tomorrow evening (A)/my uncle, Ravi, (B)/would reach (C)/the United States (D)/No error (E).
(a) B (b) A (c) D (d) C (e) E

9. We did not (A)/go out (B)/as it (C)/was still rain.(D)/No error (E).
(a) A (b) B (c) C (d) D (e) E

10. Sachin has (A)/scored a century (B)/a week (C)/ago. (D)/ No error (E).
(a) B (b) C (c) D (d) A (e) E

Directions (Q. Nos. 11-20) *In the following questions, a sentence is given which is divided into four parts labelled (a), (b), (c) and (d). Read each sentence to find out whether there is any error in any part and indicate your response against the corresponding letter. If you find no error, your response should be indicated as (e).*

11. When I called on her she doing her assignment.
(a) When I (b) called on her
(c) she doing (d) her assignment
(e) No error

12. My cousin has been owning this property for the last twenty years.
(a) My cousin
(b) has been owning
(c) this property
(d) for the last twenty years
(e) No error

13. I could not attend the board's meeting as I was unwell.
(a) I could not
(b) attend the board's
(c) meeting as
(d) I was unwell
(e) No error

14. India has won freedom in the year 1947.
(a) India has
(b) won freedom
(c) year 1947
(d) in the
(e) No error

15. I used to go to the park everyday when I were young.
(a) When I were young
(b) I used to
(c) go to the
(d) park everyday
(e) No error

16. The news of Sushant's death has not been declared yet.
(a) The news of
(b) Sushant's death
(c) declared yet
(d) has not been
(e) No error

17. A sum of ₹ 2.5 crore has sanctioned to the Wildlife Institute of India by the Ministry of Forest.
(a) A sum of ₹ 2.5 crore
(b) has sanctioned
(c) to the Wildlife Institute of India by
(d) the Ministry of Forest
(e) No error

18. Lauri Marker, founder-head of Cheetah Conservation in Namibia, visited India lasted February.
(a) visited India lasted February
(b) Lauri Marker, founder-head
(c) in Namibia
(d) of Cheetah Conservation
(e) No error

19. The National Bird destroyed crops at a nascent stage and cause huge losses to the farmers.
(a) The National Bird destroyed
(b) crops at a nascent stage
(c) and cause huge losses
(d) to the farmers
(e) No error

20. The Asiatic Cheetahs, which once roamed in different parts of India, are now finding in Iran.
(a) are now finding in Iran
(b) The Asiatic Cheetahs
(c) which once roamed
(d) in different parts of India
(e) No error

Exam Practice

Directions (Q. Nos. 1-3) *Each question in the exercise has a sentence with three underlined parts labelled (a), (b) and (c). Read each sentence and find out if there is any error in any underlined part and indicate your response against the corresponding letter. If there is no error, your response should be indicated as (d).*

1. She said that she was understanding (a) his point of view (b) very well. (c) No error. (d)

2. He had gone (a) home three weeks ago and was expected (b) to be back yesterday, but he has not come (c) yet. No error. (d)

3. The scientists in America (a) are trying for long (b) to discover the genes responsible for ageing. (c) No error. (d) **NDA 2016**

Directions (Q. Nos. 4-17) *Each sentence in this question is broken into four parts. Find out the error part from the given options and indicate your response from the options given on the answer sheet.*

4. A closed economy is identified as a human community which produces all it consumes and consumed all it produces. **CDS 2019**

(a) A closed economy is identified
(b) as a human community
(c) which produces all it consumes
(d) and consumed all it produces

5. You look as if you have ran all the way home. **CDS 2019**

(a) You look as if
(b) you have ran
(c) all the way home
(d) No error

6. No struggle can ever succeeded without women participating side by side with men. **CDS 2019**

(a) No struggle can ever succeeded
(b) without women participating
(c) side by side with men
(d) No error

7. The big bad wolf gobbled up the little lamb so fast that a bone was stick in his throat. **SBI Clerk 2015**

(a) The big bad wolf gobbled
(b) up the little lamb so fast
(c) that a bone was stick
(d) in his throat
(e) No error

8. Harsh Vardhan said he was looking forward to serve his roots, as he had spend the first 15 years of his life in the streets of Old Delhi. **SBI Clerk 2016**

(a) Harsh Vardhan said he was looking forward
(b) to serve his roots, as he had spend
(c) the first 15 years of his life
(d) in the streets of Old Delhi
(e) No error

9. We have finished our work three hours ago and have been waiting for you since then. **SSC CGL 2015**

(a) three hours ago and have been waiting
(b) We have finished our work
(c) for you since then
(d) No error

10. The Ministry was considered several proposals for the development of small and medium enterprises during Budget discussions. **SSC CGL 2015**

(a) The Ministry was considered several proposals
(b) for the development of small and medium enterprises
(c) during Budget discussions
(d) No error

11. I have reached the office before the rain started. **SSC CGL 2015**

(a) I have reached
(b) the office
(c) before the rain started
(d) No error

12. The government granted relief payments of ₹ 5000 each to those who injured in the fire incident. **SSC CGL 2015**

(a) The government granted
(b) relief payments of ₹ 5000 each
(c) to those who injured in the fire incident
(d) No error

13. By May next year, I have been working in this college for twenty years. **SSC CGL 2015**

(a) for twenty years
(b) By May next year
(c) I have been working in this college
(d) No error

14. I shall look forward to being with you sometime next month. **SSC CGL 2015**

(a) to being with you
(b) sometime next month
(c) I shall look forward
(d) No error

15. He has ruined his eyesight by not using his spectacles regularly. **SBI PO 2015**

(a) He has ruined his eyesight
(b) by not using
(c) his spectacles regularly
(d) No error

16. While the country spend about $ 800 million on fireworks every year, at a cost of only $ 74 million it is set to launch a rocket into space to orbit Mars and gather data about the planet. **SBI PO 2016**

(a) While the country spend about $ 800 million on fireworks
(b) every year, at a cost of only $ 74 million it
(c) is set to launch a rocket into space to
(d) orbit Mars and gather data about the planet.
(e) No error

17. Santosh succeed due to the encouragement of friends, relatives and well-wishers. **IBPS PO/MT 2015**

(a) Santosh succeed
(b) due to the encouragement
(c) of friends, relatives
(d) and well-wishers
(e) No error

Answers

Work Book Exercise A

1. run **2.** get **3.** dances **4.** leaves **5.** does not have

Work Book Exercise B

1. is not working, is playing **2.** is leaving **3.** are you reading, am reading
4. are having, is catching **5.** am doing

Work Book Exercise C

1. have just seen **2.** have ever and **3.** have you known
4. have gone **5.** has not mended

Work Book Exercise D

1. (a) have taken (b) took
2. (a) have prepared (b) prepared
3. (a) haven't seen (b) have seen (c) saw
4. opened
5. (a) have known (b) knew

Work Book Exercise E

1. heard **2.** celebrated **3.** caught
4. did not find **5.** did not arrive

Work Book Exercise F

1. was wearing **2.** were playing, were swimming
3. was working **4.** was climbing
5. were doing

Work Book Exercise G

1. had left **2.** had typed **3.** had finished
4. had belonged **5.** had left

Work Book Exercise H

1. will meet/am meeting **2.** will join/are joining
3. will come/will be coming **4.** will come/is coming
5. will speak/will be speaking

Work Book Exercise I

1. will be working/will work **2.** shall be living
3. will be behaving **4.** will not be drinking/will not drink
5. will be smoking

Work Book Exercise J

1. will have completed **2.** will have qualified
3. will have left **4.** will have lost
5. will have known

Work Book Exercise K

1. had been sitting, had been reading
2. had been playing
3. had owned
4. had been searching
5. had been barking
6. has known
7. has owned
8. has been studying
9. has not eaten
10. has been raining
11. will have they been staying
12. will have been living
13. will have been sleeping
14. will have been working
15. will have known

Revision Exercise

1. (a) Use 'is' in place of 'are'.
2. (e) E
3. (a) Remove 'had'.
4. (a) E
5. (c) Replace 'completed' by 'complete'.
6. (a) Replace 'opened' by 'open'.
7. (c) E
8. (d) Use 'will have reached' in place of 'would reach'.
9. (d) Use 'raining' in place of 'rain'.
10. (d) Remove 'has'.
11. (c) Add 'was' after 'she'.
12. (b) Use 'has owned' in place of 'has been owning'.
13. (e) No error.
14. (a) Remove 'has'
15. (a) Use 'was' in place of 'were'
16. (e) No error
17. (b) Add 'been' after 'has'
18. (e) Use 'last' in place of 'lasted'
19. (a) Use 'destroys' in place of 'destroyed'
20. (a) Use 'found' in place of 'finding'.

Exam Practice

1. *(a)* 'was understanding' would be changed to 'had understood'.
2. *(a)* 'had gone' will be changed to simple past tense 'went'.
3. *(b)* 'are trying for long' will be change to Present Perfect Continuous Tense. i.e. 'have been trying for long'.
4. *(d)* The statement describes a fact, so Simple Present Tense will be used here. Hence, we will change 'and consumed all it produces' to 'and consumes all it produces'.
5. *(b)* 'you have ran' will be change to 'you ran'.
6. *(a)* The sentence is in Present Tense. So, we will change 'succeeded' to 'succeed'.
7. *(c)* The sentence describes a past event. So, 'stick' will be change to its past form i.e. 'stuck'.
8. *(b)* As the sentence is in Past Tense, 'spend' will be changed to 'spent'.
9. *(b)* 'We have finished our work' will be changed to 'We finished our work'.
10. *(d)* As the given sentence is in Simple Past Tense, use 'The Ministry considered several proposals' instead of 'The Ministry was considered several proposals.'
11. *(a)* When both events happen in the past, the event that happens earlier should be expressed in Past Perfect Tense. So, 'I have reached' would be changed to 'I had reached'.
12. *(c)* The sentence expresses an activity in the past. So, 'were' will be added after 'who'.
13. *(c)* The sentence describes a situation that will be continuing in the future, so Future Continuous Tense will be used here.
    Hence, we will use 'I shall have been working in this college'.
14. *(c)* 'I shall look forward' will be changed to 'I look forward' or 'I am looking forward'.
15. *(d)* No error
16. *(a)* 'Spend' will be changed to 'spends' (Simple Present) as the sentence expresses a fact.
17. *(a)* The sentence describes a past event, so 'succeed' will be replaced by 'succeeded'.

Voice

A verb may tell us about what a person or a thing does. Therefore, a verb is said to be an action on the part of a doer/subject. *For example*

(i) They will **do** the work.

(ii) The teacher **has punished** the boy.

The verbs 'do, punish' are transitive. The actions of the subjects 'They, The teacher' passes over to the objects 'work, the boy'. Therefore, these verbs are called transitive.

The verb may **also tell us what** is done to a person or a thing.

Now read the following sentences

(iii) The work **will be done** by them. *(Passive Voice)*

(iv) The boy **has been punished** by the teacher. *(Passive Voice)*

How to Define a Voice?

(a) In active voice a sentence begins with a subject (They, The teacher) sentence (i) & (ii).

(b) In passive voice a sentence begins with an object (The work, The boy) sentences (iii) & (iv).

Note Sentences only with **transitive verbs** admit of passive expressions.

Now study the following sentences

(v) Jaya **came** here. *(vi)* Father is **going** out.

The verbs 'come, go' are **intransitive** because these verbs do not have objects. The effect of the action does not pass over to any object. Therefore, these verbs are called intransitive. Since they are not used with an object, they do not admit of passive expression.

Therefore, before making a sentence, a student must note carefully whether the sentence is beginning with subject or object.

How to Make a Passive Voice?

(a) The passive voice of an active voice is formed by using the verb **'to be'** and by converting, the original active verb into **Past Participle**.

(b) Object is generally placed before the verb in passive expressions.

Now study the examples.

The forms of 'Be' as used in passive voice are explained in the table below.
In conclusion, the construction of these sentences may be represented as follows

(a) (i) Subject + Transitive verb + Object *(Active)*

(ii) Subject + Intransitive verb. *(Active)*

(b) Object + To be + PP of Transitive verb + Subject *(Passive Voice)*

[Passive voice — Sentences (iii) and (iv)]

The Verb 'To be'

*The verb '**To be**' has following two uses*

1. As an **auxilliary verb** it is used with other verbs both in active and passive voice.
2. As an **ordinary/regular verb** it is used in 'No verb' sentences.

The forms of 'to be'	Tenses	The forms of verb in passive voice	No verb
be	Infinitive, Modals, Future Indefinite	PP (Past Participle) of Transitive verb	Noun Pronoun Adjective Adverb
is, am, are,	Present Indefinite,		
was, were	Past Indefinite		
been	Perfect (Present, Past, Future)		
being	Continuous (Present, Past), Participle/Gerund		

*The use of '**To be**' in the passive sentences*

Object + be + PP of Transitive Verb + by Subject

A. **Infinitive**

B. **Modals**

C. **Future Indefinite**

Active Subject + will + $(\text{verb})_1$ + Object

Passive Object + will/shall be + $(\text{verb})_3$ + Subject

(i) He will be punished for his misbehaviour.

(ii) My letter will be posted by this little boy.

(iii) These papers will not be signed by her.

D. **Present Indefinite—is, am, are**

1. **Present Indefinite Tense**

Active Subject + $(\text{Verb})_1$ /$(\text{Verb})_3$ + Object

Passive Subject + is/am /are + $(\text{Verb})_3$+ by + Object
(Objective Case) (Subjective Case)

(i) She is taught English daily by her class teacher.

(ii) I am often invited to attend party by my friends.

(iii) Elections are held every five years.

E. **Past Indefinite—was, were**

Active Subject + $(\text{Verb})_2$ + Object

Passive Subject + $\frac{\text{was}}{\text{were}}$ + $(\text{Verb})_3$ + by + Object

(Objective Case) (Subjective Case)

(i) She was punished for her negligence.

(ii) Both the friends were selected for senior hockey team.

F. **Perfect** (Present, Past, Future)—**been**

Active Subject + has/ have + $(\text{Verb})_3$ + Object

Passive Subject + has/ have + been + $(\text{Verb})_3$ + by + Object

(Objective Case) (Subjective Case)

Active Subject + had + $(\text{Verb})_3$ + Object

Passive Subject + had + been + $(\text{Verb})_3$ + by + Object

(Objective Case) (Subjective Case)

Active Subject + will/ shall + have + $(\text{Verb})_3$ + Object

Passive Subject + will/shall + have been + $(\text{Verb})_3$ + by + Object

(Objective Case) (Subjective Case)

(i) He has just been elected as a member of the Committee.

(ii) She had already been admitted to hospital.

(iii) My friend will have been married by now.

G. **Continuous** (Present, Past)—**being**

Active Subject + is/ am/ are + (Verb) + ing + Object

Passive Subject + is/ am / are+ being + $(\text{Verb})_3$ + by + Object

(Objective Case) (Subjective Case)

Active Subject + was/were + (Verb) + ing + Object

Passive Subject + was/ were + being + $(\text{Verb})_3$ + by + Object

(Objective Case) (Subjective Case)

(i) The match is being telecast now on Sony TV.

(ii) The match was being telecast yesterday on Sony TV.

H. **Participle/Gerund—being**

(i) Nobody likes being cheated.

(ii) The murderer escaped being hanged.

(iii) I saw her being taken to hospital.

NOTE **Future continuous** and **perfect continuous** tenses do not admit of passive voice expressions.

Work Book Exercise A

Directions *Use the verbs given in brackets either in active or passive voice as the case may be.*

1. The teacher .... with the students yesterday for their misbehaviour. *(annoy)*
2. The criminals should .... at the earliest. *(punish)*
3. I .... then that he .... working hard. *(convince, be)*
4. Prohibition in many states .... lately by the State Governments. *(enforce)*
5. His parents .... when he did not arrive at the function. *(disappoint)*
6. Our leaders ought to .... honestly in the interest of common people. *(behave)*
7. Children should ...... with responsibility to make them feel responsible. *(entrust)*
8. I .... to see my Aunt when I reached home. *(amaze)*
9. My father .... when he sees my brother's report card. *(please)*
10. The eldest son .... the burden of the whole family these days. *(bear)*

Some Tips for Making Passive Voice

(I) **The objects used in the following sentences are used with verbs which do not agree with the common rules of verbs. Such nouns are given in chapter on Nouns under Rule (iv) & (v).**

Study the following sentences

(i) He gave me spectacles.
Spectacles were given to me by him.

(ii) They play Billiards.
Billiards is played by them.

In these sentences the noun 'spectacles' is followed by plural verb and 'Billiards' by singular verb. Students should take note of such misleading nouns.

(II) **Carefully study the use of interrogative pronouns while changing active sentences into passive.**

'Which, what', etc. are placed as they are.

However, when 'What/Which' is used as a subject, it is changed into 'By what' or 'By which', 'Who' is changed into 'By whom' and 'Whom' is changed into 'Who'.

(i) What are you writing?
What is being written by you?

(ii) What makes you angry?
By what are you made angry?

(iii) Who teaches you English?
By whom are you taught English?

(iv) Whom are you teaching?
Who is being taught by you?

(v) Which girl helped you?
By which girl were you helped?

(III) (a) **When the subjects are indefinite/(vague pronouns or nouns)** , it is not necessary to use them in passive voice as 'by somebody'.

(i) Somebody has picked my pocket.
My pocket has been picked.

(ii) They will declare the result soon.
The result will be declared soon.

(b) **Sentences beginning with negative indefinite pronouns are converted into negative passive sentences.**

For example

(i) Nobody can change destiny.
Destiny cannot be changed.

(ii) None saw her in the parlour.
She was not seen in the parlour.

(IV) **When principal clause is followed by a Noun clause as object, the passive voice is made as follows.**

(i) People consider that he is honest.
It is considered that he is honest.

(ii) We hope that he will pass.
It is hoped that he will pass.

Study these verbs carefully 'consider, believe, understand, suspect, report, say, claim, know, expect, allege, find, learn, require, suppose (appear, seem)'.

They are followed by Noun clause as objects.

(V) **Verbs with Two Objects** Sometimes verbs are used with two objects in active voice sentences. Passive Voice of such sentences can be made with either of the objects.

(i) He gave me a book.
(a) I was given a book by him.
(b) A book was given to me by him.

(ii) They made him King.
(Complement; King is complement of the verb 'make')
He was made King.

(VI) **'By' is not used with certain verbs when making a passive voice. Instead we use at, with, in, to etc.**

(i) I know him.
He is known to me.

(ii) Her sudden arrival surprised everyone.
Everybody was surprised at her sudden arrival.

(VII) **Infinitives**

(i) She is to write a letter.
A letter is to be written by her.

(ii) They were to complete the work.
The work was to be completed by them.

(iii) My sister has to buy a new car.
A new car has to be bought by my sister.

(iv) There is nothing to lose.
There is nothing to be lost.

(v) I would like someone to help me.
I would like to be helped.

(vi) I am not to blame for the loss.
I am not to be blamed for the loss [*Passive sense (responsible for)*]

(VIII) **Participles/Gerund**

(i) I remember my mother taking me to doctor.
I remember being taken to doctor by my mother.

(ii) I found his friends laughing at him.
I found him being laughed at by his friends.

(IX) **If a preposition or an adverb is used with a verb to convey specific meaning, it should not be removed while making a passive voice.**

For example

(i) Mothers **look after** their children.
Children are looked after by their mothers.

(ii) You should not **look down upon** the poor.
The poor should not be looked down upon.

(X) **The Verbs, 'Let, bid, make, help, feel, see, watch, hear', are used with direct infinitive (without to) in active voice.**

In passive voice these verbs are used with Infinitive (to + verb)

'Let' is an exception. 'Let' is followed by direct infinitive both in active & passive voice sentences.

For example

(i) I bade him go.
He was bidden to go.

(ii) I have made her sing a song.
She has been made to sing a song.

(iii) She let me go.
I was let go by her.

(XI) **Imperative Sentences**

1. **Command and Order**

(a) When object is given, use Let + object + be + Past Participle in passive voice.

(i) Bring a book
Let a book be brought.

(ii) Turn Payal out
Let Payal be turned out.

(b) When no object is given, begin the sentence with
You are ordered/commanded to......... in passive voice.

(i) Go out at once
You are ordered to go out at once.

(ii) Don't stay here.
You are ordered not to stay here.

2. Permission, Request, Advice

(a) When only only an object is given, make passive voice as.
Object + Should + Past Participle

(i) Obey parents.
Parents should be obeyed.

(ii) Listen to me.
I should be listened to.

(iii) Prepare for war.
You should be prepared for war.
Or Be prepared for war.

NOTE Use of **let** is avoided in this type of sentences.

(b) When an no object is given, begin the sentence with
You are allowed, requested or advised.......... in passive voice.

(i) Please come soon.
You are requested to come soon.

(ii) Please don't talk loudly.
You are requested not to talk loudly.

(XII) **Sentences Beginning with Let** (Permission & Suggestion)

(a) When object is given make, passive voice as follows.

(i) Let me play here (Permission)
I may be allowed to play here.

(ii) Let us help him. (Suggestion)
He should be helped.

(b) When no object is given, begin the passive sentence, with
It is suggested.....................

(i) Let us stay here (Suggestion)
It is suggested that we should stay here.

(ii) Let us sleep here.
It is suggested that we should sleep here.

(XIII) **'To be' is often allowed in the sense of 'have' in passive voice sentences of the following verbs**

'Fall, rise, come, arrive, go, lose.'

(i) Mighty Caeser is fallen. *(has fallen)*
(ii) Summer is come. *(has come)*
(iii) The book is lost. *(has been)*
(iv) The sun is risen. *(has risen)*
(v) Golden days are gone. *(have gone)*

(XIV) **Miscellaneous Sentences**

Study these sentences carefully

1. The police arrested a millitant and sent him to jail. *(Active)*
   A millitant was arrested by police and (was) sent to jail. *(Passive)*
2. It is necessary to help the poor. *(Active)*
   The poor are required to be helped. *(Passive)*
3. It is time to wind up business. *(Active)*
   It is time for the business to be wound up. *(Passive)*
4. The fruit tastes sweet. *(Active)*
   The fruit is sweet when (it is) tasted. *(Passive)*
5. I have to stay here. *(Active)*
   I am obliged to stay here. *(Passive)*
6. It is your duty to help your children. *(Active)*
   You are supposed (bound in duty) to help your children. *(Passive)*
7. It is impossible to do. *(Active)*
   It is impossible to be done. *(Passive)*

The Use of 'TO BE' (As An Ordinary/Regular Verb)

As an ordinary verb, it is used to denote **state, condition, existence, quality, time, distance, weather, etc.**

There is no action in this kind of sentences.

(i) She **is** a naughty child.
(ii) She **was** healthy.

In these sentences, **'To be'** verb has been used alone. It is itself an ordinary verb. For our convenience we may call them 'No verb sentences'.

Work Book Exercise B

Directions *Complete the sentences using 'To be' as ordinary verbs.*

1. I wonder where Atul .... lately. *(be)*
2. Where .... you an hour ago? *(be)*
3. Of late there .... great improvements in the city. *(be)*
4. Mr. Bhargava .... our family doctor since long. *(be)*
5. My friend .... in Mumbai for ten years when I .... there last month. *(be, transfer)*
6. Everybody presumes that she may .... present at the time of her brother's marriage next month. *(be)*
7. He .... ill for the last ten days when his wife .... him yesterday. *(be, visit)*
8. He .... 20 now, next year he .... an adult. *(be, be)*
9. The milkman .... absent since last Sunday. *(be)*
10. He .... in Delhi for ten years when I went there. *(be)*

Revision Exercises

Exercise A

Directions *Change the voice according to the corresponding rules.*

Rule I

1. He bought new scissors.
2. They have brought news for you.
3. The minister has issued orders for his transfer.
4. I received summons yesterday.
5. He has repaired his quarters.

Rule II

1. Which book do you like most?
2. Who did this work?
3. What are you teaching?
4. Whom do you like most?
5. Who has taught you English?

Rule III

1. Nobody can mend this wall.
2. Nobody saw him going out.
3. Somebody has stolen my books.
4. One should do one's duty.
5. Somebody told us to wait outside.

Rule IV

1. They hope that he will pass.
2. People believe that he will return soon.
3. We decided that we would leave early.
4. Nobody knows how rich he is.
5. He expects that he will pass.

Rule V

1. He has given me a book.
2. They will ask me a question.
3. They made him Captain.
4. She told me a story.
5. He bought me a scooter.

Rule VI

1. I do not expect it from you.
2. The angry mob thronged the roads.
3. A blow of lathi killed the dog.
4. Do you know the lady?
5. The book contains much information.
6. The servant annoyed the master.
7. His behaviour surprised everyone.
8. His insolence has annoyed the teacher.
9. Their jokes disgusted me.
10. Material life always disgusts him.

Rule VII and VIII

1. Arnav is to help his sister.
2. Shaurya has to distribute sweets.
3. They saw the police chasing a terrorist.
4. She was to write a book on animals.
5. They found him helping the poor.

Rule IX

1. What are you listening to?
2. They were searching for the lost book.
3. The Government cannot dispense with computers.
4. I have never heard of such an accident.
5. All his friends will laugh at him.

Rule X 1. I made him write a letter. 2. She let me stay in her home. 3. She bade me leave the room. 4. They heard her sing a song. 5. I let him go.

Rule XI 1. Obey your teacher. 2. Do it as early as possible. 3. Do not go out. 4. Prevent him from going out. 5. Please enter by this door.

Rule XII 1. Let me sleep here. 2. Let them watch the match. 3. Let us watch TV. 4. Let us not hurt anybody. 5. Let us go now.

Exercise B

Directions *Below are given sentences in active/passive voice. Out of the four alternatives suggested, select one which best expresses the same sentence in passive/active voice.*

1. The waiter filled the glasses with water.
   (a) The glasses filled with water by the waiter
   (b) The glasses were filled with water by the waiter
   (c) The waiter was filled the glasses with water
   (d) The water were filled on the glasses by waiter
2. She took the dog for a walk.
   (a) The dog was taken for a walk by her (b) The dog took her for a walk
   (c) The dog was took for a walk (d) The dog took a walk by her
3. He was driving the car so fast that it skidded on the snowy road.
   (a) The car was driven by him so fast that it skidded on the snowy road
   (b) The car was being driven by him so fast that it skidded on the snowy road
   (c) The car had been driven by him so fast that it skidded on the snowy road
   (d) The car has been driven by him so fast that it skidded on the snowy road
4. They will laugh at you.
   (a) You can be laughed at by them (b) You may be laughed at by them
   (c) You will be laughed at by them (d) You will have been laughed at by them
5. Then her face was bowed.
   (a) Then she was being bowed her face (b) Her face was bowed by then
   (c) Then she bowed her face (d) Then her face has been bowed
6. The walls had not been decorated by us.
   (a) We have he not been decorating the walls
   (b) We had not been decorating the walls
   (c) We have not decorated the walls
   (d) We had not decorated the walls
7. I shall have written the letter.
   (a) The letter will be written by me
   (b) The letter has been written by me
   (c) The letter is being written by me
   (d) The letter will have been written by me
8. We must endure what we cannot cure.
   (a) What we cure must be endured
   (b) What cannot be cured must be endured
   (c) What cannot cured must endured
   (d) What could be cure must be endured

9. A fresh batch of eggs was collected by the farmer's wife.
(a) The farmer's wife was collecting a fresh batch of eggs
(b) The farmer's wife collected a fresh batch of eggs
(c) The farmer's wife had collected a fresh batch of eggs
(d) The farmer's wife will be collecting a fresh batch of eggs

10. They are going to build a new airport near the old one.
(a) A new airport going to be built near the old one
(b) A new airport is being built near the old one
(c) A new airport will be built near the old one
(d) A new airport is going to be built near the old one

11. Rosemary was moved to tears at the sight of the miserable beggar.
(a) The sight of the miserable begger moved Rosemary to tears
(b) The sight of the miserable beggar has moved Rosemary to tears
(c) The sight of the miserable beggar moves Rosemary to tears
(d) The sight of the miserable beggar has moved Rosemary to tears

12. Could you pass the salt?
(a) Could the salt been passed? (b) Could the salt be passed by anyone?
(c) Could the salt be past? (d) Could the salt be passed?

13. Don't subject the animals to cruelty.
(a) The animals are not to be subjected to cruelty
(b) The animals shall not be subjected to cruelty
(c) The animals will not be subjected to cruelty
(d) The animals should not be subjected to cruelty

14. Who asked you to draft this letter?
(a) By who you are asked to draft this letter?
(b) By who have you been asked to draft this letter?
(c) By whom were you asked to draft this letter?
(d) By whom you were asked to draft this letter?

15. The lightning caused a serious forest fire and damaged many nearby houses.
(a) A serious forest fire has been caused by lightning and many nearby houses have been damaged
(b) A serious forest fire was caused by lightening and many houses are damaged
(c) A serious forest fire had been caused by lightning and many nearby houses had been damaged
(d) A serious forest fire was caused by lightning and many nearby houses were damaged

16. Today I accomplished my task successfully.
(a) Today my task is accomplished successfully
(b) Today my task has been accomplished successfully
(c) Today my task accomplished successfully
(d) Today my task was accomplished successfully

17. Look! They have painted the door.
(a) Look! The door's being painted (b) Look! The door had been painted
(c) Look! The door has been painted (d) Look! The door was painted

18. She was advised 15 days' rest after her surgery.
(a) The doctor was advised her 15 days' rest after her surgery
(b) The doctor has advised her 15 days' rest after her surgery
(c) The doctor advised her 15 days' rest after her surgery
(d) The doctor had advised her 15 days' rest after her surgery

19. When did he return my books?
(a) When were my books returned by him?
(b) When will my books be returned by him?
(c) When has he returned my books?
(d) When are my books returned by him?

20. We had to stop all other work to complete our assignment.
(a) All other work has to be stopped by us to complete our assignment
(b) All other work had stopped by us to complete our assignment
(c) All other work had to be stopped by us to complete our assignment
(d) All other work was stopped by us to complete our assignment

21. Gandhiji started the Quit India Movement in 1942.
(a) The Quit India Movement was started by Gandhiji in 1942
(b) The Quit India Movement was been started by Gandhiji in 1942
(c) The Quit India Movement had been started by Gandhiji in 1942
(d) The Quit India Movement started by Gandhiji in 1942

22. Gagan Narang and Vijay won bronze medals in the London Olympics.
(a) Bronze medals won by Gagan Narang and Vijay in the London Olympics
(b) Bronze medals had been won by Gagan Narang and Vijay in the London Olympics
(c) Bronze medals were won by Gagan Narang and Vijay in London Olympics
(d) Bronze medals have been won by Gagan Narang and Vijay in the London Olympics

23. The modern means of communication have made life so much easier.
(a) Life had been made so much easier by the modern means of communication
(b) Life is being so much easier by the modern means of communication
(c) Life has been made so much easier by the modern means of communication
(d) Life was made so much easier by the modern means of communication

24. Thick clouds have overcast the sky.
(a) The sky has been overcast by thick clouds
(b) The sky overcast by thick clouds
(c) The sky is overcast by thick clouds
(d) The sky is being overcast by thick clouds

25. One should not give unsolicited advice.
(a) Unsolicited advice is not to be given (b) Unsolicited advice can't be given
(c) Unsolicited advice may not be given (d) Unsolicited advice should not be given

Exam Practice

Directions (Q. Nos. 1-5) *Each item in this section has a sentence in active voice followed by four sentences, one of which is the correct passive voice statement of the same. Select the correct one and mark it in the answer sheet accordingly.*

1. The Members of the Parliament elect their group leader either by consensus or by voice vote. **CDS 2018**
(a) The group leader is elected by the Members of the Parliament either by consensus or by voice vote

(b) The group leader was elected by the Members of the Parliament either by consensus or by voice vote
(c) The group leader has been elected by the Members of the Parliament either by consensus or by voice vote
(d) The Members of the Parliament are elected by their group leader either by consensus or by voice vote

2. All the examinees have answered one particular question in the long answer writing section. **CDS 2018**
(a) One particular question is answered by all the examinees in the long answer writing section
(b) One particular question was answered by all the examinees in the long answer writing section
(c) All the examinees answered one particular question in the long answer writing section
(d) One particular question has been answered by all the examinees in the long answer writing section

3. The writer who passed away recently has authored a dozen novels and a number of poetry collections. **CDS 2018**
(a) A dozen novels and a number of poetry collections have been authored by the writer who passed away recently
(b) A dozen novels and a number of poetry collections has been authored by the writer who passed away recently
(c) A dozen novels and a number of poetry collections were authored by the writer who passed away recently
(d) A dozen novels and a number of poetry collections had been authored by the writer who passed away recently

4. Shut the door. **CDS 2018**
(a) Shut the door
(b) Let the door be shut
(c) The door be shut
(d) The door is shut

5. India won freedom with the blood and sweat of hundreds and thousands of Indians. **CDS 2018**
(a) India had won freedom with the blood and sweat of hundreds and thousands of Indians
(b) Freedom had been won by India with the blood and sweat of hundreds and thousands of Indians
(c) Freedom was won by India with the blood and sweat of hundreds and thousands of Indians
(d) Freedom was won by hundreds and thousands of Indians with their blood and sweat

6. *In the following question, a sentence has been given in Active/Passive voice. Out of the four alternatives suggested, select the one which best expresses the same sentence in Passive/Active voice.* **SSC CGL 2017**

I will wash the car every Sunday.
(a) The car is washed by me every Sunday.
(b) Every Sunday by me the car is to be washed.
(c) Every Sunday by myself the car is to be washed.
(d) The car will be washed by me every Sunday.

7. Select the correct passive form of the given sentence. **SSC CGL 2018**
The sailors had never encountered such a rough sea.
(a) Such a rough sea was never encountered by the sailors.
(b) Such a rough sea had never been encountered by the sailors.
(c) Such a rough sea has never been encountered by the sailors.
(d) Such a rough sea is never encountered by the sailors.

8. Select the correct active form of the given sentence.
We all will be greatly benefitted by this scheme. **SSC CGL 2018**
(a) This scheme has greatly benefitted us all.
(b) This scheme would greatly benefit we all.
(c) This scheme will greatly benefit us all.
(d) This scheme is going to greatly benefit us all.

9. Select the correct active form of the given sentence. **SSC CGL 2018**
He was given a book for his birthday.
(a) She gave him a book for his birthday.
(b) She will be giving him a book for his birthday.
(c) She has gave him a book for his birthday.
(d) She give a book to him for his birthday.

10. Select the correct passive voice of the given sentence. **SSC CGL 2018**
The artist played the violin.
(a) The violin is being played by the artist.
(b) The violin will be played by the artist.
(c) The violin had been played by the artist.
(d) The violin was played by the artist.

11. Select the correct active form of the given sentence. **SSC CGL 2020**
The thief was being arrested by the police.
(a) The police arrested the thief.
(b) The police had arrested the thief.
(c) The police was arresting the thief.
(d) The police has arrested the thief.

Directions (Q.Nos. 12-21) *Below are given sentences in active/passive voice. Out of the four alternatives suggested, select one which best expresses the same sentence in passive/active voice.* **SSC CGL 2011**

12. Our task had been completed before sunset.
(a) We completed our task before sunset
(b) We have completed our task before sunset
(c) We complete our task before sunset
(d) We had completed our task before sunset

13. The government has launched a massive tribal welfare programme in Jharkhand.
(a) A massive tribal welfare programme is launched by the government in Jharkhand
(b) A massive tribal welfare programme has been launched by the government in Jharkhand
(c) Jharkhand government has launched a massive tribal welfare programme
(d) The government in Jharkhand has launched a massive tribal welfare programme

14. The burglar destroyed several items in the room. Even the carpet has been torn.
(a) Several items were destroyed in the room by the burglar. Even the carpet he has torn
(b) Several items in the room were destroyed by the burglar. Even the carpet was torn
(c) Including the carpet, several items in the room have been torn by the burglar
(d) The burglar, being destroyed several items in the room, also carpet has torn

15. Has anybody answered your question?
(a) Your question has been answered? (b) Anybody has answered your question?
(c) Has your question been answered? (d) Have you answered your question?

16. The shopkeeper lowered the prices.
(a) The prices lowered the shopkeeper
(b) The prices were lowered by the shopkeeper
(c) Down went the prices
(d) The shopkeeper got down the prices

17. One must keep one's promises.
(a) One's promises are kept (b) One's promises must kept
(c) One's promises were kept (d) One's promises must be kept

18. They have published all the details of the invention.
(a) All the details of the invention have been published by them
(b) The publication of the details of invention was done by them
(c) All the details have been invented by the publishers
(d) All the inventions have been detailed by them

19. Please shut the door and go to sleep.
(a) The door is to be shut and you are to got to sleep
(b) Let the door be shut and you be asleep
(c) You are requested to shut the door and go to sleep
(d) The door is to be shut and you are requested to sleep

20. It is impossible to do this.
(a) Doing this is impossible (b) This is impossible to be done
(c) This must not be done (d) This can't be done

21. We must take care of all living species on Earth.
(a) All living species on Earth are taken care of by us
(b) All living species on Earth must be taken care of by us
(c) All living species on Earth had been taken care of by us
(d) All living species on Earth will be taken care of by us

Directions (Q.Nos. 22-30) *Below are given sentences in active/passive voice. Out of the four alternatives suggested, select one which best expresses the same sentence in passive/active voice.*

22. It is being read by us.
(a) We are reading it (b) It will be read by us
(c) We can read it (d) We have to read it

23. He had committed a mistake.
(a) A mistake had committed by him (b) A mistake was committed by him
(c) A mistake had been committed by him (d) A mistake has been committed by him

24. The most useful training of my career was given to me by my boss.
(a) My boss has been giving me the most useful training of my career
(b) My boss giving me the most useful training
(c) My boss is given me the most useful training
(d) My boss gave me the most useful training of my career

25. Why did she break the garden wall?
(a) Why the garden wall was broken by her?
(b) Why had the garden wall been broken by her?
(c) Why was the garden wall broken by her?
(d) Why will the garden wall be broken by her?

26. The students were laughing at the old man.
(a) The old man was being laughed at by the students
(b) The old man was laughed at by the students
(c) The old man was being laughed by the students
(d) The old man is laughing at the students

27. Can we send this big parcel by air?
(a) Can this big parcel be sent by air?
(b) Can this big parcel sent by air?
(c) Could this big parcel be sent by air?
(d) Could this big parcel sent by us by air?

28. The government is planning a new road near my school.
(a) A new road is being planned by the government near my school.
(b) A new road planned by the government near my school.
(c) A new road was planned by the government near my house.
(d) A new road was being planned by the government near my house.

29. Picasso was painting a boy at that time.
(a) A boy were being painted by Picasso at that time
(b) A boy was being painted by Picasso at that time
(c) A boy was painted by Picasso at that time
(d) A boy was painting Picasso at that time

30. This house was built in 1960 by my grandfather.
(a) My grandfather builds this house in 1980
(b) My grandfather build this house in 1960
(c) My grandfather built this house in 1960
(d) My grandfather building this house in 1960

Directions (Q. Nos. 31-38) *Each item in this section has a sentence in passive voice followed by four sentences one of which is the correct active voice of the given sentence. Select the correct one and mark it in the answer sheet.*

31. The doors have been cleaned.
(a) Someone cleans the doors
(b) Someone have cleaned the doors
(c) One has cleaned the doors
(d) Someone has cleaned the doors

32. Ritika was sent a cheque.
(a) Someone sends her a cheque
(b) Someone has sent Ritika cheque
(c) Someone sent Ritika a cheque
(d) Cheque has been sent

33. The plenary meeting was postponed.
(a) Someone postponed the plenary meeting
(b) They postpones the plenary meeting
(c) One has postponed the plenary meeting
(d) They postponed the plenary meeting

34. The boy killed the dogs.
(a) The dogs was killed by the boys
(b) The dogs were killed by the boy
(c) The dogs were killed
(d) The dogs were being killed by the boys

35. Her money was stolen by her husband.
(a) Her husband stole her money
(b) The husband stole her money
(c) Her husband steals her money
(d) Her husband's stole her money

36. The students are taught by Mrs. Bedi.
(a) Mrs. Bedi teach the students
(b) Mrs. Bedi teaches the student
(c) Mrs. Bedi taught the students
(d) Mrs Bedi teaches the students

37. A grand dinner is going to be made by Rashi tonight.
(a) Rashi would make a grand dinner tonight
(b) Rashi makes a grand dinner tonight
(c) Rashi is going to make a grand dinner tonight
(d) Rashi will make a grand dinner

38. India Gate has been visited by many tourists.
(a) Many tourists have been visiting India Gate
(b) Many a tourist has visited India Gate
(c) Many tourists have visited the India Gate
(d) A number of tourists have visited the India Gate

Answers

Work Book Exercise A

1. was annoyed	**2.** be punished
3. was convinced, was	**4.** has been enforced
5. were disappointed	**6.** behave
7. be entrusted	**8.** was amazed
9. will be pleased	**10.** is bearing

Work Book Exercise B

1. has been	**2.** were	**3.** have been	**4.** has been
5. had been, was transferred		**6.** be	**7.** had been, visited
8. is, will be	**9.** has been	**10.** had been	

Revision Exercise

Exercise A

Rule I

1. New scissors were bought by him.
2. News has been brought for you by them.
3. Orders for his transfer have been issued by the minister.
4. Summons was received by me yesterday.
5. His quarters have been repaired by him.

Rule II

1. Which book is liked most by you?
2. By whom was this work done?
3. What is being taught by you?
4. Who is liked most by you?
5. By whom have you been taught English?

Rule III

1. This wall cannot be mended.	**2.** He was not seen going out.
3. My books have been stolen.	**4.** Duty should be done.
5. We were told to wait outside.	

Rule IV

1. It is hoped that he will pass.
2. It is believed that he will return soon.
3. It was decided that we would leave early.
4. It is not known how rich he is.
5. It is expected that he will pass.

Rule V

1. (a) I have been given a book by him. (b) A book has been given to me by him.
2. I will be asked a question by them.
3. He was made captain.
4. A story was told to me by her.
5. A scooter was bought for me by him.

Rule VI

1. It is not expected of you by me.
2. The roads were thronged with the angry mob.
3. The dog was killed with a blow of lathi.
4. Is the lady known to you?
5. Much information is contained in the book.
6. The master was annoyed with the servant.
7. Everyone was surprised at his behaviour.
8. The teacher has been annoyed at his insolence.
9. I was disgusted at their jokes.
10. He is always disgusted with material life.

Rule VII

1. Arnav's sister is to be helped by him.
2. Sweets have to be distributed by Shaurya.

Rule VIII

3. A terrorist was seen being chased by the police.
4. A book on animals was to be written by her.
5. The poor were found being helped by him.

Rule IX

1. What is being listened to by you?
2. The lost book was being searched for by them.
3. Computers cannot be dispensed with by the Government.
4. Such an accident has never been heard of.
5. He will be laughed at by all his friends.

Rule X

1. He was made to write a letter by me.
2. I was allowed to stay in her home.
3. I was bidden to leave the room by her.
4. Her song was heard by them.
5. He was let go by me.

Rule XI

1. Your teacher should be obeyed.
2. It should be done as early as possible.
3. (a) You are ordered not to go out.
   (b) You are forbidden to go out.
4. He should be prevented from going out.
5. You are requested to enter by this door.

Rule XII

1. I may be allowed to sleep here. 2. They may be allowed to watch the match.
3. TV should be watched by us. 4. Nobody should be hurt by us.
5. It is suggested that we should go now.

Exercise B

1. *(b)* The glasses were filled with water by the waiter.
2. *(a)* The dog was taken for a walk by her.
3. *(b)* The car was being driven by him so fast that it skidded on the snowy road.
4. *(c)* You will be laughed at by them.
5. *(c)* Then she bowed her face.
6. *(d)* We had not decorated the walls.
7. *(d)* The letter will have been written by me.
8. *(b)* What cannot be cured must be endured.
9. *(b)* The farmer's wife collected a fresh batch of eggs.
10. *(d)* A new airport is going to be built near the old one.
11. *(a)* The sight of the miserable beggar moved Rosemary to tears.
12. *(d)* Could the salt be passed?
13. *(d)* The animals should not be subjected to cruelty.
14. *(d)* By whom you were asked to draft this letter?
15. *(d)* A serious forest fire was caused by lightning and many nearby houses were damaged.
16. *(d)* Today my task was accomplished successfully.
17. *(c)* Look! The door has been painted.
18. *(c)* The doctor advised her 15 days' rest after her surgery.
19. *(a)* When were my books returned by him?
20. *(c)* All other work had to be stopped by us to complete our assignment.
21. *(a)* The Quit India Movement was started by Gandhiji in 1942.
22. *(c)* Bronze medals were won by Gagan Narang and Vijay in the London Olympics.
23. *(c)* Life has been made so much easier by the modern means of communication.
24. *(a)* The sky has been overcast by thick clouds.
25. *(d)* Unsolicited advice should not be given.

Exam Practice

1. *(a)* As the sentence describes a fact (Simple Present Tense), its correct passive voice is given in option (a).
2. *(d)* 'have' in active voice will be changed to 'has been' in passive voice. So, option (d) gives the correct passive voice of the sentence.
3. *(a)* The given sentence is in Present Perfect Tense, so its correct passive voice is given in option (a).
4. *(b)* An imperative sentence in Passive Voice has the following structure: Let + object + be + Past Participle. So, option (b) gives the correct passive voice.
5. *(c)* The given sentence is in Simple Past Tense. So, option (c) gives its correct passive voice.
6. *(d)* Option (d) gives the correct passive voice of the given sentence as the sentence is in future tense.
7. *(b)* Option (b) gives the correct passive voice of the given sentence.
8. *(c)* The correct active voice of the given sentence will be 'This scheme will greatly benefit us all'.
9. *(a)* Option (a) gives the correct active voice of the given sentence.
10. *(d)* 'The violin was played by the artist,' is the correct passive voice of the given sentence.
11. *(c)* The sentence is in Past Continuous Tense. So, option (c) gives the correct active voice of the sentence.
12. *(d)* Option (d) gives the correct active voice of the sentence.
13. *(b)* Option (b) is the correct passive voice of the sentence as the given sentence is in Present Perfect Tense.

14. *(a)* Option (a) gives the correct passive voice of the sentence.
15. *(c)* 'Has your question been answered?' is the appropriate passive voice of the given sentence.
16. *(b)* 'lowered' will be changed to 'were lowered' in the passive voice.
17. *(d)* 'One's promises must be kept' is the correct passive voice of the given sentence.
18. *(a)* Option (a) gives the appropriate passive voice of the given sentence.
19. *(c)* Option (c) is the correct option here.
20. *(b)* 'This is impossible to be done' is the correct conversion of the given sentence.
21. *(b)* 'must take care' will be changed into 'must be taken care of' in passive voice.
22. *(a)* 'We are reading it' is the correct active voice of the given sentence.
23. *(c)* 'had' will be changed to 'had been' in passive voice.
24. *(d)* 'My boss gave me the most useful training of my career' is the correct active voice of the given sentence.
25. *(c)* Option (c) gives the correct passive voice of the given sentence.
26. *(a)* 'were laughing' will be changed to 'was being laughed' in the passive voice.
27. *(a)* Option (a) gives the correct conversion of the given sentence.
28. *(a)* Option (a) gives the correct conversion of the given sentence.
29. *(b)* 'was painting' will change to 'was being painted' in passive voice.
30. *(c)* 'My grandfather built this house in 1960' is the correct active voice of the given sentence.
31. *(d)* 'Someone has cleaned the doors', is the correct active voice of the sentence.
32. *(c)* Option (c) gives the correct active voice of the given sentence.
33. *(d)* 'They postponed the plenary meeting' is the correct active formation of the given sentence.
34. *(b)* Option (b) gives the correct transformation of the sentence.
35. *(a)* 'Her husband stole her money', is the correct active voice of the sentence.
36. *(d)* 'Mrs. Bedi teaches the students', is the correct active voice of the sentence.
37. *(c)* Option (c) gives the correct active transformation of the sentence.
38. *(c)* Option (c) gives the correct active transformation of the sentence.

3

Modals

There are two classes of verbs.

(i) Ordinary/Regular verbs

(ii) Auxiliary verbs

Auxiliary verbs are of two kinds

(a) Primary Auxilary
Be, do, have

(b) Modal Auxiliary
May, might, should, must, will, etc.

What is Modal Auxilary?

A verb used to express the mood (mode) or attitude of a speaker is called Modal Auxiliary. *For example*

(i) You **should** regularly go for a morning walk.

(ii) They **must** attend tomorrow's meeting.

(iii) **May** I use your pen please?

(iv) You **can** park the car in front of our house.

(v) You **may** take these books home.

(vi) **Could** you open the door please?

Most Commonly Used Modals

Can	Could	May	Might
Should	Would	Must	Ought to
Am/Was to	Have/Had to	Used to	Need
Dare	Shall, Will		

All these Modals Suggest

(A) Permission

(B) Ability

(C) Possibility

(D) Suggestion, Advice

(E) Promise

(F) Intention

(G) Request

(H) Necessity, Compulsion

(I) Prohibition

(J) Wish or Prayer

(K) Duty, Obligation

Different Uses of Modals

1. **May & Might** These are used to express

(A) **Possibility**

(i) It *may/might* rain.

(ii) He *may/might* go to Delhi tomorrow.

(iii) You *may* fall.

(iv) Teena said that she *might* go there.

(B) **Permission**

(i) *May* I come in? *(ii)* Yes, you *may* come in.

(C) **Wish or Prayer**

(i) *May* you enjoy marital happiness!

(ii) *May* you live long!

(D) **Purpose**

(i) She works hard so that she *may* pass.

(ii) She came so that she *might* see me.

(E) **Remote Possibility**

'Might' is used in place of 'may' to express remote possibility.

(i) It *might* rain.

(ii) He *might* be sleeping now.

Normally, both 'May & Might' can be used to express possibility regarding present and future. However, 'might' is used when the reporting verb is in the past. See sentence no. (iv) in (A) and sentence no. (ii) in (D).

(F) **May/Might+Have** They are used to express possibility/desirability relating to the past action. *For example*

(i) He *may/might* have left yesterday. *(It is possible he left)*

(ii) He *might* have failed. *(It is possible he failed)*

(iii) Better, you *might* not *have* revealed the secret. *(It is possible that secret was revealed)*

NOTE Sometimes **'May/Might have'** give the opposite sense of the action.

2. **Can & Could** (Able to) They are used to express

(A) **Ability** (Present, Past & Future)

(i) She *can* write English well. (is able to)

(ii) Meetu *could* play cards. (was able to)

(iii) She will be able to help me. (future of 'can')

(iv) I have been able to do it. (perfect of 'can')

(B) **Polite Request**

(i) *Could* you please do it for me? ('would' is also used while making polite requests)

(ii) *Could* you please lend me some money?

(C) **Permission/Order**

(i) Yes, you *can* go now.

(ii) You *can* take my book. (Here 'can' is an alternative to 'may')

(D) **Prohibition/Offer**

(i) You *cannot* enter the room. (Prohibition)

(ii) *Can* I get you some fruits? (Offer)

(iii) *Can* I help you? (Offer)

(E) **Possibility**

(i) Who is she with him?
She *could* be his wife. (possibly, she is)

(ii) How old is she?
She *could* be sixteen. (possibly, she is)

(F) **Could + Have** This form is used for past ability while indicating that the action did not take place. *For example*

(i) I *could have* revealed the secret. (but I did not)

(ii) You *could have* borrowed some money. (but you did not)

(iii) The police *could have* arrested him. (but they did not)

NOTE In all these sentences **the action** did not take place.

3. **Should** It is used to express

(A) **Duty/Obligation**

(i) You *should* stand by your brother. *(ii)* I *should* leave now.

(iii) Promises *should* be kept. *(iv)* He *should* be present here.

(B) **Future in the Past**

(i) I told him that I *should* go there.

(ii) Did I not tell you that I *should* qualify?

(C) **Purpose**

Walk carefully lest you *should* fall.

(D) **Condition**

Should you work hard, you will get success. ('should' is used in the sense of 'if')

(E) **Should + Have** This form is used to express obligation in the past. It may imply the non-performance of the action. *For example*

(i) You *should have* stood by your brother.

(ii) He *should have* left a message.

(iii) He *should have* been present at the party.

(iv) My brother *should have* replied politely.

4. **Must** It expresses

(A) **Necessity or Obiligation** (in place of 'should')

(i) You *must* follow instructions.

(ii) I *must* leave now.

(B) **Order of the Speaker**

(i) You *must not* leave now. *(ii)* They *must not* play here.

(C) **Strong Possibility** (in place of 'may')

(i) It is ten. The teacher *must* be in the class.

(ii) She *must* be working in the office now.

(D) **Determination**

I *must* help him.

(E) **Deduction, Inference**

(i) He has a big house. He *must* be rich.

(ii) She reads a lot. She *must* be learned.

(F) **Must + Have** This form is used for a past action or situation indicating non-performance of action. *For example*

(i) You *must* have followed instructions.

(ii) You *must* have left them.

(iii) I *must* have helped him.

5. **Ought to** It expresses

(A) **Duty or Moral Obligation** It is normally used for 'should & must', when there is strong sense of moral duty, advice or indication of **correct action.** *For example*

(i) You *ought to* serve your motherland.

(ii) You *ought* not to take fatty food.

(iii) You *ought to* take food before leaving.

(B) **Ought to + Have** This construction is used in relation to past action of duty that was not fulfilled or an action that was neglected in the past.

(i) You *ought to have* taken care of your wife.

(ii) You *ought to have* served your parents.

(iii) He *ought to have* been present at the wedding of his friend.

(iv) He *ought* not *to have* smoked in the bus.

6. **To be + Infinitive** This expression is used to

(A) **Express plan**

(i) I am to make a speech tomorrow.

(ii) She is to leave for the States after marriage.

(iii) I was to make a speech yesterday.

(iv) She was to leave for the States for higher study.

The last two sentences do not state expressively about the implementation of the plan.

(B) **Express Order** (In the sense of 'must')

(i) Students are to wait outside.

(ii) The servant is to remain in the house till we return.

(C) **Obligation/Duty**

(i) I am to help my ailing brother.

(ii) My friend was to send money to his sister.

(D) **To be + have** This expression is used to express an action that could not take place according to the plan.

(i) He was to have attended marriage but fell ill.

(ii) Deepu was to have appeared at the examination but she gave up the plan.

7. **To have + Infinitive** This expression is used to express compulsion as is expressed with **'Must'**. It also expresses obligation (In the Present, Past and Future).

(i) I have to leave for Delhi today.

(ii) I don't have to meet him now. *(need not)*

(iii) I will have to get up early in the morning.

(iv) I had to leave for Delhi yesterday.

(v) I did not have to meet him there. *(need not have)*

8. **Used To** They are used

(A) **To Denote Habitual Action or the Past Routine of the Subject**

(i) He *used to* go to Delhi by car.

(ii) Dina *used to* study at noon.

(iii) She *used to* go out with me in the morning.

(B) **To Denote Discontinued Action**

(i) He *used to* play hockey. *(now he has stopped)*

(ii) She *used to* work in office before marriage. *(not now)*

(C) **'Used to' is also used as an adjective** (be used to) It is equal to 'accustomed to' as

(i) He is *used to* getting up early.

(ii) I was *used to* driving through crowded streets.

(iii) He will be *used to* taking dinner early.

(iv) We are *used to* hot noons in the plains.

9. **Would** It is used in the following cases

(i) *Would* you please help my son? *(polite request)*

(ii) She told me that she *would* give me money. *(future in the past)*

(iii) I *would*/should like to play now. *(wish)*

(iv) I *would*/should be glad to help you. *(wish)*

(v) I would rather stay. *(wish)*

(vi) Who is she? She *would* be his sister. *(possibly she is)*

(vii) She *would* be sixteen. *(possibly she is)*

(viii) If only you *would* stay with me. *(wish)*

(ix) He *would* go to Delhi by car. *(habitual)*

(x) Diana *would* go to library. *(past routine)*

10. **Need & Need Not** 'Need' can be treated as an **auxiliary or as an ordinary verb**. As an auxiliary verb, it is used mainly in the negative and the interrogative forms with direct infinitive. It has no past tense.

(A) **Need Not** As an auxiliary verb, it is used for an action which is not necessary.

For example

(i) He *needs* to work hard. *(Ordinary verb)*
(ii) *Need* I write to him? *(Auxiliary verb)*
(iii) He *need* not go there again. *(Auxiliary verb)*
(iv) Rohit *need* not phone her now. *(Auxiliary verb)*
(v) You do not need to work now. *(Ordinary verb)*
(vi) Do you need to work now? *(Ordinary verb)*

(B) **Need Not + Have** This form is used for an action which was not necessary but was performed.

For example

(i) You *need not have* gone there.
(ii) Rohit *need not have* phoned her yesterday.

11. **Dare** 'Dare' can be treated as an auxiliary or as an ordinary verb. As an auxiliary verb, it is used mainly in the negative and the interrogative forms with direct infinitive.

(i) She *dared* her sister to touch her. *(Challenge, Ordinary verb)*
(ii) He does not *dare* me to fight. *(Challenge, Ordinary verb)*
(iii) I *dare* to go outside now. *(To have courage, Ordinary verb)*
(iv) He *dares* to abuse his rivals. *(To have courage, Ordinary verb)*
(v) I *dare* not go outside now. *(Auxiliary verb)*
(vi) He *dare* not abuse his rivals. *(Auxiliary verb)*
(vii) *Dare* you go outside now? *(Auxiliary verb)*
(viii) *Dare* he say so? *(Auxiliary verb)*
(ix) He *dared* not go outside then. *(Auxiliary verb)*
(x) I *dare* say she will cheat you. *(I suppose)*

NOTE 'S' is not used with **dare & need** as auxiliary verbs.

Work Book Exercise A

Directions *Complete the sentences with suitable alternatives.*

May & Might

1. She expects that her son ....
(a) can return (b) may return (c) should return

2. If we request her she .... to college.
(a) must give a lift (b) might give a lift (c) can give a lift

3. It is possible Marlowe .... plays for Shakespeare.
(a) may write (b) might have written (c) might write

4. All felt that he .... a cheat.
(a) may be (b) can be (c) might be

5. .... I go out? asked her son.
(a) Should (b) May (c) Must

6. "Yes, you ....", the mother answered.
(a) should go (b) may go (c) must go

7. The son asked his mother if he ....
(a) can go out (b) may go out (c) might go out

8. .... our king live long!
(a) May (b) Must (c) Should

9. We eat so that we .... live.
(a) may (b) might (c) can

10. He went there so that he .... borrow money.
(a) may (b) can (c) might

Should

11. She advised that I .... curtail expenditure.
(a) should (b) shall (c) should have

12. You .... him that gambling would ruin him.
(a) should warn (b) should have warned (c) must warn

13. We enjoyed the movie, you .... there.
(a) should have been (b) can be (c) should be

14. .... you work hard, you will pass.
(a) Would (b) Will (c) Should

15. I told him that I .... leave next day.
(a) should (b) should have (c) could

16. Make haste lest you .... late.
(a) should get (b) should not get (c) may not got

Must

17. She .... work hard if she wants to top the merit list.
(a) must have *(b)* must *(c)* must not

18. She .... alone as it was raining heavily.
(a) must not leave *(b)* must not have left *(c)* should not leave

19. Principal to a student : You .... with bad girls.
(a) must not mix *(b)* cannot mix *(c)* may not mix

20. She .... alone as it is raining heavily.
(a) must not leave *(b)* must not have left *(c)* should not have left

21. There .... something wrong with the cooker today.
(a) must be *(b)* should have been *(c)* must have been

22. Swati is gentle, her sister .... it.
(a) should have done *(b)* must have done *(c)* should do

23. I am sure the Principal .... in his room.
(a) should be *(b)* can be *(c)* must be

Ought to

24. You .... obey your parents.
(a) should *(b)* ought to *(c)* must

25. You .... stood by your sister, when she was in difficulties.
(a) ought to *(b)* ought to have *(c)* should have

Work Book Exercise B

Directions *Complete the sentences with suitable alternatives.*

Can, Could

1. Since the keys are with my brother, I .... you money.
(a) will not lend *(b)* cannot lend *(c)* may not lend

2. She told me that she .... English fluently and was very happy.
(a) could speak *(b)* could have spoken *(c)* can speak

3. .... you please help my son?
(a) Can *(b)* Was able to *(c)* Could

4. After we had changed the punctured tyre we .... continue our journey.
(a) can *(b)* was able *(c)* were able to

5. My friend did not help me though he .... helped.
(a) could *(b)* could have *(c)* should

To Be + Infinitive

6. He .... catch the first train tonight.
(a) is to *(b)* was to have *(c)* is to have

7. How are you here? You .... her marriage.
(a) are to attend (b) were to attend (c) were to have attended

8. She .... the first flight so she hurried to the airport in a taxi.
(a) was to catch (b) am to catch (c) was to have caught

Would, Used to, Be used to

9. She told me that she .... go to Mumbai next month.
(a) will (b) should (c) would

10. He .... go to college daily by bus in his college days.
(a) should (b) would (c) will

11. .... you please help my son?
(a) Should (b) Can (c) Would

12. My friend .... visit me every Sunday when I was ill.
(a) used to (b) is used to (c) was used to

13. Deepu .... getting up early in the morning.
(a) used to (b) is used to (c) accustomed to

Need not

14. My sister .... to Delhi in such circumstances.
(a) need not go (b) need not to have gone (c) need not to go

15. She .... here last night as her friend was better then.
(a) need not have stayed (b) need not stay (c) should not have stayed

16. You .... your note books from tomorrow.
(a) need not bring (b) need not to bring (c) need not have brought

17. .... there while my father had forbidden me?
(a) Do I need go (b) Need I go (c) Need I have gone

Dare

18. Yesterday she .... her sister to touch her.
(a) dares (b) does not (c) dared

19. He dares .... his rivals.
(a) abuse (b) to abuse (c) abusing

20. I dare not .... outside now.
(a) go (b) to go (c) going

Revision Exercise

Directions (Q. Nos. 1-9) *Fill in the blanks by choosing the appropriate modal from the options.*

1. You .... be serious. You want me to go out without wearing a helmet.
(a) won't (b) shouldn't (c) couldn't (d) can't

2. One .... worry all the time. It leads to serious health problems.
(a) should (b) couldn't (c) mayn't (d) shouldn't

3. I .... be really mean to Divya, but I don't want to treat her like that.
(a) need (b) could (c) could have (d) have

4. Sumer .... go to the wedding. He has a shift that day.
(a) could have (b) need (c) can't (d) haven't

5. I .... go to New Delhi this week.
(a) don't have (b) need (c) have (d) might

6. When Sucheta won the prize,she .... speak for a moment.
(a) should (b) must (c) couldn't (d) could

7. Do you .... to work on Sundays?
(a) have (b) need (c) must (d) has

8. .... I have your permission to leave the office early?
(a) Would (b) Wouldn't (c) Can (d) May

9. You .... to finish this on time because you have no choice.
(a) may have (b) could have (c) have (d) needn't

Directions (Q. Nos. 10-17) *Read the following sentences to find out if there is any error in them. The error, if any, will be in one part of the sentence. That part is the answer. If there is no error, mark 'No error' as your answer.*

10. Don't worry/they/should eventually/succeed, I assure you.
(a) Don't worry (b) succeed, I assure you
(c) they (d) should eventually
(e) No error

11. You should/take an umbrella/with you as/it will rain later.
(a) it will rain later (b) You should (c) with you as (d) take an umbrella
(e) No error

12. I say to myself/each morning/I really must/write that letter.
(a) I say to myself (b) each morning (c) write that letter (d) I really must
(e) No error

13. I know/I would/do it/as I have done it before.
(a) as I have done it before (b) I know
(c) I would (d) do it
(e) No error

14. One must/follow the rules/or one/will go to jail.
(a) One must (b) follow the rules (c) or one (d) will go to jail
(e) No error

15. You should be/angry with Nikki,/it's not/her fault.
(a) it's not (b) You should be (c) angry with Nikki (d) her fault
(e) No error

16. One/could obey/one's/teachers.
(a) teachers (b) one (c) could obey (d) one's
(e) No error

17. Do you think you/should come over at/6 pm tomorrow so we/can go to the party?
(a) Do you think you (b) 6 pm tomorrow so we
(c) should come over at (d) can go to the party?
(e) No error

Directions (Q. Nos. 18-25) *In the following questions, some part of the sentence may have an error. Find out which part of the sentence has an error and select that part as your answer. If a sentence is free from error, select the option which says 'No error'.*

18. Sarah may (A)/be exhausted (B)/as she (C)/ran 20 kms today. (D)/ No error (E)
(a) B (b) A (c) C (d) D (e) E

19. I hope you (A)/can come (B)/to play (C)/the match. (D)/No error (E)
(a) E (b) A (c) B (d) C (e) D

20. Bismillah would (A)/play the shehnai(B)/when he (C)/was very young. (D)/No error (E)
(a) E (b) D (c) C (d) B (e) A

21. That can't (A)/be Peehu's coat. (B)/It is (C)/too small. (D)/No error (E)
(a) A (b) B (c) C (d) D (e) E

22. He will call (A)/at 5 O'clock. (B)/He could (C)/have got home by then. (D)/No error (E)
(a) A (b) B (c) D (d) C (e) E

23. Amit must have (A)/been very angry/if he had (C)/seen you. (D)/No error (E)
(a) A (b) B (c) C (d) D (e) E

24. You can't (A)/borrow my (B)/pen if (C)/you like. (D)/No error (E)
(a) E (b) D (c) C (d) A (e) B

25. Ravi shouldn't go (A)/out as (B)/COVID is spreading (C)/very fast. (D)/No error (E)
(a) B (b) A (c) C (d) E (e) D

Exam Practice

Directions (Q. Nos. 1-6) *Each question in this section has three underlined parts labelled (a), (b) and (c). Read each sentence to find out whether there is any error in any underlined part and indicate your response against it. If you find no error, your response should be indicated as (d).*

1. She told her teacher that she (a) could not be able to attend the class (b) the previous day because of heavy rains. (c) No error (d) **CDS 2016**

2. As I was leaving for Delhi, (a) he asked me whether (b) I could buy a tape recorder for him. (c). No error (d) **CDS 2016**

3. He couldn't (a) find (b) an answer. (c) No error (d) **CDS 2017**

4. The guards (a) dare not (b) to harm him. (c) No error (d) **NDA 2016**

5. Work hard (a) lest you do not (b) fail. (c) No error (d) **NDA 2019**

6. If the scheme would have been implemented effectively (a) all affected (b) would have benefitted. (c) No error (d) **CDS 2020**

Directions (Q. Nos. 7-15) *Read the sentence to find out whether there is any error in it. The error, if any, will be in one part of the sentence. That part is the answer. If there is no error, mark 'No error' as the answer.*

7. Had this notification/been amended earlier/we should have stopped/the transfer of funds.
(a) Had this notification (b) been amended earlier
(c) we should have stopped (d) the transfer of funds

8. Tendulkar would/bat even at/the age of three.
(a) Tendulkar would (b) bat even at
(c) the age of three (d) No error

9. We shall/respect our/elders.
(a) We shall (b) respect our
(c) elders (d) No error

10. I shall go to Dehradun tomorrow morning.
(a) I shall go (b) to Dehradun
(c) tomorrow morning (d) No error

11. You can listen to what the teacher says.
(a) listen to (b) what the teacher says
(c) You can (d) No error

12. One must not drink alcohol.
(a) drink alcohol (b) One must
(c) not (d) No error

13. I'm not sure. Kavita should be in Dehradun.
(a) I'm not sure. (b) Kavita should
(c) be in Dehradun (d) No error

14. Pragya is only wearing a T-shirt and it's 9 degrees. She may be freezing.
(a) Pragya is only wearing a T-shirt (b) and it's 9 degrees
(c) she may be freezing (d) No error

15. That lady mustn't be Mohini's mother as she looks just like her.
(a) just like her (b) That lady mustn't be
(c) Mohini's mother as she (d) No error

Directions (Q. Nos. 16-20) *In the following questions, some part of the sentence may have an error. Find out which part of the sentence has an error and select the appropriate option. If a sentence is free from error, select the option which says 'No error'.*

16. Will you (A)/mind if (B)/I ride with (C)/you to work? (D)/No error (E)
(a) E (b) A (c) B (d) C
(e) D

17. This isn't a difficult (A)/task, so you mustn't be (B)/able to complete it (C)/by Sunday. (D)/No error (E)
(a) A (b) C (c) B (d) E
(e) D

18. Nikhat could (A)/be crazy. (B)/He wants to go out (C)/without wearing a mask. (D)/No error (E)
(a) E (b) D (c) B (d) A
(e) C

19. Sameera wouldn't give me(A)/a straight answer. (B)/She avoided my questions (C)/the whole time. (D)/No error (E)
(a) A (b) B (c) C (d) E
(e) D

20. I wouldn't understand (A)/him because (B)/I don't (C)/speak German. (D)/No error (E)
(a) E (b) D (c) C (d) A
(E) B

Answers

Work Book Exercise A

1. (b)	**2.** (b)	**3.** (b)	**4.** (c)	**5.** (b)	**6.** (b)	**7.** (a)	**8.** (a)
9. (a)	**10.** (b)	**11.** (a)	**12.** (b)	**13.** (a)	**14.** (c)	**15.** (a)	**16.** (a)
17. (b)	**18.** (b)	**19.** (a)	**20.** (a)	**21.** (a)	**22.** (b)	**23.** (c)	**24.** (b)
25. (b)							

Work Book Exercise B

1. (b)	**2.** (a)	**3.** (c)	**4.** (c)	**5.** (b)	**6.** (a)	**7.** (b)	**8.** (a)
9. (c)	**10.** (b)	**11.** (c)	**12.** (a)	**13.** (b)	**14.** (a)	**15.** (a)	**16.** (a)
17. (b)	**18.** (c)	**19.** (b)	**20.** (a)				

Revision Exercise

1. *(d)* can't
2. *(d)* shouldn't
3. *(b)* could
4. *(c)* can't
5. *(d)* might
6. *(c)* couldn't
7. *(a)* have
8. *(d)* may
9. *(c)* have
10. *(d)* Replace 'should' by 'will'.
11. *(a)* Replace 'will' by 'may'.
12. *(e)* No error
13. *(c)* Use 'can' in place of 'would'.
14. *(e)* No error
15. *(b)* Use 'shouldn't' in place of 'should'.
16. *(c)* Use 'must' or 'ought to' in place of 'could'.
17. *(c)* Replace 'should' by 'can'.
18. *(b)* Use 'must' in place of 'may'.
19. *(a)* E
20. *(e)* Replace 'would' by 'could'.
21. *(e)* E
22. *(d)* Use 'will' in place of 'could'.
23. *(a)* Use 'would' in place of 'must'.
24. *(d)* Use 'can' in place of 'can't'.
25. *(d)* E

Exam Practice

1. *(b)* 'could' should be replaced by 'would'.
2. *(d)* No error
3. *(d)* No error
4. *(c)* 'to' is not needed in the sentence as 'dare' by itself conveys a negative meaning. Remove 'to'.
5. *(b)* 'lest' goes with 'should'. So, replace 'do not' with 'should'.
6. *(a)* Replace 'If the scheme would have' by 'Had this scheme'.
7. *(c)* Replace 'should' by 'would'.
8. *(a)* Replace 'would' by 'could'.
9. *(a)* Replace 'shall' by 'should' or 'must'.
10. *(d)* No error
11. *(c)* Replace 'can' by 'must'.
12. *(d)* No error
13. *(b)* Replace 'should' by 'may'.
14. *(c)* Use 'must' in place of 'may'.
15. *(b)* Use 'must' in place of 'mustn't'.
16. *(b)* Use 'Would' in place of 'Will'.
17. *(c)* Use 'should' in place of 'mustn't'.
18. *(d)* Replace 'could' by 'must'.
19. *(d)*
20. *(d)* Use 'couldn't' in place of 'wouldn't'.

Unit II

4

Kinds of Sentences and Clauses

What is a Clause?

A group of words that forms a part of a sentence and has a subject and a verb of its own is called a **clause**. *For example*

(i) When she wakes up. *(ii)* When the moon shone.
(iii) Who lived in a neighbouring village.

Generally, there are two types of clauses as mentioned below

(a) **Independent clause** It is a clause that can stand alone as a sentence. *For example*

(i) Even though I made millions, **I am still grounded**.
(ii) After he dies, **he'll be forgotten**.

(b) **Dependent clause** It is a clause that is usually a supporting part of a sentence. *For example*

(i) **Even though I made millions**, I am still grounded.
(ii) **After he dies**, he'll be forgotten.

Kinds of Sentences

There are three kinds of sentences as mentioned below

I. Simple sentence **II. Complex sentence** **III. Compound sentence**

I. **Simple Sentence** A sentence which has only one verb or one independent cause is a simple sentence. *For example*

(i) She is walking. *(ii)* He has written a letter to help his son.
(iii) Mary likes tea. *(iv)* The earth goes round the sun.

II. **Complex Sentence** A complex sentence consists of a principal/main clause with one or more subordinate clauses. It means that a complex sentence consists of an independent clause and a dependent clause. Sub-ordinate clauses are joined by sub-ordinating conjunctions.

For example

(i) I know that he is a good man.

(ii) I know the man who was here last month.

(iii) We missed our plane because we were late.

III. **Compound Sentence** A compound sentence consists of two or more principal or independent clauses. These clauses are joined by co-ordinating conjunctions such as
'and, but, so, therefore, otherwise, or, else, nor, while, for, whereas, still, yet, nevertheless, however, as well as, all the same, indeed but'.

The clauses of a compound sentence are called co-ordinate clauses. *For example*

(i) My brother came **and** he handed over money to me.

(ii) She is rich **but** she is not vain.

(iii) Speak **or** you will die.

(iv) She is ill **so** she will not come.

(v) She is intelligent **while** her sister is dull.

(vi) It was dark, **however** we went out.

(vii) He was convicted **as well as** fined.

(viii) I was feeling tired **all the same still** I went to office.

(ix) It is cold **indeed, but** I will go out.

More About a Complex Sentence

A Principal clause with one or more sub-ordinate clauses forms a complex sentence. There are three kinds of sub-ordinate clauses joined by their respective sub-ordinating conjunctions. *For example*

(a) I know that he is a good boy.

(b) I know the man who was here yesterday.

(c) He left in a hurry, after he got a phone call.

These sentences represent three kinds of sub-ordinate clauses,

1. **Noun Clause** In the sentence (a) 'I know' is a principal clause, 'that he is a good boy' is a noun clause.
   Noun clause explains the verb, noun and pronoun of the main or some other clause. (Explanation)
2. **Adjective Clause** In the sentence (b) 'I know the man' is a principal clause, 'who was here yesterday' is an adjective clause.
   Adjective clause qualifies an antecedent (noun or pronoun) as the case may be. (Qualification)
3. **Adverb Clause** In the sentence (c) 'He left in a hurry' is a principal clause, 'after he got a phone call' is an adverb clause.
   Adverb clause is required to modify a verb, adverb or adjective in the main or some other clause. (Modification)

More about Sub-ordinate Clauses

1. Noun Clause

Take care of the rules given below while writing a noun clause

(a) Use the conjunctions **'that, if, whether, when, where, how, why, what (whatever), who (whoever), whose, whom, which.'**

(b) Tense of the noun clause should be in the past if the verb of the main clause is in the past. If the tense is in present or future tense, the tense of the verb does not change. The tense of **universal truth** does not change.

(c) Noun clause should never be expressed in interrogative form.

Work Book Exercise A

Directions *Complete the following sentences with Noun clause.*

1. ***Object to a Transitive Verb***

1. I say ....
2. I said ....
3. I cannot say ....
4. She hinted ....
5. I don't know what ....
6. I know what ....
7. I wonder ....
8. I doubt ....
9. I am certain ....
10. The police suspected ....

NOTE When noun clause begins with interrogative pronouns (conjunctions of noun clause) and is followed by principal clause, 'that' is used before interrogative pronouns : 'what, when, where' etc.

For example

(i) She says that when he will come is uncertain.

(ii) She said that whether she would pass was doubtful.

2. ***The Case in Apposition to a Noun or a Pronoun*** *(Apposition means placing near)*

1. She never believed in his statement ....
2. No one heard the news ....
3. It is true ....
4. It is not known ....

3. ***The Subject of a Verb***

Noun clause as a subject is used in place of pronouns **'it, this, that'**?

For example

It is true **what he knows.**

What he knows is true.

1. What you are doing ....
2. Whether he will come ....
3. How she disappeared ....
4. That he is honest ....

NOTE Some other examples include

(i) Where she came from or where she lived is difficult to tell.

(ii) What he says and what he does are difficult to tell.

4. ***Object of Infinitive, Participle and Preposition***

1. I was pleased by .... **2.** Listen to ....

3. Everybody was pleased to note ....

4. Good students ought to realise ....

5. She kept on asking ....

5. ***Complement of a Verb***

1. The hope is .... **2.** The fact is ....

NOTE Noun clause following the verbs—**'to be, become, seem, appear, grow, taste, smell, prove, look, make'**, etc.—perform the function of a complement of these verbs (in place of predicate).

2. Adjective Clause

While writing an adjective clause, observe the following rules

(a) Adjective clause should be placed after the **antecedent** (noun/pronoun) qualified by the adjective clause. **'Those' is used for 'They' and 'Them' as an antecedent.**

(b) The verb of the adjective clause should be (singular/plural) in accordance with the antecedent.

(c) Use of **connectives** (relative pronouns)

Who, whose, whom	for living beings.
Which, of which	for non-living things and animals.
'That' may be used	for 'who & which'. **But** 'that' is usually used if the **antecedent** is preceded by **'the same, all, only, nothing, little, few, superlative degree, interrogative pronoun, some, any.'**
'As' is used	after **'the same or such' in place of who or which**. [Refer to Note (2) under the Box]
'Why' is used 'When' is used 'Where' is used 'How' is used	after **reason** as an antecedent. after **time** as an antecedent. after **place** as an antecedent. after **manner** as an antecedent.

NOTE

1. Conjunctions '**when, why, where, how**', used in adjective clause are **relative adverbs.** They express their meanings as follows
   1. I remember the year **when** she was married. *(in which year)*
   2. She explained the reason **why** she had to tell a lie. *(for which reason)*
   3. Has he told you the place **where** the accident took place? *(at which place)*
   4. She told me **how** her sister completed the work. *(in which manner)*
2. **The use of 'As' and 'That' with the 'Same'** *(is what way/manner)*

   (I) **'That' is used when 'The same'** is used with a noun both in the case of qualification and resemblance.

   (i) I shall buy the same perfume that my friend bought. *(resemblance)*

   (ii) She is the same girl that asked me for books yesterday. *(qualification)*

(II) **'As' is used when 'The same'** is used either without a noun or when the verb is unexpressed in the case of resemblance.

(i) Just do the same as I do. *(resemblance)*

(ii) I like the same perfume as she. (likes) *(resemblance)*

Work Book Exercise B

Directions *Complete the following sentences with Adjective clause.*

1. I know the man ....
2. This is my pen ....
3. I don't know any man ....
4. He is a man ....
5. I have met all the boys ....
6. This is the best book ....
7. I have invited Mohan whose ....
8. I have invited Mohan whom ....
9. He is the man whose leg ....
10. It is the table the leg of which...... .

3. Adverb Clause

Adverb clause does the work of an adverb. It modifies some verb, adverb or adjective in the main clause. Adverb clause may be classified as follows:

(A) Adverb Clause of Time
(B) Adverb Clause of Condition
(C) Adverb Clause of Purpose
(D) Adverb Clause of Place
(E) Adverb Clause of Result
(F) Adverb Clause of Reason
(G) Adverb Clause of Concession or Contrast
(H) Adverb Clause of Manner
(I) Adverb Clause of Comparison

(A) Adverb Clause of Time

(a) This clause is introduced by conjunctions of time such as **'when, whenever, as soon as, as, while, before, after, by the time, until, till, since, ever since, as long as.'**

(b) One should be careful in distinguishing between simultaneous and preceding / succeeding actions. Preceding action should be expressed in perfect tense as the case may be.

NOTE Future tense in an adverb clause becomes **Present**.

Study the following sentences carefully

(i) When she will arrive, she will tell us about the expedition. *(Change 'will arrive' to 'arrives')*

(ii) When he completed the letter, he posted it. *(Change 'completed' to 'had completed')*

(iii) As the teacher arrived, the students stood up. *(Correct)*

(c) **Avoid the use of 'not' in the clause beginning with 'until'.**
Please do not go until I return. *(Correct)*

(d) Clause beginning with 'since, ever since' should be in Past Indefinite/Past Perfect tense and the main clause should be according to the rules of time expression. (Perfect tense or perfect continuous) *For example*

(i) Since she came to Nagpur, she has not met me.

(ii) Since I returned from America, I have been working here.

Study the following sentences carefully

(i) I can't say when he will go. *(Noun clause)*

(ii) I know the time when he will go. *(Adjective clause)*

(iii) I shall give you money when you return my book. *(Adverb clause)*

(iv) It has been a long time since we met. *(Correct)*

(v) It had been a long time since I had met her. *(Correct)*

(B) Adverb Clause of Condition

(a) There are three types of conditional clauses. Each kind contains a different pair of sequences as follows

Condition	Conditional Clause	Principal Clause
(i) Present likely condition	Present Indefinite	Shall/will
(ii) Present unlikely condition/ Regret, wish	Subjunctive mood	Should/would
(iii) Past condition	Past Perfect	(Would, should, could, might) + have

Present Likely

(i) If he runs, he will get here soon.

(ii) You will pass if you work hard.

Present unlikely/Regret, wish

(i) If I had a stamp, I would give it to you.

(ii) If I were rich, I would help you.

(iii) I wish I were a queen.

(iv) If I knew her address, I woud send her a message.

Past Condition

(i) If she had written the letter, she would have replied yesterday.

(ii) If she had brought money, she could have enjoyed the picnic.

(b) Conditional clauses are introduced with following connectives **'If, unless, I wish, would that, I would, if only, suppose, on condition that, provided, in case.** *For example*

(i) If you come by car, we will take you to temple.

(ii) In case you don't waste time, you can live here.

(c) Sometimes sub-ordinate conjunction 'if' is omitted in adverb clause of condition. (**'Should, were, had'** are used instead.) *For example*

(i) **Should** you work hard, you will pass. *(Present condition)*

(ii) **Were** she intelligent, she would not do it. *(Present unlikely condition)*

(iii) **Had** I done it, I would not have repented. *(Past condition)*

(d) **Avoid the use of 'not' in the clause beginning with 'unless'.**
You will not pass unless you work hard.

(e) **'Would that, I wish, I would and if only'** are used to express regret or dissatisfaction with the present. Such expressions are expressed in **subjunctive mood**. *For example*

(i) Would that he could have listened to his father.
(ii) I wish I had money now.
(iii) If only I hadn't met her last year.
(iv) I wish I had money then.

NOTE **'Would'**, should be used when the subjects of the clauses differ, *e.g.*,
I wish you would help my brother.

(C) Adverb Clause of Purpose

Adverb clause of purpose is introduced by the conjunctions **'that, so that, in order that, lest'**. *For example*

(i) He goes to Delhi every month **so that** he may see his ailing father.
(ii) She came **in order that** she might borrow money.
(iii) Work hard **lest** you should fail.

NOTE **'Not'** is avoided in a clause beginning with **lest**

(D) Adverb Clause of Place

Adverb clause of place is introduced by the conjunctions **'where & wherever'** but it does not qualify any place given in the main clause.
For example

(i) I shall go to Delhi where my father lives. (It is an adjective clause because it qualifies the noun 'Delhi')
(ii) I shall follow you wherever you go. *(Adverb clause)*
(iii) I do not know where he lives. *(Noun clause)*

(E) Adverb Clause of Result

Adverb clause of result is expressed by **'that'** in the adverb clause preceded by **'so'**, **'such'** in the main clause. *For example*

(i) He was **so** late **that** he had to miss the dinner.
(ii) He is **such** an intelligent boy **that** he can easily pass.

(F) Adverb Clause of Reason

Adverb clause of reason is introduced by **'because, since, as, now that, that.'**

(i) I did it because my father told me to do it.
(ii) As he was absent, he was punished.
(iii) Since she came late, so she was fined. *(Remove 'so')*
(iv) I am happy that you are successful. *('That' means because)*

NOTE '**So**' and '**therefore**' should be avoided in the main clause.

(G) Adverb Clause of Concession or Contrast

Adverb clause of contrast is introduced by **'Although, though, even if, however, whatever, no matter what, no matter how, no matter where, no matter that etc., notwithstanding that, admitting that, as, whether, even though, much as, come what may, say what you will'.**

For example

(i) Though she is rich, she is unhappy.
(ii) Rich as she is, she is not happy.
(iii) Even if it is cold, I shall go.
(iv) Though he was intelligent, he failed.
(v) No matter what I say, nobody listens to me.
(vi) I shall do it whether you like it or not.
(vii) Much as I like to give you money, I can't do so.
(viii) However rich he may be, he is not kind.

NOTE The main clause following the adverb clause of contrast should not begin with **'but, nevertheless and still'.** A student may write the main clause with **'yet'**.

(H) Adverb Clause of Manner

Adverb clause of manner is introduced by **'as, as if and as though'.**

Conjunctions **'as if'** and **'as though'** are used to express **a contrary to fact statement. Subjunctive mood** is used in this kind of statements.

For example

(i) She did it as she was advised.
(ii) She talks as if she were the landlady.
(iii) She talks as if she had belonged to a very rich family before her marriage.
(iv) He looks as if he is my brother.

NOTE *In sentence (iv), manner clause is not a contrary to fact statement. It means that he looks* ***like*** *my brother. (Resemblance)*

(I) Adverb Clause of Comparison

Adverb clause of comparison is introduced by **'than'** and **'as'**.

Comparison should be made **between the same cases of pronouns or between two persons or things being** compared.

For example

(i) She is as good as he is. *(Affirmative)*
(ii) She is not so active as they are. *(Negative)*
(iii) She is as intelligent like her brother. *('like' is a preposition, use 'as')*
(iv) He is wiser than me. *(Use 'I' in place of 'me')*
(v) My house is larger than her. *(Use 'hers'/'her house' in place of 'her')*
(vi) The price of my book is less than your book. *(Insert 'that of' after 'than')*
(vii) I found her smarter than he. *(Use 'him' in place of 'he')*

Work Book Exercise C

Directions *Fill up the proper forms of verbs/alternatives to make Adverb clause.*

1. When you ……… the book, I shall help you. *(write)*

2. I will do this work when you ……… me to do it. *(ask)*

3. As I ……… the bus stand, the bus arrived. *(reach)*

4. As soon as the teacher ……… the classroom, the boys stand up. *(enter)*

5. When you ……… your exams, I shall take you to hill station. *(take)*

6. When she ……… the letter, she posted it. *(write)*

7. My brother ……… before we took our dinner. *(come)*

8. My brother ……… by the time we took our dinner. *(come)*

9. After we ……… our dinner, my brother came. *(take)*

10. My brother will come after we ……… our dinner. *(take)*

11. We ……… our dinner when the guest arrived. *(take)*

12. Since my father ………for Mumbai, he has not written to me. *(leave)*

13. Since she arrived, she ………from cold. *(suffer)*

14. She ………ill since she arrived. *(be)*

15. While it ……… ,no one went out. *(rain)*

16. He will not come until you ………this place. *(leave)*

17. As long as you ……… in the town, he will not return. *(be)*

18. Many students ………by the time the match begins. *(arrive)*

19. Many students ……… by the time the match began. *(arrive)*

20. Please wait till I ……… . *(go)*

21. If you ………hard, you will pass. *(work)*

22. If it ………tomorrow, we shall not sail. *(rain)*

23. Unless you ……… hard, you will not pass. *(work)*

24. If I ……… his address, I would tell you now. *(know)*

25. If I ……… money, I would give you. *(have)*

26. If it ……… possible, I would help him. *(be)*

27. I wish I ……… present there tomorrow. *(be)*

28. Were I a doctor, I ………him. *(treat)*

29. If I ……… his address, I would have told you then. *(know)*

30. If I ……… money , I would have given you. *(have)*

Revision Exercises

(Based on Noun, Adjective and Adverb Clauses)

Exercise A

(Based on Noun and Adjective Clauses)

Directions *Correct the following sentences*

1. He believed that he will turn out to be a cheat.
2. Why he came is difficult to understand.
3. I cannot say that he has passed.
4. It was difficult to pretend that I am penniless.
5. We did not see that man in the room who was standing in the corner.
6. Please go and ask him that he is going there.
7. I did not know that why is he not staying there.
8. No such boy who is living here will do this.
9. You should follow the same method which he does.
10. Let us help them who are in greater need than he.
11. What you did it cannot be pardoned.
12. All the books what you bought are not upto the mark.
13. There was every reason to believe that he has changed.
14. Tell me the reason that they could not marry.
15. It is better to write with a pen whose nib is smooth.
16. The boy who you know is not going there.
17. He gave me a book and which I like very much.
18. He told me that he saw his father last month.
19. I doubt that you can pass the examination.
20. I cannot say as to why he was annoyed.

Exercise B

(Based on Adverb Clause)

1. I shall do this work when you will pay me.
2. I shall lend you my car if you will not misuse it.
3. I would have believed if I saw with my own eyes yesterday.
4. If I were you, I shall never help him.
5. If she had a book yesterday, she would not have refused to give.
6. Nothing is so good like we think.
7. You have done it because I forbade you.
8. Carry it carefully lest it will break.
9. Let us not behave as though we are indifferent to others.

10. When you complete this work, I shall buy you sweets.
11. By the time the sun set he typed all letters.
12. I have not seen her since she has come back from Delhi.
13. Unless she does not mends her behaviour, I shall send her out.
14. After you go through the book, please return it to me.
15. As she is obstinate so she will not obey you.
16. The child is out since her mother went to market.
17. Though he ran fast still he could not escape from the police.
18. He is a good student but I have much pleasure in granting him scholarship.
19. He started early because he might not get late.
20. He had reached office before it started raining.

Exercise C

(Based on Miscellaneous Clauses)

1. I know something what my mother told you.
2. I cannot say what is she doing these days.
3. Maruti is one of those motor car which are liked very much.
4. I doubt that my father will help you.
5. She was singing which I did not like it.
6. Don't go out until you are not well.
7. Sanskrit is one of the oldest languages that was spoken by the Aryans.
8. Have you ever met such a boy who has not travelled by train?
9. She behaves with her neighbour as though she is the landlady.
10. He said that what he was doing was not correct.
11. I shall come back by the time you get up.
12. It is the tree whose fruit is not sweet.
13. Though he ran fast still he could not escape from the police.
14. When she will marry, she will invite you.
15. Who knows that when will the result be out?
16. When you complete your service, you will be retired on pension.
17. You must carry on so that you will succeed.
18. Twelve years passed since his uncle has died.
19. He cannot see clearly unless he will wear his glasses.
20. Don't go out until you complete the work.

Answers

Work Book Exercise A

Object to a Transitive Verb

1. I say that she is intelligent.
2. I said that he was very smart.
3. I cannot say if/whether she will go.
4. She hinted that she would not go.
5. I don't know what she is doing these days.
6. I know what you like.
7. I wonder what she is doing.
8. I doubt whether/if she will marry at all.
9. I am certain that she will marry him.
10. The police suspected that he was the culprit.

The case in Apposition to a Noun or a Pronoun

1. She never believed in his statement that he would get her a job.
2. No one heard the news that the Prime Minister had resigned.
3. It is true that she will succeed.
4. It is not known how she arrived.

The Subject of a Verb

1. What are you doing is not desirable.
2. Whether he will come is not certain.
3. How she disappeared is a mystery.
4. That he is honest is known to us.

Object of Infinitive, Participle and Preposition

1. I was pleased by what she did for us.
2. Listen to what your teacher tells you.
3. Everybody was pleased to note that she looked cheerful at the party.
4. Good students ought to realise that hard work is the key to success.
5. She kept on asking where I was going.

Complement of a Verb

1. The hope is that his son will return.
2. The fact is that he is honest.

Work Book Exercise B

1. I know the man who came here.
2. This is my pen which I gave you.
3. I don't know any man that is present here.
4. He is a man who will never cheat you.
5. I have met all the boys that have been admitted to the hostel.
6. This is the best book that I have ever read.
7. I have invited Mohan whose father is a famous doctor.
8. I have invited Mohan whom all of us admire.
9. He is the man whose leg is amputed.
10. It is the table the leg of which is broken.

Work Book Exercise C

1. write
2. ask
3. reached
4. enters
5. had taken
6. had written
7. had come
8. had come
9. had taken
10. have already taken
11. had already taken
12. left
13. has been suffering
14. has been
15. was raining

16. leave
17. are
18. will have arrived
19. had arrived
20. go
21. work
22. rains
23. work
24. knew
25. had
26. were
27. were
28. would treat
29. had known
30. had had

Revision Exercises

(Based on Noun, Adjective and Adverb Clause)

Exercise A

1. 'would' in place of 'will'
2. No error.
3. 'if/whether' in place of 'that'
4. 'was' in place of 'am'
5. Place 'in the room' before 'we'
6. 'if' in place of 'that'
7. Say 'why he was not staying there'
8. 'as' in place of 'who'
9. 'that' in place of 'which'
10. 'those' in place of 'them'
11. Drop 'it'
12. 'that' in place of 'what'
13. 'had' in place of 'has'
14. 'why' in place of 'that'
15. 'the nib of which' in place of 'whose nib'
16. 'whom' in place of 'who'
17. Delete 'and'.
18. 'had seen' in place of 'saw'
19. 'if' in place of 'that'
20. Drop 'as to'

Exercise B

1. Drop 'will'
2. 'do not' in place of 'will not'
3. 'had seen' in place of 'saw'
4. 'should' in place of 'shall'
5. 'if she had had' in place of 'if she had'
6. 'as' in place of 'like'
7. 'although' in place of 'because'
8. 'should' in place of 'will'
9. No error
10. 'will have completed' in place of 'complete'.
11. 'had typed' in place of 'typed'
12. 'came' in place of 'has come'
13. Drop 'does not'
14. 'have gone' in place of 'go'
15. Drop 'so'
16. 'has been' in place of 'is'
17. Drop 'still'
18. 'and' in place of 'but'
19. 'so that' in place of 'because'
20. No error

Exercise C

1. 'that' in place of 'what' or remove 'something'
2. 'she is doing' in place of 'is she doing'
3. 'cars' in place of 'car'
4. 'if' in place of 'that'
5. 'and' in place of 'which'
6. Drop 'not'
7. No error
8. No error
9. 'were' in place of 'is'
10. No error
11. 'shall have' in place of 'shall'
12. 'the fruit of which' in place of 'whose fruit'
13. Drop 'still'
14. 'marries' in place of 'will marry'
15. Drop 'that' and 'will' after 'result'.
16. 'have completed' in place of 'complete'
17. 'may' in place of 'will'
18. Insert 'have' after 'years' and remove 'has'
19. 'wears' in place of 'will wear'
20. 'have completed' in place of 'complete'

5

Clause Analysis

As already stated in chapter on clauses a number of finite verbs in a sentence determine a number of clauses. Here, remember that Non- finite verbs are not considered for the purpose of clause analysis.

1. In a **simple sentence**, there is one finite verb and hence only one clause.
For example
(i) She **is writing** a novel.
(ii) Pearl **will examine** a patient.

2. In a **complex sentence**, there is more than one clause as follows
(a) Principal/Main clause
(b) Sub-ordinate clauses
(i) Noun clause,
(ii) Adjective clause and
(iii) Adverb clause.

These sub-ordinate clauses are joined by sub-ordinating conjunctions (Look up chapter 4, based on clauses)

3. In a **compound sentence**, there are more than one principal clause/co-ordinate clause related to each other.

Co-ordinate clause is joined by co-ordinating conjunctions (Look up chapter 4, based on clauses)

NOTE However, when a co-ordinating conjunction joins two sub-ordinate clauses, the sentence remains a complex sentence. *For example*
(i) I told her that she was polite and her sister was humble. (*Complex*)
(ii) I told her that she was not polite and advised her to improve her behaviour. (*Compound*)

How to Find out Clauses?

Now let us study how to analyse a sentence by pointing out the clauses separately and defining their functions.

1. Principal/Main Clause

While analysing a sentence, a student is required to find out a **Principal clause**. It is easy to do so because the principal clause is not introduced by any joining conjunction.

Having found out the **principal clause** a student is expected to break up the rest of the sentence into **sub-ordinate /co-ordinate clauses.**

2. Sub-ordinate Clauses

(i) Noun clause, *(ii)* Adjective clause and
(iii) Adverb clause.

3. Co-ordinate Clause

NOTE Refer to Chapter 4 (on Clauses) for the detailed study of the clauses before attempting the following questions.

The Manners of Conjunctions

Some of the conjunctions, denoting different meanings, have been used in the following sentences. As a result of this they form different clauses

1. I asked him **when he would go there.** *(Noun clause)*
2. I know the time **when he will come.** *(Adjective clause)*
3. He will give me money **when I go to Mumbai.** *(Adverb clause)*
4. I shall not tell you **where he lives.** *(Noun clause)*
5. I shall go to the place **where my friend lives.** *(Adjective clause)*
6. I shall go **where my friend lives.** *(Adverb clause)*
7. I do not know **if he will come.** *(Noun clause)*
8. You will pass **if you work hard.** *(Adverb clause)*
9. I do not know **who came here last night.** *(Noun clause)*
10. I know the boy **who came here last night.** *(Adjective clause)*
11. I know the man **whom every body likes.** *(Adjective clause)*
12. I do not know **whom she is teaching.** *(Noun clause)*
13. I cannot say **whose book this is.** *(Noun clause)*
14. I have invited my friends **whose parents are in India.** *(Adjective clause)*
15. Do you know **which his house is.** *(Noun clause)*
16. I know the house **which he got built last year.** *(Adjective clause)*
17. He gave me the same book **that I wanted.** *(Adjective clause)*
18. I know **that he will come.** *(Noun clause)*
19. I know the boy **that lives there.** *(Adjective clause)*
20. I am happy that **she is successful.** *(Adverbs clause)*
21. We come here **that we may study.** *(Adverb clause)*

22. He is so weak **that he cannot run.** *(Adverb clause)*
23. He is such a weak boy **that he cannot run.** *(Adverb clause)*
24. He is such a boy **who does not help anybody.** *(Adjective clause)*
25. Since my brother came, he has been teaching. *(Adverb clause)*
26. Since she is ill, she cannot go out. *(Adverb clause)*
27. As I arrived at the station, the train left. *(Adverb clause)*
28. As he was late, he missed the bus. *(Adverb clause)*
29. She is as intelligent **as her brother is.** *(Adverb clause)*
30. Rich as he is, he is not happy. *(Adverb clause)*
31. She did it **as I advised her to do.** *(Adverb clause)*
32. My house is the same as **yours(is).** *(Adjective clause)*
33. I shall do **whatever he says.** *(Noun clause)*
34. I shall do it **whatever you may say.** *(Adverb clause)*
35. I cannot say **what he is talking about.** *(Noun clause)*
36. He told me **what his father had told him.** *(Noun clause)*
37. I do not know **whether he will come tomorrow.** *(Noun clause)*
38. I shall do it **whether you like it or not.** *(Adverb clause)*
39. While it was raining, nobody went out. *(Adverb clause)*
40. She is intelligent **while her brother is dull.** *(Co-ordinate clause)*
41. I do not know **why he will not come.** *(Noun clause)*
42. This is the reason **why he has not passed.** *(Adjective clause)*
43. It was dark, however we went out.
44. However honest he may be he is not respected.

Work Book Exercise A

Directions *Find out the **Noun clause** and mention the function as explained in the foregoing examples. Translate them in your mother language as well.*

1. I say that she is intelligent.
2. I cannot say if she will go.
3. I did not know whether she would go.
4. It is certain that she will marry him.
5. I do not know what she is doing these days.
6. I shall not do what you want me to do.
7. What he says is not correct.
8. I was pleased by what she did for us.
9. She never believed in his statement that he would get her a job.
10. Everybody was pleased to note that she looked cheerful at the party.

Work Book Exercise B

Directions *Below are given the sentences for the students to find out* ***Adjective clause*** *stating the Noun or Pronoun qualified by them. Translate them in your own mother tongue as well.*

1. I know the man who came here.
2. This is my pen which I gave you.
3. I don't know any man that is present here.
4. He is such a man who will never cheat you.
5. The boys that have been admitted to the hostel belong to Bhopal.
6. This is the best book that I have ever read.
7. I have invited Mohan whose father is a famous doctor.
8. I have invited Ashok whom all of us admire.
9. The table the leg of which is broken is very costly.
10. The news he gave is wrong.

Work Book Exercise C

Directions *Each of the following sentences contain an Adverb clause. Pick out the* ***Adverb clause*** *stating its kind and the word it modifies. Translate them in your own mother tongue as well.*

1. When you write the book, I shall help you.
2. My brother had come before we took our dinner.
3. After we had taken our dinner, my brother came.
4. Since she arrived, she has been suffering from cold.
5. He will not come until you leave this place.
6. Please wait till I go.
7. He works hard so that he may stand first.
8. Walk carefully lest you should fall.
9. She worked so hard that she could get first class.
10. If you work hard, you will pass.

Miscellaneous Exercise

Directions *Analyse the following sentences pointing out the kind of clauses. Also state their functions.*

1. The boy stated that his brother would not come.
2. The boy who lives here said that his brother would not come.
3. The boy who lives here told us that his brother who was a doctor and whom they had called would not come.
4. We don't know how our ancestors led their lives in great difficulties when there were no comforts of life.
5. We, who live in the present age do not know how our ancestors led their lives in ancient India.
6. We do not know whether our ancestors led their lives in great difficulties but we are certain of their problems.
7. The house that was constructed by me has been rented to the student who came yesterday.
8. The persons who do wrong to others are always humiliated by those whom they wrong.
9. Once he said that he could not do the work his brother was doing as he was illiterate.
10. He told us that he had read the book which was written by Tagore.
11. He was ordered that he would not go out until the rain had stopped.
12. Those who do not respect others don't know that others will not respect them unless they respect others.
13. I doubt if he said that those who would not come in time would not get food.
14. We cannot say anything about any religion unless we agree that all the religions teach us to be compassionate.
15. Those who do not help others unless their motive is fulfilled are called selfish.
16. I did not tell him that I would not help those boys who did not work hard.
17. I don't know how this came to be so although I must confess that if I had inquired I could have found out why he acted so selfishly.
18. He tells everybody that nobody will help and give him money because nobody believes him.
19. She told me that if I gave her book she would be grateful to me.
20. Satya knows very well that when her husband returns from office she will be asked to leave the house.
21. Will you ever forget her who stood by you when you were in trouble and will not write to her?
22. She hoped that she would inherit the property of her sister who had no offspring.
23. The statement that she was absent when the police came was not believed by her friends who suspected her complicity in the crime.
24. Hardy believed that the forces that govern human destiny were still in the making.
25. The robbers warned him that if he informed the police of the happening he would be in trouble again.
26. History is a witness to the fact that there had never been a strong central authority to rule over our country that remained under foreign domination for ages.
27. I have no pity for a man who, you know very well, told me that he had lost courage when disaster befell him.
28. Mr. Patel asked his party men to find out if they could launch agitation when the British Government was torn with internal problems.

29. He told the little girl that throwing banana onto a pavement was a bad habit because any pedestrian could slip on it.

30. You should be content and pleased with what you have these days since to complain of high prices does not speak well of you.

Miscellaneous Exercise

1. (a) The boy stated..........Principal clause.
(b) that his brother would not come..........Noun clause, object to the transitive verb 'stated'. *(The sentence is complex.)*

2. (a) The boy (...) said..........Principal clause.
(b) who lives here..........Adjective clause, qualifying the noun 'the boy'.
(c) that his brother would not come..........Noun clause, object to the transitive verb 'said'. *(The sentence is complex.)*

3. (a) The boy told us..........Principal clause.
(b) who lives here..........Adjective clause, qualifying the noun 'the boy'.
(c) that his brother (...) would not come..........Noun clause, object to the transitive verb 'told'.
(d) who was a doctor........Adjective clause, qualifying the noun 'brother'.
(e) and whom they had called.......Co-ordinate clause to 'd'. *(The sentence is complex.)*

8. (a) The persons (...) are always humiliated by those..........Principal clause.
(b) who do wrong to others..........Adjective clause, qualifying the noun 'persons'.
(c) whom they wrong..........Qualifying the pronoun 'those'. *(The sentence is complex.)*

12. (a) Those (...) don't know..........Principal clause.
(b) who do not respect others..........Adjective clause, qualifying the pronoun 'those'.
(c) that others will not respect them—Noun clause, object to the transitive verb 'know'.
(d) unless they respect others..........Adverb clause of condition, modifying the verb 'respect'. *(The sentence is complex.)*

17. (a) I don't know..........Principal clause.
(b) how this came to be so..........Noun clause, object to the transitive verb 'know'.
(c) although I must confess..........Adverb clause of contrast, modifying the verb 'don't know'.
(d) that (...) I could have found out..........Noun clause, object to the transitive verb 'confess'.
(e) If I had inquired..........Adverb clause of condition, modifying the verb 'found'.
(f) why he acted so selfishly..........Noun clause, object to the transitive verb 'found'. *(The sentence is complex.)*

19. (a) She told me..........Principal clause.
(b) that she would be grateful to me..........Noun clause, object to the verb 'told'.
(c) If I gave her a book..........Adverb clause, modifying 'would be grateful'.

23. (a) The statement (...) was not believed by her friends..........Principal clause.
(b) that she was absent..........Noun clause, Apposition to the noun 'the statement'.
(c) when the police came..........Adverb clause of time, modifying the verb 'was'.
(d) who suspected her complicity in the crime—Adjective clause, qualifying the noun 'the friends'. *(The sentence is complex.)*

30. (a) You should be content..........Principal clause.
(b) and pleased with..........Co-ordinate to principal clause.
(c) what you have these days..........Noun clause, object to the preposition 'with'.
(d) since to complain of high prices does not speak well of you.......... Adverb clause of reason, modifying the verb 'should be'. *(The sentence is compound.)*

Answers

Work Book Exercise A

1. that she is intelligent ....'Noun Clause', object to the verb 'say'.
2. if she will go.........'Noun Clause', object to the verb 'say'.
3. whether she would go ....'Noun Clause', object to the verb 'know'.
4. that she will marry him ....'Noun Clause', In apposition to 'it'.
5. what she is doing ....'Noun Clause', object to the verb 'know'.
6. what you want me to do ....'Noun Clause', object to the verb 'do'.
7. what he says ....'Noun Clause', subject of the verb 'is'.
8. what she did for us ....'Noun Clause', object to the preposition 'by'.
9. that he would get her a job ....'Noun Clause', case in apposition to the 'statement'.
10. that she looked cheerful at the party ....'Noun Clause', object to infinitive 'to note'.

Work Book Exercise B

1. who came here ....'Adjective Clause' qualifying the noun 'man'.
2. which I gave you ....'Adjective Clause' qualifying the noun 'pen'.
3. that is present here ....'Adjective Clause' qualifying the noun 'any man',
4. as will never cheat you ....'Adjective Clause' qualifying the noun 'such a man'.
5. that have been admitted to the hostel ....'Adjective Clause' qualifying the noun 'all the boys'.
6. that I have ever read ....'Adjective Clause' qualifying the noun 'the best book'.
7. whose father is a famous doctor.........'Adjective Clause' qualifying the noun ' Mohan'.
8. (Whom) all of us admire ....'Adjective Clause' qualifying the noun 'Ashok'.
9. the leg of which is broken ....'Adjective Clause' qualifying the noun 'the table'.
10. (That) he gave ....'Adjective Clause' qualifying the noun 'the news'.

Work Book Exercise C

1. when you write the book ....'Adverb Clause' of time, modifying the verb 'help'.
2. before we took our dinner.........'Adverb Clause' of time, modifying the verb 'had come'.
3. after we had taken our dinner.........'Adverb Clause' of time, modifying the verb 'came'.
4. since she arrived ....'Adverb Clause' of time, modifying the verb 'suffering'.
5. until you leave this place ....'Adverb Clause' of time, modifying the verb 'come'.
6. till I go ....'Adverb Clause' of time, modifying the verb 'wait'.
7. so that he may stand first ....'Adverb Clause' of purpose, modifying the verb 'work hard'.
8. lest you should fall ....'Adverb Clause' of purpose, modifying the verb 'walk'.
9. that she could get first class ....'Adverb Clause' of result, modifying the verb 'worked'.
10. If you work hard ....'Adverb Clause' of condition, modifying the verb 'pass'.

6

Question Tags

Definition

Question tags are not complete questions in itself. These are a form of questions attached with a statement. They acts as a confirmation to the statements. Question tags are also used in everyday life conversations in order to seek the attention of the listener.

Types

(a) **Positive Question Tags** Tags are said to be positive if they are attached to negative statements. *For example*

(i) She is not working, is she?
  - She is not working ⇒ Negative statement
  - is she? ⇒ Positive tag

(ii) They had not gone there, had they?
  - They had not gone there ⇒ Negative statement
  - had they? ⇒ Positive tag

(b) **Negative Question Tags** Tags are said to be negative if they are attached to positive statements. *For example*

(i) We are reading, aren't we ?
  - We are reading ⇒ Positive statement
  - aren't we ? ⇒ Negative tag

(ii) You will do this job, won't you?
  - You will do this job ⇒ Positive statement
  - won't you? ⇒ Negative tag

NOTE **Statement Positive** Tag Negative
Statement Negative Tag Positive

Structure of Tags

(a) Structure of a positive tag
Auxiliary + Subject + ?

(b) Structure of a negative tag
Auxiliary + not + Subject + ?

Work Book Exercise A

Complete the following by using suitable tags

1. He isn't going to do it, ...
2. You enjoyed that, ...
3. He doesn't write very well, ...
4. We love it, ...
5. It doesn't work, ...
6. They don't live in Liverpool, ...
7. She works in sales, ...
8. It looks perfect there, ...
9. We went there last year, ...
10. I don't know him, ...

Rules Regarding the Formation of Tags

Rule **1** Subject of a tag can never be a noun. It is always a pronoun. *For example*

(i) Ram is doing maths, isn't he ?
Ram ⇓ Noun; he ⇓ Pronoun

(ii) Parul has not eaten, has she ?
Parul ⇓ Noun; she ⇓ Pronoun

Rule **2** Question tag never starts with a capital letter.

Rule **3** The auxiliary that is to be used in the formation of a tag must be in the contracted form. This holds good only in the case of a negative tag.

Here is the list of those contracted auxiliaries

do + not = don't	does + not = doesn't
did + not = didn't	is + not = isn't
are + not = aren't	has + not = hasn't
have + not = haven't	had + not = hadn't
was + not = wasn't	were + not = weren't
shall + not = shan't	will + not = won't
can + not = can't	may + not = mayn't
could + not = couldn't	might + not = mightn't
should + not = shouldn't	would + not = wouldn't
ought + not = oughtn't	must + not = mustn't
used + not = usedn't	need + not = needn't
dare + not = daren't	

Exception *'Am I'* not is not written as 'amn't I' but it is written as *'aren't I'*.

Rule **4** In case auxiliary is not there in the statement then [do/does/did] is used in the tag. *For examples*

(i) She plays chess beautifully.

In the above sentence, there is no auxiliary used. When we are to make its tag then we shall use one out of the three auxiliaries (do/does/did). *For example*

She plays chess beautifully, doesn't she?
⇓
Auxiliary

(ii) We play fair.

We play fair, don't they?
⇓
Auxiliary

(iii) They went to the park.

They went to the park, didn't they?
⇓
Auxiliary

NOTE $(\text{Verb})_1 \rightarrow \text{Do} + (\text{Verb})_1$
$(\text{Verb})_1 + \text{s / es} \rightarrow \text{Does} + (\text{Verb})_1$
$(\text{Verb})_2 \rightarrow \text{Did} + (\text{Verb})_1$

Apply the above method in writing tags for those sentences that don't have an auxiliary with them.

Rule **5** Statements that use the following are considered negative and hence, tag to these statements will be positive

Barely, Hardly, No, Neither, None, Nobody, No one, Nothing, Seldom, Scarcely, Rarely.

For example

(i) He had nothing, had he?
Negative word ⇓ — Positive tag ⇓

(ii) She seldom weeps, does she?
Negative word ⇓ — Positive tag ⇓

Rule **6** If the statement has an introductory subject with it then the subject of the tag becomes as follows

Subject of Statement	Subject of Tag
This	It
That	It
These	They
Those	They

One | One
There | There
It | It

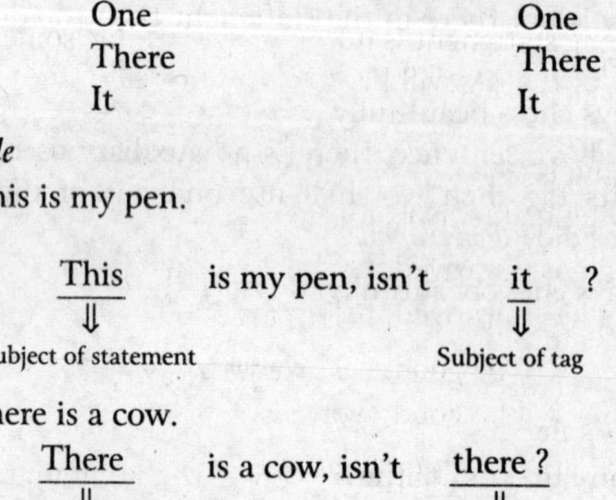

For example

(*i*) This is my pen.

This is my pen, isn't it ?
(This ⇓ Subject of statement; it ⇓ Subject of tag)

(*ii*) There is a cow.

There is a cow, isn't there ?
(There ⇓ Subject of statement; there ⇓ Subject of tag)

Rule **7** If the statement has demonstrative or distributive adjectives with it then the subject of the tag will be chosen as per the number, gender and person of the noun being qualified by the adjective.

For example

(*i*) This girl was dancing.

This girl was dancing, wasn't she ?
(This ⇓ Demonstrative adjective; girl ⇓ Noun; she ⇓ Subject of tag)

(3rd person, Feminine, Singular)

(*ii*) One man can do this.

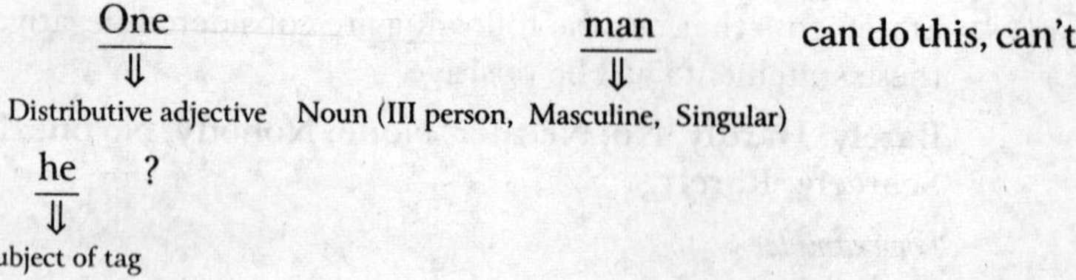

One man can do this, can't he ?
(One ⇓ Distributive adjective; man ⇓ Noun (III person, Masculine, Singular); he ⇓ Subject of tag)

Rule **8** If the subject of the statement is an indefinite pronoun then the subject of the tag will be 'they'.

For example

(*i*) Somebody invited me.

Somebody invited me, didn't they ?
(Somebody ⇓ Indefinite pronoun; they ⇓ Subject of tag)

(*ii*) None can ruin me.

None can ruin me, can they ?
(None ⇓ Indefinite pronoun; they ⇓ Subject of tag)

Rule **9** If the subject of the statement is nothing, everything, something or anything then the subject of the tag will be 'it'.

For example

(i) Everything is fine.
Everything is fine, isn't it?

(ii) Nothing has improved.
Nothing has improved, has it?

(iii) Something will be good.
Something will be good, won't it?

Rule **10** Some expressions that use objective case of the pronoun and are used as the subjects in the statement then the subject of the tag will be the subjective case of the pronoun.

For example

(i) All of you are convicts.
All of you are convicts, aren't you?

(ii) None of us have gone there.
None of us have gone there, have we?

(iii) Neither of them is good.
Neither of them is good, are they?

Rule **11** Statements that begin with 'let' take their subject of tag in different ways.

Statement with 'Let'	Subject of Tag
Let us	We
Let him	You
Let them	You
Let her	You

For example

(i) Let us go.
Let us go, shall we?

(ii) Let him dance.
Let him dance, will you?

Rule **12** If the imperative sentence is written with positive sense then the tag will be either 'will you' or ' won't you'.

Also, if the imperative sentence is written with negative sense, then the tag will be 'will you'.

For example

(i) Open the gate.
Open the gate, will you?

(ii) Open the door.
Open the door, won't you?

(iii) Mind your business.
Mind your business, won't you?

(iv) Don't break the glass.
Don't break the glass, will you?

Rule **13** If the imperative sentence expresses annoyance or irritation then the tag used is 'can't you'.

For example

(i) Shut up.
Shut up, can't you?

(ii) Keep your mouth shut.
Keep your mouth shut, can't you?

Work Book Exercise B

Complete the following by using suitable tags

1. There isn't an answer, ... ?
2. He's really good-looking, ... ?
3. It isn't any good, ... ?
4. There's a pub on the corner, ... ?
5. They weren't enjoying it, ... ?
6. She isn't here, yet .... ?
7. It's the last one, ... ?
8. She's leaving tomorrow, ... ?
9. It isn't what we wanted, ... ?
10. He isn't very happy with it, ... ?

Revision Exercises

1. *Match the tags with the statements*

1. You haven't got one,	(a) should she?
2. It can't be them,	(b) mustn't he?
3. We should do it now,	(c) can't he?
4. He has told you,	(d) can it?
5. They can't have finished yet,	(e) shouldn't we?
6. She shouldn't have said anything,	(f) have you?
7. He must have seen it,	(g) can they?
8. Let's do that,	(h) mustn't it?
9. It must be him,	(i) shall we?
10. He can do it,	(j) hasn't he?

2. *Match the tags with the statements*

1. You enjoyed that, didn't you?	(a) Actually she doesn't. She's in accounts now.
2. He doesn't write very well, does he?	(b) No, we didn't. It was the year before.
3. We love it, don't we?	(c) Yes, I did. Very much.
4. It doesn't work, does it?	(d) No,he doesn't. I don't like his books.
5. They don't live in Liverpool, do they?	(e) No, you don't. He's new to the job.
6. She works in sales, doesn't she?	(f) Yes, they do. They've been there for years.
7. It looks perfect there, doesn't it?	(g) No, it doesn't. It never did.
8. We went there last year, didn't we?	(h) Yes, It does. It looks great.
9. I don't know him, do I?	(i) Yes, we do. It's great.
10. He didn't say that, did he?	(j) I'm afraid he did

3. *Choose the correct option for the questions given below*

1. Do as I say, ... ?
(a) didn't you (b) won't you (c) needn't you (d) shan't you

2. Now you can make question tags, ... ?
(a) can you (b) won't you (c) can't you (d) will you

3. I am working hard on this book, ... ?
(a) don't I (b) won't I (c) aren't I (d) can't I

4. He was asleep , ... ?
(a) was he *(b)* wasn't he
(c) didn't he *(d)* did he

5. Let us start now, ... ?
(a) shall we *(b)* should we
(c) could we *(d)* would we

Directions (Q. Nos. 1-5) *Each question in this section has three underlined parts labelled (a), (b) and (c). Read each sentence to find out if there is any error in any underlined part and indicate your response in the Answer Sheet against the corresponding letter. If you find no error, your response is (d).*

1. Ramesh doesn't want (a) to go to (b) college today, does she? (c) No error (d)

2. Let's pray (a) to God (b) to save us from this epidemic, should we? (c) No error (d)

3. You had (a) met me before (b) Haven't you? (c) No error (d)

4. We couldn't (a) go outside (b) because of the bad weather, couldn't we? (c) No error (d)

5. Delhi is not (a) very for away (b) from Meerut. Is it? (c) No error (d)

Directions (Q. Nos. 6-8) *In the following sentences, identify the segment which contains the grammatical error.*

6. Everybody was watching the TV, won't they?
(a) won't they (b) Everybody was (c) Watching (d) the TV

7. Something must be done for the poor. mustn't it?
(a) Something must be (b) done for the
(c) poor mustn't it (d) No error

8. You always have your lunch at 12 O' clock, don't you.
(a) You always (b) at 12 O' clock
(c) don't you (d) have your lunch

Direction (Q. No. 9-10) *Read each sentence to find out whether there is any grammatical or idiomatic error in it. The error, if any, will be in one part of the sentence. The alphabet corresponding to that part is your answer. If there is 'No error', the answer is (e).*

9. Miss Madhuri does (A)/not play (B)/chess regularly.(C)/does she? (D)/No Error (E)
(a) A (b) B (c) C (d) D
(e) E

10. You should (A)/not drink(B)/wine (C)/Should you?(D)/No error (E)
(a) B (b) C (c) A (d) D
(e) E

Exam Practice

Directions (Q. Nos. 1-10) *Each question in this section has three underlined parts labelled (a), (b) and (c). Read each sentence to find out if there is any error in any underlined part and indicate your response in the Answer Sheet against the corresponding letter. If you find no error, your response is (d).*

1. You are (a) just sixteen years old (b) isn't it? (c) No error (d) **CDS 2017**

2. Sanvi has (a) two friends (b) does she? (c) No error (d)

3. I went (a) to the mall (b) yesterday, didn't I?(c) No error(d)

4. Mr. Trump is (a) from the United States (b) is he? (c) No error (d)

5. Naman has (a) been to Bengaluru recently (b) hasn't he? (c) No error (d)

6. My father (a) has got infected with Corona (b) has he? (c) No error (d)

7. You must (a) wear a mask when you go out (b) must you? (c) No error (d)

8. Yesterday was (a) so much fun (b) wasn't it?(c) No error (d)
9. I don't need (a) to go to work today (b) do I. (c) No error(d)
10. They couldn't (a) see me (b) would they? (c) No error (d)

Directions *(Q. Nos. 11-15) In the following questions, one part of the sentence may have an error. Find out which part of the sentence has an error and select the appropriate option. If the sentence is free from error, select 'No error'.*

11. Namrata is a (a)/doctor by (b)/profession, isn't he? (c)/No error (d)
12. The buses (a)/never come on (b)/time, did they ? (c)/No error (d)
13. Nobody has (a)/called for (b)/Nutan, have they (c)/ No error (d)
14. Peehu is (a)/ working on that project (b)/ wasn't she?(c)/No error(d)
15. The mobile (a)/is switched off, (b)/isn't it? (c)/No error (d)

Directions (Q. Nos. 16-18) *In the following sentences, identify the segment which contains the grammatical error.*

16. Mansi's parents have shifted to Mumbai, haven't they.
(a) haven't they (b) Mansi's parents
(c) have shifted (d) to Mumbai
17. It was raining heavily yesterday, was it?
(a) raining heavily (b) was it
(c) It was (d) yesterday
18. This cat likes to eat cheese, isn't it?
(a) isn't it? (b) This cats (c) likes to (d) eat cheese

Directions (Q. Nos. 19-25) *Read each sentence to find out whether there is any grammatical or idiomatic error in it. The error, if any, will be in one part of the sentence. The alphabet corresponding to that part is your answer. If there is 'No error', the answer is (e).*

19. I'm going to get (A)/a letter with complete details (B)/about the project (C)/amn't I? (D)/No error (E)
(a) A (b) C (c) B (d) D
(e) E
20. Shweta didn't say(A)/much after she (B)/failed in the test.(C)/did she? (D)/No error (E)
(a) A (b) B (c) C (d) D
(e) E
21. We should (A)/switch off our (B)/vehicles at (C)/red lights, should we? (D)/ No error(E)
(a) B (b) C (c) D (d) E
(e) A
22. None of the (A)/photocopiers are (B)/working properly/(C) are they? (D)/No error(E)
(a) B (b) E (c) A (d) D
(e) C
23. I'm going (A)/the next (B)/presentation on 'saving water'. (C)/Amn't I? (D)/No error (E)
(a) B (b) C (c) E (d) D
(e) A
24. Kripa and Samarth had (A)/been seeing (B)/each other for years, (C)/been they? (D)/No error (E)
(a) D (b) B (c) C (d) A
(e) E

25. Prisha could (A)/have bought (B)/a new car (C)/couldn't she? (D)/No error (E)
(a) E (b) C (c) D (d) A
(e) B

Answers

Work Book Exercise A

1. is he? **2.** didn't you? **3.** does he? **4.** don't we?
5. does it? **6.** do they? **7.** doesn't she? **8.** doesn't it?
9. didn't we? **10.** do I?

Work Book Exercise B

1. is there **2.** isn't he **3.** is it **4.** isn't there
5. were they **6.** is she **7.** isn't it **8.** isn't she
9. is it **10.** is he

Revision Exercises

1. **1.** (f) **2.** (d) **3.** (e) **4.** (j) **5.** (g) **6.** (a) **7.** (b)
8. (i) **9.** (h) **10.** (c)

2. **1.** (c) **2.** (d) **3.** (i) **4.** (g) **5.** (f) **6.** (a) **7.** (h)
8. (b) **9.** (e) **10.** (j)

3. **1.** (b) **2.** (c) **3.** (c) **4.** (b) **5.** (a)

4. **1.** (c) Replace 'she' by 'he'. **2.** (c) Replace 'should' by 'shall'.
3. (c) Use 'Hadn't you?' in place of 'Haven't you?'
4. (c) Use 'could' in place of 'couldn't' **5.** (d) No error
6. (a) Use 'weren't' in place of 'won't'. **7.** (c) Use 'Mustn't' in place of 'mustn't'.
8. (c) Add '?' in place of '.' **9.** (d) use 'Does' in place of 'does'.
10. (e) No error

Exam Practice Questions

1. (c) Replace isn't it? by 'aren't you?' **2.** (c) Use 'doesn't' in place of 'does'
3. (*d*) No error **4.** (c) Replace 'is' by 'isn't'
5. (*d*) No error **6.** (c) Replace 'has' by 'hasn't'
7. (c) Use 'Mustn't' in place of 'Must' **8.** (*d*) No error
9. (*d*) Use '?' in place of '.' **10.** (c) Replace 'would' by 'could'.
11. (*c*) 'he' should be changed to 'she'.
12. (*c*) 'did they?' should be replaced by 'do they?'
13. (*c*) '?' should be added after 'they' to complete the question tag.
14. (*c*) 'wasn't' should be replaced by 'isn't'.
15. (*d*) No error
16. (*a*) '?' should be used in place of '.'
17. (*b*) 'wasn't' should be used in place of 'was'.
18. (*a*) Replace 'isn't it' with 'dont they?'
19. (*d*) 'amn't' should be replaced by 'aren't'.
20. (*e*) No error
21. (*c*) 'shouldn't we?' should be used in place of 'should we?'
22. (*b*) No error
23. (*d*) 'Amn't I?' should be changed to 'Aren't I?'
24. (*a*) 'been they?' should be changed to 'hadn't they?'
25. (*a*) No error

7

Non-Finite Verbs

(Infinitives, Gerunds, Participles)

Study the following sentences carefully

(i) I have given him money.

(ii) I like to give him money today.

In the sentence (i) the verb 'have given' has 'I' as its subject. The verb 'have given' is limited by the number and person of its subject. It is, therefore, called a **finite verb**.

In sentence (ii) 'like' is a finite verb. But the verb 'to give' has no separate subject and is not limited by the number and person. It is, therefore, called a **Non-finite verb**.

Forms of Non-Finite Verbs

The Non-finite verbs are divided into three forms

1. Infinitives 2. Gerunds 3. Participles

1. Infinitives

Infinitives are a kind of noun with certain features of a verb. 'To' is used with infinitives. However, it can be omitted sometimes.

Forms of Infinitives

As used in the following sentences

(i) She comes here **to study**. *(Purpose)*

(ii) Everyone desires **to be admired**. *(Passive voice)*

(iii) He admitted **to have abused** him. *(Perfect infinitive)*

(iv) He admitted **to have been arrested** last year. *(Perfect passive)*

(v) He seems **to be running** out of money. *(Continuous infinitive)*

(vi) He admitted **to have been spying** for the enemy for sometime. *(Perfect continuous, time expression)*

(vii) Everyone desires **to be popular**. *('Be' as an ordinary verb)*

(viii) **To err** is human. *(Subject)*

Rules of Infinitives

Rule I

(A) **(Verb/Adjective/Noun) + Infinitive**

(i) She comes here to study. *(Active voice)*
(ii) Nobody likes to be cheated. *(Passive voice)*
(iii) Everyone desires to be rich. *(No verb)*
(iv) To err is human. (It is human to err). *(Subject)*

(B) **Some of the verbs and adjectives are followed by infinitives.** They are Agree, happy, desire, need, dare, hope, expect, decede, want, wish, refuse, eager, fail, glad, happy, heard, easy.

(C) **How + Infinitives**
When infinitives are used to express manner, the full form of infinitives is 'how to'. The verbs implying manner/method are
'know, learn, explain, teach, discover, wonder, show, ask, remember, forget, etc. *For example*

(v) He knows how to write English.
(vi) We taught him how to cook food.

Rule II Difference between 'To' and 'For'

Study the following sentences carefully

I went to see him. *[Correct (purpose)]*
I went for seeing him. *(Incorrect)*
'for seeing' cannot be used for purpose implying future because

(A) For + Gerund is used for actions showing cause. (Action in the past).
For example

(i) He will punish you for breaking the pen.
(ii) He punished you for coming late.

(B) For + Gerund is used for showing purpose for which the subject is used.
For example

(i) This book is for reading.
(ii) This machine is for measuring height.

(C) For + Noun is used for purpose in place of **to + verb** when verb is made to serve as noun. *For example*

(i) We come here for a drive.
(ii) Sameer requested for a rest.
(iii) Esha went for a walk.

(D) To + Gerund is also used with certain verbs and phrases. *For example*

(i) She is used to swimming at dawn.

Rule III Direct Infinitives

In certain cases the infinitives without 'to' is used. We may call it infinitive without 'to' or Direct Infinitives.

Direct Infinitives is used after

(A) 'Need' and 'Dare' in the negative and interrogative sentences only when they are used as auxiliaries. *For example*

(i) You need to work hard. *(Affirmative)*
(ii) You do not need to work hard. *(Negative as ordinary)*
(iii) He need not work hard. *(Negative as auxiliary)*
(iv) Do you need to work there now? *(Interrogative as ordinary)*
(v) Need he work there now? *(Interrogative as auxiliary)*
(vi) He dares to go outside in dark. *(Affirmative)*
(vii) He does not dare to go in dark. *(Negative as ordinary)*
(viii) He dare not go in dark. *(Negative as auxiliary)*
(ix) Does he dare to go in dark? *(Interrogative as ordinary)*
(x) Dare he go in dark? *(Interrogative as auxiliary)*

NOTE '**s**' is not used with **dare/need** when they are used as auxiliary verbs.

(B) 'Direct Infinitives' are used after the verbs—**'let, bid, make, know, help, feel, hear, watch, see'.**

'Direct Infinitives' are used only when these verbs are **used in active voice** (not in passive voice except the verb 'let'.) The verb '**let**' is followed by direct infinitives both in active and passive voice. *For example*

(i) I made the student write an essay.
(ii) The student was made to write an essay. *(Passive voice)*
(iii) The teacher let him go out.
(iv) He was let out by the teacher. *(Passive voice)*

(C) The following phrases are also used with Direct Infinitives 'had better, had rather, would rather, would better, as soon, sooner than (prefer)'. *For example*

(i) I would/had better leave your house at once.
(ii) She would/had rather stay than leave now.
(iii) They had sooner stay than leave.
(iv) I would as soon stay at home as go. *(with equal willingness)*

(D) Direct Infinitives are used with, **'but, than, and, except, as, or'**. *For example*

(i) He did nothing but cry. *(correct)*
(ii) She did no more than sleep the whole day. *(correct)*
(iii) She had nothing to eat except to drink water. *(remove 'to')*
(iv) Do you wish to watch TV or to go to bed early. *(remove to)*

(E) Direct Infinitives are used with phrases, 'Why not and Why'. *For example*

(i) Why not rest now? *(Suggestion)*
(ii) Why not stay here? *(Suggestion)*
(iii) Why stay here? *(Question)*

(F) 'Have + object' (used in the sense of 'wish') is followed by direct infinitive.
For example

(i) I will have him **believe** it. *(I wish him to believe it)*
(ii) She will have me **recite** this poem.

(G) 'Won't' + have + object + gerund (Used in the sense of won't allow).
For example

(i) I won't have you talking like that.
(ii) I won't have you staying at Meerut.

Rule IV Perfect Infinitives

(A) Perfect infinitives should be used if the action expressed by the infinitives precede the action of the finite verb. *For example*

(i) Yesterday I intended to have gone to Delhi. *(Incorrect, say 'to go')*
(ii) He admitted to have uttered these words against me. *(Correct)*

In the above sentence (ii) the action 'uttered' is prior to the action of the finite verb. Hence, the use of perfect infinitive is justified.

(B) The verbs where perfect infinitives may be, if needed, used.

'Deny, confess, admit, recollect, remember, recall, claim, regret, seem, appear, report, believe, understand, say, allege, suspect' learn, require, suppose, etc. *For example*

(i) She denied to have seen him yesterday.
(ii) He appears to have been rich earlier.
(iii) I still remember to have met you in Shimla last year.
(iv) He appears to be poor these days.

NOTE (i) She denied seeing him yesterday. *(Correct - as 'seeing' is an earlier action)*
(ii) She denied having seen him yesterday. *(Correct)*

Rule V

Use of infinitives after **Adjective and Noun** in active voice should be taken care of

(A) **Adjective 'enough'** is used after adjective and **'very'** before adjective when infinitives express affirmative meaning.

'too' is used before adjective when infinitives express negative meaning.

(i) She is too ill **to go out**. *(cannot go out)*
(ii) She is good enough **to help me**. *(can help me)*

(B) **Noun** Preposition should be used, if required, after the infinitives when the infinitives qualify the noun. *For example*

(i) These days no airlines is safe to travel. *(Use 'by' after 'travel')*
(ii) I gave him a pen to write. *(Use 'with' after 'write')*
(iii) He gave me a paper to read. *(No preposition)*
(iv) I have no house to live. *(Use 'in' after 'live')*
(v) I have no book to read. *(No preposition)*

Rule VI Split Infinitives

'To' should not be separated from its verb by inserting any adverb between the two. **The split infinitives** thus are grammatically wrong. *For example*

(i) You are requested to kindly stay for sometime. *(Use 'kindly' to stay)*
(ii) You are required at least to obey your parents. *(Correct)*
(iii) I advised him to carefully carry the bag. *(Say to 'carry the bag carefully')*
(iv) The students were required to seriously study for examination. *(Say 'to study seriously')*

Rule VII Continuous Infinitives

Continuous Infinitives can be used with the following verbs and Modal auxiliaries.

(a) appear, seem, believe, consider, think, report, happen, arrange, hope, pretend, say etc.

(b) may be, might be, should be, could be, must be, etc. *For examples*

(i) Malini appears to be running temperature. *It appears that.........*
(ii) I happened to be sitting with my daughters. *When I was sitting.........*
(iii) She is reported to be working at Chandigarh. *It is reported.........*
(iv) She is said to be always cursing her fate. *It is said that.........*
(v) She pretended not to be overhearing our talk *She pretended as if.........*
(vi) I hope to be living in a large house in a few years. *I hope that I shall.........*
(vii) She may be coming tomorrow. *Perhaps will come*
(viii) She may be sleeping now *Perhaps is sleeping*
(ix) He thought she might be waiting for her. *Perhaps was waiting*
(x) She could be going by car. *(deduction)*
(xi) She must be waiting for her husband. *(deduction)*
(xii) You should be sleeping now instead of watching T.V. *(Advice)*

2. **Gerund** (Verbal Noun)

Gerund is a verb form which functions as a noun. It is formed by adding 'ing' to a verb. It is used in place of Infinitive in certain cases. *For example*

(i) I do not believe **in talking** rubbish. *(Preposition + gerund)*
(ii) I do not like **riding**. *(Direct gerund)*
(iii) She is used **to swimming**. *(To + gerund)*
(iv) **Smoking** is not good for health. *(Subject)*

NOTE

1. Infinitives and gerunds are easily replaceable. However, certain rules have to be followed for replacing **infinitives and gerunds** by each other. *For example*

(i) I like **to swim** today. *(At a particular time)*
(ii) I like **swimming.** *(General/habitual statement)*

2. The difference between **participle and gerund**

Gerund is a kind of noun like the infinitives. Participle is a verb/adjective (an action in progress). *For example*

(i) I saw him **smoking** in the cinema hall. *(Participle)*
(ii) **Smoking** is injurious to health. *(Gerund)*
(iii) I am tired **of working** in this place. *(Gerund)*
(iv) We found him **working** even after the sun had set. *(Participle)*
(v) He was punished **for playing** carelessly. *(Gerund, showing 'reason')*

NOTE The verbs, **'need, require, want'**, are followed by gerund in place of passive voice infinitives.

Rules of Gerund

Rule I Preposition + Gerund

Gerund is used after certain verbs/phrases that are followed by appropriate prepositions instead of 'to'.

In case of, for + gerund refer to rule II on Infinitives.

Let us study a few of them

desirous of	intent on	justified in
disqualify from	bent on	hesitate in
refrain from	keen on	a hope of
prevent from	aim at	hope to (infinitives)
debar from	confident of	fortunate in
desist from	confidence in	harm in
restrain from	insist on	assist in
prohibit from	persist in	a chance of
dissuade from	succeed in	fond of
abstain from	successful in	take/feel pleasure in
point in	sense in	give pleasure to (infinitives)
deter from	interested in	

For example

(i) I prohibited him to go there. *(Use 'from going' in place of 'to go')*
(ii) She is bent to harm her friend. *(Use 'on harming' in place of 'to harm')*
(iii) She is confident to get success. *(Use 'of getting' in place of 'to get')*
(iv) She insisted to pay money to her mother. *(Use 'on paying' in place of 'to pay')*

Rule II Direct Gerunds

(A) The following phrases and certain verbs are followed by **direct gerunds**.

'Avoid, mind, detest, can't help, can't bear, resist, enjoy, resent, stop, start, postpone, defer, worth, prefer, consider, practise, finish, risk, pardon, excuse, forgive, it is no use/good, propose, miss, imagine, regret, means, anticipate, love, like, hate, dislike.'

(B) Phrasal verbs are also followed by direct gerunds such as **'give up, put off, set about'**, etc. *For example*

(i) We stopped to write. *(Say 'writing' for 'to write')*
(ii) He has given up to play hockey. *(Say 'playing')*
(iii) She enjoyed to ride on the hills. *(Use 'riding' in place of 'to ride')*
(iv) You should avoid to spend extra money. *(Use 'spending' in place of 'to spend')*
(v) She cannot help to tell a lie. *(Use 'telling' in place of 'to tell')*
(vi) Suhani does not mind helping me. *(Correct)*
(vii) It is no use/good waiting for her. *(Correct)*
(viii) There is no use/good of spending on luxuries. *(Correct)*

NOTE Sentence (v) can also be written as 'She cannot help but tell a lie.' (but tell = telling)

Rule III To + Gerunds

Note the use of gerunds correctly with

'be used to, accustomed to, averse to, with a view to, addicted to, devoted to, in addition to, look forward to, object to, owing to, given to, taken to, disposed to, prone to' *For example*

(i) He is addicted to smoke heavily. *(Use 'smoking' for 'smoke')*
(ii) We go there with a view of study Science. *(Use of 'studying' for 'study')*
(iii) He is used to getting up early in the morning. *(Correct)*
(iv) She used to dance before her marriage. *(Correct habit in the past)*

Rule IV

The noun or pronoun before a Gerund (verbal noun) should be in the possessive case. *For example*

(i) I don't like him wasting time. *(Use 'his' for 'him')*
(ii) Geeta insisted on Rohan going with her. *(Say 'Rohan's' for 'Rohan')*
(iii) I saw him wasting time. *('wasting' is participle)*

3. Participles

Participles are the form of verb that ends with **ing, ed, en, t.**

(A) It is used both as a verb (progressive) and an adjective.

Present	Past	Past Participle	Present Participle	Perfect Participle
Burn	burnt	burnt	burning	having burnt

For example

(i) We found a candle **burning.** *(Verb, Present Participle)*
(ii) A **burning** candle was extinguished. *(Adjective, Present Participle)*
(iii) A **burnt** paper was discovered. *(Adjective, Past Participle)*
(iv) She returned **disappointed.** *(Past Participle)*
(v) **Having taken food** she left for office. *(Perfect Participle)*

(B) Past participles are used as passive voice of present participle. It is also used to make perfect participles.

A burning candle	—	That is burning.	*(Adjective)*
A burnt paper	—	That is burnt.	*(Adjective)*
Having burnt paper	—	After burning paper.	*(Verb)*
Having been burnt	—	Passive voice.	*(Verb)*

Rules of Participles

Rule I

Participle Clause/Absolute Phrase (Nominative Absolute)

A participle is used as participle clause. It is a kind of clause containing participle in place of a finite verb.

Absolute Phrase/Nominative Absolute It is a kind of participle with a Noun/Pronoun before it.

(i) **Walking in the garden** I came across an old friend. *(Present Participle, Active voice)*

(ii) **Surprised at the news** I rushed to the airport. *(Past Participle, Passive voice)*

(iii) **Having taken food** I left for office. *(Perfect Participle, Active voice)*

(iv) **Having been arrested the thief** was taken to prison. *(Perfect Participle, Passive voice)*

(v) **The Sun having risen**, we left the town. *(Absolute Phrase)*

Rule II

Participles can be changed into following clauses

(a) Adverb Clause of Time
(b) Adverb Clause of Condition
(c) Adverb Clause of Reason
(d) Adverb Clause of Contrast
(e) Adjective Clause
(f) Co-ordinate Clause

(a) **Adverb Clause of Time** (while, having, on)

(i) As I was wandering in the street, I met my old friend.
(While) wandering in the street I met my old friend.

(ii) After I had passed High school, I got a job.
Having passed High school I got a job.

(iii) When she saw me, she called me.
(On) seeing me she called me.

(b) **Adverb Clause of Condition** (by, without, but for)

(i) If you go out, you will catch cold.
By going out you will catch cold.

(ii) If you don't work hard, you will not pass.
Without working hard you will not pass.

(iii) If you had not worked hard, you would have failed.
But for working hard you would have failed.

(c) **Adverb Clause of Reason** (owing to, because of, on account of)

(i) As she ran very fast, she was able to overtake me.
On account of running very fast she was able to overtake me.

(ii) Since she was late, she was punished.
Being late she was punished.

(d) **Adverb Clause of Contrast** (Inspite of, despite, notwithstanding, for all)

(i) Although she came late, she was not punished.
Inspite of coming late she was not punished.

(ii) Though she is rich, she is not happy.
Despite being rich she is not happy.

(iii) Though she was punished, she did not feel sorry.
Inspite of being punished she did not feel sorry.

(e) **Adjective Clause**

(i) I saw a girl who was singing a song.
I saw a girl singing a song.

(ii) The students who are studying English here will be successful.
The students studying English here will be successful.

(iii) The book which was presented to me by my mother is very interesting.
The book presented to me by my mother is very interesting.

(iv) A burning candle fell off the table.
A candle that was burning fell off the table.

(f) **Co-ordinate Clause**

A participle can replace a co-ordinate clause

(i) He returned and he was smiling.
He returned smiling.

(ii) She went out and she was disappointed.
She went out disappointed.

Rule III

Present participles should be used only to express an action which coincides with the action of the finite verb.

He left for Mumbai on Monday, reaching there on Tuesday. (Incorrect, 'reaching' is not a simultaneous action)

He left for Mumbai on Monday and reached there on Tuesday. *(Correct)*

Rule IV Misrelated/Unrelated Participles

When the participle clause/phrase is not followed by a subject of its own, the participle is called **misrelated, dangling or unattached.**

(i) Wandering in the street a dog bit him. *(Incorrect)*

(ii) Wandering in the street he was bitten by a dog. *(Correct)*

NOTE 'Wandering' should have a proper subject **'he'** and not **'a dog'**.

How to Correct a Misrelated Participle?

Misrelated participle can be corrected in three ways.

1. Expand the participle into a clause. *(Already explained in Rule II)*
2. Bring the proper subject immediately after the participle. *(by changing voice)*
3. Place the proper subject before the participle. *(only before 'being' and 'having')*

Let us study the problem by working out some questions.

1. Walking along the road a scooter knocked him down. *(Incorrect)*
   (i) While he was walking along the road a scooter knocked him down. *(Correct)*
   (ii) Walking along the road he was knocked down by a scooter. *(Correct)*
2. Having taken food my father sent me to market. *(Incorrect)*
   (i) When I had taken food, my father sent me to market. *(Correct)*
   (ii) I having taken food my father sent me to market. *(Absolute Phrase)*
   (iii) Having taken food I was sent to market by my father. *(Correct)*
3. Being cloudy we enjoyed picnic. *(Incorrect)*
   (i) As it was cloudy, we enjoyed picnic. *(Correct)*
   (ii) It being cloudy we enjoyed picnic. *(Absolute Phrase)*
4. Being honest the teacher rewarded him. *(Incorrect)*
   (i) As he was honest, the teacher rewarded him. *(Correct)*
   (ii) He being honest, the teacher rewarded him. *(Correct)*
   (iii) Being honest he was rewarded by the teacher. *(Correct)*
5. Possessing huge wealth people do not like him. *(Incorrect)*
   (i) Although he possesses huge wealth, people donot like him. *(Correct)*
   (ii) Possessing huge wealth he is not liked by people. *(Correct)*

Rule V

Participles such as

'regarding, concerning, considering, speaking', do not refer to any particular subject. They can do without agreement with any noun or pronoun.

(i) Considering his problems he was advised to leave Jalgaon. *(Correct)*
(ii) Roughly speaking two hundred persons died in the earthquake. *(Correct)*

In these sentences the unexpressed subject is indefinite. Therefore, participle need not be in agreement with the Noun or Pronoun it refers to.

Some Important Uses of Non-Finites

Study the following sentences carefully and note the difference in their sense.

1. I regret being late/to be late. *(Present Infinitive)*
2. I regret to have been late/having been late. *(Perfect Infinitive)*
3. She prided herself on being Indian. *('Pride' is verb here)*
4. Take Pride in serving your motherland. *('Pride' is noun here)*
5. I feel pleasure in inviting you to dinner tonight. *(No difference in meaning)*

6. It gives me pleasure to send you greetings. *(No difference in meaning)*
7. Leaving home is difficult. *(Experience)*
8. To leave home is difficult. *(Opinion)*
9. I would like to attend marriage tomorrow. *(Enjoy)*
10. I would like you to study. *(Think it right)*
11. I like to get myself examined. *(Think it wise)*
12. I like attending marriages. *(Habit)*
13. My mother loves telling us stories. *(Habit)*
14. I would love to do it for your sake. *(Enjoy)*
15. I propose to go there. *(Intend)*

Work Book Exercise A

(Based on Infinitive & Gerund)

Directions *Spot the errors, if any, in the following sentences.*

1. The teacher made the students to solve their problems.
2. His aim is no more than to use unfair means to attain success in life.
3. He goes every Sunday to Delhi with a view to buy raw material.
4. The teacher asked them to stop write as soon as the bell rang.
5. She can't help to visit her sister every Sunday.
6. He is rich today but he appears to be poor in the past.
7. The scientists claim to discover cure for AIDS and the medicine will be put on sale very soon.
8. She started to cry when she was left alone.
9. She did not dare enter the room without his permission.
10. I always resent my brother wandering about and doing nothing.

Work Book Exercise B

Directions *Use the most suitable form of Infinitive/Gerund in the following sentences.*

1. Today everyone wishes .... money quickly.
   (a) earn *(b)* to earn *(c)* for earning
2. She is very keen .... modelling.
   (a) to take up *(b)* on taking up *(c)* taking up
3. The director made the officers .... longer than usual.
   (a) to wait *(b)* wait *(c)* waiting
4. My brother is interested .... in the Army.
   (a) to serve *(b)* in serving *(c)* to serving
5. The boys in the hostel are averse .... part in the strike.
   (a) to take *(b)* to taking *(c)* for taking
6. He never minds .... the deserving persons.
   (a) to help *(b)* helping *(c)* in helping

7. She resented .... late at night.
   (a) my returning *(b)* me returning *(c)* against my returning
8. I feel pleasure .... you of my success.
   (a) to inform *(b)* to informing *(c)* in informing
9. I don't remember .... in Kashmir last year.
   (a) to meet you *(b)* to have met you *(c)* of meeting you
10. Throughout the day she did nothing but .... illness.
   (a) feigning *(b)* feign *(c)* to feign
11. She intended .... in the teaching profession.
   (a) to have gone *(b)* to go *(c)* for going
12. For modern man there are a number of diseases ....
   (a) to suffer from *(b)* for suffering *(c)* to suffer
13. You had better .... in her house overnight.
   (a) not stayed *(b)* not stay *(c)* not to stay
14. You must know .... in society.
   (a) to conduct yourself *(b)* how to conduct yourself *(c)* to conduct
15. It gives me immense pleasure .... you of her engagement.
   (a) to inform *(b)* in informing *(c)* to informing
16. She comes .... me daily in the evening.
   (a) for seeing *(b)* seeing *(c)* to see
17. His mother always forbids him .... with Nisha.
   (a) from speaking *(b)* to speak *(c)* not to speak
18. The carpet needs .... before we use it.
   (a) to clean *(b)* cleaning *(c)* to be cleaned
19. The police officer denied .... callous to the undertrial.
   (a) to be *(b)* being *(c)* to have been
20. I have ever looked forward .... the President of the District Rotary Club.
   (a) to be *(b)* to being *(c)* to have been

Work Book Exercise C

Directions *Use these Participle Clauses/Absolute Phrase correctly.*

1. Writing a letter a beggar disturbed her.
2. Being fine we decided to go on picnic.
3. Being late the teacher punished her.
4. But for working hard she would have passed.
5. Inspite of being late the teacher did not punish her.
6. Climbing up the stairs her sandal broke and she fell.
7. Having passed B.A. examination he offered me a job.
8. Inspite of being a miser everybody likes to spend money on her.
9. While taking admission to a school, a birth certificate must be shown.
10. Cooking my dinner in the kitchen a strange sound attracted my attention.

Revision Exercise

Directions (Q. Nos. 1-5) *Each question in this section has three parts labelled (a), (b) and (c). Read each sentence to find out whether there is any error in any underlined part and indicate your response in the Answer Sheet against the corresponding letter. If you find no error, your response should be indicated as (d).*

1. You should always (a) / aim to achieve (b) / higher goal to succeed in life. (c) / No error (d)

2. She was (a) / confident to qualify (b) / the examination (c) / No error. (d)

3. The civilians were (a) / prohibited to attend (b) / the shooting competition in the military area. (c) / No error. (d)

4. You are requested to (a) / carefully carry the bag (b) / because it contains fragile material. (c) / No error. (d)

5. She was (a) / allowed (b) / to do whatever she liked. (c) / No error (d)

Directions (Q. Nos. 6-7) *In the following questions, some parts of the sentence may have errors. Find out which part of a sentence has an error. If a sentence is free from error, your answer will be no error.*

6. Last night Rupali intended to have left.
(a) Last night Rupali
(b) intended to
(c) have left
(d) No error

7. The Principal can't tolerate anybody talking nonsense.
(a) can't tolerate
(b) anybody talking nonsense
(c) The Principal
(d) No error

Directions (Q. Nos. 8-10) *Identify which part of the following sentences has an error.*

8. How dare (A)/he (B)/ to abuse (C)/my friend. (D)/No error(E)
(a) A
(b) B
(c) C
(d) D
(e) E

9. Mehak was forbidden (A)/from moving out (B)/with her (C)/friends at night (D)/No error(E)
(a) E
(b) B
(c) D
(d) C
(e) A

10. We expected (A)/to have been (B)/invited to the party (C)/organised by our neighbours. (D)/No error (E)
(a) A
(b) E
(c) B
(d) D
(e) C

Directions (Q. Nos. 11-20) *Use the most suitable form of Infinitive/Gerund to fill the blanks in the given sentences.*

11. She has given up ……… on her friend's advice.
(a) smoke (b) smoking (c) to have smoked

12. Remember, this is not a safe road ……….
(a) to travel (b) to travel by (c) travelling

13. Classical music is worth ……… .
(a) to listen (b) to listen to (c) listening to

14. The officer always made me ……… fast.
(a) work (b) to work (c) to working

15. He is reported ……… Mumbai for good last year.
(a) to leave (b) leaving (c) to have left

16. My mother always detests ……… with shady children.
(a) in dealing (b) dealing (c) to deal

17. How dare you ……… to your teachers like this?
(a) to talk (b) talk (c) talking

18. They need not ……… for their turn.
(a) to wait (b) have waited (c) wait

19. You don't need ……… here any more in the sun.
(a) to stand (b) standing (c) stand

20. Lalita seems ………… a lot of Kho-Kho during her school days.
(a) to play (b) to playing (c) to have played

Exam Practice

Direction (Q. Nos. 1-16) *In the following questions, some parts of the sentences may have errors and some are correct. Find out which part of a sentence has an error. If a sentence is free from error, your answer will be "No error".*

1. I really do regret not to learn to play the violin when I had so many opportunities to learn and practice in school. **SSC CGL 2015**
(a) to learn and practice in school
(b) when I had so many opportunities
(c) I really do regret not to learn to play the violin
(d) No error

2. The tourism industry of the state feels that the facility of visa on-arrival should be made available to keeping the industry vibrant. **SBI Clerk 2016**
(a) The tourism industry of the state
(b) feels that the facility of visa-on-arrival
(c) should be made available
(d) to keeping the industry vibrant

3. Six people fainted on board in an international flight promptly the emergency crew to check the plane for hazardous materials. **SBI Clerk 2016**
(a) Six people fainted (b) on board in an international flight
(c) promptly the emergency crew to check (d) the plane for hazardous materials
(e) No error

4. To be short-listed for the competition the children have to fill up a contest form that their respective schools will provide. **SBI Clerk 2016**
(a) To be short-listed for the competition (b) the children have to fill up
(c) a contest form that their
(d) respective schools will provide
(e) No error

5. The students of the school would be send to the zoo on a study tour to gain first-hand experience. **SBI Clerk 2016**
(a) The students of the school (b) would be send to the zoo
(c) on a study tour (d) to gain first-hand experience
(e) No error

6. A family office has to execute all tasks related to manage the wealth of the upper-rich family. **SBI Clerk 2016**
(a) A family office has to (b) execute all tasks related to
(c) manage the wealth of (d) the upper-rich family
(e) No error

7. Millie was a mouse who had a cousin named Tora living in the city. **SBI Clerk 2015**
(a) Millie was (b) a mouse who had
(c) a cousin named Tora (d) living in the city
(e) No error

8. New purchasing power will increasingly come from Asia and Africa where the demographics are still favourable for high income growth. **SBI Clerk 2019**
(a) New purchasing power will increasingly
(b) come from Asia and Africa
(c) where the demographies are still favourable
(d) for high income growth
(e) No error

9. Over half of China's 1.4 billion population lives in villages and the most pressing problem faces the country today is the lack of rural reforms. **SBI PO 2016**
(a) Over half of China's 1.4 billion population
(b) lives in villages and the most pressing
(c) problem faces the country today
(d) is the lack of rural reforms
(e) No error

10. The government plans to launch a new healthcare system which consists of a website where people can register for insurance, a data centre which stores, records, and an interface which provides insurance companies with information. **SBI PO 2016**
(a) The government plans to launch a new healthcare system
(b) which consists of a website where people can register for insurance
(c) a data centre which stores, records and an interface
(d) which provides insurance companies with information
(e) No error

11. The two-part documentary is a critique of the education system and its impacting on upliftment of women. **IBPS PO/MT 2015**
(a) The two-part documentary
(b) is a critique of the education system
(c) and its impacting
(d) on upliftment of women
(e) No error

12. She held something at her side which was totally hiding by the folds of her sari. **IBPS PO 2018**
(a) She held something
(b) at her side
(c) which was totally hiding
(d) by the folds of her saree
(e) No error

13. The movement, which aims to raise awareness about climate change, hopes to bring people together to think about what they can do for reduce harmful pollution.
(a) The movement, which aims to
(b) raise awareness about climate change, hopes
(c) to bring people together to think about
(d) what they can do for reduce pollution
(e) No error

14. My friend (a)/was habitual to drive a car (b)/at very high speed (c)/No error(d) **NDA 2016**
(a) My friend
(b) was habitual to drive a car
(c) at very high speed
(d) No error

15. If you are wanting to watch (a)/the birds nesting (b)/you must not let them see you. (c)/No error (d) **NDA 2016**
(a) If you are wanting to watch
(b) the birds nesting
(c) you must not let them see you
(d) No error

16. I asked him (a)/what had brought(b)/him there (c)/No error (d) **NDA 2016**
(a) I asked him
(b) what had brought
(c) him there
(d) No error

Answers

Work Book Exercise A

1. Drop 'to' before 'solve'
2. Drop 'to' before 'use'
3. 'of buying' in place of 'buy
4. 'writing' in place of 'write'
5. 'visiting' in place of 'to visit'
6. 'to have been' in place of 'to be'
7. 'to have discovered' in place of 'to discover'
8. 'crying in place of 'to cry'
9. 'to enter' in place of 'enter'
10. 'brother's' in place of 'brother'

Work Book Exercise B

1. (b)	**2.** (b)	**3.** (b)	**4.** (b)	**5.** (b)	**6.** (b)	**7.** (a)
8. (c)	**9.** (b)	**10.** (b)	**11.** (b)	**12.** (a)	**13.** (b)	**14.** (b)
15. (a)	**16.** (c)	**17.** (b)	**18.** (b)	**19.** (c)	**20.** (b)	

Work Book Exercise C

1. While she was writing a letter, the beggar disturbed her.
2. Place 'it' before 'being'.
3. Place 'She' before 'being' or she was punished by the teacher after 'being late'.
4. Place 'not' after 'would
5. She was not punished by the teacher after inspite of being late.
6. While she was climbing, her sandal broke and she fell.
7. Place 'I' before 'having'
8. Although she is a miser everyone like to spend money on her.
9. 'When one takes' in place of 'While taking'
10. While I was cooking my dinner, a strange sound attracted my attention.

Revision Exercise

1. (b) Use 'at achieving' in place of 'to achieve'.
2. (b) Use 'of qualifying' in place of 'to qualify'.
3. (b) Use 'from attending in place of 'to attend'.
4. (b) Use 'carry the bag carefully' in place of 'carefully carry the bag'.
5. (d) No error
6. (c) Use 'leave' in place of 'have left'.
7. (d) No error
8. (c) Remove 'to'
9. (b) Use 'to move' in place of 'from moving'.
10. (b) No error

11. (b) **12.** (b) **13.** (c) **14.** (a) **15.** (c) **16.** (b)
17. (b) **18.** (c) **19.** (a) **20.** (c)

Exam Practice

1. (*c*) 'to learn' will be changed to 'learning'.
2. (*d*) 'keeping' should be changed to 'keep'.
3. (*c*) 'prompting' should be used in place of 'promptly'
4. (*e*) No error
5. (*b*) 'sent' should be used in place of 'send'.
6. (*c*) 'managing' should be used in place of 'manage'.
7. (*e*) No error
8. (*e*) No error
9. (*c*) 'faces' should be changed to 'facing'.
10. (*a*) Change 'plans' to 'is planning'.
11. (*c*) 'impact' should be used in place of 'impacting'.
12. (*c*) 'hidden' will be used in place of 'hiding'.
13. (*d*) 'reducing' will be used in place of 'reduce'.
14. (*b*) 'to drive' should be changed to 'of driving'.
15. (*a*) 'are wanting' should be changed to 'want'.
16. (*d*) No error

Verb

What is a Verb?

A verb is a word that is used to describe an action or talk about something that happens.

(a) What a person or a thing does *(Active)*

(i) She teaches in our school.

(ii) He often visited his village.

(b) What is done to a person or a thing. *(Passive)*

(i) He was punished.

(ii) Shikha was taught a lesson.

(c) What a person or a thing is *('Be' as a regular/ordinary verb)*

(i) She is a pretty village girl.

(ii) My brother is a chemist.

There are two classes of verbs

(A) The auxiliary verbs (B) The ordinary/regular verbs

(A) **The auxiliary verbs are of two types**

I. **Primary auxiliaries**

(i) To be is, are, am, was, were, been, being.

(ii) To have has, have, had.

(iii) To do do, does, did.

II. **Modal auxiliaries** will, must, should, may, etc.

(B) **The ordinary verbs**

to work, to play, to write, etc.

The Use of 'To Be'

(1) **As an auxiliary verb.**

(i) She is writing a letter. *(Active)*

(ii) Arjun was called back. *(Passive)*

(2) **As an ordinary/regular verb.**

(i) She is a doctor.

(ii) She was present.

(For further details look up the chapter on Voice.)

Kinds of Verbs

1. Finite verbs 2. Non-finite verbs

1. **Finite Verbs** Finite verb has a subject of its own and is limited by the person and the number of the subject. *For example*

   (i) She is **playing** Tennis.

   (ii) They were **watching** television.

   (a) **Transitive Verbs** Transit means 'to move'. The action of transitive verbs passes over to the object. *For example*

   (i) She **writes** a letter. *(ii)* She **teaches** me.

   (b) **Intransitive Verbs** The action of the intransitive verbs does not pass over to the object. It goes back to the subject. *For example*

   (i) She **cried** a lot. *(ii)* She **came** on time.

NOTE

Transitive verbs alone can be used in passive voice.

2. **Non-finite Verbs** Non-finite verbs are not limited by the person and the number of any subject. They are used without mentioning any subject.
   Non-finite verbs are of three kinds.

   (a) Infinitive (b) Gerund (c) Participle

   For example

   (i) She comes here to **study**. *(ii)* We saw them **waiting for** the bus.

   (iii) She likes **reciting** poems.

Rules of Verbs

Rule I

When two or more subjects are joined by **'as well as, like, unlike, besides, in addition to, with, together with, along with, and not, rather than, no less than, except, nothing but, more than one'**, the verb is used according to the first subject. *For example*

(i) The director as well as the dancers were honoured by the public. *(Use 'was' in place of 'were')*

(ii) The mother, and not her children have been arrested for committing theft. *(Use 'has' in place of 'have')*

(iii) More men than one were absent yesterday. *(Correct)*

(iv) Nothing but truth is immortal. *(Correct)*

(v) My mother no less than my father is strict. *(Correct)*

Rule II

When two or more subjects are connected by **'not only-but also, neither-nor, either-or, none-but'** the verb is according to the nearest subject. *For example*

(i) Neither the students nor their guide were found present in the common room. *(Use 'was' in place of 'were').*

(ii) No one but the leaders of our country is responsible for this state of affairs. *(Use 'are' in place of 'is')*

(iii) One or two books are needed. *(Correct)*

(iv) I or he is to be rewarded. *(Correct)*

(v) Am I or he to be rewarded? *(Correct)*

Rule III

(a) **'Neither, either, none, anyone, each, every' used as pronoun or adjective** should be followed by third person singular verbs. *For example*

(i) Neither of the two boys have done it. *(Use 'has' in place of 'have')*

(ii) Each of the students are obedient. *(Use 'is' in place of 'are')*

(iii) Either of us has done his work. *(Correct)*

(iv) Every boy and every girl has been invited. *(Correct)*

(b) When **None** is used with countable nouns both singular and plural verbs are correct. But with an uncountable noun, singular verb is correct.

(i) None of the boys has/have done home work. *(Correct)*

(ii) None of the work is completed. *(Correct)*

(c) When 'each' is used after the subject, the verb is plural. *For example*

(i) We each have taken our bags.

(ii) They each are honest.

Rule IV

When plural nouns explain specific **'amount, sum, distance, quantity, time, period'** as a whole the verb should be singular. *For example*

(i) Four miles are not a long distance. *(Use 'is' in place of 'are')*

(ii) Two hundred rupees were a large amount fifty years ago. *(Use 'was' in place of 'were').*

(iii) Two hundred rupees were lost. *(Correct)*

Rule V

The expression **'many a/an, more than one'** should be followed by a singular noun and singular verb. *For example*

(i) Many accidents have recently taken place. *(Correct)*

(ii) Many an accidents have recently taken place. *(The correct usage is 'many an accident has')*

(iii) More than one man was absent. *(Correct)*

(iv) More men than one were burnt. *(Correct. Refer to Rule I)*

Rule VI

In a **compound sentence** both auxiliary verbs and principal verbs should be mentioned separately if they differ in **number, form** or **voice**. In such cases one verb cannot act for both the clauses. *For example*

(i) He has not and will not marry in near future. *(Place 'married' after 'has not')*

(ii) She is intelligent but her sisters dull. *(Place 'are' after 'sisters') (iii)* He surrendered before the court and sent to jail. *(Use 'was' before 'sent')*

(iv) She disappeared last month and found dead near a well last night. *(Place 'was' after 'and')*

(v) She is intelligent but her sister dull. *(Correct)*

(vi) I did not and will not go there. *(Correct)*

Rule VII

The inverted form of the verb is used in the following cases

(A) When the sentence is introduced by an adverb.

(B) When the verb is meant to express a wish or prayer.

For example

(i) So quickly did she finish her work that we were surprised. *(Correct)*

(ii) May you succeed in life. *(Correct)*

(iii) Hardly/scarcely had I reached the airport when the plane arrived. *(Correct)*

(iv) No sooner did she arrive than she started laughing. *(Correct)*

Rule VIII

The verb in the following cases is used in singular form.

(A) When two singular nouns refer to the same person denoted by one article.

(B) In certain phrases or idiomatic pair of words suggesting the same meaning, though not synonyms. *For example*

(i) The Collector and District Magistrate are on a visit to the Tehsil today. *(Use 'is' in place of 'are')*

(ii) What is the aim and object of his costly plan? *(Correct)*

(iii) The sum and substance of the passage is given below. *(Correct)*

(iv) Bread and butter are sold here. *(Correct)*

(v) Bread and butter is difficult to earn. *(Correct)*

(vi) Two and two is/are four. (makes four) *(Correct)*

(vii) No student and no teacher was present. *(Correct)*

(viii) Three fives are fifteen. *(Correct)*

(ix) Five times ten is fifty. *(Correct)*

(x) Slow and steady wins the race. *(Correct)*

(xi) Time and tide wait for none. *(Correct)*

Rule IX

(a) **When the sentence begins with 'It'** the verb is according to the subject 'It'.

(b) **In the case of a sentence beginning** with **'there'** and **Interrogative pronouns,** the verb is according to the predicate/complement.

However, verb should not be used according to complement in other than these cases. *For example*

(i) It is the stars that guide our destiny. *(Correct)*

(ii) It is I who am helping you. *(Correct)*

(iii) There was a boy in the classroom. *(Correct)*

(iv) There were a boy and a teacher in the classroom. *(Correct)*
(v) There lives a boy who is my best friend. *(Correct)*
(vi) What evidence are these acts? *(Correct)*
(vii) What have the boys thought about this plan? *(Correct)*

Rule X

(A) A singular or a plural verb with the nouns in the following cases is used according to the sense which they convey.

(a) Number (b) Means, wages

(c) Variety, plenty, rest, deal of, a lot of (lots of), a heap of, two thirds of, most of, some of, a half of, per cent of.

(a) **Number**

1. A large number of boys were absent on account of bad weather. *(Correct)*
2. The number of admissions have gradually fallen off. *(Use 'has')*

(b) **Means, Wages**

3. She could not continue her study because her means were poor. *(Correct)*
4. A fair means is always preferable to the foul one. *(Correct)*
5. Means are more important than the ends. *(Correct)*
6. The wages in India are quite meagre. *(Correct)*
7. "Wages of sin is death", says the Bible. *(Correct)*

(c) **Variety, Plenty, etc.**

8. A variety of books on the subject are available in the market. *(Correct)*
9. A variety of food is available in this hotel. *(Correct)*
10. Plenty of milk is available in this part of the country. *(Correct)*
11. Plenty of books were donated to the library by him. *(Correct)*
12. The rest of the lesson has been completed. *(Correct)*
13. The rest of the students have left for their homes. *(Correct)*
14. A lot of (lots of) guests were attended upon by the host. *(Correct)*
15. A lot of work is yet to be done. *(Correct)*
16. A great deal of labour is required to complete the job. *(Correct)*
17. A good deal of boys have joined our club. *(Correct)*
18. Two thirds of the actors are unsuccessful. *(Correct)*
19. Two thirds of the book is easy to read. *(Correct)*
20. The seventy per cent of the students are hard working. *(Correct)*
21. The seventy per cent of our population is poor. *(Correct)*

NOTE (a) But with 'percentage' in the subject the verb is singular. *For example*
The percentage of successful candidates is very high.

(b) A singular verb is used with collective nouns when they denote unity/a group.
"A set of books, a pair of spectacles, a bouquet of flowers, a kind of, a series of events, a gang of robbers," etc. *For example*
(i) The pair of spectacles is broken. (Correct)
(ii) A series of matches is likely to be played next month. (Correct)

Rule XI Unreal Past/Subjunctive Mood

A wish, a regret, unlikely condition and contrary to fact statements are expressed in subjunctive mood.

(A) In subjunctive mood (present situation) we may use 'was/were', though 'were' is the more correct form. (Simple past plural)

(a) **To express regret/wish for a present situation.** (at the time of speaking)

(i) I wish I had a house of my own now = I am sorry I don't have a house.

(ii) I wish I were rich now = I am sorry I am not rich.

NOTE I wish = would that, I would, If only.

(b) **To express unlikely condition.** *For example*

(i) If I had a house, I would not hire yours.

(ii) If I were a teacher, I would help you.

(c) **'As if/as though'**

The subjunctive can be used in a clause beginning with 'as if/as though' to express a statement contrary to the fact. *For example*

She behaves as if she were the landlady.

(B) After **'It is high time'** *For example*

It is high time you did something now. *(In the sense of 'should')*

(C) After **'would rather/had rather' + Clause**

These phrases are followed by a clause in a subjunctive mood. Otherwise direct infinitives are used. *For example*

(i) I would rather you helped my brother.

(ii) I had rather you stayed with me. *(Say 'would stay')*

(iii) I would rather go to Mumbai. *(Direct Infinitive)*

(D) In subjunctive mood referring to Past situation use Past Perfect Tense.
For example

(i) I wish I had a gun then. *(Past situation)*

(ii) I wish I had a gun now. *(Present situation)*

(iii) I wish I had not met her last year. *(Regret for a past situation)*

Rule XII

The use of causative verbs. (Make, Get, Have Cause)

(i) I made my friend write a letter.

(ii) My friend was made to write a letter.

(iii) He got his house painted by expert painters.

(iv) He had a house demolished.

NOTE In sentence (i) the causative verb 'make' is followed by direct infinitive 'write'. In sentence (ii) 'make' is followed by 'to write' because it is in passive voice.

But we can say **'They caused him to leave India'**.

[Refer to Rule II (b) on Non-finite verbs.]

Rule XIII

When negative ideas are introduced in a noun clause with the following verbs in principal clause, it is advisable to make principal clause in negative.

'imagine, think, believe, suppose'.

NOTE This rule doesn't apply to 'I hope'. *For example*

(i) I don't think he will pass. *(Correct)*
I think he will not pass. *(Incorrect)*

(ii) I don't suppose she will pass. *(Correct)*
I suppose she will not pass. *(Incorrect)*

Rule XIV

The position of verb in the clause beginning with 'As' and 'Than', when the subject is hidden can be understood through the examples given below

(i) The guests came on time **as were hoped**. *[say, (it) was hoped]*

(ii) The guests came more in number **than was expected**. *[say, (they) were expected]*

(iii) There were more mangoes than were expected. *[say, (it) was expected]*

(iv) There were more servants than was required. *[say, (they) were required]*

Rule XV

Verbs Often Confused

The Base Form (Present)	Past	Past Participle (PP)
1. Swing	Swung	Swung
2. Wring	Wrung	Wrung
3. Sting	Stung	Stung
4. Find	Found	Found
5. Found	Founded	Founded
6. Fall	Fell	Fallen
7. Fell	Felled	Felled
8. Befall	Befell	Befallen
9. Fly	Flew	Flown
10. Blow	Blew	Blown
11. Flow	Flowed	Flowed
12. Strike	Struck	Struck
13. Stick	Stuck	Stuck
14. See	Saw	Seen
15. Saw	Sawed	Sawed/Sawn
16. Flee	Fled	Fled
17. Affect	Affected	Affected
18. Effect	Effected	Effected
19. Rend	Rent	Rent
20. Rent	Rented	Rented

The Base Form (Present)	Past	Past Participle (PP)
21. Awake	Awoke	Awoke/Awaken
22. Wake	Woke	Woken
23. Lie	Lied	Lied
24. Lie	Lay	Lain
25. Lay	Laid	Laid
26. Hang	Hanged	Hanged
27. Hang	Hung	Hung
28. Cast	Cast	Cast
29. Telecast	Telecast	Telecast
30. Forecast	Forecast	Forecast
31. Cost	Cost	Cost
32. Lose	Lost	Lost
33. Rise	Rose	Risen
34. Raise	Raised	Raised
35. Arise	Arose	Arisen
36. Rouse	Roused	Roused
37. Bind	Bound	Bound
38. Bound	Bounded	Bounded
39. Practise	Practised	Practised
40. Advise	Advised	Advised
41. Devise	Devised	Devised
42. Prophesy	Prophesied	Prophesied
43. Grind	Ground	Ground
44. Ground	Grounded	Grounded
45. Bear	Bore	Borne
46. Bear	Bore	Born
47. Wind	Wound	Wound
48. Wound	Wounded	Wounded
49. Forego	Forewent	Foregone
50. Forgo	Forwent	Forgone

Work Book Exercise A

Directions *Spot the error, if any, in the following sentences.*

1. None but cowards is afraid of fighting.
2. Many a bride have been burnt and killed for dowry.
3. Each of these players have been warned not to repeat the silly mistake.
4. Lime and soda is a digestive drink.
5. The mother as well as her children were brought to the police station for interrogation.
6. His benevolence and kindness are admired by his friends.
7. She never has and never will allow her only son to join Army.
8. Three parts of the lesson are yet to be completed.
9. She is intelligent but her sister dull.
10. Intelligence, as well as knowledge of the subject are required to grasp the meaning of the book.
11. Twenty officers have been dismissed and thirty left on their own.
12. Every word and every line in the poems of Wordsworth sings about the blessings of nature.
13. So honestly he worked that he was rewarded by the chairman of the company.
14. Riches and not character bring you respect these days.
15. The sum and substance of the passage is beyond my understanding.

Work Book Exercise B

Directions *Spot the error, if any, in the following sentences.*

1. In old age neither of his two sons are prepared to come to his help.
2. I don't think ten thousand rupees are a large sum for the work you are going to undertake.
3. It were the students who wanted the teacher to declare holiday.
4. So fast did he drive the motor car that even the best driver could not overtake him.
5. Each one of the new Nursing Homes coming up in the urban areas need a lot of improvement.
6. Never I have come across a man who is foolish to such an extent.
7. He will be likely to take part in the wedding ceremony of his brother provided he is granted leave.
8. Two thirds of the members are needed to pass the resolutions for the impeachment of the President.
9. During freedom struggle many a patriot were fired with patriotism and sacrificed everything for the sake of the motherland.
10. There are a dozen of history books lying in the shelf of my personal library and you can use them whenever you like.

11. The number of amendments to our constitution have been very large since independence.
12. Just outside the village is a *Panchayat* House with dedicated workers working here.
13. Just to the North of India is the Himalayas that were once impregnable.
14. Who does go there nowadays?
15. Our source of information was the spies captured during the raid.

Work Book Exercise C

(Based on verbs often confused)

Directions *Choose the most suitable alternative to make the sentence logical*

1. The police......... into action on receiving the telephone call yesterday.
   (a) swang (b) swung (c) swing
2. Being a philanthropist, he .... this institution.
   (a) founded (b) was founded (c) found
3. No one is allowed to .... the trees in the forest.
   (a) fall (b) fell (c) fallen
4. When calamity .... the family, he faced it boldly.
   (a) fell (b) fall (c) befell
5. I think she .... the clock this week.
   (a) wounded (b) wind (c) wound
6. The bridge .... up by the terrorists only last week.
   (a) blowed (b) was blowed (c) was blown
7. During rainy season this stream ....
   (a) overflowed (b) overflow (c) overflown
8. When he was ....with stone he did not retaliate.
   (a) strike (b) striked (c) struck
9. The woodcutter .... the log of the wood to make a cot.
   (a) saw (b) sew (c) sawed
10. When the robbers had put all the money in the bag they.........
    (a) fled (b) fleed (c) flee
11. When the village was attacked, loud cries .... the air.
    (a) rended (b) rented (c) rent
12. She is always .... by illness, when she is asked to study.
    (a) affects (b) effects (c) effected
13. Indian Government is planning to .... many changes in the constitution.
    (a) affect (b) effect (c) effected
14. Hard work is bound to ....your health.
    (a) effect (b) affect (c) effected
15. Corruption has tremendous .... on our political system.
    (a) effect (b) affect (c) affected

Revision Exercise

Directions (Q. Nos 1-5) *Each sentence in this section has three parts labelled as (a), (b) and (c). Read each sentence to find out whether there is any error in any part and indicate your response on the Answer Sheet. If you find no error, your response should be indicated as (d).*

1. None but those (a)/ with honest record (b) / needs to come to me for help (c)/ No error (d)

2. Four miles are (a)/ not a long distance (b)/ for a young person like you (c)/ No error (d)

3. No sooner he was (a)/ brought here (b)/ than he began to feel uneasy (c)/ No error (d)

4. Not only will she (a)/ go there (b)/ but also she will stay (c)/ No error (d)

5. He, like the other members of his family, (a)/ were left shelterless as (b)/ a result of floods in the town (c)/ No error (d)

Directions (Q. Nos 6 and 7) *Read the sentences that have parts, out of which one may have an error. Choose that part as your answer. If the sentence is without error, then choose (e).*

6. I had been to Delhi (a)/ last month to meet (b)/ my ailing father (c)/ who was admitted in a hospital (d)/ No error (e)

7. Either Zara or you (a)/ are to blame (b)/ for the mismanagement (c)/ of the domestic affairs (d)/ No error (e)

Directions (Q. Nos. 8-10) *In the following questions, a sentence is divided into five parts. One part of the sentence may have an error. Find out which part of the sentence has an error, and select the appropriate option. If a sentence is free from error, select 'No error'.*

8. It were the children (A)/ that caused a lot of problems (B)/ to their parents (C)/ during the long railway journey. (D)/No error (E)

(a) A (b) B (c) C (d) D
(e) E

9. Rajnish will be likely (A)/ to leave for the States (B)/ last year to (C)/ visit his wife. (D)/ No error (E)

(a) B (b) C (c) D (d) E
(e) A

10. The soldiers along with the Commander (A)/ was court-martialled (B)/ for defying the orders (C)/ of the Army High-Command (D)/ No error (E)

(a) A (b) C (c) B (d) E
(e) D

Directions (Q. Nos. 11-25) *Choose the most suitable alternative to make the sentence logical.*

11. She .... the child on the bed to keep him warm.

(a) laid (b) lain (c) lay (d) lied

12. My mother asked me to ...... down and take some rest for sometime.

(a) lay (b) lain (c) laid (d) lie

13. The executioner .... her till she died.

(a) hanged (b) hung (c) hang (d) hangs

14. Bhagat Singh .... his life for his motherland.

(a) lie down (b) lay down (c) lied down (d) laid down

15. As soon as we arrived in the dormitory we .... our pullovers.

(a) hang (b) hanged (c) hung (d) hungs

16. This LED TV .... me ₹ 15,000 last year.
(a) costed (b) cost (c) had costed (d) has costed

17. Nobody could have .... the election results correctly.
(a) forecast (b) forcast (c) forecasted (d) forcasting

18. Remember .... your temper even when provoked.
(a) not to loose (b) not to lose (c) not losing (d) not to loss

19. The traders suddenly .... the prices of crude oil last year.
(a) rose (b) rised (c) rise (d) raised

20. Mihir .... suddenly and knocked Tupur down.
(a) arose (b) raised (c) rose (d) rises

21. Difficulty after difficulty .... in his way to success.
(a) arose (b) rose (c) roused (d) raise

22. When the villagers were attacked, they were .... to violent acts.
(a) raised (b) rose (c) rised (d) roused

23. .... our freedom is in danger.
(a) Arise (b) Rise (c) Raise (d) Arose

24. The noise in the bedroom .... me up.
(a) awoke (b) awake (c) woke (d) woked

25. One is .... in duty to help the ageing parents.
(a) bound (b) bounded (c) binding (d) binded

Exam Practice

Directions (Q.Nos. 1-26) *In the following questions, a sentence has been given in parts, out of which a part contains an error. The part with the error is your answer. In case there is no error, then your answer is 'No error'.*

1. Many a man want to be rich quickly. **SSC 2015**
(a) want to be (b) many a man
(c) rich quickly (d) No error

2. The Russian ambassador's whereabouts is not known to anyone. **SSC 2015**
(a) whereabouts is (b) not known to anyone
(c) The Russian ambassador's (d) No error

3. A study is going underway to determine the exact quantity of lead in the water supply. **SSC CGL 2015**
(a) to determine the exact quantity (b) A study is going underway
(c) of lead in the water supply (d) No error

4. Everyone of us should realise that any act of negligence will cause a great harm to our country's security. **SSC CGL 2015**
(a) any act of negligence will cause
(b) Everyone of us should realise that
(c) a great harm to our country's security
(d) No error

5. A large consignment of books are expected. **SSC CGL 2016**
(a) A large (b) consignment of books
(c) are expected (d) No error

6. Cows are amongst the gentlest of animals; none shows more passionate tenderness towards their young. **SSC CGL 2018**
(a) Cows are amongst
(b) towards their young
(c) none shows more
(d) the gentlest of animals

7. The cost of fruits and vegetables have risen abnormally this month. **SSC CGL 2018**
(a) have risen
(b) the cost of fruits and vegetables
(c) this month
(d) abnormally

8. Ten kilometers are a long distance to cover on foot for a child. **SSC CGL 2018**
(a) Ten kilometers are
(b) to cover on foot
(c) a long distance
(d) for a child

9. The Prime Minister along with other ministers have left for America. **SSC CGL 2020**
(a) the other ministers
(b) for America
(c) the Prime Minister along with
(d) have left

10. The mother asked the child why did she cry out in her sleep. **NDA 2016**
(a) The mother asked the child
(b) why did she cry out
(c) in her sleep
(d) No error

11. I asked him that why he was angry but he did not answer. **NDA 2016**
(a) I asked him that
(b) why he was angry
(c) but he did not answer
(d) No error

12. I can fly if I will be a bird. **NDA 2017**
(a) I can fly (b) if I will be (c) a bird (d) No error

13. Never I have seen such a town. **NDA 2017**
(a) Never
(b) I have
(c) seen such a town
(d) No error

14. The owner as well as his servants is honest. **NDA 2018**
(a) The owner
(b) as well as his servants
(c) is honest
(d) No error

15. In my younger days I could run four miles at a stretch. **NDA 2018**
(a) In my younger days
(b) I could run four miles
(c) at a stretch
(d) No error

16. A great part of Arabia is desert. **NDA 2019**
(a) A great part
(b) of Arabia
(c) is desert
(d) No error

17. If Ramesh will be promoted he will get a higher salary. **NDA 2019**
(a) If Ramesh will be promoted
(b) he will get
(c) a higher salary
(d) No error

18. This building comprises of six houses, three parking lots and one basement. **NDA 2020**
(a) This building comprises of six houses
(b) three parking lots
(c) and one basement
(d) No error

19. I am glad that you are here. **CDS 2016**
(a) I am
(b) glad
(c) that you are here
(d) No error

20. Sita with all her sisters were here. **CDS 2016**
(a) Sita with (b) all her sisters (c) were here (d) No error

21. Every student should be asked to give their ideas on the subject. **CDS 2017**
(a) Every student
(b) should be asked
(c) to give their ideas on the subject
(d) No error

22. Emperor Ashoka have conquered Kalinga before he embraced Buddhism. **CDS 2017**
(a) Emperor Ashoka (b) have conquered Kalinga
(c) before he embraced Buddhism (d) No error

23. The students' test results were pleasant. **CDS 2018**
(a) The students (b) test results
(c) were pleasant (d) No error

24. There have been a tornado watch issued for Texas country until 11 o' clock tonight. **CDS 2018**
(a) There have been a tornado watch (b) issued for Texas country
(c) until 11 o'clock tonight (d) No error

25. Children are not allowed to use the swimming pool unless they are with an adult. **CDS 2019**
(a) Children are not allowed (b) to use the swimming pool
(c) unless they are with an adult (d) No error

26. The real voyage of discovery consist not in seeking new landscapes, but in having new eyes. **CDS 2019**
(a) The real voyage of discovery
(b) consist not in seeking new landscapes
(c) but in having new eyes
(d) No error

Directions (Q. Nos. 27-34) *Read each sentence to find out whether there is a grammatical error in it, The error, if any, will be in one part of the sentence. The alphabet corresponding to that part is your answer. If there is 'No Error' the answer is (e).*

27. The priest together with (A)/ his followers were totally injured (B)/ in the accident which occurred last night (C)/ near the unmanned railway crossing. (D)/ No error (E) **SBI Clerk 2018**
(a) A (b) B (c) C (d) D
(e) E

28. The young woman who is watching television in that room (A)/ lived here for more than (B)/ a year, but she has never created (C)/ any problem for us. (D)/ No error (E) **SBI Clerk 2018**
(a) A (b) B (c) C (d) D
(e) E

29. Each of the employees, (A)/ whom the company has chosen to take part (B)/ in the international seminar to be conducted (C)/ in the City Hall, are up to the mark. (D)/ No error (E)
(a) A (b) B (c) C (d) D
(e) E

30. Tribal angst over economic issues (A)/ leading to the scapegoating of non-tribal longtime residents (B)/ reflects the continued failure (C)/ to forge a more inclusive politics in Meghalaya. (D)/ No error (E)
(a) A (b) B (c) C (d) D
(e) E

31. Yesterday I met (A)/ an old friend (B)/ when I am going (C)/ to the market. (D)/ No error (E) **SBI Clerk 2019**
(a) A (b) B (c) C (d) D
(e) E

32. It is widely believe (A)/ that the village which is situated on the (B)/ eastern coast of India will be wiped out (C)/ within a decade (D)/ No error (E) **SBI Clerk 2019**

(a) A (b) B (c) C (d) D
(e) E

33. Not only the (A)/ students, but also (B)/ the principal were (C)/ laughing at the joke he cracked. (D)/No error (E) **SBI Clerk 2019**

(a) A (b) B (c) C (d) E
(e) E

34. FATF strongly urges (A)/ Pakistan to swiftly complete its action plan (B)/ by October 2019 to stop (C)/ terror funding in the country. (D)/ No error (E). **SBI Clerk 2019**

(a) A (b) B (c) C (d) D
(e) E

Answers

Work Book Exercise A

1. Use 'are' in place of 'is'
2. Use 'has' in place of 'have'
3. Use 'has' in place of 'have'
4. No error
5. Use 'was' in place of 'were'
6. Use 'is' in place of 'are'
7. Insert 'allowed' after 'has'
8. No error
9. No error
10. 'is' in place of 'are'
11. Insert 'have' before 'left'
12. No error
13. Use 'did he work' in place of 'he worked'
14. No error
15. No error

Work Book Exercise B

1. Use 'is' in place of 'are'
2. Use 'is a large sum' in place of 'are a large sum'
3. Use 'was' in place of 'were'
4. No error
5. Use 'needs' in place of 'need'
6. Use 'Never have I' in place of 'Never I have'
7. Use 'is' in place of 'will be'
8. No error
9. Use 'was' in place of 'were'
10. Use 'is' in place of 'are'
11. Use 'has' in place of 'have'
12. No error
13. Use 'are' in place of 'is'
14. Use 'goes' for 'does go'
15. No error

Work Book Exercise C

1. (b) **2.** (a) **3.** (b) **4.** (c) **5.** (c) **6.** (c) **7.** (a)
8. (c) **9.** (c) **10.** (a) **11.** (c) **12.** (c) **13.** (b) **14.** (b)
15. (a) **16.** (b) **17.** (c) **18.** (a) **19.** (b) **20.** (a)

Revision Exercise

1. (c) Use 'need' in place of 'needs'.
2. (a) Replace 'are' by 'is'.
3. (a) Use 'was he' in place of 'he was'.
4. (d) No error
5. (b) Use 'was' in place of 'were'.
6. (a) Use 'went' in place of 'had been'.
7. (e) No error
8. (a) Use 'was' in place of were'.
9. (e) Use 'was' in place of 'will be'.
10. (c) Use 'were' in place of 'was'.

11. (a) **12.** (d) **13.** (b) **14.** (d) **15.** (c) **16.** (b) **17.** (c)
18. (b) **19.** (d) **20.** (c) **21.** (a) **22.** (d) **23.** (a) **24.** (c)
25. (a)

Exam Practice

1. (a) 'wants' should be used in place of 'want'.
2. (d) No error
3. (b) 'going' is not needed. Remove 'going'.
4. (d) No error
5. (c) Here 'A large consignment of books' is a singular noun, so 'is' will be used in place of 'are'.
6. (c) 'show' will be used in place of 'shows'.
7. (a) Here 'fruits and vegetables' are taken as a whole. So, a singular verb 'has' will be used in place of 'have'.
8. (a) 'is' will be used in place of 'are'.
9. (d) 'Prime Minister' is a singular noun. So, 'has left' will be used in place of 'have left', 'along with' agrees with the first noun in the sentence.
10. (b) 'Why she had cried out' will be used in place of 'why did she cry out'.
11. (a) 'that' is not needed here, Remove 'that'.
12. (b) 'if I were' will be used in place of 'if I will be'.
13. (b) As there is inversion in the sentence, 'have I' will be used in place of 'I have'.
14. (d) No error
15. (d) No error
16. (d) No error
17. (a) 'is' will be used in place of 'will be'.
18. (a) 'of' will not be used here. So, remove 'of'.
19. (d) No error
20. (c) 'was here' will be used in place of 'were here'.
21. (d) No error
22. (b) 'had' will be used in place of 'have'.
23. (d) No error
24. (a) 'has' will be used in place of 'have'.
25. (d) No error
26. (b) 'consists' will be used in place of 'consist'.
27. (b) 'was' should be used in place of 'were'.
28. (b) 'has been living here for more than' should be used in place of 'lived here for more than' as the sentence describes continuous activity. (Present perfect continuous Tense)
29. (d) 'Each' takes a singular verb. So, 'is' will be used in place of 'are'.
30. (e) No error
31. (c) As the sentence describes an activity that happened in the past ('yesterday'), past tense 'was' will be used in place of 'am'.
32. (a) 'believed' will be used in place of 'believe'.
33. (c) 'was' should be used in place of 'were'.
34. (e) No error

Unit III

Articles

What is an Article?

Articles are very important words in English and so is their knowledge. Articles are used before only nouns to limit or define their uses in the context of the sentence. They impart effectiveness and accuracy to the nouns. In fact, articles are used as **demonstrative adjectives and determiners before nouns.**

There are two kinds of articles.

1. **Indefinite Articles** A, An (in the sense of 'one' and 'any')
2. **Definite Articles** The (in the sense of 'this' and 'that')

Rules of Articles

The Use of Indefinite Articles 'A' and 'An'

Rule **I**

The choice between 'A' and 'An' is determined primarily by **Sound**.

(A) 'A' is used before a word beginning.

(i) With consonant. *For example*

a boy | a child
a student | a book

(ii) With a vowel giving the sound of a consonant. *For example*

a one eyed man | a university student
a European | a unique book
a uniform | a universal problem

(B) 'An' is used before a word beginning.

(i) With a vowel. *For example*

an elephant | an apple
an ass | an umbrella

(ii) With a mute 'h'. *For example*

an hour | an heir
an honourable person | an honest man
an honorary post | an hourly visit

(iii) With a consonant pronounced with the sound of a vowel. *For example*

an LL.B student an M.P.
an M.L.A. an S.P.
an X-ray an F.I.R.

Rule II

(I) Indefinite articles 'A'/'An' are used when we talk of a thing or a person that is indefinite or that is mentioned for the first time. (in the sense of 'one').

(II) Indefinite article is also used to express a class (in the sense of 'any')[Rule III (B)].

(A) Before a singular/countable common noun when it is mentioned for the first time representing no particular person or a thing. *For example*

(i) I need a book. *(one)*
(ii) Twelve inches make a foot. *(one)*
(iii) A beggar came to my door. *(one)*
(iv) Please get me a scooter. *(one)*
(v) She gave her a notebook. *(one)*

(B) Before a singular countable noun which is used to single out some person/something as a representative **of a class of things, animals and persons** [Rule III (C)]. *For example*

(i) A cow is a useful animal. *(any in the sense of class)*
(ii) A beggar cannot be a chooser. *(any in the sense of class)*
(iii) A rose is a beautiful flower. *(any in the sense of class)*
(iv) A son should be obedient. *(any in the sense of class)*

(C) To make a common noun of a proper noun to express quality.

(i) A Shylock is living in my neighbourhood. *(a cruel miser)*
(ii) He is a Vikramaditya known for his fairness. *(a just man)*
[Refer to Rule III (H)]

(D) In certain expressions of quantity with certain numbers and expressions of 'Price/Rate, Speed, Ratio'. *For example*

(i) Rupees ten a kilo. *(ii)* A dozen mangoes.
(iii) Half a dozen. *[Refer to Rule III (L)]*

(E) When 'A/An' represents a weakened form of preposition 'in'. *For example*

(i) He earns fifty thousand rupees a year.
(ii) We should brush our teeth two times a day.

(F) In exclamations with 'what' or 'how' before singular countable nouns. *For example*

(i) What a hot day! *(ii)* What a pretty girl!
(iii) What a naughty child! *(iv)* How fine a day!
(v) What a fool he is! (vi) What kind of a teacher.
(vii) What fool will believe it? [Correct (Interrogative)]

* But we don't say 'What a kind of'.

(G) Note the position of indefinite articles in the following adverbs : **'Rather, very, much, quite, so, too, such, as'** *For example*

(i) It is rather a nuisance.

(ii) It is rather a good step (or a rather good step).

(iii) He is a very good person.

(iv) He is a much hated character.

(v) He is such a nice man that everybody likes him.

(vi) It is quite an interesting story.

(vii) She is as intelligent a student as her brother is.

(viii) She is too weak a student to pass.

(ix) She is so weak a student that she can't pass.

(H) Before a person not known to the speaker. *For example*

(i) A Mr. Gupta = Some Mr. Gupta

(ii) A Mrs. Sharma = Some Mrs. Sharma

(I) Before the verbs used as nouns. *For example*

(i) For a swim | *(ii)* For a talk

(iii) For a visit | *(iv)* For a walk

(v) For a drive | *(vi)* For a rest

(vii) Have a taste | *(viii)* Have a mind

(ix) Have a pain

(J) Before certain phrases. *For example*

(i) In a hurry | *(ii)* A pity

(iii) Take a liking | *(iv)* Feel a shame

(v) Take a fancy | *(vi)* Make a noise

(vii) Tell a lie

(K) Before the words denoting numbers. *For example*

(i) A hundred | *(ii)* A dozen

(iii) A million

(L) Before the adjectives 'little' and 'few' to give the sense of 'some'.

(Rule V on Adjectives)

A little – Some (Quantity)

A few – Some (Number)

(i) I have little money to buy a house. (hardly any)

(ii) Please give me a little sugar. (some)

(iii) He has spent the little money that he had. (some but all)

(iv) There are few boys in the class. (hardly anyone)

(v) I met a few students in the university. (some)

(vi) The few students that were in the class were sitting idle. (some but all)

(M) There is no plural of 'a', 'an'. 'Some' or 'Any' is the equivalent of the plural.

A horse — some horses/any horses

An orange — some oranges/any oranges

The Use of Definite Article 'The'

Rule III

(A) When we talk of a particular person or a thing as already mentioned, known or under discussion. *For example*

(i) The book (which you mentioned) is not available in the market.
(ii) Let us study the lesson carefully. (lesson in hand)

(B) Before **proper nouns** (unique objects) when they refer to the names of historical buildings, mountain ranges, planets, rivers, oceans, gulfs, groups of islands, holy books, ordinals, descriptive names of countries, states, newspapers, magazines, deserts, superlative degree, names of trains, hotels, shops. *For example*

The Persian Gulf	The Taj Mahal	The Netherlands
The Indian Ocean	The best picture	The Sudan
The Ganges	The first man	The USA
The Himalayas	The Sahara	The Maurya Sheraton
The Ramayana	The Bay of Bengal	The Ranjit
The Vedas	The Rajdhani Express	
The Moon	The Times of India	
The Sun	The Frontline	
The Earth	The North Pole	

NOTE 'The' is not used before **Aravali** and **Everest** because they are not mountain ranges.

(C) When a singular noun expresses a class of animal or things. However, 'the' is avoided with their plural forms and persons to express a class. *For example*

(i) The dog is a faithful animal. *(ii)* The rose is a sweet flower.
(iii) The cow is economically useful. *(iv)* Dogs are faithful.
(v) The cows are economically useful. *(Delete 'the')*
(vi) The son should be obedient. *(Delete 'The', use 'A'. 'The' before a person does not express a class of persons)*

(1) In the sense of 'any' to single out a person, a thing or an animal as a representative of a class. *[Refer to Rule II (B)]*

(i) A son should be obedient. *(ii)* A cow is a useful animal.
(iii) A mango is a sweet fruit. *(iv)* Sons should be obedient.

(2) 'Man/Woman/Mankind' used in general sense to represent human race are used without article. *For example*

(i) Man is mortal. *(Used in general sense)*

(D) Before an adjective when it represents a class of persons. *For example*

(i) The rich should help the poor.
(ii) The old are respected by the young.

(E) Before musical instruments. *For example*

(i) He can play the flute.
(ii) She is fond of playing the harmonium.

(F) As an adverb with a comparative sense. (Double comparison) *For example*

(i) The sooner, the better.
(ii) The higher you go, the colder it is.

(G) Before comparative degree in case of a choice. *For example*

(i) She is the weaker of the two sisters.
(ii) Who is the more beautiful of the two sisters?

(H) Before proper noun for the sake of comparison. *For example*

(i) Surdas is the Milton of India.
(ii) Kalidas is the Shakespeare of India. *[Refer to Rule II (C)]*

(I) Before sports cups and trophies. *For example*

(i) India won the Singer Cup last year.
(ii) A number of teams are taking part in the World Cup.

(J) Before physical positions. *For example*

(i) The top of the mountain. *(ii)* The back of the house.
(iii) The centre of the market. *(iv)* The front of the house.

(K) With the cardinal points. *For example*

(i) The Sun rises in the East.
(ii) The Himalayas are to the North of India.

(L) Before a unit of measurement. *For example*

(i) Cloth is sold by the metre.
(ii) Eggs are sold by the dozen. *[Refer to Rule II (D)]*

(M) Before castes and communities. *For example*

(i) The Rajputs are brave people.
(ii) The Marathas are hard working.

(N) Before the adjectives 'same and whole' and after the adjectives 'all and both' used with plural nouns. *For example*

(i) This is the same book that you gave me.
(ii) The whole class was absent. *(iii)* All the boys were present there.
(iv) Both the brothers were honest. *(v)* All sugar is wasted.

(O) In certain idiomatic phrases. *For example*

(i) In the wrong. *(ii)* On the contrary.
(iii) In the town. *(iv)* The benefit of the doubt.
(v) In the air. *(vi)* Speak the truth.
(vii) Out of the question. *(viii)* In the right.

(P) Before a common noun to give it the force of a superlative. *For example*

(i) She is the woman. *(ii)* Netaji was the leader.
(iii) He is the man for this job.

(Q) Before a common noun to give it the sense of an abstract noun (feelings, qualities, etc.). *For example*

(i) The judge in him. *(sense of justice)*

(ii) The mother in her. *(feelings of a mother)*

(iii) The beast in him. *(cruelty of a beast)*

(R) Before inventions. *For example*

(i) The telephone.

(ii) The wireless.

(iii) The television. *(as an invention)*

(iv) He was watching the television. *('television' is used just as a set)*

(v) He was listening to the radio.

(S) Before the name of professions used collectively. *For example*

(i) The Press. *(ii)* The Bench.

(T) Before a noun, qualified by adjectives. *For example*

(i) The former President Abdul Kalam.

(ii) The immortal Shakespeare.

(iii) The late Shri S.C. Bose.

(U) Before the case in apposition. *For example*

(i) Netaji, the hero of Modern India, ought to be remembered.

(ii) Who can underestimate Mr. Vajpayee, the former Prime Minister?

(V) Before the dates. *For example*

(i) The 10th of May. *(ii)* The 5th of September.

(W) Before the organs of government. *For example*

(i) The Judiciary *(ii)* The Legislature

(X) Before the parts of a body of a person in place of possessive adjectives. *For example*

(i) He hit me on the back. *(ii)* She caught me by the arm.

(Y) Before the political parties. *For example*

(i) The BJP (ii) The Labour Party

(iii) The Janta Party

(Z) (a) Before the Armed Forces. *For example*

(i) The Army *(ii)* The Police

(iii) The Air Force

(b) Before the dynasties, empires, wars, revolutions, centuries. *For example*

(i) The Gupta Dynasty *(ii)* The British Empire

(iii) The Red Revolution *(iv)* The Middle Ages

(v) The Civil War *(vi)* The Vedic Ages

(vii) The Sixth Century

(c) Before language to signify nationality. *For example*

(i) The Chinese are hard working.

(ii) The Japanese are patriots out and out.

(d) Before nationality (plural). *For example*

(i) The Greeks *(ii)* The Indians
(iii) The Asians

NOTE But for singular nouns, we say
An Indian, An Asian, A Greek.

(e) Before little and few. *[Refer to Rule II (L)]*

(i) The little – some but all *(ii)* The few – some but all

Rule IV The Omission of Articles

The articles 'A/An, The' are omitted.

(A) Before proper nouns. *For example*

(i) Shakespeare was the greatest dramatist.
(ii) Delhi is the capital of India.

NOTE (a) When indefinite articles are used before proper nouns they become **common nouns**.
(b) 'The' before a proper noun is used for the sake of comparison. *For example*
(i) This man is a Shylock. (a miser)
(ii) Samudra Gupta was the Napolean of his age.
(The greatest General of his time.)

(B) Before names of materials. *For example*

(i) Silver is a useful metal. *(ii)* Tea grows in India.
(iii) The tea of Assam is very famous. *(particular tea)*
(iv) The water of the Ganga is sacred. *(particular water)*

(C) Before common noun used in its widest sense. *For example*

(i) Man is mortal. *(ii)* God is omnipresent.
(iii) The Gods and the Goddesses are kind to him. (in the sense of deities).

(D) Before abstract nouns as qualities, feelings and states used in general sense. *For example*

(i) Truth is a noble quality.
(ii) Love is a natural feeling.
(iii) Honesty is the best policy.

NOTE But we can say. *For example*
(i) The honesty of my brother is beyond any doubt.
(ii) He always tells a lie.
(iii) He always speaks the truth.

(E) Before noun complement. (appoint, make, elect, select, etc.) *For example*

(i) The committee appointed him Captain.
(ii) They elected him President.

(F) Before collective nouns in general sense. *For example*

(i) Life is complex. *(ii)* Society does not allow this.

(G) Before uncountable nouns. (Refer to Rule I in the chapter on Nouns). *For example*

(i) He gave me advice. *(ii)* He passed on information to me.

(H) Before languages. *For example*

(i) Chinese is a difficult language.

(ii) He knows Russian very well. *[Rule III Z(b)]*

(iii) He knows the Sanskrit language.

(I) Before **'school, college, home, church, temple, sea, work, bed, table, hospital, market, prison, court'** when their purpose is thought of rather than the actual building/place. *For example*

(i) We go to temple on Mondays. (for prayer)

(ii) The thief went to the bed. (upto the bed)

(iii) I go to bed early. (to sleep)

(iv) He was sent to prison after conviction. (as a prisoner)

(v) He went to Sea is his early youth. (as a sailor)

(vi) He went to the Sea alone. (travel & other purposes)

NOTE 'The' is used before **'office, cinema, movie, theatre, picture, circus, station, bus stop'**, etc.

(J) Before 'hobbies, professions and sports'. *For example*

(i) Dancing is her profession. *(ii)* Gardening is his hobby.

(K) Before names of diseases. *For example*

(i) Cancer is a dreaded disease. *(ii)* AIDS is spreading like wild fire.

NOTE But we can say, the Measles, the Mumps, the Rickets, the Plague, the Flu.

(L) Before regular meals except when preceded by an adjective. *For example*

(i) I take breakfast at 8 a.m. *(ii)* You should take dinner early.

(iii) They gave us a good breakfast. *(iv)* A good breakfast is necessary.

(v) A dinner in honour of the President will be held. (in the sense of Party)

(M) Before parts of the body. *For example*

Liver is the largest organ of human body.

(N) Before modes of travel. *For example*

(i) He will go by air.

(ii) A journey by road is very comfortable.

(O) Before names of relations like 'Uncle, mother, father', etc. in place of possessive adjectives. *For example*

(i) Father will go to Delhi tomorrow.

(ii) Aunt is expected any moment.

NOTE 'Father' and 'Aunt' implies 'our father' and 'our aunt'.

(P) In certain phrases. *For example*

(i) To lose heart.	*(vii)* Last but not least.
(ii) To set foot.	*(viii)* To catch fire.
(iii) To give ear.	*(iv)* To send word.
(iv) By day.	*(x)* In hand.
(v) At sunrise.	*(xi)* By name.
(vi) At home.	*(xii)* At last.

(Q) Study the following phrases carefully.

(i) In summer, winter	+	in the summer season.
(ii) From beginning to end	+	from the beginning of the day to the end of the day.
(iii) From right to left	+	keep to the left.
(iv) At dawn, at midday, at noon, at night, at dusk	+	during the day, in the afternoon, in the evening, in the night.
(v) Next week (time)	–	the next question (number).
Last week (time)	–	the last question (number).

(R) Before such nouns as
'Cattle, gentry, people', etc. When they are used in general sense.

(Refer to Rule II on Nouns)

(S) Before little, few. (in negative sense).

(i) Little sugar (hardly any)
(ii) Few students (hardly any one) *[Refer to Rule II (L)]*

Rule V

(A) When two or more connected nouns refer to the same person or thing, the article should be used before the first noun. However, the article is used before each noun if they refer to two different persons or objects. *For example*

(i) The Prime Minister and the President are visiting the town today.

(Two different persons holding two different posts.)

(ii) The Prime Minister and President of the party is on a visit to the town today.

(One person holding two posts.)

(B) Similarly, one article before the first adjective is used when two or more adjectives qualify the same noun. *For example*
She is wearing a black and a white saree. *(Omit 'a' before 'white')*

(C) If there are two articles before ordinals, use singular noun. In the case of article before one ordinal, noun should be used in plural form. *For example*

(i) The first and the second **chapter** are very difficult.
(ii) The first and second **chapters** are very difficult.

NOTE The article is not repeated with plural nouns. Verb is in plural form in the sentences given in 'C'.

Work Book Exercise A

Direction *Spot the error, if any, in the following sentences.*

1. My friend always likes to travel by the air since he is a very busy man.
2. Dr. Radha Krishnan was a more famous philosopher than a politician.
3. The Manager and the Executive Director of our hotel is a very energetic person.
4. Whenever I meet him, he always makes a mention of his father.
5. Although he has undergone a very costly treatment, he has not been cured of a headache.
6. Those in hurry should realise that speed is no key to success in life.
7. God made country and man made town.
8. It is pity that he does not behave humbly with his parents and friends.
9. Being M.A. only he could not be appointed to the post of a lecturer.
10. He always takes a heavy breakfast because he generally skips lunch.
11. Please go and find out dog so that you may not lose it forever.
12. Snake we saw was very deadly though it left the kitchen quietly.
13. Tonight I shall go to the bed early because I have to leave for Mumbai at dawn tomorrow.
14. Child needs love and affection if he is to be brought up as a healthy young man.
15. It is said that elephant is vindictive by nature and never forgets his enemy.
16. It is very difficult to get a taxi at such a hour as it is already 11 p.m.
17. Do you take a sugar and if so, how much?
18. She lives in first storey of the house and she has to come down quite often.
19. He knows how to play flute. He learnt it while he was a student.
20. What nice mother she is, because she takes care of every small need of her children.

Work Book Exercise B

Direction *Spot the error, if any, in the following sentences.*

1. He is as a weak boy as my brother.
2. It is futile to give an advice to a person who would not listen to you.
3. 'The pride hath a fall', says the Bible.
4. She is both a virtuous and a beautiful daughter of a successful working mother.
5. He has been sent to the prison several times but has not shown any sign of improvement in his conduct.
6. He was watching the television when I called him last night.
7. Prince William is a heir to the throne of the Great Britain.
8. Tea we used to get in the Scouting Camp was never to our taste.
9. It was a so hot day that it was impossible to go out shopping.
10. I shall never forget a good deed you did to me, when I was in crisis.

11. The singing is both my vocation and avocation because it is a source of joy and bread to me.
12. Surdas is often called Milton of India, although unlike Milton, Surdas had no political ambitions.
13. Higher you go, colder it is.
14. The old woman placed kettle on fire and came back to the bedroom.
15. Never give the ear to the slanderous talk of others because they are always motivated by jealousy.
16. The District Magistrate possesses both the civil and criminal jurisdiction.
17. You must enjoy classical music on radio even if you are not able to understand its true spirit.
18. I have a work to do and so I will reach late.
19. You should be true to a word because it is a characteristic of a gentleman.
20. This young man is in search of an employment because he is in a grave financial crisis.

Revision Exercise

Directions (Q. Nos. 1-10) *Each sentence in this question has three underlined parts, labelled as (a), (b) and (c). Read each sentence to find out whether there is any error in any underlined part and indicate your response on the answer sheet against the corresponding letter. If you find no error, your response should be indicated as (d).*

1. It is said that (a) he is a wise (b) man. He cannot err. Vedas may err. (c) No error (d)
2. These days only rich (a) can afford the hospitality of the costly (b) nursing homes and hospitals coming up all over the country. (c) No error (d)
3. Rajputs belong to a martial race (a) since they were organized (b) into the force to fight against the oppression of the rulers. (c) No error (d)
4. What a kind of (a) a fellow he is, (b) if his enemies are to be believed. (c) No error (d)
5. Kapil Dev bought glory (a) to India by winning (b) World Cup in 1983. (c) No error (d)
6. Although he is a hard working (a) student, his success in the (b) examination is out of question. (c) No error (d)
7. Wisdom of Vikramaditya (a) solved many riddles (b) that people bought to him for solution. (c) No error (d)

8. The Chinese is a very (a) / difficult language to understand (b) / for those who have never been to China. (c) / No error (d)

9. News you broke to his wife (a) / made her nervous (b) / and she broke down. (c) / No error (d)

10. The lions (a) / are (b) / carnivorous. (c) / No error (d)

Directions (Q. Nos. 11-13) *Read each sentence to find out whether there is any grammatical or idiomatic error in it. The error, if any, will be in one part of the sentence. The number of that part is the answer. If there is 'No error', the answer is (e).*

11. The English usually (a)/ spend their (b)/ holidays in (c)/ mountains. (d) No error (e)

12. I can't live on (a)/ the petty amount (b)/of ten thousand (c)/ a month. (d) No error (e)

13. I don't like (a)/ the cats, but (b)/ I like Shweta's (c)/ cat a lot. (d) No error (e)

Directions (Q. Nos. 14-16) *Read the following sentences to find out whether there is any grammatical/idiomatic error in it. The error, if any, will be in one part of the sentence. Mark the part as your answer. If there is no error, mark 'No error' as your answer. Ignore errors of punctuation, if any.*

14. Lal Bahadur Shastri is / the real / Indian hero / of the 20th century.
(a) Lal Bahadur Shastri is
(b) the real
(c) Indian hero
(d) of the 20th century.
(e) No error

15. Here is / the Mumbai Indians / squad for / IPL 2020.
(a) IPL 2020.
(b) squad for
(c) Here is
(d) the Mumbai Indians
(e) No error

16. Someone called/ the policeman/ when he saw/ the building on fire.
(a) Someone called
(b) when he saw
(c) the building on fire
(d) the policeman
(e) No error

Directions (Q. Nos. 17-20) *Read each sentence to find out whether there is any grammatical or idiomatic error in it. The error, if any, will be in one part of the sentence. The alphabet corresponding to that part is the answer. If there is 'No error', the answer is (e). Ignore errors of punctuation, if any.*

17. This is (A)/ the best Thar restaurant (B)/in the (C)/ North India. (D)/ No error (E)
(a) A
(b) B
(c) C
(d) D
(e) E

18. VK Krishna Menon (A)/ proposed the idea (B)/ of Universal Children's Day (C)/ to the UN General Assembly. (D)/ No error (E)
(a) A
(b) C
(c) E
(d) B
(e) D

19. All countries should (A)/ introduce the annual (B)/ event to encourage togetherness (C)/ and understanding between children all over the world. (D)/ No error (E)
(a) B
(b) A
(c) C
(d) D
(e) E

20. Kamla veered off (A)/ to the left (B)/ and leapt easily (C)/ over low wall. (D)/ No error (E)
(a) A
(b) C
(c) B
(d) E
(e) D

Exam Practice

Directions (Q. Nos. 1 and 2) *Each sentence in this question has three underlined parts labelled as (a), (b) and (c). Read each sentence to find out whether there is any error in any underlined part and mark your response to the corresponding letter. If you find no error, your response should be indicated as (d).*

1. An electrical circuit (a)/ is the complete path (b)/ traversed by electric current. (c)/ No error (d) **NDA 2017**
2. He appears (a)/ to be (b)/ a honest man. (c)/ No error (d) **NDA 2018**

Directions (Q. Nos. 3-10) *Read each sentence to find out whether there is any grammatical or idiomatic error in it. The error, if any, will be in one part of the sentence. The number of that part is the answer. If there is 'No error', the answer is (e).*

3. While residential land purchases (a)/ have benefitted many investors (b)/buying land can be risky (c)/ especially for a NRI. (d)/ No error (e) **SBI 2016**
4. The criminal was (a)/ sentenced to the (b)/ death and was (c)/ hung for his crime. (d)/ No error (e) **SBI 2019**
5. The iron (a)/ is a (b)/ heavy (c)/ metal. (d)/ No error (e) **IBPS 2015**
6. The more (a)/ you work hard (b)/ more (c)/ you would gain. (d)/No error (e) **IBPS 2015**
7. Pope is (a)/ visiting (b) Russia this (c)/ weekend. (d)/ No error (e)
8. Sumer could (a)/ play (b)/ guitar (c)/ when he was five years old. (d)/ No error (e)
9. The police are (a)/ searching for a (b)/ 14 year old (c)/ girl. (d)/ No error (e)
10. Afroz is (a)/ pupil of (b)/ the Happy School (c)/ in Daryaganj. (d)/ No error (e)

Directions (Q. Nos. 11-16) *Read the following sentences to find out whether there is any grammatical mistake/error in them. The error, if any, will be in one part of the sentence. Mark that part as your answer. If there is no error, mark 'No error' as your answer. Ignore errors of punctuation, if any.*

11. One of the/ students said, /"A teacher is/late today." **IBPS 2016**
    (a) One of the (b) students said, (c) "A teacher is (d) late today."
    (e) No error
12. My sister-in-law's/family speaks/the Polish/and English. **IBPS 2016**
    (a) the Polish (b) My sister-in-law's (c) family speaks (d) and English.
    (e) No error
13. Prisha is/learning to/play a/guitar these days. **IBPS 2017**
    (a) guitar these days. (b) Prisha is (c) learning to (d) play a
    (e) No error
14. Never in my/life have I/seen a more/perplexed driver. **IBPS 2018**
    (a) perplexed driver. (b) Never in my (c) seen a more (d) life have I
    (e) No error
15. I lived on/ the Mount Road/ when I first/ shifted to Chennai. **SBI 2019**
    (a) shifted to Chennai. (b) the Mount Road
    (c) when I first (d) I lived on
    (e) No error
16. Our neighbours are/ the owners of/ a cat/ and the dog. **NDA 2016**
    (a) the owners of (b) Our neighbours are
    (c) a cat (d) and the dog.
    (e) No error

Answers

Work Book Exercise A

1. Drop 'the' before 'air'
2. Drop 'a' before 'politician'
3. Drop 'the' before 'executive'
4. Drop 'a' before 'mention'
5. Drop 'a' before 'headache'
6. Insert 'a' before 'hurry'
7. Insert 'the' before 'country' and 'town'
8. Insert 'a' before 'pity'
9. Insert 'an' before 'MA'
10. No error
11. Insert 'the' before 'dog'
12. Insert 'the' before 'snake'
13. Drop 'the' before 'bed'
14. Insert 'A' before 'child'
15. Insert 'the' before 'elephant'
16. Replace 'a' with 'an' before 'hour'
17. Drop 'a' before 'sugar'
18. Insert 'the' before 'first'
19. Insert 'the' before 'flute'
20. Insert 'a' before 'nice'

Work Book Exercise B

1. Remove 'a'
2. Drop 'an' before 'advice'
3. Drop 'The' before 'pride'
4. Drop 'a' before 'beautiful'
5. Drop 'the' before 'prison'
6. Drop 'the' before 'television'
7. 'an' in place of 'a'
8. Insert 'The' before 'tea'
9. Insert 'a' before 'day' and drop 'a' before 'so'
10. 'the' in place of 'a'
11. Drop 'The' before 'singing'
12. Insert 'the' before 'Milton'
13. Insert 'the' before 'higher' and 'colder'
14. Insert 'the' before 'fire'
15. Drop 'the' before 'ear'
16. Insert 'the' before 'criminal'
17. Insert 'the' before 'radio'
18. Drop 'a' before 'work' or use 'a piece of work'
19. Drop 'a' before 'word'
20. Drop 'an' before 'employment'

Revision Exercise

1. (c) Add 'The' before 'Vedas'
2. (a) Add 'the' before 'rich'
3. (a) Add 'The' before 'Rajputs'
4. (a) Remove 'a'
5. (c) Add 'the' before 'World'
6. (d) No error
7. (a) Add 'The' before 'wisdom'
8. (a) Remove 'The' before 'Chinese'
9. (a) Add 'The' before 'news'
10. (a) Remove 'The'
11. (d) Add 'the' before 'mountains'
12. (e) No error
13. (b) Remove 'the' before 'cats'
14. (b) Use 'a' in place of 'the'
15. (a) Add 'the' before 'IPL'
16. (d) Use 'a' in place of 'the'
17. (c) Remove 'the'
18. (c) No error
19. (a) Use 'an' in place of 'the'
20. (e) Add 'the' before 'low'

Exam Practice

1. (c) Add 'the' before 'electric'
2. (c) Replace 'a' by 'an'
3. (c) Replace 'a' by 'an'
4. (b) Remove 'the'
5. (a) Remove 'The'
6. (c) Add 'the' before 'more' in part (c) of the sentence
7. (a) Add 'The' before 'pope'
8. (c) Add 'the' before 'guitar'
9. (e) No error
10. (b) Add 'a' before 'pupil'
11. (c) Replace 'A' by 'The'
12. (a) Remove 'the' before 'Polish'
13. (d) Remove 'a' and add 'the' in place of it
14. (e) No error
15. (e) No error
16. (d) Use 'a' in place of 'the'

Noun

What is a Noun?

A Noun is used as the name of a person, thing, place, idea and a quality of a person.

(I) **Kinds of Noun**

(a) **Common Noun** It is the name given in common to every person or thing of the same kind. It is not a name of any particular person thing or place. *For example* boy, girl, teacher, etc.

(b) **Proper Noun** It is the name given to a particular person, thing or place. *For example* Delhi, Sania, India, Jupiter, etc.

(c) **Collective Noun** It is the name of a collection of persons and things treated and spoken together as a whole.
For example fleet, audience, class, committee, crowd, mob, etc.

(d) **Abstract Noun** It is the name of a quality, idea, concept or state.
For example beauty, youth, honesty, death, etc.

(e) **Material Noun** It is the name of a material or substance from which things are made. *For example* gold, coal, wheat, tea, etc.

(II) **Number of a Noun** Singular - Plural

(III) **Gender of a Noun** Masculine - Feminine - Neuter

(IV) **Case of a Noun**

For example

(i) Mohan is my friend. *Subjective/Nominative case*

(ii) Who brought this book? *Objective/Accusative case*

(iii) She is Mohan's wife. *Possessive/Genetive case*

(iv) Help me, Mohan. *Vocative case*

Case in Apposition

Mohan, the Captain of our team, has been rewarded.

Appositon means placing near the word just as 'captain' is placed after 'Mohan'. It is a kind of descriptive expression not joined by any conjunction.

Rules of Noun

Rule I

(A) (a) Uncountable Nouns are used in singular forms only.

(b) Indefinite articles are not used before them.

(c) They are not used with plural verbs.

(d) 'Much' or 'Some' are used in place of 'Many' for denoting plurality.

Some of the important Nouns of this kind are

'Advice, information, hair, luggage, business, work, word (in the sense of promise, message, discussion), **mischief, bread, scenery, abuse, vacation, money, knowledge, evidence, employment, alphabet, poetry, food, furniture, baggage, fuel, paper, equipment, machinery, material, etc'.**

For example

(i) He gave me an information. *(Omit 'an')*

(ii) You should be true to your words. *(Use 'word' in place of 'words')*

(iii) He was punished for committing many mischiefs. *(Use 'much mischief' in place of 'many mischiefs')*

(iv) Young persons dislike the advices of the elderly people. *(Use 'advice' in place of 'advices')*

(B) These nouns may be used to denote singularity as follows

(i) a piece/a word of advice. *(ii)* a word of abuse

(iii) an act of mischief. *(iv)* a piece of work.

(v) a piece/loaf of bread. *(vi)* an article of luggage.

(C) These nouns may be used to denote plurality as follows

(i) much/some advice.

(ii) a lot of/many words/many pieces of advice.

(iii) two pieces/loaves of bread. *(iv)* words of abuse.

Rule II

There are some collective nouns which are used with plural verbs. *For example*

(a) **'cattle, gentry, peasantry, poultry, clergy, people, majority, folk.'**

(b) The nouns **'committee, jury, house, ministry, family, mob, crowd, audience, police, team, number, board, staff, public'** are used with singular verbs when they are used as a body or group.

(c) When these nouns denote members or individuals, the verb is used in Plural form.

(i) Cattles **are** grazing in the field. *(Use 'cattle' in place of 'cattles')*

(ii) Majority **is** in favour of this proposal. *(Use 'are' in place of 'is')*

(iii) The committee **is** unanimous on this issue. *(Correct)*

(iv) The committee **are** divided and there is bitterness among the members. *(Correct)*

(v) The people of all the countries should work for peace. *(Correct)*

(vi) An average Hindu family in India **consists** of four members. *(Correct)*
(vii) His family **are** not agreed on this point. *(Correct)*
(viii) The audience **was** spell-bound. *(Correct)*
(ix) The audience **were** forbidden to occupy chairs. *(Correct)*
(x) The Police **has** become insensitive. *(Correct)*
(xi) The Police **were** posted all over the route. *(Correct)*
(xii) The team **are** full of high spirits. *(Correct)*
(xiii) The team **is** at the top in this competition. *(Correct)*

Rule III

'Offspring, deer, fish, sheep' are expressed as singular or plural only by the use of verb. Both in singular and the plural they have the same form.

(i) Sheeps are economically useful. *(Use 'Sheep' in place of 'Sheeps')*
(ii) A sheep is grazing in the field. *(Correct)*

NOTE 'Fishes' may be used in the sense of different number and kind.

Rule IV

Some of the nouns (ending in 's' or 'es') are used with singular verbs.

(A) Branches of learning. *For example*
Mathematics, Physics, Mechanics, Politics, Statistics, Statics, Economics.

NOTE Statistics as subject is used with **singular verb**. Statistics when taken as a collection of data is used with **plural verb**.

(B) Diseases. *For example*
Mumps, Measles, Rickets, etc.

(C) Games and sports. *For example*
Billiards, Aquatics, Gymnastics, Athletics, etc.

(D) Titles of books. *For example*
The Three Musketeers, Gulliver's Travels, Arabian Nights, War and Peace, Tales from Shakespeare, etc.

(E) Descriptive names of countries. *For example*
United States, United Arab Emirates, United Kingdom, etc.

(F) Some other nouns are
Innings, Series, News, Summons. *For example*

(i) The measles have broken out in the town. *(Use 'has' in place of 'have')*
(ii) Politics are a dirty game. *(Use 'is' in place of 'are')*
(iii) These news are disappointing. *(Say 'This news is')*
(iv) The summons has been served on him. *(Correct)*
(v) A series of matches are being played. *(Use 'is' in place of 'are')*
(vi) Two series of matches was played last year. *(Use 'were' in place of 'was')*

Rule V

Study the uses of Nouns as singular and plural in forms.

Noun	Used as	Noun	Used as
Wood	Material	Woods	Forest
Water	Material	Waters	Sea
Asset	Quality	Assets	Property
Sand	Material	Sands	Land
Iron	Material	Irons	Chains
Cloth	Material	Clothes	Dress
Abuse	Indecent words	Abuses	Misuses
Work	Labour	Works	Literary writings
Air	Element	Airs	Behaviour
Advice	Suggestion	Advices	Bills
Custom	Habit	Customs	Tax
Effect	Result	Effects	Goods
Colour	Material	Colours	Flag
Fruit	Edible thing	Fruits	Results
Wit	Ability to talk	Wits	Intelligence
Arm	Organ	Arms	Weapons
Good	Advantage/use	Goods	Articles

Rule VI

Some nouns are generally used in plural form with plural verb.

(a) Articles of dress.
'Trousers, breeches, Jeans'

(b) Names of instruments.
'Scissors, spectacles, shears, scales'

(c) Other nouns such as
'Alms, thanks, proceeds, riches, contents, credentials, orders, refreshments, requirements, customs, rations, archives, annals, ashes, arrears, assets, stairs, spirits, statistics (data), **quarters, earnings, manners outskirts, savings, auspices** (support), **surroundings.** *For example*

(i) My scissors is not sharp. *(Use 'are' in place of 'is')*
(ii) My spectacles is very costly. *(Use 'are' in place of 'is')*
(iii) A pair of spectacles has been bought by me. *(Correct)*
(iv) Order for his transfer has been issued. *(Incorrect)*
Orders for his transfer have been issued. *(Correct)*

Rule VII

A compound noun (numerical + noun) is not used in plural if a noun does the work of an adjective. *For example*

(i) Ten-day tour
(ii) A ten-mile race
(iii) A ten-year old boy
(iv) He is a ten year old musician.
(v) A five-rupee note
(vi) Five-foot long room

Rule VIII

Nouns expressing number are used in singular with numerical adjectives.
'Two hundred, two thousand, five dozen, two score, two million, three lakh.'
For example

(i) I gave him two hundreds rupees. *(Omit 's' in 'hundreds')*
(ii) I gave him five dozens pencils. *(Omit 's' in 'dozens')*
(iii) There are hundreds of partially built houses. *(Correct)*

Rule IX

Use of Apostrophe with 's'

(A) The use of apostrophe with 's' is not correct in the case of non-living things. It is restricted only to living things, time, weight, distance, amount or personified nouns.

(i) Boy's hand.
(ii) Time's march.
(iii) A one-kilometre's journey.
(iv) A rupee's worth.
(v) A night's journey.
(vi) A metre's length.
(vii) Nature's laws.
(viii) A week's holiday.

(B) Two nouns in the possessive case denote plural form. When apostrophe with 's' is used with one noun, it expresses singular form. *For example*

(i) Sheela and Rohit's father. *(the father of both Sheela and Rohit)*
(ii) Sheela's and Rohit's fathers are meeting today. *(fathers of Sheela and Rohit)*

(C) With compound nouns apostrophe with 's' should be added only with the last word.

(i) Mother-in-law's behaviour
(ii) Maid-servant's absence.

(D) Pronouns are written by omitting apstrophe but 's' is added. *For example*

(i) Yours truly *(ii)* Its colour
(iii) Hers *(iv)* It's (It is)

(E) Possessive case is indicated by apostrophe without 's' after Plural nouns or words ending with 's'.

(i) John Keats' poems.
(ii) Girls' Hostel.
(iii) Dickens' novels.
(iv) Jesus' sake.
(v) Kalidas' works.

(F) (a) 'Else' combined with indefinite pronouns (somebody, anybody, nobody, etc.) is expressed in possessive case as **somebody else's** in place of somebody's else.

(b) The correct expression 'whose else' should be used in place of the expression 'who else's'. However 'who else' is also correct.

(i) This is not my book. This is somebody's else *(Say somebody else's)*

(ii) Who else is coming? *(Correct)*

(iii) Who else's book is this? *(Use 'whose else' in place of 'who else's')*

NOTE 'Who' should be converted into possessive 'whose'. So 'whose else' is correct.

Rule X

Two adjectives denoting different meanings and qualifying the same noun are considered plural and are used with plural verbs. *For example*

(i) Cultural and social life in India are changing.

(ii) Summer and winter vacation are compulsory in our schools.

(Look up Rule V on Articles)

Rule XI

Noun after preposition is repeated in singular form. *For example*

(i) Word for word. *(ii)* Hour after hour.

(iii) Door to door.

Rule XII

The use of fractions.

(i) One and a half years are wasted. *(ii)* One and a half hours are wasted.

(iii) A year and a half is wasted. *(iv)* An hour and a half is wasted.

Rule XIII

Study the plural forms of the nouns given below carefully.

Singular Form	Plural Form	Singular Form	Plural Form
Commander-in-chief	Commanders-in-chief	Medium	Media
Major General	Major Generals	Forum	Forums, Fora
Attorney General	Attorneys General	Stadium	Stadia
Maid servant	Maid servants	Criterion	Criteria
Looker-on	Lookers-on	Phenomenon	Phenomena
Passer by	Passers by	Formula	Formulae
Mother-in-law	Mothers-in-law	Oasis	Oases
Man servant	Men servants	Lacuna	Lacunae
Woman servant	Women servants	Erratum	Errata
M.A.	M.A.'s	Memorandum	Memoranda
Mouse	Mice	Alumnus	Alumni
Ox	Oxen	Syllabus	Syllabi
Datum	Data	Addendum	Addenda

Work Book Exercise A

Directions *Spot the error, if any, in the following sentences.*

1. Cattles are not allowed to enter this ground.
2. The enemy has received many informations regarding the activities of the army of our neighbouring country.
3. Order has been issued for his transfer to another district but he has not received them so far.
4. The hills of the Uttar Pradesh abound in beautiful sceneries and visitors are attracted to it every year.
5. Although she has studied English for almost a year, she has yet to learn the alphabets.
6. There are two scores of books which are lying unused in the library.
7. Children are prone to making mischiefs if they have nothing to do.
8. Sheeps are economically useful and so they are reared in the hills.
9. I have not gone through the letter and so I am not aware of its content.
10. Twenty cattles were found wandering on the road.
11. I shall not attend the meeting since I have many works to complete within allotted time.
12. It is difficult to find man servants in big cities because they are engaged in other profitable professions.
13. All his sister-in-laws are married and settled in the U.K.
14. You should always be true to your words if you are to succeed in life.
15. It is a pity that even five years old boys are engaged in hazardous factories.

Work Book Exercise B

Directions *Spot the error, if any, in the following sentences.*

1. Ration has run out and the District Magistrate has been informed.
2. The table's wood is infested with mite and I am likely to dispose it of.
3. The morale of the army was high because the news coming from the front were very encouraging.
4. The majority likes reading sensational stories and watching western movies.
5. A variety of books is available in the market to help the students qualify the competitive examinations.
6. Variety are the spice of life otherwise life may become dull and drab.
7. Lots of friends come to meet him whenever he visits his home town.
8. He never believes in using a fair means because they are not acceptable in this materialistic age.
9. A plenty of informations about his activities was passed on to his boss.
10. I can't come to you now because a lot of works remains to be done.
11. All the evidences against him were rejected by the High Court.
12. Commander's-in-chief orders arrived late and the forces had to retreat.
13. Have you deposited the proceed in the Bank or not?
14. You can buy the scissors that is sharp.
15. He goes fishing everyday and brings a lot of fishes that his wife cooks for him.

Revision Exercise

Directions (Q. Nos. 1-5) *Each sentence in this question has three parts labelled (a), (b) and (c). Read each sentence to find out whether there is any error in any part and indicate your response against the corresponding letter. If you find no error, you response should be indicated as (d).*

1. I wanted to get (a) a hair cut today (b) but couldn't get time. (c) No error (d)

2. In my country, maths are (a) a compulsory subject (b) until you're sixteen. (c) No error (d)

3. I don't know (a) if this table is (b) made of a wood or plastic. (c) No error (d)

4. I always carry (a) two pairs of (b) binocular with me. (c) No error (d)

5. Everything depends (a) on President Trump's (b) election results now. (c) No error. (d)

Directions (Q. No. 6-10) *Read the following sentences to find out whether there is any grammatical or idiomatic error in it. The error, if any, will be in one part of the sentence. That part is the answer. If there is no error, the answer is 'No Error'.*

6. Recently a Van Gogh/was sold/for 20 million/dollars.
(a) Recently a Van Gogh
(b) was sold
(c) for 20 million
(d) dollars
(e) No error

7. Four dozens eggs/have been sold/by me/in the market today.
(a) Four dozens eggs
(b) have been sold
(c) by me
(d) in the market today
(e) No error

8. Louse is a/small insect that/lives on the hair or skin/of people or animals.
(a) Small insect that
(b) Louse is a
(c) of people or animals
(d) lives on the hair or skin
(e) No error

9. The CEO firmly believes/that a radical change/in the structure of our/various departments are necessary.
(a) The CEO firmly believes
(b) that a radical change
(c) in the structure of our
(d) various departments are necessary
(e) No error

10. The shadow was/an expected effect/of the/floodlights in the stadium.
(a) of the
(b) floodlights in the
(c) The shadow was
(d) an unexpected effect
(e) No error

Directions (Q. Nos. 11-15) *Read each sentence to find out whether there is any grammatical or idiomatic error in it. The error, if any, will be in one part of the sentence. The alphabet corresponding to that part is your answer. If there is no error, the answer is (e). (Ignore errors of punctuation, if any)*

11. His censor was (A) appropriate as (B)/he is the (C) writer of the script. (D) No error (E)
(a) A
(b) B
(c) C
(d) D
(e) E

12. The Republic Day parade (A) will precede (B) down the (C)/designated route. (D)/ No error (E)

(a) A (b) C (c) B (d) E
(e) D

13. The volunteers went (A)/ to the (B) disaster site (C)/to rescue the trapped workers. (D)/ No error (E)

(a) A (b) E (c) C (d) B
(e) D

14. Ramesh's son-in-laws (A)/are coming (B)/to meet him (C)/this weekend. (D)/No error (E)

(a) E (b) C (c) A (d) D
(e) B

15. The website has (A)/a list of (B)/ best onlines offers (C)/for customers. (D)/No Error (E)

(a) A (b) B (c) C (d) D
(e) E

Directions (Q. Nos. 16-25) *Each of the following sentences in this section has a blank space and four words or group of words given after the sentence. Select the word or group of words you consider the most appropriate for the blank space and indicate your response on the Answer sheet accordingly.*

16. .... are tiny, wingless, parasitic insects that feed on human blood.

(a) Vice (b) Rice
(c) House (d) Lice

17. The .... created a scene outside the mall entry.

(a) divorce (b) repartee
(c) divorcee (d) resource

18. It took a lot of .... to talk to your boss like that.

(a) chutzpah (b) voice
(c) cowardice (d) summon

19. The .... are very comfortable.

(a) bus's seats (b) bus' seats (c) bus seats (d) seats of the bus

20. The tennis tournament is open to both .... and professionals.

(a) amateur's (b) matures
(c) pros (d) amateurs

21. The first .... of COVID-19 include fever and cold.

(a) symposium (b) symptom
(c) symptoms (d) seasons

22. My father attended a .... on Land Information Systems (LIS) organised by Survey of India.

(a) symposium (b) primer
(c) symbol (d) souvenir

23. The buildings reflect the elegance of a bygone ....

(a) eras (b) area
(c) era (d) ancients

24. Gandhiji was a non-smoker and a ....

(a) teatotaller (b) teetotaller
(c) romantic (d) pandemic activist

25. The soap actor is a .... and keeps herself up-to-date with all the latest trends.

(a) fashionist (b) fascist
(c) famished (d) fashionista

Exam Practice

Directions (Q. Nos. 1-3) *Each sentence in this question has three parts labelled (a), (b) and (c). Read each sentence to find out, whether there is any error in any part and indicate your response against the corresponding letter. If you find no error, your response should be indicated as (d).*

1. The King was embarrassed (a)/to find evidences (b)/against his own queen. (c)/ No error (d) **NDA 2016**
2. He waved us a good bye (a)/as he boarded the train (b)/which disappeared into the tunnel. (c)/ No error (d) **NDA 2017**
3. A small parcel (a)/of novels is (b)/better than none. (c)/No error (d) **NDA 2017**

Directions (Q. Nos. 4-20) *Each sentence in this question has three underlined parts labelled (a), (b) and (c). Read each sentence to find out whether there is any error in any underlined part and indicate your response in the Answer Sheet against the corresponding letter. If you find no error, your response should be indicated as (d).*

4. At the request of the Defence Attorney (a) the Jury were called (b) and their individual verdicts were recorded. (c) No error (d) **NDA 2018**
5. My brother goes (a) to the office (b) five day week. (c) No error (d) **NDA 2019**
6. Slow and steady (a) owns the race (b) as the wise would say. (c) No error (d) **NDA 2018**
7. We often hear people say (a) that most human beings have not evolved (b) or grow up enough to stick to truth or non-violence. (c) No error. (d) **NDA 2018**
8. A time slot of fifteen minutes (a) are allowed (b) to each speaker. (c) No error (d) **NDA 2019**
9. My friend's (a) daughter-in-laws (b) have come. (c) No error (d) **NDA 2020**
10. The writer (a) of this poetry (b) is Wordsworth. (c) No error (d) **CDS 2016**
11. One of the assistant (a) was (b) Alfred. (c) No error (d) **CDS 2016**
12. Their all belongings (a) were lost (b) in the fire. (c) No error (d) **CDS 2017**
13. The memoranda (a) are (b) on the table (c) No error (d) **CDS 2017**
14. Tell him to take (a) another photograph (b) of the group. (c) No error (d) **CDS 2017**

15. Her parents (a) has not permitted her (b) to marry Sunil. (c) No error (d) **CDS 2017**

16. The old furniture's (a) was disposed of (b) and the new ones were placed. (c) No error (d)

17. Electricity companies are (a) working throughout (b) days and nights to repair the damage. (c) No error (d) **CDS 2018**

18. Two thirds of the book (a) were (b) rubbish. (c) No error (d) **CDS 2018**

19. Because of the movement of a glacier (a) the form (b) of the Great lakes was very slow. (c) No error (d) **CDS 2018**

20. The visitor's to the zoo are requested (a) in the interest of all concerned, (b) not to carry sticks, stones or food inside and not to tease animals. (c) No error (d) **CDS 2018**

Answers

Work Book Exercise A

1. 'Cattle' in place of 'Cattles'
2. Use 'many pieces of information'/much information
3. 'Orders have' in place of 'Order has'
4. 'scenery' in place of 'sceneries'
5. 'alphabet' in place of 'alphabets'
6. 'score' in place of 'scores'
7. 'mischief' in place of 'mischiefs'
8. 'Sheep are' in place of 'Sheeps are'
9. 'contents' in place of 'content'
10. 'Twenty head of cattle' in place of 'Twenty cattles'
11. 'much work' in place of 'many works'
12. 'men servants' in place of 'man servants'
13. 'sisters-in-law' in place of 'sister-in-laws'
14. 'word' in place of 'words'
15. 'five year old boys' in place of 'five years old boys.

Work Book Exercise B

1. 'Rations have' in place of 'Ration has'
2. 'The wood of the table' in place of 'table's wood'
3. 'was very encouraging' in place of 'were very encouraging'
4. 'like' in place of 'likes'
5. 'are' in place of 'is'

6. 'is' in place of 'are'
7. No error, 'a lot' of and 'lots of' both are correct.
8. Remove 'a' before 'fair means'
9. 'information' in place of 'informations'
10. 'work' in place of 'works'
11. 'evidence' in place of 'evidences' and 'was' in place of 'were'
12. 'Commander-in-Chief's in place of 'Commander's-in-chief'
13. 'proceeds' in place of 'proceed'
14. 'are' in place of 'is'
15. 'fish' in place of 'fishes'

Revision Exercise

1. (b) Use 'haircut' in place of 'hair cut'.
2. (a) Use 'is' as maths is a 'singular subject,
3. (c) Remove 'a' before 'wood'.
4. (c) Use 'binoculars' in place of 'binocular'.
5. (d) No error
6. (e) No error
7. (a) Use 'dozen' in place of 'dozens'.
8. (e) No Error
9. (d) Use 'is' in place of 'are'.
10. (e) No Error
11. (a) Use 'censure' in place of 'censor', 'censure' means strong criticism or disapproval.
12. (c) Use 'proceed' in place of 'precede'.
13. (b) No Error
14. (c) Use 'sons-in-law' in place of 'son-in-laws'.
15. (c) Use 'online' in place of 'onlines'.

16. (d) **17.** (c) **18.** (a) **19.** (d) **20.** (d) **21.** (b) **22.** (a) **23.** (c) **24.** (b) **25.** (d)

Exam Practice

1. (b) 'evidence' is an uncountable noun. So, it does not have a plural form. Hence, we will change 'evidences' to 'evidence' to correct the sentence.
2. (a) Remove 'a' before goodbye.
3. (d) No error
4. (b) Replace 'were' with 'was'
5. (c) 'day' should be replaced by 'days a to correct the sentence.
6. (b) 'owns' does not make sense in the sentence. It should be changed to 'wins' to make the sentence meaningful.
7. (c) 'grown' should be used in place of 'grow'.
8. (b) 'are' should be changed to 'is' to correct the sentence as 'time slot of fifteen minutes' is taken as a singular noun.
9. (b) The plural of 'daughter-in-law' is 'daughters-in-law'. So, we will change 'daughter-in-laws' to 'daughters-in-law' to correct the sentence.
10. (b) 'Poetry' should be changed to 'poem' to correct the sentence.
11. (a) 'One of' uses a plural noun. So, 'assistants' will be used in place of 'assistant'.
12. (a) 'Their all' should be changed to 'All their' to correct the sentence.
13. (d) No error
14. (d) No error
15. (b) Change 'has' to 'have' as 'parents' is a plural noun.
16. (a) Change 'furniture's' to 'furniture' as 'furniture' is an uncountable noun.
17. (c) 'days and nights' should be changed to 'day and night'.
18. (b) Here 'Two thirds of the book' is taken as a whole (singular noun). So, 'were' would be replaced by 'was'.
19. (b) The word 'form' does not make sense here. It should be changed to 'formation' to make the sentence meaningful.
20. (a) 'Visitor's should be changed to 'visitors' to make the sentence meaningful.

Pronoun

What is a Pronoun?

Pronoun is a word used in place of a noun in order to avoid repetition of the latter.

Kinds of Pronoun

1. **Personal Pronouns** Words used in place of nouns referring to particular persons. These include

   'I, we, you, he, she, it, they', etc.

The Case of Personal Pronouns		Subject	Object	Possessive Adjectives	Possessive Pronouns
Singular	First Person	I	me	my	mine
Plural		We	us	our	ours
	Second Person	You	you	your	yours
Singular		She	her	her	hers
	Third Person	He	him	his	his
		It	It	Its	—
Plural		They	them	their	theirs

2. **Demonstrative Pronouns** Words used for nouns to point out the position of objects **'This, that, these, those'**, etc.

   (i) **This** is my book.
   (ii) **That** is her house.

   But in the following examples 'This' and 'That' are used as demonstrative adjectives.

   (i) This book
   (ii) That house

3. **Relative Pronouns** Words which introduces a dependent clause with the use of words such as **'who, which, that, whose, whom'**, etc.

   (i) The man **who** has just entered the room is my friend.
   (ii) The book **that** I bought is very costly.

4. **Interrogative Pronouns** Words used for nouns to ask questions. These include **Who, What, Which, Whose and Whom**

   (i) **Who** took my bag?
   (ii) **Whom** did you meet?
   (iii) **Whose** books are these?
   (iv) **What** are you doing?

(v) **What** shirt is this? *(Interrogative adjective)*
(vi) **Whose** book is this? *(Interrogative adjective)*

5. **Indefinite Pronouns** Words used for nouns that do not refer to a specific person or thing and thus are vague. These include **'everybody, nobody, somebody, either, neither, all, much, several, each, others, another'**, etc.
6. **Reflexive Pronouns** Words used to refer back to a person or thing. These include **'myself, ourselves, himself, themselves, yourself'**, etc.
7. **Distributive Pronouns** Words used to refer to person or things one at a time. **'either, neither, each, every, none, anyone'**, etc.
   (i) **Either** of the two sisters is staying here.
   (ii) **Neither** of his arms is defective.
   (iii) You can take **either** room. *(Distributive adjective)*
   (iv) You can talk to **each** boy. *(Distributive adjective)*
8. **Reciprocal Pronouns** Words used to point out mutual or reciprocal relationship. They include **'each other** and **one another'**.
   (i) Both the brothers love **each other.**
   (ii) Indians should not fight with **one another.**

Rules of Pronoun

Rule I

When the subject of the verb is the receiver of the action, the action is said to be reflected. Such verbs are used reflexively.

'Acquit, absent, avail, reconcile, amuse, resign, avenge, revenge, enjoy, exert, apply, adapt, adjust, pride, overreach, etc. are used reflexively. *For example*

(i) You should avail yourself, of every chance in life. *(Correct)*
(ii) They enjoyed the picture last evening. *(No reflexive pronoun is needed)*
(iii) They enjoyed during summer vacation. *(Place 'themselves' after 'enjoyed')*
(iv) He resigned himself to his failure. *(Correct)*
(v) The former DM acquitted very efficiently. *(Place 'himself' after 'acquitted')*
(vi) He was determined to avenge the death of his wife. *(Correct)*

Rule II

The following verbs are not used reflexively :

Keep, stop, turn, qualify, bathe, move, rest, hide, etc.
For example

(i) You should keep yourself from bad boys. *(Drop 'yourself ')*
(ii) He has qualified himself for the post. *(Drop 'himself ')*
(iii) He hid himself in the room. *(Drop 'himself ') (Int. Verb)*
(iv) The thief hid the money under the carpet. *(Correct) (Tran. Verb)*

Rule III

A reflexive pronoun cannot act as a subject or object of a verb unless it is preceded by the concerned pronoun or noun . *For example*

(i) Myself will see to it that you get your share of property. *(Change 'myself' into 'I')*

(ii) Yourself and he reached there in time. *(Change 'yourself' into 'you')*

(iii) I myself like him. *(Correct)*

(iv) Raj will do it for myself and my sister. *(Change 'myself' to 'me')*

Rule IV

(a) The verb **'to be'** should be followed by subjective form when the complement is a pronoun. *For example*

(i) It is me who have brought you home. *(Change 'me' into 'I')*

(ii) Was it her who did it for you? *(Change 'her' into 'she')*

(iii) It will be us who will buy a new house. *(Change 'us' into 'we')*

Rule V

Verbs and Prepositions are followed by the objective case of a pronoun.

(i) Between you and I, Suhani is intelligent. *(Say 'me')*

(ii) She is teaching Rohit and she. *(Say 'her')*

(iii) Let they go. *(Say 'them')*

Rule VI

(a) Good manners require that the order of singular pronouns should be **second person, third person and first person** (231).

(b) **But in plural 'we' is used before 'you' and 'they' after 'you'** (123). The latter order is also observed while referring to unpleasant acts. *For example*

(i) I and you will attend her wedding tomorrow. *(Correct use is 'You and I')*

(ii) He and you will share the mangoes. *(Use 'You and he')*

(iii) You, Mohan and I will watch a movie tonight. *(Correct)*

(iv) We, you and they are leaving for Mumbai tomorrow. *(Correct)*

(v) You and I will be punished. *(Unpleasant act, use 'I and you')*

Rule VII

Use of possessive adjectives (Possessive case of the pronoun)

(A) When two subjects are joined by

'As well as, together with, along with, and not, in addition to, like, unlike, with' rather than, except, no less than, nothing but, more (noun) **than one,** the possessive case of the pronoun (possessive adjective) is used in accordance with the first subject.

(B) When two subjects are joined by

'Either-or, neither-nor, not only-but also, none-but.'
the possessive case of pronoun (possessive adjective) is used according to the nearest subject.

(C) When the pronouns
'Each, every, neither, either, anyone' many a, more than one (possessive adjective) are used as subject, the possessive case should be third person singular. They may refer to two or more than two objects or persons.

(D) When **'one'** is used as a subject, the possessive case of the pronoun should be according to one. (*i.e.,* one's)

(E) When a pronoun is used for more than one noun or pronouns of different persons, the possessive case is in the form of first person plural (**our**) and second person plural (**your**). *For example*

(i) Each boy and each teacher is required to bring their luggage. *(Correct)*
(ii) One should do his duty sincerely. *(Use 'one's' in place of 'his')*
(iii) Neither the students nor the teacher were in their proper uniform. *(Correct)*
(iv) Reena as well as her children has returned to their home. *(Use 'her' for 'their')*
(v) Only you and I have brought your books. *(Use 'our' for 'your')*
(vi) You and he completed their work. *(Use 'your' for 'their')*
(vii) Have you received their letters? *(Use 'our' for 'their')*
(viii) Neither of the two brothers has brought their bedding. *(Correct)*
(ix) Each one of us is doing our duty properly. *(Correct)*
(x) Everyone should do one's duty. *(Use 'his' for 'one's')*
(xi) My sister along with her friends is doing her job at Delhi. *(Correct)*

Rule VIII

A noun or pronoun in the possessive case should not be used sometimes with the nouns such as
'Separation, leave, excuse, mention, report, pardon, sight, favour.' *For example*

(i) Your separation is very painful to me. *(Say 'separation from you')*
(ii) At his sight the robbers fled. *(Say 'At the sight of him')*
(iii) I beg your favour, please. *(a favour of/from you)*
(iv) She did make mention of you. *(Correct, 'your mention' is wrong)*

Rule IX

'Either, neither, each other'
are used in speaking of two persons or things.
'Anyone, none, one another'
are used while referring to more than two persons or things. *For example*

(i) Indians should never fight with each other. *(Use 'one another' in place of 'each other')*
(ii) Anyone of his eyes is defective. *(Use 'either' in place of 'anyone')*
(iii) None of his arms was wounded in the accident. *(Use 'neither' for 'none')*
(iv) Either of his four sons has sold his property after his death. *(Use 'anyone' for 'Either')*

Rule X

While writing **question tag the subject and verb must be according to the main sentence.** *For example*

(i) Our teacher is intelligent, isn't it? *(Use 'isn't he?')*
(ii) The boys are not going on picnic, are they? *(Correct)*
(iii) They went to Delhi yesterday, isn't it? *(Use 'didn't they?')*
(iv) She comes here daily, does she? *(Use 'doesn't she?)*
(v) She will help me, won't she? *(Correct)*
(vi) I shall not play, shan't I? *(shan't is not correct, use 'shall')*
(vii) He is seldom absent, isn't he? *(Correct)*
(viii) We need not worry, need we? *(Correct)*
(ix) I used to write poetry, didn't I? *(Correct)*
(x) We have a book, don't we? *(Correct)*
(xi) You have taken food, haven't you?

Imperative Sentence

(xiii) Don't close the room, will you? *(Correct)*
(xiv) Close the room, won't you/will you? *(Correct)*
(xv) Let them stay here, will they? *(Correct)*
(xvi) Let us stay here, shall we? *(Correct)*
(xvii) Let us play, shall we? *(Correct)*

Indefinite Pronouns

(xviii) Everything is settled, isn't it? *(Correct)*
(xix) Nothing is settled is it? *(Correct)*
(xx) None of your friends like her, do they? *(Correct)*
(xxi) Few students are working hard, aren't they? *(Correct)*
(xxii) Everybody can speak English, can't they? *(Correct)*
(xxiii) No one can speak English, can they? *(Correct)*
(xxiv) One of/most of/all of you will go there, won't you? *(Correct)*
(xxv) One of/most of/all of us shall go there, shan't we? *(Correct)*
(xxvi) One of/most of/all of them will go there, won't they? *(Correct)*

NOTE (i) The negative statements having words such as **'hardly, seldom, barely, scarcely', few, little**, etc. are followed by ordinary question tag. (Affirmative)
(ii) With **'everybody, everyone, somebody, someone, nobody, no one, anybody, none, neither, either'**. 'They' is used in question tag.

Rule XI Use of Both

'Both' should be followed by 'and' and not by **'as well as', Negative is avoided with 'Both'**. *For example*

(i) Both you as well as my brother are going to attend her marriage tomorrow. *(Use 'and' in place of 'as well as')*
(ii) Both of them are not going there. *(Incorrect)*
Neither of them is going there. *(Correct)*

Rule **XII**

'Which' is used in place of 'Who' when we are referring to a choice between two or more than two things or persons. *For example*

(i) Of the two sisters who is the more intelligent. *(Use 'which' in place of 'who')*
(ii) Who is your father in the crowd? *(Use 'Which' in place of 'Who')*
(iii) Who is better of the two dancers in our society? *(Place 'the' before better and change 'Who' into 'Which')*

Rule **XIII**

Possessive case We don't use noun after possessive case of a pronoun. *For example*

(i) This book is mine = This is **my** book.
(ii) This shirt is yours = This is **your** shirt.
(iii) **Our** is a populous country. *(Say 'Ours')*

Rule **XIV**

The relative pronoun should be expressed according to its relation with the verb of the adjective clause. 'Who' is used as a subject of a verb of adjective clause and 'whom' is used as an object of a verb of adjective clause. *For example*

(i) He was talking of the women who, he said, he met in America. *(Use 'whom' in place of 'who')*
(ii) She is the kind of lady whom, every body knows, is intelligent. *(Use 'who' in place of 'whom')*

Rule **XV**

The use of '**But**' as a relative pronoun. *For example*

(i) There was none but wept. *(Who did not weep)*
(ii) There is no country but is corrupt. *(Which is not corrupt)*

Rule **XVI**

The use of the 'same' as pronoun is wrong. *For example*

(i) I shall give you a book and **the same** is very useful. (Say 'it' for 'the same')
(ii) He bought a house and is living in **the same**. (Say 'it' for 'the same')

Rule **XVII**

'What' is used without an antecedent and it refers to things only. *For example*

(i) It is incredible what she said.
(ii) I don't believe in the words what she uttered. *(Use 'which'/'that' in place of 'what')*
(iii) I don't believe in what you say. (Correct)
(iv) I know which you say. (Say 'what')

NOTE For detailed study of relative pronouns look up **adjective clause** in the chapter on **Clauses**.

Work Book Exercise A

Directions *Spot the errors, if any, in the following sentences.*

1. He bought the books and put it in the bag.
2. Civil servants should acquit efficiently in the service of the common man.
3. My father always adivses me that I should keep myself from bad boys.
4. Avail every chance that comes your way lest you should repent in the long run.
5. There should be no misunderstanding between your father and she.
6. It was Mohan or her who came here last night and kept on knocking at the door.
7. Let Rohit and she complete this job as they like to do it.
8. Was it him who gave money to buy new books?
9. He and myself alone will complete this work because we don't need anyone's help.
10. You, I and he should take the examination seriously.
11. It was with great difficulty that each of the brothers could get their share of property.
12. They that hanker after fame and money are likely to be disappointed.
13. I am sad to learn that you and your brother have lost their money in the share market.
14. Both he as well as I are going to Delhi tomorrow to buy a new motorbike.
15. This is only one of her novels that have been published till date.

Work Book Exercise B

Directions *Spot the errors, if any, in the following sentences.*

1. Which we saw surprised all and one present at the function.
2. She is the woman who, I know, you can always rely upon.
3. Don't respect such persons who have no respect for elders.
4. When warned he stopped himself at once.
5. He is the same person who was present at the wedding party last night.
6. The only person who can read and write English well is my friend.
7. The Saraswati is a river whose origin has always been a matter of conjecture.
8. They that tell a lie should not be depended upon for doing anything right.
9. My friend is honest and hard working, isn't it?
10. They did not go to attend the marriage of their neighbours' daughter, didn't they?
11. Your separation is very painful to me.
12. It is difficult to say who is the better of the two sisters.
13. He is the same man who always likes to boast of his bravery.
14. All which glitters is not gold.
15. I never expected that you would provide me with such a servant that was not reliable at all.

Revision Exercise

Directions (Q. Nos. 1-10) *Fill in the blanks by selecting the correct pronouns from the options that follow.*

1. I really like watching old movies. .... are some of the best things on TV.
(a) Those (b) That (c) This (d) These

2. .... flavour do you prefer to have?
(a) What (b) Which (c) Who (d) Whom

3. I heard someone knocking at the door but wasn't sure .... it was.
(a) who (b) what (c) which (d) whom

4. Neeta slipped on the road and hurt ....
(a) himself (b) themselves (c) herself (d) her

5. The students talked to .... when the teacher had left.
(a) each other (b) themselves (c) oneself (d) one another

6. The Cabinet gave .... vote today morning.
(a) its (b) their (c) theirs (d) it's

7. He .... is down need fear no fall.
(a) whom (b) that (c) who (d) it

8. Let .... who can, save her from drowning.
(a) he (b) him (c) it (d) their

9. The CEO .... made a presentation on the topic of environmental awareness.
(a) herself (b) itself (c) her (d) herselves

10. Taruna is the receptionist .... I have employed in my new office.
(a) who (b) which (c) whose (d) whom

Directions (Q. Nos. 11-15) *Each question in this section has a sentence with three underlined parts labelled (a), (b) and (c). Read each sentence to find out whether there is any error in any underlined part and indicate your response in the Answer Sheet against the corresponding letter. If you find no error, your response should be indicated as (d).*

11. Everyone announced (a) / one's plans to celebrate Diwali (b) / in the presence of the President. (c) / No error (d)

12. She availed of (a) / the opportunity to (b) / travel all alone. (c) / No error (d)

13. The committee were (a) / divided in their opinion (b) / regarding the issue. (c) / No error (d)

14. If I were him (a) / I would not misbehave (b) / like this. (c) / No error (d)

15. Good citizens like (a) / you and she (b) / should wear a mask when going outside. (c) / No error (d)

Directions (Q. Nos. 16-20) *Read each sentence to find out whether there is any grammatical or idiomatic error in it. The error, if any, will be in one part of the sentence. The alphabet corresponding to that part is the answer. If there is 'No error' the answer is (e). (Ignore errors of punctuation, if any)*

16. Dear students (A) / enjoy yourselves (B) / during the (C) / Diwali holidays. (D) / No error (E)

(a) A (b) B (c) C (d) D
(e) E

17. Those two companies (A) / always help (B) / one another (C) / in this matter. (D) / No error (E)

(a) A (b) B (c) C (d) D
(e) E

18. I, you and he (A) / must attend (B) / the seminar (C) / on online teaching. (D) / No error (E)

(a) B (b) C (c) E (d) A
(e) D

19. The manager (A) / as well as (B) / the clerks (C) / absented themselves today. (D) / No error (E)

(a) A (b) E (c) D (d) C
(e) B

20. There is (A) / none who (B) / can help you (C) / in this time. (D) / No error (E)

(a) A (b) B (c) C (d) D
(e) E

Exam Practice

Directions (Q. Nos. 1 and 2) *Each question in this section has a sentence with three parts labelled (a), (b) and (c). Read each sentence to find out whether there is any error in any part and indicate your response against the corresponding letter. If you find no error, your response should be indicated as (d).*

1. Being a day of national mourning (a) / the offices were closed (b) / and the national flag few half mast. (c) / No error (d) **NDA 2016**

2. The Principal looks very worried (a) / because students are on strike for the last fifteen days as a protest against (b) / his disciplinary action against some miscreants. (c) / No error (d) **NDA 2016**

Directions (Q. Nos. 3-7) *Each question in this section has a sentence with three underlined parts labelled (a), (b) and (c). Read each sentence to find out whether there is any error in any grammatical part and indicate your response against the corresponding letter. If you find no error, your response should be indicated as (d).*

3. It is necessary for us to familiarise with (a) and get used to (b) the ways of people among whom we live. (c) No error (d) **NDA 2016**

4. Neither praise nor blame (a) seem (b) to affect him. (c) No error (d) **NDA 2019**

5. Every one (a) of the boys (b) love to ride. (c) No error (d) **NDA 2019**

6. He asked (a) whether either of the brothers (b) were at home. (c) No error (d) **NDA 2019**

7. I am (a) glad (b) that you are here. (c) No error (d) **CDS 2016**

Directions (Q. Nos. 8-16) *Each question in this section has been divided into three parts labelled (a), (b) and (c). Read each sentence to find out, whether there is any error in any part and indicate your response against the corresponding letter. If you find no error, your response should be indicated as (d).*

8. Being a rainy day, (a) / we did not feel like going out or doing anything (b) / except playing chess in our room. (c) / No error (d) **CDS 2017**

9. It is not difficult to believe that a man (a) / who has lived in this city for a long time (b) / he will never feel at home anywhere else in the world. (c) / No error (d) **CDS 2017**

10. All of them (a) / speak (b) / good English. (c) / No error (d) **CDS 2017**

11. Of the many problems that confront the leaders of the world (a) / none are of grave consequence (b) / than the problem of saving the normal race from extinction. (c) / No error (d) **CDS 2017**

12. No one knows (a) / as to why he did it, (b) / or who was behind his doing it. (c) / No error (d) **CDS 2017**

13. Somebody (a) / who I enjoy reading (b) / is Tagore. (c) / No error (d) **CDS 2018**

14. "I'm tired of my boys", said the mother, (a) / "Both of them keep quarreling all the time (b) / right now also they are quarreling with one another". (c) / No error (d) **CDS 2018**

15. The legendary hero has (a) / laid down his precious life (b) / for our country. (c) / No error (d) **CDS 2018**

16. Our gardener, which is very lazy (a) / says that (b) / there will be no apples this year. (c) / No error (d) **CDS 2018**

Directions (Q. Nos. 17-18) *Each a sentence has been divided into multiple parts. Find out the error part from the given options and indicate your response from the options (a), (b), (c) and (d) on the answer sheet.*

17. My sister and me are planning a trip from Jaipur to Delhi. **CDS 2019**
    (a) My sister and me are
    (b) planning a trip
    (c) from Jaipur to Delhi
    (d) No error

18. Each one of these chairs are broken. **CDS 2019**
    (a) Each one
    (b) of these chairs
    (c) are broken
    (d) No error

Answers

Work Book Exercise A

1. 'them' in place of 'it'
2. 'acquit themselves' in place of 'acquit'
3. Drop 'myself'
4. 'Avail yourself of' in place of 'Avail'
5. 'her' in place of 'she'
6. 'she' in place of 'her'
7. 'her' in place of 'she'
8. 'Was it he' in place of 'Was it him'
9. 'I' in place of 'myself'
10. 'You, he and I' in place of 'You, I and he'
11. No error
12. 'those' in place of 'they'
13. 'your' in place of 'their'
14. 'and' in place of 'as well as'
15. 'has' in place of 'have'

Work Book Exercise B

1. 'What' in place of 'which'
2. 'whom' in place of 'who'
3. no error
4. Drop 'himself'
5. 'that' in place of 'who'
6. 'that' in place of 'who'
7. 'the origin of which' in place of 'whose origin'
8. 'those' in place of 'they'
9. 'isn't he ?' in place of 'isn't it?'
10. 'did they?' in place of 'didn't they?'
11. 'Separation from you' in place of 'Your separation'
12. 'which' in place of 'who'
13. 'that' in place of 'who'
14. 'that' in place of 'which'
15. 'who' in place of 'that'

Revision Exercise

1. (a) **2.** (b) **3.** (a) **4.** (c) **5.** (d) **6.** (b) **7.** (b)
8. (a) **9.** (a) **10.** (d)
11. (b) Use 'their' in place of 'one's'
12. (a) Add 'herself ' before 'of '
13. (d) No error
14. (a) Use 'he' in place of 'him'.
15. (b) Use 'her' in place of 'she'.
16. (e) No error
17. (c) Use 'each other' in place of 'one another'.
18. (d) Use 'You, he and I' in place of 'I, you and he'.
19. (b) No error
20. (b) Use 'that' in place of 'who'.

Exam Practice

1. (a) 'It' should be added before 'Being' to correct the sentence.
2. (d) No error
3. (a) Add 'ourselves' after 'familiarise'.
4. (b) Use 'seems' in place of 'seem'.
5. (c) 'loves' should be used in place of 'love'.
6. (c) 'was' will be used in place of 'were'.
7. (d) No error
8. (a) Use 'It being' in place of 'Being'.
9. (c) Remove 'he' as it is not needed in the sentence.
10. (d) No error
11. (b) Use 'is' in place of 'are'.
12. (d) No error
13. (b) Use 'whom' in place of 'who'.
14. (c) Use 'each other' in place of 'one another'.
15. (d) No error
16. (a) Use 'who' in place of 'which'.
17. (a) Use 'I' in place of 'me'.
18. (c) Use 'is' in place of 'are'.

Unit IV

Adjective

What is an Adjective?

Adjective is a word that tells us about or adds to the meaning of a noun.

For example

(i) She is a kind lady.
(ii) I like this pen.
(iii) She lives in a large house.
(iv) He is a strong player.

There are following two classes of adjectives

(i) Descriptive adjective
(ii) Determiner adjective

Descriptive adjectives denote the quality, size, colour, shape, etc. of a noun.

Position of Adjectives Descriptive adjectives are used both attributively and predicatively while Determiner adjectives are used only before the noun.

She is an honest girl. *(Attributive use)*

The girl is honest. *(Predicative use)*

Kinds of Adjectives

(A) **Descriptive Adjectives**
Adjective of Quality — Ugly, heavy, dry, good, red

(B) **Determiner Adjectives**
(i) **Demonstrative Adjectives** — This, that, these, those
(ii) **Distributive Adjectives** — Each, every, either, neither
(iii) **Quantitative Adjectives** — Some, any, no, little
(iv) **Numerical Adjectives** — few, many all, several, one, first
(v) **Interrogative Adjectives** — Which, what, whose
(vi) **Possessive Adjectives** — My, our, your, his, her, their, its
(vii) **Present/Past Participle Adjectives** — A moving bus, a wounded driver, a burnt man, tiring journey
(viii) **Relative Adjectives** — who, which, that
(ix) **Emphatic Adjectives** — Own, such, same, very
(x) **Proper Adjectives** — Indian, Asian, American
(xi) **Exclamatory Adjectives** — What, which, how

(C) **Articles as Determiners**

A, An, The (See Chapter on Articles)

Distinction between Adjectives and Pronouns

1. **Demonstrative Adjectives and Demonstrative Pronouns**

(i) Please get me that book. *(Adjective)*

(ii) That is my book. *(Pronoun)*

2. **Possessive Adjectives and Possessive Pronouns**

(i) This is my book. *(Adjective)*

(ii) This book is mine. *(Pronoun)*

(iii) It is her vanity box. *(Adjective)*

(iv) This vanity box is hers. *(Pronoun)*

3. **Distributive Adjectives and Distributive Pronouns**

(i) Either boy has stolen my book. *(Adjective)*

(ii) Neither book will serve my purpose. *(Adjective)*

(iii) I do not like either of the sisters. *(Pronoun)*

(iv) We bought neither of the bikes. *(Pronoun)*

NOTE **Every** is only an adjective and it cannot be used as a determiner. But **Each** can be used both as an adjective and a pronoun.

(v) Every boy was present. *(Adjective)*

(vi) Each boy was present. *(Adjective)*

(vii) Each of the boys will come. *(Pronoun)*

(viii) Everyone of them is wasting money. *(Pronoun)*

Explanation of Degrees of a Few adjectives

Positive Degree	Comparative Degree	Superlative Degree
Good/well	Better	Best
Bad/ill	Worse	Worst
Much/Many	More	Most
Few	Fewer	Fewest
Little	Less	Least
Early	Earlier	Earliest
Late	Later/Latter	Latest/Last
Old	Older/Elder	Oldest/Eldest
Far	Further/Farther	Furthest/Farthest
Near	Nearer	Nearest/Next
Economical	More Economical	Most Economical
Beautiful	More Beautful	Most Beautiful

Rules of Adjective

Rule I

Generally speaking an **adjective is used when the quality of a noun and pronoun rather than the action of a verb** is expressed.

Adverb is used to modify the action of a verb, an adjective, an adverb. *For example*

(i) She is a skilful dancer. *(quality)*
(ii) She dances skilfully. *(action)*
(iii) Sonu's act was thoughtful. *(quality)*
(iv) Sonu acted thoughtfully. *(action)*

Rule II

The verbs given below are **linking verbs**

Some verbs are not modified by adverbs. 'Be, become, seem, appear, taste, smell, sound, feel, turn, get, grow, keep, look, make, prove, etc.

(i) Her voice sounds harsh.
(ii) She appears sad.
(iii) I feel sick.
(iv) She has grown wise.
(v) Mona is smart.

NOTE The distinction between the following sentences

1. (a) She **looked** calm and quiet. *(Linking verb, Correct)*
   (b) She looked at her angry husband calmly and quietly. *(In a calm and quiet manner, Correct)*
2. (a) The mangoes taste sweetly. *(Use sweet)*
   (b) She talks sweetly. *(Correct)*

Rule III

There are some adjectives which don't admit of any comparative and superlative degree. Such adjectives denote absolute position.

'Perfect, unique, ideal, chief, universal, extreme, complete, entire, excellent, absolute, impossible, eternal, supreme', etc. *For example*

(i) I have never seen a more complete book on General Studies. *(Drop 'more')*
(ii) Happiness is the chiefest aim of mankind. *(Use 'chief')*
(iii) How can divided India become the most supreme power? *(Remove 'the most')*

Rule IV

The comparative adjectives such as

'Prior, junior, senior, superior, inferior, prefer (verb), **preferable, elder'** etc. are followed by **'to' instead of 'than'**.

Also, they are not used in comparative degree.

(i) He is senior than me in service. *(Use 'to' in place of 'than')*

(ii) Lemon juice is preferable than tea. *(Use 'to' in place of 'than')*
(iii) My sister is elder than me by two years. *(Use 'to' in place of 'than')*
(iv) She prefers coffee rather than tea. *('rather than' in place of 'to' is correct)*
(v) She is comparatively smarter than her husband. *(Use smart)*
(vi) She is more senior to her boss in service. *(Remove 'more')*
(vii) Milk is more preferable to tea. *(Remove 'more')*

NOTE 'Rather than' may be used for 'to' after 'prefer'. (iv)

Rule V

Note carefully the distinction among the following adjectives

Little is used for quantity. (Little, less, least) **Little** means hardly any. (Negative sense) **A little** means not much (some). (Affirmative meaning) **The little** means not much but all.	**Few** is used for number. (Few, fewer, fewest) **Few** means hardly anyone/anything. (Negative sense) **A few** means not many (some). (Affirmative meaning) **The few** means not many but all.
Some is used in affirmative and while making request. In interrogative sentences **Some** is used as an adjective. **Somewhat** is used as an adverb.	**Any** is used for negative and interrogative sentences and in the sense of every. (**No any/Not any** are wrong expressions.) if any
Farther means more distant. *(Far, farther, farthest)*	**Further** means additional.
Other means the second of the two.	**Another** means additional one. *(More)*
Older/Oldest is used for persons *(not blood relation)* and things. *(Old, older, oldest)* It refers both to age and time.	**Elder/Eldest** is used for persons only in the case of blood relations. *(Old, elder, eldest)* It refers to age only.
Later is the opposite of earlier. (**Refers** to time) **Latest** means recent, last up to now only. *(Late, later, latest)* [*Time*]	**Latter** is the opposite of former. *(**Refers** to position)* Last means last of all. *(Late, latter, last) (Position)*

NOTE Little and few cannot qualify the words 'quantity' and 'number', 'small' is used to qualify these words.

Now study these sentences

(i) Little common sense can bring success to you. *(Use 'a little')*
(ii) Little that she did for me is unforgettable. *(Use 'The' before 'little')*
(iii) Little knowledge is a dangerous thing. *(Use 'a' before 'little')*
(iv) I requested him to bring me few books. *(Use 'a few')*
(v) Few days I passed in her company were exciting. *(Use 'The few')*
(vi) There are less passengers in the compartment today. *(Use 'fewer')*
(vii) There are five students less in the class. *(Correct)*
(viii) I have ten rupees less to pay. *(Correct)*
(ix) Could you please give me some money? *(Correct)*
(x) Have you brought some gold for her? *(Use 'any' in place of 'some')*
(xi) Little money you are earning should not be wasted *(Use 'The' before 'little')*
(xii) She was some angry. *(Use 'somewhat' in place of 'some')*
(xiii) She expressed somewhat anger. *(say 'some anger')*
(xiv) I have no any money in my pocket. *(Drop 'any')*
(xv) Moradabad is further from Delhi than Meerut. *(Use 'farther' in place of 'further')*
(xvi) No farther help from government is required. *(Use 'further' in place of 'farther')*
(xvii) I am still thirsty, please give me other glass of water. *(Say 'another' in place of 'other')*
(xviii) My oldest sister is living in Chicago these days. *(Use 'eldest' in place of 'oldest')*
(xix) My sister is elder to me. *(Correct)*
(xx) My friend is older than I. *(Correct)*
(xxi) She came latter than I. *(Use 'later' for time)*
(xxii) Reena and Heena are two sisters but the later is more intelligent than the former. *(Use 'latter' for position)*
(xxiii) Jeans are the last rage among younger generations. *(Use 'latest' in place of 'last')*

NOTE In sentence (vii) & (viii) 'less' has been used in place of 'few' (number) because 'definite numerical adjectives + plural nouns' are followed by 'less'.

Rule **VI**

When two adjectives qualify the same noun, both the adjectives should be expressed in the same degree. *For example*

(i) She is the most active and energetic social worker in our club. *(Use 'the most' before 'energetic')*
(ii) She is both cleverer and intelligent than her sister. *(Use 'more' before 'intelligent')*

Rule **VII**

Ordinal is placed before numerical adjective. *For example*

(i) You must study the two first chapters of the book. *(Use 'the first two')*
(ii) The two or last three lessons of your book are worth reading. *(Use 'The last two or three')*

Rule **VIII**

The comparative adjectives ending in 'er' (*i.e.,* cleverer) should be used as 'more clever' while comparing the two qualities of one and the same thing or a person.
For example

(i) She is cleverer than honest. *(Use 'more clever')*
(ii) She is more clever than her sister. *(Use 'cleverer' in place of 'more clever')*

Rule **IX**

The expression 'these' and 'those' should not be used with singular noun **'kind' 'type'** and **'sort'**. *For example*

(i) I will not do these kind/sort of acts. *(Use 'this kind/sort' for 'these kind/sort')*
(ii) This type of articles are not allowed into the hall. *(Use 'is' for 'are')*

Rule **X**

Note Carefully the use of 'other and else' in comparative and superlative degrees. *For example*

(i) She is a best teacher. *(Use 'a very good teacher')*
(ii) She is the most intelligent person. *(Use 'a very' in place of 'the most')*
(iii) My brother is the smartest player of all others in the team. *(Remove 'others')*
(iv) She is better than anybody in the class. *(Use 'anybody else')*
(v) The Ganga is more sacred than any river of India. *(Use 'other' after 'any')*
(vi) He is the most corrupt politician than anybody in the country. *(Use 'of all' in place of 'than anybody')*
(vii) This novel is the most interesting of any in the library. *(Use 'of all' in place of 'of any')*
(viii) No writer in India was so famous as RK Narayan. *(Use 'other' after 'No')*
(ix) His condition is good today. *(Say 'better' in place of 'good')*
(x) She is equally intelligent as my brother. *(Use 'as' in place of 'equally')*
(xi) The Nile is longer than any other river in India. *(Remove 'other')*
(xii) The Nile is longer than any other river in the world. *(Correct)*
(xiii) She is taller than any other boy in the class. *(Remove 'other')*
(xiv) The weather is as cold as last year. *(Say 'as that of' or 'last year's)*
(xv) I found this book the most interesting. *(Delete 'the')*
(xvi) Her shirt is cheaper than you. *(Say 'yours'/your shirt)*
(xvii) The climate of Chennai is warmer than Delhi. *(Say 'that of Delhi')*

Rule **XI**

The use of **'all, both and whole'** as adjectives.

(A) Place 'the' after 'all' and 'both' when used as adjectives for plural nouns. But 'the' is used before 'whole'. *For example*

(i) All the students were present. *(Correct)*

(ii) Both the boys left soon. *(Correct)*
(iii) Whole country is suffering from drought. *(Say 'The whole')*
(iv) All sugar is wasted. *(Uncountable noun, Correct)*

(B) Place possessive case after 'all' and 'both'. *For example*

(i) My all efforts ended in smoke. *(Say 'All my')*
(ii) Both my friends are honest. *(Correct)*
(iii) He is a fortunate person whose all efforts succeed. *(Say 'all whose')*

Rule XII

'Either, neither, only, both, even, but also' should be placed immediately before the words they emphasize. (qualify/ modify). *For example*

(i) She not only came to see me but also to take her old books. *(Use 'not only' before 'to see')*
(ii) Neither she is intelligent nor honest. *(Use 'neither' before 'intelligent')*
(iii) Her sister and her brother are both living with her. *(Use 'both' before 'her sister')*
(iv) Not only he likes to take coffee but also tea. *(Use 'Not only' before 'coffee')*

Rule XIII

'As' is used in the positive degree to denote equality while 'than' is used in the comparative degree. Both 'as' and 'than' are required to be used when a sentence contains adjectives in positive and comparative forms. *For example*

(i) She is as honest, if not more honest than her brother. *(Incorrect)*
She is as honest as, if not more honest than her brother. *(Correct)*
(ii) I am as strong or even stronger than my foe. *(Incorrect)*
I am as strong as or even stronger than my foe. *(Correct)*

Rule XIV

When two adjectives require different prepositions, appropriate prepositions should be used with both adjectives. *For example*

(i) He is senior and older than I. *(Use 'to' after 'senior')*
(ii) His dress is different and cheaper than mine. *(Use 'from' after 'different')*
(iii) She is stronger and younger than her sister. *(Correct)*

Rule XV

Place an adjective after noun when the noun is followed by preposition. *For example*

(i) The subject is a worthy matter of note. *(Say 'matter worthy of ')*
(ii) He is a suitable man for any post. *(Say the 'man suitable for any post')*

Rule XVI

Comparison of weight, quantity & number.

No comparison is implied in the following sentences, when there is 'time' used for comparison. So positive degree is used. *For example*

But we use comparative degree when the sentence is without 'times'

(i) My book is three times cheaper than yours. *(Say 'as cheap as')*

(ii) Your income is many times higher than Tushar's. *(Incorrect, say 'as high as')*

(iii) This book is five rupees cheaper than yours. *(Correct)*

(iv) This table is ten kilos lighter than that. *(Correct)*

Rule **XVII**

The following adjectives cannot be used before nouns (attributively), '**Afraid, asleep, due, ready, unable, alike, aware, glad, sorry, well, alone, ill, sure**', **worth.** *For example* 'Ill man, asleep boy, alone lady, afraid man, alike situation' are wrong expressions.

(i) She alone is responsible for my problems. *(Correct)*

(ii) I found a boy asleep. *(Correct)*

(iii) The man is ill. *(Correct)*

(iv) The man is afraid of my dog. *(Correct)*

(v) This book is worth reading. *(Correct)*

Rule **XVIII**

The order of adjectives qualifying a noun (S S A C N M)

Size → Shape → Age → Colour → Nationality → Material → Noun

(i) Twenty year old black American Negro.

(ii) A small Indian Stadium.

(iii) A big round black Indian plastic table.

(iv) A spacious dark cell.

(v) A large glass room.

Work Book Exercise A

Directions *Spot the errors, if any, in the following sentences.*

1. There were no less than fifty persons in the dining hall.
2. Few remarks that he made were offensive to my brother.
3. It is a worth seeing movie and you must not miss it.
4. Of all the students Rita was less worried when the date for the annual examination was announced.
5. Even the most perfect person in the world is said to have erred when there was time to act.
6. I was surprised to see every student sitting quietly in the class, even though the teacher was not present.
7. Whole of India expressed anger over the hijacking of Air India Boeing Jet by militant at Karachi.
8. I like him because he is the most interesting fellow because of his amiable nature.
9. The meeting was postponed because only the few persons were present there.
10. In the opinion of everyone she is wiser than beautiful.

Work Book Exercise B

Directions *Spot the errors, if any, in the following sentences.*

1. He is as intelligent if not more intelligent than his brother.
2. She is better than any girl that studies in our class.
3. The latest chapter of this novel is the most comprehensive of all the chapters in the book.
4. She was not punished though she came latter than I.
5. She is the best and beautiful girl of our village.
6. My book is superior than yours although it has cost me much less.
7. Of all other my neighbours he is the kindest and most considerate to others.
8. 'Arabian Nights' is the most adventurous of any books written so far.
9. The works of Shakespeare are more famous than any other English dramatist.
10. It is all the more better if you work in my company.
11. These kind of roses are very popular.
12. He doesn't need your help because he is too intelligent.
13. Modinagar is further from Dehradun than Meerut.
14. It was bitter cold and we preferred not to go out that night.
15. No animal is so sacred to the Hindus as the cow is.

Revision Exercise

Directions (Q. Nos. 1-5) *Each question in this section has a sentence with three underlined parts labelled (a), (b) and (c). Read the sentences to find out whether there is any error in any underlined part and indicate your response against the corresponding letter. If there is no error, your response should be indicated as (d).*

1. Nupur is the most honest (a) and simple girl in (b) her class. (c) No error (d)

2. I watched the IPL final (a) lively on my (b) smart TV. (c) No error (d)

3. Little knowledge (a) is a (b) dangerous thing. (c) No error (d)

4. My sister (a) is older (b) to me. (c) No error (d)

5. Arnab is the (a) most talented (b) news anchor in the team. (c) No error (d)

Directions (Q. Nos. 6-10) *Read the following sentences to find out whether there is any grammatical error in it. The error, if any, will be in one part of the sentence. Mark the part with error as your answer. If there is 'No error', mark 'No error' as your answer. (Ignore errors of punctuation, if any)*

6. The dastardly incident/took place in a /railway coach/last year.
(a) The dastardly incident
(b) took place in a
(c) railway coach
(d) last year
(e) No error

7. I took a course/in creatively writing/to improve/my writing skills.
(a) I took a course
(b) in creatively writing
(c) to improve
(d) my writing skills
(e) No error

8. It was a lazy Wednesday/afternoon that gave me a reason/to take a stroll/down the phone's contact list.
(a) It was a lazy Wednesday
(b) afternoon that gave me a reason
(c) to take a stroll
(d) down the phone's contact list
(e) No error

9. It was in 2010/that dementia stamped its/chemically footprints/all over my grandfather's neurological system.
(a) that dementia stamped its
(b) It was in 2010
(c) chemically footprints
(d) all over my grandfather's neurological system
(e) No error

10. A series of picture books/very ambiguously titled "Your Emotions"/helps younger children understand/the range of their negative feelings.
(a) helps younger children understand
(b) the range of their negative feelings
(c) A series of picture books
(d) very ambiguously titled "Your Emotions"
(e) No error

Directions (Q. Nos. 11-15) *Read each sentence to find out whether there is any grammatical or idiomatic error in it. The error, if any, will be in one part of the sentence. The alphabet corresponding to that part is your answer. If there is "No error", the answer is (e). (Ignore errors of punctuation, if any)*

11. I was asked (A)/to read the (B)/three first lines (C)/of the poem. (D)/ No error (E)
(a) A (b) B (c) C (d) D
(e) E

12. Haji Kallan was a (A)/younger orphan when he (B)/came from Peshawar (C)/to Delhi with his aunt in 1912. (D)/ No error (E)
(a) A (b) B (c) C (d) D
(e) E

13. This wraith-liked quality (A)/ is one of the reasons (B)/why the barn owl is the (C)/most successful owl species in the world. (D)/ No error (E)
(a) B (b) C (c) D (d) A
(e) E

14. Jahangir's rule was (A)/ended by rebellion (B)/but was (C)/larger peaceful. (D)/ No error (E)
(a) A (b) E (c) B (d) C
(e) D

15. Water is (A)/a most (B)/universal solvent (C)/found on Earth. (D)/No error (E)
(a) A (b) B (c) C (d) D
(e) E

Exam Practice

Direction (Q. No. 1 and 2) *The question in this section has a sentence with three parts labelled (a), (b) and (c). Read the sentence to find out whether there is any error in any part and indicate your response against the corresponding letter. If you find no error, your response should be indicated as (d).*

1. It is most essential for us (a)/to reach the station before noon (b)/lest we should miss the train. (c)/No error (d) **NDA 2016**

2. The after morning (a)/she woke up to the first ray of (b)/light through the window.(c)/ No error (d) **SSC CGL 2017**

Directions (Q. Nos. 3-10) *Each item in this section has a sentence with three underlined parts labelled (a), (b) and (c). Read each part to find out whether there is any error in any underlined part and indicate your response in Answer sheet against the corresponding letter. If you find no error, your response should be indicated as (d).*

3. Frank Lloyd Wright has been acclaimed (a) by colleagues (b) as the greater of all modern architects (c) No error (d) **NDA 2018**

4. One of most widely spread (a) bad habits (b) is the use of tobacco. (c) No error (d) **NDA 2019**

5. The price of my dress (a) is higher than that of (b) yours. (c) No error (d) **NDA 2020**

6. This box (a) is heavy than (b) the other. (c) No error (d) **CDS 2017**

7. We have to reach (a) there at ten, (b) will you please walk little faster. (c) No error (d) **CDS 2017**

8. The Department of Fine Arts has been critised (a) for not having much required courses (b) scheduled for this semester. (c) No error (d) **CDS 2017**

9. Except for few days (a) in a year during the monsoon (b) the river cannot flow on its own. (c) No error (d) **CDS 2019**

10. The auction, conducted by the bank (a) will be price based (b) using multiple priced method. (c) No error (d) **CDS 2020**

Directions (Q. Nos. 11-12) *In the sentence, identify the segment which contains the grammatical error.*

11. The modern man is busy acquiring more and more wealth and designing ways to invest it in more sense pleasures. **SSC CGL 2020**
(a) in more sense pleasures
(b) designing ways to invest it
(c) acquiring more and more wealth
(d) The modern man is busy
(e) No error

12. Mostly of the newly recruited officers have no experience in the banking sector. **SBI PO 2015**
(a) Mostly of the
(b) newly recruited officers
(c) have no experience
(d) in the banking sector
(e) No error

Direction (Q. No. 13) *Read the following sentence to find out whether there is any grammatical mistake/error in it. The error, if any, will be in one part of the sentence. Mark the part with the error as your answer. If there is no error, mark 'No error' as your answer. (Ignore errors of punctuation, if any)*

13. Hares are rather/noise animals who/love to hear/themselves talking. **SBI Clerk 2015**
(a) Hares are rather
(b) noise animals who
(c) love to hear
(d) themselves talking
(e) No error

Directions (Q. Nos. 14-16) *Read each sentence to find out whether there is any grammatical or idiomatic error in it. The error, if any, will be in one part of the sentence. The alphabet corresponding to that part is your answer. If there is 'No error', the answer is (e). (Ignore errors of punctuation, if any)*

14. The Prime Minister has great power of (A)/implementing some useful (B)/schemes but the ministers (C)/have even greatest ability to foil them. (D)/No error (E) **SBI Clerk 2018**
(a) A (b) B (c) C (d) D
(e) E

15. Lenovo has launched Think Pad XI Fold (A)/The world's first foldable (B)/laptop which is claimed/(c) to be more durable as its other devices(D)/No Error (E). **SBI Clerk 2018**
(a) A (b) B (c) C (d) D
(e) E

16. Elon Musk is determined (A)/to be success (B)/in whatever field (C)/he chooses. (D)/No error (E) **SBI Clerk 2019**

(a) A (b) B (c) C (d) D
(e) E

Direction (Q. No. 17) *Read the sentence to find out whether there is any error in it. The error, if any, will be in one part of the sentence. That part is the answer. If there is no error, mark 'No error' as the answer.*

17. We had extensively discussions/with the participants and/obtained their feedback/ regarding our new services. **IBPS Clerk 2016**

(a) We had extensively discussions (b) with the participants and
(c) obtained their feedback (d) regarding our new services
(e) No error

Directions (Q. Nos. 18-22) *In the following questions, a sentence is given which is then divided into five parts out of which the last part is correct. There is an error in three parts and only one part is correct. You have to choose the correct part as your answer.* **IBPS Clerk 2017**

18. After he had read/the first two chapters/of the novel,/he had felt like/reading the book in one sitting.

(a) After he had read (b) the first two chapters
(c) of the novel, (d) he had felt like
(e) All are incorrect

19. Temefos is organophosphate/larvicide used to treat/water infested with diseased-carrying insects/includings mosquitoes,/midges, and black larvae.

(a) Temefos is a organophosphate
(b) larvicide used to treat
(c) water infested with diseased-carrying insects
(d) includings mosquitoes
(e) All are incorrect

20. Dulkal was set up in Chennai/with a cored team of five professionals/from vary fields/including engineered,/IT and education.

(a) Dulkal was set up in Chennai (b) with a cored team of five professionals
(c) from vary fields (d) including engineered,
(e) All are incorrect

21. The Russians Sputnik V vaccine/against the noble coronavirus will/be tested in India's/on 100 volunteered,/the DGCI's head told the TOI.

(a) The Russians Sputnik V vaccine (b) against the noble coronavirus will
(c) be tested in India's (d) on 100 volunteered
(e) All are incorrect

22. Jasmine is an importance/flower crops grown/on a commerce scale and/is seriously affected by a mosquito liked insect/called the blossom ridge.

(a) Jasmine is an importance
(b) flower crops grown
(c) on a commerce scale and
(d) is seriously affected by a mosquito liked insect
(e) All are incorrect

Answers

Work Book Exercise A

1. 'fewer' in place of 'less'
2. 'The few' in place of 'Few'
3. Say 'movie worth seeing'
4. 'the least' in place of 'less'
5. Drop 'most'
6. No error
7. Insert 'the' before 'whole'
8. 'an' in place of 'the most'
9. Delete 'The' before 'few'
10. 'more wise' in place of 'wiser'

Work Book Exercise B

1. Use 'as intelligent as'
2. Insert 'other' after 'any'
3. 'the last' in place of 'latest'
4. 'later' in place of 'latter'
5. Insert 'most' before 'beautiful'
6. 'to' in place of 'than'
7. Drop 'other' before 'my neighbours'
8. 'all' in place of 'any'
9. Insert 'those of' after 'than'
10. Drop 'all the more' before 'better'
11. Say, 'This kind' and 'is'
12. 'very' in place of 'too'
13. 'farther' in place of 'further'
14. 'bitterly' in place of 'bitter'
15. Insert 'other' after 'No'

Revision Exercise

1. (b) Add 'most' before 'simple'.
2. (b) Use 'live' in place of 'lively'.
3. (a) Add 'A' before 'little'.
4. (b) Use 'elder' in place of 'older'.
5. (d) No error
6. (e) No error
7. (b) Use 'creative' in place of 'creatively'.
8. (e) No error
9. (c) Use 'chemical' in place of 'chemically'.
10. (a) Replace 'younger' by 'young'.
11. (c) Use 'first three' in place of 'three first'.
12. (b) Use 'young' in place of 'younger'.
13. (d) Use 'wraith-like' in place of 'wraith-liked'.
14. (e) Replace 'larger' by 'largely'.
15. (b) Remove 'most'.

Exam Practice

1. (a) 'very' should be used in place of 'most'.
2. (a) 'next' should be used in place of 'after'.
3. (c) 'greatest' should be used in place of 'greater'.
4. (d) No error
5. (d) No error
6. (b) As comparison is being made between two boxes, the comparative for 'heavy' i.e. 'heavier' should be used in place of 'heavy'.
7. (c) 'a little' should be used to replace 'little'.
8. (b) Replace 'much' by 'the most'.
9. (a) 'few' should be replaced by 'a few'.
10. (c) 'price' should be used in place of 'priced' to correct the sentence.
11. (a) The noun 'sense' should be replaced by the adjective 'sensual' to make the sentence meaningful.
12. (a) 'Most' should be used in place of 'Mostly'.
13. (b) The word 'noise' (noun) is inappropriately used in the sentence. It should be replaced by 'noisy' (adjective).
14. (d) 'greater' should be used in place of 'greatest'.
15. (a) 'To be as durable as' should be used in place of 'To be more durable as'.
16. (b) The noun 'success' does not fit with the context of the sentence. It should be replaced by its adjective form 'successful' to correct the sentence.
17. (a) 'extensive' must be used in place of 'extensively' to correct the sentence.
18. (b) 'the first two chapters' is correct.
19. (b) 'larvicide used to treat' is correct.
20. (a) 'Dulkal was set up in Chennai' is the correct part in the sentence.
21. (e) All are incorrect.
22. (e) All are incorrect.

Adverb

What is an Adverb?

An adverb is a word used to modify to the meaning of a verb, adjective or another adverb. *For example*

(i) She is walking slowly. *(ii)* She is very intelligent.
(iii) She is walking very slowly.

Kinds of Adverb

1. **Adverb of time** Before, ago, lately, yet, now, soon, yesterday, already, never.
2. **Adverb of frequency** Always, once, seldom, usually, rarely etc.
3. **Adverb of place** Here, everywhere, down, near, away, backward, upward.
4. **Adverb of manner** Slowly, soundly, delightfully, bravely, easily, foolishly, clearly.
5. **Adverb of affirmation and negation** Certainly, apparently, obviously, no undoubtedly.
6. **Adverb of degree** Almost, fully, very, enough, rather, quite, too, really, so.
7. **Interrogative adverb** How, what, when, why.
8. **Relative adverb** When, where, why, how.

   Relative adverbs are used to make an adjective clause.

   He was born in the year **when** I left India. *('in which/on which')*
   He does not like to stay at the hotel **where** they are staying. *('in which/at which')*
   Don't you know the reason **why** she did not marry? *('for which')*
   You are supposed to know the manner **how** they cheated you. *('in which/by which')*

Rules of Adverb

Rule I

Adjective qualifies a noun and a pronoun whereas **adverb** modifies a verb, an adjective and an adverb. *For example*

(i) Her act was remarkable. *(Correct)*

(ii) She acted remarkably to achieve success. *(Correct)*

(iii) She ran quicker than I. *(Say 'more quickly' for 'quicker')*

(iv) She is a very skillful dancer. *(Correct)*

(v) She dances very skilfully. *(Correct)*

Rule II

Adverbs of time such as
'Always, often, already, just, never, ever, sometimes, frequently, generally, recently, usually, seldom, hardly', rarely, normally, etc. are generally placed before the verb they modify. *For example*

(i) My brother comes often every Sunday. *(Place 'often' before 'comes')*

(ii) He goes usually to the movie every Friday. *(Place 'usually' before 'goes')*

(iii) He never talks ill of friends. *(Correct)*

(iv) He is always satisfied. *(Correct)*

Rule III

Adverbs of manner are placed only after the Intransitive verb. However, the adverb can be placed **either before or after the transitive verb.** *For example*

(i) He returned immediately. *(Correct)*

(ii) He briefly narrated the incident to me. *(Correct)*

(iii) He narrated to me the incident briefly. *(Correct)*

(iv) He soundly slept last night. *(Place 'soundly' after 'slept')*

Rule IV

If the sentence is introduced by an adverb, inverted form of the verb is used for the sake of emphasis. *For example*

(i) Seldom he visits his parents. *(Incorrect)*

(ii) Seldom does he visit his parents. *(Correct)*

(iii) He seldom visits his parents. *(Correct)*

(iv) Not seldom does he visit his parents. *(Correct)*

(v) Never I'll see her again. *(Incorrect)*

(vi) Never will I see her again. *(Correct)*

(vii) I'll never see her again. *(Correct)*

(viii) She no sooner reached the station **than** she met her friend. *(Correct)*

(ix) No sooner did she reach the station **than** she met her friend. *(Correct)*

(x) She had hardly reached the station **when** the train arrived. *(Correct)*

(xi) Hardly/scarcely had she reached the station **when** the train arrived. *(Correct)*

(xii) So quickly she ran that she overtook her rivals. *(Use 'So quickly did she run')*

Rule V Use of Else and Other

'Else' should be followed by 'but'.

'Other' and **'otherwise'** are followed by 'than'. *For example*

(i) It is nothing else than sheer madness. *(Use 'but' in place of 'than')*

(ii) She had no other alternative but stay here. *(Use 'than' in place of 'but')*

(iii) She has no one else to look after her except me. *(Use 'but' in place of 'except')*

Rule VI

Both **'never'** and **'not'** are adverbs. The use of 'never' for 'not' is incorrect. *For example*

(i) I never went to Ooty last year. *(Use 'did not go' in place of 'never went')*

(ii) I never remember to have said so. *(Use 'do not' in place of 'never')*

(iii) I remember never to have said so. *(Correct)*

Or

I don't remember to have said so.

(iv) I never allow my son to go out in dark. *(Correct/habitual action)*

Rule VII

Note the use of phrases.

'Seldom or never', 'seldom, if ever', 'little or nothing', 'little, if anything'.

The phrases 'seldom or ever' and 'little or anything' are wrong in use. *For example*

(i) We seldom or ever meet our relatives these days. *(Incorrect)*

(ii) We seldom or never (seldom, if ever) meet our relatives these days. *(Correct)*

(iii) We have little or anything to say. *(Incorrect)*

(iv) We have little or nothing to say. *(Correct)*

Rule VIII

Negative adverbs should not be used with the words negative in meaning. So, two negatives should be avoided.

'Seldom, nowhere, never, nothing, hardly, scarcely, neither, barely, rarely' are some of the adverbs expressing negative meaning. *For example*

(i) I rarely went to meet nobody across the road. *(Use 'anybody' in place of 'nobody')*

(ii) She hardly knows nothing about the family. *(Use 'anything' in place of 'nothing')*

(iii) I hardly know somebody in the town. *(Say 'anybody' in place of 'somebody')*

(iv) He does nothing without never consulting me. *(Use 'ever' for 'never')*

(v) They do not seldom come here. *(Remove 'do not')*

(vi) This will not help him, nothing never does. *(Use 'ever' for 'never')*

(vii) He does not write well and I do not write neither. *(Say 'either')*

NOTE **I.** Avoid the use of negative, with 'deny', 'forbid' and 'both'.

(i) She denied that she had not given him books. (Delete 'not')

(ii) (a) Both of us are not going there. (Incorrect)

(b) Neither of us is going there. (Correct)

II. Avoid the use of negative with Conjuntions **until, unless, lest**.

Rule IX

Given below are some of the examples of the words being treated as adverbs whereas they are adjectives or nouns. *For example*

(A) **Manly, masterly, slovenly, monthly, weekly, sickly, friendly, orderly, gentlemanly** are adjectives and should not be confused with adverbs.

(B) **Coward, miser, niggard** are nouns.
'Cowardly, miserly, niggardly' are adjectives.
'In a cowardly, miserly and niggardly manner' are used as adverbs.

(C) **Fast, straight, outright, direct, hard, hardly, late, light, high, safe, quiet**, etc. are used both as an adjective and adverb.

(D) **'Loudly' and 'Aloud'** are adverbs though different in meanings. 'Loud' is an adjective.

(E) **Late, lately**
Late is both an adjective and an adverb
Lately is an adverb. *(Recently)*

(F) **Hard** is both an adjective and adverb used in affirmative sense.
Hardly is an adverb used in negative meaning. *For example*

(i) A soldier is trained never to fight cowardly. *(Use 'in a cowardly manner')*
(ii) I have never come across a coward Indian soldier. *(Use 'cowardly' in place of 'coward')*
(iii) The darkness closed in even as she was returning home fastly. *(Use 'fast' in place of 'fastly')*
(iv) You must learn to behave manly in the face of danger. *(Use 'in a manly manner' in place of 'manly')*
(v) He is earning five hundred rupees monthly. *(Say 'a month')*
(vi) She is doing this work good these days. *(Say 'well' for 'good')*
(vii) Rohit always comes lately to school. *(Say 'late' for 'lately')*
(viii) He is coward. *(Use 'a' before 'coward')*
(ix) The teacher asked the students to talk loudly. *(Say 'aloud')*
(x) We must try to preserve hardly won freedom. *(Use 'hard' in place of 'hardly')*
(xi) Please keep the things in the room orderly. *(Use 'in order' or 'in an orderly manner' in place of 'orderly')*
(xii) She rejected my application outrightly. *(Say 'outright')*
(xiii) Outright rejection of my plan disappointed me. *(Correct)*

Rule X

The use of **'very, much, so, too, enough, rather'**.

(A) **'Very'** modifies present participle used as adjective, adverb and adjective in positive degree. **'Much'** is used with comparative degree and past participle.

For example

(i) It is a much interesting picture. *(Use 'very' in place of 'much')*
(ii) I was very exhausted in the evening. *(Use 'much' in place of 'very')*

(iii) She did this work very quickly. *(Correct)*
(iv) She is much wiser than her mother. *(Correct)*
(v) She is very tired after a day's work. *(Correct)*

NOTE Students should note the use of **'very'** and **'much'** in superlative degree.
For example
(i) She is **the very best** teacher in our school. *(Here 'very' means 'really')*
(ii) She is **much the best** teacher in our school. *(Here 'much' means 'decidedly')*
(iii) She is **by far the** best teacher in our college. *('by far' means 'to a large extent')*

(B) **'So'** and **'too'** should not be used without 'that' (Adverb clause) and 'to' (Infinitive) respectively.

'Very' and **'much'** may be used in the place of 'so' and 'too'.
(i) My brother is so healthy. *(Use 'very' in place of 'so')*
(ii) She is very kind. *(Here 'very' means 'to a great extent')*
(iii) She is too poor to study further. *(Correct)*
(iv) She is so poor that she cannot study further. *(Correct)*
(v) She is too healthy. *(Over healthy, say 'very' for 'too')*
(vi) It is too bad. *(Correct)*

(C) **'Enough'** is both an adjective and adverb. As an **adverb** it is always placed after the adjective it modifies.

As an **adjective** it is placed before a noun. *For example*
(i) She is enough wise to allow her son to go. *(Place 'enough' after 'wise')*
(ii) He has enough money to spend. *(Correct)*
(iii) She is too kind to help everybody. *(Say 'kind enough' in place of 'too kind')*
(iv) She is too weak to pass. *(Correct)*

(D) The use of 'rather'

(a) 'Rather' is an adverb of degree like 'fairly, quite, pretty (to some degree)'.
For example
(i) She is rather intelligent.
(ii) He is walking rather slowly.

(b) 'Rather' can also be used before a noun. *For example*
(i) It is rather a nuisance.
(ii) It is rather a good step. *(or a rather good step)*

NOTE Article 'a', 'an' should be placed before a noun. If there is an adjective with a noun, articles 'a', 'an' may be placed either before or after 'rather'.

(c) 'Rather' is also used in case of preference
'would rather, had rather, rather than' are used to express preference.
For example
(i) I'd like to play inside rather than going out with my friends.
(Refer to Rule III(c) on Infinitive)

Rule XI

Note the difference between too, as well, also.

(a) 'Too, as well, also', are used in the sense of "besides", "in addition to" in affirmative sentences. But 'also' cannot be used at end position.
  (i) She found her bag and money too/as well.
  (ii) She plays the piano and the harmonium as well/too.
  (iii) She found her bag and money also. *(say 'also money')*

(b) So + auxilary + subject is used in affirmative sentences in relation to two persons doing one action.
  (i) She won the prize and so did her sister. *(win)*
  (ii) His wife plays the piano and so does he. *(play)*

(c) Neither + auxilary + subject is used in negative sentences in realtion to two persons doing one action.
  (i) He does not write well and neither do I. *(write)*
  (ii) She will not lend money and neither will he. *(lend)*

Rule XII

While answering a question, the adverb 'yes' or 'no' should be used according to the affirmative and negative answer. *For example*
  (i) Have you taken food?
  (ii) No, I have not taken so far. *(Use 'No' in place of 'Yes')*

Rule XIII

(A) **Adverb 'as' should be used to introduce predicative of the verbs 'regard, describe, define, treat, view, know'.**

(B) **Adverb 'as' should be avoided to introduce predicative of the verbs 'name, elect, think, consider, call, appoint, make, choose.'**
For example
  (i) I regard him my brother. *(Add 'as' after 'him')*
  (ii) Science has been defined the study of nature. *(Add 'as' after 'defined')*
  (iii) She is considered as the best dancer in the town. *(Drop 'as' after 'considered')*.
  (iv) The teacher called him as stupid. *(Drop 'as')*
  (v) The principal appointed him as peon. *(Remove 'as')*
  (vi) He thinks her as a fool. *(Remove 'as')*
  (vii) He was elected as the secretary of our club. *(Remove 'as')*

Work Book Exercise A

Directions *Spot the errors, if any, in the following sentences.*

1. Although I was in Delhi last month I never met him.
2. One should face the misfortunes of life courageously.
3. When I got home I was too exhausted.
4. I did not know hardly anyone in the city and so felt lonely.
5. I rarely find something in his character that I can admire.
6. You have acted nobler than all of us.
7. He is enough kind to help everybody in need.
8. Don't stop anywhere. Go home fastly.
9. He has no time to read novels and no desire neither.
10. He has not seldom visited his parents since he left this place.
11. It was much hot yesterday and we didn't go out.
12. I meet him often near the District Library.
13. I told her as blunt as I could but she was not convinced.
14. What to talk of tea they did not offer us even water.
15. My mother works very quicker than I at embroidery.

Work Book Exercise B

Directions *Spot the errors, if any, in the following sentences.*

1. I never remember to have met a more interesting man in my life.
2. I refused to accompany him because I was so tired.
3. She did this work as good as she could do.
4. This fruit tastes more sweetly than any other fruit.
5. We seldom or ever go to the movie these days because we don't like moving out.
6. The student came to the classroom lately and was punished by the teacher.
7. He looks full of energy today because he soundly slept last night.
8. I care a fig for such a worthless fellow.
9. She had barely nothing to eat when she came to me last month.
10. Have you secured first class? Yes, I have not secured it.
11. It had been bitter cold the whole month and we preferred staying in the plains.
12. Don't be unreasonable angry with me because I understand your problem.
13. Never in the history of India there has been as brave a lady as Rani Lakshmi Bai.
14. They pay him hadsome salary and he is earning fifteen thousand rupees monthly.
15. They have got much too confusion.

Revision Exercise

Directions (Q. Nos. 1-5) *Each item in this section has a sentence with three underlined parts labelled (a), (b) and (c). Read each sentence to find out whether there is any error in any underlined part and indicate your response in the Answer Sheet against the corresponding letter. If you find no error, your response should be indicated as (d).*

1. I met Big B (a) about twelve years ago (b) and have remembered him ever for. (c) No error (d)
2. Nutan said (a) it was quite (b) all right to reject the offer. (c) No error (d)
3. I am too glad (a) to receive the invitation (b) for the Navy Ball. (c) No error (d)
4. The amount which (a) the government has paid (b) to the dependents of the dead workers is fairly unjustified. (c) No error (d)
5. When carefully examined, (a) it was found that there (b) were some missing pieces in the evidence given by him. (c) No error (d)

Directions (Q. Nos. 6-10) *Read each sentence to find out whether there is any error in it. The error, if any, will be in one of the part of the sentence which are marked as (a), (b), (c) and (d). If there is no error, the answer will be (e) i.e., No Error. (Ignore errors of punctuation, if any)*

6. The child took (a) / the lemon drink and (b) / said that it tasted (c) / real good. (d) / No error (e)
7. The presently study (a) / was initiated in June 2009 (b) / by Per Alstrom and Shashank Dalvi (c) / at high elevations of Western Arunachal Pradesh. (d) / No error (e)
8. Pfizer announced that (a) / a vaccine for the corona virus (b) / developed by Dr. Sahin and his team (c) / was more than 90% effective in preventing the disease among trial volunteers. (d) / No error (e)
9. Their songs were (a) / striking different. (b) / although no definite (c) / morphological differences were detected in the field. (d) / No error (e)
10. The doctor was quiet convinced (a) / that the corona virus (b) / which was spreading quickly in parts of China. (c) / would explode into a full-blown pandemic. (d) / No error (e).

Directions (Q. Nos. 11-15) *Read each sentence to find out whether there is any grammatical or idiomatic error in it. The error, if any, will be in one part of the sentence. The alphabet corresponding to that part is the answer. If there is 'No error', the answer is (e) (Ignore errors of punctuation, if any)*

11. I was (A) / fined by the traffic police (B) / for driving fast (C) / on the Ring Road. (D) / No error (E)
(a) A (b) B (c) C (d) D
(e) E

12. The CEO usually (A) / arrives early (B) / for the (C) / annually board meetings. (D) / No error (E)
(a) A (b) C (c) D (d) B
(e) E

13. Sonali looked happily (A) / when I spotted (B) / her in the (C) / old school photograph. (D) / No error (E)
(a) A (b) E (c) D (d) B
(e) C

14. I ever go (A) / to the supermarket (B) / with my mother (C) / on weekdays. (D) / No error (E)
(a) B (b) C (c) D (d) A
(e) E

15. The weather (A) / isn't never (B) / sunny in the (C) / month of December in Delhi. (D) / No error (E)
(a) A (b) C (c) E (d) B
(e) D

Directions (Q. Nos. 16-20) *Each sentence is divided into multiple parts. Find out the error part from the given options and indicate your response from the options (a), (b), (c) and (d) on the answer sheet.*

16. Sukanya could not hardly hear what her teacher was saying.
(a) Sukanya could not (b) hardly hear
(c) what her teacher (d) was saying
(e) No error

17. Prerna looks active today as she soundly slept last night.
(a) active today as she (b) soundly slept
(c) last night (d) Prerna looks

18. Shaan is surely a great singer and no other singer is a match for him.
(a) a great singer (b) is a match for him
(c) and no other singer (d) Shaan is surely
(e) No error

19. Mahatma Gandhi tried to eradicate social evils tooth and nail.
(a) Mahatma Gandhi tried (b) to eradicate social
(c) evils (d) tooth and nail
(e) No error

20. I often met him nearly India Gate in the evenings.
(a) I often met him (b) nearly India Gate
(c) in the (d) evenings
(e) No error

Exam Practice

Directions (Q. Nos. 1-12) *Each sentence is divided into underlined parts labelled as (a), (b) and (c). Read each sentence to find out whether there is any error in any underlined part and indicate your response in the Answer Sheet against the corresponding letter i.e., (a) or (b) or (c). If you find no error, your response should be indicated as (d).*

1. Dispose off (a) the garbage (b) from the shelves. (c) No error (d) **NDA 2020**

2. For young Donald, (a) peace in Vietnam (b) was almost terrible as war. (c) No error (d) **CDS 2016**

3. Mr. Joshi was, however, sure (a) that the idea would never work (b) in practice. (c) No error (d) **CDS 2016**

4. It is almost difficult (a) in case impossible (b) to keep awake late after dinner. (c) No error (d) **CDS 2016**

5. Are you (a) through with (b) that newspaper (c) ? No error (d) **CDS 2017**

6. All the boys (a) returned back home (b) well in time for lunch. (c) No error (d) **CDS 2017**

7. Considering about these facts (a) the principal has offered (b) him a seat. (c) No error (d) **CDS 2017**

8. Nandita asked me (a) if I was working (b) hardly these days. (c) No error (d) **CDS 2017**

9. This hardly won liberty (a) was not to be (b) lightly abandoned. (c) No error (d) **CDS 2019**

10. Since the 15 minutes that she drive, (a) she confessed that she felt like (b) a woman with wings. (c) No error (d) **CDS 2019**

11. Scrolling thorough my social media timeline, (a) I hovered over a video (b) of a minor road traffic accident, (c) No error (d) **CDS 2020**

12. Evolutionary biology leave us (a) distinctly pessimistic about the possibility (b) that altruism can arise naturally among humans. (c) No error (d) **CDS 2020**

Answers

Work Book Exercise A

1. 'did not meet' in place of 'never met'
2. No error
3. 'much' in place of 'too'
4. Remove 'hardly'
5. 'anything' in place of 'something'
6. 'more nobly' in place of 'nobler'
7. 'kind enough' in place of 'enough kind'
8. Say 'fast'
9. 'either' in place of 'neither'
10. Drop 'not'
11. 'very' in place of 'much'
12. Place 'often' before 'meet'
13. 'bluntly' in place of 'blunt'
14. Add 'when' before they
15. 'more quickly' in place of 'very quicker'

Work Book Exercise B

1. 'don't' in place of 'never'
2. 'very' in place of 'so'
3. 'well' in place of 'good'
4. 'sweeter' in place of 'more sweetly'
5. 'never' in place of 'ever'
6. 'late' in place of 'lately'
7. 'slept soundly' in place of 'soundly slept'
8. Add 'don't' after 'I'
9. 'anything' in place of 'nothing'
10. Remove 'not'
11. Say 'bitterly cold'
12. 'unreasonably' in place of 'unreasonable'
13. 'has there been' in place of 'there has been'
14. 'a month' in place of 'monthly'
15. Use 'too much' in place of 'much too'.

Revision Exercise

1. (c) Use 'since' in place of 'for'.
2. (c) Remove 'all'.
3. (a) Use 'very' in place of 'too'.
4. (c) Use 'rather' or 'highly' in place of 'fairly'.
5. (a) Change 'carefully examined' to 'examined carefully'.
6. (d) Use 'really' in place of 'real'.
7. (a) Use 'present' in place of 'presently'.
8. (e) No error
9. (b) Change 'striking' to 'strikingly'.
10. (a) Use 'quite' in place of 'quiet'.
11. (e) No error.
12. (c) Use 'annual' in place of 'annually'.
13. (a) Change 'happily' to 'happy'.
14. (d) Change 'ever' to 'never'.
15. (d) Use 'is' in place of 'isn't'.
16. (a) Remove 'not' as it does not come with 'hardly'.
17. (b) Use 'slept soundly' in place of 'soundly slept'.
18. (e) No error
19. (e) No error
20. (b) Use 'near' in place of 'nearly'.

Exam Practice

1. (d) No error.
2. (c) Add 'as' before 'terrible'.
3. (d) No error
4. (b) Replace 'in case' by 'but in no case'.
5. (d) No error
6. (b) Remove 'back' as it is not used with 'returned'.
7. (a) Remove 'about' as it is not used with 'considering'.
8. (c) Use 'hard' in place of 'hardly'.
9. (a) Use 'hard' in place of 'hardly'.
10. (a) 'For' should be used in place of 'Since'.
11. (a) Use 'through' in place of 'thorough'.
12. (a) Use 'leaves' in place of 'leave'.

14

Prepositions

What is a Preposition?

The word **Preposition** (as is indicated by Prefix **'Pre'**) is a word or a group of words that is placed before a noun or pronoun to indicate direction, method, place, source, etc. In other words, the noun or pronoun is shown to have a kind of relation with regard to the other parts of a sentence with the help of a Preposition. *For example*

(i) The Preposition may join one noun to another.
Sheena was in the **kitchen**. *('Sheena' and 'kitchen')*

(ii) It may join noun to a verb.
She **slipped** off the **stairs**. *('slipped' and 'stairs')*

(iii) It may join noun to an adjective.
We are **proud** of our **country**. *('proud' and 'country')*

1. **'At, in, on, of, off, through, below, with'**, etc. are some of the prepositions.
2. The noun or pronoun used with the preposition is in the **accusative case**.
For example
(i) The book is on the **table**.
(ii) I did not talk to **him**.
Here **'table'** and **'him'** have been used in the accusative case because these words are the objects of the preposition.
3. A Preposition sometimes may have more than one object. *For example*
(i) I gave money to Ritu and her brother.
(ii) Distribute the mangoes among the boys and the girls.
Here 'Ritu' and 'her brother' are objects in (i) and 'boys' and 'girls' are objects in (ii).
4. A clause can also be the object to a preposition. *For example*
(i) I was pleased with what she did for me.
(ii) Pay attention to what your parents say.
Here, 'what she did for me' and 'what your parents say' are the clauses.
5. Adverbs of time and place can also be the object of preposition. *For example*
(i) I don't like to go from here. *(ii)* She had returned by then.
In the sentences given above, 'here' and 'then' are adverbs of place and time respectively.

6. When verbs are placed after prepositions (other than 'to') they should be in the gerund form except when they are used in infinitive form. *For example*

(i) I am confident of winning her love.

(ii) She does not believe in wasting time.

(iii) She insisted on going to Pune.

Here, 'winning' and 'wasting' are verbs in the gerund form. They are followed by the prepositions 'of ' and 'in' respectively.

Prepositions before Particular Words

(A) **Travel, movement**

(a) From, to, at, in, by, on, into, onto, off, out, out of. *For example*

We travel daily from Meerut to Delhi.

(b) Arrive at/in, get to (reach). *For example*

(i) They arrived in India in March. *(ii)* I arrived at Patel Bridge.

(iii) I got to the Bus stand late.

(c) Home (Without preposition) *For example*

(i) They went home. *(Without Preposition)*

(ii) She returned to her home late. *(With Preposition)*

(B) **Above and over**

(a) Above gives the sense of 'vertically higher than'. The surface of both object are then not in contact. *For example*

(i) The flags waved above our heads.

(ii) The helicopters flew above the flooded fields.

(b) But 'over' can also mean 'covering on the other side of', across, from one side to the other and in every part of the region. *For example*

(i) We put a sheet over his body. *(ii)* There is a bridge over the river.

(iii) He has friends all over the world.

(C) **Under, below beneath**

(a) 'Below', 'under', mean lower than, but 'under' can indicate contact. *For example*

(i) She kept money under the bed.

(ii) The old man was crushed under the car.

(iii) The book is kept below the dictionary.

(b) However, 'below' is used when there is a space between the two surfaces. *For example*

(i) They live below us. *(We live above them)*

(ii) There was a beautiful lake below us in the valley.

(c) 'Under' can mean junior in ranks. *For example*

(i) He is under me. *(I am his superior, below doesn't have this meaning)*

(d) 'Beneath' has the same meaning as under, but it is better to use it for abstract meanings. *For example*

(i) He would think it beneath him to do such a small work. *(Unworthy of him)*

(D) **Time and date** (Uses of At, On, By, In)

(a) At 'At' usally denotes a definte point in time likethe time of clock, exact time of the parts of the day, names of festivals and celebrations, etc. such as at Five O'clock, at 11:45, at Midnight, at lunchtime, at diwali, at sunset, at the End of the Meeting. *For example*

(i) We left on the evening of the sixth at 5:30 p.m.

(b) In 'In' is used before parts of the day, month, year season such as; in October, in 1998, in the 18th century, in the 1990s, in (the) winter, in the middle ages, in (the) future, etc.

(c) On 'On' is used for days and dates on Tuesday, on 18 May 2010, on Christmas day, on my birthday, on Tenth of December, etc.

(d) By 'By' denotes the latest time at which an action will be over (would not extend the Mentioned time)

(i) They will return by 5 p.m.

(E) **On time, in time, in good time**

(a) 'On time' (at time arranged, neither before nor after) *For example*
The 12:45 train left on time. (It left at 12:45)

(b) 'In time' (not late) *For example*
Passengers should be in time for their train.

(c) 'In good time' (with comfortable margin) *For example*
I arrived at the theatre in good time.

(F) **At the beginning/at the end, in the beginning/in the end, at first, at last**

(a) At the beginning of a book, there is a foreword. (Literally at the beginning)

(b) At the end, there may be an index.

(c) 'In the beginning/at first' = In the early stage. It implies that later there was a change. *For example*
In the beginning we used hand tools, later we had machines.

(d) 'In the end/At last' = eventually/after sometime. *For example*
At first he opposed marriage, but in the end he gave his consent.

(e) in, on, at, the back of

(i) What is there at the back of the table. *(behind)*

(ii) There is glossary at the back of the book. *(few pages)*

(iii) There is a room on the back of the house. *(back of as part/area)*

(iv) He was stabbed in the back.

(G) **By, before**

By time/date (not later than)

(i) Please be at home by 8.00 p.m.

(ii) By the end of this year my study will have finished.

Rules of Preposition

Rule I

A preposition is usually placed before its object but sometimes it is placed after it in the following cases

(A) When the object in the interrogative pronoun is understood. *For example*

(i) To whom are you talking? *(Incorrect)*
Who are you talking to? *(Correct)*
Whom are you talking to? *(Correct)*

(ii) About what are you talking? *(Incorrect)*
What are you talking about? *(Correct)*

(iii) For what are you looking? *(Incorrect)*
What are you looking for? *(Correct)*

(iv) For what are you waiting? *(Incorrect)*
What are you waiting for? *(Correct)*

(B) When the object of the preposition is a relative pronoun 'that'. *For example*

(i) This is the book for that I have been looking. *(Incorrect)*
This is the book that I have been looking for. *(Correct)*

(ii) This is the picture of that she always talks. *(Incorrect)*
This is the picture that she always talks of. *(Correct)*

(C) When an infinitive qualifies a noun, the preposition should be placed after the infinitive, if required. *For example*

(i) It is not a safe place to live. *(Say 'live in')*
(ii) He gave me a pen to write. *(Say 'write with')*
(iii) He gave me money to spend. *(Correct)*

Rule II

(A) As a rule no preposition is placed after the following verbs when these verbs **are used in active voice.**
'Stress, emphasise, discuss (matter), investigate, comprise, accompany, consider, violate, demand, resemble, pervade, precede, succeed, reach (at), **resign** (post), **attack, invade, resist, enter** (come into), **eschew, befall, order, direct, join, sign, affect, ensure, board, describe, await, lack, regret, concern**. *For example*

(i) The police are investigating into the case. *(Drop 'into')*
(ii) The teacher emphasised on the need of discipline in life. *(Drop 'on')*
(iii) I have ordered for his transfer. *(Drop 'for')*
(iv) I shall discuss about the problem with you. *(Drop 'about')*
(v) Soni resembles with her mother. *(Drop 'with')*
(vi) Our college comprises of class rooms. *(Drop 'of')*
(vii) India has never attacked on any country. *(Drop 'on')*
(viii) She promised to accompany with me to the park. *(Drop 'with')*
(ix) The Committee comprised of five members. *(Correct)*

(B) Omission of 'to' **with verbs of communication before the object, 'advise, tell, ask, beg, command, encourage, request, inform, order, urge.**
For example
(i) I advised to him to go. *(Drop 'to')*
(ii) I informed to the police of the accident. *(Drop 'to')*
(iii) I enquired of him. *(Correct)*

Rule III

Use of preposition in relation to its object

(A) Omission of preposition before Indirect Object.
Study the following verbs.
'bring, give, lend, promise, leave, sell, buy, show, take, fetch, tell, hand, send, sing, read, cost, play (an instrument), **find, get, ask, offer,** etc.' *For example*

(i) I shall fetch you books from market.
Or
I shall fetch books for you from market.

(ii) Her father left him large property.
Or
Her father left large property to him.

(iii) I shall buy you this necklace.
Or
I shall buy this necklace for you.

(iv) I shall find Robin a nice job.
Or
I shall find a nice job for Robin.

(v) Will you sing me a song?
Or
Will you sing a song for me?

(B) Note the placement of proper object (Direct/Indirect) with the use of the following verbs with special reference to the preposition.
The use of verbs **'provide, supply, furnish, entrust, present'**. *For example*
I provided him money. *(Incorrect)*
I provided him with money. *(Correct)*
Or
I provided money to him. *(Correct)*

(C) The correct use of **'rob, fine, inform, explain, recommend, compensate, suggest, propose'**, in relation to objects. *For example*
(a) Rob a person of something.
(b) Fine someone (ten rupees etc.).
(c) Inform someone of something.
(d) Explain something to a person.
(e) Recommend/Suggest/Propose something/some-body to others.
(f) Compensate someone for something.

Examples worked out

(i) He robbed the old woman of all her ornaments.
(ii) The teacher fined him ten rupees.
(iii) We informed the police of the accident.
(iv) The teacher explained the meaning of the poem to us.
(v) He recommended me for promotion to the Principal.
(vi) He recommended this book to his students.
(vii) I shall compensate you for the loss.

Rule IV

A student should take special note of the following Prepositions

(A) **'Than & but'** as Preposition

'Than & but' are usually conjunctions. However, they may be sometimes used as Prepositions. *For example*

(i) I did not see any other person than your brother.
(ii) I did not see any body else but your brother.

(B) **'A'** in the following sentences has been used as a Preposition, though in a weakened form of (in) *For example*

(i) He earns fifty rupees a day.
(ii) She visits me once a month.

(C) **Between, Among**

'Between' is used while referring to two persons/things. It may also be used for two or more in choice.

'Among' is used while referring to more than two persons/things. *For example*

(i) The two brothers divided the property between themselves.
(ii) The two brothers and their sisters divided the property among themselves.

NOTE Between the students in the class which is the best?
(between is correct in choice for more than two)

(D) **Beside, Besides**

'Beside' means 'by the side of '. **'Besides'** means 'in addition to'.

For example

(i) Besides studying he is also working somewhere.
(ii) She sat beside him at the party.

(E) **By, With**

'By' is used for 'doer' of the action. **'With'** is used to denote the instrument.

For example

(i) He struck the dog with a stick. *(ii)* A dog was struck by him.

(F) **Since** *(as a preposition)*

(a) **Since is used for Time Expression** *(time from the past to the present.)*

Since is used for a definite time in the past or some past occasion. *For example,* since birth, since last Sunday, since Diwali, since 2'o clock.

(i) I have not met him since last month. *(From last month till now)*

(ii) She has been doing homework since morning. *(From morning till now)*

(b) **Since as a Conjunction**

(i) I didn't go there since I had no time. *(Here meaning of 'since' is 'because')*

(ii) Since he has never came late, they have promoted him.

(c) **Since as an Adverb**

(i) She went to the USA in 2003 and I have not seen her since. *(From 2003 till now)*

(ii) It was indeed a shock but she has since recovered from it. *(long before now)*

(G) **'For'** is used for time expression (indefinite), a specific period of time (for two months/six years/two hours etc.), purpose, exchange and change.

For example

(i) I shall go to Delhi for two weeks. *(Period of time)*

(ii) She has been sleeping for two hours. *(Time Expression)*

(iii) The drowning man shouted for someone to help him. *(Purpose)*

(iv) Who will pay for the food? *(Refer Exchange)*

(H) **From, Between**

'**From**' is normally used for origin/source, sender and used with 'to/till/until'. 'Between' is used with '**and**'. *For example*

(i) Many Rivers originate from the Himalayas. *(Here 'Himalayas' is origin)*

(ii) Ram borrowed ₹ 500 from Shyam. *(Here 'Shyam' is sender)*

(iii) He works in the office from Ten to Five.

(iv) The Reception will be held between 5 p.m. and 9 p.m.

(I) **Before, Ago**

'**Before**' denotes the preceding action and '**Ago**' refers to the past action.

For example

(i) She left India two days ago/before.

(ii) She had left India before she was married. (Conjunction) (Preceding action)

(J) **In, At**

'**In**' refers to towns, cities and countries in a wider sense while '**at**' is used for speaking of comparatively smaller places. *For example*

(i) He lives in Delhi. *(ii)* He lives at Rohini in Delhi.

(K) **In, Into**

'**In**' denotes position whereas '**into**' shows movement and entrance. *For example*

(i) The students are in the classroom.

(ii) The students came into the classroom.

(L) **On, Upon**

'**On**' denotes position, '**upon**' denotes movement. *For example*

(i) The book is on the table. *(ii)* He threw the book upon the table.

(M) **Within, In**

'Within' means before the end of time, **'In'** means at the end of time while denoting a period of time. *For example*

(i) He will return in ten minutes.

(ii) He will return within ten minutes.

(iii) The train is running on time. *(Neither before nor after)*

(N) **Till, To** (upto)

(a) 'Till' is used to indicate time. *For example*
He studied till 11 p.m.

(b) To (upto) is used of place/distance. *For example*
I went upto Rani Bagh.

(O) **Across, Through**

Both given the sense of 'crossing over' and reaching the other side.

(i) There is a temple across this river.

(ii) The train passed through the tunnel.

(P) **Towards**

Towards gives the sense of 'in the direction of the destination'. *For example*

(i) We went towards the school. (in the direction of the school)

(Q) **Of, Off**

'Of' is generally used for possession and relation while, 'Off' shows seperation. *For example*

(i) The Minister of Education refused the allegation

(ii) He fell off the chair.

Rule V

When two words or adjectives require different prepositions, appropriate prepositions should be used with both the words. *For example*

(i) He is senior and older than I. *(Use 'to' after 'senior')*

(ii) His dress is different and cheaper than mine. *(Use 'from' after 'different')*

(iii) She is younger and taller than her sister. *(Correct)*

Important Prepositional Phrases

Preposition

1.	**Abound in** (V)	(*rich in*) Uttar Pradesh *abounds in* water resources.
2.	**Abound with** (*Adj*)	(*full of*) The forest is *abound with* streams. (*teeming with*)
3.	**Absolve from**	(*declare free from guilt, obligation or punishment*) The court has *absolved* him *from* the crime.
4.	**Absorb in**	(*busy in work*) He is completely *absorbed in* his work.
5.	**Abstain from**	(*hold oneself back, used for food habits*) His doctor asked him to *abstain from* drinking.
6.	**Abstemious in**	(*moderate in eating and drinking*) Those who are *abstemious* in food habits enjoy good health.
7.	**Accede to**	(*to agree to a request or a demand*) He *acceded to* my request.
8.	**Access to**	(*means of reaching, approaching*) There is no *access* to the basic health facilities in the rural areas.
9.	**Adhere to**	(*stick to*) We decided to *adhere to* the programme already agreed upon.
10.	**Approve of**	(*give one's approval*) She *approved of* my proposal in no time.
11.	**Assent to**	(*official agreement e.g., to a proposal*) The President has given *assent to* the Bill.
12.	**Abhorrent to**	(*to dislike something very much*) Racism is *abhorrent to* a majority of people.
13.	**Acquaint with**	(*familiar with*) I am not *acquainted with* the new rules.
14.	**Addicted to**	(*unable to stop from taking*) He is *addicted to* alcohol.
15.	**Assured of**	(*positive about*) I am *assured of* his help in need.
16.	**Attain to**	(*arrive at a position/post*) He *attained to* this status after hard struggle.
17.	**Attracted to**	(*thing or person*) He was *attracted to* her at first sight.
18.	**Avail of**	(*take advantage of*) She *availed* herself *of* this opportunity and got success.
19.	**Aloof from**	(*stay away from*) Keep *aloof from* bad boys.
20.	**Advance for**	(*mature*) He is *advanced for* his years.
21.	**Advance by**	(*prepone by*) The visit of the President has been *advanced by* two days.
22.	**Abide by**	(*rules, comply with*) You should *abide by* the rules laid down by the committee.
23.	**Accused of**	(*a crime, charge with*) He was *accused of* theft and convicted.

24. **Acquit of** (*crime, fault*) He was *acquitted of* the crime.
25. **Admit to** (*get admission*) He was *admitted to* the school on merit.
26. **Admit of** (*scope for*) Your crime does not *admit of* any excuse.
27. **Admit into** (*admittance*) He was *admitted into* the room of the Principal.
28. **Alight on** (*notice*) His eyes alighted on the item in question.
29. **Alight from** (*a bus, car, train*) When he *alighted from* the car, he was welcomed with open arms.
30. **Annoy with** (*be slightly angry*) Noddy was *annoyed with* his friends on account of their misbehaviour.
31. **Annoy at** (*an act*) Suhani was *annoyed at* the misbehaviour of her friends.
32. **Aspire to** (*to aim to achieve something or to be successful*) All the candidates *aspire to* the post of commissioned officers.
33. **Amuse at** (*mock at, laugh at*) Everyone was greatly *amused at* his awkward behaviour during the ceremony.
34. **Amuse with** (*enjoy*) They *amused* themselves *with* playing video games.
35. **Answer to** (*a person*) What will you *answer to* your father?
    (a) She did not *answer* my question.
    (*b*) She did not give *answer to* my question. (*Used as a noun*)
36. **Answer for** (*explain, account for*) You will have to *answer for* your misdeeds.
37. **Account for** (*explain*) You should *account for* your absence from the office.
38. **Antipathy to** (*a strong feeling of not liking someone or something*) I have great *antipathy to* wine.
39. **Antipathy against** (*a person*) We should not have *antipathy against* the poor.
40. **Ask for** (*demand*) I *asked* him *for* help but he refused.
41. **Affiliated to** (*a university or board*) Agra college is *affiliated to* the B.R. Ambedkar University.
42. **Affiliated with** (*a party*) Indian Communists are *affiliated with* the Communist Parties of Russia & China.
43. **Attend to** (*pay attention to*) He did not *attend to* what his mother advised him to do.
44. **Attend upon** (*serve, wait upon*) He has no servant to *attend upon* him in old age.
45. **Antidote to** (*Something that counteracts the effect of poison*) There is no effective *antidote to* poison.

46. **Antidote against** (*cure for*) Quinine is an effective *antidote against* Malaria.
47. **Agree with** (*a person*) I do not *agree with* you.
48. **Agree on** (*a point*) After much discussion they *agreed on* the terms of partnership.
49. **Agree to** (*views*) He *agreed to* all my views but his father did not.
50. **Afflicted with** (*to suffer from a disease, problem, mental trouble*) India is *afflicted with* extreme poverty.
51. **Allowance for** (*allow for*) Always make *allowance for* the mistake of others and pardon them.
52. **Atone for** (*to show that you are sorry for doing something bad or wrong*) The Hindus go to the Ganga to *atone for* their sins.
53. **Aptitude for** (*talent*) He shows some *aptitude for* languages.
54. **Alliance with** (*joined or united*) China has entered into *alliance with* Pakistan against India.
55. **Acquiesce in** (*accept passively*) I had no alternative but to *acquiesce in* his unfair demand.
56. **Apprise of** (*inform*) I *apprised* him *of* the serious food situation in the state.
57. **Act upon** (*comply with*) Always *act upon* the advice of your elders.
58. **Adept in** (*proficient in*) He is *adept in* the art of dancing.
59. **Adept at** (*proficient in*) My brother is *adept at* classical music.
60. **Adapt to** (*make suitable*) You must *adapt* yourself *to* new situations for attaining to high position in life.
61. **Accustomed to** (be used to) I am *accustomed to* early rising.
62. **Akin to** (*similar to*) Your behaviour of indifference is *akin to* jealousy.
63. **Alien to** (*foreign to*) French is *alien to* me because I have never studied it.
64. **Alive to** (*aware of*) He is fully *alive to* the danger of the situation.
65. **Amenable to** (*willing to do something or to agree with someone*) Nowadays majority of the students are not *amenable to* discipline.
66. **Analogous to** (*similar to*) Jahanara's wisdom was *analogous to* her beauty.
67. **Aware of** (*know about*) I am *aware of* your success.
68. **Beware of** (*cautious*) *Beware of* dogs lest you should be bitten.
69. **Blush at** (*to feel embarrassed or ashamed*) She *blushed at* the mention of her qualities.
70. **Blind in** (*to be unable to see from*) He is *blind in* left eye and needs a major surgery.

71. **Blind to** (*to ignore*) We should not be *blind to* the fault of our children.

72. **Born of** (*a child of*) She was *born of* a beautiful mother/parents.

73. **Born to** (*passive voice*) A son was *born to* her.

74. **Bearing on** (*relation to*) Your speech has no *bearing on* the subject we are discussing.

75. **Beset with** (*surrounded with*) India is *beset with* many problems these days.

76. **Believe in** (*to have faith*) I *believe in* him because he is honest.

77. **Benefit by** *(Verb)* You should *benefit by* the experience of others.

78. **Benefit from** (*Noun*) You should derive *benefit from* the experience of others.

79. **Compensate for** (*give something to make up*) He *compensated* me *for* the damage to my scooter.

80. **Cure of** (*rid of*) He is *cured of* his illness after long treatment.

81. **Cure for** (*treatment*) There is no *cure for* AIDS yet.

82. **Compete with** (*person*) He will *compete with* me for the first position in the college.

83. **Compete for** (*trophy etc.*) Our team will not *compete for* the Roman Trophy.

84. **Conformity with** (*in agreement with*) I acted in *conformity with* the opinion of the majority.

85. **Conformity to** (*according to*) I did that in *conformity to* the traditions of the family.

86. **Cling to** (*to hold tight*) The child was *clinging to* her mother.

87. **Comply with** (*act in accordance with*) You must *comply with* the rules laid down by the committee.

88. **Condemn to** (*punishment*) The accused was *condemed to* death.

89. **Congratulate on** (*success*) Arnav *congratulated* his friend *on* his success.

90. **Certain of** (*sure of*) Those who work hard should be *certain of* their success.

91. **Confident of** (*success*) My sister is always *confident of* success.

92. **Count on** (*depend on*) You should never *count on* unreliable persons.

93. **Charge of** (*Noun*) (*crime*) *Charge of* murder was framed against him.

94. **Charge with** *(Verb)* (*crime*) He was *charged with* the murder of his neighbour.

95. **Cope with** (*manage work*) My advocate cannot *cope with* heavy court work.

96. **Contrast to** (*Noun*) Her character is a *contrast to* her husband's.

97. **Contrast with** (Verb) *They tried to contrast* the character of their father *with* mine.

98. **Cash in on** (*avail of*) Everybody of them was trying to *cash in on* the reservation of posts announced for the community.

99. **Contribute to** (*add to a thing*) Every Indian should *contribute to* the success of the Indian economy.

100. **Complain against** (*a person*) He *complained to* the Principal *against* me.

101. **Complain of** (*a thing*) The teacher *complained of* his rude behaviour.

102. **Cordone off** (*to block an area*) The Police cordoned off a part of the city centre.

103. **Commit to** (*a promise, pledge, sentence*) He has *committed* himself *to* the service of the society.

104. **Confide in** (*to trust someone with secrets*) I have always *confided in* him and he has never deceived me.

105. **Confide to** (*to tell a secret*) Do not *confide* your secrets *to* unreliable friends.

106. **Consist in** (*remain*) Beauty *consists in* the character of a person.

107. **Consist of** (*comprise*) The house *consists of* four rooms.

108. **Commence** (*to start on a day, at time, in a month*) The examinations will *commence* on monday at 10 o'clock.

109. **Commence with** (*to start*) He *commenced with* grammar when he started teaching English.

110. **Clamour for** (*demand*) The labourers are *clamouring for* the rise in their wages.

111. **Clamour against** (*complain against*) The residents are *clamouring against* the negligence of the police.

112. **Cause for** (*reason for*) There is no *cause for* anxiety.

113. **Cause of** (*result from*) The *cause of* Cancer is still unknown.

114. **Concerned for** (*worried*) I am greatly *concerned for* the safety of his money.

115. **Concerned with** (*have anything to do*) I am not *concerned with* his business.

116. **Condole with** (*express grief or sympathy*) I *condoled with* my friend for the death of his father.

117. **Disappoint of** (*to fail to satisfy someone or their hopes, wishes, etc.*) I was *disappointed of* my success in the new venture.

118. **Despair of** (*lose hope*) The shipwrecked sailors despaired of being rescued.

119. **Dabble in/at** (*art, politics etc.*) Though he belonged to the family of politicians, he never *dabbled in* politics.

120. **Destined for** (*intended for a particular purpose*) He is *destined for* the post of D.M. and is expected to be promoted soon.

121. **Disgrace on** (*dishonourable*) He is a *disgrace on* his family.

122. **Dwell on/upon** (*speak/write in detail*) The teacher *dwelt on* the need of discipline.

123. **Die of** (*a disease*) He *died of* malaria after a few days' illness.

124. **Die from** (*some cause*) He *died from* overwork because hard work had affected his health adversely.

125. **Differ with** (*to disagree with a person in views*) I *differ with* you on the views of life.

126. **Differ from** (*be unlike or dissimilar*) She *differs from* me both in habits and looks.

127. **Deal in** (*trade in*) My friend *deals in* cloth.

128. **Deal with** (*to give attention to someone or something*) You must learn how to *deal with* customers.

129. **Dispense with** (*to remove, to do without*) You cannot *dispense with* the use of a fan in summer.

130. **Dispense** (*to deal out, distribute*) As a judge he *dispenses* equal justice to all and one.

131. **Dispose of** (*sell*) I shall *dispose of* my old furniture and buy new one.

132. **Disposed to** (*inclined to*) He is *disposed to* travelling abroad.

133. **Decamp with** (*to leave a place quickly*) The robbers had *decamped with* the booty before the police arrived.

134. **Disgust with** (*to show strong disapproval*) Being spiritual he is *disgusted with* material things in life.

135. **Disgust at** (*disapproval of an act*) Every one felt *disgusted at* his jokes.

136. **Discriminate against** (*not to treat well*) No one should *discriminate against* the poor.

137. **Discriminate between** (*difference between*) We should always *discriminate between* right and wrong.

138. **Embark on** (*venture, undertake*) He has decided to *embark on* a new business undertaking.

139. **Enter into** (*alliance, agreement*) India and America have *entered into* various agreements.

140. **Enter upon/on** (*undertake*) My brother has decided to *enter upon* the expansion programme of his business.

141. **Enlarge on/upon** (*write or say more*) I need not *enlarge on* the problem and waste your time.

142. **Endowed with** (*gifted with*) His wife is *endowed with* both charms and talents.

143. **Enamoured with** (*like/love something very much*) Rosalind was *enamoured with* Orlando at first sight.

144. **Enamoured of** (*to admire*) Though it was their first meeting, he was *enamoured of* her talents.

145. **Enrage at** (*to get angry at an act*) The teacher was *enraged at* the student's insolence.

146. **Enrage with** (*to get angry at a person*) The teacher was *enraged with* the student for his insolence.

147. **Exult over** [*enjoy (bad sense*] The spectators *exulted over* the defeat of the Pakistani team.

148. **Exult at** (*enjoy*) The spectators *exulted at* the victory of Indian team.

149. **Eligible for** (*to be suitable*) Only graduates are *eligible for* the post.

150. **Familiar to** (*to know*) Her face is quite *familiar to* everyone.

151. **Familiar with** (*knowledge*) I am not very *familiar with* botanical names of plants.

152. **False of** (*dishonest*) He is not *false* of heart.

153. **False to** (*friends or principles*) We should not be *false to* our friends.

154. **Fascinated by** (*attracted*) The children were *fascinated by* all the toys in the shop windows.

155. **Fascinated with** (*a person*) I was *fascinated with* her because of her admirable manners.

156. **Fly into** (*to suddenly get angry*) On hearing my remarks, she *flew into* a rage.

157. **Feed on** (*live on*) Carnivorous animals *feed on* flesh.

158. **Fondness for** (*liking for*) He has *fondness for* classical music.

159. **Fond of** (*liking for*) He is *fond of* classical music.

160. **For lack of/For want of/For short of/** (*something*) *For lack of* money, he could not continue his studies further.

161. **Grieve for** (*to feel sorrow*) He *grieved for* the victims of the storm.

162. **Grieve over** (*a thing*) He *grieved over* the loss of money in business.

163. **Grieve at** (*an event*) He *grieved at* my father's death when I informed him of my personal tragedy.

164. **Guard against** (*to be cautious against mistakes, temptations*) You should *guard against* the wrong use of words.

165. **Guard from** (*a danger, of a thing etc.*) You should *guard from* him because he is false of heart.

166. **Glance at** (*take a quick look*) He *glanced at* her face and started noting down her address.

167. **Glance through** (*go through*) He *glanced through* the letter in a hurry and handed it back to me.

168. **Good at** (*expert*) He is *good at* the piano.

169. **Hear from**	(*a person*) I have not *heard from* you for a long time.
170. **Hear of**	(*something*) I *heard of* this event in Mumbai and rushed back to Delhi.
171. **Hear by**	(*post, through communication*) I *heard by* a letter about his uncle's death.
172. **Hard by**	(*near*) The college is *hard by* so I go on foot.
173. **Hard up**	(*financially tight*) He is *hard up* these days.
174. **Hanker after**	(*run after, hunger after*) Don't *hanker after* money and fame.
175. **Healed of**	(*cured of*) He is *healed of* the illness after long treatment.
176. **Infer from**	(*statement*) You cannot *infer* anything *from* his statement.
177. **Insight into**	(*reality, situation*) Wise persons have *insight into* the reality of life.
178. **Impress upon**	(*advice*) The Principal *impressed upon* the students the need of discipline.
179. **Impress with**	(*to gain admiration and respect*) He *impressed* me very much *with* his good manners.
180. **Inquire for/about**	(*to ask*) He has just gone to *inquire for* the supply of rations.
181. **Inquire after**	(*welfare, ask after*) I *inquired after* his father's health.
182. **Inquire of**	(*ask a person*) I *inquired of* him the name of his father.
183. **Inquired into**	(*investigate*) The police are *inquiring into* the case.
184. **Interfere in**	(*come in between*) Don't *interfere in* my private affairs.
185. **Interfere with**	(*hinder*) Refrain from *interfering with* the course of justice.
186. **Invest with**	(*authority*) The Principal was *invested with* powers to deal with this problem.
187. **Influence with**	(*a person*) He has immense *influence with* the police.
188. **Influence over**	(*the people*) The P.M. has great *influence over* the people of tribal regions.
189. **Influence on**	(*a thing*) The *influence* of books *on* young children is great.
190. **Intrude into**	(*to go into a place or situation in which you are not wanted or expected to be*) He *intruded into* the room but was turned out.
191. **Intrude on**	(*privacy*) Don't *intrude on* the privacy of anyone.
192. **Intimate with**	(*friendly*) She is *intimate with* my family.
193. **Irritated at**	(*feel frustrated*) He seems greatly *irritated at* my refusal.
194. **Incensed at**	(*thing*) He was greatly *incensed at* his conduct.
195. **Indignant at**	(*angry and surprised because you feel insulted or unfairly treated*) Instead of being happy, he is *indignant at* my offer.

196.	**Judge of**	(*give opinion*) Don't *judge of* things by their outward appearance.
197.	**Judge by**	(*test by*) He was *judged by* his academic qualifications.
198.	**Jump to**	(*conclusion*) Dont *jump to* conclusion without giving due consideration to the facts.
199.	**Jump at**	(*an offer*) He *jumped at* the offer and was highly pleased.
200.	**Jeer at**	(*make rude or mocking remarks*) The spectators *jeered at* their team on their fourth defeat.
201.	**Jest at**	(*make fun of*) Never *jest at* those who are in trouble.
202.	**Known to**	(*passive voice*) You are *known to* her very well.
203.	**Known by**	(*recognize*) A man is *known by* the company he keeps.
204.	**Known for**	(*a quality*) Arnav is well-*known for* his benevolence.
205.	**Knocked at**	(*the door*) I *knocked at* the door but there was no reply.
206.	**Knock on** (*Noun*)	Mala heard a *knock on* the door.
207.	**Key to**	(*success*) Hard work is the *key to* success.
208.	**Lean on**	(*depend on*) I had to *lean on* him in difficulties.
209.	**Lean to**	(*inclined towards*) He seems to *lean* more *to* his daughter than his son.
210.	**Live in**	(*region, area, country*) He is *living in* America.
211.	**Live at**	(*indicate the place*) He is *living at* Agra.
212.	**Live on**	(*food*) He *lives* entirely *on* vegetables these days.
213.	**Live by**	(*livelihood, manner*) I have to *live by* the labour of my own hands.
214.	**Live off**	(*source*) Nowadays he is *living off* his rental income.
215.	**Listen to**	(*advice*) You should *listen to* my advice.
216.	**Liable for**	(*responsible for*) I hold you *liable for* the murder.
217.	**Liable to**	(*deserve*) He is *liable to* imprisonment and fine.
218.	**Laugh with**	(*enjoy with others*) It is better to *laugh with* than to laugh at others.
219.	**Laugh at**	(*an act, person*) Never *laught at* the old persons.
220.	**Lacking in**	(*something, wanting in*) Even educated persons were *lacking in* table manners.
221.	(Have) **Liking for**	(*a person, a thing*) She has a great *liking for* children.
222.	(Take) **Liking to**	(*a person, a thing*) My friend took *liking to* Arnav and married him.
223.	**Likeness between**	(*similarity*) There is *likeness between* the Chinese and the Koreans.
224.	**Limit to**	(*extent*) There is always a *limit to* friendship.

225. **Move to** (*tears*) On listening to the tale of my sufferings, Pearl was *moved to* tears.

226. **Move with** (*pity*) Pearl was *moved with* pity at the beggar's plight.

227. **Move by** (*affected by*) We were *moved by* her pathetic condition.

228. **Married to** Arnav was *married to* a famous doctor.

229. **Mix with** (*a thing*) Please don't mix water with milk.

230. **Menace to** (*threat to*) Terrorists are *a menance to* the security of the country.

231. **Match for** (*a person in quality*) His father is no *match for* my uncle.

232. **Mock at** (*an act, a person*) Never *mock at* the poverty of others.

233. **Meditate on** (*to think of a past act*) She was in tears when she *meditated on* her humiliation.

234. **Meditate** (*future act*) She is *meditating* revenge for her humiliation.

235. **Neglectful of** (*ignorant of a person, work, a thing*) He has been *neglectful of* his business.

236. **Negligent in** (*careless in duty*) Don't be *negligent in* your duty.

237. **Need for** (*something*) There is no *need for* further action in the matter.

238. **(In) need of** (*something*) I am not in *need of* money (*feelings*).

239. **Originate in** (*place as a source*) Modern civilisation *originated in* Europe.

240. **Originate with** (*a person*) This scheme *originated with* the Finance Minister.

241. **Occupied in** (*doing a thing*) I am just now *occupied in* solving the problems.

242. **Occupied with** (*a thing*) My father is *occupied with* the expansion of his business.

243. **Operate on/upon** (*in the sense of operation*) The doctor decided to *operate on* her leg immediately.

244. **Oblivious of** (*having no memory, ignorant of*) *Oblivious of* danger, they kept on marching ahead.

245. **Offend at** (*felt hurt*) He was *offended at* my words.

246. **Offend with** (*person*) Please don't get *offended with* her as she is honest.

247. **Overwhelm with** (*feelings*) Her mother was *overwhelmed with* love for his son.

248. **Overwhelm by** (*defeated by*) The enemy was *overwhelmed by* our army.

249. **Part with** (*to get seperated from a thing*) A miser cannot *part with a* single penny.

250. **Part from** (*a person*) I *parted from* my friend in Delhi.

251. **Preface to** (*a book*) He wrote a *preface to* his book.

252	**Profit by**	(*learn*) You will *profit by* your experience at the hotel.
253.	**Profit from**	(*gain*) We may *profit from* the new pension policy.
254.	**Partiality for**	(*a thing, liking*) She has *partiality for* sweets.
255.	**Partiality to**	(*a person's favour*) He always shows *partiality to* his relatives.
256.	**Prone to**	(*inclined to*) Thickly populated areas are *prone to* riots and diseases.
257.	**Perish by**	(*destroy, famine, sword*) The tyrants *perish by* sword.
258.	**Perish with**	(*suffer from*) They are *perishing with* starvation.
259.	**Prevail against**	(*face*) They *prevailed against* all odds in life.
260.	**Prevail on/upon**	(*to compel*) I have *prevailed on* him to come to attend the function.
261.	**Point out**	(*reveal*) I *pointed out* his errors and he got annoyed with me.
262.	**Point at**	(*blame*) No one can *point at* his character because he is quite honest.
263.	**Point to**	(*refer to*) His speech *pointed to* a few problems relating to poverty.
264.	**Preside at**	(*a party, chief guest*) The Governor *presided at* the feast.
265.	**Preside over**	(*meeting, president*) *He presided over* the meeting in the absence of the chairman.
266.	**Provided against**	(*adversity*) We should always *provide against* a rainy day.
267.	**Provided for**	(*arrange what is necessary*) He died without *providing for* his family.
268.	**Popular for**	(*known for*) He is *popular for* his honesty.
269.	**Popular with**	(*the people*) He is *popular with* the students of the class.
270.	**Pine for**	(*crave for a person*) She is *pining for* the return of her lost son.
271.	**Pine away**	(*die away with grief*) She *pined away* in the memory of her lost son.
272.	**Play at**	(*cards*) We are *playing at* cards.
273.	**Play upon**	(*a musical instrument*) She is *playing upon* the piano.
274.	**Partake of**	(*share any thing*) They *partook of* our food and were satisfied.
275.	**Prey on**	(*exploit*) The rich *prey on* the poor.
276.	**Passion for**	(*strong desire*) He has a *passion for* writing poetry.
277.	**Peculiar to**	(*particular*) This habit is *peculiar to* my father.
278.	**Pity for** (*Noun*)	We should feel *pity for* the poor.
279.	**Pity on** (*Noun*)	He should take *pity on* the poor.

280.	**Pity** *(Verb)*	We should *pity* the poor.
281.	**Pride on** *(Verb)*	They *prided* themselves *on* their wealth.
282.	**Pride in** (*Noun*)	They take *pride in* their wealth.
283.	**Proud of**	We should be *proud of* our country.
284.	**Prompt in**	(*quick in*) You should be *prompt in* doing your duty.
285.	**Quick at**	(*a thing*) The dog is *quick at* smelling.
286.	**Quick in**	(*doing a thing*) The boy is *quick in* working out the problems.
287.	**Quick of**	(*understanding*) The child is very *quick of* understanding.
288.	**Quarrel over**	(*to fight over*) They *quarrelled over* the division of their ancesteral property.
289.	**Quarrel with**	(*a person*) Don't *quarrel with* your friends over trifles.
290.	**Reputation for**	(*a quality*) My brother has a *reputation for* honesty.
291.	**Remorse for**	(*wrongdoing*) She felt *remorse for* neglecting her old parents.
292.	**Respite from**	(*relief from*) People have felt no *respite from* the cold wave.
293.	**Replace by**	(*a new object*) Old furniture will be *replaced by* new one.
294.	**Repent of**	(*an action*) He *repented of* the misdeeds of his youth.
295.	**Recourse to**	(*resort to, adopt as means*) They took *recourse to* wrong means for success.
296.	**Revenge oneself on** *(Verb)*	(*a person*) He *revenged himself on* his enemy for the murder of his brother.
297.	**Revenge for** (*Noun*)	(*an injury*) She took *revenge on* him for his misdeeds.
298.	**Reconcile oneself to**	(*a thing*) You must *reconcile yourself to* the circumstances and endure them.
299.	**Reconcile with**	(*a person*) He has not yet been *reconciled with* his wife.
300.	**Reason with**	(*to explain*) I *reasoned with* him but could not bring him round.
301.	**Reckon on/upon**	(*depend on*) You can safely *reckon upon* the books for advice.
302.	**Remonstrate with**	(*a person*) The players *remonstrated with* the umpire against his L.B.W. decision.
303.	**Remiss in**	(*duty*) Those found *remiss in* duty will be punished.
304.	**Sure of**	(*a thing*) We are *sure of* victory in the game.
305.	**Smile at**	(*mock at*) All his friends *smiled* mockingly *at* his failure.
306.	**Smile on**	(*favour*) At last fate *smiled on* him and he was successful.
307.	**Slow at**	(*doing something*) On account of her old age, she is *slow at* cooking.
308.	**Substitute for**	(*be replaced with*) New furniture will be *substituted for* old one.

309.	**Scare of**	(*afraid of*) I got *scared of* the sound of bomb blast.
310.	**Shoot at, strike at, catch at, Hit at**	(*unsuccessful attempt*) The police *shot at* the thief who escaped in darkness.
311.	**Shoot at, Strike at, Catch at, Hit at**	(*successful in attempt*) The police *shot* the robber dead.
312.	**Speak for**	(*favour*) I shall *speak for* you to the Commander.
313.	**Speak of**	(*praise*) There is no scenic spot here to *speak of.*
314.	**Start on**	(*journey*) He *started on* journey for Mumbai though he did not have enough money.
315.	**Strive for**	(*try for*) It is futile to *strive for* permanent joy in life.
316.	**Strive with**	(*compete with*) Don't *strive with* the rich and the powerful.
317.	**Side with** *(Verb)*	(*favour*) He would never *side with* those who are unjust.
318.	**Search for**	(*a thing*) He is still *searching for* a good house.
319.	**Seek after**	(*in demand*) He is much *sought after* actor these days.
320.	**Seek for**	(*try to win*) He always *sought for* his aim in his life.
321.	**Seething with**	(*anger, discontent*) The residents of the locality were *seething with* anger over the apathy of the police.
322.	**Suffer from**	(*disease*) He is *suffering from* cancer and is not likely to survive long.
323.	**Show off**	(*display*) The modest persons do not *show off* their wealth.
324.	**Sentence to**	(*punishment*) Madho was *sentenced to* death by the judge.
325.	**Spark off**	(*give rise to, trigger off*) Communal speech will *spark off* riots in the town.
326.	**Think of**	(*remember a subject*) *Think of* a plan and let me know by tomorrow.
327.	**Think over**	(*to consider*) I will *think over* your case after sometime.
328.	**Tantamount to**	(*equal in effect*) His remarks are *tantamount to* insult.
329.	**Tired of**	(*sick of, fed up with, weary*) I am *tired of* listening to his flattering words.
330.	**Treat of**	(*a subject, deal with*) You should *treat of* this problem patiently.
331.	**Tresspass on**	(*encroach on, land*) Do not *tresspass on* government land.
332.	**Tresspass against**	(*law*) He was punished for *tresspassing* the rules of the road.
333.	**Triumph over**	(*to win over*) At last he *triumphed over* his difficulties.
334.	**Trifle with**	(*make fun of*) Don't *trifle with* the feelings of the poor.
335.	**Usher in**	(*begin, bring out*) Globalisation has *ushered in* an era of market economy.
336.	**Verse in**	(*expert in*) She is *versed in* the art of cooking.
337.	**Vote for**	(*a person*) I don't *vote for* worthless politicians.

338.	**Vote on *(Verb)***	The members *voted on* the resolution which was passed by majority.
339.	**Vote to**	(*win*) He was *voted to* power with thumping majority.
340.	**Venture upon**	(*an undertaking*) He did not dare to *venture upon* a new enterprise.
341.	**Vain of**	(*proud of*) Though rich, she is not *vain of* her wealth.
342.	**Vexed with**	(*person*) Don't get *vexed with* me.
343.	**Vexed at**	(*a thing*) I am *vexed at* my brother's absence.
344.	**Wait upon**	(*attend upon, to serve*) Who is *waiting on* this table?
345.	**Wait for**	(*person, thing*) He is *waiting for* her.
346.	**Weary of**	(*a thing*) He was *weary of* study and retired to bed.
347.	**Warn against**	(*fault, danger*) I have already *warned* you *against* your carelessness.
348.	**Warn of**	(*danger*) He *warned* the nation of financial crisis.
349.	**Wish for**	(*a thing*) I dont *wish for* anything in life.
350.	**Worthy of**	(*praise*) Your remarks are really *worthy of* note.
351.	**Wanting in**	(*lacking in*) She is *wanting in* common sense.
352.	**Ward off**	(*keep at a distance*) Hindus believe in many rituals to *ward* the evils *off*.
353.	**Wary of**	(*be cautious of*) We should be *wary of* strangers.
354.	**Yearn for**	(*acute desire, long for*) She *yearned for* the return to her own home.
355.	**Zealous for/about**	(*a thing*) A good soldier is always *zealous for* his country's honour.

Work Book Exercise A

Directions *Spot the errors, if any, in the following sentences.*

1. We should always listen the advice of our well wishers.
2. He closely resembles with his father in facial features.
3. While taking examinations, always write with dark ink.
4. The Insurance Company has promised to compensate the damage to my house.
5. You must revise your answer sheet again.
6. He suffered from heart attack last year.
7. Everybody complains against callous treatment of the police.
8. She is very popular among her friends and relatives.
9. The highway robbers robbed all their belongings.
10. Would you please ring me up on next Monday?

Work Book Exercise B

Directions *Spot the errors, if any, in the following sentences.*

1. In a democratic society no one should be discriminated because of caste and creed.
2. A summons was served to him last week.
3. As a responsible officer you should dispense with justice to the poor and the needy.
4. Whenever she goes out her chaperon accompanies with her.
5. The meeting began at about 2 p.m. and he had arrived quite earlier.
6. The news of the Prime Minister's death spread in all over the country.
7. He always travelled in second class with a view to understanding the pulse of his countrymen.
8. She was admitted in the hospital when she met with a serious accident.
9. After his death, his wife and children died of misery and starvation.
10. While going to college, I met my old friends in the way.

Work Book Exercise C

Directions *Spot the errors, if any, in the following sentences.*

1. She is very arrogant because she comes from a rich family.
2. He has not come to meet me although he came back before a week.
3. I saw him climbing on the tree to pluck mangoes.
4. Everybody knows what for Kanpur is famous.
5. He has never wished any reward although he has served suffering humanity throughout his life.

6. Do you know he will be operated tomorrow in a Delhi hospital?
7. Six teams are competing the Singer World Cup.
8. They were talking something but I don't know what they were talking.
9. She prays God everyday for the safe return of her son.
10. In a short time the new staff will be substituted by those who are on long leave.

Work Book Exercise D

Directions *Fill up the blanks with suitable prepositions from the alternatives given under each sentence.*

1. His professional ability proves that he is cut .... for this job.
   (*a*) out (*b*) up (*c*) down
2. The history of Hindu religion dates .... ancient times.
   (*a*) from (*b*) since (*c*) for
3. Now government servants have the day .... every Saturday.
   (*a*) out (*b*) off (*c*) since
4. Nothing can deter him .... pursuing his aim of life.
   (*a*) for (*b*) from (*c*) in
5. After the death of his father the responsibility has devolved .... him.
   (*a*) on (*b*) at (*c*) from
6. In accordance with the advice of a doctor she is .... diet.
   (*a*) on (*b*) at (*c*) off
7. Normally he stays .... until 11 p.m. these days.
   (*a*) up (*b*) out (*c*) on
8. No one believes him because he is false .... heart.
   (*a*) to (*b*) at (*c*) of
9. The officials have the habit of fawning .... ministers.
   (*a*) above (*b*) at (*c*) on
10. The problem of communal harmony cannot be glossed .... by government.
    (*a*) at (*b*) on (*c*) over

Work Book Exercise E

Directions *Fill up the blanks with suitable prepositions from the alternatives given under each sentence.*

1. You cannot expect respect from him because he is lost .... sense of shame.
   (*a*) in (*b*) to (*c*) into
2. You have not to get up because the book is lying .... hand.
   (*a*) at (*b*) in (*c*) on

3. After all hard work has come to tell .... your health.
(a) on (b) upon (c) at

4. Dishonesty is always detrimental .... progress in life.
(a) to (b) for (c) in

5. He made insulting remarks that are derogatory .... his reputation.
(a) for (b) to (c) in

6. In the long run, drinking proved fatal both .... his reputation & health.
(a) for (b) to (c) of

7. The rich are not inured .... manual labour.
(a) of (b) on (c) to

8. Disintegration of the country is inimical .... the progress of the people.
(a) to (b) for (c) from

9. The court has absolved him .... all the charges levelled against him.
(a) of (b) from (c) to

10. Children, by the force of habit, are attracted .... anything that glitters.
(a) by (b) to (c) with

Work Book Exercise F

Directions *Fill up the blanks with suitable prepositions from the alternatives given under each sentence.*

1. As a step to renovation he has decided to replace old furniture ...... new one.
(a) with (b) by (c) for

2. During the course of speech the Principal enlarged .... the need of improving college library.
(a) upon (b) to (c) in

3. He was in a hurry and just glanced .... the letter.
(a) over (b) at (c) through

4. Nowadays rich people enjoy influence .... the police authorities.
(a) with (b) over (c) on

5. Nobody likes anyone to intrude .... his privacy.
(a) in (b) into (c) on

6. Think over the matter. Please don't jump .... conclusions in a hurry.
(a) to (b) at (c) for

7. The scheme of Rozgar Yojna originated .... the Prime Minister.
(a) in (b) with (c) by

8. We must not show partiality .... our relatives.
(a) to (b) for (c) of

9. The Hindus believe in many rituals to ward .... evils.
(a) against (b) off (c) out

10. There is no limit .... the wants of man.
(a) for (b) to (c) of

Work Book Exercise G

Directions *Fill up the blanks with appropriate preposition.*

1. Disruptive forces in the country are fatal .... the integrity of the nation.
2. Politeness is a quality that is alien .... Mrs. Kapoor.
3. Liquor is not the best means to gain respite .... sufferings in life.
4. I think his long silence is tantamount .... a refusal.
5. Never in life has he been beset .... grave financial problems.
6. Heedless .... consequences he remained deaf .... her request.
7. Temperance in life is conducive .... health.
8. As a literary artist he is indifferent .... praisc or blame.
9. There is no need .... helping a reckless fellow like him.
10. For want .... experience he was easily taken in by his sweet words.

Work Book Exercise H

Directions *Fill up the blanks with appropriate prepositions.*

1. He is always distrustful .... the prejudicial motives of his partners.
2. The attitude of the fanatics is always prejudicial .... other religion.
3. The way she uses cosmetics is offensive .... good taste.
4. The competitive exams should never be allowed to coincide .... university examinations.
5. At the end of his life he was bereft .... wealth and home.
6. Extremism is detrimental .... the progress of a country.
7. The Minister has decided to sue the newspaper .... libellous writing.
8. You have no right to trespass .... the law of the land.
9. The government has decided to impose enhanced excise duty .... luxury goods.
10. Aurangzeb divested Shahjahan .... royal powers.

Work Book Exercise I

Directions *Fill up the blanks with appropriate preposition.*

1. Don't side .... those who act contrary .... national interests.
2. She took exception .... his oblique reference to her parents.
3. Mr. Narayan has been overwhelmed .... grief since his young son met with a fatal accident.
4. At last she acceded .... his proposal of marriage after long courtship.
5. The team was elated .... joy .... their victory.
6. Despite financial programme they could not adhere .... it.

7. The emergency meeting of the college staff approved .... the budget proposals for the coming year.
8. They have apprised the authorities concerned .... the failure of the plan.
9. Never judge .... a metal .... its glitter as all that glitters is not gold.
10. My guest had to pay for lunch since I had no money .... me.

Revision Exercise

Directions (Q.Nos. 1-15) *Some of the following sentences are grammatically incorrect and some are correct. Find out which part of a sentence has an error and mark that part. If there is no error mark that part as your answer.*

1. He does not seem (a) to be (b) aware (c) as to (d) his merits. No error (e)
2. Between every blow (a) of the hammer (b) the blacksmith (c) looked up at (d) the door. No error (e)
3. As (a) we see, she appears (b) to be unreasonable (c) anxious about (d) pleasing her husband. No error (e)
4. The landscape of Kashmir (a) is (b) by far (c) more enchanting of all (d). No error (e)
5. She stated to me (a) as blunt as (b) she could the reasons why (c) she was opposed (d) to my thoughtless suggestion. No error (e)
6. They were (a) charged of having (b) sheltered (c) anarchists (d). No error (e)
7. It was barely (a) midnight when I arrived home (b) but I found them both sitting (c) at the table waiting on me (d). No error (e)
8. She can (a) understand Marathi (b) but she cannot speak (c) it proper or fluent (d). No error (e)
9. Hardly (a) any other monument (b) in the world is beautiful (c) as the Taj Mahal (d). No error (e)
10. She was noticeably (a) upset by (b) how indignant (c) he responded to her final question (d). No error (e)
11. I don't know why (a) he has been (b) unreasonably anxious (c) to solve this problem (d). No error (e)
12. The two or three first chapters (a) of most of (b) the novels (c) are dull reading (d). No error (e)

13. He had (a) / no other wish (b) / but to see his son (c) / fixed up in a steady job (d). / No error (e)

14. This widely publicised (a) detergent is not much (b) different than (c) the one which I have been using (d). No error (e)

15. Lata (a) parted with her mother (b) with tears but the journey (c) to Delhi amused her (d). No error (e)

Directions (Q. Nos. 16-20) *Each sentence in this section has multiple parts in it. Find out the error part from the given options and indicate your response from the options (a), (b), (c) and (d) on the answer sheet.*

16. Merely speeches made from all sorts of public platforms cannot bring about an economic revolution.
(a) Merely speeches made from (b) all sorts of public platforms
(c) cannot bring about (d) an economic revolution

17. Do you insist that we meet at least once tomorrow to discuss about the subject?
(a) Do you insist that we meet (b) at least once tomorrow
(c) to discuss about (d) the subject?

18. Our people must work hard with a view to improving our national economy.
(a) Our people must (b) work hard with
(c) a view to improving (d) our national economy

19. The tallest among them expressed a keen desire to sit under the shade of a tree.
(a) The tallest among them (b) expressed a keen desire
(c) to sit under (d) the shade of a tree

20. Except he and possibly our mother, all others have agreed to come back soon.
(a) Except he and possibly (b) our mother
(c) all others have agreed (d) to come back soon

Directions (Q. Nos. 21-25) *Read each sentence to find out whether there is any grammatical or idiomatic error in it. The error, if any, will be in one part of the sentence. The alphabet corresponding to that part is your answer. If there is no error, the answer is (e).*

21. Believe me (A)/ I couldn't hardly believe (B)/ what anyone of (C)/ them had said. (D)/ No error (E)
(a) A (b) B (c) C (d) D (e) E

22. The Socialist Party (A)/ is as good if not better (B)/ than any other (C)/political party. (D)/ No error (E)
(a) A (b) B (c) C (d) D (e) E

23. I got much less (A)/ marks in my History paper (B)/ which I had offered as (C)/ an alternative to Economics. (D)/ No error (E)
(a) B (b) E (c) A (d) C (e) D

24. The Principal (A)/forbade us (B)/ not to use (C)/ the entire central hall. (D)/ No error (E)
(a) A (b) C (c) E (d) B (e) D

25. The interviewer asked (A)/ the candidate (B)/ to what district (C)/ he came from. (D)/ No error (E).
(a) C (b) A (c) B (d) E (e) D

Exam Practice

Directions (Q. Nos. 1-2) *Each sentence in this section has been divided into three underlined parts labelled as (a), (b) and (c). Read each sentence to find out whether there is any error in any underlined part and indicate your response on the Answer Sheet against the corresponding letter. If you find no error, your response should be indicated as (d).*

1. All the houses having been washed away (a) by the floods, (b) the villagers sought shelter in the panchayat office. (c) No error (d) **NDA 2016**
2. We must sympathise (a) for others (b) in their troubles. (c) No error (d) **NDA 2016**

Directions (Q. Nos. 3-5) *Each question in this section has a sentence with three parts labelled (a), (b) and (c). Read each sentence to find out, whether there is any error in any part and indicate your response against the corresponding letter. If you find no error, your response should be indicated as (d).*

3. As I prefer coffee than tea (a)/ my friends always take the trouble (b)/ to get me a cup of coffee whenever I visit them. (c)/ No error (d) **NDA 2016**
4. As soon as (a)/ the train arrived (b)/ the passengers entered the compartments. (c)/ No error (d) **NDA 2017**
5. He goes to his office (a)/ by bicycle (b)/ everyday. (c)/ No error (d) **NDA 2017**

Directions (Q. Nos. 6-7) *Each sentence in this section has three underlined parts labelled (a), (b) and (c). Read each sentence to find out whether there is any error in any underlined parts. If you find no error, your response should be indicated as (d).*

6. One of the members (a) expressed doubt if (b) the Minister was an atheist. (c) No error (d) **NDA 2018**
7. The Eastern Ghats are home of 2600 plant species (a) and this habitat fragmentation (b) can pose a serious threat to endemic plants. (c) No error (d) **NDA 2019**

Directions (Q. Nos. 8-14) *Each sentence in this section has three underlined parts labelled (a), (b) and (c). Read each sentence to find out whether there is any error in any underlined part and indicate your response in the Answer Sheet against the corresponding letter. If you find no error, your response should be indicated as (d).*

8. Opening his letters, (a) reading them carefully and sending for his clerk, (b) he dictated answers with them. (c) No error (d) **NDA 2019**
9. He was my school-friend, (a) but becoming a great man, (b) he has grown proud enough to forget his old friends. (c) No error (d) **NDA 2019**

10. The art of printing was introduced into England (a) during the reign of Edward IV (b) by William Caxton, a native of Kent. (c) No error (d) **NDA 2019**

11. From thirty years (a) he devoted himself to public affairs (b) without taking a holiday. (c) No error (d) **NDA 2019**

12. I cannot (a) cope up (b) with this pressure. (c) No error (d) **NDA 2020**

13. I came (a) to this place (b) by walk. (c) No error (d) **NDA 2020**

14. What is (a) the time (b) in your watch. (c) No error (d) **NDA 2020**

Directions (Q. Nos. 15 and 16) *Each question in this section has a sentence with three parts labelled (a), (b) and (c). Read each sentence to find out whether there is any error in any part and indicate your response against the corresponding letter. If you find no error, your response should be indicated as (d).*

15. I do not understand why (a)/ in spite of my best efforts to please him (b)/ my boss is so angry at me. (c) No error (d) **CDS 2017**

16. I prefer (a)/ this book (b)/ than that one. (c) / No error (d) **CDS 2017**

Directions (Q. Nos. 17-20) *Each sentence in this section has three underlined parts labelled (a), (b) and (c). Read each sentence to find out whether there is any error in any underlined part and indicate your response in the Answer Sheet against the corresponding letter. If you find no error, your response should be indicated as (d).*

17. The best way in which you can (a) open the bottle is (b) by putting it into hot water first. (c) No error (d) **CDS 2018**

18. You will be (a) answerable for the court with (b) any lies you have told. (c) No error (d) **CDS 2018**

19. The fruit (a) can be made (b) to jam. (c) No error (d) **CDS 2018**

20. Gandhi ji always regretted for the fact (a) that people gave him adulation while what he wanted (b) was acceptance of his way of life. (c) No error (d) **CDS 2018**

Directions (Q. Nos. 21-25) *Each sentence in this section has three parts labelled as (a), (b) and (c). Read each sentence to find out whether there is any error in any part and indicate your response in the answer sheet against the corresponding letter. If you find no error, your response should be indicated as (d).*

21. Parents of LGBT community members (a)/ are coming in (b)/ with a little help from NGOs. (c)/ No error (d) **SSC CGL 2017**

22. Tilak rowed (a)/ through the river (b)/ and tied his boat on the other side. (c)/Nor error (d). **SSC CGL 2017**

23. Being apprised with our approach (a)/ the whole neighbourhood (b)/ came out to meet the minister. (c)/ No error (d) **CDS 2019**

24. The celebrated grammarian Patanjali (a)/ was (b) a contemporary to Pushyamitra Sunga. (c)/ No error (d) **CDS 2019**

25. His appeal for funds (a)/ met (b)/ a poor response. (c) No error (d) **CDS 2019**

Directions (Q. Nos. 26 and 27) *Read the sentences that have parts, out of which one may have an error. Choose that part as your answer. If the sentence is without error, then choose 'e'.*

26. Innovations especially into the field of/information technology can help to increase/the wages of the workforce provided/workers have the necessary skills. **SBI PO 2016**
(a) Innovations especially into the field of
(b) information technology can help to increase
(c) the wages of the workforce provided
(d) workers have the necessary skills.
(e) No error

27. Over eighty percent from us/feel that if we had taken/some corrective measures earlier/the crisis could have been averted. **IBPS PO/MT 2016**
(a) over eighty percent from us
(b) feel that if we had taken
(c) some corrective measures earlier
(d) the crisis could have been averted.
(e) No error

Directions (Q. Nos. 28 and 29) *In the following questions, a sentence is divided into four parts. Choose the part of the sentence which contains grammatical or contextual error in it. If the given sentence is both grammatically correct and contextually meaningful, choose option (5) i.e., "No error" as your answer.*

28. Although of good (A)/rains the production (B)/of food (C)/grains fell (D) **IBPS CWE 2018**
(a) A (b) B (c) C (d) D
(e) No error

29. No wonder then that for some time now, (A)/ media and technology companies for the world (B)/ have looked at (C)/ Artificial Intelligence (AI)-led algorithms as the saviour-the demon-slayers (D).
(a) A (b) B (c) C (d) D
(e) No error

Answers

Work Book Exercise A

1. listen to
2. Drop 'with'
3. write in dark ink
4. compensate for damage
5. Drop 'again'
6. drop 'from'
7. 'of' in place of 'against'
8. No error
9. robbed them all of the belongings
10. Drop 'on'

Work Book Exercise B

1. Use 'against' in place of 'because of'
2. 'on' in place of 'to'
3. Remove 'with'
4. Remove 'with'
5. Use either began at 2 p.m. or about 2 p.m.
6. Remove 'in'
7. Remove 'in'
8. Use 'to' in place of 'in'
9. Use 'from' in place of 'of'
10. Use 'on' in place of 'in'

Work Book Exercise C

1. 'of' in place of 'from'
2. a week before/ago
3. 'up' in place of 'on'
4. what Kanpur is famous for
5. Insert 'for' after 'wished'
6. 'on/upon' after 'operated'
7. Insert 'for' after 'competing'
8. Insert 'about' after 'talking' on both the cases.
9. Insert 'to' after 'prays'
10. No error

Work Book Exercise D

1. (a) **2.** (a) **3.** (b) **4.** (b) **5.** (a) **6.** (a) **7.** (a)
8. (c) **9.** (c) **10.** (c)

Work Book Exercise E

1. (b) **2.** (a) **3.** (b) **4.** (c) **5.** (b) **6.** (b) **7.** (c)
8. (a) **9.** (b) **10.** (b)

Work Book Exercise F

1. (b) **2.** (a) **3.** (c) **4.** (c) **5.** (c) **6.** (a) **7.** (b)
8. (a) **9.** (b) **10.** (b)

Work Book Exercise G

1. to **2.** to **3.** from **4.** to **5.** with **6.** of, to **7.** to
8. to **9.** for **10.** of

Work Book Exercise H

1. of **2.** to **3.** to **4.** with **5.** of **6.** to **7.** for
8. against **9.** on **10.** of

Work Book Exercise I

1. with, to **2.** to **3.** with **4.** to **5.** with, over **6.** to **7.** of
8. with **9.** of, by **10.** on

Revision Exercise

1. (d) 'of' for 'as to'
2. (a) Say 'after' for 'between'
3. (c) Say 'unreasonably anxious'
4. (d) Use 'the most enchanting'
5. (b) Say 'bluntly'
6. (b) Use 'charged with'
7. (d) Say 'waiting for'
8. (d) Say 'properly or fluently'
9. (c) Add 'as' before 'beautiful'
10. (c) Say 'indignantly'
11. (e) No error
12. (a) Say 'The first two or three'
13. (c) Use 'than' for 'but'
14. (c) Use 'from'
15. (b) Say 'part from'
16. (a) Use 'Mere' in place of 'Merely'
17. (c) Remove 'about'
18. (c) Use 'of' in place of 'to'
19. (c) Use 'in' in place of 'under'
20. (a) Use 'him' in place of 'he'
21. (b) Replace 'couldn't' by 'could'
22. (b) Add 'as' after 'good'
23. (c) Use 'fewer' in place of much 'less'
24. (b) Remove 'not'
25. (a) Remove 'to'

Exam Practice

1. (b) Replace 'by' with 'in'
2. (b) Use 'with' in place of 'for'
3. (a) Use 'to' in place of 'than'
4. (d) No error
5. (b) Use 'on' in place of 'by'
6. (b) Replace 'if ' by 'that'
7. (a) Use 'to' in place of 'of '
8. (c) Use 'to' in place of 'with'
9. (b) Add 'after' between 'but' and 'becoming'.
10. (a) Use 'in' in place of 'into'
11. (a) Use 'for' in place of 'from'
12. (b) Remove 'up' as it is not used with 'cope'
13. (c) Replace 'by walk' with 'on foot'
14. (c) Use 'by' in place of 'in'
15. (c) Use 'with' in place of 'at'
16. (c) Use 'to' in place of 'than'.
17. (d) No error
18. (b) Use 'to' in place of 'for'
19. (c) Use 'into' in place of 'to'.
20. (a) Remove 'for'.
21. (b) Use 'out' in place of 'in'
22. (b) Here 'across the river' should be used in place of 'through the river'
23. (a) Use 'of' in place of 'with'.
24. (c) Use 'of ' in place of 'to'.
25. (c) Add 'with' before 'a'.
26. (a) Use 'in' in place of 'into'
27. (a) Use 'of' in place of 'from'
28. (a) Use 'Inspite of' in place of 'Although of'
29. (b) Use 'of' in place of 'for'

Unit V

15

Phrasal Verbs

What are Phrasal Verbs?

English language abounds in the use of verbs with prepositions or adverbs to obtain a variety of meanings. The verbs used with prepositions, adverbs or both are defined as phrasal verbs and they denote idiomatic meaning only **when taken as a whole**. These prepositions and adverbs are known in grammar as Particles.

For example

(i) Set in .... start. *(verb + preposition)*

(ii) Set up .... establish. *(verb + adverb)*

(iii) Put up with .... tolerate. *(verb + adverb + preposition)*

When particle is separated from its verb, both verb & particle revert to their individual meanings separately.

(i) Set, in *(ii)* Set, up

(iii) Put, up, with

There are two types of expressions of phrasal verbs

1. Transitive expressions 2. Intransitive expressions

1. Transitive Expressions

I. Nouns (as direct objects) are usually placed at the end of transitive expressions or immediately after the verb & before the particle.

(i) She **took off** her apron. *(ii)* She **took her apron** off.

II. Pronoun objects are more often used after the verb or before the short words 'off, on, up, down, in, out, away' etc.

(i) I went to **see him off.** *(ii)* She **brought him up.**

III. Pronoun objects are placed at the end of such expressions when verbs cannot be split such as 'look for, account for, call at, call on, look after', etc.

(i) I am **looking for** him.

(ii) You should **look after** her.

(iii) I **called on** him yesterday.

(iv) You have to **stand by** me.

2. Intransitive Expressions

Intransitive expressions of phrasal verbs **do not** admit of any object.

(*i*) She **broke down** in the court.

(*ii*) His father **came round** at last.

(*iii*) Their marriage **comes off** next month.

(*iv*) The meeting **broke up** suddenly.

Now, study the following phrasal verbs that are currently in use.

1. **Account for** (*explain the reason, answer for*) I can't *account for* his unusual behaviour in this matter.
2. **Ask after** (*ask about the welfare, inquire after*) I met your brother at the party, he *asked after* you.
3. **Ask for** (*request for*) She *asked for* a glass of water.
4. **Back out** (*withdraw from promise*) He agreed to help but *backed out* at the last moment.
5. **Be in for** [about to take place (*unpleasant*)] On account of his bad habits, he *is in for* trouble.
6. **Bear away** (*win*) Suhani *bore away* the first prize in the dance competition.
7. **Bear on/upon** (*relevant*) Your remarks have no *bearing on* the main problem.
8. **Bear out** (*support the argument, corroborate*) I am sure my classmates will *bear out* my statement.
9. **Bear with** (*to show patience, co-operate*) In view of the heavy losses suffered by the company, the shareholders were requested to *bear with*.
10. **Blow out** (*extinguish*) The candle *blew out* as the gust of wind came in.
11. **Blow over** (*pass off without harm, come to an end*) Don't worry, the crisis is likely to *blow over*.
12. **Blow up** (*explode, start suddenly*) The plan of the enemy to *blow up* the flyover was foiled by the police.
13. **Break down** (*emotional collapse, stop functioning*) While giving evidence in the court, she *broke down*.
14. **Break into** (*enter by force*) The robbers *broke into* his house last night.
15. **Break off** (*come to an end*) *The talks between India and China broke off*.
16. **Break out** [*spread (war, epidemic, fire, riots*)] The fear that AIDS has *broken out* in India is not unfounded.
17. **Break through** (*major achievement*) There is no hope of a *break through* in the murder case of the famous actor, Sushant.
18. **Break up** [terminate (*meeting, school, session*)] The college will *break up* next week for summer vacation.
19. **Break up with** (*quarrel*) After a long and fruitful friendship, the two friends have *broken up with* each other.
20. **Break open** (*open by force*) The theif *broke open* the lock and stole the money.

21. **Bring about** (*cause to happen*) The administration helped to *bring about* a peaceful settlement.
22. **Bring out** (*explain the meaning*) When asked to explain, she could not *bring out* the meaning of the poem.
23. **Bring round** (*to make one agree, bring to senses*) I was able to *bring* my mother *round* to my views with great difficulty.
24. **Bring up** (*rear, educate*) Fathers are beginning to play a bigger role in *bringing up* their children.
25. **Call at** (*visit a place to meet*) I *called at* the residence of my boss yesterday.
26. **Call for** (*neccssary, require*) For the unity of the country, discipline among the people is *called for*.
27. **Call in** (*send for help*) The police were *called in* without delay by the residents.
28. **Call off** (*suspend or abandon*) We decided to *call off* the strike.
29. **Call on** (*go and visit a person*) It is a tradition for the Prime Minister to *call on* the President.
30. **Call out** (*ask to come for help*) The National Guards has been *called out* to render help in the flood affected areas.
31. **Call up** (*to telephone, recall*) Many of my friends *called* me *up* to congratulate me.
32. **Call upon** (*appeal, exhort*) He was *called upon* to prove the correctness of the press reports.
33. **Carry away by** (*lose control*) On hearing the news of his success, he was *carried away by* joy.
34. **Carry on** (*continue*) Now it is difficult to *carry on* this business in the teeth of stiff competition.
35. **Carry out** (*implement, obey, execute*) It is not likely that your father will *carry out* the threat of disinheriting you.
36. **Cast away** (*throw away as useless*) We usually give our servants the old clothes which we *cast away*.
37. **Cast down** (*dejected, down cast*) Nowadays he is *cast down* as a result of his failure in the examination.
38. **Cast off** (*release, remove*) An organisation must *cast off* its old fashioned practices in order to survive.
39. **Catch up with** (*make up for deficiency, overtake*) He remained ill for many days but *caught up with* the pending work very soon.
40. **Come about** (*happen*) It is not good that such an unfortunate accident *came about*.
41. **Come across** (*meet or discover by chance*) I *came across* my old friend in the market yesterday.
42. **Come by** (*get*) How have you *come by* such a precious diamond?
43. **Come of** (*belong to*) Reeta *comes of* a family of freedom fighters.

44. **Come off** (*take place as arranged, fade, get separated*) I was surprised to see that the plaster had *come off* the walls.
45. **Come over** (*to suddenly experience a strong feeling*) I don't know what *came over* me when I hit my best friend.
46. **Come round/around** (*around, agree, recover from illness*) My father at first refused to let me continue my studies but he *came round* in the end.
47. **Come upon** (*get by chance*) My friend *came upon* the evidence when he was searching his old papers.
48. **Cope with** (*manage*) They *coped with* all their problems cheerfully.
49. **Cut down** (*curtail, reduce*) Since you are out of job these days, you must *cut down* your expenditure.
50. **Cut off** (*discontinue, die, remove*) Gas supplies have now been *cut off*.
51. (Be) **Cut out for** (*suitable*) He is *cut out for* an administrative career.
52. **Cut out** (*to take a piece from the whole*) He *cut out* a piece of the cake and put it in my plate.
53. **Cut up** (*distressed, cut into small pieces*) She was *cut up* because she had been scolded by her teacher.
54. **Die down** [gradually disappear (*riots, excitement, storm, etc.*)] The wind has *died down*.
55. **Die out** (*become out of use or existence*) He thought that the custom of dowry had *died out* a long time ago.
56. **Dispose of** (*sell off*) She has decided to *dispose of* her old house.
57. **Dispose to** (*willing, inclined favourably*) My friend is *disposed to* discussing the problems thoroughly.
58. **Do away with** (*eradicate*) We should *do away with* social evils.
59. **Do for** (*serve the purpose*) This book will *do for* the SSC examination.
60. **Done with** (*have no relation*) I am *done with* him because of his dishonesty.
61. **Do without** (*to manage without*) We cannot *do without* a fan in summer.
62. **Done for, done in** (*be ruined*) He appears to be *done for* since he has lost heavily in gambling.
63. **Draw up** (*to write, compose, draft*) I was busy *drawing up* plans for the new online course.
64. **Draw on or upon** (*to use a part of a supply such as money*) He was able to *draw on* his savings when he was jobless.
65. **Drop in** (*to pay a short visit*) I thought I'd just *drop in* and see how you were.
66. **Drop out** (*retire in the midst of doing something*) She could not qualify for the selection as she *dropped out* while the race was in progress.
67. **Fall back** (*retreat*) The rioters *fell back* when the police arrived.
68. **Fall back on** (*depend on*) You must save money *to fall back on* it in old age.

69. **Fall off** (*decrease in number, get separated*) In the wake of the corona epidemic, the admissions in the school have *fallen off*.
70. **Fall out** (*quarrel*) The two friends appear to have *fallen out* over a minor issue.
71. **Fall in with** (*agree with*) Instead of challenging the lie, she *fell in with* their views.
72. **Fall through** (*to remain incomplete, fail*) For want of sufficient funds, your new project is likely to *fall through*.
73. **Follow up** (*pursue after the first attempt*) The idea has been *followed up* by a group of researchers.
74. **Get ahead** (*go forward*) You can *get ahead* of your rivals only by hard work.
75. **Get along** (*be friendly*) They just can't *get along* together because of their temperamental differences.
76. **Get at** (*reach, understand*) It is very difficult to *get at* the truth in the ongoing scandal.
77. **Get away** (*escape*) The thieves *got away* on a scooter.
78. **Get away with** (*without being punished or with little punishment*) Although his fault was serious, he *got away with* a light punishment.
79. **Get on** (*progress*) How is your son *getting on* with his studies?
80. **Get on with** (*live together*) Both husband and wife are *getting on* well *with* each other.
81. **Get over** (*recover from an illness or shock, come over*) He is still trying to *get over* the financial crisis.
82. **Get through** (*pass through, succeed*) It is not possible to *get through* any examination without working hard.
83. **Get up** (*rise from bed, dressed*) The woman *got up* from her chair with the baby in her arms.
84. **Give away** (*distribute*) She has *given away* jewellery worth thousands of rupees to help the poor.
85. **Give in** (*surrender, agree*) At first she was adamant but at last she *gave in* to the request of her friend.
86. **Give out** (*announce verbally, emit*) It was *given out* that she had failed.
87. **Give up** (*stop, abstain from*) He *gave up* smoking to regain his health.
88. **Give way** (*collapse under pressure, break*) The contractor was charged with negligence when the roof of a new building built by him *gave way*.
89. **Given to** (*accustomed to*) He is *given to* smoking.
90. **Go back on** (*withdraw, back out*) One should not *go back on* one's promise.
91. **Go down** (*be believed*) Your excuse of being unwell will not *go down* as you were seen playing with your teacher today morning
92. **Go in for** (*buy, practise, to enter a contest*) I thought of *going in for* teaching.
93. **Go off** (*explode and be discharged*) When he was cleaning his gun, it *went off* and killed him.

94. **Go on** (*continue*) There is no need to *go on* arguing about it.
95. **Go over** (*examine carefully, look over*) On *going over* the balance sheet of the company, the auditors have found serious mistakes.
96. **Go through** (*read hurriedly, endure*) He didn't lend me the newspaper because he was *going through* it.
97. **Go up** (*rise, increase*) As a result of a sharp rise in prices of chemicals, the price of washing soap has *gone up*.
98. **Hand out** (*distribute*) *Hand out* the books to the students.
99. **Hand over** (*give charge or authority*) He has not *handed over* charge to the new manager.
100. **Hang about** (*stay waiting, roam about*) The boys *hanging about* the girls' hostel were punished by the police.
101. **Hold on** (*carry on, bear difficulties, persist*) Inspite of financial difficulties, he *held on* and succeeded in the long run.
102. **Hold out** (*resist*) When the robbers ran short of ammunition, they could no longer *hold out*.
103. **Hold over** (*postpone*) Most of the bills are *held over* till the next session of the Parliament.
104. **Hold up** (*to stop in order to rob, delay*) The terrorists *held up* the motor car and kept the ladies as hostages.
105. **Jump at** (*accept happily*) He *jumped at* the offer of his boss to accept the job abroad.
106. **Jump to** (arrive suddenly [*conclusion*]) You should never *jump to* conclusions.
107. **Keep from** (*refrain from, not to mix with*) Always *keep from* selfish people because they can harm you anytime.
108. **Keep off** (*keep at a distance*) There was a notice at the site, "*Keep off* the bushes."
109. **Keep on** (*continue*) She *kept on* crying inspite of my assurance of help.
110. **Keep up** (*maintain*) Always try to *keep up* the standard of life even in the face of crises.
111. **Keep up with** (*try to move with, not to fall behind*) Young men should *keep up with* the latest developments in the international field.
112. **Lay by** (*save money*) The wise men always *lay by* money for their old age.
113. (Be) **Laid up with** (*confined to bed*) She is not going out as she is *laid up with* the flu.
114. **Lay down** (*establish a rule, sacrifice, surrender*) The conditions *laid down* by the Department of Health were violated by the nursing homes.
115. **Lay off** (*to discontinue work or get dismissed temporarily*) The workers have been *laid off* for want of raw material.
116. **Lay out** (*plan building, garden, etc.*) A number of gardens were *laid out* by the Moghuls.
117. **Let down** (*humiliate, to lower down*) We should never *let down* our friends.

118. **Let into** (*allow to enter*) After repeated requests, he was *let into* the classroom.
119. **Let off** (*to free from punishment, pardon*) She was *let off* by the Principal with light punishment.
120. **Let** (somebody) **in on** (*share a secret*) I will not *let* her *in on* my plans.
121. **Let up** (*cessation, respite*) There is no *let up* in heat during May.
122. **Live on** (*depend for food*) The lion is carnivorous and *lives on* flesh.
123. **Live by** (*means/manner*) You must learn to *live by* honest means.
124. **Live off** (*source of income*) They were *living off* their rental income as they had lost their jobs in the lockdown.
125. **Look about** (*in search of, on the watch*) The thirsty crow was *looking about* water here & there.
126. **Look after** (*take care of*) In her old age, she has no one to *look after* her.
127. **Look at** (*see carefully*) The boys are *looking at* the sky.
128. **Look back on** (*to think of the past*) People can often *look back* and reflect *on their* happy childhood memories.
129. **Look for** (*search for a person or lost thing*) She was *looking for* her lost books.
130. **Look down upon** (*hate, despise*) It is folly on your part to *look down upon* the poor students.
131. **Look into** (*investigate a matter*) A committee was set up to *look into* the issue of child labour in Delhi.
132. **Look on** (*to see as a spectator*) His parents *looked on* with a triumphant smile when he performed on the annual day.
133. **Look over** (*examine carefully, go over*) The examiner has yet to *look over* the practice note books.
134. **Look out** (*watch out*) *Look out*! there is a snake under the bush.
135. **Look out for** (*in search of, on the watch*) He is *looking out for* a decent job.
136. **Look to** (*rely upon, be careful*) The poor *look to* financial help from the government.
137. **Look up** (*consult some book for a word, rise*) Please *look up* this word in the dictionary.
138. **Look up to** (*to admire or respect someone*) His younger brother *looks up to* him and obeys his every order.
139. **Look upon** (*consider, regard*) We must *look upon* social evils as a nuisance.
140. **Make off with/away with** (*run away, destroy*) They *made off with* the cash and fled.
141. **Make out** (*understand the meaning*) The police could not *make out* the coded message they had intercepted.
142. **Make over** (*transfer possession, convert*) Since she had no legal heir, she *made over* her house in charity.

143. **Make up** (to end (*a quarrel*), compose) You should make an effort to *make up* with your friend.
144. **Make up for** (*compensate for*) After her long illness, she is trying her best to *make up for* her deficiency in studies.
145. **Pass away** (*die, expire*) On the *passing away* of his father, I sent him a message of condolence.
146. **Pass for** (*regarded to be*) The Tatas *pass for* philanthropists in the country.
147. **Pass off** (*take place*) The elections are likely to *pass off* peacefully.
148. **Pass oneself off** (*show off*) The hypocrites always *pass themselves off* as honest persons.
149. **Pass through** (*go through, undergo, endure*) He is *passing through* financial difficulties these days.
150. **Pass out** (*leave after completing education*) The cadets will *pass out* next month after completing their training.
151. **Pull down** (*demolish a structure*) The municipality *pulled down* the shops that were encroaching on government land.
152. **Pull off** (*succeed*) India *pulled off* victory in the last stage of the match.
153. **Pull through** (*recover from illness*) I think she'll *pull through* her serious illness very soon.
154. **Pull up** (*stop, scold*) The students were *pulled up* by the Principal for their misbehaviour with the class teacher.
155. **Pull with** (*live together, get on with*) He is *pulling* well *with* his wife these days.
156. **Put down** (*crush, keep down*) The riots were *put down* by the local police.
157. **Put off** (*postpone, avoid, discourage*) The meeting had to be *put off* because the President could not come.
158. **Put on** (*wear, pretend*) It is difficult to *put on* the appearance of innocence for a long time.
159. **Put out** (*extinguish*) The fire was *put out* suddenly.
160. **Put up** (*stays*) He is *putting up* at a hostel these days.
161. **Put up with** (*tolerate patiently*) For an honourable person it is difficult to *put up with* the haughty behaviour of the Directors.
162. **Round up** (*arrest*) The police *rounded up* anti-social elements last night.
163. **Run after** (*pursue, hanker after*) We should not *run after* money.
164. **Run down** (*criticise, to stop working*) One mustn't keep *running* oneself *down.*
165. **Run into** (*come across, meet by chance*) While walking along the roadside, I *ran into* my old schoolmates.
166. **Run out** (*come to an end*) When the rations *ran out*, the head office was informed.
167. **Run over** (*crush under*) He was *run over* by a speeding car.

168. **Run through** (*waste money*) It is a pity that he has *run through* his fortune over gambling and drinking.
169. **See off** (*to escort a guest for his/her departure*) His friends were present at the station to *see* him *off*.
170. **See through** (*discover something hidden, motive*) Man has grown so clever that it is difficult to *see through* his tricks.
171. **Send for** (*summon*) She *sent for* a doctor when her husband fell ill.
172. **Set about** (*start doing*) As soon as she reached home, she *set about* calling up her friends.
173. **Set aside** (*allocate, strike down, turn down*) The High Court *set aside* the verdict of the lower court in this sensitive matter.
174. **Set in** (*begin*) As soon as the summer *sets in*, the reptiles come out of hibernation.
175. **Set off** (*to start a series of events, process, improve*) Privatisation has *set off* the process of liberalisation in foreign trade.
176. **Set up** (*establish*) The factory was *set up* by his uncle.
177. **Set forth** (*start on a journey, explain*) The party will *set forth* its views on globalisation at a public rally.
178. **Set out** (*start on a journey, set forth*) No sooner was the hunter informed of a lion's presence in the forest than he *set out.*
179. **Sit back** (*relax*) He believes that he has the right to *sit back* while others should work hard.
180. **Sit up** (*stay up*) She *sat up* till her son returned.
181. **Stand by** (*support, help*) Although he promised to *stand by* me in difficulties, he did not live up to it.
182. **Stand for** (*represent*) T.E.C. *stands for* Technical Education Certificate.
183. **Stand out** (*to be different*) She *stood out* from the crowd because of her amiable manners.
184. **Stand up for** (*defend*) It is your duty to always *stand up for* the poor.
185. **Strike off** (*remove from the list*) His name has been *struck off* the admission list.
186. **Take after** (*resemble*) She always reminds me of her mother since she *takes after* her.
187. **Take down** (*write*) She was busy in *taking down* the dictation which the teacher was giving.
188. **Take off** (*remove, leave the ground, improve*) It is difficult for the Indian economy to *take off* in the absence of heavy investment.
189. **Take over** (*take up responsibility*) The environmental agency tried to *take over* the task of cleaning the Ganges.
190. (Be) **Taken to** (*form a habit*) He *took to* wearing black leather jackets.
191. **Take up** (*start a hobby or study, occupy*) He has *taken up* modelling as a career.

192. **Tell upon** (*affect adversely*) I have warned him that heavy work will *tell upon* his health.
193. (Be) **Taken in** (*be deceived*) For all your intelligence you are likely to be *taken in* by impostors.
194. **Take for** (*suppose to be, identify*) I *took* the scoundrel *for* a noble person.
195. (Be) **Taken aback** (*be surprised*) I was *taken aback* to hear of the news of his failure.
196. **Talk over** (*discuss a matter*) I agreed to go home and *talk over* the matter.
197. **Turn down** (*reject, strike down*) I *turned down* the request of my friend to go to Simla.
198. **Turn off** (*stop, switch off*) Please make it a point to *turn off* the water taps before you go out.
199. **Turn on** (*switch on, start*) She *turned on* the shower to take bath.
200. **Turn over** (*change, capsize, upset*) Ten persons got drowned when the boat *turned over.*
201. **Turn out** (*prove, reveal, expel*) Nothing ever *turned out* right for me in life.
202. **Turn up** (*arrive, take place*) Who can say what will *turn up* next?
203. **Watch out** (*look out, be careful*) If you do not *watch out*, the snake might harm you.
204. **Wipe away** (*cleanse, remove*) The marks of blood were *wiped away* by the accused.
205. **Wipe out** (*destroy completely*) We must try to *wipe out* poverty from the country.
206. **Wind up** (*bring to an end*) We were forced to *wind up* the business on account of heavy loss.
207. **Work out** (*solve the problem*) He is very intelligent and can *work out* any difficult problem.
208. **Work up** (*incite, instigate*) The politicians should not try to *work up* communal frenzy among the people.
209. **Work upon** (*influence*) The leader tried to *work upon* the mob.

Addenda

210. (Get the) **Hang of something** (*learn about*) As I entered the conference hall, I got the hang of the conspiracy.
211. **Hang together** (*fit together*) Your present statement does not *hang together* with the one that you gave earlier.
212. **Hang round with** (*spend time together*) I used to *hang round with* my friends on the Mall road.
213. **Pull in** (*enter*) As the train *pulled in*, the passengers ran to board it.
214. **Set to** (*determined*) If we really *set to,* we can get the work done within time.
215. **Break with** (*to stop following old customs*) It is very difficult to *break with* the custom of gender inequality in India.

Phrasal Verbs used as Nouns, Verbs, Adjectives

Break

Breakout (*noun*)	escape from prison The news of prison *breakout* has been confirmed.
Outbreak (*noun*)	beginning The *outbreak* of the Third World War will prove to be a universal disaster.
Breakdown (*noun*)	of machinery, mental collapse The *breakdown* of the car delayed our departure.
Break-through (*noun*)	major achievement There is no sign of any *break-through* in the making of a vaccine for corona virus.

Beat

Offbeat (*adj.*)	different, unusual They like *offbeat* themes of the novels.

Bring

Upbringing (*noun*)	bringing up of a person. His *upbringing* has been very simple.

Call

Call-up (*noun*)	a summons for military service. He avoided *call-up* pretending illness.

Come

Outcome (*noun*)	result of an action We are not aware of the *outcome* of the meeting.
Overcome (*verb*)	solve problem, succeed, defeat Have you *overcome* your financial problems?

Fall

Fall-out (*noun*)	dangerous radioactive dust, unexpected result The *fallout* of globalisation has not proved to be a blessing for the common man.

Hold

Hold-up (*noun*)	attempt for robbery The news of *hold-up* made us change our route.
Uphold (*verb*)	support what is right, confirm We should *uphold* the dignity of our profession.

Keep

Upkeep (*noun*)	maintenance The *upkeep* of my office costs me a lot these days.

Let

Outlet (*noun*)	way of expressing or getting rid of strong feelings, a place for selling goods.
	Children must have an *outlet* for spending their energy.

Lay

Layout (*noun*)	The way a building or book is planned
	He does not like the *layout* of this building.
Outlay (*noun*)	expenditure
	The *outlay* on the plan is exorbitant.
Lay-off (*noun*)	a period when labour is unemployed, an account of no work.
	There is a six month *lay-off* in our sugar factory.

Look

Look-out (*noun*)	on watch
	He is on the *look-out* for a good job.
Outlook (*noun*)	attitude to life and the world
	You must have an optimistic *outlook*.
Overlook (*verb*)	fail to see, pardon
	He was kind enough to *overlook* my fault.

Make

Make-up (*noun*)	use of cosmetics
	It takes her long to put on her *make-up*.

Mix

Mix-up (*noun*)	confusion
	The *mix-up* of the luggage in the cloak room caused the confusion.

Round

Round-up (*noun*)	bringing people together, arrest
	The government ordered a *round-up* of the miscreants on the eve of the new year.

Run

Runaway	one who has escaped.
(Noun)	The *runaways* from the prison were arrested again.
(Adjective)	The *runaway* prisoners were arrested again.

Sell

Sell-out (*noun*)	To sell all the supply that you have of something
	The new edition of the look has been a complete *sell-out*.

Set

Outset (*noun*)	start, beginning
	The trainees were warned of the danger at the *outset*.

Offset (*verb*)	to make the effect of something less strong or noticeable The rise in income is generally *offset* by the rising taxes.
Upset (*noun, verb*)	an unexpected situation, unhappy, anxious
Noun	The *upset* in the semi-finals has completely dashed our hopes.
Verb	The behaviour of her daughter has *upset* her.

Take

Intake (*noun*)	The quantity or number taken in a period. The famous institute in our city has an yearly *intake* of 1,500 students.
Take-off (*noun*)	leaving ground (plane) The *take-off* of the aeroplane has been delayed.
Take-over (*noun*)	an offer to buy company The *take-over* of Air India has been finalised.
Overtake (*verb*)	to go past a vehicle *Overtaking* heavy vehicles can sometimes prove fatal.

Turn

Turnover (*noun*)	amount received for sale He has a *turnover* of about 50 lakhs a year.
Overturn (*noun*)	capsize The boat *overturned* and sank.
Turn-out (*noun*)	attendance There was a heavy *turn-out* for the US elections.

Work Book Exercise A

Directions *Fill up the blanks with suitable phrasal verbs from the alternatives given below.*

1. How have you .... such a precrous and beautiful shroud.
(*a*) come across (*b*) come upon (*c*) come by

2. We usually give our old things that we .... to charity.
(*a*) cast off (*b*) cast aside (*c*) cast away

3. He was .... to prove the thesis he had submitted.
(*a*) called up (*b*) called on (*c*) called upon

4. The partners .... due to financial tiff.
(*a*) fell down (*b*) fell out (*c*) fell into

5. The thienes ....with all thewedding jewellery.
(*a*) made out (*b*) made off (*c*) made for

6. Please make it a point to .... water tap before you go out
(*a*) turn down (*b*) turn about (*c*) turn off

7. The teenage boys were .... by the police for manhandling the old lady.
(*a*) pulled up (*b*) pulled for (*c*) pulled off

8. Seema .... a family of army men.
(a) comes of (b) comes by (c) comes from

9. We should try to .... the evil practices in our society.
(a) do with (b) do away with (c) do away

10. RMC is still trying to .... their debts.
(a) get on (b) get off (c) get over

11. The dogs were .... well with each other.
(a) getting on (b) getting up (c) getting over

12. As a result of long illness, she has .... a lot
(a) run out (b) run down (c) run over

13. I can't understand how these undesirable events ....
(a) came over (b) came of (c) came about

14. The court sessions had .... the verdict.
(a) held onto (b) held over (c) held out

15. The detectives arrested him while he was .... counterfeit currency notes.
(a) palming off (b) palming over (c) palming by

Revision Exercise

Directions (Q. Nos. 1-5) *Read each sentence to find out whether there is any grammatical or idiomatic error in it. The error, if any, will be in one part of the sentence. The alphabet corresponding to that part is your answer. If there is 'No error', the answer is (e). (Ignore errors of punctuation, if any)*

1. Some people (A)/look down at (B)/the poor and (c) the illiterate. (D)/No error (E)
(a) A (b) B (c) C (d) E (e) E

2. I look up to (A)/my father (B)/because he (C)/has been successful in his life. (D)/No error (E)
(a) B (b) C (c) E (d) A (e) D

3. Many friends of (A)/Nupur say (B)/that she takes over (c)/her mother. (D)/No error (E)
(a) A (b) C (c) B (d) E (e) D

4. You can (A)/always count (B)/in your true friends(C)/in times of a crisis. (D)/No error (E)
(a) A (b) B (c) C (d) D (e) E

5. The new CEO (A)/will bring over (B)/changes in (C)/our company's outdated policies. (D)/No error (E)
(a) A (b) B (c) C (d) D (e) E

Directions (Q. Nos. 6-20) *Fill in the blanks by choosing the correct word/s from the given options.*

6. Put your shoes .... , it's too cold to walk barefoot.
(a) of (b) on (d) off (d) over

7. Kashish wanted to .... the new trousers.
(a) try over (b) try off (c) try out (d) try on

8. The music teacher urged Lata to not to .... singing as she was very talented.
(a) give down (b) get down (c) give off (d) give up

9. My mother asked me to write the phone number .... for her.
(a) up (b) down (c) off (d) over

10. My pet dog likes to .... of his kennel to chase squirrels.
(a) break down (b) break over (c) break off (d) break out

11. The scientists are having some trouble .... the solution to the issue of air pollution.
(a) working out (b) working over (c) going over (d) going off

12. We must .... a life jacket before getting into a boat.
(a) put over (b) put up (c) put on (d) put into

13. Will you be able to .... this month with the little you have?
(a) get with (b) get by (c) get over (d) get under

14. I don't like people who .... their wealth publicly.
(a) show on (b) show over (c) show off (d) show of

15. His candidature for the post was cancelled as he did not .... for the interview on time.
(a) show up (b) show over (c) show on (d) show off

16. Many trees in our area were .... by the strong winds.
(a) blown over (b) blown up (c) blown off (d) blow above

17. Have you ever .... such an amazing piece of art?
(a) come over (b) come up (c) come above (d) come across

18. .... for a cup of coffee sometime.
(a) Drop over (b) Drop into (c) Drop off (d) Drop in

19. The police asked the lady to .... her mask to check her identity.
(a) take over (b) take of (c) take off (d) take across

20. The manager of the company wants the sales team to hand .... their reimbursement documents by Monday.
(a) across (b) out (c) in (d) over

Exam Practice

Directions (Q Nos. 1-22) *Each of the following sentence has a blank space and four words are given after the sentence. Select which word you consider the most appropriate for the blank space and indicate your response.*

1. She has been lying in bed for the last fortnight. I hope she will .... **NDA 2016**
(a) come out (b) pull out (c) pull through (d) go out

2. The path of progress is beset .... difficulties. **NDA 2016**
(a) with (b) by (c) through (d) along

3. The lecture was not very interesting. In fact I .... in the middle of it. **NDA 2019**
(a) showed off (b) put off (c) dozed off (d) plugged off

4. A woman got into the car and .... **NDA 2019**
(a) drove off (b) broke down (c) rode in (d) drove in

5. I ran .... John yesterday, and it was a pleasant surprise. **NDA 2020**
(a) by (b) off (c) beside (d) into

6. He visits the needy to relieve them .... their sufferings and poverty. **NDA 2020**
(a) from (b) off (c) of (d) on

7. The clouds of suspicion will clear .... soon. **CDS 2017**
(*a*) up (*b*) away (*c*) off (*d*) by

8. The teachers said that they were no longer prepared to .... the ways of the new Headmaster. **CDS 2017**
(*a*) put over with (*b*) put on with (*c*) put up with (*d*) put up to

9. I hope that the rain will .... for our picnic tomorrow. **CDS 2018**
(*a*) keep off (*b*) put off (*c*) set back (*d*) stay out

10. After the marathon, some of the competitors felt completely .... **CDS 2018**
(*a*) cut up (*b*) done in (*c*) done out (*d*) run out

11. I do not think he will ever .... the shock of his wife's death. **CDS 2018**
(*a*) get by (*b*) get off (*c*) get through (*d*) get over

12. It is no use in crying over .... **CDS 2018**
(*a*) spoiled milk (*b*) spirited milk (*c*) split milk (*d*) spilt milk

13. The new student found it difficult to .... with his classmates. **CDS 2018**
(*a*) get along (*b*) get among (*c*) get well (*d*) get up

14. The visiting Diplomat .... the Prime Minister. **CDS 2018**
(*a*) called in (*b*) called at (*c*) called on (*d*) called upon

15. The football match had to be .... because of the weather. **CDS 2019**
(*a*) called on (*b*) called off (*c*) called out (*d*) called over

16. Nobody believed Ram at first but he .... to be right. **CDS 2019**
(*a*) came out (*b*) carried out (*c*) worked out (*d*) turned out

17. How are you...... in your new job? Are you enjoying it? **CDS 2019**
(*a*) keeping on (*b*) going on (*c*) getting on (*d*) carrying on

18. I parked my car in a no-parking zone, but I .... it. **CDS 2019**
(*a*) came up with (*b*) got away with (*c*) made off with (*d*) got on with

19. You were going to apply for the job and then you decided not to. So what .... ? **CDS 2019**
(*a*) put you off (*b*) put you out (*c*) turned you off (*d*) turned you away

20. The police could not establish how the accident .... **CDS 2020**
(*a*) came off (*b*) came about (*c*) came on (*d*) came out

21. I .... my old friend after twenty years. **CDS 2020**
(*a*) ran into (*b*) ran in (*c*) run in (*d*) run on

22. On his way to the capital, the minister .... the eminent social worker at his residence. **CDS 2020**
(*a*) called on (*b*) called (*c*) calling for (*d*) call off

Answers

Work Book Exercise A

1. (a)	**2.** (a)	**3.** (c)	**4.** (b)	**5.** (b)	**6.** (c)	**7.** (a)
8. (c)	**9.** (b)	**10.** (c)	**11.** (a)	**12.** (b)	**13.** (c)	**14.** (b)
15. (b)						

Revision Exercise

1. (b) 'at' will be replaced by 'on'. 'look down on someone' means to think that someone is less important than you or does not deserve your respect.
2. (c) No error
3. (b) Replace 'over' by 'after'. 'Take after somebody' means to look or behave like an older relative.
4. (c) Replace 'in' by 'on'. 'Count on/upon somebody/something' means to depend on somebody or something, especially in a difficult situation.
5. (b) Use 'about' in place of 'over'. 'Bring about' means to make something happen, especially to cause changes in a situation.

6. (b)	**7.** (c)	**8.** (d)	**9.** (b)	**10.** (d)	**11.** (a)	**12.** (c)
13. (b)	**14.** (c)	**15.** (a)	**16.** (a)	**17.** (d)	**18.** (d)	**19.** (c)
20. (c)						

Exam Practice

1. (c) 'pull through' means to manage to stay alive after you have been very ill or very badly injured.
2. (a) 'beset with' means having to deal with a lot of something that causes problems.
3. (c) 'dozed off' means to start to sleep, especially during the day without intending to.
4. (b) 'break down' means to be unable to control your feelings and start to cry.
5. (c) 'run into someone' means to meet someone by chance.
6. (c) 'relieve' means to make pain or another bad feeling less unpleasant. So, 'of ' is suitable to fill the blank as it goes with 'relieve'.
7. (a) 'clear up' means to solve a problem or a mystery.
8. (c) 'put up with something' means to accept someone or something unpleasant in a patient way.
9. (a) 'Keep off ' means (of bad weather) fail to occur.
10. (d) 'run out' means completely tired.
11. (d) 'get over something' means to begin to feel better after a very upsetting experience.
12. (d) The idiom 'cry over spilt milk' means to waste time feeling sorry about an earlier mistake or problem that cannot be changed.
13. (a) 'get along' means to deal with a situation, usually successfully.
14. (c) 'call on someone' means to go and visit a person.
15. (b) 'call off ' means to decide that something will not happen.
16. (d) 'turn out' means to happen in a particular way or to have a particular result, especially an unexpected one.
17. (c) 'get on with something' means to make progress with a particular activity, plan, etc.
18. (b) 'get away with something' means to not be caught or punished when you have done something wrong.
19. (a) 'Put off ' means to make someone not want to do something, or to make someone not like someone or something.
20. (b) 'come about' means to happen.
21. (a) 'run into someone' means to meet someone accidentally.
22. (a) 'call on' means to visit someone for a short time.

16

Idioms and Phrases

The command of idiomatic expressions in any language is pre-requisite for expressive writing and comprehension. Phrasal verbs, idiomatic adjectives and noun phrases and idiomatic pairs of nouns, adjectives and adverbs comprise such a vast portion of idiomatic expressions that it is nearly impossible to deal with them comprehensively in such a short space. However, this chapter contains the most important idioms and phrases that are indispensable for any competitive examination. Students would do well to consult the dictionary for further improvement in this field.

1. **At one's wit's end** (*perplexed*) Sohan was **at his wit's end** to find that his younger brother has taken poison.
2. **At one's fingertips** (*complete knowledge*) All the rules of synthesis are **at his fingertips.**
3. **At the spur of the moment** (*without delay*) In an interview we must reply **at the spur of the moment.**
4. **All in all** (*most important*) As he was the only son in a big family, he was **all in all** in his home.
5. **At close quarters** (*close examinations*) Many of my friends proved selfish **at close quarters.**
6. **Apple-pie order** (*in perfect order*) On the eve of inspection everything was kept in **apple-pie order.**
7. **Above board** (*honest and straightforward*) He is known for his **above board** conduct.
8. **Above all** (*before everything else*) **Above all**, he is blunt and dare devil.
9. **As fit as a fiddle** (*strong and healthy*) He has recovered from illness and now he is **as fit as a fiddle.**
10. **At random** (*aimlessly*) The militants fired **at random** killing a lot of innocent persons.
11. **At a loose end** (*unoccupied, idle*) Now-a-days he is **at a loose end** because he has wound up his business.

12. **At loggerheads** (*to be at strife*) The partners of our firm are **at loggerheads** these days.
13. **At odds** (*in dispute*) The members of the group were **at odds** over the selection procedure.
14. **An apple of discord** (*cause of quarrel*) Ancestral property is **an apple of discord** between the two sisters.
15. **At cross purposes** (*have conflicting intentions*) How can there be peace in their family when husband and wife are **at cross purposes.**
16. **After one's own heart** (*to one's liking*) When Deepa met a man **after her own heart**, she got married to him.
17. **At the bottom of** (*to be mainly responsible for*) It was found later that Shanu was **at the bottom of** the whole trouble.
18. **At a loss** (*to be unable to decide*) I am **at a loss** to know what to do.
19. **At dagger's drawn** (*to have bitter enmity*) The quarrel between the two brothers has grown more bitter now and they are **at dagger's drawn.**
20. **At large** (*abscond, to keep unchained*) People keep their dogs **at large** at night.
21. **At sea** (*applied to a person confused*) My sister is quite **at sea** in Maths; she cannot solve a single problem.
22. **Add fuel to the flame or fire** (*to make matter worse*) The attempt to suppress the agitation of the strikers only **added fuel to the flame.**
23. **At sixes and sevens** (*in disorder*) There was a robbery in our neighbourhood last night and when I entered the house to inquire, everything was **at sixes and sevens.**
24. **Assume airs** (*to pretend superiority*) The rich are in the habit of **assuming air** in the presence of their poor relations.
25. **Argus eyed** (*careful, observant*) As a politician, he is **argus eyed** and never overlooks even a small matter.
26. **At a stone's throw** (*very close*) My friend's house is **at a stone's throw** from mine.

B

1. **By hook or by crook** (*by one means or another*) He is determined to obtain first division in his class **by hook or by crook.**
2. **Bear the brunt of** (*to bear the main shock of*) The poor have to **bear the brunt of** increasing prices.
3. **Bell the cat** (*to take first step at personal risk*) Many people can boast of their bravery, but very few can **bell the cat.**
4. **Bid defiance** (*to ignore*) Rohan **bade defiance** to his father's wish of becoming a doctor and instead became an engineer.
5. **Blow one's trumpet** (*to praise oneself*) No one likes to talk to those who are always **blowing their own trumpet.**

6. **Break the news** (*to give bad news*) He **broke the news** of her husband's death very gently so as to lessen the intensity of the shock.
7. **Burn a hole in one's pocket** (*money spent quickly*) Money given to a spendthrift only **burns a hole in his pocket.**
8. **Bury the hatchet** (*to make peace*) India and Pakistan must **bury the hatchet** to bring about peace to the region.
9. **Beside oneself** (*to feel excessively*) Due to the accidental death of his wife he was **beside himself** with grief.
10. **Bad blood** (*bitter relations*) The riots have created **bad blood** between the two communities in India.
11. **Black and blue** (*to beat mercilessly*) The thief was beaten **black and blue** by the police.
12. **Beat about the bush** (*to talk in a round about manner*) We should always come to the point and not **beat about the bush.**
13. **Beat the air** (*to make useless efforts*) Some speakers merely **beat the air** in speech while preaching.
14. **Build castles in the air** (*to make visionary schemes*) Many people who live in dreams only **build castles in the air** and do not succeed in life.
15. **Break the ice** (*to speak first after prolonged silence*) In the meeting Rajesh **broke the ice** and suggested the plan to solve the problem.
16. **Bring to book** (*to punish, to call to account*) The manager was **bought to book** for his negligence.
17. **Breathe one's last** (*to die*) He **breathed his last** in the prime of his life.
18. **Back stairs influence** (*by unfair means*) These days many people are given good posts through **back stairs influence.**
19. **Bird's eye view** (*concise view*) We had a **bird's eye view** of the whole fair from the top of a giant wheel.
20. **Bolt from the blue** (*sudden or unexpected shock*) The news of her husband's death in the air crash came to her as a **bolt from the blue.**
21. **Burn one's boats** (*point of no return*) We had **burnt our boats** by declaring that we were not going to sign C.T.B.T.
22. **By the by** (*by the way*) **By the by**, what is your age?
23. **Be upto** (*to be obliged to do*) He **is upto all** the tricks of the trade to grind his own axe.
24. **Bated breath** (*in anxiety, expectancy*) The fate of the match hung in balance and everybody waited for the result with **bated breath.**
25. **Bandy words** (*to be rude or argumentative*) Obedient children don't use **bandy words** with their parents when they are advised.
26. **Bee in one's bonnet** (*to be fussy*) She seems to have a **bee in her bonnet** because she is always finding faults with others.

27. **Bite the dust** (*to be defeated*) Pakistan had to **bite the dust** in the final of the World Cup.
28. **Blue stocking** (*educated but pedantic lady*) No body likes to mix with her because she is a **blue stocking.**
29. **Bookworm** (*a person in the habit of pouring over books*) He has no time for social activities because he is a **bookworm.**
30. **Bring down the house** (*receive applause*) Though it was his maiden speech, he **brought down the house** because of his oratory skill.
31. **Brow beat** (*to bully*) The President of the college union always tries to **brow beat** the students opposed to him.
32. **Bad egg** (*worthless*) He comes of a noble family but he himself is a **bad egg**.
33. **Beside the mark** (*irrelevant*) No body agreed with him because his arguments were **beside the mark.**
34. **Burn one's fingers** (*to get into trouble*) Those who interfere in the affairs of others, often **burn their fingers.**
35. **Brown study** (*reverie, day-dream*) He could not follow the significance of my offer. He was in **brown study.**
36. **Bank on** (*depend on, count on*) The rich always **bank on** money to get things done.
37. **Blaze the trail** (*to start a movement*) Surinder Nath Bannerjee **blazed the trail** of Indian National Movement.
38. **Bull in a China shop** (*one who causes damage*) Most of the leaders of the freedom struggle have proved **bulls in a China shop.**
39. **By the rule of thumb** (*according to practical experience*) In older times business was run **by the rule of thumb.**
40. **Big draw** (*a huge attraction*) The match between India and Pakistan is always a **big draw.**
41. **Broken reed** (*support that failed*) When he needed help, his friend proved a **broken reed.**
42. **By the skin of the teeth** (*narrowly*) He escaped death in the accident **by the skin of the teeth.**
43. **Bone of contention** (*cause of quarrel*) Since India got independence, Kashmir problem has been a **bone of contention** between India and Pakistan.
44. **Bit/piece of one's mind** (*to scold*) My father wrote to my brother giving a **piece of his mind** about his insulting conduct.
45. **Born with silver spoon** (*to be born in a rich family*) My friend does not have to worry about spending any amount of money as she is **born with a silver spoon** in her mouth.
46. **Burn candle at both ends** (*to survive with difficulty*) After the death of his father, he is **burning candle at both ends.**

47. **By fits and starts** (*irregularly*) If we study **by fits and starts** we can never be successful in our exams.
48. **By dint of** (*by force of*) He achieved success in life **by dint of** hard work.
49. **Blow hot and cold** (*to speak in favour and against at the same time*) Do not trust those who **blow hot and cold** in the same breath.
50. **By and by** (*gradually*) He is recovering **by and by** after a long illness.
51. **Blue blood** (*aristocratic blood*) Though my friend has **blue blood,** yet her conduct is very mean and vulgar.

1. **Carry matters with a high hand** (*to deal with a person strictly*) The owner of the industry **carried matters with a high hand** and expelled two workers who were caught doing mischief in the office.
2. **Clip one's wings** (*to limit someone's ability to do or say things*) My elder sister is very ambitious but my mother will surely **clip her wings.**
3. **Come home to** (*to understand*) Seema wanted to be a teacher in the college but soon it **came home to** her that she was not fit for the job as she was only a graduate.
4. **Come to a standstill** (*come to a sudden stop*) When we were going to Mussourie yesterday, our car **came to a standstill** right in the middle of the journey.
5. **Come off with flying colours** (*to come out successfully*) The final football match was very crucial but finally we won and **came off with flying colours.**
6. **Cross one's mind** (*to occur to oneself*) In the examination hall it **crossed my mind** that I had left my pen outside on the table.
7. **Cry for the moon** (*to wish for something impossible*) The hope of winning the lottery amounting to lakhs of rupees is simply **crying for the moon.**
8. **Curry favour with** (*win favour of somebody*) Neena gave a lot of costly presents to her science teacher to **carry favour with** her.
9. **Call a spade a spade** (*to speak plainly*) People often get angry when one **calls a spade a spade.**
10. **Carry the day** (*to win a victory*) After initial setback India **carried the day** in the Test match.
11. **Cut a sorry figure** (*to give a poor show*) The speaker **cut a sorry figure** in the meeting.
12. **Cry over spilt milk** (*repent*) Careless students often have to **cry over spilt milk** during the exams.
13. **Cut one's coat according to one's cloth** (*to live wihtin one's means*) A wise man always **cuts his coat according to his cloth** if he wants to be successful in his life.

14. **Call names** (*to abuse*) Neeta **called** me **names,** so she was severely punished by the teacher.
15. **Curtain lecture** (*a reproof by wife to her husband*) My brother never pays any attention to his wife's **curtain lecture** and does what he thinks.
16. **Chip of the old block** (*resembling one's parents in habits*) My friend is quite helpful like her father, so she is a **chip of the old block.**
17. **Cave in** (*yield*) Although our team fought bravely, yet had to **cave in** before the superior power play of the opposite team.
18. **Cloven hoof** (*the evil intention*) The Chinese showed the **cloven hoof** in 1962.
19. **Cut throat** (*tough*) It is very difficult for Indian Industry to survive in the teeth of international **cut throat** competition.
20. **Call in question** (*doubt*) You should not **call in question** my honesty.
21. **Cheek by jowl** (*close together*) In metropolitan cities it is common that affluence and poverty exist **cheek by jowl.**
22. **Come to a pass** (*a difficult situation*) The things have **come to** such a pretty **pass** that he is financially ruined.
23. **Close shave** (*a narrow escape*) As he was driving recklessly in a crowded street, he had a **close shave.**
24. **Cut and dried** (*readymade form*) There is no **cut and dried** formula for success in life.
25. **Clinch the issue** (*decide the matter*) When he agreed to leave the house for good, it **clinched the issue** in favour of his wife.
26. **Carry one's point** (*win approval*) After heated discussion he was able to **carry his point.**
27. **Chequered/Checkered career** (*full of ups and downs*) Politicians have a generally **chequered career** all along.
28. **Cut both ends** (*argue in favour of both sides*) He is ambiguous because he always **cuts both ends.**
29. **Cocksure** (*very sure and certain*) He was so **cocksure** of his success that he applied for the job before the declaration of the result.
30. **Cock a snook** (*to show impudent contempt*) She is so proud of her wealth that she always **cocks a snook** at the acts of her husband.
31. **Chapter and verse** (*in full detail, to give proof*) He has such a sharp memory that he can narrate the story **chapter and verse.**
32. **Cool one's heels** (*to be kept waiting*) He had to **cool his heels** before he could meet the President of the party.
33. **Carrot and stick policy** (*reward and punishment*) A successful businessman follows the **carrot and stick policy** towards his employees.
34. **Come in handy** (*to be useful*) Take some woollen clothes. They may **come in handy** in Simla.

1. **Dig the grave** (*to tarnish, to destroy*) By taking side of the culprit he **dug the grave** of his reputation.
2. **Draw the long bow** (*exaggerate*) By calling him the best politician of the world, his followers **draw the long bow.**
3. **Die in harness** (*die while working*) Our Principal **died in harness.**
4. **Dutch courage** (*bravery under alcoholic influence*) Drunkards often indulge in **Dutch courage** and boast of their imaginary qualities.
5. **Dare devil** (*fearless person*) Only a **dare devil** can face the land mafia.
6. **Dead broke** (*penniless*) On account of reckless spending he is **dead broke** these days.
7. **Down and out** (*without money, a job, or a place to live*) After a slump in share market he is **down and out** these days.
8. **Draconian law** (*extremely severe law*) During emergency in 1975 the government imposed **Draconian laws** to subdue opposition.
9. **Die-hard** (*persistent in struggle*) He is a **die-hard** person and will not easily surrender.
10. **Days of reckoning** (*time to answer for one's actions*) You may commit crime after crime but **days of reckoning** are never far off.
11. **Down in the mouth** (*out of elements*) Now-a-days he is **down in the mouth** because he has suffered heavy loss in business.
12. **Dog in the manger** (*a person who prevents others from enjoying what he himself cannot*) By disrupting the Parliament Session the Congress is following a **dog in the manger** policy.
13. **Damp squib** (*complete failure*) The visit of our Foreign Minister to China proved a **damp squib** on border issue.

1. **Eat humble pie** (*to apologize*) Inspite of his constant bragging he lost the match and had to **eat humble pie.**
2. **Eat one's words** (*take a statement back*) I warned my friend to be very careful in her speech otherwise she would have to **eat her own words.**
3. **End in smoke/fiasco** (*come to nothing*) He spoke a lot about his new film but it all **ended in smoke** as it flopped on box office.
4. **Egg on** (*to urge somebody*) The Captain **egged** the players **on** to continue to play foul till the end of the match.
5. **Eke out** (*supplement income*) To **eke out** his income he also works as a part time accountant in the evening.

6. **Every dog has his day** (*good fortune comes sooner or later*) Don't be disappointed. It is truly said that **every dog has his day.**
7. **Ever and Anon** (*now and then, sometimes*) He visits his parents **ever and anon.**
8. (An) **eye wash** (*a pretence*) My friend's promise to help me just proved an **eye-wash.**

1. **Flesh and blood** (*human nature*) People in some villages are so poor that their sufferings are more than a **flesh and blood** can endure.
2. **Fish in troubled waters** (*to take advantage of the trouble of others*) Shrewd businessmen **fish in troubled waters** when there is scarcity of things.
3. **Follow suit** (*to act in a like manner*) If you do not obey your elders, your children will **follow suit.**
4. **Fall flat** (*to have no effect*) The minister's speech **fell flat** on the audience.
5. **Fight shy of** (*to attempt to avoid a thing or a person*) I generally **fight shy of** confronting my elder sister as she is in the habit of making sickening comments.
6. **Fabian policy** (*policy of delaying decisions*) Politicians generally follow a **Fabian policy** in order to keep everyone satisfied.
7. **For no rhyme or reason** (*without any logical or obvious reason*) Seema did not appear for her final examinations **for no rhyme or reason.**
8. **Fight to the finish** (*fight to the end*) Indian Army has vowed to **fight to the finish** and turn every intruder out of Indian territory.
9. **Few and far between** (*very rare*) His visits to his home town are **few and far between** because of his expanding business.
10. **Flog a dead horse** (*to revive interest in old matters*) The rivals always **flog a dead horse** to insult their enemies.
11. **Fool's errand** (*useless undertaking*) His visit to the States to earn money proved to be a **fool's errand.**
12. **Fall foul of** (*to quarrel*) They were once bosom friends but now they have **fallen foul of** each other.
13. **Fly off the handle** (*to lose one's temper*) When his father questioned him about money, he **flew off the handle.**
14. **French leave** (*to be absent without permission*) Those who take **french leave** should not be pardoned.
15. **Fair and square** (*upright, an honest way*) My father advised me to be **fair and square** in business dealings.
16. **Feather one's own nest** (*to provide first for one self*) Our leaders are busy **feathering their own nests** and have no concern for the poor.

17. **From pillar to post** (*rush in all directions and suffer much harassment*) You may rush **from pillar to post,** but you stand no chance of getting what you want without a bribe.
18. **Foot the bill** (*bear expenses*) Although he hosted the feast, his brother had to **foot the bill.**
19. **Fair weather friend** (*selfish friend*) A **fair weather friend** will never stand by you in difficulty.
20. **Flash in the pan** (*something that happened only once or for a very short time and was not repeated*) The success of Indian cricket team is never constant and steady. It is generally a **flash in the pan.**
21. **Fit to hold a candle to** (*match for, equal in quality*) He is the son of a famous writer but he is not **fit to hold a candle to** his father.
22. **The Fourth Estate** (*the press*) The newspaper is regarded as **the Fourth Estate** of the state.
23. **Feather in one's cap** (*additional success*) His success in his M.A. exams has added a new **feather in his cap.**
24. **Fly in the face of** (*to defy*) It is disobedience on their part to **fly in the face** of the orders of the Principal.

1. **Gain ground** (*to succeed slowly & steadily*) The belief in the abolition of dowry system is **gaining ground.**
2. **Get off scotfree** (*to escape without punishment*) A murderer can also very easily **get off scotfree** for lack of evidence.
3. **Grease the palm** (*to bribe*) Nowadays if you want to get your work done, you will have to **grease the palm** of someone or the other.
4. **Gird up the loins** (*to prepare for hard work*) Indians must **gird up the loins** to face any foreign attack on their country.
5. **Go to the dogs** (*to be ruined*) The rich industrialist will **go to the dogs** because of his son's bad habits.
6. **Get oneself into a mess** (*to drift into trouble*) Due to sheer ignorance, Vijay seems to have **got himself into a mess** in his office.
7. **Give a wide berth** (*to avoid*) We should always **give a wide berth** to all selfish and mean persons.
8. **Gentleman at large** (*an unreliable person*) We must not believe a **gentleman at large.**
9. **Good Samaritan** (*one who helps strangers*) He is a **good Samaritan** because he always comes to the help of the old and the children in difficulties
10. **Give a good account of oneself** (*to act creditably*) As the eldest son of his family he **gave a good account of himself** when calamity befell the family.

11. **Give the devil his due** (*give credit to a worthless person for his good qualities*) We should **give the devil his due** for his good qualities.
12. **Greenhorn** (*inexperienced*) Though a **greenhorn** in political field, he appears to have a bright future.
13. **Give up the ghost** (*pass away, die*) After long illness he **gave up the ghost** last week.
14. **Go the whole hog** (*to do something thoroughly*) You will have to **go the whole hog** to come out of this mess.
15. **Get into a scrape** (*awkward situation*) He **got into a scrape** when his wife refused to let him help his sister.
16. **Go broke** (*become bankrupt*) As a result of heavy gambling he had to **go broke** in the long run.
17. **Get into hot waters** (*get into trouble*) He **got into hot waters** by marrying a girl of another caste.
18. **Give currency** (*to make publicly known*) The Government has refused to **give currency** to a number of scams.
19. **Great hand** (*expert*) He is a **great hand** at organising social parties.
20. **Get down to brass tacks** (*to deal with the matter straight*) Instead of wasting time in discussion, please **get down to brass tacks.**
21. **Give one a long rope** (*to let someone commit mistakes*) He never **gives his employees a long rope.**
22. **Good turn** (*an act of kindness*) He did me a **good turn** by recommending me for the post of Vice-President.

1. **Hold water** (*appear to be valid, sound or reasonable*) His statement will not **hold water** as it is not based on facts.
2. **Hang together** (*support one another*) The two statements delivered by the leader of the party do not **hang together.**
3. **Hope against hope** (*hope inspite of disappointment*) Sohan's case is very weak and everybody knows that finally he will lose, but he is still **hoping against hope.**
4. **Have an axe to grind** (*to have a selfish interest*) Reema is very selfish but the way she is being polite with everyone gives the impression that she **has an axe to grind.**
5. **Have the gift of the gab** (*art of speaking*) Meena is not highly qualified but she **has the gift of the gab.**
6. **Hit below the belt** (*to strike unfairly*) We should always face the enemy boldly and never **hit him below the belt.**
7. **Hold one's tongue** (*to keep quiet*) We should always **hold our tongue** before our elders.

8. **Herculean task** (*very difficult*) It is a **Herculean task** to root out corruption in India.
9. **Haul over the coals** (*to take to task*) She was **hauled over the coals** by her parents for her misconduct.
10. **Have one's finger in everyone's pie** (*to partake of something*) My best friend likes to **have her finger in everyone's pie** as she is in the habit of meddling with the affairs of others.
11. **Halcyon days** (*peaceful days*) The days we spend in our school life are the **halcyon days** of our life.
12. **Have an iron will** (*strong will*) If we have to live among the mean and selfish people, we must **have an iron will.**
13. **Hold out an olive branch** (*offer of peace*) The terrorists are not prepared to **hold out an olive branch** to the Government of India.
14. **Hanky panky** (*jugglery*) None of this **hanky panky**, tell me the truth.
15. **Have feet of clay** (*full of faults*) The C.B.I. inquiry has revealed that many ministers **have feet of clay.**
16. **Heart and soul** (*devotedly*) He took part in the annual function with **heart and soul.**
17. **Hard and fast** (*strict*) No **hard and fast** rule is laid down about being regular in the college.
18. **Hang fire** (*remain unsolved*) Kashmir problem has been **hanging fire** for many years.
19. **High and dry** (*a difficult situation*) He was left **high and dry** by his business partners.
20. **Hit the nail on the head** (*to do the right thing at the right time*) He **hit the nail on the head** by resigning his job.
21. **Hobson's choice** (*no alternative*) The employees in the private sector have **Hobson's choice** because they are forced to accept what they are ordered to do.
22. **Have too many irons in the fire** (*doing many things at a time*) He is fickle minded and **has too many irons in the fire.**
23. **Hold in abeyance** (*postpone*) For lack of funds the district administration has **held** the construction of road **in abeyance.**
24. **High and mighty** (*proud persons*) The **high and mighty** forget that everything in the world is transient.
25. **Hard nosed attitude** (*aggressive*) I don't know why my teacher always has a **hard nosed attitude** towards me.
26. **Hold in leash** (*to restrain*) As a responsible leader of a party you must **hold** criticism of party workers **in leash.**
27. **Head and shoulders** (*superior*) The new CEO is **head and shoulders** above his predecessors.

28. **Hold a brief** (*to defend someone*) It is very improper for parents to **hold a brief** for their children who are in the wrong.
29. **Hush money** (*a bribe*) He managed to escape punishment by paying **hush money.**
30. **Hold at bay** (*to prevent enemy from coming*) Maharana Partap could not **hold** the Mughal army **at bay** for long.
31. **Hit the jack pot** (*unexpected success*) He **hit the jack pot** by investing his money in shares.
32. **Helter skelter** (*here and there*) When the police arrived the rioters ran **helter skelter.**
33. **Have a brush with** (*to have encounter*) Our principal **had a brush with** the Vice Chancellor over the appointment of a lecturer.
34. **Hornet's nest** (*raise controversy*) The speaker stirred up a **hornet's nest** by referring to impending changes in the rules.
35. **Hold somebody to ransom** (*to demand concession by making someone captive*) It is a pity that a handful of militants are **holding the nation to ransom.**
36. **Hole and corner** (*secret*) I have come to know of your **hole and corner** method of dealing with people.

1. **Ill at ease** (*uncomfortable*) A student is often **ill at ease** when he has to see the Principal after he has done something wrong.
2. **In a fix** (*In a dilemma*) The whole police department is **in a fix** about the threatening letters written by the kidnappers.
3. **In a fair way** (*hopeful*) The doctor feels that patient is **in a fair way** on to recovery.
4. **In the good books of** (*to be in favour with a person*) Sunita's brilliant success in her final examination has led her to be **in the good books of** her teachers.
5. **In tune** (*in a mood*) The teacher asked the students if they were **in tune** for study.
6. **In the lurch** (to leave a friend in difficulty) You must never leave your best friend **in the lurch.**
7. **Ins and outs** (secrets) The servants are generally familiar with the **ins and outs** of the family.
8. **In the blues** (*in dumps, depressed*) After his failure in the Examination, he is **in the blues** these days.
9. **In the red** (*in debt*) Most of our Public Sector Undertakings are **in the red** for lack of efficient administration.
10. **In the limelight** (*prominent*) After being out of favour with the leader of the party he is again **in the limelight** these days.

11. **In the teeth of** (*inspite of bitter opposition*) Hindu Code Bill was passed **in the teeth of** opposition by various organizations.
12. **In a tight corner** (*in a difficult situation*) After losing in gambling heavily, he is **in a tight corner.**
13. **In cold blood** (*to do something deliberately*) The child was murdered **in cold blood.**
14. **In doldrums** (*to be depressed*) After his failure in the examination he is **in doldrums** these days.
15. **In the family way** (*pregnant*) She has been advised complete rest because she is **in the family way.**
16. **Ivory tower** (*imaginary world*) Those who talk of non-violence as a useful tool in international politics live in **ivory tower.**
17. **In the dumps** (*in low spirits*) Her visit cheered me up as I was **in the dumps** before her visit.
18. **In a flutter** (*excited*) My sister is **in a flutter** today because she is going for the interview.

1. **Jaundiced eye** (*prejudice*) You must not evaluate the success of your rivals with a **jaundiced eye.**

1. **Keep body and soul together** (*to maintain life*) These days because of rising prices it is difficult to **keep body and soul together.**
2. **Keep at an arm's length** (*to keep at a distance*) Selfish people should always be **kept at an arm's length.**
3. **Keep the wolf from the door** (*to avoid starvation*) In India millions of people struggle hard to **keep the wolf from the door.**
4. **Kith and kin** (*blood relation*) If we have no love for our **kith and kin,** we cannot be expected to love humanity.
5. **Knit the brow** (*to frown*) Her mother-in-law always **knits the brow** at everything she does.
6. **Kick the bucket** (*to die*) He **kicked the bucket** after long illness in the prime of his life.
7. **Keep up appearances** (*to maintain outward show*) Though he is in financial crisis, he is able to **keep up appearances.**
8. **Keep one's fingers crossed** (*to wait expectantly*) We had to **keep our fingers crossed** till the last ball was bowled.
9. **Keep the pot boiling** (*earn hardly enough for living*) He is earning only to **keep the pot boiling.**

10. **Kick one's heels** (*to waste time in waiting*) As the train was late we had to **kick our heels** at the station.
11. **Keep abreast of** (*not to fall behind*) It is very important for young persons to **keep abreast of** political developments in the country.

L

1. **Lost in the clouds** (*confused*) My psychology teacher is often **lost in the clouds** as she sometimes is unable to explain the questions clearly.
2. **Lose ground** (*fail to keep position*) The belief in prophecies and horoscopes is **losing ground** these days.
3. **Laugh in one's sleeves** (*to laugh secretly*) The students **laughed in their sleeves** at the teacher's ignorance of the subject.
4. **Leave no stone unturned** (*to make all possible efforts*) The minister assured the poor that he shall **leave no stone unturned** to uplift their condition.
5. **Leap in the dark** (*to take a risk deliberately*) You must not **leap in the dark** by entering the business without experience.
6. **Look sharp** (*to make haste*) **Look sharp,** the bus is moving.
7. **Let the cat out of the bag** (*to disclose*) Sunita has, at last, **let the cat out of the bag,** by confessing that she had stolen her brother's money.
8. **Live in a fool's paradise** (*false hope*) My brother is **living in a fool's paradise** if he thinks that he can be a rich man without working hard.
9. **Lion's share** (*large part*) Generally the sons as compared to daughters have a **lion's share** of their mother's affection.
10. **Loaves and fishes** (*material benefit*) Most of the ministers are more concerned with the **loaves and fishes** of office than the service of man.
11. **Live-wire** (*energetic*) India needs **live-wire** political leaders who can put the country on the right track.
12. **Look a gift horse in the mouth** (*criticize a gift*) One should not **look a gift horse in the mouth** because it is given out of love and regards.
13. **Lose one's head** (*to be carried away*) One should not **lose one's head** even in such a victory.
14. **Long and short** (*in brief*) The **long and short** of the principal's speech was that examination would be held on time.
15. **Latin and Greek** (*incomprehensible*) The speech of literary persons is always **Latin and Greek** to illiterate persons.
16. **Last nail in the coffin** (*causing ruin*) Second world war proved to be a **last nail in the coffin** of British imperialism.
17. **Lead up the garden path** (*to cheat*) The traders **lead** the credulous customers **up the garden path** by assuring them of warranty.

18. **Leaps and bounds** (*rapidly*) In comparison to India, China has progressed by **leaps and bounds** in every field.
19. **Last straw** (*the final trial of patience*) The Rowlatt Act was the **last straw** on the Camel's back and the whole India rose in protest against the British rule.
20. **Let the grass grow under feet** (*to delay the matters*) We are bound to suffer if we **let the grass grow under feet** by postponing action.

1. **Make both ends meet** (*to live within one's means*) As my uncle has to bring up five children, he finds it difficult to **make both ends meet.**
2. **Mend one's fences** (*to make peace*) It is high time for the two brothers to bury the hatchet and **mend their fences.**
3. **Make a clean breast** (*to confess*) When asked by the Magistrate sternly, the thief **made a clean breast** of the whole crime.
4. **Make amends** (*to give compensation*) The government **made amends** to the family for the loss of their earning member in the war.
5. **Make the most of** (*to utilize time*) Students should **make the most of** their time if they want to get an administrative job.
6. **Move heaven and earth** (*to try utmost*) Ramesh **moved heaven and earth** to gain his end but failed.
7. **Make sure** (*to ascertain*) We went to the office to **make sure** if our exams would start in the next week.
8. **Make neither head nor tail** (*not to understand*) The students can **make neither head nor tail** of what Mr. Dev teaches them.
9. **Moot point** (*a debatable point, undecided*) The question of abolition of child marriage is a **moot point** as far as Indians are concerned.
10. **Meet one's Waterloo** (*to face final defeat*) Tipu Sultan **met his Waterloo** in the fourth battle of Mysore.
11. **Man of letters** (*literary person*) Dr. Radhakrishnan was a **man of letters.**
12. **Make light of** (*not to care*) He is in the habit of **making light of** the advice of his parents.
13. **Midas touch** (*a touch which turns anything into gold*) Our manager seems to be gifted with **Midas touch** because he is capable of selling every product.
14. **Man of parts** (*a man of qualities*) Our Principal is a **man of parts** and is respected by all and one.
15. **Mealy mouthed** (*afraid to speak frankly or straight forwardly*) Our local government is filled with mealy-mouthed politicians and self-serving bureaucrats.
16. **Man of straw** (*a weak person*) The king being a **man of straw**, his orders were often disobeyed.

17. **Mince matters** (*hide the truth and pretend*) Tell the truth to your parents because it does not pay **to mince matters.**
18. **Mare's nest** (*a false invention*) The involvement of teachers in the scheme proved to be **a mare's nest.**

1. **Null and void** (*ineffective*) Strangely, the laws made by the British in India are not yet **null and void.**
2. **Next to nothing** (*almost nothing*) The thieves made off with everything from the kitchen and there was **next to nothing** left.
3. **Neck and crop** (*completely*) The decoits finished him off **neck and crop** beyond recognition.
4. **No love lost** (*intense dislike*) There is **no love lost** between the two neighbours.
5. **Nip in the bud** (*to destroy in the very beginning*) The evils of the society must be **nipped in the bud.**
6. **Not worth one's salt** (*not deserving*) We should not help the persons who are **not worth their salt.**

1. **Off hand** (*without preparation or delay*) I am very poor in English grammar & can't answer all the questions **off hand.**
2. **Over head and ears** (*excessively*) Mohan is **over head and ears** in love with Neena.
3. **Out of the question** (*unlikely, uncertain*) His success is **out of the question** because he is not working hard these days.
4. **Out of the woods** (*out of danger*) The patient is not **out of the woods** yet.
5. **Order of the day** (*in fashion*) It is difficult to get any work done without bribery because it is the **order of the day.**
6. **On the score of** (*on the grounds of*) He was debarred from appearing in the examination **on the score of** indiscipline.
7. **On that score** (*for the reason*) You need not worry **on that score.**
8. **Over and above** (*moreover, besides*) I shall lend you books **over and above** what I have promised to give you in cash.
9. **Out and out** (*completely*) Shri Bhagat Singh was a patriot **out and out.**
10. **Off and on** [occasionally (*now & then*)] Since she is over busy these days, she visits me **off and on.**
11. **One's Achilles heel** (*a weak point*) Howsoever powerful a person may be, he is vulnerable because of **his Achilles' heel.**

12. **Off colour** (*not in usual form*) Once a glamorous actress, she is **off colour** these days.
13. **Odds and ends** (*scattered things*) The thief made away with the **odds and ends** lying about the drawing room.
14. **Off the hook** (*out of trouble*) He is not yet **off the hook** because Income Tax department is making a thorough inquiry into his financial status.
15. **Oily tongue** (*flattering words*) He has often won over the enemies by his **oily tongue.**
16. **On the horns of dilemma** (*in a fix*) He is **on the horns of dilemma** in the matter of his marriage.
17. **One's cup of tea** (*to one's liking*) Teaching is not **my cup of tea.**
18. **Out of sorts** (*to be unwell*) Sohan had been **out of sorts** the whole day and could not do his office work properly.
19. **On its last legs** (*about to collapse*) In many sections of Indian society the system of child marriage is **on its last legs.**
20. **On the carpet** (*to be under consideration*) What is **on the carpet** these days is in the newspapers.

1. **Past master** (*an expert*) He is a **past master** in befooling the people by his oily tongue.
2. **Palmy days** (*prosperous, affluent days*) We still remember the **palmy days** of our life when we had nothing much to do and still got everything to fulfil our needs.
3. **Part and parcel** (*inseparable part*) Every Indian citizen must regard himself as **part and parcel** of a larger whole.
4. **Pass the buck** (*to blame each other*) Political parties **pass the buck** on to one another for failure on economic front.
5. **Pay off old scores** (*to take revenge*) The way he is treating his younger brother makes it quite obvious that he is **paying off old scores.**
6. **Pay through one's nose** (*to pay dearly*) A hapless customer has to **pay through his nose** when there is shortage of goods in the market.
7. **Pay lip service** (*insincere expression of friendship, admiration, support, etc.*) Most of the political parties **pay lip service** to the plight of the poor.
8. **Pay one back in the same coin** (*tit for tat*) We should not hesitate in **paying** China and Pakistan **back in their own coins.**
9. **Pin-money** (*allowance given to housewife for personal use*) She is frugal and saves even out of **pin-money.**
10. **Pell-mell** (*great confusion*) After the thieves had ransacked the house, every thing was **pell-mell.**

11. **Play fast and loose** (*repeatedly change one's attitude*) No one can trust Rohan as he is used to **playing fast and loose** with his friends.
12. **Play second fiddle to** (*to play a subordinate part*) A self-respecting man can never **play second fiddle** to anyone.
13. **Play truant** (*to be absent from duty without permission*) It is a very bad habit of the employees to **play truant** from office.
14. **Play to the gallery** (*to gain cheap popularity*) The speeches of our leaders are not sincere; they are intended to **play to the gallery.**
15. **Play ducks and drakes** (*to squander money*) After the death of his father he got into heavy debt by **playing ducks and drakes** with money.
16. **Play foul** (*to do something wrong*) Don't **play foul** with your well-wishers.
17. **Plough the sands** (*futile labour*) He cannot make money because he appears to be **ploughing the sands.**
18. **Pour oil on troubled waters** (*to pacify the matters*) The two good friends exchanged hot words but the intervention of their teacher **poured oil on troubled waters.**
19. **Pull a long face** (*to look sad*) Seema **pulled a long face** when she was scolded by her teacher for her carelssness.
20. **Pull one's socks up** (*work hard*) You must **pull your socks up** to get over financial problems.
21. **Pull strings** (*to exercise influence secretly*) He managed his promotion by **pulling strings.**
22. **Put heads together** (*consult seriously*) Our leaders should **put their heads together** to solve national problems.
23. **Put a spoke in a wheel** (*to obstruct*) He would not like me to succeed; so he **put a spoke in a wheel.**
24. **Put the cart before the horse** (*to do wrong thing first*) Our leaders **put the cart before the horse** by neglecting villages in the name of industrial progress.
25. **Pros and cons** (*for and against a thing*) We must always consider the **pros and cons** of any new project that we take in hand.
26. **Pyrrhic victory** (*victory at a high cost*) Greek victory over Trojans proved to be a **pyrrhic victory.**
27. **Pick holes** (*to find fault with*) He is always **picking holes** in every project.

1. **Queer fish** (*strange person*) One cannot make anything out of Sohan's attitude as he is such a **queer fish.**
2. **Quixotic project** (*foolishly ideal*) Being not worldly wise he wasted his money in **quixotic projects.**

R

1. **Rise to the occasion** (*to act as the occasion demands*) To face critical situations boldly you should **rise to the occasion.**
2. **Run short of** (*shortage*) These days due to some financial crises my friend is **running short of** money.
3. **Rank and file** (*common man*) If we want our country to progress in every field, we must improve the economic lot of the **rank and file.**
4. **Red tapism** (*official delay*) **Red tapism** is a bane of Indian bureaucracy.
5. **Rest on one's laurels** (*complacent, self satisfied*) Ambitious persons never **rest on their laurels** because they dream of unending achievements.
6. **Rock the boat** (*upset the balance*) If your party withdraws the support from the Government, it may **rock the boat.**
7. **Red herring** (*something to distract attention*) The demand of inquiry into his conduct is just a **red herring** as there is no truth in it.
8. **Rip up old sores** (*to revive forgotton quarrel*) Rahul and his wife can't live in peace; they are always **ripping up old sores.**
9. **Read between the lines** (*to understand the hidden meaning*) If her essay **is read between the lines,** we will find that she has made comments against the Government.
10. **Rule the roost** (*to dominate*) Today the rich **rule the roost.**
11. **Red rag to a bull** (*anything that provokes*) The law against the dowry system is, for the greedy persons, like a **red rag to a bull.**
12. **Ride roughshod over** (*to treat in a high handed fashion*) Don't **ride roughshod over** a person when he is down and out.
13. **Rub one the wrong way** (*annoy*) If you **rub him the wrong way,** he is bound to react.

1. **Sit on the fence** (*not to commit oneself*) When the party split Ramesh was accused of **sitting on the fence.**
2. **Smell a rat** (*to be suspicious*) I **smelt a rat** in the bargain that my uncle made with my father.
3. **Shed crocodile tears** (*to show false sorrow*) The mother **shed crocodile tears** on the death of her step daughter.
4. **Split hair** (*to indulge in over refined arguments*) We should not try to **split hair** with our elders.
5. **Stand in good stead** (*to be helpful in need*) During the time of distress the advice of elders always **stands in good stead.**
6. **Show white feather** (*to show cowardice*) Brave people never **show white feather** in the face of difficulties.

7. **See eye to eye** (*to agree*) Neema could never **see eye to eye** with her elder brother.
8. **Set store by** (*to value*) I have always **set store by** my father's opinion.
9. **Snap one's fingers at** (*to show contempt*) The industry owner feels that he may **snap his fingers at** the demands of his workers, but he is greatly mistaken.
10. **Speak volumes for** (*to have abundant proof*) The amount of sacrifice made by Reena's friend **speaks volumes for** her true love for her friend.
11. **Steal a march** (*to get ahead secretly*) Rohan **stole a march** on my brother in business and is very rich today.
12. **Steer clear of** (*to avoid*) Everyone, if possible, should **steer clear of** selfish people.
13. **Swan song** (*last creation*) 'Lament' was **the swan song** of Shelley.
14. **Snake in the grass** (*a secret enemy*) The country is always betrayed by the **snakes in the grass.**
15. **Sword of Damocles** (*facing imminent danger*) A **sword of Damocles** is always hanging over the head of a soldier in the event of war.
16. **Sail under false colours** (*a hypocrite*) We should not believe our leaders because they **sail under false colours.**
17. **Spartan life** (*life of ascetic*) Swami Vivekanand led a **spartan life** for promoting health of mind and body.
18. **Save one's face** (*to avoid disgrace*) He is making lame excuses to **save his face** because he could not qualify the examination.
19. **A scarlet woman** (*a woman with loose morals*) Being **a scarlet woman** she is looked down upon by her neighbours.
20. **Set people by ears** (*to incite people*) The communal speeches **set people by ears.**
21. **To set the Thames on fire** (*to achieve something impossible*) Qualifying Civil Services examination for you is like **setting the Thames on fire.**
22. **Sweat of the brow** (*hard labour*) The honest persons live by **sweat of the brow.**
23. **Steal someone's thunder** (*make a better impression*) The young actor performed so well that he **stole his rival's thunder.**
24. **Straight from the shoulders** (*candidly*) My lawyer told me **straight from the shoulders** that my case was weak.
25. **Spick and span** (*in order*) Her house looked **spick and span** because everything was in its place.
26. **Shot in the arm** (*encouraging*) A victory in Kargil war proved a **shot in the arm** of our Defence Forces.
27. **Something up one's sleeve** (*a secret plan*) She is quite a mischievous lady. There is always **something up her sleeve.**

28. **Send about one's business** (*to dismiss*) His employees **sent him about his business** when he behaved insolently.
29. **Stand one's ground** (*remain firm*) He did not yield to pressure and **stood his ground** till the end.
30. **Small fry** (*insignificant person*) Who cares for him, he is a **small fry** in the office.
31. **Seamy side of life** (*immoral side of society*) The picture depicts realism and presents the **seamy side of life** in modern India.
32. **Sow wild oats** (*irresponsible pleasure seeking*) After **sowing his wild oats** Ram has decided to work hand in future.
33. **Spill the beans** (*to give information*) Continuous interrogation finally made the man **spill the beans** and the disaster was averted.
34. **A stalking horse** (*pretence*) The trade union's seemingly rightful demand is only **a stalking horse** to black-mail the management.

1. **Turn the tables** (*to reverse the condition*) A batsman often **turns the table** on the opposite team by his good batting.
2. **Turn up one's nose** (*to take lightly with contempt*) Meena has failed twice in her class and yet she **turns up her nose** at my advice.
3. **Turn coat** (*one who changes political affiliations*) Anti-defection bill is aimed at checking the evil practices indulged in by **turn coats.**
4. **Take up the cudgels** (*to support or defend*) One of my lawyer friends **took up the cudgels** on my behalf to defend me.
5. **Turn the corner** (*to pass a critical stage*) After long illness at last my friend **turned the corner** and was completely out of danger.
6. **Tall talk** (*exaggerate the matters*) No one likes to be in the company of Neema as she always indulges in **tall talk.**
7. **Tooth and nail** (*violently*) All the students revolted **tooth and nail** against the partiality of the teachers towards some students.
8. **Throw in a towel** (*to be defeated*) When the wrestler could not resist the opponent, he had to **throw in a towel.**
9. **Take with a pinch of salt** (*to accept with doubt*) Everybody **takes** Rahul's problems **with a pinch of salt** because he is an unreliable person.
10. **Turn a hair** (*show any reaction*) Although his friends provoked him against Rohit, he did not **turn a hair** and remained calm.
11. **Tall stories** (*exaggerated stories*) Since he retired from Army, he has been famous for his **tall stories** which regale the villagers.

12. **Take the floor** (*make a speech*) When the Prime Minister **took the floor** in the cabinet meeting there was pin drop silence.
13. **Take lying down** (*accept insult*) It is impossible for me to **take** his remarks **lying down.** It amounts to meek surrender.
14. **Turn to account** (*turn to advantage*) The brave **turn** their failures **to account.**
15. **Take heart** (*feel bold*) You must **take heart** and face life boldly.
16. **Take to heart** (*feel excessively*) He **took** his failure **to heart** and lost interest in worldly affairs.
17. **Take the bull by the horns** (*to meet the danger boldly*) You can succeed in life only if you have courage to **take the bull by the horns.**
18. **Through and through** (*entirely*) He was drenched in the rain **through and through.**
19. **To the back bone** (*thoroughly*) We need leaders who are selfless **to the back bone.**
20. **Take wind out of another's sails** (*to gain advantage by anticipation*) Farsighted Generals can win war by **taking wind out of enemy's sails.**
21. **Throw down the glove/gauntlet** (*to challenge*) China had **thrown down the glove** by not recognising Sikkim as part of India.
22. **Take leaf out of somebody's book** (*to emulate*) The young should **take leaf out of great men's books.**
23. **Take people by storm** (*to surprise unexpectedly*) The successful launching of GSLV-1 **took the nation by storm.**
24. **Tall order** (*something difficult*) It is a **tall order** to check population explosion in India.
25. **Throw a spanner** (*to sabotage a plan*) He refused to finance my project and so **threw a spanner** in it.
26. **Take to task** (*punish, ask for explanation, to scold*) I **took** my younger sister **to task** for not obeying her elders.
27. **Turn a deaf ear** (*not to pay attention to, refuse to listen*) All the party members **turned a deaf ear** to their leader.
28. **Throw out of gear** (*not working properly*) Many of our small scale industries have been **thrown out of gear** because of lack of finance.
29. **Take to heels** (*to run away*) The students making mischief **took to** their **heels** on seeing the Principal.
30. **Throw cold water** (*to discourage*) Instead of encouraging me my business partner **threw cold water** on my plans.
31. **Turn over a new leaf** (*to be entirely changed*) After the sudden death of his father Rajesh **turned over a new leaf** and took all the responsibilities of the family on himself.
32. **Take somebody for a ride** (*to deceive a person*) The traders **take** the **customers for a ride** by selling fake foreign goods to them.

33. **Take up arms** (*to fight*) The tribals of this region have **taken up arms** against the government.
34. **To and fro** (*forward and backward*) He was strolling in the garden **to and fro.**
35. **Throw up the sponge** (*surrender*) He never **threw up the sponge** and at last got over his problems.

1. **Uphill task** (*difficult task*) The problem of holding exams on time is an **uphill task** for the V.C. of the college.
2. **Ups and downs** (*change in fortune*) My uncle has experienced many **ups and downs** in his furniture business.
3. **Under the rose** (*secretly*) When the parents of Amul did not agree to the marriage of their son,, he married Meeta **under the rose.**
4. **Up and doing** (*active*) A labourer should be **up and doing** daily if he has to earn his living.
5. **Under a cloud** (*to be under suspicion*) His secret connections with the smugglers have brought him **under a cloud.**
6. **Upto the mark** (*as good as should be*) Your speech was **upto the mark.**

1. **With open arms** (*cordially, warmly*) When my cousin came back from England after ten years he was welcomed **with open arms** by all the relatives.
2. **Win laurels** (*to win distinction*) Dr. Tagore **won laurels** in the world of literature.
3. **White elephant** (*anything with less utility and more expenditure*) The Public Sector Undertakings have proved **white elephants** to our economy.
4. **Well disposed to** (*friendly or helpful to somebody*) One is always **well disposed to** those who are honest and hard working.
5. **Writing on the wall** (*signal, warning*) The factory owner read the **writing on the wall** and closed down the factory.
6. **When the crunch comes** (*the moment of decision*) Brave persons never despair **when the crunch comes.**
7. **Willy-Nilly** (*whether one wishes or not*) **Willy-Nilly,** she has to agree to the views of her husband all the time.
8. **Window shopping** (*to look at goods displayed but not for buying*) Though I did not have any mind to make purchases, I just went out **window shopping** in the evening.
9. **Wear and tear** (*damage caused by use*) **Wear and tear** of the machinery is known as depreciation in accountancy.

10. **Weal and woe** (*joy and sorrow*) We must learn to bear **weal and woe** of life patiently.
11. **Wash hands of** (*to have nothing to do*) I have **washed hands of** your affairs because you do not take me seriously.
12. **Wide berth** (*keep away*) We should give a **wide berth** to bad characters.
13. **Will o' the wisp** (*elusive, unreal*) To Romantic poets reality appears to be **will o' the wisp.**
14. **Wry face** (*disappointed look*) He made a **wry face** when he was refused admission to the college of his choice.
15. **Win hands down** (*win easily*) Australia **won hands down** in the Davis Cup finals.
16. **Within an ace of** (*close to something*) When our team was **within an ace of** victory, Iraq scored a last minute goal to draw the game.
17. **Wear the trousers** (*dominant*) It is Leena who **wears the trousers** and her husband simply obeys her.
18. **Wee hours** (*at dawn*) The old couple was murdered in the **wee hours** of the day.
19. **With a high hand** (*oppressively*) He was a king who ruled his subjects **with a high hand.**
20. **Wet blanket** (*any person that dampens enthusiasm*) The principal proved a **wet blanket** while the students were on picnic.
21. **Wild-goose chase** (*unprofitable*) All the efforts of the government to remove illiteracy in India is like a **wild-goose chase.**
22. **Wind fall** (*sudden gain*) The legacy left by his uncle proved a **wind fall** for Arnav.
23. **Wrangle over an ass' shadow** (*to quarrel over trifles*) Their long friendship ended because they **wrangled over an ass' shadow.**

1. **Yellow press** (*newspaper publishing sensational news*) In recent times there is a spurt of sensational newspapers making **yellow press** popular.
2. **Yeoman's service** (*excellent work*) Sardar Patel did a **Yeoman's service** by welding numberless States into one strong nation.

Work Book Exercise A

Directions *In each of the following questions an idiomatic phrase is given followed by four alternatives. Choose the alternative that best expresses the meaning of the expression.*

1. Hang together
(*a*) confirm each other
(*b*) live together
(*c*) hang with each other
(*d*) go together

2. Hard boiled
(*a*) boiled hard
(*b*) extremely hot
(*c*) hardened
(*d*) hardly boiled

3. Get cold feet
(*a*) to run for life
(*b*) to get cold
(*c*) to be afraid
(*d*) to become discourteous

4. Make no bones about
(*a*) to make no effort
(*b*) to admit something readily
(*c*) to make fuss about
(*d*) to create no hindrance

5. Turn out crabs
(*a*) end in failure
(*b*) to be successful
(*c*) to bring up crabs
(*d*) to be victorious

6. Devil's Advocate
(*a*) an advocate of a Devil
(*b*) an advocate like a Devil
(*c*) present a counter argument
(*d*) one who is against religion

7. Between the Devil and the Sea
(*a*) in a fix
(*b*) a Devil in the sea
(*c*) in a worse situation
(*d*) a compromising situation

8. Dance attendance upon
(*a*) to flatter
(*b*) to dance with a partner
(*c*) to attend upon
(*d*) to attend to

9. Go abegging
(*a*) go in vain
(*b*) go for begging
(*c*) beg for going
(*d*) request for something

10. A Gala day
(*a*) a day of success
(*b*) a day of merry-making
(*c*) an eventful day
(*d*) a day of singificance

11. Go hot & cold
(*a*) get angry
(*b*) get irritated
(*c*) get out of cold
(*d*) sudden feeling of fear and anxiety

12. Gird up one's Loins
(*a*) get ready for a job
(*b*) leave bag & baggage
(*c*) hunt for lions
(*d*) a loin cloth

13. Pocket an insult
(*a*) bear insult without protest
(*b*) not to take any action
(*c*) sit over a resolution
(*d*) ignore a case

14. In pretty pass
(*a*) problems of a passage
(*b*) in difficulties
(*c*) in a difficult way
(*d*) caught in heavy traffic

15. Small talk
(*a*) light conversation
(*b*) gossip
(*c*) back biting
(*d*) whispering

16. Plough a lonely furrow
(*a*) work single handedly
(*b*) plough the field
(*c*) plough the sands
(*d*) work in a furrow

17. Rub shoulders with
(*a*) come in contact with
(*b*) quarrel with a person
(*c*) rub shoulders of someone
(*d*) have a cause to fight

18. Run the gauntlet
(*a*) lash with gauntlet
(*b*) run away with gauntlet
(*c*) face criticism
(*d*) accept a challenge

19. Rest on one's oars
(*a*) take rest after working long
(*b*) tired of working
(*c*) tired of boating
(*d*) rest with oars

20. Join the majority
(*a*) on the side of majority
(*b*) to die
(*c*) a turn coat
(*d*) have the majority

21. Wash dirty linen in public
(*a*) to criticise
(*b*) make personal quarrels public
(*c*) to talk dirty things in public
(*d*) to wash clothers

22. Augean stables
(*a*) to remove an evil
(*b*) to clean the stables
(*c*) a place for horses
(*d*) stables for Augean horses

23. At the helm of
(*a*) at the helm of the ship
(*b*) at the main situation
(*c*) in the centre of a storm
(*d*) in the centre of the ship

24. An apple of discord
(*a*) the cause of a contention
(*b*) sour apple
(*c*) a quarrel
(*d*) a fight for an apple

25. Call one's shot
(*a*) make intentions clear
(*b*) call with a shot
(*c*) shoot at a call
(*d*) to show determination

26. Few and far between
(*a*) very small in number
(*b*) very small in distance
(*c*) very small in quantity
(*d*) between near and far

27. Force an issue
(*a*) make an issue
(*b*) force a decision
(*c*) solve an issue
(*d*) bring an issue

28. To lose face
(*a*) to look angry
(*b*) to be humiliated
(*c*) to be helpless
(*d*) to look vacant

29. Much ado about nothing
(*a*) to make a noise
(*b*) to make a fuss over small matter
(*c*) a play by Shaw
(*d*) talk about nothing

30. Make the best of a bad bargain
(a) to turn failure to best advantage
(b) to make a bad bargain
(c) to make the best bargain
(d) to make a bargain

31. Chapter and verse for a thing
(a) to produce proof
(b) to praise a thing
(c) to make publicity
(d) to attach value to a thing

32. Bid fair
(a) have a good prospect
(b) to be just
(c) try in a fair manner
(d) fair effort

33. Talk shop
(a) talk about shop
(b) talk in shop
(c) talk business
(d) talk to the point

34. Tread on one's toes
(a) to give offence
(b) walk on toes
(c) tread with toes
(d) flatter someone

35. Carry the can
(a) accept the blame
(b) get into trouble
(c) face the repercussions
(d) share the responsibility

36. Take time by the forelock
(a) forecast on event
(b) forecast time
(c) talk one's own time
(d) prepare for action before time

37. All agog
(a) all happy
(b) rife with rumours
(c) restless
(d) playful

38. Toe the line
(a) mark the line
(b) cross the line
(c) hit on the toe
(d) follow others

39. Throw up one's cards
(a) accept defeat
(b) spoil the card's game
(c) throw cards in the air
(d) throw away the game

40. Turn tail
(a) run like a coward
(b) one who changes ideas
(c) run with a tail
(d) run at the end

Work Book Exercise B

Directions *For each of the following sentences four alternatives are given. You are required to choose the correct meaning of the Idioms given in* **bold** *in the sentences.*

1. We should give a **wide berth** to bad characters.
(*a*) keep away from
(*b*) publicly condemn
(*c*) give publicity to
(*d*) not sympathise with

2. Sumit had to look **high and low** before he could find his scooter key.
(*a*) nowhere (*b*) always
(*c*) everywhere (*d*) somewhere

3. You may *rush from* **pillar to post**, but you stand no chance of getting what you want without a bribe.
(*a*) be very busy
(*b*) rush in all directions and suffer much harassment.
(*c*) go to all post offices.
(*d*) go to many offices and post letters.

4. At a party, he is always in **high spirits**.
(*a*) talkative (*b*) cheerful (*c*) drunk (*d*) uncontrollable

5. She rejected his proposal of marriage **point blank**.
(*a*) directly (*b*) pointedly (*c*) absurdly (*d*) briefly

6. We should guard against our **green-eyed** friends.
(*a*) rich (*b*) jealous
(*c*) handsome (*d*) enthusiastic

7. It was clearly a case of the **pot calling the kettle black** when Jagjit said that Ramu was a thief.
(*a*) Someone criticizing another for a fault which he himself has.
(*b*) A person accusing another of being black.
(*c*) A person blaming another for something, he has not done.
(*d*) Both are guilty of the same mistake.

8. The sight of the accident made my **flesh creep**.
(*a*) worried me (*b*) frightened me
(*c*) confused me (*d*) drew my attention

9. He is **a queer fish**. I have failed to understand him.
(*a*) funny person (*b*) sensitive person
(*c*) strange person (*d*) quarrelsome person

10. The involvement of teachers in the scheme of education proved to be a **mare's nest**.
(*a*) a false invention (*b*) a noble thing
(*c*) a successful (*d*) a timely sleep

11. Chandu used very ugly words against his kind uncle; he **threw down the gauntlet** before him.
(*a*) abused and insulted (*b*) threw the challenge
(*c*) behaved as an important person (*d*) put conditions

12. The present undergraduate syllabus leaves very little **elbow room** for teachers to be innovative.
(*a*) room for elbow (*b*) space
(*c*) freedom (*d*) ground

Work Book Exercise C

Directions *For each of the following sentences four alternatives are given. You are required to choose the correct meaning of the Idioms given in* **bold** *in the sentences.*

1. Komal was left ***high and dry*** by her friends when she lost all her money.
(*a*) isolated (*b*) rejected
(*c*) wounded (*d*) depressed

2. The party stalwarts have advised the president to take it **lying down** for a while.
(*a*) to show no reaction (*b*) to take rest
(*c*) to be on the defensive (*d*) to be cautious

3. A movement for the world unity is **in the offing**.
(*a*) at the end (*b*) about to start
(*c*) on decline (*d*) in the air

4. Sita is not **cut out** for this kind of work.
(*a*) trained (*b*) suitable
(*c*) recommended (*d*) considered

5. His most trusted friend proved to be **a snake in the grass.**
(*a*) cowardly and brutal (*b*) an unreliable and deceitful person
(*c*) a hidden enemy (*d*) low and mean

6. The politician was able to sway the mob with **his gift of the gab**.
(*a*) fluency of speech (*b*) flattering words
(*c*) abundance of promises (*d*) political foresight

7. The speaker gave a **bird's eye view** of the political conditions in the country.
(*a*) a detailed presentation (*b*) a biased view
(*c*) a general view (*d*) a personal view

8. After **sowing his wild oats** Ram has decided to stick to the straight and narrow path in future.
(*a*) becoming a gardener
(*b*) becoming a farmer
(*c*) a period of wildness
(*d*) going through a period of irresponsible pleasure seeking

9. When he tells stories about himself, he **is inspired to draw the long bow**.
(*a*) get excited (*b*) exaggerate
(*c*) get emotional (*d*) underrate

10. He was a king who ruled his subjects **with a high hand**.
(*a*) oppressively (*b*) kindly
(*c*) conveniently (*d*) sympathetically

11. He **did me a good turn** by recommending me for the post of Vice-president.
(*a*) became suddenly good
(*b*) improved my prospects
(*c*) did an act of kindness
(*d*) returned my kindness

12. Being an introvert, he will only **eat his heart out**.
(*a*) eat too much (*b*) keep brooding
(*c*) invite trouble (*d*) suffer silently

Work Book Exercise D

Directions *For each of the following sentences four alternatives are given. You are required to choose the correct meaning of the Idioms given in* **bold** *in the sentences.*

1. Caesar was **done to death** by the conspirators.
(*a*) attacked (*b*) removed
(*c*) eliminated (*d*) murdered

2. His boss was always **breathing down** his neck.
(*a*) abusing and ill-treating him (*b*) watching all his actions closely
(*c*) shouting loudly at him (*d*) giving him strenuous work

3. He is **not worth his salt** if he fails at this juncture.
(*a*) quite worthless (*b*) very proud of himself
(*c*) quite depressed (*d*) very strange

4. After having finished the last project, I find myself at **a loose end.**
(*a*) happy (*b*) on vacation
(*c*) free of troubles (*d*) with nothing to do

5. It was such a strange affair that I would not make **head or tail of it**.
(*a*) face it (*b*) tolerate it
(*c*) remember (*d*) understand it

6. She exhibited remarkable **sangfroid** during the crisis.
(*a*) temper (*b*) irritation
(*c*) composure (*d*) anger

7. My father **strained every nerve** to enable me to get settled in life.
(*a*) worked very hard (*b*) spent a large amount
(*c*) tried all tricks (*d*) bribed several persons

8. Though she herself was **as ugly as sin**, she had the audacity to criticise the looks of her companion.
(*a*) sinfully ugly (*b*) very ugly
(*c*) exceptionally ugly (*d*) quite ugly

9. He has become **a dab hand at** Internet and software.
(*a*) always telling non-sense (*b*) hearing a fake intentiion
(*c*) ready to listen to other people's (*d*) skilled in particular area

10. He does not like to be friendly with Sarla. He always gives **her a cold shoulder**.
(*a*) pushes her with his shoulder wherever they meet
(*b*) insult her in the presence of others
(*c*) tries to be unfriendly by taking no notice of her
(*d*) argues with her on any issue

11. It was he who **put a spoke in my wheel.**
(*a*) tried to cause an accident (*b*) helped in the execution of the plan
(*c*) thwarted the execution of the plan (*d*) destroyed the plan

12. The captain played with determination because the honour of the team was **at stake.**
(*a*) very tense (*b*) at the top
(*c*) in danger (*d*) appropriate

13. His promotion is **on the cards**.
(*a*) due (*b*) evident
(*c*) certain (*d*) probable

Revision Exercise

Directions (Q.Nos. 1-20) *In these questions, four alternatives are given for the idiom/phrase given in* **bold** *in the sentence. Choose the alternative which best expresses the meaning of the idiom/phrase.*

1. He **put across** his ideas to the minister.
(a) made available (b) effectively conveyed
(c) strongly expressed (d) laid aside

2. George and I are neighbours, but we don't **see eye to eye** with each other.
(a) like (b) interact
(c) agree (d) fight

3. People were **dropping like flies** in the intense heat.
(a) collapsing in large numbers
(b) getting infected with many diseases
(c) taking leave in large numbers
(d) sitting down in the shade

4. The officer **called for** an explanation form the cashier for the shortage of cash.
(a) asked (b) begged
(c) served a notice (d) demanded

5. The actress **took cue from** her brother and became successful.
(a) some help (b) a hint
(c) some money (d) learnt acting

6. We wanted the gift to be a surprise for my mother, but my sister **gave the game away**.
(a) lost the game (b) gave out the secret
(c) gave away the gift (d) withdrew from the plan

7. Let us have a **heart to heart talk** to solve this problem.
(a) good talk (b) emotional talk
(c) frank talk (d) loving talk

8. His speech **fell short** on the audience.
(a) had no effect (b) moved the audience
(c) impressed the audience (d) was quite short

9. As a businessman, my father always maintained that his transactions constituted **an open book**.
(a) an account book always open (b) a book of open confessions
(c) an opening for new ventures (d) straight-forward and honest dealings

10. The project advanced by **leaps and bounds**.
(a) rapidly (b) slowly
(c) sharply (d) simply

11. She is **too fond of her own voice**.
(a) loves singing (b) very selfish
(c) does not listen properly to anyone else (d) very talkative

12. Indian Police is, on the whole, **high handed** in dealing with citizens.
(a) kind (b) overbearing
(c) prompt (d) adept

13. **Birds of the same feather**
(a) persons of same caste (b) persons of same colour
(c) birds with same type of feather (d) persons of same character

14. To call a spade a spade
(a) to be frank (b) to be sly
(c) to be rude (d) to be diplomatic

15. A white elephant
(a) an extinct species of elephant found in Burma
(b) a report by the government to give information
(c) huge and colossal waste of human energy
(d) costly and troublesome possession useless to its owner

16. To miss the bus
(a) to miss, the bus that one regularly takes
(b) to miss an opportunity
(c) to have something to fall back upon
(d) to find fault with others

17. To look down one's nose
(a) to show anger (b) to retaliate
(c) to insult in the presence of others (d) to regard with contempt

18. To shed crocodile tears
(a) to weep profusely (b) to pretend grief
(c) to grieve seriously (d) to mock something

19. By putting two and two together
(a) to mix several things (b) to make an arithmetical calcualtion
(c) to keep people in pairs (d) to deduce from given facts

20. To go scot-free
(a) to walk like a native of Scotland (b) to get something free
(c) to escape without punishment (d) to save tax

Directions (Q.Nos. 21-33) *In these questions, four alternatives are given for the idiom/ phrase given below. Choose the alternative which, best expresses the meaning of the idiom/phrase.*

21. To bring to light
(a) to reveal (b) to conceal
(c) to provide luminescence (d) to appeal

22. To hit the jackpot
(a) to gamble (b) to get an unexpected victory
(c) win a lot of money (d) to make money quickly

23. To burn the candle at both ends
(a) to spend cautiously (b) to be stingy
(c) to be extravagant (d) to survive with difficulty

24. Status quo
(a) unchanged position (b) excellent place
(c) unbreakable statue (d) long queue

25. By fair means or foul
(a) without using common sense (b) without difficulty
(c) in any way honest or dishonest (d) having been instigated

26. At one's beck and call
(a) to attend a call (b) to be helped by someone
(c) to be useful to someone (d) to be dominated by someone

27. To explore every avenue
(*a*) to search all streets
(*b*) to scout the wilderness
(*c*) to find an adventure
(*d*) to try every opportunity

28. A red letter day
(*a*) a dangerous day in one's life
(*b*) a sorrowful day in one's life
(*c*) an important or joyful occasion in one's life
(*d*) both a dangerous and sorrowful day in one's life

29. On the spur of the moment
(*a*) to act at once
(*b*) to ride a horse in a race
(*c*) to act deliberately
(*d*) to act at the appointed time

30. Build castles in the air
(*a*) waste time
(*b*) daydream
(*c*) build houses
(*d*) work hard

31. Sought after
(*a*) highly paid
(*b*) pursued by
(*c*) in great demand
(*d*) with great talent

32. To hit below the belt
(*a*) to punish
(*b*) to tie with a belt
(*c*) to hit with a belt
(*d*) to attack unfairly

33. Pot-luck dinner
(*a*) dinner where everybody brings something to eat
(*b*) dinner where everybody pays for his food
(*c*) dinner where only soup is served
(*d*) dinner where people eat and play games of the same time.

Directions (Q.Nos. 34-39) *In these questions, four alternatives are given for the idiom/ phrase given in* **bold** *in the sentence. Choose the alternative, which best expresses the meaning of the idiom/phrase.*

34. I had to **pull strings** to put up a good show.
(*a*) play music
(*b*) use personal influence
(*c*) use the instrument
(*d*) play a song

35. You can easily overcome this situation if you **keep your head clear.**
(*a*) keep faith in
(*b*) remain calm
(*c*) believe in
(*d*) trust the others

36. It is clear that the ideas of both reformers **ran in the same groove**.
(*a*) promoted each other
(*b*) clashed with each other
(*c*) moved in harmony
(*d*) moved in different directions

37. There was a job for me to **cut my teeth on**.
(*a*) to gain experience
(*b*) to try
(*c*) to sharpen my wits
(*d*) to earn a decent salary

38. The **carrot and stick** policy pays dividends in every organisation.
(*a*) fair and foul
(*b*) continuous vigilance
(*c*) democratic
(*d*) reward and punishment

39. Unless you **grease his palms,** he will not do your work.
(*a*) talk to him
(*b*) flatter him
(*c*) beat him
(*d*) bribe him

Directions (Q.Nos. 40-49) *Four alternatives are given for the meaning of the given Idiom/Phrase given below. Choose the alternative which best expresses the meaning of the Idiom/Phrase .*

40. To take to heart
(*a*) to be encouraged (*b*) to grieve over
(*c*) to like (*d*) to hate

41. Yeoman's service
(*a*) medical help (*b*) excellent work
(*c*) social work (*d*) hard work

42. To face the music
(*a*) to enjoy a musical recital (*b*) to bear the consequences
(*c*) to live in a pleasant atmosphere (*d*) to have a difficult time

43. To put up with
(*a*) to accommodate (*b*) to adjust (*c*) to understand (*d*) to tolerate

44. To call it a day
(*a*) to conclude proceedings (*b*) to initiate proceedings
(*c*) to work through the day (*d*) None of these

45. A damp squib
(*a*) rainy weather (*b*) a disappointing result
(*c*) a skirt in a laundry (*d*) None of these

46. In cold blood
(*a*) angrily (*b*) deliberately (*c*) excitedly (*d*) slowly

47. To take someone for a ride
(*a*) to give a ride to someone (*b*) to deceive someone
(*c*) to be indifferent (*d*) to disclose a secret

48. To move heaven and earth
(*a*) to cause an earthquake (*b*) to try everything possible
(*c*) to pray to all Gods (*d*) to travel in a rocket

49. To smell a rat
(*a*) to smell foul (*b*) to see a rat
(*c*) to chase a rat (*d*) to be suspicious

Directions (Q.Nos. 50-64) *In these questions, four alternatives are given for the Idiom/Phrase given in* ***bold*** *in the sentence. Choose the alternative which best expresses the meaning of the Idiom/Phrase.*

50. His **utopian idea** was entertaining but not acceptable.
(*a*) unworthy idea (*b*) imaginary idea
(*c*) classic idea (*d*) intelligent idea

51. He has the habit of **getting into a row** over trivial matters.
(*a*) getting a right path (*b*) giving unwanted advice
(*c*) seeking the help (*d*) picking up a fight

52. A small fry
(*a*) unimportant (*b*) weak (*c*) little (*d*) important

53. Do not **lose your head** in public.
(*a*) get angry (*b*) get a headache
(*c*) be embarrassed (*d*) shave your hair

54. A good sportsman cannot afford to have a **fit of the blues** before the game.
(*a*) steroids or drugs (*b*) depression
(*c*) stimulants (*d*) entertainment

55. The project is carried over to this year and we need **to keep the ball rolling**.
(*a*) to continue the work (*b*) more information
(*c*) to do better (*d*) new strategies

56. The host team **bore the palm** in the league matches.
(*a*) played quite well (*b*) was victorious
(*c*) was defeated (*d*) played a very boring match

57. Just **keep your wig on.** Everything will be alright.
(*a*) hold on to your wig, so it won't fall off (*b*) get another haircut
(*c*) calm down (*d*) take off your wig

58. Parents pay **through their nose** for their children's education.
(*a*) by taking loans (*b*) an extremely high price
(*c*) grudgingly (*d*) willingly

59. Monica's habit of **picking holes** in every relationship is very irksome.
(*a*) admiring people (*b*) finding fault
(*c*) criticizing people (*d*) arguing with people

60. She didn't realize that the clever salesman was **taking her for a ride.**
(*a*) forcing her to go with him. (*b*) trying to trick her
(*c*) taking her in a car (*d*) pulling her along

61. I **jumped out of my skin** when the explosion happened
(*a*) was angry (*b*) was in panic
(*c*) was excited (*d*) was nervous

62. There is no point in discussing the new project with him as he always **pours cold water on** and new ideas.
(*a*) postpones (*b*) puts off (*c*) dislikes (*d*) disapproves of

63. His speech has **taken the wind out of my sails.**
(*a*) made me remember my past (*b*) made my words or actions ineffective
(*c*) made me depressed (*d*) made me think of the future

64. Regardless of what her parents said, she wanted to **let her hair down** that night.
(*a*) work till late (*b*) really enjoy (*c*) wash her hair (*d*) comb her hair

Directions (Q.Nos. 65-69) *In the following questions, four alternatives are given for the Idiom/Phrase given in* **bold** *in the sentence. Choose the alternative which best expresses the meaning of the Idiom/Phrase.*

65. What **egged you on** to become a social worker?
(*a*) urged (*b*) dampened (*c*) hindered (*d*) discouraged

66. Many politicians in India are **not fit to hold a candle** to Mahatma Gandhi.
(*a*) superior (*b*) equal (*c*) inferior (*d*) indifferent

67. She must **be paying through the nose** for the face left.
(*a*) paying less than necessary (*b*) paying too much
(*c*) paying the right amount (*d*) paying reluctantly

68. He is **putting the cart before the horse** by purchasing furniture before buying a house.
(*a*) doing a thing in the wrong way (*b*) doing a thing in the right way
(*c*) committing a great crime (*d*) doing things meticulously.

69. **Casting pearls before swine**
(*a*) speaking nice words and convincing them
(*b*) offering good things to underserving people
(*c*) uplifting the needy for their welfare
(*d*) doing worthwhile things to unknown people

Exam Practice

Directions (Q. Nos. 1-10) *Given below are some idioms/phrases followed by four alternative meanings to each. Choose the response (a), (b), (c) or (d) which is the most appropriate meaning.*

1. Be over the hill **NDA 2019**
(a) To be on a mountain top (b) To travel in the jungle
(c) To be too old to do things (d) To do something in the most complete way

2. Bite your tongue **NDA 2019**
(a) To stop yourself from saying something because it would be better not to
(b) To bite off your tongue while eating
(c) To feel sorry
(d) To ask someone something that you want

3. Turn a blind eye **NDA 2019**
(a) To run away
(b) To begin to be have in a more positive manner
(c) To change a situation
(d) To choose to ignore behaviour that you know is wrong

4. Yellow journalism **NDA 2019**
(a) Paid storytelling
(b) Government reports published on yellow coloured papers
(c) Writings in newspapers that try to influence people's opinion by using strong language and false information
(d) Journalism which agrees completely with the policies of the government and capitalists

5. To be in seventh heaven **NDA 2019**
(a) To fly in the air (b) To be extremely happy
(c) To be completely alone
(d) To visit a place which is in the lit of the seven wonders of the world.

6. A dark horse **NDA 2019**
(a) A black coloured horse
(b) A person who wins a race or competition although no one expected him to
(c) A person who keeps secrets
(d) An ignorant person

7. A show-stopper **NDA 2019**
(a) Someone who stops the show (b) Someone who organises the show
(c) A performance that is extremely good (d) A fashionable person

8. A jack of all trades **NDA 2019**
(a) Someone who has many skills (b) A confident and not very serious young man
(c) Someone who has hit the jackpot (d) A great businessman

9. Fight tooth and nail **NDA 2019**
(a) To quarrel with someone (b) To attack someone with a lot of force
(c) To try hard to prevent something from happening
(d) To try very hard to achieve something

10. Fair and square **NDA 2019**
(a) In an honest way (b) In a critical way
(c) Neither very good nor very bad (d) In a foolish way

Directions (Q. Nos. 11-24) *Given below are some idioms/phrases followed by four alternative meanings to each. Choose the response (a), (b), (c) or (d) which is the most appropriate meaning.*

CDS 2019

11. Dirt cheap
(a) Extremely cheap
(b) Extremely costly
(c) Very cheap person
(d) Very cheap item

12. A shrinking violet
(a) A lean person
(b) A shy person
(c) A happy person
(d) A sad person

13. Gordian knot
(a) Undoable job
(b) A difficult problem
(c) A different problem
(d) Doable job

14. Fall in heap
(a) To be at the mercy of someone else
(b) To be thinking about someone
(c) To lose control of one's own feelings
(d) To be in control of one's own feelings

15. Have a conniption fit
(a) To be very angry
(b) To be very happy
(c) To be very sad
(d) To be a jubilant person

16. Catch 22 situation **CGL 2017**
(a) A paradoxical situation from which an individual cannot escape
(b) Close to winning line
(c) Able to achieve the target
(d) Grabbing the oppartunity on time

17. Hand in glove
(a) Working separately
(b) Working together
(c) Working for someone
(d) Not willing to work

18. Nip in the bud
(a) Prevent a small problem before it becomes severe
(b) Prevent the big problems
(c) Make it severe
(d) Beating the problem

19. Like a shag on a rock
(a) Completely alone
(b) Completely idle
(c) Completely silence
(d) Completely happy

20. Jog someone's memory **CGL 2017**
(a) An important piece of news
(b) To cause someone to remember something
(c) An important thing for life
(d) Describe someone

21. A match made in heaven
(a) A marriage that is solemnised formally
(b) A marriage that is unsuccessful
(c) A marriage that is likely to be happy and successful
(d) A marriage of convenience

22. A culture vulture
(a) Someone who is very keen to experience art and literature
(b) Someone who wants to defend ancient culture
(c) Someone who is ashamed of one's own culture
(d) Someone who looks at her/his culture critically

23. A death blow
(a) To be nearly dead
(b) To be deeply afraid of death
(c) To beat someone to death
(d) An action or event which causes something to an end or fail

24. The jewel in the crown
(a) Someone who has many skills
(b) Something that one wants
(c) The most valuable thing in a group of things
(d) The jewel in the crown of the king

Directions (Q. Nos. 25-32) *Given below are some idioms/phrases followed by four alternative meanings to each. Choose the response (a), (b), (c) or (d) which is the most appropriate expression and mark your response in the Answer Sheet accordingly.* **CDS 2020**

25. A paper tiger
(a) Person or organisation that appears powerful, but actually is not
(b) Person or organisation that acts like a tiger
(c) People who campaign for the protection of tigers
(d) A daredevil

26. Lily-livered
(a) Brave and courageous (b) Not brave
(c) Comical (d) Outrageous

27. Eat like a bird
(a) Eat fast (b) Eat very little
(c) Eat a lot (d) Pretending to be eating

28. The dog days
(a) Days celebrating dogs (b) The bitter days
(c) The hottest days (d) The coldest days

29. A banana republic
(a) A small or poor country with a weak government
(b) a small or poor country which produces banana
(c) A country which has been occupied by a big country
(d) A country without any government

30. The pros and cons
(a) The good and bad parts of a situation (b) Like and dislike of a situation
(c) A bad experience in an event (d) A good moment of an event

31. Prime the pump
(a) To do something in order to make something succeed
(b) To do good things to succeed in life
(c) To do something in order to get bad things done
(d) Asking people to do things to make something succeed

32. The green-eyed monster
(a) Feeling of being joyous (b) Feeling of being jealous
(c) Feeling bad about happenings (d) Feelings lucky about something

Directions (Q. Nos. 33 and 34) *Select the most appropriate meaning of the given idioms.* **SSC CGL 2020**

33. On shank's mare
(a) On a lion (b) On a bicycle (c) On foot (d) On an elephant

34. A snake in the grass

(a) A secret enemy (b) A good friend
(c) Difficult to find (d) A well-wisher
(e) emerge

Answers

Work Book Exercise A

1. (a)	2. (c)	3. (c)	4. (b)	5. (a)	6. (c)	7. (a)
8. (a)	9. (a)	10. (b)	11. (d)	12. (a)	13. (a)	14. (b)
15. (a)	16. (a)	17. (a)	18. (c)	19. (a)	20. (b)	21. (b)
22. (a)	23. (b)	24. (a)	25. (d)	26. (a)	27. (b)	28. (b)
29. (b)	30. (a)	31. (a)	32. (a)	33. (c)	34. (a)	35. (a)
36. (d)	37. (c)	38. (d)	39. (a)	40. (a)		

Work Book Exercise B

1. (a)	2. (c)	3. (b)	4. (b)	5. (a)	6. (b)	7. (a)
8. (b)	9. (c)	10. (a)	11. (b)	12. (c)		

Work Book Exercise C

1. (a)	2. (a)	3. (b)	4. (b)	5. (c)	6. (a)	7. (c)
8. (d)	9. (b)	10. (a)	11. (c)	12. (d)		

Work Book Exercise D

1. (d)	2. (b)	3. (a)	4. (d)	5. (d)	6. (c)	7. (a)
8. (c)	9. (d)	10. (c)	11. (c)	12. (c)	13. (c)	

Revision Exercise

1. (b)	2. (c)	3. (a)	4. (d)	5. (b)	6. (b)	7. (c)
8. (a)	9. (d)	10. (a)	11. (c)	12. (b)	13. (d)	14. (a)
15. (d)	16. (b)	17. (d)	18. (b)	19. (d)	20. (c)	21. (a)
22. (b)	23. (d)	24. (a)	25. (c)	26. (d)	27. (d)	28. (c)
29. (c)	30. (b)	31. (c)	32. (d)	33. (a)	34. (b)	35. (b)
36. (c)	37. (a)	38. (d)	39. (d)	40. (b)	41. (b)	42. (b)
43. (d)	44. (a)	45. (b)	46. (b)	47. (b)	48. (b)	49. (d)
50. (b)	51. (d)	52. (a)	53. (a)	54. (b)	55. (a)	56. (b)
57. (c)	58. (b)	59. (b)	60. (b)	61. (b)	62. (d)	63. (b)
64. (b)	65. (a)	66. (c)	67. (b)	68. (a)	69. (b)	

Exam Practice

1. (c)	2. (a)	3. (d)	4. (c)	5. (b)	6. (b)	7. (c)
8. (a)	9. (d)	10. (a)	11. (a)	12. (b)	13. (b)	14. (c)
15. (a)	16. (a)	17. (b)	18. (a)	19. (a)	20. (b)	21. (c)
22. (a)	23. (d)	24. (c)	25. (a)	26. (b)	27. (b)	28. (c)
29. (a)	30. (a)	31. (a)	32. (b)	33. (c)	34. (a)	

Unit VI

17

Spotting Errors (Miscellaneous)

Exercise A

Directions (Q. Nos 1-5) *Each sentence in this section has multiple parts. Find out the error part from the given options and indicate your response from the options (a), (b), (c) and (d) on the Answer Sheet.*

1. Another baffling change that I notice in him nowadays is that he avoids to speak to me.
(a) Another baffling change
(b) that I notice in him nowadays
(c) is that he avoids
(d) to speak to me

2. I asked him how could he go out if it started raining.
(a) I asked him
(b) how could he go
(c) out if
(d) it started raining

3. One of the state in which Satyagraha was offered was Rajkot, where he had spent his youth.
(a) One of the state
(b) in which satyagraha
(c) was offered was Rajkot,
(d) where he had spent his youth

4. Hardly the inspector had arrived there to investigate the crime when the house was set ablaze.
(a) Hardly the inspector had
(b) arrived there to investigate
(c) the crime when
(d) the house was set ablaze

5. Since his arrival at his native town he is trying to the best of his ability to spread education among the poor masses.
(a) Since his arrival at his
(b) native town he is trying
(c) to the best of his ability
(d) to spread education among the poor masses

Directions (Q. Nos 6-10) *Read each sentence to find out whether there is any gramatical error in it. The error, if any, will be in one part of the sentence. The alphabet corresponding to that part is your answer. If there is No error, the answer is (e). (Ignore errors of punctuation, if any)*

6. Needless to say (A)/ no sooner had all these large and rather expensive operations finished (B)/ when the main electricity was brought in (c)/ and the turbine became obsolete (D)/ No Error (E)
(a) A
(b) B
(c) C
(d) D
(e) E

7. He lay the watch (A)/ on the table (B)/ and then forgot all about it (C)/ when he went out (D)/ No error (E)
(a) A (b) B (c) C (d) D
(e) E

8. Although he draws a reasonably (A)/ good salary, he has (B)/ a large family to support, and he finds (C)/ difficult to make both ends meet (D)/ No error (E)
(a) A (b) B (c) C (d) D
(e) E

9. While it is apparent (A)/ that biotechnology offers (B)/ significant benefits, adequate attention (C)/ has not been focused to this vital area. (D)/ No error (E)
(a) B (b) A (c) D (d) C
(e) E

10. The reason for (A)/ his failure is (B)/ because he (C)/ did not work hard. (D)/ No error (E)
(a) E (b) D (c) C (d) B
(e) A

Direction (Q. Nos. 11-25) *Each sentence in this section has four underlined parts labelled as (a), (b) (c) and (d). Read each sentence to find out whether there is any error in any underlined part and indicate your response on the answer sheet against the corresponding letter. If you find 'No error' your response should be indicated as (d).*

11. We had to cancel our trip to Delhi (a) because when we reached the railway station, (b) the train left. (c) No error (d)

12. Many a student (a) has failed in the Mathematics test (b) but Dilip has scored 100 per cent. (c) No error (d)

13. The General with over 1000 officers and soldiers (a) have surrendered to the Indian (b) troops who are patrolling the valley. (c) No error (d)

14. If he wrote the examination faster (a) and had answered one more question (b) he would have scored better. (c) No error (d)

15. For decades (a) there have been (b) a debate on whether schizophrenia is a psychological condition. (c) No error (d)

16. Mohan is the one (a) who always finds (b) fault with whatever Ram does. (c) No error (d)

17. There is a need (a) to revising Government policies (b) on controlling unauthorized constructions. (c) No error (d)

18. We know where it begins (a) but we don't know (b) that where it ends. (c) No error (d)

19. The simplest method (a) of welding two pieces of metal together (b) in known as pressure welding. (c) No error (d)

20. One of the important benefits (a) of machine age (b) is that our standard of life has improved. (c) No error (d)

21. There is sense of urgency (a) in locating alternative sources of water (b) to augment the dwindling supply. (c) No error (d)

22. Although there is virtually no production in India (a) the 'Encyclopaedia Britannica' estimate (b) that India has perhaps the largest accumulated stocks of silver in the world. (c) No error (d)

23. Neither the severe earthquake (a) or the subsequent famine (b) could demoralize the people of the country. (c) No error (d)

24. As soon as I shall reach New Delhi (a) I shall send you the file (b) you have asked for. (c) No error (d)

25. All the furnitures have been (a) replaced by the owner of the house (b) before shifting. (c) No error (d)

Exercise B

Direction (Q. Nos. 1-5) *Read each sentence to find out whether there is any grammatical or idiomatic error in it. The error, if any, will be in one part of the sentence. The letter of that part is the answer.*

1. Beware of a fare weather friend who is neither a friend in need nor a friend indeed.
(a) Beware of a fare weather (b) friend who is
(c) neither a friend in need (d) nor a friend indeed

2. Copernicus proved that Earth moves round the Sun.
(a) Copernicus proved (b) that Earth
(c) moves round (d) the Sun

3. Seldom we have been treated in such a rude manner by a police personnel.
(a) Seldom we have been treated (b) in such a rude maner
(c) by the (d) police personnel

4. Some men are born great, some achieve greatness and some had greatness thrust on them.
(a) Some men are born great (b) some achieve greatness
(c) and some (d) had greatness thrust on them

5. The property was divided among the two sisters.
(a) The property (b) was divided
(c) among (d) the two sisters

Direction (Q. Nos. 6-10) *Read each sentence to find out whether their is any grammatical error in it. The error if any will be in one part of the sentence. The alphabet corresponding to that part is your answer. If there is 'No error' the answer is (e). (Ignore errors of Punctuation, if any)*

6. I am quite (A) / certain that the lady (B)/ is not only greedy (C)/ but miserly. (D)/ No Error (E)
(a) A (b) B (c) C (d) D
(e) E

7. There are a number of reasons (A)/ I do not like him (B)/ but his selfishness (C)/ is intolerable. (D)/ No error (E)
(a) A (b) B (c) C (d) D
(e) E

8. I have read an interesting book (A)/ yesterday and underlined (B)/ the new words (C)/ which are simple but effective. (D)/ No error (E)
(a) B (b) A (c) D (d) C
(e) E

9. He cannot be trusted (A)/ with important informations, (B)/ otherwise I would have (C)/ made him my assistant. (D)/ No error (E)
(a) E (b) C (c) A (d) B
(e) D

10. Neither praise (A)/ nor blame (B)/ seem to (C)/ affect him. (D)/ No Error (E)
(a) E (b) C (c) A (d) D
(e) B

Direction (Q. Nos. 11-25) *Each sentence in this section has four underlined parts labelled as (a), (b), (c) and (d). Read each sentence to find out whether there is any error in any underlined part and indicate your response on the answer sheet against the corresponding letter. If you find 'No error' your response should be indicated as (d).*

11. During the final minutes of the speech (a) the speaker requested to (b) the audience to have patience. (c) No error (d)

12. He is running temperature since last Friday (a) and doctors suspect (b) that he is down with typhoid. (c) No error (d)

13. Travel agents around the world have come to rely on computers (a) to book seats (b) in air flights or rooms in hotels, either today or a year from now. (c) No error (d)

14. She expressed her gratitudes (a) to all those (b) who had supported her. (c) No error (d)

15. When the meeting was over, (a) he was very tired (b) so that he went home immediately. (c) No error (d)

16. Modern man must pull himself off together (a) and act his part in life (b) as God's own most favourite creature. (c) No error (d)

17. There would be fewer follies, (a) and happiness and good feeling all round (b) if we applied the scientific attitude for all our affairs. (c) No error (d)

18. Heera told to the teacher (a) that she couldn't come for the rehearsals (b) the next day. (c) No error (d)

19. I am told that Anjali has been (a) suffering from fever (b) since ten days. (c) No error (d)

20. The armed forces have been working around the clock (a) to bring a semblance of (b) normality (c) in the flood affected areas. (d) No error (e)

21. Just when Alfred Nobel's discoveries were beginning to bring him rewards, (a) which were to make him one of the richest man of his day, (b) an anti-Nobel campaign was started in France. (c) No error (d)

22. This is the second communication we have sent (a) and we are much surprised (b) at receiving no answer. (c) No error (d)

23. Several guests noticed Mr. Sharma (a) falling back in his chair (b) and gasping for breath. (c) No error (d)

24. Long life is good (a) if one be happy (b) and has friends. (c) No error (d)

25. His assistants have (a) and are still doing (b) excellent work for the organization. (c) No error (d)

Exercise C

Directions (Q. Nos 1-5) *Each question in this section has a sentence with four parts labelled (a), (b), (c) and (d). Read each sentence to find out, whether there is any error in any part and indicate your response against the corresponding letter.*

1. None of the diplomats at the conference was able neither to comprehend or solve the problem.
(a) None of the diplomats (b) at the conference was
(c) able neither to comprehend (d) or solve the problem

2. Rather than go with Amit he decided to stay at home.
(a) Rather than go (b) with Amit
(c) he decides (d) to stay at home

3. Tushar always practice justice and cares for moral principles.
(a) Tushar always (b) practice justice
(c) and cares (d) for moral principles

4. The whole block of flats including two shops were destroyed in fire.
(a) The whole block (b) of flats including
(c) two shops (d) were destroyed in fire

5. She feels her troubles as much or even more than they.
(a) She feels her (b) troubles as much
(c) or even more (d) than they

Directions (Q. Nos 6-10) *Read each sentence to find out whether there is any grammatical error in it. The error if any, will be in one part of the sentence. The alphabet corresponding to that part is your answer. If there is 'No error' the answer is (e). (Ignore errors of punctuation, if any)*

6. Such rules (A)/ do not apply (B)/ to you (C)/ and I. (D)/ No error (E)
(a) A (b) B (c) C (d) D
(e) E

7. It is (A)/ a quarter (B)/ to ten (C)/ by my watch (D)/ No error (E)
(a) A (b) B (c) C (d) D
(e) E

8. I like (A)/ reading more (B)/ than to play (C)/ games (D)/ No error (E)
(a) A (b) B (c) C (d) D
(e) E

9. The sum (A)/ and substance (B)/ of this poem (C)/ is as follows (D)/ No error (E)
(a) B (b) A (c) D (d) E
(e) C

10. The teams (A)/ was now in (B)/ the field (C)/ and about to take their place (D)/ No error (E)
(a) E (b) D (c) C (d) B
(e) A

Direction (Q. Nos. 11-25) *Each sentence in this section has four underlined parts labelled as (a), (b), (c) and (d). Read each sentence to find out whether there is any error in any underlined part and indicate your response on the answer sheet against the corresponding letter. If you find 'No error' your response should be indicated as (d).*

11. Perhaps you know (a) that I have passed (b) the examination in 1990 (c). No error (d)

12. The teacher (a) kept advising us (b) to work hard. (c) No error (d)

13. At a very young age (a) he died with (b) heart disease. (c) No error (d)

14. The average age (a) at which people (b) begin to need (c) eye-glasses are increasing. (d) No error (e)

15. He is trying (a) to earn money (b) for myself (c) and him. (d) No error (e)

16. We Indians (a) don't understand that (b) driving vehicles (c) require care and skill. (d) No error (e)

17. Indians are (a) wedded in the (b) democratic way (c) of life in a peaceful manner. (d) No error (e)

18. The present President of (a) the United States (b) is thinking of (c) becoming the most supreme leader of the world. (d) No error (e)

19. Although the truck was (a) moving very fast (b) the driver stopped it (c) in a skilfully manner. (d) No error (e)

20. Although (a) he achieved great success (b) but he (c) could not win fame. (d) No error (e)

21. I pretended as if (a) interested in the conversation (b) but really it was very boring. (c) No error (d)

22. I don't usually like staying at hotels, (a) but last summer we spent a few days (b) at a very nice hotel by sea. (c) No error (d)

23. I will try to be on time (a) but do not worry (b) when I am late. (c) No error (d)

24. The teacher remarked that (a) they all had (b) done it very badly. (c) No error (d)

25. The train is supposed (a) to arrive at 10 a.m. yesterday (b) but it was an hour late. (c) No error (d)

Exercise D

Direction (Q. Nos. 1-5) *Read each sentence to find out whether there is any grammatical or idiomatic error in it. The error if any will be in one part of the sentence. The letter of that part is the answer.*

1. Ritu will be surprised as she hears the news.
(a) Ritu will (b) be surprised (c) as she (d) hears the news

2. I asked two persons the way to the station but none of them knew it.
(a) I asked two (b) persons the way
(c) to the station (d) but none of them knew it

3. Despite of a good monsoon this year, the production of food grains in the country did not go up.
   (a) Despite of a good monsoon this year (b) the production of
   (c) food grains in (d) the country did not go up

4. Anywhere in the world there is a conflict women and children suffer the most.
   (a) Anywhere in the world (b) there is a conflict
   (c) women and children (d) suffer the most

5. His friends feel that he will be suspended unless he does not report for duty immediately.
   (a) unless he does not (b) His friends feel that
   (c) report for duty immediately (d) he will be suspended

Directions (Q. Nos. 6-10) *Each sentence in this section has four parts labelled (a), (b), (c) and (d). Read each sentence to find out, whether there is any error in any part and indicate your response against the corresponding letter. If you find 'No error' your response should be indicated as (d).*

6. Today, the cost of living (a)/ is such higher that many people (b)/ find it difficult to keep their hearth burning (c)/ No error (d)

7. Rina was trying for admission in a medical college (a)/even though her parents (b)/ wanted her to take up architecture. (c)/ No error (d)

8. Yavanika is one of the latest (a)/ additions to good drama (b)/ which appeared in recent times (c)/ No error (d)

9. Children visiting the park (a)/ are amused by the monkeys (b)/ play in the cages (c)/ No error (d)

10. I am better acquainted (a)/ with the country (b) / than you (c)/ No error (d)

Direction (Q.Nos. 11-15) *Read each sentence to find out whether there is any grammatical error in it. The error if any will be in one part of the sentence. The alphabet corresponding to that part is your answer. If there is 'No error', the answer is (e) (Ignore errors of punctuation if any)*

11. Being occupied (A)/ with important matters (B)/ he had no leisure (C)/ to see us (D) / No error (E)
    (a) A (b) B (c) C (d) D
    (e) E

12. He was not promoted (A)/ to the rank of a Colonel (B)/ till for a few months (C)/ of his resignation (D)/ No error (E)
    (a) A (b) B (c) C (d) D
    (e) E

13. The man who is perpetually (A)/ hesitating in deciding which of (B)/ the two things he will do first (C)/ will ultimately do either (D)/ No error (E)
    (a) B (b) C (c) D (d) A
    (e) E

14. No other hill station is as (A)/ beautiful as Darjeeling (B)/ with its (C)/ scenic beauties (D)/ No error (E)
    (a) D (b) A (c) B (d) E
    (e) C

15. Being a well known neurologist, (A)/ Dr. Garg was invited (B)/ to deliver a lecture (c)/ on this topic. (D)/ No error (E)
    (a) A (b) B (c) C (d) D
    (e) E

Direction (Q. Nos. 16-25) *Each sentence in this section has four underlined parts labelled as (a), (b), (c) and (d). Read each sentence to find out whether there is any error in any underlined part and indicate your response on the answer sheet against the corresponding letter. If you find 'No error' your response should be indicated as (d).*

16. The chief idea of every common type (a) of traveller is to see as (b) many objects of interest as he possibly could. (c) No error (d)

17. He was hard down (a) for money and was (b) being harassed by his creditor. (c) No error (d)

18. If we really set to (a) we can get the whole house (b) cleaned in an afternoon. (c) No error (d)

19. The main reason (a) for his fiscal success (b) is that (c) he is hardworking. (d)

20. Since the two parties each won (a) the same number of seats, (b) the minority party holds the balance of power. (c) No error (d)

21. It's arrogant for you (a) to assume you'll (b) win every time. (c) No error (d)

22. We've paid for our travel and accommodation, (a) so we need only to take (b) some pocket-money with us. (c) No error (d)

23. There's no evidence to show (a) that information technology secrets are more (b) vulnerable in India than Britain or the U.S. (c) No error (d)

24. It is shameful that hunting (a) is still considered sport (b) by some unscrupulous people in the civilised world. (c) No error (d)

25. The vacancy was filled by Mr. Rao (a) who the manager (b) thought worthy of promotion. (c) No error (d)

Exercise E

Directions (Q Nos. 1-5) *Read each sentence to find out whether there is any grammatical or idiomatic error in it. The error if any will be in one part of the sentence. The letter of that part is the answer.*

1. She was taller than either of her five sisters.

(a) She was taller (b) than either
(c) of her (d) five sisters

2. Treasure Island is one of the best pirate stories that was ever written.
(a) Treasure Island is one (b) of the best
(c) pirate stories (d) that was ever written

3. The population of Kolkata is greater than in any town in England.
(a) The population of Kolkata (b) is greater than
(c) in any town (d) in England

4. He has a scheme of his own which he thinks more preferable to that of any person.
(a) He has a scheme of his own (b) which he thinks
(c) more preferable to (d) that of any person

5. Some people complain when they encounter a small misfortune in their thorough happy life.
(a) Some people compain (b) a small misfortune
(c) when they encounter (d) in their thorough happy life

Direction (Q. Nos 6-10) *Read each sentence to find out whether there is any grammatical error in it. The error, if any, will be in one part of the sentence. The alphabet corresponding to that part is your answer. If there is 'No error', the answer is (e). (Ignore errors of punctuation, if any).*

6. The new model (A)/ costs twice (B)/ more than (C)/ last year's model. (D)/ No error (E)
(a) A (b) B (c) C (d) D
(e) E

7. No student (A)/ is as (B)/ intelligent as (C)/ Ananya's son. (D)/ No error (E)
(a) A (b) B (c) C (d) D
(e) E

8. The boy's parents (A)/ pleaded with the Principal (B)/ that they were too (C)/ poor to pay his tuition fee. (D)/ No error (E)
(a) A (b) E (c) D (d) C
(e) B

9. The most important (A)/ feature of our product (B)/ are that (C)/ they are developed in house. (D)/ No error (E)
(a) A (b) C (c) E (d) B
(e) D

10. When I finished writing (A)/ the letter, I could not help (B)/ admiring myself to have (C)/ achieved the impossible. (D)/ No error (E)
(a) A (b) B (c) C (d) D
(e) E

Direction (Q. Nos.11-15) *Each question in this section has a sentence with four parts labelled (a), (b), (c) and (d). Read each sentence to find out whether there is any error in any part and indicate your response against the corresponding letter. If you find 'No error' your response should be indicated as (d).*

11. The principal along (a)/ with the (b)/ students have gone to Ladakh. (c)/ No error (d)

12. When you have gone (a)/ through my book (b)/ give the same to me. (c)/ No error (d)

13. He said a number of lies (a)/ and then went without (b)/ saying me goodbye. (c)/ No error (d)

14. Not only we saw (a)/ the Education Minister but (b)/ also the Chief Minister. (c)/ No error (d)

15. I came directly (a)/ to my residence (b)/ from the airport (c)/ No error (d)

Direction (Q. Nos. 16-25) *Each question in this section has a sentence with four underlined parts labelled as (a), (b), (c) and (d). Read each sentence to find out whether there is any error in any underlined part and indicate your response on the answer sheet against the corresponding letter. If you find 'No error' your response should be indicated as (d).*

16. I signed on the receipt (a) in the morning but the pay (b) has not been disbursed to me. (c) No error (d)

17. This is the same story (a) which I heard (b) from him yesterday. (c) No error (d)

18. What to speak of (a) food even water (b) was not available. (c) No error (d)

19. It was difficult to get out (a) because the street was full of people (b) from one end to another. (c) No error (d)

20. He gave such a long speech (a) but everybody (b) felt bored. (c) No error (d)

21. She does not hardly (a) know what (b) happened yesterday. (c) No error (d)

22. In my opinion (a) a pencil is always (b) more preferable to a pen. (c) No error (d)

23. The salesman tried (a) to mislead me (b) with a talk of amazing savings on heating bills. (c) No error (d)

24. He is well up (a) these days despite (b) having ill health (c) No error (d)

25. He regarded his marriage (a) as a mean to an end; (b) he just wanted his wife's wealth. (c) No error (d)

Exercise F

Direction (Q. Nos 1-5) *Each question in this section has a sentence with four parts labelled (a), (b), (c) and (d). Read each sentence to find out whether there is any error in any part and indicate your response against the corresponding letter. If you find 'No error' your response should be indicated as (d).*

1. Their offspring (a)/ are all (b)/ very inquisitive. (c)/ No error (d)

2. Their distress had (a)/ no affect on him (b)/ as he was determined to have his pound of flesh. (c)/ No error (d)

3. Today should (b)/ be saluted for the (b)/ beginning of a new era. (c)/ No error (d)

4. Such considerations are (a)/ secondary with our main aim (b)/ of improving efficiency. (c)/ No error (d)

5. Ostensibly he was on a business trip (a)/ but he spent (b)/ most of time on the beach. (c)/ No error (d)

Direction (Q.Nos 6-10) *Read each sentence to find out whether there is any grammatical error in it. The error if any will be in one part of the sentence. The alphabet corresponding to that part is your answer. If there is 'No error', the answer is (e) (Ignore errors of punctuation, if any)*

6. I can't do (A)/ the fourth and fifth questions (B)/ but I have done (C)/ all the others (D)/ No error (E)
(a) A (b) B (c) C (d) D
(e) E

7. After a year without defeat, (A)/ the team now reigns (B)/ over supreme as (C)/ the finest in the country. (D)/ No error (E)
(a) A (b) E (c) D (d) B
(e) C

8. The question of (A)/ finance is subsidiary to (B)/ the question whether (C)/ the project will be approved. (D)/ No error (E)
(a) A (b) E (c) D (d) C
(e) B

9. They've surcharged us (A)/ 10 per cent on the price (B)/ of the holiday because of (C)/ a rise of air fares. (D)/ No error (E)
(a) A (b) B (c) C (d) D
(e) E

10. She's all the sweetness and lightness (A)/ provided you're (B)/ doing what (C)/ she wants. (D)/ No Error (E)
(a) E (b) D (c) C (d) B
(e) A

Direction (Q.Nos 11-15) *Read each sentence to find out whether there is any grammatical or idiomatic error in it. The error if any will be in one part of the sentence. The letter of that part is the answer.*

11. Unemployment has reached a level that would have been not thinkable two years ago.
(a) Unemployment has reached (b) a level that
(c) would have been not (d) thinkable two years ago

12. The smell of cooking told them there was a meal in the offing
(a) of cooking (b) told them there
(c) was a meal in the offing (d) The smell

13. I told him outrightly what I thought of his behaviour.
(a) I told him (b) what I thought
(c) outrightly (d) of his behaviour

14. You may be a bit upset, but it's really nothing else than unreasonable anxiety.
(a) You may be a bit upset, (b) nothing else than
(c) unreasonable anxiety (d) but it's really

15. She would resign sooner then take part in such dishonest business deals.
(a) business deals (b) She would resign
(c) take part in such dishonest (d) sooner then

Direction (Q. Nos. 16-25) *Each question in this section has a sentence with four underlined parts labelled as (a), (b), (c) and (d). Read each sentence to find out whether there is any error in any underlined part and indicate your response on the answer sheet against the corresponding letter. If you find 'No error' your response should be indicated as (d).*

16. Don't apply for that job: (a) you're in danger of (b) over-reaching yourself. (c) No error (d)

17. Weather conditions were bad enough (a) even to give a pause to (b) the most experienced climbers. (c) No error (d)

18. We had a lot of difficulty (a) to find (b) the house. (c) No error (d)

19. Patience as well as perseverance (a) are necessary (b) for success. (c) No error (d)

20. The passer-by told us (a) where was the marriage hall (b) and even led us to it. (c) No error (d)

21. The increase in consumption is directly (a) proportional to the increase (b) in income. (c) No error (d)

22. In Singapore (a) my brother-in-law with his wife (b) were present at the function. (c) No error (d)

23. Scarcely had (a) I arrived than (b) the train left. (c) No error (d)

24. The reason why (a) he was rejected (b) was because he was too young. (c) No error (d)

25. Teachers of various schools (a) met to discuss about (b) how to improve the standard of English. (c) No error (d)

Exercise G

Direction (Q. Nos. 1-10) *Each question in this section has a sentence with four underlined parts labelled as (a), (b), (c) and (d). Read each sentence to find out whether there is any error in any underlined part and indicate your response on the answer sheet against the corresponding letter. If you find 'No error' your response should be indicated as (d).*

1. His tradition-bound attitude (a) was a constant source of dissatisfaction (b) among the younger members of the family. (c) No error (d)

2. The two first to arrive (a) were the lucky recipients (b) of a surprise gift. (c) No error (d)

3. Adults suffering chicken pox (a) can develop (b) all kinds of complications. (c) No error (d)

4. The well-known pianist (a) had to practice for several hours a day (b) even after he rose to fame. (c) No error (d)

5. The Prime Minister was asked (a) to write a forward (b) to the book. (c) No error (d)

6. I must complement you (a) on your good manners (b) and your impeccable behaviour. (c) No error (d)

7. The young men from Japan (a) found the assent of the mountain (b) hard going. (c) No error (d)

8. Even today (a) it is incredulous to think (b) that men have walked on the moon. (c) No error (d)

9. The firemen wore (a) inflammable clothing (b) for protection. (c) No error (d)

10. Beside food (a) the pilgrims carried (b) some medicines. (c) No error (d)

Direction (Q. Nos 11-15) *Read each sentence to find out whether there is any grammatical or idiomatic error in it. The error if any will be in one part of the sentence. The letter of that part is the answer.*

11. The sweets were shared between the four girls.
(a) The sweets
(b) were shared
(c) between
(d) the four girls

12. The long distance train which met with an accident was carrying some army personal.
(a) The long distance train
(b) which met with an
(c) accident was carrying
(d) some army personal

13. I have seen her only once but I am liking her a lot.
(a) I have seen
(b) but I am liking
(c) her a lot
(d) her only once

14. I told Shweta that we missed him very much at the party.
(a) at the party
(b) I told Shweta
(c) him very much
(d) that we missed

15. The greatest merit of democracy is that everyone feels free and can pursues his/her interest.
(a) The greatest merit of
(b) democracy is that
(c) everyone feels free and
(d) can pursues his/her interest

Direction (Q. Nos. 16-20) *Read each sentence to find out whether there is any grammatical error in it. The error if any will be in one part of the sentence. The alphabet corresponding to that part is your answer. If there is 'No error', the answer is (e) (Ignore errors of punctuation, if any)*

16. Two hours have (A)/ passed since he (B)/ have fallen (C)/ asleep. (D)/ No Error (E)
(a) A (b) B (c) C (d) D
(e) E

17. Having broken down (A)/ the driver sent (B)/ the car (C)/ to the garrage. (D)/ No Error (E)
(a) A (b) E (c) D (d) B
(e) C

18. Arnab is one of (A)/ those journalists (B)/ who has won acclaim (C)/ the world over. (D)/ No Error (E)
(a) A (b) E (c) B (d) C
(e) D

19. The mason will (A)/ not do the work (B)/ except give (C)/ the order. (D)/ No Error (E)
(a) A (b) B (c) C (d) D
(e) E

20. When students are ill (A)/ they find that (B)/ they have a lot of work (C)/ to catch up when they return. (D)/ No Error (E)
(a) E (b) D (c) C (d) A
(e) B

Direction (Q. Nos 21-25) *Each question in this section has a sentence with four parts labelled (a), (b), (c) and (d). Read each sentence to find out, whether there is any error in any part and indicate your response against the corresponding letter. If you find 'No error', your response should be indicated as (d).*

21. Learning many languages (a)/ promotes linguistic, cultural and social harmonies (b)/ among people speaking different languages. (c)/ No error (d)

22. All stake holders of education (a)/ have the right to ask for accountability (b)/ in every aspects of its implementation (c)/ No error (d)

23. Prabhat asked me (a)/ if I was interested (b)/ to joining the group for the volunteering activities. (c)/ No error (d)

24. He has been (a)/ one of the most revered (b)/ member of the choir. (c)/ No error (d)

25. After making me wait for two agonising hours (a)/ the great man called me in (b)/ and asked me what do I want. (c)/ No error (d)

Exercise H

Direction (Q. Nos. 1-10) *Each question in this section has a sentence with four underlined parts labelled as (a), (b), (c) and (d). Read each sentence to find out whether there is any error in any underlined part and indicate your response on the answer sheet against the corresponding letter. If you find 'No error' your response should be indicated as (d).*

1. The ebb and flow of the tides / are / now understood. / No error
a b c d

2. The green paint on the wall / provides a suitable contrast
a b
with the yellow doors. / No error
c d

3. Either of the roads / lead / to the park. / No error
a b c d

4. I went to the temple / with my parents, / my aunts and my cousins. / No error
a b c d

5. I have passed / the examination / two years ago. / No error
a b c d

6. The earth moves / round the sun, / Isn't it? / No error
a b c d

7. Unless you do not give / the keys of the safe / you will be shot. / No error
a b c d

8. Of the billions of stars in the galaxy, / how much are / suitable for life. / No error
a b c d

9. The value of the dollar (a) declines as the rate (b) of inflation raises. (c) No error (d)

10. One of my desires (a) are to become (b) a doctor. (c) No error (d)

Direction (Q.Nos. 11-15) *Read each sentence to find out whether there is any grammatical error in it. The error if any will be in one part of the sentence. The alphabet corresponding to that part is your answer. If there is 'No error', the answer is (e) (Ignore errors of punctuation, if any)*

11. A hot and (A)/ a cold spring (B)/ was found near (C)/ each other. (D)/ No Error (E)
(a) A (b) B (c) C (d) D
(e) E

12. All doubts (A)/ are cleared (B)/ between you (C)/ and me. (D)/ No Error (E)
(a) A (b) E (c) D (d) B
(e) C

13. India never (A)/ has and (B)/ never will (C)/ take such strong measure. (D)/ No Error (E)
(a) E (b) D (c) B (d) C
(e) A

14. I forget (A)/ if I had (B)/ to pay (C)/ the bill today. (D)/ No Error (E)
(a) A (b) E (c) D (d) C
(e) B

15. Ruchi has been working (A)/ on the problem (B)/ for a long time but is (C)/ still not able to solve it. (D)/ No Error (E)
(a) A (b) B (c) C (d) D
(e) E

Directions (Q. Nos 16-20) *Each question in this section has a sentence with four parts labelled (a), (b), (c) and (d). Read each sentence to find out, whether there is any error in any part and indicate your response against the corresponding letter. If you find 'No error', your response should be indicated as (d).*

16. Standing on the top of the light house (a)/ the distant ships (b)/ are clearly visible. (c)/ No error (d)

17. The train came (a)/ at 2 O' clock (b)/ in the next morning. (c)/ No error (d)

18. It is (a)/ high time you buy (b)/ that car. (c)/ No error (d)

19. I and my brother (a)/ live with my parents (b)/ and work in the farm. (c)/ No error (d)

20. Few scientists changed people's idea as much as Charles Darwin (a)/ with his theory of evolution, (b)/ yet as a boy he showed little sign of becoming a great scientist. (c)/ No error (d)

Direction (Q. Nos 21-25) *Read each sentence to find out whether there is any grammatical or idiomatic error in it. The error if any will be in one part of the sentence. The letter of that part is the answer.*

21. The Prime Minister's good looks won him the election but he has still to prove that he's not a just pretty face.
(a) that he's not a just pretty face
(b) The Prime Minister's good looks won him
(c) the election but he still
(d) has to prove

22. The two books are the same except for the fact that this has an answer book in the back.
(a) except for the fact that
(b) this has an answer book
(c) The two books are the same
(d) in the back

23. He estimated his income tax bill by extrapolation over figures submitted in previous years.
(a) He estimated his income tax bill (b) by extrapolation over figures
(c) submitted in (d) previous years

24. The modern office block sticks out like a sour thumb among the old building in the area.
(a) The modern office block (b) sticks out like a sour thumb
(c) among the old buildings (d) in the area

25. I have not been to New York before and neither my sister.
(a) I have not been (b) before and
(c) to New York (d) and neither my sister

Exercise 1

Direction (Q. Nos. 1-10) *Each question in this section has a sentence with four underlined parts labelled as (a), (b), (c) and (d). Read each sentence to find out whether there is any error in any underlined part and indicate your response on the answer sheet against the corresponding letter. If you find 'No error' your response should be indicated as (d).*

1. A major contribution of Mathura sculptors (a) of that period were the creation and popularization (b) of the Buddha's image in human form. (c) No error (d)

2. I had hoped that (a) I would see you the other day (b) but unfortunately I fell ill. (c) No error (d)

3. Mahavira was an advocate of non-violence and vegetarianism, (a) who revived and recognized the Jain doctrine (b) and established rules for their monastic order. (c) No error (d)

4. Microwaves are the principle carriers of television, (a) telephone and data transmissions (b) between stations on earth and also between the earth and satellites. (c) No error (d)

5. An unit is an abstract idea, (a) defined either by reference to a randomly chosen (b) material standard or to a natural phenomenon. (c) No error (d)

6. She stood off (a) from the crowd (b) because of her height and flaming red hair. (c) No error (d)

7. The data on (a) the divorce case is (b) on the judge's desk. (c) No error (d)

8. There is a beautiful moon out tonight (a) and Neeta and I are going for a stroll; (b) would you like to come along with she and I? (c) No error (d)

9. Your husband doesn't (a) believe that you are older (b) than I. (c) No error (d)

10. You should be cautious (a) and make a few discreet enquiries about (b) the firm before you sign anything. (c) No error (d)

Directions (Q. Nos 11-15) *Each question in this section has a sentence with four parts labelled (a), (b), (c) and (d). Read each sentence to find out, whether there is any error in any part and indicate your response against the corresponding letter. If you find 'No error', your response should be indicated as (d).*

11. You must make up the (a)/ time you wasted this afternoon (b)/ by working late over tonight (c)/ No error (d)
12. I am going to bed (a)/ and you would be well (b)/ advised to do likely. (c)/ No error (d)
13. On the land turtle (a)/ is ungainly (b)/ but in the water it is very agile. (c)/ No error (d)
14. Your argument was clear (a)/ to us from the start (b)/ there's no need to labour the point. (c)/ no error (d)
15. The fact that I do not like (a)/ your fiance is neither here nor there (b)/ what matters is what you feel. (c)/ No error (d)

Direction (Q. Nos. 16-20) *Read each sentence to find out whether there is any grammatical or idiomatic error in it. The error if any will be in one part of the sentence. The letter of that part is the answer.*

16. "Here is coming my parents", exclaused Parul when she was anxious.
    (a) "Here is coming my parents" (b) exclaused Parul
    (c) when she (d) was anxious
17. The Minister has put a different glass on recent developments in the Middle East.
    (a) in the Middle East (b) The Minister has put
    (c) on recent developments (d) a different glass
18. She certainly has gone up in my estimation since she told the manager what she thought of him.
    (a) She certainly has gone up (b) in my estimation
    (c) since she told the manager (d) what she thought of him
19. The plans have been under discussion for a year now but no decision has reached.
    (a) The plans have been under (b) now but no decision
    (c) discussion for a year (d) has reached
20. Unless their paths diverged Lennon and MC Cartrey wrote many hits together.
    (a) Unless their paths diverged (b) Lennon and MC Cartrey
    (c) wrote many (d) hits together

Exercise J

Directions (Q. Nos 1-5) *Each question in this section has a sentence with four parts labelled (a), (b), (c) and (d). Read each sentence to find out, whether there is any error in any part and indicate your response against the corresponding letter. If you find 'No error', your response should be indicated as (d).*

1. Amit needs marry (a) / a down-to-earth person (b)/who will organize his life for him. (c)/ No error (d)
2. As soon as (a) / the clock strike five, (b)/ they down tools and off they go. (c)/ No error (d)
3. A careful driver watches the road and goes slowly or quickly (a)/depending upon the condition of the road (b) / the visibility and the traffic. (c)/ No error (d)
4. Despite some past experiences (a)/with averse publicily (b)/ she is usually gracious to reporters. (c) No error (d)
5. According to a spokesman for the government (a)/the charge of corruption is a contemptuous lie (b)/ inspired by political motives. (c) No error (d)

Directions (Q. Nos 6-10) *Read each sentence to find out whether there is any grammatical error in it. The error if any will be in one part of the sentence. The alphabet corresponding to that part is your answer. If there is 'No error', the answer is (e) (Ignore errors of punctuation, if any)*

6. If I would have arrived (A)/ sooner, I would (B)/ not have (C)/ missed the train. (D)/ No Error (E)
   (a) A (b) B (c) C (d) D
   (e) E
7. Unless two or more members object (A)/ to him joining the club (B)/ we shall have to accept (C)/ his application. (D)/ No Error (E)
   (a) A (b) B (c) C (d) D
   (e) E
8. The prospective buyer (A)/ of the house (B)/ left the premises because he was asked to pay a (C)/ considerable higher price than he could afford. (D)/ No Error (E)
   (a) A (b) B (c) C (d) D
   (e) E
9. You are being quite cynical (A)/ when you say that (B)/ the reason why we have such a large turnout is (C)/ because we are serving refreshments. (D)/ No Error (E)
   (a) A (b) B (c) C (d) D
   (e) E
10. We can't hardly believe (A)/ that the situation (B)/ is so serious as to (C)/ justify such precautions as you have taken. (D)/ No Error (E)
    (a) A (b) C (c) B (d) E
    (e) D

Directions (Q. Nos 11-25) *Each question in this section has a sentence with four underlined parts labelled as (a), (b), (c) and (d). Read each sentence to find out, whether there is any error in any underlined part and indicate your response on the answer sheet against the corresponding letter. If you find 'No error', your response should be indicated as (d).*

11. Although I am playing cricket (a) for more than three years (b) I have not been able to score a century. (c) No error (d)

12. If I have to make a choice between Aryan, Amit and Abhishek (a) I think I'll select Aryan (b) because of his commanding personality. (c) No error (d)

13. Man's happiness or misery (a) are in a great measure (b) in his own hands. (c) No error (d)

14. I feel bad about the present conflict (a) because I do not know how to resolve it (b) without hurting either you or him. (c) No error (d)

15. Cows are amongst the gentlest of breathing creatures; (a) none shows more passionate (b) tenderness to their young. (c) No error (d)

16. He is not the kind of a person (a) who accepts such treatment passively; (b) he is certain to seek revenge. (c) No error (d)

17. The rise and fall (a) of the tide are due (b) to lunar influence. (c) No error (d)

18. I was surprised and pleased (a) when I was informed of me (b) winning the contest. (c) No error (d)

19. Many a man (a) has succumbed (b) to this temptation. (c) No error (d)

20. The street lights (a) come in at dusk and (b) go off at dawn. (c) No error (d)

21. Two of the mountain climbers (a) were suffering (b) with frost-bite. (c) No error (d)

22. Although there was still (a) a faint heart beat, the patient was (b) for all intents and purposes dead. (c) No error (d)

23. When the rules for police procedure (a) were laid up (b) a lot of grey areas remained. (c) No error (d)

24. Anurag is eclipsed by his wife, (a) who is much clever and (b) more amusing than he is. (c) No error (d)

25. The company took a gamble by (a) cutting the price of its products, (b) and it paid up. (c) No error (d)

Exercise K

Direction (Q. Nos. 1-5) *Read each sentence to find out whether there is any grammatical or idiomatic error in it. The error if any will be in one part of the sentence. The letter of that part is the answer.*

1. The Indian farmers have been reeling under the weight of illiteracy for time immemorial.
   (a) The Indian farmers have been
   (b) reeling under the weight of
   (c) illiteracy
   (d) for time immemorial
2. It's difficult to make friends with her, she's constantly in the offensive.
   (a) It's difficult
   (b) to make friends
   (c) with her
   (d) she's constantly in the offensive
3. I needed that money so desperately, it was like manna from heaven when it arrived.
   (a) when it arrived
   (b) it was like manna from heaven
   (c) so desperately
   (d) I needed that money
4. I can't see much likelihood between him and his father.
   (a) I can't see
   (b) much likelihood
   (c) between him
   (d) and his father
5. The world today is totally different than we have seen in the last century.
   (a) The world today
   (b) is totally different
   (c) than we have seen
   (d) in the last century

Direction (Q. Nos 6-10) *Each question in this section has a sentence with four parts labelled (a), (b), (c) and (d). Read each sentence to find out, whether there is any error in any part and indicate your response against the corresponding letter. If you find 'No error', your response should be indicated as (d).*

6. Of all the teacher I have ever met (a)/Dr. Subramaniam is the (b)/ most remarkable teacher. (c) No error (d)
7. The moral of the entire novel (a)/ is how money doesn't (b)/ make you happy. (c)/ No error (d)
8. That store (a) / hadn't hardly (b)/any of those goods. (c)/ No error (d)
9. In this lockdown period every worker (a)/in the factory (b)/has started bring their own lunch. (c)/No error (d)
10. Everyone of the films (a)/ you suggested (b)/ are not worth seeing. (c)/ No Error (d)

Directions (Q. Nos 11-25) *Each question in this section has a sentence with four underlined parts labelled as (a), (b), (c) and (d). Read each sentence to find out, whether there is any error in any part and indicate your response on the answer sheet against the corresponding letter. If you find 'No error', your response should be indicated as (d).*

11. The Secretary and the Principal of the college (a) are attending (b) the District Development Council Meeting at the collectorate (c). No error (d)
12. No sooner had the hockey match started (a) when it began (b) to rain (c). No error (d)
13. The secretariat (a) comprises of (b) many air-conditioned rooms (c). No error (d)

14. It is high time (a) he stood on his own (b) two legs. (c) No error (d)

15. You should avoid (a) to travel (b) in the rush hour. (c) No error (d)

16. There is (a) only one of his novels (b) that are interesting. (c) No error (d)

17. He denied (a) to have (b) been there. (c) No error (d)

18. Knowledge of (a) at least two languages (b) are required to pass the examination. (c) No error (d)

19. The members of the opposition party in the Parliament (a) shout upon the minister (b) if he makes a wrong statement. (c) No error (d)

20. It is about time (a) you have taken your children (b) to school. (c)

21. You will find it difficult (a) to explain of your use (b) of such offensive language. (c) No error (d)

22. Because of the (a) extenuating circumstances (b) the court acquitted him out of the crime. (c) No error (d)

23. The carpet was badly stained (a) to such an extent (b) that you could not tell its original colour. (c) No error (d)

24. It is greatly to Amit's credit (a) that he gave back the money he found; (b) his honesty does him for credit. (c) No error (d)

25. The company has (a) set off itself some stiff production (b) goals for this year. (c) No error (d)

Exercise 1

Direction (Q. Nos. 1-10) *Each question in this section has a sentence with four parts labelled as (a), (b), (c) and (d). Read each sentence to find out whether there is any error in any underlined part and indicate your response on the answer sheet against the corresponding letter. If you find 'No error' your response should be indicated as (d).*

1. A senior doctor (a) / expressed concern (b) / about physicians recommended the vaccine. (c)/ No error (d)
2. We have discussing (a) / all the known mechanisms (b) / of physical growth. (c) / No error (d)
3. Children enjoy listening to (a) / ghosts stories (b) / especially on Halloween night. (c) / No error (d)
4. I (a) / have (b) / many works to do. (c) / No error (d)
5. There are so many filths (a) / all around (b) / the place. (c) / No error (d)
6. A great many student (a) / have been declared (b) / successful. (c) / No error (d)
7. We are going to launch (a) / this three-crores project (b) / within the next few months. (c)/ No error (d)
8. I hope to go to shopping (a) / this weekend (b) / if the weather permits. (c) / No error (d)
9. The lawyer asked (a) / if it was worth to take (b) / the matter to court. (c) / No error (d)
10. After a carefully investigation (a) / we discovered (b) / that the house was infested with termites. (c)/ No error (d)

Direction (Q. Nos. 11-15) *Read each sentence to find out whether there is any grammatical error in it. The error if any will be in one part of the sentence. The alphabet corresponding to that part is your answer. If there is 'No error', the answer is (e) (Ignore errors of punctuation, if any)*

11. We are meeting (A)/ today afternoon (B)/ to discuss the matter (C)/ and reach a compromise. (D)/ No error (E)
    (a) A (b) B (c) C (d) D
    (e) E
12. Either Ram or (A)/ you is responsible (B)/ for his (C)/ actions. (D)/ No error (E)
    (a) A (b) B (c) C (d) D
    (e) E
13. The student (A)/ finally denied (B)/ that he had copied (C)/ in the examination hall. (D)/ No error (E)
    (a) A (b) B (c) C (d) D
    (e) E
14. By the time (A)/ you arrive tomorrow (B)/ I have finished (C)/ my work. (D)/ No error (E)
    (a) A (b) B (c) C (d) D
    (e) E
15. The speaker stressed (A)/ repeatedly on (B)/ the importance of (c)/ wearing a mask when going outside. (D)/ No error (E)
    (a) A (b) B (c) C (d) D
    (e) E

Direction (Q. Nos. 16-50) *Each question in this section has a sentence with four underlined parts labelled as (a), (b), (c) and (d). Read each sentence to find out whether there is any error in any underlined part and indicate your response on the answer sheet against the corresponding letter. If you find 'No error' your response should be indicated as (d).*

16. The captain with the members of his team (a) / are returning (b) / after a fortnight. (c) / No error (d)

17. After returning from (a) / an all-India tour (b) / I had to describe about it. (c) / No error (d)

18. The teacher asked his students (a) / if they had gone through (b) / either of the three chapters included in the prescribed text. (c) / No error (d)

19. Although, they are living in the country (a) / since they were married (b) / they are now moving to the town. (c) / No error (d)

20. Do you know (a) / how old were you (b) / when you came here? (c) / No error (d)

21. Young school students now-a-days (a) / are subjected to intense pressure from peers and parents alike (b) / to fetch high marks in public examinations. (c) / No error (d)

22. The candidate's performance (a) / was not upto mark (b) / in the interview. (c) / No error (d)

23. After a successful tour of Europe (a) / my old parents returned back to India (b) / on New Year's day. (c) / No error (d)

24. The global economy, slaved by (a) / stagnation in Europe and Japan, is being (b) / further hampered by England's decelerating growth. (c) / No error (d)

25. Though, death is a daily fact (a) / it is a wonder that people should (b) / behave to be immortal. (c) / No error (d)

26. It would be more better (a) / If you could paint (b) / the gate green. (c) / No error (d)

27. Being his sole companion (a) / I was the one to who (b) / he naturally looked for help. (c) / No error (d)

28. He came to report that the work went very slowly (a) / because the X-ray machine was not working very good (b) / that morning. (c) / No error (d)

29. The principal objected (a) to them wearing short skirts (b) at the function. (c) No error (d)

30. I spent nearly four and half years (a) at Harrow (b) of which three were in the Army class. (c) No error (d)

31. The scientist was seemed (a) to be excited (b) over the result of his experiment. (c) No error (d)

32. The student could not answer the teacher (a) when he was asked to explain (b) why he was so late that day. (c) No error (d)

33. John could not come (a) to school (b) as he was ill from cold. (c) No error (d)

34. Though, she has aptitude in Mathematics (a) I won't allow her to take it up as a subject of study for the Master's Degree (b) because I know the labour involved will tell upon her health. (c) No error (d)

35. I am not familiar with (a) all the important places in this town, (b) although I have been living here since two years. (c) No error (d)

36. If I would be a millionaire (a) I would not be wasting my time (b) waiting for a bus. (c) No error (d)

37. Until you begin to make a better use of your time, (a) I shall not stop (b) finding fault in you. (c) No error (d)

38. Neither of the two boys (a) is sensible (b) enough to do this job. (c) No error (d)

39. They left (a) their luggages (b) at the railway station. (c) No error (d)

40. You will get (a) all the informations (b) if you read this booklet carefully. (c) No error (d)

41. She sang (a) very well, (b) isn't it? (c) No error (d)

42. He is working (a) in a bank in New Delhi (b) for the past several months. (c) No error (d)

43. There is no question (a) of my failing (b) in the examination. (c) No error (d)

44. He is going everyday (a) for a morning walk (b) with his friends and neighbours. (c) No error (d)

45. Her relatives could not explain to us (a) / why did not she come for the wedding (b) / as she was expected. (c) / No error (d)

46. None of the applicants have turned up (a) / for the interview (b) / on time. (c) / No error (d)

47. Her mother did not reply (a) / when I asked her (b) / why was she weeping. (c) / No error (d)

48. The oxygen content of Mars is not (a) / sufficient enough to support life (b) / as we know it. (c) / No error (d)

49. He told his friends that (a) / each of them (b) / should be able to carry out the order oneself. (c) / No error (d)

50. If the police would have worked (a) / in time (b) / the riot would not have occurred.. (c) / No error (d)

Exercise Ⓜ

Direction (Q. Nos. 1-25) *Each question in this section has a sentence with parts labelled as (a), (b), (c) and (d). Read each sentence to find out whether there is any error in any part and indicate your response against the corresponding letter. If you find 'No error' your response should be indicated as (d).*

1. I am glad (a) / that the news (b) / are good. (c) / No error (d)
2. The judge tested the accused (a)/ to see if he would (b)/ read English. (c) / No error (d)
3. I have neither visited (a)/ or intend (b) / to visit hill stations. (c) / No error (d)
4. Kamala is not (a) / inferior than Geetha (b)/ in her studies. (c) /No error (d)
5. Some of the people (a) / Awere standing on the street (b)/watch cricket match, while others were sitting. (c) / No error (d)
6. These are the ideas and ideals (a) / which have shaped (b)/ our economic thought in the past. (c) / No error (d)
7. India's problems are not similar with (a) / those of other countries (b)/ in several ways. (c)/ No error (d)
8. He had lost a ring in the sand and (a) /I helped him search for it, (b) / but it was like a look for a needle in a haystack. (c) /No error (d)
9. The Ganges and (a) / it's tributaries constitute (b) / one of the largest river-systems in the world. (c)/ No error (d)
10. The sudden change (a) / of place (b) / affected her health. (c)/ No error (d)
11. There are a number of people (a) /of every class and nationality (b)/ who doubts the truth of his statement. (c)/ No error (d)
12. I like this book because the writer has explained (a) /the reasons (b) /of his failure truly. (c) / No error (d)

13. She is very weak in the subject (a) /and does not understand things (b) / though the teacher explains her repeatedly. (c) /No error (d)

14. The speaker from the Fifth Avenue, (a) / who was a rich banker's wife (b) /was simple and compassionate. (c) / No error (d)

15. There was no any piece of paper (a) / in my pocket (b) / as I had expected. (c) / No error (d)

16. Neither the teacher (a) /or the student (b) / is keen on joining the dance. (c) / No error (d)

17. My neighbour Deepak (a) / is a person (b) / that will help anyone. (c)/ No error (d)

18. I'll ask that man (a) / which of the roads (b) /are the one we want. (c) / No error (d)

19. Now we have banks (a) / and people deposit there money there, (b) / and draw it out by cheques. (c) / No error (d)

20. Apart government agencies, (a) / a number of private organisations too (b) / have been making use of satellites. (c) / No error (d)

21. What sorts of a drug this is (a) / that no one seems to be able to predict its long-term effects (b) / with any certainty? (c) / No error (d)

22. You will lose (a) / your dog (b) / if you did not tie it up. (c) / No error (d)

23. In view of the fact that almost all varieties of rural games and sports (a) / are fast gaining national importance it is desired (c) / that the rules of such games are strictly adhered. (c) / No error (d)

24. More than one (a) / workmen (b) was killed. (c) / No error (d)

25. The parties disagreed (a) / on the two first clauses (b) / in the agreement. (c) / No error (d)

Direction (Q. Nos. 26-50) *Each question in this section has a sentence with four underlined parts labelled as (a), (b), (c) and (d). Read each sentence to find out whether there is any error in any underlined part and indicate your response on the answer sheet against the corresponding letter. If you find 'No error' your response should be indicated as (d).*

26. Instead of being (a) helpful he was (b) being hindrance. (c) No error (d)

27. Where (a) have I (b) to deposit fees? (c) No error (d)

28. By the time she had finished her work (a) I had nearly given up (b) all hope of arriving at the party in time. (c) No error (d)

29. Some categorically suspected (a) having seen the (b) guard and the thief together. (c) No error (d)

30. He was (a) not in position to state (b) the speed the ship travelled. (c) No error (d)

31. The NCC commandant along with his cadets (a) are going to Delhi (b) to participate in the Republic Day Parade. (c) No error (d)

32. World is producing enough (a) for every citizen but still there is hunger and malnutrition (b) and it is continuing year after year. (c) No error (d)

33. Many of the famous (a) advertising offices (b) are located at Madison Avenue. (c) No error (d)

34. Nature has denied us (a) the power of closing our ears (b) which she gave in respect of our eyes. (c) No error (d)

35. He did not succeed (a) to get the job (b) though he tried his level best. (c) No error (d)

36. Let us (a) bring this discussion (b) to close. (c) No error (d)

37. Each of them (a) have a different version (b) of the crime. (c) No error (d)

38. I and Gopal (a) went to the meeting (b) together. (c) No error (d)

39. Latin is not only hard to write (a) but also (b) to read. (c) No error (d)

40. In most villages (a) the roads are rough (b) isn't it? (c) No error (d)

41. Despite of continuing pain (a) she worked at her temporary summer job (b) most of the week. (c) No error (d)

42. As soon the film started (a) I developed (b) an irritating headache. (c) No error (d)

43. He applied for an employment (a) in (b) an office. (c) No error (d)

44. Though we drove fast, the train left (a) before we could reach (b) the station. (c) No error (d)

45. One Indian virtue that has impressed me greatly (a) and touched me deeply (b) was the Indian people's freedom of rancour. (c) No error (d)

46. Lack of winter rains (a) have delayed the sowing of (b) wheat crop in this area. (c) No error (d)

47. The teacher let the boy off (a) with a warning (b) though he was convinced with his guilt. (c) No error (d)

48. Although I prepared myself (a) for appear strong to my mother, (b) my heart ached and cried. (c) No error (d)

49. He has been going to the office (a) for a year now, (b) and he even can't understand its working. (c) No error (d)

50. He boasts of having visited Europe many times. (a) but he can neither speak English (b) nor he can speak French. (c) No error (d)

Answers

Exercise A

1. (d) Say 'speaking' instead of 'to speak'
2. (b) Say 'he could go'
3. (a) Say 'One of the states'
4. (a) Say 'had the inspector'
5. (b) Say 'has been trying'
6. (c) Use 'that' in place of 'when'
7. (a) Say 'laid' for 'lay'
8. (e) No error
9. (c) Use 'on' in place of 'to'
10. (c) Say 'that' instead of 'because'
11. (c) Say 'the train had left'
12. (c) Say 'full marks' instead of '100 per cent'
13. (b) Use 'has' in place of 'have'
14. (a) Say 'had written'
15. (b) Say 'there has been'
16. (d) No error
17. (b) Say 'to revise' instead of 'to revising'
18. (c) Remove 'that'
19. (b) Remove 'together'
20. (b) Say 'the machine age'
21. (a) Add 'a' before 'sense'
22. (b) Say 'estimates'
23. (b) Use 'nor' in place of 'or'
24. (a) Remove 'shall'
25. (a) Say 'furniture has been'

Exercise B

1. (a) Use 'fair' in place of 'fare'
2. (b) Say 'the Earth'
3. (a) Say 'have we been'
4. (d) say 'have' inplace of 'had'
5. (c) Say 'between' inplace of 'among'
6. (d) Say 'but also'
7. (b) 'why I do not like him'
8. (b) Remove 'have'
9. (d) Say 'information'
10. (b) Use 'seems' in place of 'seem'
11. (b) Delete 'to'
12. (a) Say 'has been running'
13. (b) Use 'on air flights'
14. (a) Say 'gratitute'
15. (c) Remove 'that' after 'so'
16. (a) Remove 'off'
17. (c) Use 'to' in place of 'for'
18. (a) Remove 'to'
19. (c) Use 'for' in place of 'since'
20. (a) Say 'round the clock'
21. (b) Say 'men' for 'man'
22. (d) No error
23. (d) No error
24. (b) Say 'if one is happy'
25. (a) Say 'have done'

Exercise C

1. (d) Use 'nor' in place of 'or'
2. (a) Use 'going' in place of 'go'
3. (b) Use 'practises'
4. (d) Use 'was' in place of 'were'
5. (b) Say 'as much as'
6. (d) Say 'you and me'
7. (b) Remove 'a'
8. (c) Say 'playing' in place of 'to play'
9. (d) No error
10. (d) Say 'The team were'
11. (b) Delete 'have'
12. (b) Add 'on' after 'kept'
13. (b) Use 'of' in place of 'with'
14. (d) Use 'is' in place of 'are'
15. (c) Say 'for me'
16. (e) No error
17. (b) Use 'to' in place of 'in'
18. (d) Delete 'most'
19. (d) Say 'in a skilful manner'
20. (c) Remove 'but'
21. (b) Say 'I was interested'
22. (c) Say 'by the sea'
23. (c) Say 'if' for 'when'
24. (d) No error
25. (a) Say 'was supposed'

Exercise D

1. (c) Say 'when' for 'as'
2. (d) 'neither of them' in place of 'none'
3. (a) 'Despite' for 'Despite of'
4. (a) Use 'Whenever' in place of 'Anywhere'
5. (a) Use 'if' in place of 'unless'
6. (b) Say 'so high'
7. (d) No error
8. (b) Use 'which have appeared' in place of 'which appeared'
9. (c) 'playing' for 'play'
10. (c) Say 'you are' in place of 'you'
11. (e) No error
12. (c) Use 'where they have'
13. (c) 'neither' in place of 'either'
14. (a) 'beauty' in place of 'beauties'
15. (e) No error
16. (c) Use 'can' in place of 'could'
17. (a) 'hard up' in place of 'hard down'
18. (c) Use in the afternoon
19. (b) Say 'fiscal' for 'financial'
20. (a) 'have won' in place of 'won'
21. (a) Say 'arrogant of' for 'arrogant for'
22. (b) 'to take only' in place of 'need only'
23. (c) 'than those of Britain' in place of 'than Britain'
24. (b) 'a sport' for 'sport'
25. (b) Use 'whom' in place of 'who'

Exercise E

1. (b) Use 'anyone' in place of 'either'
2. (d) 'were' in place of 'was'
3. (c) 'that of any' in place of 'in any'
4. (c) Use 'is more preferable than'
5. (d) 'thoroughly' for 'thorough'
6. (c) Use 'as much as' in place of 'more than'
7. (a) Add 'other' after 'No'
8. (b) No error
9. (b) Use 'is' in place of 'are'
10. (a) Use 'after' in place of 'When'
11. (c) Use 'has gone to Ladakh'
12. (c) Use 'it' in place of 'the same'
13. (a) Use 'told' in place of 'said'
14. (a) Place 'not only' after 'saw'
15. (a) Say 'direct'
16. (a) Drop 'on' after 'signed'
17. (b) Use 'that' in place of 'which'
18. (a) Use 'Not to speak of' in place of 'What to speak of'
19. (c) Say 'one end to other'
20. (b) 'that' in place of 'but'
21. (a) Remove 'hardly'
22. (c) Remove 'more'
23. (d) No error
24. (a) Use 'off' for 'up'
25. (b) Use 'means' for 'mean'

Exercise F

1. (d) No error
2. (b) Use 'effect' in place of 'affect'
3. (d) No error
4. (b) Use 'to' for 'with'
5. (c) Say 'most of the time'
6. (d) Use 'all the other questions'
7. (e) Remove 'over'
8. (b) No error
9. (d) Use 'in' in place of 'of' before 'air'
10. (e) A 'light' in place of 'lightness'
11. (c) 'have not been' in place of 'have been not'
12. (b) Add 'that' after 'them'
13. (c) Use 'outright' in place of 'outrightly'
14. (b) Use 'but' for 'than'
15. (d) Use 'than' in place of 'then'
16. (d) No error
17. (a) Say 'too bad' for 'bad enough'
18. (b) Use 'in finding' for 'to find'
19. (b) Use 'is' in place of 'are'
20. (b) Place 'was' after 'hall'
21. (d) No error
22. (c) Use 'was' in place of 'were'
23. (b) Use 'when' in place of 'than'
24. (c) Use 'that' in place of 'because'
25. (b) Remove 'about'

Exercise G

1. (c) Say 'to' for 'among'
2. (a) Use 'The first two'
3. (a) Use 'suffer from'
4. (b) Use 'practise' in place of 'practice'
5. (b) 'foreword' in place of 'forward'
6. (d) No error
7. (b) Use 'ascent' for 'assent'
8. (b) Use 'incredible' for 'incredulous'
9. (b) Use 'non-inflammable' for 'inflammable'
10. (a) Use 'Besides' for 'Beside'
11. (c) Use 'among'
12. (d) Use 'personnel' for 'personal'
13. (b) Say 'I like' for 'I am liking'
14. (c) Use 'her' in place of 'him'
15. (d) Use 'pursue ' in place of 'pursues'
16. (c) Use 'fell' in place of 'have fallen'
17. (a) Use 'The car' before 'having'
18. (d) Say 'have won'
19. (d) Use 'orders' for 'order'
20. (b) Say 'catch up with'
21. (a) Use 'harmony' in place of 'harmonies'
22. (c) Use 'aspect' in place of 'aspects'
23. (c) Use 'in' in place of 'to'
24. (c) Use 'members'
25. (c) Say 'what I wanted'

Exercise H

1. (d) No error
2. (c) Use 'to' for 'with'
3. (b) Use 'leads' in place of 'lead'
4. (a) Remove 'the' before 'temple'
5. (a) Say 'passed' in place of 'have passed'
6. (c) Use 'doesn't it?' in place of 'isn't it?'
7. (a) Remove 'don't'
8. (b) Use 'how many' for 'how much'
9. (c) Use 'rises' in place of 'raises'
10. (b) Use 'is' for 'are'
11. (c) Use 'were' in place of 'was'
12. (b) No error

13. (c) Say 'has taken'
14. (e) Use 'that' for 'if'
15. (d) 'yet' in place of 'still'
16. (a) Say 'If one stands on' for 'Standing on'
17. (c) Delete 'in'
18. (b) Use 'you bought' in place of 'you buy'
19. (a) Use 'My brother and I'
20. (a) Add 'did' after 'Darwin'
21. (a) Use 'just a' in place of 'a just'
22. (d) Say 'at the back'
23. (b) Use 'from' in place of 'over'
24. (b) Use 'sore' in place of 'sour'
25. (d) Use 'neither has my sister been' in place of 'neither my sister'

Exercise I

1. (b) Use 'was' in place of 'were'
2. (d) No error
3. (c) 'Its' for 'their'
4. (a) Use 'principal' in place of 'principle'
5. (a) Use 'A unit' in place of 'An unit'
6. (a) Use 'stood out' in place of 'stood off'
7. (b) Use 'are' in place of 'is'
8. (c) Use 'her and me' in place of 'she and I'
9. (d) No error
10. (c) Say 'something'
11. (c) Remove 'over'
12. (c) 'so' in place of 'likely'
13. (a) Add 'the' before 'turtle'
14. (d) No error
15. (c) Say 'That what you'
16. (b) Use 'exclaimed' in place of 'exclansed'
17. (d) Say 'gloss' for 'glass'
18. (a) Say 'has certainly'
19. (d) Use 'has been reached'
20. (a) Use 'Until' for 'Unless'

Exercise J

1. (a) Say 'needs to marry'
2. (b) Use 'strikes' for 'strike'
3. (d) No error
4. (b) Use 'adverse' for 'averse'
5. (b) Use 'contemptable' for 'contemptuous'
6. (a) Say 'If I had arrived'
7. (b) Say 'to his joining'
8. (d) Use 'considerably' for 'considerable'
9. (d) Use 'that' in place of 'because'
10. (a) Use 'can' in place of 'can't'
11. (a) Say 'I have been playing'
12. (d) No error
13. (b) Use 'is' in place of 'are'
14. (d) No error
15. (c) Say 'young ones'
16. (d) No error
17. (a) Use 'is' in place of 'are'
18. (b) Use 'of my' in place of 'of me'
19. (d) No error
20. (b) Use 'come on' in place of 'come in'
21. (c) Say 'suffer from'
22. (c) Say 'to all intents and purposes'
23. (b) Say 'laid down'
24. (c) Use 'him' in place of 'he is'
25. (c) Say 'paid off'

Exercise K

1. (d) Use 'from/since time immemorial'
2. (d) Say 'on the offensive'
3. (b) add 'that' before 'it was'
4. (b) Say 'likeness' for 'likelihood'
5. (c) Say 'from what' for 'than'
6. (d) No error
7. (b) Say 'That how'
8. (b) 'did not have' for 'hadn't hardly'
9. (c) Use 'bringing' in place of 'bring'
10. (c) Say 'is' for 'are'
11. (d) No error
12. (a) Say 'hardly' for 'No sooner'
13. (b) delete 'of'
14. (c) Remove 'two'

15. (b) Say 'travelling'
16. (c) Say 'that is'
17. (d) No error
18. (c) Say 'is required'
19. (b) Say 'shout at'
20. (b) Say 'took' for 'have taken'
21. (b) Remove 'of'
22. (c) Remove 'out'
23. (d) No error
24. (c) Remove 'for'
25. (b) Remove 'off'

Exercise L

1. (c) Replace 'recommended' by 'recommending'
2. (a) Replace 'discussing' by 'discussed'
3. (b) Replace 'ghosts' by 'ghost'
4. (c) Replace 'many works' by 'much work'
5. (a) Replace 'many' by 'much'
6. (a) Replace 'student' by 'students'
7. (b) Replace 'three-crores' by 'three crore'
8. (a) Remove preposition 'to'
9. (b) Replace 'to take' by 'taking'
10. (a) Replace 'carefully' by 'careful'
11. (a) Replace 'meeting' by 'going to meet'
12. (b) Replace 'is' by 'are'
13. (e) No error
14. (c) Replace 'have' by 'shall have'
15. (b) Replace 'on' by 'over'
16. (b) Replace 'are' by 'is'
17. (c) Replace 'had' by 'have'
18. (c) Replace 'either' by 'anyone'
19. (a) Replace 'are' by 'have been'
20. (a) Replace 'do' by 'did'
21. (d) No error
22. (b) Add 'the' between 'upto' and 'mark'
23. (b) Remove 'back'
24. (a) Use 'enslaved' in place of 'slaved'
25. (b) Replace 'that' by 'why'
26. (a) Remove 'more'
27. (b) Replace 'who' by 'whom'
28. (b) Replace 'very good' by 'well'
29. (b) Replace 'to them' by 'their'
30. (a) Put 'a' before 'half'
31. (a) Remove 'was'
32. (d) No error
33. (c) Replace 'from' by 'with'
34. (a) Use 'for' in place of 'in'
35. (c) Use 'for' in place of 'since'
36. (a) Use 'were' in place of 'would be'
37. (c) Use 'with' in place of 'in'
38. (d) No error
39. (b) Use 'luggage' in place of 'luggages'
40. (b) Use 'information' in place of 'informations'
41. (c) Use 'didn't she' as sentence is in the past tense
42. (a) Replace 'is' by 'has been'
43. (b) Use 'failure' in place of 'failing'
44. (a) Use 'goes' in place of 'is going'
45. (b) Use 'she did not' in place of 'did not she'
46. (a) Replace 'have' by 'has'
47. (c) Replace 'why was she' by 'why she was'
48. (d) No error
49. (c) Replace 'oneself' by 'themselves'
50. (a) Replace 'would have' by 'had'

Exercise M

1. (c) Put 'is' in place of 'are'
2. (b) Put 'could' in place of 'would'
3. (b) Put 'nor' in place of 'or'
4. (b) Put 'to' in place of 'than'
5. (c) Put 'watching' in place of 'watch'
6. (b) replace 'have' by 'had'
7. (a) Replace 'with' by 'to'
8. (b) Use 'looking' in place of 'a look'
9. (b) Replace 'it's' by 'its'

10. (b) Replace 'of' by 'in'
11. (c) Replace 'doubts' by 'doubt'
12. (d) No error
13. (d) No error
14. (a) Use 'of' in place of 'from'
15. (a) Remove 'any'
16. (b) Replace 'or' by 'nor'
17. (d) No error
18. (c) Replace 'are' by 'is'
19. (b) Replace 'there' by 'their'
20. (a) Use 'from' after 'apart'
21. (a) Use 'sort' in place of 'sorts'
22. (c) Replace 'did' by 'would'
23. (b) Replace 'fast' by 'fastly'
24. (b) Replace 'workmen' by 'workman'
25. (b) Use 'two' after 'first'
26. (c) Put 'a' in place of 'being'
27. (b) Replace 'have I' by 'do have'
28. (a) Remove 'had'
29. (a) Put 'have' before 'categorically'
30. (c) Use 'at which the ship had travelled'
31. (b) Replace 'are' by 'is'
32. (a) Put 'The' before 'world'
33. (c) Replace 'located at' with 'situated in'
34. (c) Put 'has given' in place of 'gave'
35. (b) Replace 'to get' by 'in getting'
36. (c) Put 'conclusion' in place of 'close'
37. (b) Put 'has' in place of 'have'
38. (a) Use 'Gopal and I'
39. (c) Put 'hard' before 'not only'
40. (c) Put 'aren't they' in place of 'isn't it'
41. (a) Remove 'of'
42. *(a)* Put 'as' after 'soon'
43. (a) Replace 'an employment' by ' a job'
44. (a) Use 'the train had left'
45. (c) Replace 'was' by 'is'
46. (b) Replace 'have' by 'has'
47. (c) Replace 'with' by 'of'
48. (b) Use 'to' in place of 'for'
49. (c) Replace 'and' by 'but'
50. (c) Remove 'he can'

18

Sentence Improvement

The technique to attempt Sentence Improvement questions is a variation of Spotting errors. In this type of questions a sentence is given with a word or a phrase italicised, underlined or in bold letters. Under this sentence a number of substitutes are given as alternatives. An examinee is required to locate the error and find the correct answer from among the alternatives given. When the alternative has been substituted, the sentence becomes grammatically correct. If no other alternative is required, the answer is 'no improvement'.

However, this kind of questions can be attempted only if a student is comprehensively equipped with the knowledge of common errors, vocabulary, correct use of phrases and overall comprehension of rules of grammar. *For example*

1. If **I am** present there now, I would help him.

(a) I was
(b) I were
(c) I have been
(d) no improvement

As the sentence expresses regret for the present situation, subjunctive mood is required to be substitued for the italicised portion. Hence, the correct answer is (b).

2. They told me that they **had already sold** out all their belongings.

(a) has sold already
(b) have already been sold
(c) had already sold
(d) no improvement

Since the italicised portion requires no improvement, the correct answer is (d).

Work Book Exercise A

Directions *In the following questions you will find sentences, part of which are* ***bold****. Compare the bold part of each sentence with the expressions (a), (b) and (c) given below. Choose the expression which is an improvement upon the bold part. If none of the three expressions improves the sentence, then your answer is (d).*

1. I am tired as **I am working** since 7 O' clock in the morning.
(*a*) I was working (*b*) I had been working
(*c*) I have been working (*d*) no improvement

2. When it was dark they decided to **put at** an inn.
(*a*) put off with (*b*) put up at
(*c*) put out in (*d*) no improvement

3. We should be bound by a code of conduct, **isn't it**?
(*a*) Shouldn't we (*b*) is it
(*c*) aren't we (*d*) no improvement

4. A highly improved variety of seeds **is** available to the farmer these days.
(*a*) are (*b*) will be
(*c*) has been (*d*) no improvement

5. The boy **told his teacher** to explain the passage.
(*a*) asked his teacher (*b*) said to his teacher
(*c*) invited his teacher (*d*) no improvement

6. **What struck one most** was their kindness.
(*a*) What stroke one most (*b*) What struck one more
(*c*) What stroke one more (*d*) no improvement

7. You should **avoid to make** such trivial mistakes.
(*a*) avoid making (*b*) avoid to have made
(*c*) avoid make (*d*) no improvement

8. The teacher gave the students some **advice.**
(*a*) advices (*b*) advise
(*c*) advises (*d*) no improvement

9. If you come across my umbrella anywhere, bring it to me, **can you**?
(*a*) isn't it (*b*) don't you
(*c*) will you (*d*) no improvement

10. The floor of the hall was **covered by** a carpet.
(*a*) covered in (*b*) covered with
(*c*) covered upon (*d*) no improvement

11. The passengers **are waiting** for the bus outside the bus stand at the main gate for long.
(*a*) were waited (*b*) were waiting
(*c*) have been waiting (*d*) no improvement

12. Miss Pillai teaches very well, **isn't it**?
(*a*) didn't she (*b*) doesn't she
(*c*) wasn't it (*d*) no improvement

13. He has **fallen out** with the girl he wanted to marry.
(*a*) fallen off (*b*) fallen in love
(*c*) fallen for (*d*) no improvement

14. They are social insects, **living in communities,** regulated by definite laws, each member of society bearing a well-defined and separate part in the work of a colony.
(*a*) who are living in communities
(*b*) living among a community
(*c*) who lives with a community
(*d*) no improvement

15. **If the room had been brighter**, I would have been able to read for a while before bed time.
(*a*) if the room was brighter
(*b*) if rooms are brighter
(*c*) had the room brighter
(*d*) no improvement

16. I shall be grateful to you if you are *of* **help to** me now.
(*a*) help
(*b*) would help
(*c*) helped
(*d*) no improvement

17. The reason **why he wrote the letter was because** he could not contact him over the phone.
(*a*) why he wrote the letter was since
(*b*) for which he wrote the letter because
(*c*) why he wrote the letter was that
(*d*) no improvement

18. The right-to-work implies the obligation on the part of the government to give a job to **all the unemployed**.
(*a*) any of the unemployed
(*b*) every unemployed
(*c*) each of the unemployed
(*d*) no improvement

19. Most donors would seriously **protest any** effort to infer from such limited data.
(*a*) protest against
(*b*) protest at
(*c*) protest to
(*d*) no improvement

20. I hope you vividly remember the premier of the film when **I, my wife and you** were present in the hall.
(*a*) my wife, I and you
(*b*) you, my wife and I
(*c*) my wife, you and I
(*d*) no improvement

21. With a thundering roar the huge rocket **soared up** from the launching pad.
(*a*) flew up
(*b*) went upwards
(*c*) took off
(*d*) no improvement

22. My **opinion for** the film is that it will bag the national award.
(*a*) opinion to
(*b*) opinion about
(*c*) opinion on
(*d*) no improvement

23. He **sent a word** to me that he would be coming late.
(*a*) sent word
(*b*) had sent a word
(*c*) sent words
(*d*) no improvement

24. It became clear that the strangers were heading **into** a serious disaster.
(*a*) along
(*b*) towards
(*c*) for
(*d*) no improvement

25. Young men and women should get **habituated** to reading and writing about current affairs.
(*a*) used
(*b*) prepared
(*c*) trained
(*d*) no improvement

Work Book Exercise B

1. An overdose of any medicine is **enough fatal** to a plant as to a man.
(*a*) too fatal (*b*) so fatal
(*c*) as fatal (*d*) no improvement

2. There is nothing **quite miserable** than illiteracy in youth.
(*a*) as miserable (*b*) very miserable
(*c*) more miserable (*d*) no improvement

3. My brother-in-law has a house **for letting**.
(*a*) for letting out (*b*) to rent our
(*c*) to let (*d*) no improvement

4. Netaji was by far **a great man** of India.
(*a*) a very great man (*b*) too great a man
(*c*) the greatest man (*d*) no improvement

5. Hardly had he finished his lunch **than** the phone rang.
(*a*) when (*b*) then
(*c*) while (*d*) no improvement

6. A very horrifying serial **was broadcasted** ten days ago.
(*a*) has brodcast (*b*) was broadcast
(*c*) was broadcasting (*d*) no improvement

7. After a few hours the unconscious patient began to come **out**.
(*a*) round (*b*) on
(*c*) up (*d*) no improvement

8. As you are a born liar, **I don't believe** in what you say.
(*a*) I am not believing (*b*) I will not believe
(*c*) I will not be believing (*d*) no improvement

9. You must not forget to call me after you **reach** Delhi.
(*a*) will reach (*b*) will have reached
(*c*) have reached (*d*) no improvement

10. Rohan died **of a wound and not from cancer**.
(*a*) from a wound and not of cancer
(*b*) of a wound and not of cancer
(*c*) from a wound and not from cancer
(*d*) no improvement

11. All criminal attitudes must be **nipped at the bud**.
(*a*) nipped on the bud (*b*) nipped in the bud
(*c*) nipped off the bud (*d*) no improvement

12. Each village adopted by the club was **provided by** electric supply.
(*a*) provided with (*b*) provided for
(*c*) provided (*d*) no improvement

13. Every man must **look up** the future and find ways of providing for his needs.
(*a*) look for (*b*) look to
(*c*) look in (*d*) no improvement

14. When Seema was fourteen, she **sat** the entrance examination for Senior Secondary school.
(*a*) sat in (*b*) sat at
(*c*) sat for (*d*) no improvement

15. The mother could not help but **cry** at his behaviour.
(a) crying (b) cry
(c) but crying (d) no improvement

16. Galileo escaped **from burning** for heresy because he apologized and withdrew his previous statements.
(a) from being burnt (b) being burnt
(c) from having been burnt (d) no improvement

17. Unless efforts are made and the population growth **stabilised** environmentalists predict a world-wide starvation by 2020 A.D.
(a) stabilises (b) will stabilise
(c) must stabilise (d) no improvement

18. It is the time the three years old **is learning** how to read and write.
(a) was learning (b) has learned
(c) learnt (d) no improvement

19. All the people are supposed **to take out** their shoes when they enter a place of worship.
(a) to take off (b) to put off
(c) to put away (d) no improvement

20. They served **a summons** on the Member of Parliament to appear in the court of law.
(a) a summon (b) the summon
(c) summons (d) no improvement

21. If I **had** money, I would send to you.
(a) had had (b) have had
(c) have (d) no improvement

22. This house **is belonging** to me for two years.
(a) belongs (b) has been belonging
(c) has belonged (d) no improvement

23. All my friends **are waiting** for me since morning.
(a) have been waiting (b) were waiting
(c) wait (d) no improvement

24. Amit is extraordinarily **clever at mimicking** his friends.
(a) clever for mimicking (b) clever in mimicking
(c) clever to mimick (d) no improvement

25. He has got many friends because he had got **much money**.
(a) enough money (b) a lot of money
(c) bags of money (d) no improvement

Work Book Exercise C

1. If a person or an animal **eats** much his body changes the extra carbohydrates and Proteins into fat and stores it.
(a) can eat (b) will eat
(c) eat (d) no improvement

2. Socrates was **one of the wisest man** that ever lived.
(a) one of the wisest men (b) one wise man
(c) one of the wise men (d) no improvement

3. We must not think that people belonging to **few castes** are superior to others.
   (a) many castes (b) high castes
   (c) some castes (d) no improvement
4. **If he studied more**, he would have been able to get a distinction.
   (a) if he were studying more (b) If he had to study more
   (c) if he had studied more (d) no improvement
5. He has very good command **on** English.
   (a) over (b) in
   (c) of (d) no improvement
6. The people in the village **are deprived** of essential commodities for the past two weeks.
   (a) are being deprived (b) had been deprived
   (c) have been deprived (d) no improvement
7. The farmer's way of life can be **contrasted to** that of the factory worker.
   (a) contrasted with (b) contrasted against
   (c) contrasted on (d) no improvement
8. The enthusiastic voters **were queuing up** outside the polling station since morning.
   (a) queued up (b) had queued
   (c) had been queuing up (d) no improvement
9. The brochure, which is being enclosed with the application form will give you **information** that you need.
   (a) the information (b) an information
   (c) informations (d) no improvement
10. Mr. Patel and the other dissident leaders **have taken shelter** at the Church last month after the authorities ordered their arrest.
   (a) took shelter (b) are taking shelter
   (c) had taken shelter (d) no improvement
11. He came to the cave uphill as the evening mist rose and drew a deep breath and looked **up the valley**.
   (a) across the valley (b) into the valley
   (c) down the valley (d) no improvement
12. The child spent two mornings with his parents and on the third he insisted **for accompanying** his grandmother on her rounds in the city.
   (a) in accompanying (b) on accompanying
   (c) to accompanying (d) no improvement
13. With the hubble space telescope astronomers expect to learn the age and size of the universe and to **probe** its origin, evolution and ultimate fate.
   (a) probe for (b) probe in
   (c) probe after (d) no improvement
14. The police **are** trying to solve the mystery.
   (a) is (b) was
   (c) has been (d) no improvement
15. We have been caught in **a rat race**.
   (a) rat race (b) the rat race
   (c) this rat race (d) no improvement
16. Can I exchange **my book for yours**?
   (a) my book with you (b) my book with yours
   (c) our book with your (d) no improvement

17. He **shook hand with me** after receiving the prize.
(*a*) shook my hand (*b*) shook hands with me
(*c*) shook my hands (*d*) no improvement

18. I would like that **you finish the project on time**.
(*a*) you finished the project on time
(*b*) that you would finish the project on time
(*c*) you finishing the project on time
(*d*) no improvement

19. There are sufficient funds to meet the requirements of **the entire schools** in our zone.
(*a*) schools (*b*) all of the schools
(*c*) all the schools (*d*) no improvement

20. It is **long since** I saw you last.
(*a*) long ago (*b*) long time
(*c*) long before (*d*) no improvement

21. The angry boys **were** arguing with the Principal since morning.
(*a*) have been (*b*) was
(*c*) has been (*d*) no improvement

22. He has been absent **for the past** few months.
(*a*) since the past (*b*) since the last
(*c*) for past (*d*) no improvement

23. You will be punished **if you will** come to my class.
(*a*) if you come (*b*) if you shall come
(*c*) if you came (*d*) no improvement

24. The good fortune **of being your student** in my younger days had helped me greatly in my life.
(*a*) of my being your student (*b*) of my having been your student
(*c*) of myself being your student (*d*) no improvement

25. A good house has been **alloted** to him.
(*a*) aloted (*b*) allotted
(*c*) alotted (*d*) no improvement

Work Book Exercise D

1. There is plenty of time **to catch** the train.
(*a*) to get (*b*) to reach
(*c*) to hold (*d*) no improvement

2. Hundreds of people were killed **by** the earthquake.
(*a*) in (*b*) from
(*c*) of (*d*) no improvement

3. He **insisted on** he was innocent.
(*a*) insisted on that (*b*) insisted that
(*c*) insists that (*d*) no improvement

4. John, who **studies** medicine at present, hopes to go abroad after graduation.
(*a*) is studying (*b*) will study
(*c*) studied (*d*) no improvement

5. The warehouse is infested **of** snakes.
(a) by (b) with
(c) off (d) no improvement

6. He **is having** three cars.
(a) has (b) was
(c) got (d) no improvement

7. He goes **to cinema** every Sunday.
(a) a cinema (b) in cinema
(c) to the cinema (d) no improvement

8. **Would** you find me absent, please don't forget to leave a message behind.
(a) Should (b) Unless
(c) As (d) no improvement

9. My mother always **finds fault** with the maid servant.
(a) is finding faults (b) has found fault
(c) find faults (d) no improvement

10. You ought not to **have gone** there, but you did.
(a) to go (b) to have been
(c) to be going (d) no improvement

11. Mary met with an accident, she did not just twist her leg, She **has broken it**.
(a) had broken it (b) break it
(c) broke it too (d) no improvement

12. What is needed **are** not large houses but small cottages.
(a) was (b) were
(c) is (d) no improvement

13. It was hard to believe that he **was dead** for two years.
(a) has been dead (b) is dead
(c) had been dead (d) no improvement

14. Do not take another step, else your life **will face** great peril.
(a) might be thrown into (b) will be in
(c) would be placed in great (d) no improvement

15. I **would gladly accompany** your sister if you had asked me.
(a) would have gladly accompanied (b) was to have gladly accompanied
(c) will gladly accompany (d) no improvement

16. He was likely to win the elections **by the sweeping majority.**
(a) with the sweeping majority (b) by a sweeping majority
(c) with sweeping a majority (d) no improvement

17. It is sheer folly to believe that you can improve the situation by **doing away** people.
(a) doing with (b) doing away with
(c) doing it to (d) no improvement

18. Governments in developing countries are under increasing pressure **for the recruiting and training** teachers to meet the demands of their rapidly expanding systems of education.
(a) in the recruiting and training of (b) to recruit and train
(c) so as to recruit and train (d) no improvement

19. Last evening I went to the optician and bought **spectacles**.
(a) a spectacle (b) two spectacles
(c) a pair of spectacles (d) no improvement

20. As John dived off the spring board, he was horrified to see that the water **was drained from** the pool the night before.
(*a*) was drained (*b*) had drained away
(*c*) had been drained off (*d*) no improvement

21. The situation remained the same, rather got worse, **all his efforts not withstanding**.
(*a*) with all his efforts notwithstanding (*b*) in spite of all his efforts notwithstanding
(*c*) for all his efforts not withstanding (*d*) no improvement

22. One can live and work in a town without being aware of the daily march of the sun across the sky without **never** seeing the moon and stars.
(*a*) seldom (*b*) hardly
(*c*) ever (*d*) no improvement

23. Being a handicapped youth, he **was put hard to** complete his military course.
(*a*) was hard put to (*b*) was put to it hard
(*c*) was hardly put to (*d*) no improvement

24. She **cut a sad figure** in her first performance on the stage.
(*a*) made a sorry figure (*b*) cut a sorry face
(*c*) cut a sorry figure (*d*) no improvement

25. **No sooner I saw** the tiger, than I ran away.
(*a*) As soon as I saw (*b*) No sooner I had seen
(*c*) No sooner did I see (*d*) no improvement

Work Book Exercise E

1. Hoping not to be disturbed, I sat down in my easy chair to read the book I **won as a prize**.
(*a*) I had to win as a prize (*b*) I have won as prize
(*c*) I had won as a prize (*d*) no improvement

2. Practically **every part** of the banana tree is used by man.
(*a*) each part (*b*) any part
(*c*) most part (*d*) no improvement

3. If you are living near a market place you should be ready **to bear** the disturbance caused by traffic.
(*a*) to bear upon (*b*) to bear with
(*c*) to bear away (*d*) no improvement

4. Please remind me **of posting** these letters to my relatives.
(*a*) by posting (*b*) to post
(*c*) for posting (*d*) no improvement

5. Whenever my students come across new words, I ask them **to look for them** in the dictionary.
(*a*) to look it up (*b*) to look them up
(*c*) to look at them (*d*) no improvement

6. His father won't be able to leave for Varanasi **until they have arrived.**
(*a*) until they arrive (*b*) until they will have arrived
(*c*) until they will arrive (*d*) no improvement

7. The company goes to great length to ensure that employees **can be comfortable** in their work environment.
(*a*) are comfortable (*b*) will be comfortable
(*c*) should be comfortable (*d*) no improvement

8. I knew he could not be trusted, he **let off the cat from the bag.**
(*a*) let the cat out of the bag (*b*) let the cat from the bag
(*c*) let the cat jump out of the bag (*d*) no improvement

9. The mother has not seen the child for several months and now eagerly **looks forward** to seeing him.
(*a*) look a head to (*b*) look for
(*c*) looks into (*d*) no improvement

10. I am definitely late. The train **will have left** the station by the time I reach there.
(*a*) will leave (*b*) will be leaving
(*c*) would have left (*d*) no improvement

11. It is unreasonable to **distort** the statement of a man simply because he does not agree to your opinions.
(*a*) bend (*b*) denounce
(*c*) discourage (*d*) no improvement

12. Scarcely had he entered the room **than** the phone rang.
(*a*) as (*b*) when
(*c*) while (*d*) no improvement

13. **As soon as** I walked into the building, I could hear the sound of a celebration in progress.
(*a*) no sooner had (*b*) sooner than
(*c*) hardly (*d*) no improvement

14. The teacher **saw through the game** and punished him.
(*a*) saw into the game (*b*) saw at the game
(*c*) saw the game (*d*) no improvement

15. This is the **least expensive** of the two cars.
(*a*) last expensive (*b*) less expensive
(*c*) lessen expensive (*d*) no improvement

16. The train **left** before I reached the station.
(*a*) will have left (*b*) leaves
(*c*) had left (*d*) no improvement

17. I do not take any cognizance **on** what he says.
(*a*) about (*b*) for
(*c*) of (*d*) no improvement

18. In a few minutes time when the clock strikes six, **I shall be waiting** for her for three quarters of an hour.
(*a*) I would have been waiting (*b*) I would have waiting
(*c*) I shall have waited (*d*) no improvement

19. I **have been writing** ten letters since breakfast.
(*a*) am writing (*b*) have written
(*c*) wrote (*d*) no improvement

20. If you **call to him** to explain your problem he will help you.
(*a*) call in him (*b*) call at him
(*c*) call upon him (*d*) no improvement

21. He enjoys nothing more than **drawing** swords with others.
(*a*) playing (*b*) crossing
(*c*) clashing (*d*) no improvement

22. This beautiful shirt which I bought for my birthday **costed** only ₹ 150.
(*a*) was costed (*b*) cost
(*c*) was cost (*d*) no improvement

23. I noticed that **the opposite man** was staring at me.
(*a*) the man opposite (*b*) the opposed man
(*c*) man opposite (*d*) no improvement

24. Do you think any man has a right **to break in** his neighbour's house ?
(*a*) to break through (*b*) to break into
(*c*) to break open (*d*) no improvement

25. They **are waiting** for her since morning.
(*a*) have been waiting (*b*) were waiting
(*c*) wait (*d*) no improvement

Work Book Exercise F

1. He plays cricket and tennis **also**.
(*a*) both (*b*) besides
(*c*) too (*d*) no improvement

2. The **need** of the hour was some fast action on the part of the leaders.
(*a*) needed (*b*) needing
(*c*) needs (*d*) no improvement

3. On seeing the lion she felt **too much** afraid.
(*a*) very much (*b*) excessively
(*c*) much (*d*) no improvement

4. No one needs to **worry** about me.
(*a*) will worry (*b*) need worry
(*c*) shall worry (*d*) no improvement

5. The teacher asked the intruder **who was he and why was he** occupying his chair.
(*a*) who he was and why he was
(*b*) who he was and why was he
(*c*) who he had been and why he had been
(*d*) no improvement

6. **It is no good to cry** over spilt milk.
(*a*) It is no good crying (*b*) It is of no good to cry
(*c*) It is of no good crying (*d*) no improvement

7. The actress said that it sometimes took her two hours to **put** her make-up.
(*a*) put over (*b*) put up
(*c*) put on (*d*) no improvement

8. He has been working **off and on** for several years to compile a dictionary.
(*a*) on or off (*b*) on and off
(*c*) regularly (*d*) no improvement

9. He has been growing weaker and his life now **hangs like a thread.**
(*a*) hangs with threads (*b*) hangs by a thread
(*c*) hangs on a thread (*d*) no improvement

10. She did not ask **any question to him.**
(*a*) any question from him (*b*) him any question
(*c*) to him any question (*d*) no improvement

11. Rohit assured Sunita that he **would look at** her work while she was on leave.
(a) would overlook
(b) would look after
(c) will look
(d) no improvement

12. No sooner had the umpire given the batsman out **than the crowd** rushed into the field.
(a) but the people
(b) when the crowds
(c) and the crowd
(d) no improvement

13. Newton wanted to **know why did the apple fall** to the ground.
(a) know that why did the apple fall
(b) know why the apple fell
(c) know that why the apple fell
(d) no improvement

14. Having finished the book, **it was put away by him**.
(a) he put it away
(b) it was being put away by him.
(c) it was putting away by him
(d) no improvement

15. He was extremely unhappy because of **the inordinately delay.**
(a) the inordinate delaying
(b) the inordinate delay
(c) the inordinately delaying
(d) no improvement

16. She says she's already paid me back but I can't remember, so I'll have **to take her word**.
(a) to take her word true
(b) to take her at her word
(c) to take her word for it
(d) no improvement

17. When the clock struck six I **was waiting** here for an hour.
(a) had waited
(b) had been waiting
(c) shall have waited
(d) no improvement

18. When the soldier returned home after the war was over, his wife received him **with open hands**.
(a) with open arms
(b) with unfolded hands
(c) with an open heart
(d) no improvement

19. By the end of this century, scientists surely **have discovered** a cure for cancer.
(a) are discovering
(b) will have discovered
(c) must discover
(d) no improvement

20. **There is no room** for you in this compartment.
(a) There is no more accommodation
(b) There is no more space
(c) There is no more seat
(d) no improvement

21. It is time **to immediately put the work in hand**.
(a) to put the work immediately in hand
(b) to put the work in hand immediately
(c) There is no more seat
(d) no improvement

22. When he arrived to attend the wedding of his brother, he **had been dressed** in dark suit.
(a) dressed
(b) was dressed
(c) had dressed
(d) no improvement

23. He gave **witness** at the sensational trial.
(a) evidence
(b) proof
(c) advice
(d) no improvement

24. As soon as our plan is approved I shall favour **its'** adoption.
(a) our
(b) it's
(c) its
(d) no improvement

25. I can always **count on him** in times of difficulty.
(a) count at him
(b) count on he
(c) count him on
(d) no improvement

Work Book Exercise G

1. Each of our **students pay their** tuition fee at the beginning of the month.
(*a*) student pay their (*b*) students pays their
(*c*) students pays his (*d*) no improvement

2. It is essential **to thoroughly clean** the machine after each use.
(*a*) to thorough clean (*b*) to clean thoroughly
(*c*) to clean thorough (*d*) no improvement

3. I told him clearly that he **hadn't ought to do** that to me.
(*a*) ought not to have done (*b*) ought not done
(*c*) ought not has done (*d*) no improvement

4. When a man has to give evidence he must **have a clean breast** of the whole matter.
(*a*) make a clean breast (*b*) obtain a clean breast
(*c*) possess a clean breast (*d*) no improvement

5. The fast train **came a halt to before** crossing the bridge.
(*a*) came before to a halt (*b*) came to a halt before
(*c*) came to halts before a (*d*) no improvement

6. Do you know **who she is going to marry**?
(*a*) who she is married? (*b*) who is she going to marry?
(*c*) whom she is going to marry? (*d*) no improvement

7. I took the cycle **which he has bought yesterday.**
(*a*) that he bought yesterday (*b*) that he had bought yesterday
(*c*) that which he had bought yesterday (*d*) no improvement

8. Even the people in authority agree that corruption has become **today's order**.
(*a*) the order of the day (*b*) the order of today
(*c*) the day's order (*d*) no improvement

9. Most of the employees from Rajan's factory were not **inclination to using** the new technology.
(*a*) inclined to be use (*b*) incline to use
(*c*) inclined to use (*d*) no improvement

10. All the allegations **levelled against** him were found to be baseless.
(*a*) levelled for (*b*) level with
(*c*) level against (*d*) no improvement

11. He **did many mischiefs.**
(*a*) made many a mischiefs. (*b*) made much mischief
(*c*) committed many mischiefs (*d*) no improvement

12. He has said so out of affection, do not take **it to heart**
(*a*) in heart (*b*) it in the heart
(*c*) by the heart (*d*) no improvement

13. Sumit **would have been looked** smart in traditional dress.
(*a*) was looked (*b*) would have looked
(*c*) had looking (*d*) no improvement

14. People are **tiring** very soon in an activity which they don't like.
(*a*) tried (*b*) tyring
(*c*) tired (*d*) no improvement

15. Is there any **place** for me to sit ?
(a) space (b) room
(c) area (d) no improvement

16. They felt humiliated because they realised that they **had cheated**.
(a) had been cheated (b) have been cheated
(c) were to be cheated (d) no improvement

17. Sri Pashupatinath is **worth seeing temple** in Kathmandu.
(a) a temple worth seeing (b) a temple to see its worth.
(c) one of the worth seeing temples (d) no improvement

18. The practical importance of the role of the industrialist in the establishment of the new order is greater than **the economist and the politician.**
(a) of the economist and politicians
(b) that of the economists and the politicians
(c) that of the economist and the politician
(d) no improvement

19. Poor Tom **laid** in the shade of a tree before he could not walk further.
(a) lied (b) lain
(c) lay (d) no improvement

20. Tell your leader that I grant him permission **of stay** in my kingdom.
(a) about stay (b) to stay
(c) for stay (d) no improvement

21. He could not **cope up with** the heavy rush.
(a) cope upto (b) cope by
(c) cope with (d) no improvement

22. He opened the letter without **caring** to read the address on the envelope.
(a) thinking (b) bothering
(c) worrying (d) no improvement

23. We were still standing in the queue when the **film was beginning**.
(a) film begins (b) film had begun
(c) film began (d) no improvement

24. It was so hot during the school parade that several of the weaker pupils passed **by**.
(a) out (b) through
(c) over (d) no improvement

25. When the train finally **came into** the station, the lonely traveller seemed relieved.
(a) pulled in (b) will pull into
(c) have pulled into (d) no improvement

Revision Exercise

Exercise A

Directions (Q.Nos. 1-50) *In the questions sentence/ a part of the sentence is bolded. Below are given alternatives, to the* ***bolded*** *part at (a), (b),(c). Which may improve the sentence. Choose the correct alternative. In case no improvement is needed your answer is (d).*

1. I did not expect an award for **assisting him with help**.
(a) helping him
(b) I had helped him
(c) I did help him
(d) no improvement

2. She gave him a cup **that contained** tea.
(a) of
(b) containing
(c) which had
(d) no improvement

3. He has finished his lunch **now and was satisfied**.
(a) and is satisfied now
(b) then and is satisfied
(c) now and is satisfied
(d) no improvement

4. The two thieves divided the loot **between themselves**.
(a) among themselves
(b) amongst themselves
(c) with themselves
(d) no improvement

5. Tell me **what is his name**?
(a) what name is he
(b) what name is his
(c) what his name is
(d) no improvement

6. The two parties **broke off relation with one another** in 1980.
(a) broke away from the party
(b) parted ways
(c) broke down several times during the speech
(d) no improvement

7. He will revise it **when he is comes back**.
(a) when he come back
(b) on coming back
(c) when he came back
(d) no improvement

8. The members of the student's union **did not give** the examination in protest.
(a) did not write
(b) did not sit for
(c) did not show up for
(d) no improvement

9. **I feel out of sort today**.
(a) I feel of sort today
(b) I feel out of sorts today
(c) I feel out of sort this day
(d) no improvement

10. An increase in crimes against women **have been reported** in the newspapers recently.
(a) are being reported
(b) has been reported
(c) has been written
(d) no improvement

11. The labourers are **bent at** getting what is due to them.
(a) bent for
(b) bent upon
(c) bent in
(d) no improvement

12. Although the goal-keeper was responsible for the defeat in the important football match, **nobody blamed him**.
(a) still nobody blamed him
(b) nevertheless nobody blamed him
(c) yet nobody blamed him
(d) no improvement

13. Would it be impertinent **to ask why you are leaving**?
(a) If asking why you are leave *(b)* for asking why you are leave
(c) to asking why you are leave *(d)* no improvement

14. We **have to know that** we can achieve things slowly and gradually, not overnight.
(a) would know that *(b)* had to know that
(c) must know that *(d)* no improvement

15. Rajesh's **ability to use** the local language surprised me.
(a) knowing of *(b)* confidence with
(c) familiarity with *(d)* no improvement

16. I usually **did not take** sugar in my tea.
(a) do not take *(b)* do not takes
(c) have not taken *(d)* no improvement

17. **Unless they modify the system**, our future generations will suffer.
(a) Unless the system is modified *(b)* Unless the system will be modified
(c) If the system will not be modified *(d)* no improvement

18. **To contact the police he tried hard.**
(a) He tried to contact the police hard *(b)* He tried hard to contact the police
(c) He tried the police to contact hard *(d)* no improvement

19. **Its not possible to judge a man by his appearance.**
(a) It's not possible to judge a man by his appearance
(b) Its impossible to judge a man by his appearance
(c) Its' not impossible to judge a man by his appearance
(d) no improvement

20. Mrs Roy **keeps an open house** on Saturday evening parties - you'll find all kinds of people there.
(a) welcomes all members *(b)* welcomes a select group of people
(c) keeps the doors of the house open *(d)* no improvement

21. **The police cordoned off the area** after the explosion.
(a) The police filled the whole area *(b)* The police isolated the area
(c) The police checked everyone in the area *(d)* no improvement

22. The manager hesitated to assign the job to the newcomer as he was **wet behind the ears**.
(a) drenched in the rain *(b)* unpunctual and lethargic
(c) stupid and slow witted *(d)* no improvement

23. She is quite well now, **except a slight cold.**
(a) except have a slight cold *(b)* except for a slight cold
(c) excepting a slight cold *(d)* no improvement

24. **If I had the money I would have bought the house**.
(a) If I had the money I would have bought the house
(b) If I have the money I would have bought the house
(c) If I have had the money I would have bought the house
(d) no improvement

25. **I wish I knew what is wrong with my car.**
(a) I wish I had known what is wrong with my car
(b) I wish I know what is wrong with my car
(c) I wish I knew what was wrong with my car
(d) no improvement

26. Just before he died, Amar, who is a poet, wrote this poem.
(a) Just before he died, Amar, who was a poet, wrote this poem
(b) Amar, who is a poet, wrote this poem just before he died
(c) Amar wrote this poem, who is a poet, just before he died
(d) no improvement

27. The flag will be risen on the 15th of August.
(a) The flag will be roused on the 15th of August
(b) The flag will be rising on the 15th of August
(c) The flag will be raised on the 15th of August
(d) no improvement

28. Sushma has wisdom, charm and **she has a good sense of humour**.
(a) Sushma had a good sense of humour *(b)* a good sense of humour
(c) has a good sense of humour *(d)* no improvement

29. They **knocked down** ten houses when they built the new road.
(a) ruptured *(b)* removed
(c) pulled down *(d)* no improvement

30. The game is more important than the winning of the prize.
(a) The gaming is more important than the winning of the prize
(b) The game is more important than winning the prize
(c) Gaming is more important than winning of the prize
(d) no improvement

31. The actor is out of jail **and not exactly a free man,** since he will be under house arrest for an additional 90 days.
(a) but not exactly a free man *(b)* though exactly a free man
(c) if not exactly a free man *(d)* no improvement

32. Some players in the team suffer from chronic knee problems and will not play in the next playoff.
(a) Some player on the team suffered *(b)* Some player on the team suffer
(c) Some players on the team suffers *(d)* no improvement

33. Students will have to **take the test** again tomorrow.
(a) apply the test *(b)* avoid the test
(c) retain the test *(d)* no improvement

34. He was **given a lot of pressure** to sign the deed.
(a) told *(b)* forced
(c) asked *(d)* no improvement

35. If he smokes less he might get rid of his cough.
(a) If he smoked less he would get rid of his cough
(b) If he had smoked less he might get rid of his cough
(c) If he smokes less he might have got rid of his cough
(d) no improvement

36. He compensated the loss to me.
(a) He compensated the loss for me
(b) He compensated me to the loss
(c) He compensated me for the loss
(d) no improvement

37. The climate of Karnataka **is cooler than** Tamil Nadu.
(a) is cooler to *(b)* is cooler than of
(c) is cooler than that of *(d)* no improvement

38. **I gave to** Sana the keys.
(a) I gave (b) I gave to the
(c) I gave the (d) no improvement

39. All nations must first **become agricultural strong.**
(a) become agriculturally strong (b) become strong agriculture
(c) become agriculture strong (d) no improvement

40. An orangutan's intelligence **is as superior to** that of man.
(a) is more superior to (b) is superior to
(c) is superior than that of (d) no improvement

41. As employees, we are **accountable for** our stakeholders.
(a) accountable with (b) accountable to
(c) accountable against (d) no improvement

42. **Recently he had insured for** a mediclaim policy.
(a) He had recently insured for (b) Recently he insured for
(c) He insured recently for (d) no improvement

43. Everyday, **we usually had** lunch at 1.30 pm.
(a) we have had usually (b) we have usually
(c) we usually have (d) no improvement

44. The young servant **goes about** with the old master.
(a) moves around (b) goes around
(c) tries to know more about (d) no improvement

45. Complete the **formalities of registration of** the workshop before you enter the hall.
(a) formalities of registration for (b) formalities to registering for
(c) formalities to register for (d) no improvement

46. Officials were asked to examine the **likelihood** of providing banking facilities in the area.
(a) probability (b) possibility
(c) profit (d) no improvement

47. **Being a rainy day**, we had to abandon the match.
(a) Having been a rainy day (b) It being a rainy day
(c) It been a rainy day (d) no improvement

48. Rahul gave me **an old scissor**.
(a) an old scissors (b) a pair of old scissors
(c) a pair of old scissor (d) no improvement

49. When **I shall go** to Agra, I shall visit the Taj Mahal.
(a) have gone (b) shall travel
(c) go (d) no improvement

50. The minister agreed **will answer** questions on television.
(a) to answer (b) for answering
(c) with answering (d) no improvement

Exercise B

Directions (Q.Nos. 1-50) *In the questions, a sentence/part of the sentence is bolded. Below are given alternatives to the **bolded** part at (a),(b) and (c). Which may improve the sentence. Choose the correct alternative. In case no improvement is needed, your answer is (d).*

1. I **give key to** my wrist watch everyday.
(*a*) wind down (*b*) wound up
(*c*) wind (*d*) no improvement

2. We **did** a test when the lights went out.
(*a*) have been doing (*b*) were doing
(*c*) had done (*d*) no improvement

3. He **put up** a lot of work on that article.
(*a*) put in (*b*) put down
(*c*) put over (*d*) no improvement

4. The man whom I thought was thoroughly honest proved to be a swindler.
(*a*) The man whom I thought was thoroughly honest proved a swindler
(*b*) The man who I thought was throughly honest proved to be a swindler
(*c*) The man to whom I thought was thoroughly honest proved to be a swindler
(*d*) no improvement

5. No sooner had the dividend been declared, the notices were sent out.
(*a*) The company had hardly declared the dividend till the notices were sent for mailing
(*b*) They had no sooner declared the dividend than the notices were sent out
(*c*) Hardly had the dividend been declared when the notices were sent out
(*d*) no improvement

6. Riding upon his horse, the tiger jumped at him.
(*a*) Riding upon the tiger, the horse jumped at him
(*b*) The tiger jumped at him while he was riding upon his horse
(*c*) The tiger rode at him while he was jumping upon his horse
(*d*) no improvement

7. I in black and white must have your terms down.
(*a*) I must have in black and white your terms down
(*b*) I must have your terms in black and white down
(*c*) I must have your terms down in black and white
(*d*) no improvement

8. When we came out of the restaurant it was half past eleven.
(*a*) When we had come out of the restaurant
(*b*) After we came out of the restaurant
(*c*) When we have come out of the restaurant
(*d*) no improvement

9. What do you for go to school?
(*a*) For what do you go to school? (*b*) What do you go for to school?
(*c*) What do you go to school for? (*d*) no improvement

10. He pleased the directors and this completed his report in good time.
(*a*) He pleased the directors in good time and this completed his report
(*b*) He completed his report in good time and this pleased the directors
(*c*) He pleased the directors and completed his report and this in good time
(*d*) no improvement

11. The courtiers used to tell the king how efficient an administrator he was all day long.

(a) The courtiers all day long used to tell the king how efficient an administrator he was
(b) The courtiers used all day long to tell the king how efficient an administrator he was
(c) The courtiers used to tell the king all day long how efficient an administrator he was
(d) no improvement

12. We had a grand party and we enjoyed very much.

(a) We had a grand party and enjoyed very much
(b) We had a grand party to enjoy very much
(c) We had a grand party and we enjoyed ourselves very much
(d) no improvement

13. He has for good left India.

(a) He has left for good India
(b) He has left India for good
(c) Good he has left India
(d) no improvement

14. We are credibly informed that the murderer has given himself up.

(a) We are informed that the murderer has credibly given himself up
(b) We are informed that the murderer has given credibly him self-up
(c) We are informed that credibly the murderer has given up himself up
(d) no improvement

15. We generally select **one of the most intelligent student of the school for this award.**

(a) one of the most intelligent students of the school
(b) one of the intelligent most students of the school
(c) one of the intelligent most student of the school
(d) no improvement

16. My friend lives in a nearby street **whose name** I have forgotten.

(a) the name of which
(b) which name
(c) of which name
(d) no improvement

17. He both won a medal and a scholarship.

(a) He won a medal and a scholarship both
(b) Both he won a medal and a scholarship
(c) He won both a medal and a scholarship
(d) no improvement

18. A taller Sikh rushed forward than any of his comrades.

(a) A Sikh, taller than any of his comrades, rushed forward
(b) A Sikh rushed forward taller than any of his comrades
(c) A Sikh rushed forward than any of his comrades taller
(d) no improvement

19. An author in the reign of Queen Anne who was famous lived in cottage.

(a) An author in the reign, who was famous, of Queen Anne lived in a cottage
(b) In the reign of Queen Anne an author lived in a cottage who was famous
(c) An author who was famous in the reign of Queen Anne lived in a cottage
(d) no improvement

20. In the absence of your support he would have lost the election.

(a) Lacking your support, he would have lost the election
(b) But for your support, he would have lost the election
(c) He would have lost the election, if you had not supported him
(d) no improvement

21. My uncle is enough rich to buy a car.
(a) My uncle is rich enough to buy a car.
(b) My uncle is richer enough to buy a car.
(c) My uncle is enough richer to buy a car.
(d) no improvement

22. Walking along the road, an old man ran over the lorry.
(a) Walking along the road an old man ran behind the lorry.
(b) Running along the road, the lorry ran over an old man.
(c) The lorry ran over an old man walking along the road.
(d) no improvement

23. I visited my aunt just **before a week.**
(a) a week before *(b)* a week earlier
(c) a week ago *(d)* no improvement

24. Foreigner often **come across with** serious difficulties in studying English.
(a) have to come across with *(b)* come cross with
(c) come across *(d)* no improvement

25. He **work hard** will succeed.
(a) who will work hard *(b)* who will be working hard
(c) who works hard *(d)* no improvement

26. The advancements in medical science **has provide** to be a boon for all of us.
(a) has proven *(b)* had proven
(c) have proved *(d)* no improvement

27. He received **many praises** for his latest invention.
(a) great many praises *(b)* much praise
(c) too much praises *(d)* no improvement

28. If was you I would not sign the document.
(a) If I have been you *(b)* If I were you
(c) If I had been you *(d)* no improvement

29. I prefer **to ride than to walk.**
(a) ride to walk *(b)* riding than walking
(c) riding to walking *(d)* no improvement

30. I have not finished **to paint** the door.
(a) painting *(b)* the paint of
(c) the painting *(d)* no improvement

31. She usually does not leave for work until she **finished** all her chores.
(a) finishes *(b)* has finished
(c) had finished *(d)* no improvement

32. The article should not **exceed more than** hundred words.
(a) exceed beyond *(b)* exceed than
(c) exceed *(d)* no improvement

33. Geeta said that she had never **viewed across** a book she liked so much.
(a) come across *(b)* come through
(c) come round *(d)* no improvement

34. I will be **giving** blood in the hospital at 9.00 am tomorrow.
(a) exchanging *(b)* contributing
(c) donating *(d)* no improvement

35. The fishermen **are fishing** in the sea from sunrise and will continue to do so until sunset.
(*a*) have fished (*b*) have been fishing
(*c*) were fishing (*d*) no improvement

36. Which newspaper do you **subscribe for?**
(*a*) subscribe in (*b*) subscribe at
(*c*) subscribe to (*d*) no improvement

37. His friends could not tell me **why he did not come** to college yesterday.
(*a*) why had he not come (*b*) why did he not come
(*c*) why not had he come (*d*) no improvement

38. The festival **is likely to fall** in December.
(*a*) will likely to fall (*b*) will be likely to fall
(*c*) will likely for fall (*d*) no improvement

39. I asked the traveller **where is he going.**
(*a*) where he is going (*b*) where was he going
(*c*) where he was going (*d*) no improvement

40. The bird sanctuary is **about 10 kms inside** from Central Delhi.
(*a*) was about 10 kms over (*b*) is about 10 kms on top
(*c*) is about 10 kms away (*d*) no improvement

41. This is **so important a** matter.
(*a*) such an important (*b*) very important
(*c*) quite important (*d*) no improvement

42. When Rahul **handed his home work**, he forgot to give the teacher the last page.
(*a*) handed in his homework (*b*) handed down his homework
(*c*) hand over his homework (*d*) no improvement

43. Although he was tired he **went out for playing.**
(*a*) goes out for playing (*b*) goes out to play
(*c*) went out to play (*d*) no improvement

44. Rakesh **didn't knew** my address.
(*a*) didn't known (*b*) didn't have
(*c*) didn't know (*d*) no improvement

45. It was quite clear that the runner **could be able** to improve upon his own record.
(*a*) will be able (*b*) should be able
(*c*) would be able (*d*) no improvement

46. The cheapest **electronic good** are manufactured in China.
(*a*) electronical good (*b*) electrical good
(*c*) electrical goods (*d*) no improvement

47. The stranger asked the little girl **what is her name.**
(*a*) what her name is (*b*) what her name was
(*c*) what was her name (*d*) no improvement

48. **Beside being** a poet, he is also a famous singer.
(*a*) Besides being (*b*) Besides becoming
(*c*) Beside becoming (*d*) no improvement

49. All the students have **passed out of** the final examination.
(*a*) passed on (*b*) passed away
(*c*) passed (*d*) no improvement

50. This is one of the best novels **that have** appeared this year.
(a) that
(b) that has
(c) to have
(d) no improvement

Exercise C

Directions (Q.Nos. 1-5) *Which of the phrases (a), (b), (c) and (d) given below each statement should be placed in the blank space provided so as to make a meaningful and grammatically correct sentence? If none of the sentences is appropriate, mark (e) i.e., 'None of the above' as the answer.*

1. Overlooking the fact that water scarcity intensifies during summer, ...
(a) the government issued guidelines to all builders to limit their consumption to acceptable limits
(b) provision for rainwater harvesting has been made to aid irrigation in drought prone area
(c) the water table did not improve even after receiving normal monsoon in the current year
(d) many residential areas continue to use swimming pools, wasting large quantities of water
(e) None of the above

2. Refuting the rationale behind frequent agitations for formation of separate states, a recent report ....
(a) proved that such agitations result in loss of governmental property
(b) indicated that the formation of small states does not necessarily improve the economy
(c) suggested that only large scale agitations have been effective in bringing out desired change in the past
(d) recommended dividing large states into smaller ones to improve governance
(e) None of the above

3. Achieving equality for women is not only a laudable goal, ...
(a) political reforms are also neglected preventing women from entering legislatures and positions of power
(b) the problem is also deep rooted in the society and supported by it
(c) their empowerment is purposefully hampered by people with vested interests in all sections of the society
(d) it is also equally difficult to achieve and maintain for a long term
(e) None of the above

4. He has lost most of his life's earning in the stock market but ....
(a) he still seems to be leading his life luxuriously and extravagantly
(b) he could not save enough to repay his enormous debts
(c) stock market is not a safe option to invest money unless done with caution
(d) experts have been suggesting to avoid investments in stock market because of its unpredictable nature
(e) None of the above

5. .... or else they would not keep electing him year after year.
(a) The party leader gave a strong message to the mayor for improving his political style
(b) Owing to numerous scandals against the mayor, he was told to resign from the post immediately
(c) The mayor threatened the residents against filing a complaint against him
(d) The residents must really be impressed with the political style of their mayor
(e) None of the above

Directions (Q.Nos. 6-14) *In the following questions, a sentence/part of the sentence is bolded. Below are given alternatives to the **bolded** sentence/part of the sentence at (a), (b) and (c) which may improve the sentence. Choose the correct alternative. In case no improvement is needed, your answer is (d)*

6. 20 km **are not a great distance** in these days of fast moving vehicles.
(a) is not a great distance
(b) are not too great a distance
(c) aren't proving a great distance
(d) no improvement

7. **I adapted** a new method to solve the problem.
(a) I have been adopted
(b) I adopted
(c) I was adapted
(d) no improvement

8. Meera, the top honcho, in the **account** department listened patiently to our problem.
(a) accounts *(b)* accounting *(c)* accounted *(d)* no improvement

9. Just **bear over** me till I complete this assignment
(a) bear upon
(b) bear with
(c) bear over
(d) no improvement

10. The more they earn, **more they spend** on luxury items.
(a) more they should spend
(b) the more they spend
(c) the more they ought to spend
(d) no improvement

11. You have come here with a view **to insult me.**
(a) to insulting me
(b) of insulting me
(c) for insulting me
(d) no improvement

12. A little rail-road engine **was employed by a station yard** for doing small pieces of work.
(a) was made by a station yard
(b) was used at the station yard
(c) was employed at the station yard
(d) no improvement

13. **From an aesthetic point of view, the painting did not appeal to me.**
(a) From the viewpoint of aesthetics, the painting did not appeal to me
(b) The painting had no aesthetic appeal to me
(c) From an aesthetic point of view, the painting had a little appeal to me
(d) no improvement

14. **The child tossed in bed burning with fever.**
(a) The child in bed, burning with fever tossed
(b) The child burning with fever, tossed in bed
(c) The child burning in bed tossed with fever
(d) no improvement

Directions (Q.Nos. 15-27) *Look at the bolded part of each sentence. Below each sentence, three possible substitutions for the **bolded** part are given. If one of them (a), (b) or (c) is better than the **bolded** part, indicate your response on the Answer Sheet against the corresponding letter. If none of these substitutions improves the sentence, indicate (d) 'No improvement' as your response on the Answer Sheet.*

15. She told the children **not to stop** the work.
(a) not stopping
(b) don't stop
(c) not stopping of
(d) no improvement

16. He succeeded **by dint of** hard work.
(a) by means of
(b) by doing
(c) by virtue of
(d) no improvement

17. You **have read** that book for ages.
(*a*) have been reading (*b*) had read
(*c*) will be reading (*d*) no improvement

18. The only bit of relief for the victims **has been** the increase in compensation.
(*a*) were (*b*) have been
(*c*) was that they were given (*d*) no improvement

19. I am not sure why **she is wanting** to see him.
(*a*) she wants (*b*) does she want
(*c*) is she wanting (*d*) no improvement

20. It has been two years **since I have seen him** last.
(*a*) when I have seen him (*b*) since I had seen him
(*c*) since I saw him (*d*) no improvement

21. He wanted an apartment of his **owning**.
(*a*) owns (*b*) own
(*c*) owned (*d*) no improvement

22. His **flute recitation** was highly appreciated.
(*a*) flute recital (*b*) flute play
(*c*) flute singing (*d*) no improvement

23. She must try **at making him understand**.
(*a*) to make him to understand (*b*) to make him understand
(*c*) to make his understanding (*d*) no improvement

24. These are your new shoes, **aren't they**?
(*a*) isn't it ? (*b*) is it so ?
(*c*) are they ? (*d*) no improvement

25. He told **to us everything he knew**.
(*a*) us everything he knew (*b*) us everything he is knowing
(*c*) us everything he was knowing (*d*) no improvement

26. Unless you **do not work hard**, you won't succeed in life.
(*a*) cannot work hard (*b*) will not work hard
(*c*) work hard (*d*) no improvement

27. As I am tired, I **cannot be able** to climb this hill now.
(*a*) can be able (*b*) will not be able
(*c*) will not be possible (*d*) no improvement

Directions (Q.Nos. 28-32) *Which phrase should replace the phrase given in **bold** in the sentence to make it grammatically correct? If the sentence is correct as it is given, then mark 'No correction required' as your answer.*

28. We asked her **that how she got** time to write all these books.
(*a*) that how did she got (*b*) that how she was getting
(*c*) how did she get (*d*) how she got
(*e*) no correction required

29. Studies in the past have shown that those who limit their activity span during the day in winters are **more likely to** suffer from depression.
(*a*) more likely for (*b*) mostly likely to
(*c*) most likely for (*d*) most likeliest for
(*e*) no correction required

30. In some cases, factors like low salary, lack of growth prospects and lack of motivation **compel all employee** to look for a change.

(a) compel those employees *(b)* compelling all employees
(c) compelling the employee *(d)* compel employees
(e) no correction required

31. Living with compassion and contributing to others lives **would helping us** add happiness to our lives as well.

(a) will helping us *(b)* will help us
(c) would helped them *(d)* will helped us
(e) no correction required

32. The **easiest way for** prevent stress caused by work or home pressures is to indulge in high levels of physical activity.

(a) easily way to *(b)* easier ways for
(c) easiest way to *(d)* easier way from
(e) no correction required

Directions (Q.Nos. 33-37) *Which of the phrases (a), (b), (c) and (d) given below each sentence should replace the word/phrase printed in* ***bold*** *in the sentence to make it grammatically correct? If the sentence is correct as it is given and no correction is required, mark (e) as the answer.*

33. US secretary of state made it clear that time **running out** for diplomacy over Iran's nuclear programme and said that talks aimed at preventing Tehran from acquiring a nuclear weapon would resume in April.

(a) runs out *(b)* was running out
(c) ran out *(d)* run
(e) no correction required

34. While the war of the generals **rage on**, somewhere in small town India, wonderful things are happening, quietly and minus fanfare.

(a) rage *(b)* raging
(c) rages on *(d)* raged on
(e) no correction required

35. According to WWF, the small Island nation of Samoa was **the first in switch off** its lights for Earth Hour.

(a) first to switch off
(b) the first to switch off
(c) the first of switch off
(d) first in switch off
(e) no correction required

36. The campaign is significant **because not just** the youths are directly appealing to the world but because their efforts challenge the chimera of normalcy in the area.

(a) not just because *(b)* just not because
(c) not just *(d)* because just
(e) no correction required

37. The doctor's association has threatened indefinite strike **support** of their teachers.

(a) on supporting to *(b)* to supporting
(c) for support *(d)* in support of
(e) no correction required

Directions (Q.Nos. 38 and 39) *In these questions, a part of the sentence is **bold** which may need improvement. Alternatives are given at (a), (b) and (c) below, one of which may be a better-option. In case of no improvement is needed your answer is (d).*

38. The children **break into a sweat** when they heard strange noises coming from the bedroom.
(a) breaking into a sweat *(b)* broke into a sweat
(c) broke upon a sweat *(d)* no improvement

39. The boy wanted to ask his father for money, but waited for a **propitious** occasion.
(a) protective *(b)* prophetic
(c) prospective *(d)* no improvement

Directions (Q.Nos. 40 and 41) *In these questions a part of the sentence is bolded. Below are given alternatives to the **bolded** part at (a), (b), (c) which may improve the sentences. Choose the correct alternative. In case no improvement is needed your answer is (d).*

40. He has lost **his nearly all many pets**.
(a) all his nearly many pets *(b)* his many pets nearly all of them
(c) nearly all his many pets *(d)* no improvement

41. **Can any spiritually dead man be so as to have no love for his native country**?
(a) Can any dead man be so as to have no spiritual love for his native country?
(b) Can any man be so spiritually dead as to have no love for his native country?
(c) Can any native man be so dead as to have no love for his spiritual country?
(d) no improvement

Directions (Q.Nos. 42-46) *Which of the phrases (a), (b), (c) and (d) given below should replace the phrase given in **bold** in the following sentence to make the sentence grammatically meaningful and correct. If the sentence is correct as it is and 'No correction is required', mark (e) as the answer.*

42. **In terms with** seating capacity, it is the third largest stadium in India.
(a) On terms with *(b)* As far as
(c) In respective to terms with *(d)* In terms of
(e) no correction required

43. That actor can double for the star, **if needed be.**
(a) if need *(b)* if need be
(c) while it is needed *(d)* whenever needed be
(e) no correction required

44. The 1982, Asian Games **brought about** a major change in India.
(a) brought after *(b)* bring after
(c) best resulted *(d)* bring around
(e) no correction required

45. Tourism, surely has suffered **given the huge** social unrest in the country.
(a) giving the huge *(b)* because to
(c) as the huge *(d)* taken the huge
(e) no correction required

46. **Combining** the ongoing crisis in Europe, the data does make a case for a pause in the rate hike.
(a) Together *(b)* Apart with
(c) Combined with *(d)* Combination of
(e) no correction required

Directions (Q.Nos. 47-50) *Look at the bolded part of each sentence. Below each sentence, three possible substitutions for the* ***bolded*** *part are given. If one of them (a), (b) or (c) is better than the bolded part, indicate your response on the Answer Sheet against the corresponding letter. If none of these substitutions improves the sentence, indicate (d) 'No improvement' as your response on the Answer Sheet.*

47. Why not **pamper you** after a hard day?
(*a*) pamper yourself (*b*) pamper your
(*c*) pampers yourself (*d*) no improvement

48. Not a word **they spoke** to the unfortunate wife about it.
(*a*) did they speak (*b*) they will speak
(*c*) they had spoken (*d*) no improvement

49. The poor villagers **have waited** in bitter cold for more than four hours now.
(*a*) have been waiting (*b*) had waited
(*c*) has been waiting (*d*) no improvement

50. If he **had** time he will call you.
(*a*) would have (*b*) would have had
(*c*) has (*d*) no improvement

Exam Practice

Directions (Q. Nos. 1-13) *In this section, look at the underlined part of each sentence. Below each sentence are given three possible substitutions for the underlined part. If one of then (a), (b) or (c) is better than the underlined part, indicate your response agaist the corresponding letter. If none of the substitutions improves the sentence, indicate (d) as your response. Thus, a 'No improvement' response will be signified by the letter (d).*

1. When he heard the rhetorical speech of the leader, he was carried along by his enthusiasm. **NDA 2016**
(a) carried aloft (b) carried down
(c) carried away (d) No improvement

2. After the heavy rains last week, the water in the lake raised another two feet. **NDA 2016**
(a) rose another two feet (b) arisen another two feet
(c) would raise another two feet (d) No improvement

3. One can live and work in a town without being aware of the daily march of the sun across the sky without never seeing the moon and stars. **NDA 2016**
(a) seldom (b) hardly
(c) ever (d) No improvement

4. If I don't know the meaning of a word, I look it after in the dictionary. **NDA 2017**
(a) look it out (b) look it for
(c) look it up (d) No improvement

5. Mr. and Mrs. Rao stay in their home every evening. **NDA 2017**
(a) at home (b) inside home
(c) within their home (d) No improvement

6. When we saw him last, he ran to catch a bus. **NDA 2017**
(a) has run (b) had run
(c) was running (d) No improvement

7. We are doing this in the interest of the poors. **CDS 2016**
(a) in the interests of the poors (b) in the interests of the poor
(c) for the interests of the poor (d) No improvement

8. He reached his destination at night. **CDS 2016**
(a) destination (b) at his destination
(c) on his destination (d) No improvement

9. One is often pleased with himself. **CDS 2016**
(a) with one's self (b) with themselves
(c) with oneself (d) No improvement

10. The man disappeared after he was rescuing a boy from drowning. **CDS 2017**
(a) was rescued (b) has been rescued
(c) had rescued (d) No improvement

11. I shall be obliged if you could grant me an interview. **CDS 2017**
(a) give (b) allow
(c) permit (d) No improvement

12. By 8.00 in the morning he wrote four letters to his friends. **CDS 2017**
(a) had written (b) had been writing
(c) was writing (d) No improvement

13. But for one witness the accused ought to have been sent to jail. **CDS 2017**
(a) would have (b) had
(c) should have (d) No improvement

Directions (14-23) *A sentence/ a part of the sentence is underlined. Below are given alternatives to the underlined part which may improve the sentence. Choose the correct alternative. In case no improvement is needed choose 'No improvement'.* **SSC CGL 2015**

14. We have been retracing our steps to the long cabin ten minutes ago.
(a) will be retracing (b) have to retrace
(c) had to retrace (d) No improvement

15. I was struck by his singular appearance.
(a) struck by how he singularly appears (b) struck by his single appearance
(c) had stricken his single appearance (d) No improvement

16. John decided to go to the Advocate General to clear his name of the accusation.
(a) to wash his name. (b) to clean his name
(c) to cleared his name (d) No improvement

17. They were being commanded to wait till the signal was given.
(a) commanded (b) given command
(c) command (d) No improvement

18. He could not be able to think logically because of his illness.
(a) cannot be able (b) can be unable
(c) was not able (d) No improvement

19. River Damodar in West Bengal carry the effluents from the Durgapur Industrial complex for miles.
(a) carried the effuents (b) carries the effluents
(c) carries the effluence (d) No improvement

20. He bowed down at the altar.
(a) next to the altar (b) infront of the altar
(c) before the altar (d) No improvement

21. I hope you will be able to steer ahead of the anti-social elements..
(a) steer free
(b) steer clear
(c) steer our
(d) No improvement

22. The climate of Shillong is somewhat like Kohima.
(a) like Kohima's
(b) as Kohima's
(c) as Kohima
(d) No improvement

23. The blue whale was thriving in all of the worlds's oceans until the turn of the century, at which time they became hunted to the point of extinction
(a) At the turn of the century, blue whales were thriving in all of the world's oceans
(b) Blue whales were thriving in all of the world's oceans until the turn of the century
(c) The blue whale was thriving in all of the world's oceans up until the turn of the century
(d) No improvement

Directions (Q. Nos. 24-33) *In the following questions, a sentence/a part of the sentence is underlined. Below are given alternatives to the underlined part which may improve the sentence. Choose the correct alternative. In case no improvement is needed, you answer will be 'No improvement'.*

SSC CGL 2015

24. Drinking tea is a English habit.
(a) convention
(b) custom
(c) tradition
(d) No improvement

25. Its high time that you go home.
(a) gone
(b) went
(c) are going
(d) No improvement

26. He lives far from the station
(a) a long way from the station
(b) away from the station
(c) off the station
(d) No improvement

27. Mr. Mukherjee knows ten languages, isn't it?
(a) hasn't he
(b) doesn't Mukherjee
(c) doesn't he
(d) No improvement

28. They spoke about the weather.
(a) talked
(b) expressed
(c) said
(d) No improvement

29. He is wanting in a little common sense.
(a) lacks
(b) is lacking in
(c) needs some
(d) No improvement

30. Mumbai is famous because of its textiles.
(a) in
(b) at
(c) for
(d) No improvement

31. The old man has acquired experience through age.
(a) developed experience
(b) got experience
(c) experienced
(d) No improvement

32. Water and soil pollutants find their entry into the body through ingestion of contaminated water or food.
(a) Passage of contaminated
(b) digestion of contaminated
(c) injection of contaminated
(d) No improvement

33. The second pigeon flew just as the first pigeon had flown.
(a) one had flown away
(b) had done
(c) one had done
(d) No improvement

Directions (Q. Nos 34 and 35) *In these questions, a part of sentence is underlined. Below are given alternatives to the underlined part, which may improve the sentence. Choose the correct alternative. In case to improvement is needed, mark 'No improvement' as you answer.* **SSC CGL 2016**

34. What you have been doing since the workshop last month?
(a) have you done (b) you have done
(c) have you been doing (d) No improvement

35. Corruption is the most serious problem in India.
(a) the more serious (b) very serious
(c) serious (d) No improvement

Direction (Q Nos 36-43) *In the following questions, out of the four alternatives, select the alternative which will improve the bracketed part of the sentence. In case no improvement is needed, select 'No improvement'.* **SSC CGL 2017**

36. What would you like (to do it) for your birthday?
(a) to do (b) doing
(c) does (d) No improvement

37. You must (be mistake)
(a) be mistakenly (b) be mistaken
(c) be mistook (d) No improvement

38. Select the most appropriate option to substitute the underlined segment in the given sentence. If no substitution in required select 'No improvement'.
Applications are to be sent to the Principal before May 30. **SSC CGL 2018**
(a) were being send to (b) No improvement
(c) will be send to (d) are sending to

39. Select the most appropriate option to substitute the underlined segment in the given sentence. If no substitution is required, select 'No improvement'. **SSC CGL 2018**
Meera has a friends who parents live in Dubai
(a) Have a friend whom parents live (b) No improvement
(c) has a friend whose parents live (d) has a friend which parents live

40. Select the most appropriate option to substitute the underlined segment in the given sentence. If no substitution is required, select 'No improvement'. **SSC CGL 2018**
Knowing the particular things that motivate each person help you add power to their motivation.
(a) No improvement (b) help you to add power
(c) helps you add power (d) help you adding power

41. Select the most appropriate option to substitute the underlined segment in the given sentence. **SSC CGL 2018**
If no substitution is required, select 'No improvement'.
Your coming home to dinner on time should be a rule rather the exception
(a) shall be a rule rather than a exception
(b) No improvement
(c) Should be a rule rather being the exception
(d) should be the rule rather than the exception

42. Select the most appropriate word to substitute the underlined segment of the given sentence. If no substitution is required, select 'No improvement'.
There is a great degrade in values in modern age. **SSC CGL 2020**
(a) demostration from values (b) No improvement
(c) degradation of values (d) deliberation for values.

43. Select the most appropriate segment to substitute the underlined segment of the given sentence. If no substitution is required select 'No improvement'. **SSC CGL 2020**
A. man in need pleaded for help.
(a) requested for helping
(b) No improvement
(c) promised for help
(d) commanded to help

Direction (Q. Nos 44-48) *Which of the phrase (a), (b), (c) and (d) given below each sentence should replace the phrase printed in bold in the sentence to make it grammatically correct? If the sentence is correct as it is given and 'No correction' required, mark (e) as the answer.* **IBPS Clerk 2015**

44. From among various alternatives we should choose the one which **is viable and consumes less** time.
(a) is viable and consuming
(b) is viability and consumes less
(c) being viable and consumes
(d) has viable and consuming less
(e) No correction required

45. We **are looking forward for** good rains this year.
(a) are looking forward to
(b) have looked forward for
(c) have been looking forward at
(d) should look forward with
(e) No correction required

46. Had we been alone we would have contended ourselves with any plain food **that give us strength**.
(a) that gives us strength
(b) that gave us strength
(c) which give us strength
(d) which give strength to us
(e) No correction required

47. The officer has triggered a controversy **by charging his superiors by inquiring** his warning.
(a) by charging his superiors with ignoring
(b) with charging his superior by ignoring
(c) by charging his superiors after ignored
(d) for charging his superior on ignoring
(e) No correction required

48. Please take delivery of material and **acknowledgement at the earliest**.
(a) sent acknowledgement at the earliest
(b) acknowledge at the earliest
(c) acknowledge the earliest
(d) early acknowledged
(e) No correction required

Directions (Q.Nos. 49-53) *The following questions consist of a sentence with a highlighted phrase which may or may not be grammatically or contextually correct. Choose the most suitable option that will replace the incorrect highlighted phrase to form a grammatically correct and meaningful sentence. If the given highlighted phrase is correct, choose option (e) i.e. 'no replacement required' as your answer choice.* **IBPS Clerk 2018**

49. India has suffered from terrorism. So has Pakistan. And **it turns out**, now the first world too is not immune.
(a) turning out to
(b) it turns to
(c) it turned out to be
(d) it turning out
(e) No replacement required

50. The advocate declared in the court that his client **has prepared to** surrender.
(a) was prepared to
(b) has been preparing for
(c) was prepared at
(d) has prepared for
(e) No correction required

51. Any step that the Prime Minister takes to remove violence in the country **will be appreciate**.

(a) will appreciated
(b) will have appreciated
(c) was appreciating
(d) will be appreciated
(e) were appreciating

52. If this is freedom of speech, then it **must been curtailed** immediately.

(a) have being curtailing
(b) must be curtailed
(c) must have been curtailed
(d) have been curtailed
(e) No correction required

53. Then the police started asking questions, the suspect **clammed up**.

(a) camped down
(b) clamped
(c) clam out
(d) clamed off
(e) No Correction Required

Directions (Q.Nos. 54-58) *In the question given below, there is a sentence in which one part is given in bold. The part given in bold may or may not be grammatically correct. Choose the best alternative among the four given which can replace the part in bold to make the sentence grammatically correct. If the part given in bold is already correct and does not require any replacement, choose option (e), i.e. 'No replacement required' as your answer.* **SBI Clerk 2018**

54. **Despite of being most efficient** method ever, it is still highly inefficient and this inefficiency inspires hope.

(a) Despite being the mostly efficient
(b) Despite of being a most efficient
(c) Despite of being the most efficient
(d) Despite being the most efficient
(e) No replacement required

55. **A satisfactorily number of contestant** must register for the contest in order for it to take place.

(a) satisfactory number of contestants
(b) satisfaction of number of contestants
(c) satisfaction in the number of contestants
(d) satisfactory number of contestant
(e) No replacement required

56. The next class of wave or oscillation detector is the magnetic detector **depending in the powers of** electric oscillations to affect the magnetic state of iron.

(a) depend on the power in
(b) depending upon the power of
(c) depends upon the power in
(d) deepening upon the power of
(e) No replacement required

57. James **had teaching** at the university for more than a year before he left for Asia.

(a) was taught
(b) had been taught
(c) had been teaching
(d) has beeen teaching
(e) No replacement required

58. His tail was short and scraggly and his harness **had been broken in** many places and fastened together again with cords and bits of wire.

(a) was broke from
(b) has broke from
(c) have been broken in
(d) have been breaking on
(e) No replacement required

Answers

Workbook Exercise A

1. (c)	**2.** (b)	**3.** (a)	**4.** (d)	**5.** (a)	**6.** (d)	**7.** (a)
8. (d)	**9.** (c)	**10.** (b)	**11.** (c)	**12.** (b)	**13.** (d)	**14.** (d)
15. (d)	**16.** (a)	**17.** (c)	**18.** (c)	**19.** (a)	**20.** (b)	**21.** (c)
22. (b)	**23.** (a)	**24.** (b)	**25.** (d)			

Workbook Exercise B

1. (c)	**2.** (c)	**3.** (c)	**4.** (c)	**5.** (a)	**6.** (b)	**7.** (a)
8. (d)	**9.** (d)	**10.** (a)	**11.** (b)	**12.** (a)	**13.** (b)	**14.** (c)
15. (d)	**16.** (b)	**17.** (a)	**18.** (c)	**19.** (a)	**20.** (d)	**21.** (d)
22. (c)	**23.** (a)	**24.** (d)	**25.** (b)			

Workbook Exercise C

1. (d)	**2.** (a)	**3.** (c)	**4.** (c)	**5.** (a)	**6.** (c)	**7.** (a)
8. (c)	**9.** (a)	**10.** (a)	**11.** (a)	**12.** (b)	**13.** (d)	**14.** (d)
15. (b)	**16.** (b)	**17.** (b)	**18.** (d)	**19.** (c)	**20.** (d)	**21.** (a)
22. (d)	**23.** (a)	**24.** (b)	**25.** (b)			

Workbook Exercise D

1. (d)	**2.** (a)	**3.** (b)	**4.** (a)	**5.** (b)	**6.** (a)	**7.** (c)
8. (a)	**9.** (d)	**10.** (d)	**11.** (c)	**12.** (c)	**13.** (c)	**14.** (b)
15. (a)	**16.** (b)	**17.** (b)	**18.** (b)	**19.** (c)	**20.** (c)	**21.** (d)
22. (c)	**23.** (a)	**24.** (c)	**25.** (c)			

Workbook Exercise E

1. (c)	**2.** (d)	**3.** (d)	**4.** (b)	**5.** (b)	**6.** (a)	**7.** (a)
8. (a)	**9.** (d)	**10.** (d)	**11.** (b)	**12.** (b)	**13.** (d)	**14.** (d)
15. (b)	**16.** (c)	**17.** (c)	**18.** (c)	**19.** (b)	**20.** (c)	**21.** (d)
22. (b)	**23.** (a)	**24.** (b)	**25.** (a)			

Workbook Exercise F

1. (c)	**2.** (d)	**3.** (a)	**4.** *(d)*	**5.** (a)	**6.** (a)	**7.** (c)
8. (b)	**9.** (b)	**10.** (b)	**11.** (b)	**12.** (d)	**13.** (b)	**14.** (a)
15. (b)	**16.** (c)	**17.** (c)	**18.** (a)	**19.** (b)	**20.** (d)	**21.** (a)
22. (b)	**23.** (a)	**24.** (c)	**25.** (d)			

Workbook Exercise G

1. (c)	**2.** (d)	**3.** (a)	**4.** (a)	**5.** (b)	**6.** (c)	**7.** (a)
8. (a)	**9.** (c)	**10.** (d)	**11.** (b)	**12.** (d)	**13.** (b)	**14.** (c)
15. (d)	**16.** (a)	**17.** (a)	**18.** (c)	**19.** (c)	**20.** (b)	**21.** (c)
22. (b)	**23.** (c)	**24.** (a)	**25.** (a)			

Revision Exercise A

1. (a)	**2.** (a)	**3.** (a)	**4.** (d)	**5.** (c)	**6.** (b)	**7.** (b)
8. (b)	**9.** (b)	**10.** (b)	**11.** (b)	**12.** (c)	**13.** (d)	**14.** (c)
15. (c)	**16.** (a)	**17.** (a)	**18.** (b)	**19.** (a)	**20.** (a)	**21.** (d)
22. (c)	**23.** (d)	**24.** (d)	**25.** (c)	**26.** (a)	**27.** (c)	**28.** (b)
29. (c)	**30.** (b)	**31.** (a)	**32.** (d)	**33.** (d)	**34.** (b)	**35.** (a)
36. (c)	**37.** (c)	**38.** (a)	**39.** (a)	**40.** (b)	**41.** (b)	**42.** (a)
43. (c)	**44.** (b)	**45.** (c)	**46.** (c)	**47.** (b)	**48.** (b)	**49.** (c)
50. (a)						

Revision Exercise B

1. (c)	2. (b)	3. (a)	4. (d)	5. (c)	6. (b)	7. (c)
8. (d)	9. (c)	10. (b)	11. (c)	12. (c)	13. (b)	14. (d)
15. (a)	16. (a)	17. (c)	18. (a)	19. (c)	20. (c)	21. (a)
22. (c)	23. (c)	24. (c)	25. (c)	26. (c)	27. (b)	28. (b)
29. (c)	30. (a)	31. (a)	32. (c)	33. (a)	34. (c)	35. (b)
36. (c)	37. (d)	38. (d)	39. (c)	40. (c)	41. (a)	42. (a)
43. (c)	44. (c)	45. (c)	46. (c)	47. (b)	48. (a)	49. (c)
50. (d)						

Revision Exercise C

1. (d)	2. (b)	3. (e)	4. (a)	5. (a)	6. (a)	7. (b)
8. (a)	9. (b)	10. (b)	11. (a)	12. (b)	13. (d)	14. (b)
15. (d)	16. (d)	17. (a)	18. (d)	19. (a)	20. (c)	21. (b)
22. (a)	23. (b)	24. (d)	25. (a)	26. (c)	27. (b)	28. (d)
29. (e)	30. (d)	31. (b)	32. (c)	33. (b)	34. (c)	35. (b)
36. (a)	37. (d)	38. (b)	39. (d)	40. (c)	41. (b)	42. (d)
43. (b)	44. (e)	45. (e)	46. (c)	47. (a)	48. (a)	49. (a)
50. (c)						

Exam Practice

1. (c)	2. (a)	3. (c)	4. (c)	5. (a)	6. (c)	7. (b)
8. (d)	9. (c)	10. (c)	11. (d)	12. (a)	13. (a)	14. (c)
15. (d)	16. (d)	17. (a)	18. (c)	19. (b)	20. (c)	21. (b)
22. (a)	23. (b)	24. (b)	25. (b)	26. (d)	27. (c)	28. (a)
29. (a)	30. (c)	31. (d)	32. (d)	33. (c)	34. (c)	35. (d)
36. (a)	37. (b)	38. (b)	39. (c)	40. (c)	41. (d)	42. (c)
43. (b)	44. (e)	45. (a)	46. (b)	47. (a)	48. (a)	49. (e)
50. (a)	51. (d)	52. (b)	53. (e)	54. (d)	55. (a)	56. (b)
57. (c)	58. (e)					

19

Selecting the Correct Sentences

In this part of section each set comprises four alternatives where different forms of sentences are given on the same theme and subject. A student is required to select a sentence which is the most suitable in respect of meaning and grammatical correctness. The correct alternative is supposed to give the exact meaning besides being grammatically correct.

Work Book Exercise A

Directions *Each set of the following sectences comprises four alternatives labelled as 'A', 'B', 'C' and 'D'. Candidate is required to select the most suitable alternative which conveys the exact meaning in accordance with the correct grammatical rules.*

1. A. To be intelligent is more essential than being hard working.
B. Being intelligent is more important than to be hard working.
C. For one to be intelligent is more important than being hard working.
D. Being intelligent is more essential than being hard working.

2. A. If he wins the prize I would be very happy.
B. If he were to win the prize I'll be very happy.
C. If he was to win the prize I would be very happy.
D. If he were to win the prize I would be very happy.

3. A. Our school had won the match if only we have concentrated.
B. Our school would have won the match if only we would have concentrated.
C. Our school would have won the match if only we had concentrated.
D. Our school had won the match if only we would have concentrated.

4. A. My sister had left for America last week.
B. My sister has been left for America last week.
C. My sister has left for America last week.
D. My sister left for America last week.

5. A. It is high time he will start earning.
B. It is high time he started earning.
C. It is high time he starts earning.
D. It is high time he has started earning.

6. A. It is a pleasure to see an alligator basking in the sunshine on a river bank as long as ninety feet.
B. It is a pleasure to see an alligator as long as ninety feet basking in the sunshine on a river bank.
C. It is a pleasure to see an alligator basking in the sunshine as long as ninety feet on a river bank.
D. It is a pleasure to see an alligator basking as long as ninety feet in the sunshine on a river bank.

7. A. The villagers were enjoying the winter evening around the fire.
B. The villagers were enjoying the winter evening around a fire.
C. The villagers were enjoying winter evening around fire.
D. The villagers were enjoying winter evening round fire.

8. A. When he had lost the book he searched it everywhere.
B. When he lost the book he searched for it everywhere.
C. When he lost the book he had searched for it everywhere.
D. When he lost the book he searched it up everywhere.

9. A. This was the ideal book available in the market.
B. This was most ideal book available in the market.
C. This was a most ideal book available in the market.
D. This was the most ideal book available in the market.

10. A. An one-eyed person was seen roaming about the streets.
B. A one-eyed person was seen roaming about the streets.
C. The one-eyed person was seen roaming about the streets.
D. One-eyed person was seen roaming about the streets.

11. A. It is the duty of a house-wife to wait on the guest.
B. It is the duty of a house-wife to wait for the guest.
C. It is the duty of a house-wife to wait the guest.
D. It is the duty of a house-wife to await the guest.

12. A. You are not working hard so your success is out of a question.
B. You are not working hard so your success is out of the question.
C. You are not working hard so your success is out of question.
D. You are not working hard so your success is not out of the question.

13. A. You cannot win my confidence without ever believing me.
B. You cannot win my confidence without never believing me.
C. You cannot win my confidence without not believing me.
D. You cannot win my confidence with ever believing me.

14. A. It is strange that you don't know swimming.
B. It is strange that you don't know how to swim.
C. It is strange that you don't know how to swimming.
D. It is strange that you don't know to swim.

15. A. The receptionist must answer courteously the questions that are asked by the callers.
B. The receptionist must answer courteously the questions of all the callers.
C. The receptionist should answer courteously the questions of the callers.
D. The receptionist courteously should answer the question of callers.

16. A. As he was sick, he was quite enthusiastic.
B. Since he was sick, he was quite enthusiastic.
C. As sick he was, he was quite enthusiastic.
D. Sick as he was, he was quite enthusiastic.

17. A. Both my brother and my sister love me but I should say that she loves me more than he.
B. Both my brother and my sister love me but I should say that she loves more than him.
C. Both my brother and my sister love me but I should say that she loves me more than him.
D. Both my brother and my sister love me but I should say that she loves I more than he.

18. A. I am an optimist and therefore I generally differ with you.
B. I am an optimist and therefore I generally differ from you.
C. I am an optimist and therefore I generally differ in you.
D. I am an optimist and therefore I generally differ you.

19. A. Neena can do it alone and no body else can do it.
B. Neena alone can do it and nobody else can do it.
C. Neena can alone do it and nobody else can do it.
D. Alone Neena can do it and no body else can do it.

20. A. Due to want of rain the wells have gone dry.
B. Because of want of rain the wells have gone dry.
C. For want of rain the wells have gone dry.
D. Owing to want of rain the wells have gone dry.

Revision Exercise

Exercise A

Directions *Each set of the following sentences comprises four alternatives labelled as 'A', 'B', 'C' and 'D'. Candidate is required to select the most suitable alternative which conveys the exact meaning in accordance with the correct grammatical rules.*

1. A. As the train which was my usual was missing I had to travel.
B. Having missed the train which I usually catch and had to travel.
C. I missed the train which I usually catch and had to travel by the next.
D. I missed not only the train which I usually catch but had to travel on the next.

2. A. He may be poor now but he appears to have been rich in his youth.
B. He may be poor now but he appears to be rich in his youth.
C. He may be poor now but he appears being rich in his youth.
D. He may be poor now but he appears to rich in his youth.

3. A. By June next year Ajay will be twenty years working in the office.
B. Till June next year Ajay will work in the office for twenty years.
C. Till June next year Ajay will work in the office for twenty years.
D. By June next year Ajay will have been working in the office for twenty years.

4. A. He went to the wholesale market and bought the cheap rations.
B. He went to the wholesale market and bought the rations cheap.
C. He went to the wholesale market and bought rations cheaply.
D. He went to the wholesale market and cheaply bought rations.

5. A. I went yesterday to the bank to collect the pass book.
B. I went to the bank yesterday to collect the pass book.
C. Yesterday to collect the pass book I went to the bank.
D. To collect the pass book yesterday I went to the bank.

6. A. The principal appointed him as a peon in the college.
B. The principal appointed him a peon in the college.
C. As a peon the principal appointed him in the college.
D. The principal as a peon appointed him in the college.

7. A. The team is confident to win the match.
B. The team is confident of winning the match.
C. The team is confident of win the match.
D. The team is confident for winning the match.

8. A. He is one of the best policeman who has ever lived.
B. He is one of the best policeman who have ever lived.
C. He is one of the best policemen that have ever lived.
D. He is one of the best policeman that has ever lived.

9. A. My sister is the poet and the philosopher.
B. My sister is a poet and the philosopher.
C. My sister is a poet and a philosopher.
D. My sister is a poet and philosopher.

10. A. Meena seldom or ever refuses an invitation.
B. Meena seldom or always refuses an invitation.
C. Meena seldom or never refuses an invitation.
D. Meena seldom if never refuses an invitation.

11. A. There is no meaning in what you say.
B. There is no meaning in that you say.
C. There is no meaning as to what you say.
D. There is no meaning that you say.

12. A. I hope you will excuse my leaving early.
B. I hope you will excuse me leaving early.
C. I hope you will excuse mine leaving early.
D. I hope you will excuse leaving early.

13. A. I am ready to say this at her face.
B. I am ready to say this on her face.
C. I am ready to say this in her face.
D. I am ready to say this to her face.

14. A. On account of shortage of time both of them cannot finish their work.
B. On account of shortage of time none of them can finish their work.
C. On account of shortage of time neither of them can finish his work.
D. On account of shortage of time neither of them cannot finish his work.

15. A. Many problems are staring at my face.
B. Many problems are staring in my face.
C. Many problems are staring me into my face.
D. Many problems are staring me in my face.

16. A. The cow does not eat anything else. It lives on grass and leaves.
B. The cow does not eat anything else. It lives at grass and leaves.
C. The cow does not eat anything else. It lives in grass and leaves.
D. The cow does not eat anything else. It lives for grass and leaves.

17. A. As one of his arms was amputated on account of an accident, the company will compensate the loss to him.
B. As one of his arms was amputated on account of an accident, the company will compensate him for the loss.
C. As one of his arms was amputated on account of an accident, the company will compensate him in the loss.
D. As one of his arms was amputated on account of an accident, the company will compensate his loss.

18. A. Now I have cancelled my meeting though I was to go there.
B. Now I have cancelled my meeting though I have to go there.
C. Now I have cancelled my meeting though I am to go there.
D. Now I have cancelled my meeting though I was to have gone there.

19. A. She insisted on me to stay there. B. She insisted on me staying there.
C. She insisted on my staying there. D. She insisted in my staying there.

20. A. You can meet my father only when he goes to prison.
B. You can meet father only when he goes into prison.
C. You can meet my father only when he goes in prison.
D. You can meet my father only when he goes to the prison.

Exercise B

Directions *Each set of the following sentences comprises four alternatives labelled as 'A', 'B', 'C' and 'D'. Candidate is required to select the most suitable alternative which conveys the exact meaning in accordance with the correct grammatical rules.*

1. A. Since the dividend being declared then the notices were prepared for mailing.
B. No sooner had the dividend being declared then the notices were prepared for mailing.
C. No sooner had the dividend been declared than the notices were prepared for mailing.
D. Scarcely had the dividend being declared than the notices were sent out.

2. A. He did not report for work today. He must has gone to the party.
B. He did not report for work today. He must have gone to the party.
C. He did not report for work today. He must go to the party.
D. He did not report for work today. He must had gone to the party.

3. A. She is not as wise as his brother.
B. She is not equally wise as his brother.
C. She is not as wise like his brother.
D. She is not so wise as his brother.

4. A. There will be a meeting in the long room at 4 o'clock of all the boys who play cricket and football.
B. There will be in the long room at 4 o'clock a meeting of all the boys who play cricket and football.
C. In the long room at 4 o'clock there will be a meeting of all the boys who play cricket and football.
D. There will be a meeting of all the boys who play cricket and football at 4 o'clock.

5. A. The teacher made it a point to explain him the situation.
B. The teacher made it a point to explain the situation him.
C. The teacher made it a point explain him about the situation.
D. The teacher made it a point to explain the situation to him.

6. A. The landlady made the servant to run to market to fetch her sweets.
B. The landlady made the servant run to market to fetch her sweets.
C. The landlady made to the servant to run to market to fetch her sweets.
D. The landlady made to the servant run to market to fetch her sweets.

7. A. The audience looked at him while he spoke.
B. The audience looked at him while he had spoken.
C. The audience looked at him while he was speaking.
D. The audience looked at him while he had been speaking.

8. A. Your answers are better than Mohan.
B. Your answers are better than Mohan's.
C. Your answers are better than those of Mohan's.
D. Your answers are better than answered by Mohan.

9. A. Everybody knows that Rahul is nothing else but a cheat.
B. Everybody knows that Rahul is nothing else than a cheat.

C. Everybody knows that Rahul is nothing else except a cheat.
D. Everybody knows that Rahul is nothing but for a cheat.

10. A. The manager asked him how he would avail this opportunity.
B. The manager asked him how he would avail of this opportunity.
C. The manager asked him how he would avail himself of this opportunity.
D. The manager asked him how he would avail himself this opportunity.

11. A. The teacher asked the students to thoroughly study this book.
B. The teacher asked the students thoroughly to study this book.
C. The teacher asked thoroughly the students to study this book.
D. The teacher asked the students to study thoroughly this book.

12. A. The important lessons are following.
B. The important lessons are as following.
C. The important lessons are as follows.
D. The important lessons are as follow.

13. A. The teacher asked the student with a frown on his face to leave the room.
B. The teacher asked with a frown on his face the student to leave the room.
C. With a frown on his face the teacher asked the student to leave the room.
D. The teacher asked the student to leave the room with a frown on his face.

14. A. The typists had corrected the errors had they known that the supervisors would have seen the report.
B. The supervisors reprimanded the typists whom they believed had made careless errors.
C. The errors in the typed reports were so numerous that they could hardly be over-looked.
D. The typist would have corrected the errors had they known that the supervisor would see the reports.

15. A. He carried the little child and me on his shoulders.
B. It was me that gave away the prizes.
C. All what he said had no effect on me.
D. They who did this thing should be punished.

16. A. In order to solve the murder case a C.B.I. officer is looking about the matter.
B. It is high time that you went to bed.
C. Though he looked innocent he turned into be cheat.
D. The majority of the workers was divided on the issue.

17. A. You cannot win my confidence until you are sincere.
B. When he lost the book he searched it everywhere.
C. She was intent to harm her friends.
D. I have not met my friend for the last five days.

18. A. He started to work hard lest he might starve in old age.
B. He started working hard lest he should not starve in old age.
C. He started to work hard lest he should starve in old age.
D. He started working hard lest he should starve in old age.

19. A. If I had money I would have bought the new house tomorrow.
B. If I had had money I would have bought a new house tomorrow.
C. If I had had money I would buy a new house tomorrow.
D. If I had money I would buy a new house tomorrow.

20. A. Taking my food I left for college.
B. While I was taking my food I left for college.
C. Having taken my food, I left for college.
D. Taking my food I shall leave for college.

Exercise C

Directions *Each set of the following sentences comprises four alternatives labelled as 'A', 'B', 'C' and 'D'. Candidate is required to select the most suitable alternative which conveys the exact meaning in accordance with the correct grammatical rules.*

1. A. The harassed wife shot herself after bidding her husband the last good bye with a gun.
B. The harassed wife with a gun shot herself after bidding her husband the last good bye.
C. The harassed wife shot herself with a gun after bidding her husband the last good bye.
D. With a gun the harassed wife shot herself after bidding her husband the last good bye.

2. A. He repeated the essay word by word.
B. Being a rainy day he did not go out.
C. She is senior but not more efficient than I.
D. All his friends are very sincere.

3. A. She had waited long before her husband had returned.
B. She waited long when her husband returned.
C. She had waited long after her husband returned.
D. She had waited long before her husband returned.

4. A. Even if intelligent he may be he can't succeed.
B. If intelligent he may be he can't succeed.
C. However intelligent he may be he can't succeed.
D. Even intelligent he may be he can't pass.

5. A. Had I been you I would help him.
B. If I had been you I would help him.
C. Should I you I would help him.
D. Were I you I would help him.

6. A. I realised later on that he cheated me.
B. I had realised later that he cheated me.
C. I had realised later that he had cheated me.
D. I realised later on that he had cheated me.

7. A. They arrived early because they may not miss the train.
B. They arrived early that they may not miss the train.
C. They arrived early when they miss the train.
D. They arrived early so that they might not miss the train.

8. A. I was rather impressed by the manner of the speaker than by his matter.
B. I was impressed by the manner of the speaker rather than by his matter.
C. Rather I was impressed by the manner of the speaker than by his matter.
D. I was impressed rather by the manner of the speaker than by his matter.

9. A. He is vain as though he were a millionaire.
B. She acted as if her mother asked her to do.
C. She carried the child carefully lest it should not fall.
D. I don't relish the food whose taste is sour.

10. A. The nature of my brother is the same as yours.
B. This is one of those novels which is admired all over the world.
C. He is such a friend that will sacrifice for me.
D. I wish he comes everyday.

11. A. So quickly he returned from market that I was surprised.
B. So quickly did he returned from the market that I was surprised.
C. So quickly did he return from the market that I was surprised.
D. So quickly did he return from the market that I had been surprised.

12. A. Would you help my brother I shall get you a decent job.
B. Had you helped my brother I shall get you a decent job.
C. Did you help my brother I shall get you a decent job.
D. Should you help my brother I'll get you a decent job.

13. A. A summon has been served on him.
B. A summons have been served on him.
C. A summons has been served on him.
D. A summon have been served to him.

14. A. You are not allowed to enter into the house.
B. You are not allowed to enter the house.
C. You are not allowed to enter in the house.
D. You are not allowed to enter on the house.

15. A. Little care was needed to avert the accident.
B. The little care was needed to avert the accident.
C. A little care was needed to avert the accident.
D. Less care was needed to avert the accident.

16. A. Could you please help me with any money?
B. Could you please help me with some money?
C. Would you please help me with any money?
D. Can you please help me with some money?

17. A. Leena is a most intelligent student in the class.
B. Leena is the most intelligent student in the class.
C. Leena is a most intelligent student.
D. Leena is most intelligent student in the class.

18. A. She is more intelligent than any other boy in the class.
B. She is more intelligent than any girl in the class.
C. She is more intelligent than any other girl in the class.
D. She is the most intelligent than any other girl in the class.

19. A. The teaching staff must take their lectures regularly when are asked by the Principal.
B. The teaching staff would have taken lectures regularly had they known that the Principal would know about it.
C. The teaching staff had taken the lectures regularly had they known that the Principal would come to know about it.

D. Many irregularities were found in their lectures by the Principal and he could not be disregarded them.

20. A. Anita was sitting with her husband on the steps of the temple with her lap full of newspapers when Bunty and Bitto came up.
B. Anita with her lap full of newspapers was sitting with her husband on the steps of the temple when Bunty and Bitto came up.
C. With her lap full of newspapers Anita was sitting with her husband on the steps of the temple when Bunty and Bitto came up.
D. Anita was sitting with her husband on the steps of the temple when Bunty and Bittu came up with her lap full of newspapers.

Exercise D

Directions *Each set of the following sentences comprises four alternatives labelled as 'A', 'B', 'C' and 'D'. Candidate is required to select the most suitable alternative which conveys the exact meaning in accordance with the correct grammatical rules.*

1. A. As he is careless he will not hear what the teacher says.
B. As he is careless he will not hear to what the teacher says.
C. As he is careless he will not listen what the teacher says.
D. As he is careless he will not listen to what the teacher says.

2. A. Shikha has been known by me for five years.
B. Shikha is known by me for five years.
C. Shikha is known to me for five years.
D. Shikha has been known to me for five years.

3. A. As soon as holidays be begin than this beach will become very crowded.
B. Since the holidays being started this beach becomes very crowded.
C. As soon as the holidays begin, this beach will become very crowded.
D. No sooner did the holiday begin than this beach will become very crowded.

4. A. You must aspire for the post according to your capability.
B. You must aspire to the post according to your capability.
C. You must aspire after the post according to your capability.
D. You must aspire the post according to your capability.

5. A. A good teacher provides a student all the useful information.
B. A good teacher provides to a student all the useful information.
C. A good teacher provides a student with all the useful information.
D. A good teacher provides to student with all the useful information.

6. A. Nobody will want to play in his team if he does not treat people kindly.
B. If he will not treat people kindly nobody will want to play in his team.
C. Nobody will treat people kindly if he does not want to play in his team.
D. Nobody will want to treat people if he does not play in his team kindly.

7. A. The priest read to the dying man couplets from the scriptures.
B. The priest read the dying man the couplets from the scriptures.
C. The priest read for the dying man the couplets from the scriptures.
D. The priest read the couplets from the scriptures for the dying man.

8. A. I do not understand to whom she is talking.
B. I do not understand whom she is talking about.
C. I do not understand who she is talking to.
D. I do not understand whom she is talking.

9. A. The boy regretted that with a plastered leg he had spent a greater part of his vacation in the chair.
B. The boy regretted that he had spent a greater part of his vacation in the chair with a plastered leg.
C. With a plastered leg, the boy regretted that he had spent a greater part of his vacation in the chair.
D. The boy with a plastered leg regretted that he had spent a greater part of his vacation in the chair.

10. A. In thirty-seven bomb blasts, fortunately only five lives were lost.
B. In thirty-seven bomb blasts, only five lives were fortunately lost.
C. In fortunately thirty-seven bomb blasts only five lives were lost.
D. Fortunately, in thirty-seven bomb blasts, only five lives were lost.

11. A. She is annoyed with you. You ought not to tell her secrets to her mother.
B. She is annoyed with you. You ought not to have told her secrets to her mother.
C. She is annoyed with you, you ought to tell her secrets to her mother.
D. She is annoyed with you. You ought to have told her secrets to her mother.

12. A. It is the best which she could do for me.
B. It is the best what she could do for me.
C. It is the best that she could do for me.
D. It is best that she could for me.

13. A. The early age of three or four years, would begin our first recollection of the world, for many of us.
B. Our first recollection of the world, for many of us, would be early age of three or four years.
C. For many of us, our first recollection of the world is from the early age of only three or four years.
D. For many of us, our first recollection of the world has been the early age of only three or four years.

14. A. Nowadays singing is a very profitabe profession.
B. Nowadays the singing is a very profitable profession.
C. Nowadays singing is very profitable profession.
D. Nowadays the singing is very profitable profession.

15. A. The report was useless to them because there was no needed information.
B. Since the report lacked needed information would have not been useful to them.
C. Since the report did not control the needed information it was not really useful to them.
D. Since the report lacked the needed information it was of no use to them.

16. A. Men are rather impressed by beauty than by character.
B. Men are impressed rather by beauty than by character.
C. Rather men are impressed by beauty than by character.
D. Men are impressed by beauty than by character.

17. A. So quickly she ran upstairs that she over took me.
B. So quickly did she ran upstairs that she over took me.
C. She ran so quickly upstairs that she had overtaken me.
D. So quickly did she run upstairs that she overtook me.

18. A. He wasn't rich by any means, although he never turned down anyone who needed help.
B. Being not rich by any means he never turned away, anyone who needed help.
C. He wasn't rich by any means but he never turned away anyone who needed help.
D. Since he wasn't rich by any means, he never turned away anyone who needed help.

19. A. Some people consider Karan the valorous hero of all the characters in the Mahabharata.
B. Some people consider Karan as the most valorous hero of all the characters in the Mahabharata.
C. Some people consider Karan the most valorous hero of all the other characters in the Mahabharata.
D. Some people consider Karan the most valorous hero of all the characters in the Mahabharata.

20. A. Neither she comes nor she writes.
B. Neither does she comes nor she writes.
C. Neither does she come nor writes.
D. Neither does she come nor does she write.

Exam Practice

Directions (Q. Nos. 1-7) *Read each of the following four sentences A, B, C and D to find out whether there is any grammatical error in it. Choose the sentence with no grammatical error as the correct answer. If all the given sentences are grammatically correct, mark 'No error' as your answer.* **IBPS Clerk 2017**

1. A. John Wonamaker, founder of the stores that bear his name, once confessed, I learnt 30 year ago that it is foolish to scold.
B. Whether rich or poor, American or Indian, we all have the same emotions deep with us.
C. This research indicate that we can no longer avoid significant warning during this century.
D. Every modern society depends on the trust in the skills and ethics of a variety of institutions such as schools and colleges, hospitals and markets.
(a) A (b) C (c) D (d) B
(e) No error

2. A. Many of us have learnt not make a public display of our emotions, particularly when they are negative.
B. Though Indians have been increasingly taking up corner office in the international companies, Rahul is the first one Indian to lead one of the top four accounting firms globally.

C. Democracy was suspended not because it came under existential threat but because it has become an obstacle to political ambitions trotted out as the nation's solution.

D. A virtual takeover of a bankrupt civil society be a coterie or individuals whom cornered tremendous power by being able to represent the state.

(a) A (b) B (c) D (d) C
(e) No error

3. A. Indian has decided do away with the practice of put each imported consignment through lab checks and switch to the international norm of random and risk based inspections.

B. SP Sumit Singh, along with Devesh Pandey, and DSP Hasan, headed separate terms that include cops from six police stations and investigators from the district police crime cell.

C. Our emissions standards are one-tenth that of global averages and far more stringent than even Europe.

D. The university has received about 500 applicants for the course; out of them 50 will be shortlisted for the programme.

(a) B (b) A (c) C (d) D
(e) No error

4. A. The RBI lifted the ban upon imports of gold coins and medallions by banks and trading houses.

B. President Pranab Mukherjee inaugurated Indian International Tradefair 2016 in Pragati Maidan in New Delhi.

C. Three Indian, two women and one man were among the shortlisted 100 applicants whom were chosen for one-way trip to Marks under one mission.

D. Fasting not only detoxifies the system but also gives a person training in endurance, a spirit of acceptance and self-control.

(a) A (b) B (c) C (d) D
(e) No error

5. A. The Reserve Bank of India (RBI) has notified that rescheduling of payment period of education loans by banks due to unemployment of borrower will not be treated as restructured accounts for computing NPAs.

B. China has started the operations of longest East-West high speed raiways.

C. Former Serbian professional tennis player Ana Ivanovic announced her retirement from tennis at the age of 29 years.

D. The Union Ministry of Sports has suspended the Indian Olympic Association (IOA) on December 30, 2016.

(a) A (b) B (c) C (d) D
(e) No error

6. A. One women, close to hysterical, grabbed my arm.

B. She has wrote eight books for young childrens.

C. Her latest book, Guddu's Photo, is about a little boy Guddu.

D. The book Rani Lakshmibai won the first prize in the children's book category.

(a) A (b) B (c) C (d) D
(e) No error

7. A. Tunisia is located along the Mediterranean Sea.
B. It is considered to be the northernmost country in Africa.
C. The capital and largest most city of Tunisia is Tunis.
D. Tunisia is predominantly Arabic in culture and tradition.
(a) A (b) B (c) C (d) D
(e) No error

Directions (Q.Nos. 8-10) *Choose the incorrect sentences from the given options.* **IBPS Clerk 2018**

8. A. Our teachers wants us to dress up as Gandhiji.
B. We'll have to do something to make you look bald.
C. You'll tell me what a great man Gandhiji was.
D. Gandhiji was teased about being small and thin.
(a) A (b) B (c) C (d) D
(e) No error

9. A. I am the Indian Navy, the naval branch of the Indian Armed Forces.
B. The President's of India belongs to be my supreme commander.
C. Till 1830, I was known as the Colonial Navy.
D. Later, I was named His Majesty's Navy.
(a) D (b) C (c) B (d) A
(e) No error

10. A. On January 23, 2003 Tarangini began circumnavigating the world to foster good relations with various other nations.
B. It came back to India in May 2004, after having visited 36 ports in 18 nations.
C. My sub-surfaced fleet includes one nuclear-powered attack submarine, two ballistic submarine and 15 conventionally-powered attack submarine's.
D. INS Vikramaditya means 'brave as the sun' and is a modified Kiev-class aircraft carrier.
(a) C (b) B (c) A (d) D
(e) No error

Directions (Q. Nos. 11-15) *In the following question, four sentences are given which may or may not contain grammatical or contextual errors. Following are the five alternatives reflecting the sentences that are devoid of all grammatical errors. If all the given sentences are correct, choose, option (e) i.e., "all are correct" as your answer choice.* **IBPS Clerk 2019**

11. (I) The Trump administration is committed to saving coal, when what it really needs to do is save the planet.
(II) In case if Hillary Clinton wins the electron in 2008, then she will become the first female President.
(III) Both of Tom's parents died when he was just a baby, so he doesn't remember either one of them.
(IV) Not only the investigation is one that is continuing and worldwide but also one that we expect to continue for quite sometime.
(a) Only (I) is correct (b) Only (IV) is correct
(c) Both (II) and (III) are correct (d) Both (I) and (III) are correct
(e) All are correct

12. (I) Mountains in the north, the country's highest point–Jebel ech Chambi–is located here.
(II) The Dorsal, an extension to the Atlas Mountains, runs across the country in a north easterly direction.
(III) In the east, along the Mediterranean Sea, is a fertile coastal plain famous for olive cultivation.
(IV) The central part is an arid desert closer to the Sahara.
(a) Only (I) is correct
(b) Both (II) is (IV) are correct
(c) Both (I) and (II) are correct
(d) Only (III) is correct
(e) All are correct

13. (I) Several rare species of birds, animals and plants call this region home.
(II) The dromedary camel is commonly found in the Tunisian Sahara.
(III) Other interesting animals include the Addax and the Fennec fox.
(IV) The Ichkeul National Park is one of the eighth UNESCO Heritage sites in the country and a stopping point for many migration birds.
(a) Both (II) and (III) are correct
(b) Both (I) and (II) are correct
(c) Only (III) is correct
(d) Only (IV) is correct
(e) All are correct

14. (I) There is a special guest in our skys, and now is the perfect time to catch a glimpse.
(II) Comets are dusty snowballs that orbit the sun just like planets does.
(III) They contain frozen gases, rock and dust, and are basically leftovers from the formation of the solar system.
(IV) There are probably millions of planets orbitting the sun.
(a) Only (I) is correct
(b) Both (I) and (II) are correct
(c) Both (III) and (IV) are correct
(d) Only (III) is correct
(e) All are correct

15. (I) Comet NEOWISE was discovered on March 27, 2020 by NASA.
(II) Its nucleus is about 5 kilometers in diameter.
(III) Its dust tail and gas tail stretch hundreds of thousands to millions of Kilometers.
(IV) The comet is brightest to be visible from the Northern Hemisphere in about a quarter century.
(a) Only (I) is correct
(b) Only (II) is correct
(c) Both (I) and (II) are correct
(d) Both (II) and (IV) are correct
(e) All are correct

Answers

Work Book Exercise A

1. (d)	**2.** (d)	**3.** (c)	**4.** (d)	**5.** (b)	**6.** (b)	**7.** (a)
8. (b)	**9.** (a)	**10.** (b)	**11.** (b)	**12.** (c)	**13.** (a)	**14.** (b)
15. (a)	**16.** (d)	**17.** (c)	**18.** (b)	**19.** (b)	**20.** (c)	

Revision Exercise

Exercise A

1. (c)	**2.** (a)	**3.** (d)	**4.** (a)	**5.** (b)	**6.** (b)	**7.** (b)
8. (c)	**9.** (d)	**10.** (c)	**11.** (a)	**12.** (a)	**13.** (d)	**14.** (c)
15. (d)	**16.** (a)	**17.** (b)	**18.** (d)	**19.** (c)	**20.** (d)	

Exercise B

1. (c)	**2.** (b)	**3.** (a)	**4.** (c)	**5.** (d)	**6.** (b)	**7.** (c)
8. (c)	**9.** (a)	**10.** (c)	**11.** (a)	**12.** (c)	**13.** (a)	**14.** (c)
15. (a)	**16.** (b)	**17.** (d)	**18.** (d)	**19.** (d)	**20.** (c)	

Exercise C

1. (c)	**2.** (d)	**3.** (d)	**4.** (c)	**5.** (d)	**6.** (d)	**7.** (d)
8. (d)	**9.** (a)	**10.** (a)	**11.** (c)	**12.** (d)	**13.** (a)	**14.** (b)
15. (c)	**16.** (b)	**17.** (b)	**18.** (c)	**19.** (b)	**20.** (b)	

Exercise D

1. (d)	**2.** (d)	**3.** (c)	**4.** (a)	**5.** (c)	**6.** (a)	**7.** (b)
8. (c)	**9.** (d)	**10.** (a)	**11.** (b)	**12.** (c)	**13.** (c)	**14.** (a)
15. (d)	**16.** (b)	**17.** (d)	**18.** (c)	**19.** (d)	**20.** (d)	

Exam Practice

1. (c) D	**2.** (a) A	**3.** (a) B	**4.** (d) D	**5.** (a) A	**6.** (c) C	**7.** (e)
8. (a) A	**9.** (c) B	**10.** (a) C	**11.** (a)	**12.** (d)	**13.** (a)	**14.** (d)
15. (e)						

PART B

Verbal Ability

Verbal ability is synonymous with Word Power. A student's comprehension skill, writing skill and communication skill depend on his verbal ability. In written examinations the verbal ability of an examinee is tested by way of comprehension skills.

This section of the book provides students with a large number of words and expressions. It would be presumptuous to claim that the words and expression included in the book are sufficient. However we have taken every care to avoid superfluity. There is no tendency on our part of include a word just because no body has ever heard of it. Only such words and their figurative expressions as are currently in vogue have been dealt within the ensueing chapters to help students meet with the challenge confidently in this sphere.

1

Paronyms and Homonyms

Confusion is often caused in understanding the meanings of certain words because they are either similar in meaning and form or similar in their sound of pronunciation. The words which are different in meaning or use but are similar in form or derivations are called **Paronyms**. On the other hand **Homonyms** are similar in their sound or pronunciation but different in meaning. They are also called **Homophones** (different in spelling and meaning but pronounced alike). In Modern English, Paronyms and Homonyms (Homophones) are not much distinguished.

1. **Access** — (*approach*) It is very difficult to have an *access* to the Prime Minister.
   Accession — (*coming to throne*) The *accession* of the prince to the throne was welcomed by the people.
   Excess — (*more than desired*) *Excess* of everything is bad.
2. **Accept** — (*to take*) The teachers *accepted* the invitation of the students on the Teachers' Day.
   Except — (*leaving out*) Everybody *except* Rahul was invited to the party.
   Expect — (*hope*) I never *expected* that my friends would desert me.
3. **Alter** — (*change*) Mohan is so obstinate that no one can *alter* his views.
   Altar — (*place of worship*) When I visited temple, I saw him kneeling at the *altar*.
4. **Assent** — (*agree*) I got *assent* of my father to study in a boarding school.
   Ascent — (*climbing up*) The *ascent* to Kargil hills is very arduous.
5. **Adopt** — (*take up*) One should not *adopt* the bad habits of others.
   Adapt — (*adjust*) One must learn to *adapt* oneself to the circumstances of life.
   Adept — (*expert*) Shruti is *adept* in the art of dancing.

6. **Amicable** (*friendly*) Finally, the two brothers came to an *amicable* settlement.

Amiable (*lovable, obliging*) Being an *amiable* housewife she is liked by her kith and kin.

7. **Accede** (*accept*) The director was kind enough to *accede* to the request of the labourers.

Exceed (*surpass*) Your essay should not *exceed* three hundred words.

Concede (*agree*) The prisoner did not *concede* to the argument of the jailor.

8. **Alteration** (*change*) There is no *alteration* in the programme yet.

Altercation (*a noisy argument*) There was *altercation* between the shopkeeper and my brother.

9. **Apposite** (*suitable*) Her remarks about the character of her friends are quite *apposite*.

Opposite (*contrary*) Sita's behaviour is *opposite* to that of her brother.

10. **Affect** (*verb*) (*to influence, to pretend*) Continuous attack of asthma has *affected* his health.

Effect (*noun*) (*influence*) Excessive hard work in life had an adverse *effect* on her health.

11. **Allusion** (*reference*) The poem is explained properly by the help of many *allusions*.

Illusion (*unreal*) According to the Vedantists, life is an *illusion*.

12. **Ail** (*suffer*) Rohit is getting weaker day by day and we don't know what *ails* him.

Ale (*intoxicating drink*) He visits the *ale* house daily against the advice of doctors.

13. **Apprehend** (*fear, perceive, arrest*) The soothsayer *apprehended* the day of Rohit's death.

Comprehend (*understand*) She could not *comprehend* the meaning of the passage.

14. **Admission** (*to get admitted, acceptance*) These days in order to get *admission* to convent schools you must give a lot of money.

Admittance (*entry*) These was a notice otside the DM's office which said, "No *admittance* without permission".

15. **Antique** (*of ancient times*) There are many *antique* pieces in the museum.

Antic (*odd, tricks*) *Antics* of the juggler regaled the children.

16. **Alternate** (*by turns*) We have a moral science class every *alternate* day.

Alternative (*one of the two choices*) There is no *alternative* to honesty in dealing with the people.

17. **Artful** (*clever*) She was able to change the behaviour of her in laws towards her by *artful* means.

Artistic (*pertaining to art*) Everybody admires her for her *artistic* temperament.

18. **Artist** (*one who practises fine art*) He is a great *artist*.
Artiste (*performing*) There was no security for the *artiste*, who had come to perform for the charity show.
Artisan (*one who does skilled work with their hands*) The *artisans* of Moradabad are very skilful.

19. **Affection** (*love, kindly feeling*) My mother is held in high *affection* and respect by all the members of the family.
Affectation (*unnatural behaviour, pretence)* I always feel vexed at her *affectation*.

20. **Abstain** [keep from things (*eating, drinking, voting*)] We should *abstain* from drinking.
Refrain (*keep from bad habits*) You should *refrain* from telling a lie.

21. **Avenge** (*just punishment*) Hamlet delayed *avenging* the murder of his father.
Revenge (*to punish out of personal grudge*) He *revenged* himself on his enemy by abducting his minor child.

22. **Adulteration** (*making impure*) The owners of the milk dairy were charged with *adulteration* of milk.
Adultery (*having extramarital relations*) Her husband accused her of *adultery* and deserted her.

23. **Aspersion** (*slander*) We should not cast *aspersions* on our friends.
Aspiration (*ambition, desire*) You can attain your *aspiration* only by hard work.

24. **Avert** (*to check or stop*) A little common sense *averted* a major mishap.
Advert (*refer to*) He *adverted* to the problem of Indian Security in his speech.

25. **Birth** (*to be born*) The exact date of *birth* of a person is known from his birth certificate.
Berth (*a seat in a train*) I booked two *berths* in the Rajdhani Express.

26. **Bridle** (*reins*) It is very difficult to control a horse without a *bridle*.
Bridal (*of bride*) The *bridal* dress must have cost a lot.

27. **Barbaric** (*savage*) He was selected to play the part of a village monster because of his *barbaric* nature.
Barbarous (*inhuman*) The Muslim invaders were *barbarous* in their wars.

28. **Barbarity** (*cruelty*) Hitler's *barbarity* is too terrible to be related.
Barbarism (*uncivilised conditions*) *Barbarism* still prevails in most of the tribal regions of the world.

29. **Beneficial** (*useful*) Nutritious food is *beneficial* for health.
Beneficent (*kind*) Everybody paid a rich tribute to the king as he was *beneficent* to all and sundry.

30. **Beside** (*by the side of*) He sat *beside* her father.
Besides (*in addition to*) *Besides* English, she is also learning French.

31. Bear (*tolerate, carry, give birth*) Mohan cannot *bear* being insulted by his boss.

Bare (*naked*) He was bitten by a snake as he was *bare* foot.

32. Borne (*carried*) The dead body was *borne* by his friends.

Born (*take birth*) Pearl was *born* at Ashwini Hospital at Mumbai.

33. Bail (*security*) His application for release on *bail* was rejected.

Bale (*bundle of cloth*) He was carrying a *bale* of cotton on his head.

34. Beatific (*feeling joy & peace*) The saints are always in a *beatific* state of mind.

Beatitude (*state of bliss, blessedness*) He experienced *beatitude* before he died.

35. Caste (*class of society*) In ancient times people were divided into different *castes* according to the work they did.

Cast (*throw*) We *cast* away old clothes and buy new ones.

Cost (*price*) The *cost* of living has risen a lot.

36. Childlike (*simple, innocent as a child*) Her *childlike* face has won over many hearts.

Childish (*silly*) Nobody likes him for his *childish* habits.

37. Canvass (*propagate*) Because of approaching elections people are *canvassing* for their candidates.

Canvas (*rough cloth*) While jogging he always wears *canvas* shoes.

38. Cite (*to quote*) The advocate *cited* many examples to prove his case.

Site (*place*) It is a very spacious *site* for constructing a nursing home.

Sight (*scene*) The mutilated body of a child was a ghastly *sight*.

39. Continuous (*without break*) He has been sleeping for an hour *continuously*.

Continual (*continuity with break*) It has been drizzling *continually* since last night.

40. Cemetery (*burial place*) The dead body was taken to the *cemetery* for burial.

Symmetry (*quality of harmony or balance in size and design*) The building looks exquisite only because of its remarkable *symmetry*.

41. Career (*vocation, profession*) If we want to make a good *career* we must work hard.

Carrier (*that one carries*) The goods were taken to the destination on a public *carrier*.

42. Confident (*certain, sure*) I am very *confident* of my friend's success in the interview.

Confidant (*a person you trust and share your feelings and secrets with*) Once his *confidant*, now Dinesh is the arch enemy of his mentor.

43. Compliment (*a remark of admiration*) I *complimented* my friend on her success.

Complement (*that completes*) Both husband and wife are *complement* to each other.

44. Cannon (*big gun*) Hundreds of *cannons* were shot in the battlefield.
Canon (*principle, a law*) *Canons* of any religion are not easy to follow.

45. Creditable (*praiseworthy*) It is really *creditable* for a village boy to have topped the university.
Credible (*believable*) Your excuse is not *credible*.
Credulous (*simple, artless*) Children are *credulous* by nature.

46. Coma (*state of unconsciousness*) After the accident, my friend had been in state of *coma* for several hours.
Comma (*a mark of punctuation*) *Comma* is a very important part of learning punctuation.

47. Corporal (*physical*) In our school the children are not given *corporal* punishment.
Corporeal (*having body, material*) Ghosts are not *corporeal* beings.

48. Comprehensive (*exhaustive, extensive*) *Comprehensive* steps have been taken to meet with unforeseen emergency.
Comprehensible (*understandable*) The talk of the new student in our class was not *comprehensible* to us at all.

49. Contagious (*that spreads by contact*) Covid-19 is a *contagious* disease.
Contiguous (*adjacent*) New Delhi and Noida are *contiguous*.

50. Censure (*blame, criticize*) *Censure* motion tabled by the opposition fell through.
Censor (*examination of films and plays*) The film 'The Bandit Queen' has not been approved of by the *censor* board.

51. Collision [striking against (*face to face*)] Due to heavy fog the car met with a *collision*.
Collusion (*nexus*) There was a *collusion* between the smugglers and the political leaders.

52. Contemptible (*deserving contempt*) The conduct of the taxi driver was highly mean and *contemptible*.
Contemptuous (*expressing contempt*) She dismissed the servant with *contemptuous* gesture.

53. Considerable (*large, to great extent*) The industrialist spent a *considerable* amount of money to uplift the living conditions of his workers.
Considerate (*thoughtful of others*) He is beneficent and *considerate* to his subordinates.

54. Ceremonious (*formal*) The bride was looking splendid and ceremonious in her wedding gown.
Ceremonial (*of ceremony*) I could not attend the *ceremonial* function of his marriage.

55. Complaisant (*pleasing, obliging*) He is popular with his friends on account of his *complaisant* nature.
Complacent (*self satisfied*) Most of the students of my class are *complacent* in their outlook and will not revolt against the principal.

56. Conscious (*aware*) We should always be *conscious* of what is going on around the world.

Conscience (*inner voice*) I always act according to my *conscience.*

Consensus (*general agreement*) Government should be run by *consensus.*

Conscientious (*honest, scrupulous*) Being a *conscientious* worker, he never shirks work.

57. Coherent (*intelligible*) She was so nervous that her words were not *coherent.*

Inherent (*inborn quality*) Sincerity is *inherent* in her character.

58. Collaborate (*work together*) Indian industries are compelled to *collaborate* with multinational companies for survival.

Corroborate (*confirm*) The principal *corroborated* the teacher's statement made to the police.

59. Casual (*occasional*) He is on a *casual* leave today.

Causal (*relating to a cause*) There is definite *causal* relationship between population and poverty.

60. Council (*an assembly*) The legislative *council* has passed the Bill.

Counsel (*advice*) His *counsel* proved very beneficial in the end.

61. Councillor (*member of a local government*) He is a *councillor* of the Legislative Council.

Counsellor (*adviser*) I have engaged a noted *counsellor* to defend my case.

62. Corpse (*dead body*) A mutilated *corpse* was found in a locked house.

Corps (*body of troops*) He is serving in the Army Ordnance *Corps.*

Carcass (*dead body of animal*) A *carcass* of a dog was lying on the road.

63. Coarse (*rough*) Though he is quite rich, he uses coarse language.

Course (*line of action*) The online training course will start next week.

64. Century (*one hundred*) Twentieth *century* is known as the age of science.

Centenary (*100th anniversary*) *Centenary* of the Indian National Movement was celebrated in 1985 AD.

65. Conservation (*preservation*) *Conservation* of forests is very important for our survival.

Conservatism (*the quality of not usually liking or trusting change, especially sudden change*) I am quite liberal and do not believe in *conservatism.*

66. Conform (*adhere to*) You must *conform* to the rules laid down by your company.

Confirm (*ratify*) I shall *confirm* my programme by tomorrow.

67. Capacity (*ability to contain*) The hall has a seating *capacity* for five hundred students.

Capability (*power of doing things*) My friend has the *capability* to do any difficult task.

68. Commonplace (*not unusual*) It is now commanplace for students to attend online classes.

Common place (*place for all*) The street is a *common place* for everyone.

69. Commandeer (*seize for military purpose*) When martial law was imposed in Pakistan huge area of vacant land was *commandeered* for building air strip.

Commander (*one who commands*) The *commander* of the army ordered the soldiers to capture the fort.

70. Disease (*illness*) My friend is suffering from an incurable *disease*.

Decease (*death*) On account of the *decease* of his father, the burden of the family fell on his shoulders.

71. Deny [refers to past (*action, knowledge*)] She *denied* that she had gone to the movie last night.

Refuse [refers to future (*request, order*)] Meeta *refused* to return the money.

72. Duel (*fight between two persons*) In ancient times, many *duels* were fought in order to settle disputes.

Dual (*double*) She follows a *dual* policy and misguides her husband.

73. Deference (*regards*) All children should have *deference* for their elders.

Difference (*distinction*) There is no *difference* among the basic concepts of all the religions.

Deferment (*postponement*) His application for *deferment* of hearing was turned down by the court.

74. Decent (*right and suitable*) She always wears *decent* clothes.

Descent (*coming down*) The *descent* of the hill is very dangerous.

Dissent (*disagreement*) Only a few members expressed *dissent* to my suggestion.

75. Desert (*noun*) (*sandy land*) The government has greatly solved the problem of getting pure drinking water in the *desert*.

Desert (*verb*) (*leave*) She was *deserted* by her husband.

Dessert (*sweet dish*) *Dessert* was served after dinner.

76. Dominant (*dominating*) The impact of coronavirus on the economy was the dominant theme of the conference.

Domineer (*to dominate*) Mothers in law try to *domineer* over their daughters in law.

77. Drought (*lack of rain*) Last year most of the areas of Uttar Pradesh suffered from a severe *drought*.

Draught (*current of wind, quantity of liquid*) A *draught* of cool wind was very refreshing on a hot day.

78. Defective (*having defect*) The fridge we brought is defective.

Deficient (*lacking*) Though young he is *deficient* in common sense.

79. Diverse (*different*) Two children of one family may have *diverse* temperaments.

Divers (*several*) He has consulted *divers* doctors about his disease.

80. Deduce (*infer*) It is difficult to *deduce* any conclusion from your ambiguous remarks.

Deduct (*subtract*) Two days' wages will be *deducted* from your monthly salary.

81. Deliverance (*freedom, emancipation*) Lord Buddha preached an eight fold path to attain *deliverance* from sorrows of life.

Delivery (*giving letters etc.*) The *delivery* of the letter was just in time.

82. Decry (*criticize*) The foreign policy of the Congress party has always been *decried*.

Descry (*to see or notice something or someone*) We could *descry* only a traveller in the bleak evening.

83. Defy (*violate*) How dare you *defy* my orders?

Deify (*to worship*) Swami Vivekananda is *deified* by every Indian.

84. Doze (*sleep*) The teacher caught him *dozing* in the class.

Dose (*of medicine*) You should not take a heavy *dose* of medicine.

85. Dam (*barrier built to reserve water*) A *dam* has been built on the river.

Damn (*condemn*) The book was *damned* by the critics.

86. Diversion (*change in direction*) There is a traffic *diversion* in Cannaught place.

Diversity (*variety*) *Diversity* is the chief feature of our civilisation.

87. Enviable (*causing envy*) All the people are jealous because of his *enviable* position in the society.

Envious (*feeling of envy*) Her friends were *envious* of her success in the medical entrance examination.

88. Exception (*objection*) There are always *exceptions* to the rules in every language.

Exceptional (*rare*) *In his own class, Rohit is a boy of exceptional* abilities.

Exceptionable (*objectionable*) I objected to her *exceptionable* remarks against my parents.

89. Eminent (*famous*) Shakespeare was an *eminent* playwright.

Imminent (*impending*) Third world war is *imminent*.

Immanent (*present everywhere*) Divine force is *immanent* in universe.

90. Eligible (*fit to be chosen*) Untrustworthy people are not *eligible* for responsible posts.

Illegible (*that cannot be read*) I can't read this letter as her handwriting is *illegible*.

91. Exceedingly [to a great extent (*good sense*)] One of my cousins is an *exceedingly* rich person.

Excessively [to a great extent (*bad sense*)] They spent money on the feast lavishly and *excessively*.

92. Exhausting (*tiring*) Teaching nursery classes is a very *exhausting* job.

Exhaustive (*detailed, comprehensive*) The teacher gave to the students *exhaustive* notes on English Grammar.

Exhausted (*tired*) He was *exhausted* and went to bed immediately.

93. Economical (*frugal*) A housewife should always be *economical* if she wants to run her house smoothly.

Economic (*pertaining to economy*) India is yet to cross many hurdles to overcome the *economic* crisis.

Economics (*a subject*) *Economics* is an interesting subject.

94. Elude (*escape*) Sohan was so clever that he *eluded* the police and escaped from the prison.

Allude (*refer, cite*) The speaker *alluded* to many examples from the Gita to make his point clear.

95. Excite (*stir up feelings*) The people got very *excited* when the police refused to take any action against the culprits.

Incite (*rousing to action*) The communal speech of the leader *incited* the mob to violence.

Insight (*ability to see the truth*) India needs leaders of great *insight.*

96. Envelop (*cover, wrap*) As the dark clouds covered the sky, the whole town was *enveloped* in darkness.

Envelope (*a letter cover*) Please put the letter in the *envelope.*

97. Expeditious (*quick, prompt*) Dattu is very *expeditious* in answering letters.

Expedient (*practical, contrary to principles*) Selfish persons are always *expedient* in their approach to life.

Expedition (*a journey to unknown place*) They will go on an *expedition* to *Everest*.

98. Esteem (*respect*) Mr Bachchan is held in high *esteem* by fellow actors.

Estimate (*calculate*) Can you give me the *estimate* of the cost of the repairs at the house?

Estimation (*opinion, judgement*) In my *estimation,* he is the fool of the first water.

99. Exposure (*reveal, exposed to heat or cold*) One should always limit one's exposure to the sun.

Exposition (*explanation*) Tilak's *exposition* of the Gita is remarkable.

100. Egotist (*one who talks a lot of oneself*) It is difficult to stand the company of an *egotist*.

Egoist (*one who believes in self interest, proud*) An *egoist* is moved only by self-interest while helping others.

101. Emerge (*come out*) It is hoped that he will *emerge* successful out of these trying conditions.

Immerse (*plunge into, absorb in*) Being a man of contemplative nature, he is always *immersed* in pensive mood.

102. Eruption (*bursting*) The *eruption* of the volcano caused heavy destruction on the island.

Irruption (*attack*) The *irruption* of Pakistan Army was successfully repulsed.

103. Elemental (*of nature, elements*) Inspite of an *elemental* hardships, Columbus discovered America.

Elementary (*beginning, introductory*) You must have an *elementary* knowledge of science.

104. Excursion (*picnic*) The students will go on an *excursion* tomorrow.

Incursion (*sudden attack*) *Incursions* by Pakistan and China into our borders speak of our weakness.

105. Entrance (*opening, gate*) The *entrance* to the fair by this route has been blocked up.

Entry (*coming into*) The *entry* of student leaders into the college premises is banned.

106. Expensive (*costing much money*) She bought a less *expensive* dress.

Valuable (*useful*) The book provides *valuable* data for further study.

107. Fatal (*causing death*) On his way to school, he met with an accident and received a *fatal* wound in the leg.

Fateful (*very significant*) The formation of I.N.A. was a *fateful* event.

Fatalist (*believer in fate*) Indians are *fatalists* by nature.

108. Forceful (*strong and powerful*) Netaji had a *forceful* personality.

Forcible (*by force, compulsion*) He was evicted from the house *forcibly*.

109. Feign (*pretend*) In order to save himself the accused *feigned* madness in the court.

Fain (*gladly*) She would *fain* do anything for her friends.

110. Forgo (*give up*) Parents *forgo* their own comforts for the sake of their children.

Forego (*go before*) This point has been dealt with in detail in the *foregoing* passage.

111. Facility (*convenience, dexterity*) The hotel provides all kinds of *facilities* to its customers.

Felicity (*apt expression, joy*) May God bless you with *felicity*!

112. Facilitate (*make easy*) The new agreement will *facilitate* the development of the trade.

Felicitate (*to congratulate*) I *felicitated* him on his success.

113. Fair (*a show, just, colour*) Let us go to Nauchandi *fair*.

Fare (*passage money, meal*) There is a steep rise in railway *fare*.

114. Formality (*show ceremony*) True friends never observe *formality* with each other.

Formalism (*observance of rites*) Swami Dayanand taught the Hindus to shun *formalism* in religion.

115. Fiscal (*of public revenue*) Government is trying to bring down the *fiscal* deficit in the next budget.

Financial (*monetary*) He suffered huge *financial* loss in the business.

116. Gentle (*not harsh*) We should be *gentle* and polite to our elders.

Genteel (*well mannered, of the upper class*) People belonging to middle class try to maintain the style of *genteel* class of society.

117. Gamble (*to play for stake*) On the occasion of Diwali people *gamble* and thus are sometimes ruined.

Gambol (*to run and jump in a playful way*) It is a beautiful sight to see a deer *gamboling* in a forest.

118. Graceful (*moving in a smooth, relaxed, attractive way*) She has a *graceful* gait.

Gracious (*kind, merciful*) God is *gracious*.

119. Gate (*door*) The dacoits entered the house through the main *gate*.

Gait (*a particular way of walking*) Her *gait* is graceful.

120. Gravitation (*pulling towards, attracting*) The theory of *gravitation* was invented by Newton.

Gravity (*quality of being serious*) One must observe *gravity* on solemn occasions.

121. Hoard (*amass, to store*) As he is a smuggler, he has a *hoard* of gold and silver in his house.

Horde (*a gang*) A *horde* of militants intruded into the Indian territory.

122. Historic (*likely to be famous in history*) Kapil Dev scored a *historic* victory by winning the World Cup in 1983.

Histrionic (*art of acting*) Rekha is known for her *histrionic* talents.

Historical (*of history*) I visited many *historical* buildings in Delhi while I was in school.

123. Humility (*politeness*) *Humility* in victory is a rare virtue.

Humiliation (*insult, disgrace*) All respectable persons prefer death to *humiliation*.

124. Honorary (*unpaid*) My sister taught in a college as an *honorary* tutor.

Honourable (*deserving honour*) He is regarded *honourable* member of the club.

125. Human (*race of man*) On account of ecological disturbances, the existence of *human* beings is endangered.

Humane (*showing kindness, care and sympathy towards others*) Doctors are supposed to be considerate and *humane*.

126. Hail (*belong to, welcome, frozen rain*) Those *hailing* from Bangladesh are living illegally in our country.

Hale (*healthy*) He is *hale* and hearty and enjoys life to the fullest.

127. Healthy (*having health*) Inspite of his old age he is quite *healthy*.

Healthful (*promoting health*) The climate of hill stations is *healthful*.

128. Hypocritical (*guilty of hypocrisy*) I do not like his *hypocritical* attitude towards his friends.

Hypercritical (*too critical*) It does not pay in life to be *hypercritical* of trivial matters.

129. Humanity (*mankind, quality of being kind*) One must act in the larger interest of *humanity*.

Humanism (*devotion to human interest*) Any act of *humanism* is always appreciated.

130. Hollow (*not solid, with a hole, false*) The stick is *hollow;* nothing is inside it.

Hallow (*ed*) (*sacred*) The *hallowed* shrine is visited by the devotees throughout the year.

Halo (*circle of light around the head*) Holy men are painted with *halo* around their heads.

131. Industrial (*pertaining to industry*) *Industrial* progress in India has not been rapid.

Industrious (*hard working*) My friend is an *industrious* man and thus he has achieved success in life.

132. Impossible (*that is not possible*) If we make up our mind and work hard nothing is *impossible* in this world.

Impassable (*that cannot be passed through*) Many places in the Himalayas are *impassable* during winter.

133. Ingenious (*skilful, clever*) She devised an *ingenious* scheme to trick the police.

Ingenuous (*frank, innocent*) Children are liked for their *ingenuous* nature.

134. Imaginary (*fanciful, unreal*) Don't be daunted by *imaginary* troubles.

Imaginative (*contemplative*) Poets and artists are *imaginative* by temperament.

135. Intelligible (*understandable*) Your remarks are not *intelligible* to me.

Intelligent (*wise and sensible*) Only *intelligent* students are found to succeed in this world of stiff competition.

136. Immoral (*not according to morality*) An *immoral* person suffers in the long run.

Unmoral (*non-moral, amoral*) *Unmoral* persons are not concerned with morality or the immorality of an action.

137. Incomparable (*so good or great that nothing or no one else could achieve the same standard*) Madhuri is a damsel of *incomparable* beauty.

Uncomparable (*having no similarity*) The security problems of India and Pakistan are *uncomparable*.

138. Invert (*to put upside down*) Put this statement in *inverted* commas.

Inert (*passive*) *Inert* gases are without active chemical properties.

139. Inept (*incompetent*) *Inept* handling of the situation resulted in riots.

Inapt (*unsuitable*) The title of the story is *inapt*.

140. **Incidental** (*happening as natural or a part of*) The risk of loss is always *incidental* to any business.

Accidental (*by chance*) It was just an *accidental* meeting between the two school mates.

141. **Jealous** (*full of jealousy*) All his friends are *jealous* of him.

Zealous (*enthusiastic*) My brother is very *zealous* about his new appointment.

142. **Judicious** (*wise, thoughtful*) We must be *judicious* in the choice of our career.

Judicial (*pertaining to judiciary*) He was sent to *judicial* lock-up by the Magistrate.

143. **Kindly** (*acts, feelings*) I shall never forget your *kindly* act.

Kind (*tender, pitiful*) He is a *kind* man who helps every body.

144. **Lightning** (*flash of light*) *Lightning* struck his house and set the whole house on fire.

Lightening (*make light*) He is always interested in *lightening* the financial burden of his father.

145. **Luxurious** (*pertaining to luxury*) As she is the daughter of a rich industrialist, she lives a very *luxurious* life.

Luxuriant (*rich in growth*) The hills of Uttarakhand are teeming with *luxuriant* forests.

146. **Loathe** (*detest*) The rich should not *loathe* the poor.

Loth (loath) (*unwilling*) She was *loth* to go with him alone.

147. **Limit** (*extent*) You must spend within your *limits*.

Limitation (*shortcomings*) There are many *limitations* in the Parliamentary form of government in backward countries.

148. **Loud** (*making a lot of noise*) Everyone was alarmed when there was a *loud* blast in the locality.

Loudly (*in a loud manner*) The teacher forbade them to speak *loudly*.

Aloud (*audible*) The students requested the teacher to speak *aloud*.

149. **Learned** (*erudite, educated*) He is not only rich but also *learned* and wise.

Learnt (*past of learn*) He *learnt* his lesson very well.

150. **Literal** (*expressed in words*) Most of the words in the poem are used in *literal* as well as figurative sense.

Literary (*of literature*) He is a *literary* man and reads a lot of books.

151. **Maze** (*winding paths*) The walled city is full of *mazes*.

Maize (*a kind of corn*) *Maize* grows in abundance in Africa.

152. **Memorable** (*worthy of remembering*) In the plays of Shakespeare, we find a lot of *memorable* quotations.

Memorial (*statue or anything in the memory of*) We collected money to erect a *memorial* in the memory of war heroes.

Immemorial (*existing or traditional for an extremely long time) The religious rites of the Hindus are an immemorial* tradition.

153. Momentary (*short lived*) One should not run after the wordly pleasures as they are *momentary*.

Momentous (*very important*) Operation *'Shakti'* at Pokhran was a *momentous* event in the history of independent India.

154. Morale (*the state of spirit, confidence*) The *morale* of the army should always be high.

Moral (*sense of right and wrong, lesson*) We are advised to pursue a *moral* course of life.

155. Maritime (*connected to human activity at sea*) Once Britain was a great *maritime* power.

Marine (*related to the sea or sea transport*) India should develop *marine* trade to earn foreign exchange.

156. Manifest (*obvious, evident*) It should be *manifest* to all by now that China and Pakistan are inciting trouble on our borders.

Manifestation (*act or desire that makes obvious*) Indiscipline among the youth is just a *manifestation* of a serious national evil.

157. Negligible (*unimportant*) The dacoits attacked his house yesterday night but his loss is *negligible*.

Negligent (*careless in duty*) We should not be *negligent* in our duty.

Neglectful (*careless*) He is so *neglectful* that he doesn't care for his family's interest.

158. Notable (*creditable*) India has made a *notable* progress in the field of agriculture.

Noticeable (*easy to notice*) There is a *noticeable* improvement in the patient.

Notorious [famous (*unfavourable*)] Our political leaders are *notorious* for their apathy to public interest.

Noted (*famous*) The leader is *noted* for his honesty.

159. Observance (*compliance*) In order to remain healthy *observance* of certain simple rules is required.

Observation (*notice*) Children have a very keen *observation* power.

160. Ordinance (*a government order*) The government has issued an *ordinance* against the people who do not pay the taxes on time.

Ordnance (*a gun*) There is an *ordnance* factory at Kanpur.

161. Official (*pertaining to office*) You are bound to maintain *official* secrecy.

Officious (*too ready to tell people what to do and having too high an opinion of your own importance*) Beware of *officious* fellows.

162. Organisation (*institution*) He is working in a non-government *organisation*.

Organism (*living beings with parts working together*) A human being is a complex *organism*.

Organic (*natural, close to nature*) Doctors have advised him to eat *organic* food.

163. Petrol (*fuel*) *Petrol* is very costly these days.

Patrol (*go round*) The *patrol* van is regularly moving on the highway day and night for our protection.

164. Providential (*divine*) My friend's *providential* escape at the critical moment saved his life.

Provident (*frugal, thrifty*) She is quite *provident* and economical in her household expenses.

Providence (*divine force*) Trust in *providence* for good days.

165. Practical (*not theoretical*) The scientist gave a *practical* demonstration of his experiment.

Practicable (*capable of being practised*) Only *practicable* schemes are adopted by our Managing Director.

166. Proscribe (*ban, prohibit*) Indecent books are generally *proscribed* by the government.

Prescribe (*recommend, advise*) A doctor has *prescribed* a very efficacious medicine for the treatment of the Corona Virus.

167. Popular (*admirable*) As Mrs. Neena is a very kind teacher, she is very *popular* with her students.

Populous (*thickly populated*) China is the most *populous* country in the world.

168. Pale (*bloodless, yellowish*) Due to his prolonged sickness he looks very *pale* now.

Pail (*container*) A *pail* full of milk was lying in the kitchen.

169. Pair (*double of a thing*) I gave a *pair* of new shoes to my brother on his birthday.

Pare (*trim*) Please *pare* your finger nails regularly.

170. Pane (*window glass*) Our window *pane* was broken by the children who were playing cricket outside our house.

Pain (*suffering of mind or body*) She was feeling *pain* in her neck.

171. Peel (*to remove the skin*) Please wash the mangoes before you *peel* them.

Peal (*a loud sound*) On hearing his jokes all of us went into a *peal* of laughter.

172. Personal (*private*) We were asked to express our *personal* views on this subject in the debate.

Personnel (*the people who are employed in a company, organization or one of the armed forces*) The *personnel* department has issued termination notice to Sachin.

173. Punctual (*at fixed time*) *Punctual* students alone deserve a splendid success.

Punctilious (*very careful in duty*) We are taught to be very *punctilious* in our work in the school.

174. Prudent (*wise, careful, having foresight*) It is *prudent* on her part to break with selfish friends.

Prudential (*of prudent actions, policy*) The *prudential* actions of my father saved the family from financial crisis.

175. Precedent (*previous examples*) The lawyer cited many *precedents* in support of his case.

President (*Head of Institution*) The Indian *President* is only de jure head of the government.

176. Physique (*physical health*) He is a smart young man with a good *physique.*

Physic (*medicine*) No *physic* has yet been discovered to cure cancer.

Physics (*a subject*) *Physics* is my favourite subject.

177. Prey (*hunt and kill*) As our national bird, the Peacock is not a bird of *prey*.

Pray (*offer prayer*) He *prays* to God daily.

178. Proceed (*to move forward*) Inspite of difficulties he *proceeded* with his enterprise.

Precede (*to be or go before someone or something*) I have mentioned every detail in the *preceding* passage.

179. Politic (*prudent, wise*) It is not *politic* to flog a dead horse.

Political (*of politics*) The *political* parties in India have no concern for the poor.

180. Prosecute (*file a suit in the court*) You are likely to be *prosecuted* in the court for violation of rules.

Persecute (*oppress*) She was mercilessly *persecuted* for not bringing a car in dowry.

181. Pitiable (*deserving pity*) The condition of the family is *pitiable* on account of poverty.

Pitiful (*making one feel pity*) It was a *pitiful* sight to see a beggar woman suffering from cancer.

182. Polity (*form of government*) Indian *polity* is not in a healthy state these days.

Policy (*plan of action*) Honesty is the best *policy*.

183. Proscription (*prohibition*) The *proscription* of the newspaper was resented by the people.

Prescription (*recommendation*) The *prescription* of medicine by the doctor proved very useful.

184. Putrefy (*to rot*) Many unclaimed dead bodies lay *putrefying* in the field.

Petrify (*turn into stone, stun*) We were *petrified* with terror to see the ghastly sight of the carnage.

185. Righteous (*just, truthful*) The Principal's anger was *righteous* for he could not tolerate the indiscipline in the college.

Rightful (*having a just and fair claim according to the law*) He is the *rightful* owner of the property.

186. Raise (*increase*) The traders have *raised* the prices of food grains.

Raze (*wipe out*) All the huts of the poor were *razed* to the ground as the government needed land to build a five star hotel.

187. Reign (*rule*) The *reign* of the Gupta dynasty, is known as the golden period in the history of India.

Rein (*bridle of horse*) He *reined* the horse and escaped a fall.

188. Rite (*ceremony*) The marriage was performed according to the Hindu *rites.*

Wright (*give a shape*) He is a great *playwright.*

Write (*compose*) Please *write* in the note-book.

189. Rout (*to defeat an enemy completely and force them to run away*) The enemy was *routed* by Indian forces.

Route (*path*) You should not go by a long *route*.

190. Respective (*belonging to each*) After the match we left for our *respective* homes.

Respectable (*enjoying respect*) His father is a *respectable* man of the city.

Respectful (*showing respect*) You must be *respectful* to your elders.

191. Rapt (*fully attentive*) They listened to the speech of the Prime Minister with *rapt* attention.

Wrapt (*lost in, absorbed*) She did not notice my arrival as she was *wrapt* in her thoughts.

192. Recourse (*means of action*) I do not advise you to have *recourse* to legal action in this matter.

Resource (*means, raw material*) India is a land teeming with natural resources.

193. Symbol (*sign, to represent something*) Vinoba Bhave was a *symbol* of simplicity and honesty.

Cymbal (*a musical instrument*) The melodious sound of the *cymbals* impressed everybody.

194. Stationery (*writing material*) His father deals in office *stationery.*

Stationary (*static, fixed*) The Sun is *stationary.*

195. Soar (*rise, fly*) Birds are *soaring* in the sky.

Sore (*painful and uncomfortable because of injury, infection or too much use*) Having a *sore* throat is one of the symptoms of the corona virus.

Sour (*bitter*) The grapes are *sour*.

196. Suspect (*to think to be true*) The whole class *suspects* Rohan to have stolen Rita's money.

Doubt (*to think to be untrue*) I *doubt* if she will get through the examination.

197. Sociable (*fond of mixing with people*) Because of her *sociable* behaviour she is liked by all the members of her family.

Social (*pertaining to society*) Man is a *social* animal.

198. Sensual (*voluptuous, exciting senses*) We should not indulge in *sensual* pleasures or we will repent later on.

Sensuous (*that affects the senses*) John Keats' poetry is *sensuous.*

199. Spacious (*having large space*) My house contains many *spacious* rooms.

Specious (*seeming to be right or true, but really wrong or false*) Nobody was impressed with his *specious* arguments.

200. Spiritual (*opposed to material, of spirit*) Indians should not give up their *spiritual* heritage.

Spirituous (*containing intoxicating drink*) Excessive consumption of *spirituous* drinks is injurious to health.

201. Stimulant (*that which stimulates*) Tea is a *stimulant* for a worker after a day's hard work.

Stimulus (*incentive*) Man hardly acts if there is no *stimulus* before him.

202. Special (*specific*) He came here on a *special* mission to bring about reconciliation between the two parties.

Especial (*to a great degree*) It is *especially* hot these days.

203. Storey (*upper part of a building*) He lives in the second *storey* of the house.

Story (*tale*) It is a very interesting *story*.

204. Suit (*a set of clothes, a lawsuit*) He presented me with a woollen *suit*.

Suite (*a set of rooms*) He has booked a *suite* in the hotel.

205. Sham (*pretend to be, pretence)* What he says is all *sham*.

Shame (*feeling of humiliation*) He felt *shame* at having told a lie.

206. Severe (*violent, rigorous*) She is suffering from *severe* headache.

Sever (*separate*) India *severed* its diplomatic relations with Pakistan after the war.

207. Statue (*figure of animal/man in stone or wood*) The *statue* of Dr. Ambedkar was unveiled by the President.

Statute (*a law passed by law making bodies*) The *statute* was passed by the Parliament unanimously.

208. Temperance (*moderation in habits*) We should observe *temperance* in our eating and drinking habits because it leads to a healthy way of life.

Temperament (*disposition, nature*) Always keep from persons of choleric *temperament*.

209. Tolerable (*bearable*) The food that was served in his daughter's marriage was *tolerable*.

Tolerant (*liberal in ideas*) Every religion teaches us to be *tolerant* of the religious views held by others.

210. Temporal (*worldly, physical*) We should not hanker after *temporal* glory.

Temporary (*lasting for short time*) He was given the job on a *temporary* basis only.

211. Tamper (*meddle with*) Please do not *tamper* with my papers.

Temper (*the tendency to become angry very quickly*) One must not lose one's *temper*.

212. Teem (*full of*) India is a country *teeming* with natural resources.

Team (*group of players*) His name has not been included in the college cricket *team*.

213. Uninterested (*having no interest*) Gaurav is *uninterested* in the study of science.
Disinterested (*free from personal motive*) A *disinterested* leader of the party always commands respect from his followers.

214. Variation (*change*) *Variation* in his blood pressure worried the doctors.
Variance (*opposite*) My views are always at *variance* with my father's.

215. Vocation (*profession*) Singing is both his *vocation* and avocation.
Avocation (*hobby*) Gardening is a very favourite *avocation* of my father.

216. Virtuous (*having virtues*) She is a *virtuous* and devoted house wife.
Virtual (*real*) Her mother is the *virtual* head of the family.

217. Voracity (*greed*) He is detested on account of his *voracity* for wealth.
Veracity (*truthfulness*) It is very difficult to verify the *veracity* of her statement since she is very clever.

218. Vane (*weather cock*) The wind *vane* points to the direction of the wind.
Vain (*proud, useless*) She is *vain* of her *wealth*.
Wane (*decline*) His popularity as a political leader is on the *wane*.
Vein (*a blood vein*) All the *veins* carry blood to the heart.

219. Vassal (*a slave*) In ancient times, prisoners of war were made *vassals*.
Vessel (*a small ship, utensil*) Empty *vessels* make much noise.

220. Venal (*corruptible*) The *venal* leaders are the bane of Indian polity.
Venial (*to be forgiven*) The fault is so slight that it is thought to be *venial*.

221. Wreak (*take revenge*) At last, he *wreaked* vengeance by killing his enemy.
Wreck (*destroy*) The fury of the storm *wrecked* many houses.

222. Wither (*fade*) The plants kept in the shade will *wither* for want of Sun and light.
Whither (*where*) Modern man is so much confused that he does not know *whither* he is heading for.

223. Willing (*ready*) We should always be *willing* to help the needy.
Wilful (*doing exactly what you want; although the person doing it knows that it is wrong*) His marriage was a total failure on account of his *wilful* nature.

224. Wave (*sea or river wave*) The *waves* rose sky high when the storm blew up.
Waive (*remove, forgo*) Government has at last agreed to *waive* excise duty on cloth.

225. Wrest (*snatch by force*) The enemy *wrested* his gun and killed him.
Rest (*peace*) Please go and take *rest* now.

226. Womanly [of woman (*good sense*)] My mother has *womanly* virtues.
Womanish [of woman (*bad sense*)] His voice is *womanish* as it is quite shrill.

227. Whet (*increase interest*) Lemon will *whet* your appetite for more food.
Vet (*screening*) The candidates were *vetted* for security reasons.
Wet (*covered with water/liquid*) He got *wet* in the rain and is not well.

Work Book Exercise

Directions (Q. Nos. 1-20) *Choose the right word to fill the blanks.*

1. Your perfume has a wonderful ....
(a) cent (b) scent
(c) sent (d) cents

2. I banged my .... on the leg of the table.
(a) two (b) toe
(c) too (e) to

3. The teacher gave a .... test today.
(a) close (b) claws
(c) cloze (d) closed

4. The online .... starts on 20th November.
(a) sail (b) shale
(c) sales (d) sale

5. What .... do you take to work?
(a) rout (b) root
(c) routes (d) route

6. I wonder if they will change .... plans.
(a) there (b) they're
(c) their (d) theirs

7. There are only a few people who still .... letters.
(a) rite (b) wright
(c) write (d) right

8. Ritesh can play a few .... on the guitar.
(a) cords (b) chords
(c) chord (d) cord

9. I always use .... when I make rotis.
(a) flower (b) floor
(c) flora (d) flour

10. I had .... pancakes for breakfast today.
(a) fore (b) four
(c) for (d) fear

11. I .... candies with my best friend.
(a) ate, eight (b) eight, ate
(c) at, eight (d) eight, at

12. My grandfather always turns up the TV volume high so he can .... it.
(a) have (b) hear
(c) here (d) heer

13. What .... of music do you like?
(a) kinder (b) kindergarten
(c) kinds (d) kind

14. My company has got a stand at the trade ....
(a) fare (b) fair
(c) far (d) fairs

15. The interview didn't .... as long as I expected.
(a) lest (b) least
(c) lests (d) last

16. The wound took time to ....
(a) heel
(b) hell
(c) heal
(d) hail

17. He was disturbed when he saw so many casualities at the accident ....
(a) sight
(b) site
(c) cite
(d) sigh

18. Raveena got .... while preparing for her .... exams.
(a) boared, board
(b) bored, board
(c) board, bored
(d) bored, bored

19. My .... is very ....
(a) deer, dear, deer
(b) dear, dear, deer
(c) dear, deer, dear
(d) deer, deer, dear

20. The couples are .... yet ready to tie the ....
(a) knot, knot
(b) not, not
(c) not, knot
(d) knot, not

Answers

1. (b)	2. (b)	3. (c)	4. (d)	5. (d)	6. (c)	7. (c)
8. (b)	9. (d)	10. (b)	11. (a)	12. (b)	13. (d)	14. (b)
15. (d)	16. (c)	17. (b)	18. (b)	19. (c)	20. (c)	

2

One Word Substitutions

One Word Substitutions (Substitutes) may be defined as single words that are used in place of a group of words to denote a person, an object, a place, a state of mind a profession, etc. In common parlance they are termed as single words used to make an expression brief and pertinent. Polonius in 'Hamlet', a play by Shakespeare, aptly remarks

"Therefore since brevity in the soul of wit.
The tediousness the limbs and outward flourishes I will be brief".

As such the use of one word substitutions tend to obviate the repetition of unnecessary words avoiding verbosity and ambiguity. Rambling style speaks of a rambling state of mind whereas brevity conveys telling effect.

Moreover, one word substitutions are indispensable while writing a precis of a given passage. A student is required not to exceed the limit of words. They come handy in such situations. Hence, their significance cannot be gainsaid and students are advised to learn them very seriously.

A few of one word substitutes are given below for the benefit of the students.

(A) One Words Denoting Persons

1. Agnostic	one who is not sure about God's existence
2. Altruist	a person who cares about others and helps others without any benefit (*Syn.–Philanthropist*)
3. Amateur	one who does a thing for pleasure without pay and not as a profession
4. Ambidexterous	one who can use either hand with ease
5. Anarchist	one who is out to destroy all governments, peace and order
6. Apostate	a person who has changed his faith
7. Arbitrator	a person appointed by two parties to solve a dispute
8. Ascetic	one who leads an austere life
9. Atheist	a person who does not believe in God (*Ant.–Theist*)
10. Bankrupt	one who is unable to pay his debts (*Syn.–Insolvent*)
11. Bigot	one who is filled with excessive enthusiasm in religious matters (*Syn.–Fanatic*)

12. Bohemian	an uncoventional style of living
13. Cacographist	one who is bad in spellings
14. Cannibal	one who feeds on human flesh
15. Carnivorous	one who feeds on flesh of animals
16. Chauvinist	a person who is blindly devoted to an idea
17. Connoisseur	a critical judge of any art and craft
18. Contemporaries	persons living at the same time
19. Convalescent	one who is recovering after illness
20. Coquette	a girl/woman who flirts with men
21. Cosmopolitan	a person who regards the whole world as his country
22. Cynosure	one who is a centre of attraction
23. Cynic	one who sneers at the beliefs of others
24. Debonair	suave (polished and light hearted person)
25. Demagogue	a leader who sways his followers by his oratory skills
26. Dilettante	a dabbler (not serious) in art, science and literature
27. Effeminate	a man who is womanish in his habits
28. Egoist	a lover of oneself, of one's advancement
29. Egotist	one who often talks of his achievements
30. Emigrant	a person who leaves his country to settle in another country (*Ant.–Immigrant*)
31. Epicure	one who is for pleasure of eating and drinking
32. Fastidious	one hard to please (very selective in his habits)
33. Fatalist	one who believes in fate
34. Feminist	one who works for the welfare of women (*Syn.–Philogynist*)
35. Fugitive	one who runs away from justice (*Syn.–Absconding person*)
36. Gourmand	a lover of good food
37. Gourmet	a connoisseur of food
38. Henpecked	a husband ruled by his wife
39. Hedonist	one who believes that sensual pleasure is the chief good
40. Heretic	one who acts against religion
41. Herbivorous	one that lives on plants and herbs
42. Honorary	one who holds a post without any salary
43. Highbrow	a person considering himself to be superior in culture and intellect (*Syn.–Snob*)
44. Hypochondriac	one who is over anxious about his health
45. Iconoclast	one who is breaker of images and traditions
46. Illiterate	one who does not know reading or writing (*Ant.–Literate*)
47. Immigrant	a person who comes to a country from his own country for settling (*Ant.–Emigrant*)

48. Impregnable	that cannot be entered by force (*Ant.–Pregnable*)
49. Impostor	one who pretends to be somebody else
50. Indefatigable	one who does not tire easily
51. Introvert	one who does not express himself freely (*Ant.–Extrovert*)
52. Insolvent	a person who is unable to pay his debts (*Syn.–Bankrupt*)
53. Itinerant	one who journeys from place to place (*Nomadic*)
54. Invincible	one too strong to be defeated (*Ant.–Vincible*)
55. Invulnerable	one that cannot be harmed/wounded (*Ant.–Vulnerable*)
56. Libertine	a person who leads an immoral life (*Syn.–Lecher*)
57. Martyr	one who dies for a noble cause
58. Mercenary	one who does something for the sake of money (*bad sense*)
59. Misanthrope	one who hates mankind (*Ant.–Philanthropist*)
60. Misogamist	one who hates the institution of marriage
61. Misologist	one who hates knowledge (*Ant.–Bibliologist*)
62. Namesake	a person having the same name as another
63. Narcissist	lover of self
64. Novice	one who is inexperienced in anything (*Syn.–Tyro*)
65. Numismatist	one who collects coins
66. Omnivorous	one who eats everything, plants as well as flesh
67. Optimist	a person who looks at the bright side of thing (*Ant.–Pessimist*)
68. Orphan	one who has lost one's parents
69. Philanthropist	one who loves mankind (*Ant.–Misanthrope*)
70. Philogynist	one who works for the welfare of women (*Ant.–Misogynist*)
71. Polyglot	one who speaks many languages (*Syn.–Linguist*)
72. Pacifist	one who hates war, loves peace
73. Pessimist	one who looks at the dark side of life (*Ant.–Optimist*)
74. Philanderer	one who amuses oneself by love making
75. Philistine	one who does not care for art and literature
76. Posthumous	a child born after the death of father *or* a book published after the death of the author *or* an award received after the death of the recepient
77. Philatelist	one who collects stamps
78. Pedestrian	one who goes on foot
79. Recluse	one who lives in seclusion
80. Sadist	a person who feels pleasure by hurting others
81. Samaritan	one who helps the needy and the helpless
82. Somnambulist	a person who walks in sleep
83. Somniloquist	a person who talks in sleep
84. Stoic	a person who is indifferent to pain and pleasures of life

85. Swashbuckler	a person who engages in daring and romantic adventures with bravado or flamboyance
86. Teetotaller	one who does not take any intoxicating drugs
87. Termagant	a noisy quarrelsome woman, a shrew
88. Truant	one who remains absent from duty without permission
89. Toper/Sot	one who is a habitual drunkard
90. Uxorious	one extremely fond of one's wife
91. Veteran	one who has a long experience of a particular occupation
92. Versatile	one who adapts oneself readily to various situations
93. Virtuoso	one who is a very skilful performer (*specially music*)
94. Volunteer	one who offers one's services
95. Verbose	a style face of difficult words

(B) One Words Denoting General Objects

1. Abdication	voluntary giving up of throne in favour of someone
2. Almanac	an annual calendar with position of stars
3. Amphibian	animal that live both on land and sea
4. Allegory	a story that expresses ideas through symbols
5. Anomaly	departure from common rule
6. Aquatic	animals that live in water
7. Autobiography	the life history of a person written by himself
8. Axiom	a statement accepted as true without proof
9. Anonymous	bearing no name
10. Belligerent	one that is in a war-like mood (*Syn.–Bellicose*)
11. Biography	the life history of a person (*written by some other person*)
12. Biopsy	examination of living tissue
13. Blasphemy	an act of speaking against religion (*Heresy*)
14. Chronology	events presented in order of occurrence
15. Conscription	compulsory enlistment for military service
16. Crusade	a religious war
17. Drawn	a game that results neither in victory nor in defeat
18. Eatable	anything to be eaten
19. Edible	fit to be eaten
20. Encyclopaedia	a book that contains information on various subjects
21. Ephemeral	lasting for a very short time/a day
22. Epilogue	a concluding speech/comment at the end of the play (*Ant.–Prologue*)
23. Extempore	a speech made without preparation (*Syn.–Impromptu*)
24. Fable	a story relating to birds/animals with a moral in the end
25. Facsimile	an exact copy of handwriting, printing (*Syn.–Xerox*)

26. Fatal	that causes death
27. Fauna	the animals of a particular region
28. Flora	the plants of a particular region
29. Fragile	that can be easily broken
30. Gregarious	animals which live in a flock, used for human beings also (*Syn.–Sociable*)
31. Illegible	difficult to read (*Ant.–Legible*)
32. Inaccessible	a person/place that cannot be easily approached (*Ant.–Accessible*)
33. Impracticable	incapable of being practised (*Ant.–Practicable*)
34. Inaudible	a sound that cannot be heard (*Ant.–Audible*)
35. Incorrigible	incapable of being corrected (*Ant.–Corrigible*)
36. Irreparable	incapable of being repaired (*Ant.–Reparable*)
37. Indelible	a mark that cannot be erased (*Ant.–Delible*)
38. Infallible	one who is free from all mistakes and failures (*Ant.–Fallible*)
39. Inedible	not fit to be eaten (*Ant.–Edible*)
40. Inflammable	liable to catch fire easily (*Ant.–Non-inflammable*)
41. Inevitable	that cannot be avoided (*Ant.–Evitable*)
42. Indispensable	that cannot be dispensed with, removed (*Ant.–Dispensable*)
43. Interregnum	a period of interval between two regimes and governments
44. Intelligible	that can be understood (*Ant.–Unintelligible*)
45. Lunar	of the moon
46. Maiden	a speech or an attempt made by a person for the first time
47. Mammal	an animal that gives milk
48. Manuscript	a matter written by hand
49. Nostalgia	home sickness, memories of the past
50. Omnipresent	one who is present everywhere
51. Omnipotent	one who is all powerful
52. Omniscient	one who knows all
53. Parable	a short story with a moral
54. Parole	pledge given by a prisoner for temporary release not to escape
55. Panacea	a remedy for all ills
56. Pantheism	the belief that God pervades nature
57. Pedantic	a style meant to display one's knowledge
58. Plagiarism	literary theft or passing off an author's original work as one's own
59. Platonic	something spiritual (love)
60. Portable	that can be carried in hand
61. Potable	fit to drink

62. **Plebiscite** a decision made by public voting
63. **Pseudonym** an imaginary name assumed by an author
64. **Quarantine** an act of separation from a person to avoid infection
65. **Quadruped** an animal with four feet
66. **Refrendum** general vote of the public to decide a question (*Syn.–Plebiscite*)
67. **Red-tapism** official formality resulting in delay
68. **Regalia** dress with medals, ribbons worn at official ceremonies (*Syn.–Raiment)*
69. **Sacrilege** violating the sanctity of religious places/objects (*Syn.–Desecration*)
70. **Sinecure** a job with high salary but a little responsibility
71. **Soliloquy** a speech made when one is alone
72. **Soporific** a medicine that induces sleep
73. **Souvenir** a thing kept in memory of an event (*Syn.–Momento*)
74. **Swan song** the last literary work of a writer/an artist
75. **Solar** of the sun
76. **Transparent** that can be seen through (*Ant.–Opaque*)
77. **Venial** a slight fault that can be forgiven
78. **Verbatim** exactly as it was spoken or written
79. **Utopia** an imaginary land with perfect social order
80. **Zodiac** a diagram showing the path of planets

(C) One Words Denoting Places

1. **Abattoir** a place where animals are slaughtered for the market
2. **Apiary** a place where bees are kept
3. **Aquarium** a tank for fishes
4. **Arena** a place for wrestling
5. **Arsenal** a place for ammunition and weapons
6. **Asylum** a place for lunatics and political refugees
7. **Aviary** a place where birds are kept (*Syn.–Volory*)
8. **Archives** a place where government records are kept
9. **Burrow** the underground dwelling place of an animal
10. **Cache** a place where ammunition is hidden
11. **Cage** a place for birds
12. **Casino** a place with gambling tables etc
13. **Cemetery** a graveyard where the dead are burried
14. **Cloakroom** a place for luggage at a railway station
15. **Convent** a residence for nuns

16. Creche	a nursery where children of working parents are cared for while their parents are at work
17. Crematorium	a cremation ground where the last funeral rites are performed
18. Decanter	an ornamental glass bottle for holding wine or other alcoholic drinks
19. Dormitory	the sleeping rooms in a college or public institution
20. Drey	a squirrel's home
21. Elysium	a paradise with perfect bliss
22. Gymnasium	a place where atheletic exercises are performed
23. Granary	a place for storing grain
24. Hangar	a place for housing aeroplanes
25. Hive	a place for bees
26. Hutch	a wooden box with a front of wire for rabbits
27. Infirmary	a home for old persons
28. Kennel	a house of shelter for a dog
29. Lair/Den	the resting place of a wild animal
30. Mint	a place where money is coined
31. Menagerie	a place for wild animals and birds (*Sanctuary*)
32. Monastery	a residence for monks or priests
33. Morgue	a place where dead bodies are kept for identification
34. Mortuary	a place where dead bodies are kept for post-mortem
35. Orchard	a place where fruit trees are grown
36. Orphanage	a place where orphans are housed
37. Pantry	a place for provisions etc. in the house
38. Portfolio	a portable case for holding papers, drawing, etc.
39. Reservoir	a place where water is collected and stored
40. Resort	a place frequented for reasons of pleasure or health
41. Stable	a house of shelter for a horse
42. Sty	a place where pigs are kept
43. Scullery	a place where plates, dishes, pots and other cooking utensils are washed up
44. Sheath, Scabbard	a case in which the blade of a sword is kept
45. Sanatorium	a place for the sick to recover health
46. Tannery	a place where leather is tanned
47. Wardrobe	a place for clothes

(D) One Words Denoting Professions

1. **Anchor** a person who presents a radio/television programme
2. **Anthropologist** one who studies the evolution of mankind
3. **Astronaut** a person, who travels in spacecraft
4. **Calligraphist** a person who writes beautiful writing
5. **Cartographer** one who draws maps
6. **Choreographer** one who teaches art of dancing
7. **Chauffeur** one who drives a motor car
8. **Compere** one who introduces performing artists on the stage programmes
9. **Curator** one who is incharge of a museum/a cricket pitch
10. **Florist** one who deals in flowers
11. **Invigilator** one who supervises in the examination hall
12. **Lexicographer** one who compiles a dictionary
13. **Radio Jockey** one who presents a radio programme
14. **Psephologist** one who studies the pattern of voting in elections
15. **Sculptor** one who gives shape to stone
16. **Usurer** one who lends money at very high rates

(E) One Words Denoting Kinds of Governments

1. **Anarchy** absence of Government
2. **Aristocracy** Government by the nobles/lords
3. **Autocracy** Government by one person (*Syn.–Dictatorship*)
4. **Autonomy** the right of self-government
5. **Bureaucracy** Government run by officials
6. **Democracy** Government by the people
7. **Gerontocracy** Government by old men
8. **Kekistocracy** Government by the worst citizen
9. **Neocracy** Government by the inexperienced persons
10. **Ochlocracy** Government by mob (*Syn.–Mobocracy*)
11. **Oligarchy** Government by a few persons
12. **Panarchy** Government run universally
13. **Plutocracy** Government by the rich
14. **Secular** Government not by the laws of religion
15. **Monarchy** Government by a King/Queen
16. **Thearchy** Government by the Gods
17. **Theocracy** Government by the laws of religion

(F) One Words Denoting Killings/Deaths of Persons

1. **Cemetery** — a graveyard where the dead are burried
2. **Cortege** — a funeral procession comprising a number of mourners
3. **Cremation ground/Crematorium** — a place where the last funeral rites are performed
4. **Obituary** — an account in the newspaper about the funeral of the deceased
5. **Elegy** — a poem of lamentation on the death of someone loved and admired
6. **Epitaph** — words inscribed on the grave/tomb in the memory of the one burried
7. **Filicide** — murder of one's children
8. **Foeticide** — murder of a foetus
9. **Fratricide** — murder of one's brother
10. **Genocide** — murder of race
11. **Homicide** — murder of a man/woman
12. **Infanticide** — murder of an infant
13. **Matricide** — murder of one's mother
14. **Parricide** — murder of one's parents
15. **Patricide** — murder of one's father
16. **Regicide** — murder of king or queen
17. **Suicide** — murder of oneself
18. **Uxoricide** — murder of one's wife
19. **Sororicide** — murder of one's sister
20. **Mortuary** — a place where dead bodies are kept for postmortem
21. **Morgue** — a place where bodies are kept for identification
22. **Postmortem** — medical examination of a dead body (*Syn.–Autopsy*)

(G) One Words Denoting Marriages

1. **Adultery** — the practice of having extra-marital relations
2. **Alimony** — an allowance paid to wife on divorce
3. **Bigamy** — the practice of having two wives or husbands at a time
4. **Celibacy** — a state of abstention from marriage
5. **Concubinage** — live-in relationship–a man and a woman living without being married
6. **Misogamist** — one who hates marriage
7. **Matrimony** — a state of being married
8. **Monogamy** — the practice of marrying one at a time
9. **Polygamy** — the practice of marrying more than one wife at a time
10. **Polyandry** — the practice of marrying more than one husband at a time
11. **Spinster** — an older woman who is not married

(H) One Words Denoting Time Periods

1. **Annual**	happening once in a year
2. **Biennial**	happening in two years
3. **Triennial**	happening in three years
4. **Quadrennial**	happening in four years
5. **Quinquennial**	happening in five years
6. **Decennial**	happening in ten years
7. **Semicentennial**	50th anniversary
8. **Centennial** (*Centenary*)	100th anniversary
9. **Sesquicentennial**	150th anniversary
10. **Bicentennial** (*Bicentenary*)	200th anniversary
11. **Tricentennial** (*Tercentenary*)	300th anniversary
12. **Tetra centennial**	400th anniversary
13. **Pentacentennial**	500th anniversary
14. **Sexagenarian**	one who is in sixties
15. **Septuagenarian**	one who is in seventies
16. **Octagenarian**	one who is in eighties
17. **Nonagenarian**	one who is in nineties
18. **Centenarian**	one who is hundred years old
19. **Century**	a period of hundred years
20. **Millennium**	a period of 1000 years

(I) One Words Denoting Groups (People, Animals, Birds and Things)

1. **Agenda**	a list of business matters at a meeting
2. **Alliance**	a state of relationship formed between states, powers, etc.
3. **Anthology**	a collection of poems
4. **Attendance/ Retinue**	a number of servants, persons present with a person in authority
5. **Audience**	a number of people gathered to listen
6. **Band**	a group of musicians, followers
7. **Batch**	a group of pupils
8. **Battery**	a group of heavy guns
9. **Bale**	a large quantity of cotton tied in a bundle
10. **Bench**	the office of judges or magistrates
11. **Bevy**	a large group of girls/ladies
12. **Block**	a group of houses or buildings bounded by four sides
13. **Bouquet**	a bunch of flowers
14. **Brood**	a group of young birds all born at the same time
15. **Brace**	a pair of pigeons

16. Board	a decision-making body of directors
17. Cache	of arms, store house for hiding
18. Caravan	a group of people travelling with their vehicles or animals
19. Catalogue	a list of books
20. Caucus	inner circle of members of government
21. Clique	a small group of persons belonging to a body
22. Circle	a group of friends
23. Claque	a group of applauders *i.e.*, paid to clap
24. Cloud	of locusts
25. Cluster	a group of islands
26. Code	a systematic collection of laws
27. Colony/column	a group of people of one race moving in the same direction
28. Constellation	a series of stars
29. Chest	of drawers
30. Congress	a meeting of delegates
31. Convoy	a group of trucks/lorries travelling together under protection
32. Cortege	a funeral procession
33. Course	a series of lectures or lessons
34. Conference	a meeting of preachers, delegates
35. Congregation	a group of worshippers
36. Crew	of sailors manning ships
37. Drove	a flock of cattle (being driven)
38. Flight	the action of flying of birds
39. *(a)* Flotilla	a small fleet of boats
***(b)* Fleet**	a group of ships
40. Galaxy	a system of millions of stars
41. Gallery	a room that contains pictures and statues displayed for sale
42. Grove	a small orchard of trees
43. Hamlet	a group of houses in a village
44. Haul	a number of fish (in a net) caught at one time
45. Heap	a number of ruins, stones
46. Herd	a large group of animals that live together
47. Hive	(swarm) of bees
48. Host	a large number of people, reasons, considerations
49. Horde	of people, robbers
50. Jumble	an untidy collection of things
51. Litter	of young pigs, dogs at birth
52. Lock	a section of hair
53. Order	a society of knights, monks living under the same rule

54. **Panel** a small group of Inspectors, examiners for investigation
55. **Poultry** of fowls, ducks etc.
56. **Posse** a group of policemen
57. **Rosary** a string of beads
58. **School** a group of thinkers or learned men sharing similar ideas
59. **Sea** of troubles, difficulties, cares
60. **Series** a number of similar events, matches, lectures
61. **Shoal** a large number of fish swimming together
62. **Sheaf** of corn, wheat
63. **String** a sequence of similar items
64. **Stream** a continuous flow of people/visitors
65. **Suite** a set of followers, rooms, furniture
66. **Suit** a set of clothes made of same fabric
67. **Syllabus** the topics of studies
68. **Swarm** of flies or locusts, bees, ants
69. **Truss** a frame-work of rafters, posts and bars
70. **Syndicate** a group of merchants
71. **Team** a group of players, horses, oxen
72. **Throng** a large crowd of people
73. **Tissue** of lies or crimes
74. **Troupe** a group of artists, dancers or acrobats
75. **Torrent** of abusive invectives, of rain
76. **Tuft** of grass, hair
77. **Union** a political unit containing a number of states
78. **Barrage** of questions
79. **Volley** a number of arrows, stones, abuses
80. **World** of cares, troubles

(J) One Words Denoting Science and Arts

1. **Acoustics** the study of sound
2. **Aeronautics** the science or art of flight
3. **Aesthetics** the philosophy of fine arts
4. **Agronomy** the science of soil management and the production of field crops
5. **Alchemy** Chemistry in ancient times
6. **Bibliography** the study of history of a list of books on a subject
7. **Anatomy** the science dealing with the structure of animals, plants or human body
8. **Anthropology** the science that deals with the origin, physical and cultural development of mankind

9. Arboriculture	cultivation of trees and vegetables
10. Astrology	the ancient art of predicting the course of human destinies with the help of indications deduced from the position and movement of the heavenly bodies
11. Bacteriology	the study of bacteria
12. Botany	the study of plants
13. Calligraphy	the art of beautiful handwriting
14. Ceramics, Pottery	the art and technology of making objects from clay etc.
15. Chronobiology	the study of duration of life
16. Chronology	the science of arranging time in periods and ascertaining the dates and historical order of the past events
17. Chromatics	the art of making fireworks
18. Cosmogony	the science of the nature of heavenly bodies
19. Cosmography	the science that describes and maps the main features of the universe
20. Cosmology	the science of the nature, origin and history of the universe
21. Cryogenics	the science of dealing with the production control and the application of very low temperatures
22. Cypher	the art of secret writings
23. Cytology	the study of cells, especially their formation, structure and functions
24. Dactylography	the study of finger prints for the purpose of identification
25. Dactylology	the technique of communication by signs made with the fingers. It is generally used by the deaf
26. Demography	the study of human population with the help of the records of the number of births and deaths
27. Ecology	the study of the relation of animals and plants to their surroundings, animate and inanimate
28. Entomology	the study of insects
29. Epigraphy	the study of inscriptions
30. Ethnology	the study of human races
31. Ethology	the study of animal behaviour
32. Etymology	the study of origin and history of words (Morphology)
33. Eugenics	the study of production of better offspring by the careful selection of parents
34. Ergonomy	the study of effect of environment on workers
35. Ganealogy	the study of family ancestries and histories
36. Genetics	the branch of biology dealing with the phenomenon of heredity and the laws governing it
37. Geology	the science that deals with the physical history of the earth

38. Gymnastics	the art of performing acrobatics feats
39. Heliotherapy	the sun cure
40. Histology	the study of tissues
41. Horticulture	the cultivation of flowers, fruits, vegetables and ornamental plants
42. Hydropathy	the treatment of diseases by the internal and external use of water
43. Hagiology	study of the lives of saints
44. Iconography	teaching with the aid of pictures and models
45. Iconology	the study of symbolic representations
46. Jurisprudence	the science of law
47. Lexicography	the writing or compiling of dictionaries
48. Numismatics	the study of coins and metals
49. Odontology	the scientific study of the teeth
50. Ornithology	the study of birds
51. Orthoepy	the study of correct pronunciation
52. Pedagogy	the art or method of teaching
53. Petrology	the study of rocks/crust
54. Philately	the collection and study of postage/revenue stamps etc.
55. Philology	the study of written records, their authenticity etc.
56. Phonetics	the study of speech sounds and the production, transmission, reception
57. Physiognomy	the study of human face
58. Paleography	the study of ancient writings
59. Rhetoric	the art of elegant speech or writing
60. Sericulture	the raising of silk worms for the production of raw silk
61. Seismology	the study of earthquakes and the phenomenon associated with it
62. Spelelogy	the study of caves
63. Telepathy	communication between minds by some means other than sensory perception
64. Zoology	the study of animal life

(K) One Words Denoting Phobias/Mental Disorders

1. Acrophobia	high places
2. Aerophobia	fear of air
3. Aglophobia	of pain
4. Altiphobia	of altitude
5. Anorexia	fear of getting fat makes young girls stop eating resulting in harmful effect
6. Agorophobia	of public/place open
7. Androphobia	of males
8. Autophobia	of solitude
9. Bathophobia	of depths
10. Biblophobia	of books
11. Cacophobia	of ugliness
12. Catrophobia	of doctors
13. Cellophobia	extreme fear about beauty
14. Chronophobia	of time
15. Cynophobia	of dogs
16. Claustrophobia	of being confined to small place
17. Dipsophobia	of thirst
18. Dipsomania	morbid compulsion to drink
19. Demonomania	delusion of being under evil spirits
20. Entomophobia	of insects
21. Ergophobia	of work
22. Gamophobia	of marriage
23. Genophobia	of birth
24. Geraphobia	of old age
25. Gnosiophobia	of knowledge
26. Graphophobia	of writing
27. Gynaephobia	of women
28. Haemetophobia	of blood
29. Hedonophobia	of pleasure
30. Hodophobia	of travel
31. Hydrophobia	of water
32. Kleptophobia	of stealing/thieves
33. Kleptomania	a compulsive desire to steal
34. Lipophobia	of getting fat
35. Logophobia	of study
36. Logomania	mania for talking
37. Maieusiophobia	of childbirth

38. Metrophobia	of motherhood
39. Menemophobia	of old memories
40. Monophobia	of loneliness, of being alone
41. Mysophobia	of filth, contamination
42. Magalomania	delusion about one's greatness
43. Nyctophobia	of darkness
44. Ophthalmophobia	of eyes
45. Ochlophobia	of crowds/mobs
46. Paedophobia	of children
47. Pathophobia	of disease/sickness
48. Peniophobia	of poverty/money problem
49. Pharmacophobia	of medicine
50. Phasmophobia	of ghosts
51. Xenophobia	of foreigners
52. Pyrophobia	of fire
53. Thanatophobia	of death
54. Scelerophobia	of burglars
55. Theophobia	of God
56. Toxicophobia	of poison
57. Triskaidekaphobia	of number thirteen
58. Theomania	a delusion that one is God

(L) One Words Denoting Young-ones

Adult	Young-one	Adult	Young-one
1. Ass	Foal	**2. Bird**	Nestling
3. Butterfly, moth	Caterpillar	**4. Cat**	Kitten
5. Cock	Cockerel	**6. Cow**	Calf
7. Cow	Heifer	**8. Deer**	Fawn
9. Dog	Puppy	**10. Duck**	Duckling
11. Eagle	Eaglet	**12. Elephant**	Calf
13. Fowl	Chicken	**14. Frog** (toad)	Tadpole
15. Goat	Kid	**16. Goose**	Gosling
17. Hare	Leveret	**18. Hen**	Pullet
19. Horse	Foal, colt	**20. Lion, Bear, Fox**	Cub
21. Mare	Filly	**22. Owl**	Owlet
23. Pig	Piglet	**24. Sheep**	Lamb
25. Stallion (horse)	Colt or Foal	**26. Swan**	Cygnet

(M) One Words Denoting Distinctive Sounds

Animal	Sound	Animal	Sound
1. Apes	Gibber	2. Arms	Clang
3. Asses	Bray	4. A person in agony	Moan
5. Babies	Lisp	6. Bees	Hum
7. Beetles	Drone	8. Bells	Jingle/chime
9. Birds	Chirp, warble	10. Brakes	Screech
11. Cattle	Low	12. Camels	Grunt
13. Cats	Mew	14. Chains	Clank
15. Coins	Jingle/tinkle	16. Corks	Pop
17. Cocks	Crow	18. Crows	Crow, caw
19. Deer	Bell	20. Dogs	Bark
21. Doors	Creak/bang	22. Doves	Coo
23. Duck	Quack	24. Elephants	Trumpet
25. Fire	Crackle	26. Flies	Buzz
27. Frogs	Croak	28. Glasses	Tinkle
29. Goats	Bleat	30. Guns	Roar
31. Hens	Cackle	32. Hoofs	Clatter
33. Horses	Neigh	34. Silk	Rustle
35. Hyenas	Laugh	36. Jackals	Howl
37. Larks	Sing, warble	38. Leaves	Rustle
39. Lions	Roar	40. Mice	Squeak
41. Monkeys	Gibber	42. Nightingales	Sing, warble
43. Owls	Hoot	44. Oxen/cow	Low
45. Paper	Crinkle	46. Parrots	Talk
47. Pigeons	Coo	48. Pigs	Squeal
49. Ravens	Croak	50. Rain	Patter
51. Rivers	Murmur	52. Serpents	Hiss
53. Silk	Rustle	54. Teeth	Chatter
55. Tigers	Roar	56. Trees	Sigh
57. Water	Ripple	58. Whip	Crack
59. Wind	Whistle	60. Wings	Flap

(N) One Words Denoting Diminutives

'Diminutives' are the words that indicate smallness. Such words are often used as an expression, of affection or contempt. Diminutives are usually formed by the use of suffixes such as 'Let' etc. For example, the diminutive of the book may be formed by the use of 'let'—Booklet.

Word	Diminutive	Word	Diminutive
1. Ankle	Anklet	**2. Babe**	Baby
3. Ball	Ballet, Bullet	**4. Baron**	Baronet
5. Book	Booklet	**6. Brace**	Bracelet
7. Brook	Brooklet	**8. Car**	Chariot
9. Cask	Casket	**10. City**	Citadel
11. Cigar	Cigarette	**12. Corn**	Kernel
13. Crown	Coronet	**14. Dear**	Darling
15. Grain	Granule	**16. Hand bag**	Reticule
17. Hill	Hillock	**18. Home**	Hamlet
19. Ice	Icicle	**20. Isle**	Islet
21. Latch	Latchet	**22. Leaf**	Leaflet
23. Lock	Locket	**24. Nest**	Nestling
25. Nose	Nozzle	**26. Part**	Particle
27. Poet	Poetaster	**28. Pouch**	Pocket
29. Ring	Ringlet	**30. River**	Rivulet
31. Sack	Satchel	**32. Star**	Starlet, Asterisk
33. Statue	Statuette	**34. Stream**	Streamlet
35. Table	Tablet	**36. Top**	Tip
37. Tower	Turret	**38. Umbrella**	Parasol
39. Weak	Weakling		

(O) One Words Denoting Comparisons

1. As *blind* as a bat.
2. As *bitter* as gall hemlock.
3. As *cheerful* as a lark.
4. As *cunning, sly, wily* as a fox.
5. As *fair* as a rose.
6. As *fast* as a hare, light, storm, eagle.
7. As *firm* as a rock.
8. As *flat* as a board or a pancake.
9. As *free* as air.
10. As *fresh* as a daisy or a rose.
11. As *grave* as a judge.
12. As *greedy* as a dog or a wolf.
13. As *gentle* as a lamb.
14. As *hard* as a flint or a stone.
15. As *harmless* as a dove.
16. As *hungry* as a horse or a hunter.
17. As *light* as a feather.
18. As *merry* as a cricket.
19. As *obstinate* as a mule.
20. As *pale* as death or ghost.
21. As *playful* as a butterfly or a kitten or a squirrel.

22. As *proud* as a peacock.

23. As *slippery* as an eel.

24. As *soft* as butter.

25. As *silent* as the dead or stars.

26. As *tricky* as a monkey.

27. As *true* as steel.

28. As *wise* as a serpent or Solomon.

29. As *yieldling* as wax.

30. As *agile* as a cat, monkey.

31. As *far apart* as the poles.

32. As *black* as ebony/coal.

33. As *blithe* as May.

34. As *boisterous* as stormy sea winds.

35. As *bounteous* as nature.

36. As *brief* as time–as a dream.

37. As *brittle* as glass.

38. As *candid* as mirrors.

39. As *chaste* as Minerva.

40. As *constant* as the sun.

41. As *cool* as cucumber.

42. As *cosy* as the nest of a bird.

43. As *dangerous* as machine-guns.

44. As *deceptive* as the mirage of the desert.

45. As *docile* as *a* lamb.

46. As *fit* as a fiddle.

47. As *fresh* as dew, as a sea breeze, rose.

48. As *grim* as death.

49. As *haggard* as spectres, ghosts.

50. As *harsh* as truth.

51. As *heavy* as lead.

52. As *inconsistent* as the moon, as the waves.

53. As *industrious* as an ant.

54. As *inevitable* as death/fate.

55. As *mad* as a hatter, as a March hare.

56. As *mean* as a miser.

57. As *meek* as a dove, mouse.

58. As *nervous* as a mouse.

59. As *resistless* as wind.

60. As *restless* as ambition, as the sea.

61. As *secure* as the grave.

62. As *slow* as a snail.

63. As *solitary* as a tomb.

64. As *talkative* as a magpie.

65. As *transparent* as glass.

66. As *treacherous* as memory.

67. As *vain* as a peacock.

68. As *vigilant* as stars.

69. As *zig–zag* as lightning.

70. As *uncertain* as the weather.

71. As *white* as snow.

72. As *hungry* as church mouse.

73. As *dear* as life.

74. As *straight* as an arrow.

75. As *impatient* as a lover.

76. As *swift* as an arrow.

77. As *old* as hills.

78. As *cold* as marble.

79. As *sharp* as razor.

80. As *busy* as a bee.

Exercise A

Directions (Q.Nos. 1-16) *Out of the four alternatives, choose the one which can be substituted for the given words/sentences.*

1. Medicine given to counteract poison.
(a) Antibiotic (b) Antiseptic
(c) Antidote (d) Antifungal

2. One who hates marriage.
(a) Misanthrope (b) Misogamist
(c) Misogynist (d) Polygamist

3. Thawing snow.
(a) Sludge (b) Slush
(c) Slosh (d) Slash

4. One who specialises in the mathematics of insurance.
(a) A statistician (b) An actuary
(c) An agent (d) Aninrurant

5. Violation of the sanctity of the Church.
(a) Infringement (b) Irreverence
(c) Sacrilege (d) Transgression

6. Of one mind or opinion.
(a) Voluntary (b) Referendum
(c) Homogenous (d) Unanimous

7. One who is always doubting.
(a) Sceptic (b) Deist
(c) Rationalist (d) Positivist

8. A collection of slaves.
(a) Coffle (b) Crew
(c) Company (d) Cortege

9. A professional soldier hired to serve in a foreign army.
(a) Mercenary (b) Liquidator
(c) Venal` (d) Hireling

10. Not likely to be easily pleased.
(a) Fastidious (b) Infallible
(c) Fatalist (d) Communist

11. The practise of having many wives.
(a) Bigamy (b) Calligraphy
(c) Polygamy (d) Polyandry

12. Take great pleasure.
(a) Revel (b) Satisfied
(c) Uphold (d) Overhaul

13. A strong dislike.
(a) Reciprocity (b) Entreaty
(c) Animosity (d) Malice

14. The Mahabharata is a long poem based on a noble theme.
(a) Summary (b) Narration
(c) Story (d) Epic

15. A person who abstains completely from alcoholic drinks.
(a) Teetotaller (b) Derelict
(c) Subjunctive (d) Incriminatory

16. Person who files a suit.
(a) Charger (b) Suitor
(c) Plaintiff (d) Accuse

Directions (Q.Nos. 17-23) *Out of the four alternatives, choose the one which can be substituted for the given words/sentences.*

17. To free anything from germs.
(a) Cauterise (b) Sterilise
(c) Antiseptic (d) Antivirus

18. The depository where state records and documents are preserved.
(a) Museum (b) Library
(c) Emporium (d) Archive

19. A place where birds are kept.
(a) Aviary (b) House
(c) Aquarium (d) Apiary

20. Incapable of making errors.
(a) Infallible (b) Incorrigible
(c) Impervious (d) Inexplicable

21. Governed by a sense of duty.
(a) Conscious (b) Sensible
(c) Intelligent (d) Conscientious

22. An assembly of worshippers.
(a) Congregation (b) Conflagration
(c) Configuration (d) Confrontation

23. A person who lives by himself.
(a) Monk (b) Recluse
(c) Extrovert (d) Prophet

Directions (Q.Nos. 24-37) *Out of the four alternatives, choose the one which can be substituted for the given words/sentences.*

24. To reduce to nothing.
(a) Cull (b) Lull
(c) Null (d) Annul

25. An obviously true or hackneyed statement.
(a) Truism (b) Syllogism
(c) Iconic (d) Imagism

26. The act of producing beautiful handwriting using a brush or a special pen.
(a) Hieroglyphics (b) Calligraphy
(c) Stencilling (d) Graphics

27. A person of obscure position who has gained wealth.
(a) Extravagant (b) Promiscuous
(c) Parvenu (d) Sumptuary

28. A study of sounds.
(a) Semantics (b) Stylistics
(c) Linguistics (d) Phonetics

29. Property inherited from one's father or ancestors.
(a) Alimony (b) Patrimony
(c) Voluntary (d) Armistice

30. To bite like a rat.
(a) Chew (b) Cut
(c) Split (d) Gnaw

31. A style in which a writer makes display of his knowledge.
(a) Ornate (b) Pedantic
(c) Artificial (d) Showy

32. One who performs daring gymnastic feats.
(a) Athlete (b) Juggler
(c) Acrobat (d) Conjuror

33. Rebellion against lawful authority.
(a) Mutiny (b) Coup
(c) Revolution (d) Dissidence

34. Soldiers who fight on horseback.
(a) Infantry (b) Artillery
(c) Cavalry (d) Armoured

35. A man who wastes his money on luxury.
(a) Extempore (b) Thrifty
(c) Extravagant (d) Promiscuous

36. A person who is well known in an unfavourable way.
(a) Notorious (b) Obscure
(c) Conspicuous (d) Ethical

37. To write under a different name.
(a) Anonymous (b) Biography
(c) Pseudonym (d) Masquerade

Directions (Q.Nos. 38-40) *Out of the four alternatives, choose the one which can be substituted for the given words/sentences.*

38. Fluent and clear in speech.
(a) Emotional (b) Enthusiastic
(c) Articulate (d) Confident

39. Spoken or done without preparation.
(a) Verbose (b) Extempore
(c) Amateur (d) Verbatim

40. Unfair advantages for members of one's own family.
(a) Optimism (b) Plagiarism
(c) Nepotism (d) Regionalism

Exercies B

Directions (Q.Nos. 1-6) *Each of the items in this section has a sentence with a blank space and four words given after the sentence. Select whichever word you consider most appropriate for the blank space.*

1. An accomplice is a partner in ....
(a) business *(b)* crime
(c) construction *(d)* gambling

2. A person, who pretends to be what he is not is called an ....
(a) imbiber *(b)* impresario
(c) imitator *(d)* imposter

3. His .... nature would not let him leave his office before 5 pm.
(a) honest *(b)* selfish
(c) unscrupulous *(d)* conscientious

4. The committee's appeal to the people for money ....little response.
(a) evoked *(b)* provided
(c) provoked *(d)* prevented

5. Too many skyscrapers .... the view along the beach.
(a) reveal *(b)* obstruct
(c) make *(d)* clear

6. Though he has several interim plans, his .... aim is to become a billionaire.
(a) absolute *(b)* determined
(c) only *(d)* ultimate

Directions (Q.Nos. 7-13) *Out of the four alternatives, choose the one which can be substituted for the given words/sentences.*

7. An apartment building in which each apartment is owned separately by the people living in it, but also containing shared areas.
(a) Condominium *(b)* Multiplex
(c) Duplex *(d)* Caravan

8. A group of three powerful people.
(a) Trio *(b)* Tritium
(c) Trivet *(d)* Triumvirate

9. Operation of the body after death.
(a) Post-mortem *(b)* Obituary
(c) Homage *(d)* Mortuary

10. Not allowing the passage of light.
(a) Oblique *(b)* Opaque
(c) Optique *(d)* Opulant

11. Science regarding principles of classification.
(a) Taxidermy *(b)* Taxonomy
(c) Toxicology *(d)* Classicology

12. A political leader appealing to popular desires and prejudices.
(a) Dictator *(b)* Tyrant
(c) Popularist *(d)* Demagogue

13. Fear of enclosed in a small closed space.
(*a*) Closophobia (*b*) Clusterophobia
(*c*) Claustrophobia (*d*) Liftophobia

Directions (Q.Nos. 14-28) *Out of the four alternatives, choose the one which can be substituted for the given words/sentences.*

14. A person who thinks only about himself and not about others' needs.
(*a*) Egocentric (*b*) Egomaniacal
(*c*) Egoistic (*d*) Egotistic

15. Something that cannot be explained.
(*a*) Inexplicable (*b*) Unthinkable
(*c*) Impregnable (*d*) Mysterious

16. A written declaration made on oath in the presence of a magistrate.
(*a*) Document (*b*) Affidavit
(*c*) Dossier (*d*) Voucher

17. A raised place on which offerings to a God are made.
(*a*) Mound (*b*) Rostrum
(*c*) Church (*d*) Altar

18. A guide-post pointing out the way for a place.
(*a*) Last-post (*b*) Finger-post
(*c*) Lamp-post (*d*) Check-post

19. The art of preserving skin of animals, birds, fishes.
(*a*) Topology (*b*) Taxonomy
(*c*) Seismology (*d*) Taxidermy

20. Chanting of magic spells.
(*a*) Narration (*b*) Recitation
(*c*) Incantation (*d*) Utterance

21. A group of three books, films etc. that have the same subject or characters.
(*a*) Trinity (*b*) Trilogy
(*c*) Trio (*d*) Tripod

22. A study of the human race.
(*a*) Anthropology (*b*) Archaeology
(*c*) Ethnology (*d*) Etymology

23. An expert in the area of the fine or other arts.
(*a*) Neophyte (*b*) Amateur
(*c*) Connoisseur (*d*) Enthusiast

24. Flowers fastened in a circle.
(*a*) Vespers (*b*) Wreathe
(*c*) Sonorous (*d*) Scurry

25. Knowing everything.
(*a*) Omnigenous (*b*) Omnipotent
(*c*) Omnipresent (*d*) Omniscient

26. That cannot be conquered.
(*a*) Invincible (*b*) Invulnerable
(*c*) Intangible (*d*) Inevitable

27. Bitter and violent attack in words or writing.
(a) Loquacious (b) Stubborn
(c) Diatribe (d) Epicurean

28. A person eighty years of age.
(a) Septogenarian (b) Nonagenarian
(c) Octogenarian (d) Sexogenarian

Directions (Q.Nos. 29-33) *Out of the four alternatives, choose the one which can be substituted for the given words/sentences.*

29. An inscription on a tomb.
(a) Espionage (b) Epilogue
(c) Epitaph (d) Elegy

30. Feeling inside you which tells you what is right and what is wrong.
(a) Cleverness (b) Conscience
(c) Consciousness (d) Fear

31. Release of a prisoner from jail on certain terms and conditions.
(a) Parole (b) Parley
(c) Pardon (d) Acquittal

32. Loss of memory.
(a) Ambrosia (b) Amnesia
(c) Insomnia (d) Forgetting

33. To struggle helplessly.
(a) Flounder (b) Founder
(c) Fumble (d) Finger

Directions (Q.Nos. 34-38) *Out of the four alternatives, choose the one which can be substituted for the given words/sentences.*

34. Code of diplomatic etiquette and precedence.
(a) Statesmanship (b) Diplomacy
(c) Hierarchy (d) Protocol

35. To renounce a high position of authority or control.
(a) Abduct (b) Abandon
(c) Abort (d) Abdicate

36. Not to be moved by entreaty.
(a) Rigorous (b) Negligent
(c) Inexorable (d) Despotic

37. An object or portion serving as a sample.
(a) Specification (b) Spectre
(c) Spectacle (d) Specimen

38. The practice of submitting a proposal to popular vote.
(a) Election (b) Reference
(c) Popularity (d) Referendum

Revision Exercise

Directions *(Q. Nos. 1-16) Select the most appropriate word for the group of words.*

1. That which can be seen through
(a) magical (b) opaque
(c) transparent (d) invisible

2. That which cannot be taken by force
(a) impregnable (b) inapprehensible
(c) inaccessible (d) immutable

3. A large impressive house
(a) mansion (b) shack
(c) cabin (d) fort

4. An official pardon
(a) redemption (b) regicide
(c) amnesia (d) amnesty

5. One who walks on foot
(a) protagonist (b) pediatrician
(c) pedestrian (d) pauper

6. Impossible or extremely difficult to understand
(a) Inevitable (b) Incomprehensible
(c) incompatible (d) inaudible

7. Willing to be guided or controlled
(a) abominable (b) amenable
(c) adamant (d) adorable

8. A group of singers in a church
(a) band (b) host
(c) choir (d) troop

9. The original inhabitants of a country
(a) immigrants (b) aborigines
(c) residents (d) slaves

10. One who treats heart diseases
(a) radiologist (b) geologist
(c) cardiologist (d) dermatologist

11. A person or thing that has the same name as another
(a) namesake (b) relative
(c) pseudonym (d) successor

12. One who eats too much
(a) overweight (b) obese
(c) corpulent (d) glutton

13. Able to adapt to many different functions or activities
(a) surrogate (b) versatile
(c) deputy (d) expert

14. Place for collection of dried plant specimens
(a) greenhouse (b) herbarium
(c) warehouse (d) nursery

15. People who enjoy social company
(a) herbivorous (b) gregarious
(c) gorgeous (d) unanimous

16. A group of stars found close together
(a) confederation (b) constellation
(c) concoction (d) conflagration

Directions (Q. Nos. 17-25) *In the following question, out of the four alternatives, select the alternative which is the best substitute of the words/sentence.*

17. Regard something as being due to a cause
(a) adventitious (b) superfluous
(c) incidental (d) ascribe

18. Showing poor taste and quality
(a) savour (b) pike
(c) tacky (d) exquisite

19. Fix an object firmly and deeply in a surrounding mass
(a) lax (b) embed
(c) flaccid (d) asunder

20. Look forward to
(a) eschew (b) abstain
(c) obviate (d) anticipate

21. Extreme self-confidence or audacity
(a) petrified (b) abashed
(c) skittish (d) chutzpah

22. Portray in words
(a) ensconce (b) depict
(c) veil (d) obscure

23. A military or political group that rules a country after taking power by force
(a) junta (b) suffrage
(c) emancipation (d) egalitarianism

24. A person who lives outside his native country
(a) indigenous (b) natal
(c) expatriate (d) intrinsic

25. The ability to make good judgements and take quick decisions
(a) puerility (b) acumen
(c) stupor (d) sanity

Exam Practice

Directions (Q. Nos. 1-7) *In the following questions, out of the four alternatives, choose the one which can be substituted for the given words/sentences.* **SSC CGL 2015**

1. Medical study of skin and its diseases.
(a) Endocrinology (b) Gynaecology
(c) Dermatology (d) Orthopaedics

2. Not suitable for eating.
(a) Inedible (b) Uneatable
(c) Spicy (d) Tasteless

3. A story in which animals or objects speak and given wholesome moral lesson.
(a) Parable (b) Fable
(c) Allegory (d) Legend

4. A process involving too much official formality.
(a) Bureaucracy (b) Nepotism
(c) Red-tapism (d) Diplomacy

5. A person who enters without any invitation.
(a) Burglar (b) Intruder
(c) Vandal (d) Thief

6. Act of injuring anothers reputation by any slanderous communication.
(a) Aberration (b) Defamation
(c) Misrepresentation (d) Orchestration

7. A recurrent compulsive urge to steal.
(a) Kleptomania (b) Pneumonia
(c) Insomnia (d) Nymphomania

Directions *(Q. Nos. 8-14) Out of the four alternatives, choose the one which can be substituted for the given words/sentences and indicate it.* **SSC CGL 2015**

8. To die without making a will
(a) Inane (b) Indigent
(c) Inure (d) Intestate

9. One who is concerned with the welfare of others.
(a) Altruist (b) Egoist
(c) Hedonist (d) Ascetic

10. That which cannot be avoided.
(a) Unvarying (b) Unrestrained
(c) Inevitable (d) Integral

11. Opinion contrary to accepted doctrines.
(a) Controversy (b) Convention
(c) Advocacy (d) Heresy

12. A person who agrees to work for somebody in order to learn a skill.
(a) Apprentice (b) Assistant
(c) Pupil (d) Lackey

13. Make pale by excluding light.
(a) Etiolate (b) Foliate
(c) Percolate (d) Procreate

14. Someone who is designated to hear both sides of a dispute and make a judgement.
(a) Arbitrator (b) Manager
(c) Magistrate (d) Counsellor

Directions (Q. Nos. 15-17) *In the following questions, out of the four alternatives, choose the one which can be substituted for the given words/sentence.* **SSC CGL 2016**

15. Highly skilled
(a) Consummate (b) Inveterate
(c) Notorious (d) Maladroit

16. Identification with the feelings of another
(a) Sympathy (b) Empathy
(c) Apathy (d) Compassion

17. Insatiable desire for wealth
(a) Selfish (b) Avarice
(c) Egoist (d) Generosity

Directions (Q. Nos. 18 and 19) *In the following questions, out of the four alternatives, select the alternative which is the best substitute of the words/sentence.* **SSC CGL 2018**

18. Complete with regard to every detail
(a) Thorough (b) Lackadaisical
(c) Lax (d) Cursory

19. The faculty or power of using one's will
(a) Antagonism (b) Aversion
(c) Rejection (d) Volition

Directions (Q. Nos. 20-23) *Select the word which means the same as the group of words given.* **SSC CGL 2018**

20. Too unimportant to consider
(a) Dimunitive (b)Trivial
(c) Nothing (d) Noticeable

21. That which can be drawn into a thin wire.
(a) Brittle (b) Ductile
(c) Flexible (d) Smooth

22. One who is a great lover of books
(a) Bibliophile (b) Xenophile
(c) Hemophile (d) Paedophile

23. An imaginary name assumed by an author for disguise
(a) Pseudonym (b) Homonym
(c) Alibi (d) Anonymous

Directions (Q. Nos. 24 and 25) *Select one word for the following group of words.* **SSC CGL 2020**

24. A period of ten years
(a) Millennium (b) Century
(c) Fortnight (d) Decade

25. One who leaves his own country to settle in another
(a) Foreigner (b) Tourist
(c) Native (d) Emigrant

Answers

Exercise A

1. (c)	**2.** (b)	**3.** (b)	**4.** (b)	**5.** (c)	**6.** (d)	**7.** (a)
8. (a)	**9.** (a)	**10.** (a)	**11.** (c)	**12.** (a)	**13.** (c)	**14.** (d)
15. (a)	**16.** (c)	**17.** (b)	**18.** (d)	**19.** (a)	**20.** (a)	**21.** (d)
22. (a)	**23.** (b)	**24.** (c)	**25.** (a)	**26.** (b)	**27.** (c)	**28.** (d)
29. (b)	**30.** (d)	**31.** (b)	**32.** (c)	**33.** (a)	**34.** (c)	**35.** (c)
36. (a)	**37.** (c)	**38.** (c)	**39.** (b)	**40.** (c)		

Exercise B

1. (b)	**2.** (d)	**3.** (a)	**4.** (a)	**5.** (b)	**6.** (d)	**7.** (a)
8. (d)	**9.** (a)	**10.** (b)	**11.** (b)	**12.** (d)	**13.** (c)	**14.** (a)
15. (a)	**16.** (b)	**17.** (d)	**18.** (b)	**19.** (d)	**20.** (c)	**21.** (b)
22. (a)	**23.** (c)	**24.** (b)	**25.** (d)	**26.** (a)	**27.** (c)	**28.** (c)
29. (c)	**30.** (b)	**31.** (a)	**32.** (b)	**33.** (a)	**34.** (d)	**35.** (d)
36. (d)	**37.** (d)	**38.** (d)				

Revision Exercise

1. (c)	**2.** (a)	**3.** (a)	**4.** (d)	**5.** (c)	**6.** (b)	**7.** (b)
8. (c)	**9.** (b)	**10.** (c)	**11.** (a)	**12.** (d)	**13.** (b)	**14.** (b)
15. (b)	**16.** (b)	**17.** (d)	**18.** (c)	**19.** (b)	**20.** (d)	**21.** (d)
22. (b)	**23.** (a)	**24.** (c)	**25.** (b)			

Exam Practice

1. (c)	**2.** (a)	**3.** (b)	**4.** (c)	**5.** (b)	**6.** (b)	**7.** (a)
8. (d)	**9.** (a)	**10.** (c)	**11.** (d)	**12.** (a)	**13.** (a)	**14.** (a)
15. (a)	**16.** (b)	**17.** (b)	**18.** (a)	**19.** (d)	**20.** (b)	**21.** (b)
22. (a)	**23.** (a)	**24.** (d)	**25.** (d)			

3

Words with Meanings

A

1. **Adamant** *(adj.)* — *(impossible to persnade, unwilling to change an opinion or decision)* Though she was *adamant* in the beginning, she came round in the end.
2. **Adverse** *(adj.)* — *(unfavourable, hostile)* One must try to overcome *adverse* circumstances.
3. **Affected** *(adj.)* — *(artificial, pretend, influence)* She is proud and always behaves in an *affected* manner.
4. **Allay** *(v.)* — *(calm, pacify)* The mother *allayed* the fears of the child.
5. **Accord** *(n.)* — *(agreement)* There is an *accord* among the family members over this problem.
6. **Adulterate** *(v.)* — *(make impure)* Those who *adulterate* milk should be severely punished.
7. **Agility** *(n.)* — *(nimbleness, alacrity)* The police acted with *agility* and apprehended the robbers.
8. **Admonish** *(v.)* — *(warn, reprove)* The officer *admonished* his subordinates for their irregular attendance.
9. **Assuage** *(v.)* — *(ease, lessen)* The government has tried to assuage the public's fears about the new coronavirus strain.
10. **Alleviate** *(v.)* — *(relieve)* Saints are born to *alleviate* the pain and misery of mankind.
11. **Altruism** *(n.)* — *(unselfish devotion)* My friend is imbued with *altruism* and has made over his property to a charitable trust.
12. **Amass** *(v.)* — *(collect)* He has no time to do good to others and appears to be more interested in *amassing* wealth.
13. **Acrimonious** *(adj.)* — *(stinging, caustic)* There were *acrimonious* arguments between the two brothers causing loss of prestige to the family.
14. **Anomaly** *(n.)* — *(irregularity)* I assure you, it is an *anomaly* because he never behaves like this in an ordinary course of life.

15. **Aptitude** *(n.)* (*a natural ability or skill*) Scientific temper calls for *aptitude* for liberal thinking.

16. **Alimony** *(n.)* (*payment to divorced wife*) She has been fighting for *alimony* from her estranged husband for two years.

17. **Atone** *(v.)* (*make amends*) You must *atone* for the injustice you have done to innocent people.

18. **Ambiguous** *(adj.)* (*doubtful in meaning*) One must avoid the use of *ambiguous* language while writing on social problems.

19. **Abjure** *(v.)* (*give up*) You must *abjure* the pursuit of sinful acts.

20. **Adjure** *(v.)* (*to ask or order someone to do something*) The judge adjured the criminal to answer truthfully.

21. **Allege** *(v.)* (*charge without proof*) It was *alleged* by her enemies that she has misappropriated the money of the trust.

22. **Acme** *(n.)* (*top, pinnacle, apex*) Once at the *acme* of his political career, now he is at nadir.

23. **Analogy** *(n.)* (*similarity*) The *analogy* between the security problems of India and Pakistan is uncalled for.

24. **Appraise** *(v.)* (*estimate value of*) It is always difficult to *appraise* the efforts in true spirit if the results are not favourable.

25. **Allocate** *(v.)* [*earmark, set aside* (*funds*)] The Prime Minister has *allocated* a huge sum for the upliftment of those living below poverty line.

26. **Adage** *(n.)* (*wise saying, proverb*) We have often heard the *adage* 'Pride hath a fall'.

27. **Adversity** *(n.)* (*a difficult or unlucky situation or event*) *Adversity* brings out the latent qualities in a person.

28. **Affluence** *(n.)* (*abundance, wealth*) *Affluence* in his life made him forget the value of character.

29. **Ample** *(adj.)* (*abundant*) There is an *ample* stock of nuclear weapons in the arsenal of super powers.

30. **Absolve** *(v.)* (*pardon, exonerate*) At last he was *absolved* from the charge of misconduct to his officers.

31. **Abscond** *(v.)* (*hide, run secretly*) He has been *absconding* since he committed the murder.

32. **Affray** *(n.)* (*public brawl*) The timely action of the police averted serious mishap of the *affray* between the two communities.

33. **Annihilate** *(v.)* (*destroy*) The use of nuclear weapons is likely to *annihilate* humanity.

34. **Affable** *(adj.)* (*amiable, pleasing*) His *affable* manners always win him admiration in the society.

35. **Amplify** *(v.)* (*to explain something more thoroughly, to make sound louder*) The students requested the teacher to *amplify* upon the point under discussion.

36. **Amalgamate** *(v.)* — (*combine, unite in one body*) The two firms were *amalgamated* under the Chairmanship of Mr. Mukesh Ambani.

37. **Appease** *(v.)* — (*pacify, soothe*) Every political party tries to *appease* the minorities to create its own vote bank.

38. **Apprise** *(v.)* — (*inform*) The Minister was *apprised* of the dangerous situation.

39. **Arduous** *(adj.)* — (*hard, strenuous*) Journey to the Amarnath Shrine is very *arduous.*

40. **Apprehend** *(v.)* — (*arrest, to understand something*) Everybody *apprehends* trouble in the city on account of the abduction of an industrialist.

41. **Ameliorate** *(v.)* — (*improve*) Unless we *ameliorate* the conditions of the working class, we cannot expect the prosperity of our country.

42. **Adulation** *(n.)* — (*praise, flattery*) False *adulation* of the leaders by their followers is a common practice these days.

43. **Animosity** *(n.)* — (*a strong feeling of disliking someone/something*) *Animosity* between the two leaders has embittered the relations, between the two communities.

44. **Audacity** *(n.)* — (*boldness*) He is feared for his *audacity* and unyielding attitude.

45. **Amnesty** *(n.)* — (*general pardon*) On the birth day of the Prince, the King granted *amnesty* to the prisoners.

46. **Ancillary** *(adj.)* — (*accessory*) He is serving in the *ancillary* unit of a multinational company.

47. **Agrarian** *(adj.)* — (*of land, farming*) Inspite of *agrarian* reforms, Indian agriculture has not shown remarkable progress.

48. **Acumen** *(n.)* — (*the ability to make good quick decisions and judgements*) The Jews are known for their business *acumen*.

49. **Abrasive** *(adj.)* — (*offensive*) Nobody likes her for her *abrasive* and haughty behaviour.

50. **Amulet** *(n.)* — (*charm against evil*) The saint gave him an *amulet* to ward off the evil.

B

1. **Benevolent** *(adj.)* — (*generous, charitable*) He is noted for his *benevolent* nature.

2. **Biennial** *(adj.)* — (*held every two years*) The meeting of the members of the Trust is held *biennially*.

3. **Belated** *(adj.)* — (*delayed*) He was sorry for making *belated* payment.

4. **Beguile** *(v.)* — (*delude, cheat*) Don't be *beguiled* by the pleasant manners of hypocrites.

5. **Behove** *(v.)* (*suited to befit, become*) It does not *behove* our political leaders to berate one another for failure in the field of economy.

6. **Banal** *(adj.)* (*commonplace, trite*) The stories of Ruskin Bond are not *banal* because he writes about uncommon subjects.

7. **Brazen** *(adj.)* (*insolent, impudent, impertinent*) Her *brazen* behaviour at the party offended her poor relations.

8. **Bouquet** *(n.)* (*bunch of flowers*) He presented a *bouquet* to his ailing mother.

9. **Brooch** *(n.)* (*ornamental clasp*) She always wears a *brooch* on her pullover.

10. **Blatant** *(adj.)* (*openly shameless*) His behaviour was condemned as *blatant* when he blamed his father for his own misdeeds.

11. **Bantering** *(n.)* [*ridicule (good natured)*] Even his *bantering* was considered offensive.

12. **Broach** *(v.)* (*open up discussion*) The parents of the boy did not even *broach* the issue of marriage with Reena.

13. **Bereft** *(adj.)* (*deprived of, lacking*) *Bereft* of wealth and honour, he died a miserable death.

14. **Benefactor** *(n.)* (*gift giver, patron*) Lord Chesterfield did not prove *benefactor* to Dr. Johnson in the long run.

15. **Benediction** *(n.)* (*blessing, boon*) The *benediction* of the elders should always be valued more than anything else.

16. **Bleak** *(adj.)* (*dismal, gloomy*) Khyber Pass is *bleak* throughout the year.

17. **Bonanza** *(n.)* (*windfall, sudden gain*) The legacy left by his uncle proved a *bonanza* for him and his family.

18. **Belittle** *(v.)* (*disparage, underestimate*) Our adversaries always try to *belittle* our success.

19. **Bellicose** *(adj.)* (*warlike, militant, belligerent*) India must adopt a *bellicose* approach with regard to its security problems.

20. **Bereavement** *(n.)* (*death of near and dear one*) On account of *bereavement* in the family, he did not attend office for days together.

21. **Bigotry** *(n.)* (*fanaticism*) Indians are always shocked at the *bigotry* and narrow-mindedness of other races.

22. **Berate** *(v.)* (*scold strongly*) The father *berated* his son for being negligent in his study.

23. **Beneficiary** *(n.)* (*person entitled to benefits*) Those living below poverty-line are the *beneficiary* of this scheme.

24. **Betroth** *(v.)* (*engaged to marry*) She was *betrothed* to her fiance last month.

25. **Brochure** *(n.)* (*pamphlet with information*) The *brochure* supplied by the institute provides all the information that you need.

26. **Bestow** *(v.)* (*confer, give*) Nature has *bestowed* many gifts on man.

27. **Bid** *(n.)* (*effort, order, auction*) He was caught while making a *bid* on her life.

28. **Baneful** *(adj.)* (*ruinous, poisonous*) Drugs have *baneful* effect on the mind of the youth.

29. **Bravado** *(n.)* (*swagger, false courage*) Retired soldiers often assume the airs of *bravado*.

30. **Besmirch** *(v.)* (*defile*) The opposition always tries to *besmirch* the reputation of the ruling party.

31. **Bovine** *(adj.)* (*slow and stupid*) She is *bovine* by nature while her sister is haughty.

32. **Baffle** *(v.)* (*perplex, frustrate*) A wrong signal was sent to *baffle* the enemy.

33. **Berserk** *(adv.)* (*frenzied, amuck, amok*) The police went *berserk* and began to lathicharge the crowd demonstrating peacefully.

34. **Boutique** *(n.)* (*store for fashionable clothes*) My friend runs a *boutique* in the heart of the city.

35. **Breach** *(n.)* (*breaking of contract/duty, peace, rift*) Anti-social elements were rounded up for fear of *breach* of peace.

36. **Bizarre** *(adj.)* (*grotesque, awkward*) The gentry present in the club were not expected to behave in a *bizarre* manner.

37. **Bode** *(v.)* (*foreshadow, foretell, augur*) Frequent elections in the country do not *bode* well for democracy in India.

38. **Blasphemous** *(adj.)* (*impious, irreligious*) *Blasphemous* acts always lead to communal riots.

C

1. **Chide** *(v.)* (*scold*) Lata was *chided* for coming late to the meeting.

2. **Conversant** *(adj.)* (*To be familiar with and have knowledge of something*) A good citizen is supposed to be *conversant* with the rules of the road.

3. **Capricious** *(adj.)* (*fickle, unstable, faithless*) *Capricious* persons change their mind frequently without any reason.

4. **Caption** *(n.)* (*title*) Please give a suitable *caption* to this picture.

5. **Carnage** *(n.)* (*massacre*) The use of atomic weapons can cause *carnage* that is impossible for human mind to foresee.

6. **Clemency** *(n.)* (*leniency, mildness, kindness*) A judge should never dispense with *clemency* while dealing with criminals.

7. **Chaste** *(adj.)* (*pure, virtuous*) She is known for her *chaste* character.
8. **Cogent** *(adj.)* (*convincing, reasonable*) He could not offer any *cogent* reasons for his absence.
9. **Compatible** *(adj.)* (*harmonious, suitable*) They always had *compatible* relations because there was a deep understanding between them.
10. **Collusion** *(n.)* (*conspiracy, nexus*) The local M.P. was found in *collusion* with the smugglers operating in the town.
11. **Contingency** *(n.)* (*emergency*) My father always maintains a *contingency* fund to meet with unforeseen expenses.
12. **Condone** *(v.)* (*overlook, forgive*) His fault is too serious to be *condoned*.
13. **Consensus** *(n.)* (*general agreement*) A good government can be run efficiently by *consensus* among all the parties.
14. **Corroborate** *(v.)* (*confirm*) I am speaking the truth and my father is sure to *corroborate* my statement.
15. **Crestfallen** *(adj.)* (*dejected*) On account of heavy loss in business, he is *crestfallen* these days.
16. **Conclave** *(n.)* (*private meeting*) Both the enemies agreed to hold a *conclave* without the presence of a third party.
17. **Construe** *(v.)* (*interpret*) It is difficult to *construe* the working of the laws of Nature.
18. **Cryptic** *(adj.)* (*mysterious, hidden*) She was never forthcoming in her replies which were wholly *cryptic*.
19. **Calamity** *(n.)* (*natural disaster*) Though man claims to have conquered nature, he is frequently struck by *calamities*.
20. **Commensurate** *(adj.)* (*equal in proportion*) The income of Indian farmer is hardly *commensurate* with the labour he has to do.
21. **Commodious** *(adj.)* (*spacious, comfortable*) He has built a *commodious* house because his sister is likely to live with him.
22. **Capitulate** *(v.)* (*surrender*) After a long encounter the militants had to *capitulate*.
23. **Compunction** *(n.)* (*feeling of regret, remorse*) Even the hard core criminals felt *compunction* at the injustice they had done to the family of their rivals.
24. **Canine** *(adj.)* (*of dog*) The flatterers follow their masters with *canine* faithfulness.
25. **Callow** *(n.)* (*inexperienced*) Though he is a *callow* now, he will gain experience by and by.
26. **Chagrin** *(n.)* (*annoyance, disappointment*) The defeat of our team filled us with *chagrin*.
27. **Censure** *(n.)* (*blame, criticise*) *Censure* motion in the Parliament could not be tabled for want of quorum.

28. **Calibre** *(n.)* (*capacity, talent*) His *calibre* for doing work in a meticulous manner is always appreciated.

29. **Cede** *(v.)* [*transfer title (land)*] India should never *cede* an inch of land to any foreign country.

30. **Chauvinist** *(n.)* (*blindly devoted*) A *chauvinist* is incapable of realising the fault in his thinking.

31. **Celestial** *(adj.)* (*heavenly*) The study of *celestial* bodies always interests me.

32. **Clandestine** *(adj.)* (*secret*) The *clandestine* activities of the smugglers are well-known to the police.

33. **Covert** *(adj.)* (*hidden, implied*) The *covert* warning he gave to me opened my eyes to the reality of the situation.

34. **Catastrophe** *(n.)* (*calamity*) A *catastrophe* in the form of a cyclone has struck the coastal cities of India.

35. **Condolence** *(n.)* (*sympathy*) I visited my friend to offer *condolence* on the death of his uncle.

36. **Chastise** *(v.)* (*punish*) Rita was *chastised* for her unruly behaviour in the presence of the guests.

37. **Connivance** *(n.)* (*pretence of ignorance, overlook*) Criminals have been carrying on their nefarious activities with the *connivance* of the police.

38. **Contraband** *(adj.)* (*illegal goods*) Customs Department has not been able to stop traffic of *contraband* goods.

39. **Countermand** *(v.)* (*cancel, revoke*) The Election Commission has *countermanded* the election of the M.L.A. for over spending in elections.

40. **Colloquial** *(adj.)* (*used in familiar and informal conversation*) *Colloquial* language should be simple and easy.

41. **Conflagration** *(n.)* (*widespread fire*) As long as the nuclear arsenal exists in the world, there is every possibility of nuclear *conflagration*.

42. **Compliant** *(adj.)* (*docile, flexible*) He is admired for his *compliant* nature.

43. **Cliche** *(n.)* (*stereotyped phrase*) I never listen to the speeches of the leaders because they are always full of *cliches*.

44. **Condign** *(adj.)* (*adequate, rigorous*) No punishment, whatsover is *condign* for a rapist.

45. **Congregation** *(n.)* (*religious gathering*) The militants did not hesitate in throwing bombs at the *congregation* gathered in the religious place.

46. **Chary** *(adj.)* (*cautious, watchful, wary*) We should be always *chary* of the strangers.

47. **Coerce** *(v.)* (*force, repress*) She was *coerced* by her husband into bringing money from her parents.

48. **Confound** *(v.)* (*confuse*) On seeing the ghastly sight of murder, everyone was *confounded*.

49. **Cache** *(n.)* [(*hiding place* (*store*)] *A cache* of illegal arms was recovered by the police.

50. **Cavil** *(v.)* (*find fault*) Please don't *cavil* about unimportant matters.

51. **Charisma** *(n.)* (*popular charm, spiritual grace*) Swami Vivekanand always stood out in the crowd because of the *charisma* reflected on his face.

52. **Castigate** *(v.)* (*punish*) The thief was *castigated* by the police.

53. **Carping** *(adj.)* (*find fault*) *Carping* critics were responsible for the miserable life of the English poet, John Keats.

D

1. **Dauntless** *(adj.)* (*bold, brave*) Shivaji was a *dauntless* warrior.

2. **Decry** *(v.)* (*disparage*) You can't gain anything by *decrying* the success of your rivals.

3. **Devoid** *(adj.)* (*lacking*) I cannot trust him because he is *devoid* of the sense of right and wrong.

4. **Dearth** *(n.)* (*scarcity*) There is no *dearth* of talent in India but it has remained unexploited.

5. **Deference** *(n.)* (*regards for another's wish*) We are advised to act in *deference* to the wishes of our parents.

6. **Dubious** *(adj.)* (*not certain, doubtful, suspicious*) He is *dubious* about the scheme made by his friends.

7. **Deleterious** *(adj.)* (*harmful*) We should always beware of the *deleterious* effect of overeating.

8. **Defile** *(v.)* (*pollute, profane*) One should never *defile* the sanctity of religious places so as not to hurt the sentiments of others.

9. **Deterrent** *(n.)* (*discouraging*) India must possess nuclear weapons so that they may act as *deterrent* for her hostile neighbours.

10. **Dilapidation** *(n.)* (*state of ruins*) Ancient monuments in our town are in state of *dilapidation*.

11. **Disdain** *(v.)* (*treat with scorn*) He always *disdains* what he considers dishonest.

12. **Dire** *(adj.)* (*disastrous*) In the interest of National Security, we must not be intimidated by the *dire* consequences of economic sanctions.

13. **Dissipate** *(v.)* (*squander, waste*) India cannot afford to *dissipate* its forest resources.

14. **Devout** *(adj.)* (*religious, pious*) My mother is *devout* and god-fearing.

15. **Dint** *(n.)* — (*means, effort*) You can attain success by *dint* of hard work.

16. **Dormant** *(adj.)* — (*torpid, hidden, latent*) Adversity brings out *dormant* qualities in a person to overcome the problems.

17. **Divulge** *(v.)* — (*reveal, unravel*) He tried to gain my favour by *divulging* the secrets of my friends.

18. **Defunct** *(adj.)* — (*dead, no longer in use*) On account of heavy loss, the factory of my uncle is almost *defunct*.

19. **Delusion** *(n.)* — (*hallucination, false*) We should never be under *delusion* about our capability.

20. **Deplete** *(v.)* — (*reduce, dwindle*) India has recklessly *depleted* her forest resources after Independence.

21. **Debauch** *(v.)* — (*corrupt*) Some of the TV channels have *debauched* the morals and manners of the youth of our country.

22. **Dovetail** *(v.)* — (*fit together*) You can be benefitted only if you *dovetail* these two schemes to cut down the cost of the material.

23. **Decoy** *(n.)* — (*lure, bait*) A goat is often used as a *decoy* by the hunters to catch a lion.

24. **Daunt** *(v.)* — (*intimidate*) One should never be *daunted* by difficulties in life.

25. **Delete** *(v.)* — (*erase, remove*) His name has been *deleted* from the list of successful candidates.

26. **Deride** *(v.)* — (*scoff at*) He is in the habit of *deriding* the achievements of his friends.

27. **Despise** *(v.)* — (*scorn, detest*) We should not *despise* anyone for his poverty.

28. **Debacle** *(n.)* — (*down fall*) The poor batting performance resulted in the *debacle* of our team.

29. **Deployment** *(n.)* — (*spreading out troops*) The Central Government has promised the *deployment* of additional troops during elections.

30. **Diffident** *(adj.)* — (*shy, timid*) A successful teacher is not expected to be *diffident*.

31. **Dynamic** *(adj.)* — (*energetic*) At this critical juncture, India needs *dynamic* and sagacious political leaders.

32. **Dilemma** *(n.)* — (*in a fix*) He is in a *dilemma* over the choice of career.

33. **Despotism** *(n.)* — (*tyranny, cruelty*) Germans got fed up with *despotism* of Hitler very soon.

34. **Dexterous** *(adj.)* — (*skilful*) The artisans of Moradabad are *dexterous* in brass work.

35. **Detrimental** *(adj.)* — (*harmful*) The foreign aid has proved to be *detrimental* to our economy.

36. **Desecrate** *(v.)* — (*violate sanctity*) The rioters *desecrated* the religious places.

37. **Diversity** *(n.)* (*variety*) *Diversity* is the hallmark of Indian Civilization.
38. **Dulcet** *(adj.)* (*melodious to the ear/taste*) As a singer Jagjit Singh is known for his *dulcet* voice.
39. **Demise** *(n.)* (*death*) In the *demise* of Sardar Patel, India lost its most sagacious leader.
40. **Demolition** *(n.)* (*destruction*) The Municipal Corporation has started a *demolition* campaign to clear up encroachment.
41. **Deranged** *(adj.)* (*insane, mad*) None but a *deranged* person could have behaved in such an irresponsible manner.
42. **Demur** *(v.)* (*delay, hesitate*) A practical man would never *demur* to avail himself of every chance.
43. **Demure** *(adj.)* (*shy, quiet*) She is both *demure* and introvert.
44. **Dilatory** *(adj.)* (*causing delay*) Many politicians consider *dilatory* tactics as an art of politics.
45. **Deteriorate** *(v.)* (*get worse*) The condition of the patient has *deteriorated.*

E

1. **Extinct** *(adj.)* (*out of existence*) Many species of flora & fauna have become *extinct*.
2. **Emaciated** *(adj.)* (*thin and wasted*) On account of poverty and starvation most of the children are *emaciated*.
3. **Elucidate** *(v.)* (*explain, enlighten*) The Government had been asked to *elucidate* their economic policy.
4. **Engross** *(v.)* (*fully absorbed*) She did not talk to me because she was *engrossed* in writing a letter.
5. **Enormity** *(n.)* (*great wickedness*) He is a hardened criminal and is insensitive to the *enormity* of his crimes.
6. **Extant** *(n.)* (*in existence*) Many of the ancient documents, still *extant* tell us about the diversity of the Indian culture.
7. **Ecstasy** *(n.)* (*rapture, joy*) On hearing of the sudden financial wind fall, the family was in *ecstasy*.
8. **Effigy** *(n.)* (*dummy*) The *effigy* of the American President was burnt by the crowd when the unfavourable remarks against India were made by him.
9. **Exorbitant** *(n.)* (*excessive*) It is very difficult to hire taxi because of the *exorbitant* charges.
10. **Embezzlement** *(n.)* (*misappropriation*) Most of the politicians involved in the *embezzlement* of public money are still at large.
11. **Emanate** *(v.)* (*to produce a smell, light, etc. or to show a particular quality*) Mother Teresa emanated tranquility.
12. **Enamoured** *(v.)* (*in love, fascinated*) Every member of the picnic party was *enamoured* of the scenic beauty of the landscape.

13. **Exonerate** *(v.)* (*acquit, exculpate*) After a long legal battle, he was *exonerated* of murder charges.
14. **Expunge** *(v.)* (*delete, cancel*) I shall request the Principal to *expunge* the unfavourable remarks from your annual report.
15. **Extol** *(v.)* (*praise, glorify*) Every Indian *extolled* the achievement of the Government in curbing the militancy in the state.
16. **Emulate** *(v.)* (*imitate, follow*) We must *emulate* the ideals of Netaji to make our country strong and invincible.
17. **Enhance** *(v.)* (*increase, improve*) The judicious use of cosmetics *enhance* the natural charms.
18. **Estranged** *(adj.)* (*separated*) The *estranged* husband and wife are living separately.
19. **Expediency** *(n.)* (*advisable, practical*) Those who hanker after material gains are often guided by *expediency* and not by moral sense.
20. **Extraneous** *(adj.)* (*not essential, external*) Bigotry is *extraneous* to the basic tenets of Hinduism.
21. **Extort** *(v.)* (*get money by threats*) Anti-social elements are busy in *extorting* money from the businessmen with the connivance of the police.
22. **Evasive** *(adj.)* (*not frank, avoiding*) The police could not make out anything of her *evasive* replies.
23. **Ennui** *(n.)* (*mental boredom*) The modern youth suffer from feeling of *ennui* since they are not engaged in any constructive work.
24. **Exquisite** *(adj.)* (*beautiful*) The picture hanging on the wall is an *exquisite* work of art.
25. **Encomium** *(n.)* (*praise*) Every member of the family showered *encomium* on his grand success.
26. **Erode** *(v.)* (*decay*) The desire for material success has *eroded* our concern for the poor.
27. **Erudite** *(adj.)* (*learned, scholarly*) His writings are not *erudite* but they are read with keen interest.
28. **Eschew** *(v.)* (*avoid, give up*) We must *eschew* violence in dealing with national issues.
29. **Epoch** *(n.)* (*period of time, era*) The exact duration of Indus Valley Civilization *epoch* has not been determined so far.
30. **Equanimity** *(n.)* (*calmness*) We must bear the hardships with *equanimity*.
31. **Enormous** *(adj.)* (*huge, immense*) On account of fire there was *enormous* loss of goods and property.
32. **Endemic** *(adj.)* (*very common, or strongly established in a place or situation*) Goitre is *endemic* in the hilly areas for want of iodine in water.

33. **Expiate** *(v.)* (*atone for*) He is ready to *expiate* his sins by giving up his irresponsible ways of life.

34. **Embellish** *(v.)* (*decorate*) The writers generally *embellish* their style by the use of unnecessary imagery.

35. **Ecology** *(n.)* (*science of environment*) *Ecology* is the study of environment.

36. **Egregious** *(adj.)* (*of mistake, failure, problem, etc.*) It's another egregious example of favouritism when the minister hired his brother as his assistant.

37. **Exodus** *(n.)* (*departure* (*large scale*)) The *exodus* of the Hindus from Kashmir valley is deplorable.

38. **Errant** *(adj.)* (*erring from right path*) Many *errant* students were punished.

39. **Errand** *(n.)* (*short visit to fetch something*) My servant has gone on *errand* to fetch rations.

40. **Erroneous** *(adj.)* (*incorrect, mistaken*) It is *erroneous* idea on your part that he will return home at last.

41. **Envisage** *(v.)* (*foresee in mind*) It was difficult for everyone to *envisage* the loss in such a profitable venture.

42. **Emancipate** *(v.)* (*make free*) Raja Ram Mohan Roy tried to *emancipate* women from many social evils.

F

1. **Flagrant** *(adj.)* (*glaring, openly wicked*) It is not easy to pardon such *flagrant* violation of the decorum of the House.

2. **Fickle** *(adj.)* (*changeable, faithless*) *Fickle* minded persons cannot be relied upon.

3. **Filial** *(adj.)* (*of son or daughter*) Children must fulfil their *filial* duties towards their parents.

4. **Fray** *(n.)* (*brawl, contest*) The miscreants involved in the *fray* were arrested by the police.

5. **Facile** *(adj.)* (*easily achieved, effortless*) India could achieve *facile* victory in the match yesterday.

6. **Fallible** *(adj.)* (*liable to err*) Man is *fallible*.

7. **Fervent** *(adj.)* (*ardent, warm*) My friend was accorded a *fervent* welcome on his arrival.

8. **Fete** *(n.)* (*outdoor entertainment, carnival*) A charity *fete* was held in our college yesterday.

9. **Fictitious** *(adj.)* (*imaginary*) Don't believe his story because it is just *fictitious*.

10. **Foolhardy** *(adj.)* (*rash, reckless*) Many believe that trying for impossible things is *foolhardy* attempt.
11. **Fiat** *(n.)* (*command*) The Court issued a *fiat* to both the parties to maintain status quo.
12. **Finale** *(n.)* (*conclusion*) The *finale* of the match was very interesting.
13. **Fitful** *(adj.)* (*spasmodic, intermittent*) You are not going to achieve anything by pursuing *fitful* study.
14. **Fraught** *(adj.)* (*filled, threatening*) Security problem on our borders is *fraught* with danger.
15. **Fortitude** *(n.)* (*bravery, courage*) One must face the problems of life with *fortitude*.
16. **Feasible** *(adj.)* (*practicable*) We must execute a proposal that is *feasible*.
17. **Ferment** *(n.)* (*agitation, commotion*) During Quit India Movement, the whole nation was in *ferment*.
18. **Franchise** *(n.)* (*right by government to vote or trade*) The Mughals granted *franchise* to East India Company to carry on trade in India.
19. **Foible** *(adj.)* (*weakness*) Man is subject to *foibles* and frailities in life.
20. **Flaunt** *(v.)* (*display ostentatiously*) The rich are in the habit of *flaunting* their material achievements.
21. **Flout** *(v.)* (*reject, mock*) No good citizen will *flout* the rules of the road.
22. **Foment** *(v.)* (*stir up, instigate*) The decision of the Government is likely to *foment* disagreement among the opposition parties.
23. **Furtive** *(adj.)* (*secret, stealthy*) She entered the room with *furtive* steps to avoid the attention of the teacher.
24. **Frantic** *(adj.)* (*marked by fast and nervous, disordered, or anxiety-driven activity*) *Frantic* efforts are going on to decorate the place on the New Year eve.
25. **Frigid** *(adj.)* (*intensely cold*) One must not be *frigid* in one's attitude towards his near and dear ones.
26. **Flair** *(n.)* (*talent*) Our Prime Minister has a *flair* for glib talk.
27. **Faux pas** *(n.)* (*an error in manner or behaviour*) Her thoughtless remarks in the meeting were a *faux pas* and amused everyone.
28. **Flux** *(n.)* (*flowing, changing*) No foreign investor would like to invest in a country where the state of economy is in a *flux*.
29. **Fracas** *(n.)* (*noisy quarrel*) The mob gathered in the street when there was *fracas* between the two neighbours.
30. **Freak** *(adj.)* (*unusual, abnormal*) It is just an example of his *freak* behaviour because he normally doesn't behave in this manner.

31. **Fawning** *(adj.)* — (*flattering*) One must be wary of *fawning* admirers because they have always an axe to grind.
32. **Fecundity** *(n.)* — (*fruitfulness*) The *fecundity* of a poet's imagination makes a poem an exquisite work of art.
33. **Foray** *(n.)* — (*raid*) The *foray* against the enemy outpost met with an unexpected success.

G

1. **Gracious** *(adj.)* — (*kind, generous*) God is *gracious*.
2. **Grouse** *(n.)* — (*complaint*) I have no *grouse* against anyone for the misfortunes of life.
3. **Glut** *(n.)* — (*overstock*) As there is economic recession, there is a *glut* of luxury goods in the market.
4. **Guileless** *(adj.)* — (*without deceit*) She is so *guileless* that she will believe anyone.
5. **Glutton** *(n.)* — (*greedy for food*) Being a *glutton* he is base.
6. **Glib** *(adj.)* — (*fluent*) Those who have command of language are *glib* talkers.
7. **Gimmick** *(n.)* — (*trick*) The reservation policy is just a political *gimmick*.
8. **Gigantic** *(adj.)* — (*huge in size*) *Gigantic* crowd was there to listen to the speech of the Prime Minister.
9. **Glossary** *(n.)* — (*brief explanation*) You will find explanation of this in the *glossary* given at the end of the book
10. **Gaol** *(n.)* — (*jail*) He is a hardened criminal and has often been to *gaol*.
11. **Grumble** *(v.)* — (*complain, protest*) We should not *grumble* when we are required to comply with the orders of our employers.
12. **Gusto** *(n.)* — (*enjoyment, enthusiasm*) The Independence Day was celebrated in our college with *gusto*.
13. **Gainsay** *(v.)* — (*deny*) Nobody can *gainsay* the truth of my statement.
14. **Gregarious** *(adj.)* — (*flocking together, sociable*) The lion is not a *gregarious* animal.
15. **Gist** *(n.)* — (*essence*) Please write the *gist* of the paragraph in not more than fifty words.
16. **Garish** *(adj.)* — (*gaudy*) She wears *garish* clothes which don't suit her.
17. **Gait** *(n.)* — (*manner of walking*) Her *gait* is graceful.
18. **Ghastly** *(adj.)* — (*horrible, fearful*) Everybody was horrified at the sight of the *ghastly* murder.
19. **Gruesome** *(adj.)* — (*frightful, heinous, grisly*) The children cried when they saw the *gruesome* movie.
20. **Goad** *(v.)* — (*urge on*) He was *goaded* by the classmates to make fun of the teacher.

21. **Grasp** *(v.)* — (*understand, seize*) I think you have *grasped* the meaning of my statement.

22. **Grimace** *(n.)* — (*expression of pain*) When hit on the head, he cried with *grimace* on his face.

23. **Granary** *(n.)* — (*store house for grain*) A country can succeed in war only if its *granaries* as well as arsenals are well stocked.

24. **Gratis** *(adv.)* — (*free*) The company offered one silver coin *gratis* to a customer who bought two dozen of soap cakes.

25. **Gruelling** *(adj.)* — (*tiring, exhausting*) The police could elicit information from the gangster only after a *gruelling* interrogation.

H

1. **Humdrum** *(adj.)* — (*dull, monotonous*) After strenuous years of service he is not able to adapt himself to *humdrum* life of retirement.

2. **Huddle** *(v.)* — (*crowd together*) The passengers sat *huddled* in a crowded compartment.

3. **Haggle** *(v.)* — (*bargain about prices*) We *haggle* with rickshaw-pullers while with doctors we cannot.

4. **Hapless** *(adj.)* — (*unfortunate*) The *hapless* victims of tragedy were sanctioned compensation by the Government.

5. **Hamper** *(v.)* — (*obstruct, impede, a gift box*) The growth of population has *hampered* economic progress in India.

6. **Hegemony** *(n.)* — (*predominance*) Both America and China are trying for *hegemony* in Asia.

7. **Hustings** *(n.)* — (*contest, elections*) The Congress party was badly defeated at the *hustings* in 1977.

8. **Heretic** *(n.)* — (*holding unorthodox belief*) Joan of Arc was considered *heretic* by the Church.

9. **Hoodwink** *(v.)* — (*deceive*) Hypocrites cannot *hoodwink* people for long.

10. **Husband** *(v.)* — (*utilise*) India has a plethora of natural resources which she must *husband* for her progress.

11. **Hostile** *(adj.)* — (*unfriendly*) Western powers have ever been *hostile* to India for reasons best known to them.

12. **Hypothecate** *(v.)* — (*mortgage, pawn*) You can get loan from this bank by *hypothecating* house.

13. **Halcyon** *(adj.)* — (*calm, peaceful*) The poet recalled the *halycon* days of the past.

14. **Holocaust** *(n.)* — (*a thorough destruction involving extensive loss of life especially through fire*) The third world war is bound to bring about nuclear *holocaust*.

15. **Hackneyed** *(adj.)* — (*commonplace, trite*) Nowadays no one is interested in the *hackneyed* speeches of the politicians.

16. **Hazy** *(adj.)* (*slightly obscure*) I have just a *hazy* idea of my mother because she died when I was just five years old.

17. **Hypocrite** *(n.)* (*pretending virtue*) Those who praise themselves are generally *hypocrites*.

18. **Hoax** *(n.)* (*trick, practical joke*) The information that a bomb had been planted in the aeroplane just proved a *hoax*.

19. **Haggard** *(adj.)* (*lean, gaunt*) A *haggard* and pale looking old man begged for some money.

20. **Heinous** *(adj.)* (*atrocious, odious*) The *heinous* crimes by the Nazis are against every norm of civilization.

21. **Humane** *(adj.)* (*kind*) Every religion preaches to be *humane* and considerate.

22. **Haphazard** *(adj.)* (*random, by chance*) He had no time and bought the clothes *haphazardly*.

23. **Hazardous** *(adj.)* (*dangerous*) A journey to Amarnath shrine is *hazardous*.

24. **Hearsay** *(n.)* (*rumour*) One must not believe in *hearsay*.

25. **Homily** *(n.)* (*moral discourse*) A person should not deliver a *homily* unless he himself follows it.

26. **Harbinger** *(n.)* (*forerunner*) Autumn is the *harbinger* of spring.

27. **Harangue** *(n.)* (*loud and scolding talk*) In his *harangue* the commander reproved the soldiers for their unruly conduct.

I

1. **Impasse** *(n.)* (*deadlock*) At present there is *an impasse* in the talks between India and Pakistan.

2. **Ignoble** *(adj.)* (*unworthy*) His *ignoble* motives were exposed by his wicked actions.

3. **Imbroglio** *(n.)* (*complicated situation*) Kashmir problem has become a national *imbroglio* which has eluded solution.

4. **Indolent** *(adj.)* (*lazy, lethargic*) She was feeling *indolent* because of the sweltering weather in the afternoon.

5. **Imbued** *(v.)* (*filled with*) It is a pity that our political leaders are not *imbued* with the spirit of nationalism.

6. **Intrinsic** *(adj.)* (*of value within, real quality*) The *intrinsic* value of the Indian rupee is on decline.

7. **Itinerary** *(n.)* (*plan of a journey*) Delhi has been included in the *itinerary* of the American President's visit to Asia.

8. **Impeccable** *(adj.)* (*faultless*) There is no person in the world who can claim to have *impeccable* character.

9. **Impede** *(v.)* (*to hinder, hamper*) Economic crisis in the country will *impede* the industrial progress.

10. **Incite** *(v.)* — *(arouse to action)* The visit of the religious leader *incited* communal riots in the city.
11. **Inept** *(adj.)* — *(incompetent)* *Inept* handling of the foreign policy by the party has created many complicated situations for the country.
12. **Inertia** *(n.)* — *(passivity)* The modern youth is suffering from *inertia* because they are not optimistic about their future.
13. **Indigenous** *(adj.)* — *(native)* India must not depend on foreign technology for there is no lack of *indigenous* talent in the country.
14. **Innate** *(adj.)* — *(inborn)* Poets are born with an *innate* talent for writing poetry.
15. **Insular** *(adj.)* — *(narrow minded)* Fanatics have *insular* views about men and matters.
16. **Indict** *(v.)* — *(accuse, charge)* The officials of the department were *indicted* by the court for financial irregularities.
17. **Intrude** *(v.)* — *(interfere, tresspass)* I don't like if anyone tries to *intrude* on my privacy.
18. **Inkling** *(n.)* — *(clue, hint)* I had no *inkling* that she would break with her friends so soon.
19. **Impervious** *(adj.)* — *(unaffected)* He never listens to his parents and is always *impervious* to their advice.
20. **Ingenuous** *(adj.)* — *(naive, artless, credulous)* Children are *ingenuous* by nature.
21. **Inapt** *(adj.)* — *(unsuitable)* The remarks she made at the party annoyed many because they were *inapt*.
22. **Inscrutable** *(adj.)* — *(incomprehensible)* The laws of nature are *inscrutable*.
23. **Instance** *(n.)* — *(example)* There are a number of *instances* of his misbehaviour but I have always overlooked them.
24. **Ingrained** *(adj.)* — *(deeply fixed in mind)* Dishonesty appears to be *ingrained* in his character.
25. **Innocuous** *(adj.)* — *(harmless)* It is now proved that soft drinks are not *innocuous*.
26. **Inordinate** *(adj.)* — *(excessive)* I don't understand the reason for his *inordinate* delay in replying to my letter.
27. **Irksome** *(adj.)* — *(tedious)* I don't like to do any *irksome* job, however profitable it may be.
28. **Imbibe** *(v.)* — *(drink, take in ideas)* Every Indian must *imbibe* the spirit of nationalism.
29. **Impertinent** *(adj.)* — *(insolent, impudent)* She was reprimanded for her *impertinent* behaviour.
30. **Intermittent** *(adj.)* — *(irregular, continual)* Heavy damage has been caused to the buildings on account of *intermittent* rains for the last two months.

31. **Immaculate** *(adj.)* (*pure, spotless*) She is often dressed in *immaculately* white dress.

32. **Integrity** *(n.)* (*wholeness, uprightness*) The *integrity* of my brother is not to be questioned.

33. **Incessant** *(adj.)* (*uninterrupted, continuous*) We had to cancel our visit to Agra because of *incessant* rains.

34. **Indigent** *(adj.)* (*very poor*) He could not continue his studies because his parents were *indigent*.

35. **Inundate** *(v.)* (*overflow, flood*) The whole village was *inundated* with flood water.

36. **Inveterate** *(adj.)* (*deep rooted, habitual*) He is an *inveterate* liar.

37. **Inimical** *(adj.)* (*unfriendly, hostile*) I feel my friends have turned *inimical* and are working against my interests.

38. **Innovation** *(n.)* (*a new idea, method, or invention*) We cannot keep up with progress unless we introduce *innovations* in our technology.

39. **Impute** *(v.)* (*attribute, ascribe*) You can *impute* his failure in life to his fickle-mindedness.

40. **Instigate** *(v.)* (*urge, incite*) China is *instigating* trouble on our borders.

41. **Infinitesimal** *(adj.)* (*very small*) They found *infinitesimal* traces of poison in the drink.

42. **Irritate** *(v.)* (*annoy*) His insolent behaviour always *irritates* us.

43. **Impending** *(adj.)* (*imminent, approaching*) Some persons have intuition about *impending* calamity.

44. **Insipid** *(adj.)* (*tasteless*) All felt bored by his *insipid* jokes.

J

1. **Jovial** *(adj.)* (*merry, happy*) He is a much sought after person because of his *jovial* nature.

2. **Jinx** *(n.)* (*someone or something that brings bad luck*) Superstitious persons consider number thirteen a *jinx*.

3. **Jaded** *(adj.)* (*tired, exhausted*) He felt *jaded* after his return from journey.

4. **Jargon** *(n.)* (*language difficult to understand*) It is difficult to understand the *jargon* of tribal people.

5. **Jumble** *(n.)* (*mixed up*) She tried to put in order everything lying *jumbled*.

6. **Jot** *(v.)* (*write hurriedly*) The journalists were *jotting* down the speech of the Prime Minister in haste.

7. **Junk** *(n.)* (*discarded things*) He is a *junk* dealer.

8. **Judicious** *(adj.)* (*wise*) He has been successful in life because of his *judicious* planning in business.

9. **Jubilant** *(adj.)* (*extremely happy and pleased because of a success*) The crowd was *jubilant* when Indian team achieved victory over the British Team.
10. **Jolt** *(v.)* (*give a jerk*) All his hopes were *jolted* when his son could not qualify the competition.
11. **Juvenile** *(adj.)* (*of young person*) *Juvenile* delinquency is on the increase.
12. **Jiffy** *(n.)* (*few moments*) He completed the work in a *jiffy*.
13. **Jeer** *(v.)* (*jest, mock*) We should not *jeer* at the shortcomings of our friends.
14. **Jaunt** *(n.)* (*short journey for pleasure*) He is on a *jaunt* to Mumbai.
15. **Jejune** *(adj.)* (*dull, boring*) He left for Mumbai because he got tired of *jejune* life in his home town.
16. **Jingoism** *(n.)* (*blind patriotism*) The *jingoism* of the Germans resulted in the Second World War.
17. **Juncture** *(n.)* (*critical moment*) At this *juncture* of life you must be wary of strangers.
18. **Jeopardy** *(n.)* (*danger*) His reputation as a doctor is in *jeopardy* because of his unethical practice.
19. **Jocund** *(adj.)* (*cheerful, merry*) Inspite of reeling under heavy debt, Mr. Micawber was a *jocund* character.
20. **Jubilation** *(n.)* (*rejoicing*) The victory of Indian Hockey team was celebrated with *jubilation.*

K

1. **Knell** *(n.)* (*death knell, last blow*) The Second World War proved to be a *knell* for British imperialism.
2. **Kiln** *(n.)* (*brick furnace*) He is running a brick *kiln* these days.
3. **Kinship** *(n.)* (*affinity*) There is *kinship* between a tiger and a cat.
4. **Kickback** *(n.)* (*bribe*) He was charged with taking *kickback*.
5. **Kindred** *(adj.)* (*having common features*) Most of the European languages are *kindred* because they have a common source.
6. **Knack** *(n.)* (*cleverness, art*) Politicians know the *knack* of putting the people off.
7. **Kleptomania** *(n.)* (*obsession to steal*) *Kleptomania* is a psychological urge to steal.
8. **Kinetic** *(adj.)* (*relating to movement*) The dust particles in air are in *kinetic* motion.
9. **Knave** *(n.)* (*dishonest person*) Don't believe him because he is a *knave* and scoundrel.
10. **Knotty** *(adj.)* (*complicated*) Since Independence, India has not been able to solve a single *knotty* problem facing the country.
11. **Kindle** *(v.)* (*arouse feeling*) The timely arrival of my friend *kindled* in me a hope of getting proper medical treatment.

12. **Kiosk** *(n.)* — (*small booth*) He is running his business in a *kiosk* because he can't afford a shop right now.
13. **Kernel** *(n.)* — (*inner part of fruit*) The *kernel* of the fruit is always tasty.
14. **Keepsake** *(n.)* — (*memento, reminder*) She gave him a ring as a *keepsake*.
15. **Kudos** *(n.)* — (*honour, credit*) Kapil Dev won *kudos* when he brought home the World Cup in 1983.

L

1. **Longevity** *(n.)* — (*length of life*) His mother prayed for his *longevity* when he fell ill.
2. **Lieu** *(n.)* — (*instead of*) I shall give you money in *lieu* of the lost book.
3. **Lavish** *(adj.)* — (*liberal, wasteful*) He came to a grief because of his *lavish* spending habits.
4. **Lucid** *(adj.)* — (*easily understood*) He gave a *lucid* lecture on the causes of inflation.
5. **Ludicrous** *(adj.)* — (*laughable, ridiculous*) Everybody condemned her *ludicrous* remarks against her friends.
6. **Lunar** *(adj.)* — (*pertaining to moon*) *Lunar* eclipse is caused when the earth comes between the sun and the moon.
7. **Levity** *(n.)* — (*light heartedness*) His staff always treats his orders with *levity*.
8. **Languor** *(n.)* — (*lassitude, depression*) On summer afternoons, we generally feel *languor*.
9. **Laconic** *(adj.)* — (*brief*) Though her speech was *laconic*, yet it was lucid.
10. **Lethargic** *(adj.)* — (*lazy*) After busy schedule during the day he felt languid and *lethargic*.
11. **Laudable** *(adj.)* — (*commendable*) The success achieved by him in such a short period is really *laudable*.
12. **Loathe** *(v.)* — (*detest, hate*) He always *loathes* dishonest means.
13. **Lair** *(n.)* — (*den, resting place*) The tiger was in the *lair* when the hunter arrived.
14. **Lascivious** *(adj.)* — (*lustful*) The market is flooded with *lascivious* books.
15. **Lethal** *(adj.)* — (*deadly*) The proliferation of *lethal* weapons do not bode well for the future of mankind.

M

1. **Mammoth** *(adj.)* — (*huge, gigantic*) A *mammoth* rally was held to protest against the increase in the cases of kidnappings and murders.
2. **Menace** *(n.)* — (*danger, threat*) Terrorism is a potential *menace* to the integrity of a country.

3. **Mascot** *(n.)* (*an animal, person or object considered to be lucky or used as a symbol of a team or organisation*) Appu was the *mascot* of the Asian Games held in India in 1982.
4. **Magnate** *(n.)* (*person of prominence*) Jamshedji Tata was a steel *magnate* of India.
5. **Malign** *(v.)* (*speak evil of, defame*) We *malign* others because we are jealous of them.
6. **Menial** *(adj.)* (*suitable for servants, servile*) Many men consider women suitable only for *menial* jobs.
7. **Manipulate** *(v.)* (*manage with skill*) Many persons are expert in *manipulating* excuses for their failure in life.
8. **Manifesto** *(n.)* (*declaration of policy*) Most of the political parties are unable to fulfil the promises made in their election *manifestos*.
9. **Marital** *(adj.)* (*pertaining to marriage*) *Marital* happiness depends on the compatibility of the partners.
10. **Morose** *(adj.)* (*sullen, gloomy*) After his failure in the exams, he is often *morose* and depressed.
11. **Mitigate** *(v.)* (*lessen, ease*) It is the duty of every person to *mitigate* the sufferings of humanity.
12. **Momentum** *(n.)* (*speed*) Indian economy is yet to gain the *momentum* to progress in right direction.
13. **Malicious** *(adj.)* (*unkind and showing a strong feeling of wanting to hurt someone*) He is *malicious* by nature and always tries to belittle the efforts of his friends.
14. **Miscreant** *(n.)* (*rowdy element*) He was kind to the *miscreants* even though he suffered at their hands.
15. **Mundane** *(adj.)* (*worldly, dull*) Wordly people are often concerned with *mundane* matters.
16. **Melee** *(n.)* (*confused struggle, stampede*) In the Kumbh Fair many pilgrims were injured in the *melee*.
17. **Myopic** *(adj.)* (*short sighted, narrowminded*) Orthodox men and women are victims of *myopic* views about life.
18. **Mollify** *(v.)* (*appease*) After exchange of hot words the shop-keeper tried to *mollify* the customer.
19. **Martinet** *(n.)* (*strict disciplinarian*) Our Principal is a *martinet* who expects everybody to carry out his orders.
20. **Mincing** *(adj.)* (*affected manner, pretentious*) She was walking with *mincing* steps and appeared ridiculous.
21. **Mettle** *(n.)* (*courage, spirit*) During fight he showed *mettle* in the teeth of strong opposition.
22. **Malinger** *(v.)* (*pretend to be ill*) Whenever he is asked to work, he always *malingers* and shirks work.
23. **Malignant** *(adj.)* (*malicious*) AIDS is a malignant and incurable disease.

24. **Mentor** *(n.)* (*teacher*) In Mr. Kapoor he found a considerate and sympathetic *mentor.*

25. **Macabre** *(adj.)* (*gruesome, grisly*) This novel deals with the *macabre* sight of carnage.

26. **Malevolent** *(adj.)* (*wishing evil, spiteful*) Both China and Pakistan nurse *malevolent* designs against India.

27. **Mediocre** *(adj.)* (*ordinary, commonplace*) Even *mediocre* students are known to have made a mark in life.

28. **Mandatory** *(adj.)* (*obligatory, compulsory*) The limit of expenses to be made on elections has been made *mandatory* for the contestants.

29. **Meticulous** *(adj.)* (*showing great attention to detail*) One must be *meticulous* in conduct while dealing with strangers.

30. **Migratory** *(adj.)* (*wandering*) The *migratory* birds cover thousands of miles to reach warmer countries.

31. **Mishap** *(n.)* (*accident*) This *mishap* could have been averted if you had been just careful.

32. **Mandate** *(n.)* [*order* (*of the people*)] During the last elections no single party was able to secure the *mandate* of the majority.

33. **Manifold** *(adj.)* (*numerous, varied*) There are *manifold* advantages of discipline in schools and colleges.

34. **Moot** *(adj.)* (*debatable*) Whether reservation for women is justified or not is a *moot* question.

35. **Magnitude** *(n.)* (*greatness, extent*) Indians are unable to comprehend the *magnitude* of the population problem in India.

36. **Monotony** *(n.)* (*dullness, boredom*) Anonymous life in the urban areas generate *monotony* for the residents.

37. **Meddlesome** *(adj.)* (*interfering*) Many marriages are ruined because of *meddlesome* mothers-in-law.

38. **Militate** *(v.)* (*work against*) The policy of appeasing everybody in life *militates* against one's own interests.

39. **Modicum** *(n.)* (*small amount*) There is no *modicum* of truth in her statement.

40. **Memento** *(n.)* (*token, reminder, keepsake*) I gave him a book as a *memento* on his birthday.

41. **Manifest** *(adj.)* (*understandable, clear*) His evil intentions were *manifest* when he mentioned the question of dowry.

42. **Myriad** *(adj.)* (*a very large number of something*) *Myriad* stars twinkle in the sky.

N

1. **Noxious** *(adj.)* (*harmful, offensive*) Emission of *noxious* gases causes air pollution.

2. **Nadir** *(n.)* (*lowest point*) Nowadays, he is disgusted with life because he is at the *nadir* of his hopes.

3. **Nostalgia** *(n.)* (*home sickness, longing for the past*) Soldiers often suffer from *nostalgia* when they are away from their homes.

4. **Naive** *(adj.)* (*artless*) Being *naive* she believes in all that her friends tell her.

5. **Novice** *(n.)* (*beginner, tyro*) We should not expect much from him because he is just a *novice* in the field of marketing.

6. **Nonchalant** *(adj.)* (*unconcerned*) It is disgusting to note that even doctors behave *nonchalantly* towards the patients.

7. **Nocturnal** *(adj.)* (*of night*) On account of disturbance during day time, the students in our hostel are accustomed to *nocturnal* study.

8. **Nefarious** *(adj.)* (*very wicked, unlawful*) The criminals should be brought to book for their *nefarious* activities.

9. **Nepotism** *(n.)* (*favour to relatives*) Meritorious candidates always suffer on account of *nepotism* and favouritism prevading in the selection procedure.

10. **Narcissism** *(n.)* (*self love and admiration*) *Narcissism* leads to selfishness in character.

11. **Nonplussed** (*confuse*) I was *nonpulssed* when my best friend refused to stand by me in my financial crises.

12. **Nascent** *(adj.)* (*incipient, beginning*) The rapid growth of this commercial organisation in its *nascent* stage is commendable.

13. **Nexus** *(n.)* (*bond, link*) The *nexus* among criminals and politicians has brought about general erosion of moral values in our political system.

14. **Nomadic** *(adj.)* (*wandering*) *The nomadic* tribes of Rajasthan are found in every major Indian city.

15. **Non-entity** *(n.)* (*a person of no importance*) A few years back he was a *non-entity* in politics; today he is a national leader.

16. **Neophyte** *(n.)* (*beginner, a recent convert*) Though a *neophyte* in politics, he has tremendous hold over the principles of state craft.

17. **Nebulous** *(adj.)* (*hazy*) Your ideas are too *nebulous* to be understood easily.

18. **Nullify** *(v.)* (*cancel*) The agreement made by the previous government has been *nullified* by the new government.

19. **Nauseous** *(adj.)* (*abominable, loathsome*) The sight of cruel and heartless treatment of animals is always unbearable and *nauseous*.

20. **Nourishing** *(adj.)* (*nutritious*) After her long illness, she must take *nourishing* diet.

O

1. **Overt** *(adj.)* (*open*) The trampling of national flag is an *overt* act of treason.

2. **Obnoxious** *(adj.)* (*harmful, nasty*) She behaved *obnoxiously* with her daughter-in-law.

3. **Opulence** *(n.)* (*luxury, wealth*) The foreign travellers to America admire the *opulence* of that country.

4. **Obsession** *(n.)* (*fixed idea*) His *obsession* with amassing wealth has made him miserly and greedy.

5. **Ostensible** *(adj.)* (*apparent, obvious*) The *ostensible* purpose of her visit was to borrow money, though she came to see me.

6. **Ornate** *(adj.)* (*decorated*) *Ornate* style of his essay appears to be artificial.

7. **Outskirts** *(n.)* (*outlying*) The cantonment is situated just on the *outskirts* of the city.

8. **Officious** *(adj.)* (*trying to please*) Beware of *officious* subordinates because they are parasites.

9. **Opportune** *(adj.)* (*timely, well chosen*) One should wait for the *opportune* moment to strike a bargain.

10. **Obliterate** *(v.)* (*wipe out*) The whole village was *obliterated* by the continued shelling of Pakistani troops.

11. **Odious** *(adj.)* (*repulsive, contemptible*) Leaving my friends in the lurch is quite *odious* for me.

12. **Overture** *(n.)* (*a suggestion or offer that you make to someone*) The *overture* on the part of her husband for reconciliation met with no response from her.

13. **Obsolete** *(adj.)* (*out-moded*) Snobs are never interested in *obsolete* fashion.

14. **Ostracize** *(v.)* (*ex-communicate*) He was *ostracized* by the elders of the village for marrying the girl of the other community.

15. **Oblivion** *(n.)* (*forgetfulness*) The famous film-personalities of the past are forced to lead a life of *oblivion* in their old age.

16. **Obviate** *(v.)* (*make unnecessary*) The use of computers will *obviate* the need for further recruitment of the staff in the banks.

17. **Obese** *(adj.)* (*very fat*) *Obese* persons are generally prone to heart attack.

18. **Onerous** *(adj.)* (*burdensome*) The work allotted to him was so *onerous* that he needed an assistant.

19. **Ostentatious** *(adj.)* (*showy*) She is disliked for her *ostentatious* behaviour towards her friends and colleagues.
20. **Oscillate** *(v.)* (*waver*) Persons with *oscillating* nature never stick to one option.

P

1. **Penchant** *(n.)* (*strong inclination*) She has a strong *penchant* for singing and dancing.
2. **Pithy** *(adj.)* (*concise, meaningful*) The essays of Francis Bacon are read all over the world because they are *pithy* and profound in their meaning.
3. **Paltry** *(adj.)* (*insignificant, petty*) Strangely enough, the two friends quarrelled over a *paltry* amount.
4. **Pecuniary** *(adj.)* (*pertaining to money*) Besides *pecuniary* loss in business, he had to suffer humiliation in society.
5. **Perpetual** *(adj.)* (*everlasting*) Neither joys nor sorrows are *perpetual* in life.
6. **Plaintive** *(adj.)* (*mournful*) The *plaintive* notes of Nightingale were heard in the forest.
7. **Pragmatic** *(adj.)* (*practical*) India should adopt a *pragmatic* foreign policy to suit the need of the country.
8. **Pedantic** *(adj.)* (*showing off learning*) The scholars try to show off their learning by using *pedantic* ideas.
9. **Perjury** *(n.)* (*false testimony*) The American President was indicted for *perjury*.
10. **Pre-requisite** *(n.)* (*pre-condition*) Hard work is a *pre-requisite* to success in life.
11. **Paradox** *(n.)* (*contradictory*) That the virtuous don't prosper materially is a *paradox* of life.
12. **Parsimonious** *(adj.)* (*mean, frugal*) He is extravagant but his wife is *parsimonious*.
13. **Perusal** *(n.)* (*careful study*) I am sending a copy of the agreement for your *perusal*.
14. **Prodigal** *(adj.)* (*wasteful*) The sons of the rich are generally *prodigal* and waste money on luxuries of life.
15. **Prolific** *(adj.)* (*fruitful, productive*) Shakespeare was a *prolific* playwright.
16. **Pamper** *(v.)* (*spoil*) In Indian families, the only son is *pampered* and spoiled by his mother.
17. **Promulgate** *(v.)* (*official proclamation*) The ordinance for the reservation of women in legislature will be *promulgated* soon.

18. **Penury** *(n.)* — (*extreme poverty*) More than half of population in India is forced to lead a life of *penury* resulting in untold sufferings.
19. **Purview** *(n.)* — (*scope, extent*) The reasons for the murder of the gangster are not within the *purview* of the inquiry committee.
20. **Profane** *(v.)* — (*desecrate*) We must respect every religion and never try to *profane* the sanctity of holy places.
21. **Pseudonym** *(n.)* — (*assumed name*) Charles Lamb wrote his essays under the *pseudonym* of Elia.
22. **Precocious** *(adj.)* — (*mature before time*) The *precocious* children need careful bringing up by their parents.
23. **Placid** *(adj.)* — (*calm, peaceful*) The *placid* atmosphere of the hill station had salutary effect on his mind and body.
24. **Plagiarism** *(n.)* — (*theft of ideas or writing*) The Indian film directors are notorious for indulging in *plagiarism*.
25. **Posterity** *(n.)* — (*future generations*) The *posterity* will not pardon the present politicians for their acts of omission and commission.
26. **Paragon** *(n.)* — (*model of perfection*) Sita is always depicted as a *paragon* of ideal and virtuous woman.
27. **Provident** *(adj.)* — (*providing for future*) We should spend in *provident* manner so as to lay by something for future emergency.
28. **Perquisite** *(n.)* — (*perks, gain above stipulated salary*) Though the salary offered by the company is not high, the *perquisites* are quite handsome.
29. **Prone** *(adj.)* — [*inclined to* (*disorder*)] Indian farming is *prone* to uncertainty because of the fickleness of monsoons.
30. **Pandemonium** *(n.)* — (*wild disorder*) There was *pandemonium* in Parliament over the objectionable remarks made by a member of the opposition party.
31. **Parasite** *(n.)* — (*living on another*) Flatterers are considered to be *parasites* because their existence depends on sycophancy.
32. **Patrimony** *(n.)* — (*inheritance from father*) Though his father left huge *patrimony*, he squandered it within a year or so.
33. **Perennial** *(adj.)* — (*lasting for a long time*) The rivers originating in the Himalayas are *perennial*.
34. **Poignant** *(adj.)* — (*touching, sharp*) The *poignant* cries of the orphaned children moved everybody present at the funeral.
35. **Pungent** *(adj.)* — (*stinging, strong*) The cigarettes of inferior brands have *pungent* smell.
36. **Paucity** *(n.)* — (*scarcity, dearth*) Many schemes have fallen through because of the paucity of funds.

37. **Pinnacle** *(n.)* — *(peak, summit)* As he reached the *pinnacle* of his career he parted from all those who stood by him in difficulties.

38. **Pernicious** *(adj.)* — *(destructive, injurious)* Obscene magazines have *pernicious* effect on the impressionable minds of the youth.

39. **Prerogative** *(n.)* — *(privilege, unquestionable)* It is the *prerogative* of the Prime Minister to constitute his cabinet.

40. **Parochial** *(adj.)* — *(narrow in viewpoint)* All the political parties rise above *parochial* considerations when the security of the country is threatened.

41. **Precedent** *(n.)* — *(earlier example)* The speaker cited many *precedents* for not allowing the opposition member to raise a question of that nature.

42. **Piquant** *(adj.)* — *(pleasantly tasting)* The *piquant* sauce makes food always enjoyable.

43. **Preposterous** *(adj.)* — *(absurd, ridiculous)* He always offers such *preposterous* excuses that nobody believes him.

44. **Precarious** *(adj.)* — *(uncertain, risky)* The patient is in a *precarious* condition because so far he has not recovered consciousness.

45. **Predilection** *(n.)* — *(partiality for)* He is a good player but his *predilection* for scoring fast has not proved good for him.

46. **Proclivity** *(n.)* — *(inclination)* Some employees are never satisfied because they have *proclivity* to complain.

47. **Pertinent** *(adj.)* — *(suitable, to the point)* Please don't beat about the bush, come to your *pertinent* point.

48. **Precursor** *(n.)* — *(forerunner, pioneer)* Surendra Nath Bannerjee was *precursor* of Indian National Movement.

49. **Pariah** *(n.)* — *(social outcast)* When he married a girl of his own choice, he came to be considered a *pariah* by his family.

50. **Perverse** *(adj.)* — *(stubborn, intractable)* She could not pull well with her husband because of her *perverse* nature.

51. **Ponder** *(v.)* — *(think)* Before taking a hasty step you must *ponder* over the consequences of your action.

52. **Passing** *(adj.)* — *(transitory)* Don't be proud of your beauty because it is *passing* in nature.

53. **Plebeian** *(n.)* — *(of low rank)* Shakespeare treated *plebeians* with contempt in his plays.

54. **Pensive** *(adj.)* — *(thoughtful)* She was in a *pensive* mood and looked intently at the placid water of the lake.

55. **Puerile** *(adj.)* — *(silly, childish)* Though she has grown up, her *puerile* behaviour always irritates her friends.

Q

1. **Quip** *(n.)* — (*a clever remark*) She is quite intelligent and is in the habit of making *quips*.
2. **Query** *(n.)* — (*question*) He raised a *query* to find out the veracity of her statement.
3. **Quisling** *(n.)* — (*traitor*) The Mughals and the English always depended on *quislings* to defeat their indomitable enemies.
4. **Quack** *(n.)* — (*untrained doctor*) A person who dishonestly claims to have knowledge of a subject is called a *quack*.
5. **Quadruped** *(n.)* — (*having four feet*) A cow is a useful *quadruped*.
6. **Quasi** *(n.)* — (*to a certain extent*) Indian Constitution is *quasi*-federal.
7. **Quandary** *(n.)* — (*in a fix, dilemma*) Most of the students are in a *quandary* about their future plans after they have completed their education.
8. **Quest** *(n.)* — (*search*) He left home at a very early age in *quest* of a job.
9. **Quell** *(n.)* — (*suppress, crush*) India must deal with the militants with an iron hand to *quell* anti-national activities.
10. **Quintessence** *(n.)* — (*perfect example, paragon*) Everybody admires her because she is the *quintessence* of benevolence.
11. **Quarantine** *(adj.)* — (*period of separation*) She was admitted to *quarantine* ward to avoid the danger of spreading Corona to others.
12. **Quash** *(v.)* — (*set aside, strike down*) The High Court *quashed* the verdict of the lower court.
13. **Quench** *(v.)* — (*satisfy*) She needed water urgently to *quench* her thirst.
14. **Queer** *(adj.)* — (*strange*) She has a *queer* way of talking.
15. **Qualms** *(n.)* — [*feeling of doubt* (*right or wrong*)] The hardened criminals are the last to feel *qualms* while committing cruel deeds.
16. **Quietude** *(n.)* — (*peace*) Once the heaven of *quietude* Kashmir Valley is now a place haunted by terrorism.
17. **Quirk** *(n.)* — (*a strange act*) One can call his misfortune just a *quirk* of fate.
18. **Quixotic** *(adj.)* — (*generous*) He has not been successful in life because of his *quixotic* ideas.
19. **Quizzical** *(adj.)* — (*questioning*) The *quizzical* remarks often made by Rohit are appreciated by his friends.
20. **Querrulous** *(adj.)* — (*fretful*) His *querrulous* behaviour has made him unpopular with his friends.

1. **Reprieve** *(n.)* (*temporary stay*) The lawyers got him *reprieve* when he was granted bail and released from jail.
2. **Requisite** *(n.)* (*necessary requirement*) Hard work and honesty are *requisite* to success in life.
3. **Rampart** *(n.)* (*defensive wall*) The Prime Minister declared from the *ramparts* of the Red Fort that sovereignty of India is inviolable.
4. **Reciprocate** *(v.)* (*repay in kind*) It is our duty to *reciprocate* the love and regards of our children.
5. **Rendezvous** *(n.)* (*meeting place*) Once Coffee House in Connaught Place was a famous *rendezvous* for the writers and journalists.
6. **Realm** *(n.)* (*kingdom*) In recent years, India has made tremendous progress in the *realm* of nuclear weapons.
7. **Refurbish** *(v.)* (*make clean*) A person can *refurbish* his image by leading a life dedicated to his vocation.
8. **Robust** *(adj.)* (*vigorous, strong*) Only *robust* players can withstand the stress and strain of sports in modern times.
9. **Renounce** *(v.)* (*abandon, give up*) Lord Buddha *renounced* material life in search of freedom from sufferings of life.
10. **Rudimentary** *(adj.)* (*not developed, elementary*) If one wishes to learn the art of conversation, one must be aware of the *rudimentary* rules of grammar.
11. **Remonstrate** *(v.)* (*protest*) The players *remonstrated* with the umpire about the run-out decision.
12. **Repudiate** *(v.)* (*disown*) The Finance Minister *repudiated* his remarks by saying that he was quoted out of context.
13. **Rapprochement** *(n.)* (*reconciliation*) There is hardly any possibility of *rapprochement* between India and China as long as boundary dispute between them exists.
14. **Raze** *(v.)* (*destroy completely*) The whole village was *razed* to ground by constant shelling from across the border.
15. **Recrimination** *(n.)* (counter charges) When her husband advised her not to neglect her domestic obligations, there were offensive *recriminations* from her.
16. **Repercussion** *(n.)* (*reaction*) Every Indian is afraid that Kashmir problem will have serious *repercussions* both on Indian polity and economy.
17. **Rectify** *(v.)* (*correct*) The accountant was able to find out the mistake and *rectified* it in time.
18. **Relinquish** *(v.)* (*abandon*) Neither of the two brothers is ready to *relinquish* his claims to the paternal property.

19. **Retrograde** *(v.)* (*going backward*) Although we claim to have progressed in every field, in fact we have *retrograded* in upholding human values.

20. **Retrospective** *(adj.)* [*looking back on the past* (*from past effect*)] When he is in *restrospective* mood, he speaks high of halcyon days of his youth.

21. **Retaliate** *(v.)* (*hit back*) The Defence Minister warned that India would *retaliate*, if attacked.

22. **Retinue** *(n.)* (*number of attendants*) The Prime Minister arrived in the town with a *retinue* of officials.

23. **Ruthless** *(adj.)* (*pitiless*) The landlady was not only robbed but also beaten *ruthlessly*.

24. **Ramification** *(n.)* (*far reaching effect*) The interference of the President in the affairs of Central Government is fraught with dire *ramifications*.

25. **Relegate** *(v.)* (*put to lower position*) After the defeat of Indian Cricket team in the semifinals in the World Cup it has been *relegated* to seventh position in ranking.

26. **Recant** *(v.)* (*repudiate*) Inspite of the advice of the party high command he did not *recant* his observation about the leader of the party.

27. **Restive** *(adj.)* (*restless, unmanageable*) The labourers working in this factory are *restive* on account of non-payment of bonus this year.

28. **Rampage** *(n.)* (*rush in sudden violent behaviour*) The demonstrators went on the *rampage* when the Superintendent of Police refused to listen to their grievances.

29. **Rapt** *(adj.)* (*fully attentive*) The speech of the Prime Minister was listened to with *rapt* attention by the audience.

30. **Renegade** *(n.)* (*turncoat in politics, religion*) Inspite of anti-defection law *renegades* in Indian politics are having a field day.

31. **Retard** *(v.)* (*hinder, check*) Population problem has *retarded* economic progress in every field.

32. **Reprisal** *(n.)* (*retaliation*) Inspite of provocative policy of militancy pursued by Pakistan, India has done nothing by way of *reprisal*.

33. **Rancour** *(n.)* (*bitterness*) Though they had planned to marry, now there is feeling of *rancour* between them.

34. **Ravage** *(n.)* (*plunder, destroy*) The floods this year have *ravaged* the crops severely.

35. **Regime** *(n.)* (*system of government*) Every *regime* in Pakistan has survived only by arousing animosity against India.

36. **Render** *(v.)* (*deliver, give*) He is always prepared to *render* help to the needy.

37. **Recipient** *(n.)* — (*receiver*) The *recipients* of gallantry awards will be honoured on the Republic day.

38. **Repartee** *(n.)* — (*clever retort*) The discussion in the Parliament on the reservation issue was replete with *repartees*.

39. **Reiterate** *(v.)* — (*repeat*) The Principal has *reiterated* that those students who are irregular will not be allowed to take examination.

40. **Rusticate** *(v.)* — (*expel*) He was caught copying in the examination hall and was *rusticated* from the university for two years.

41. **Replenish** *(v.)* — (*fill up again*) When the food ran out, it was *replenished* by the rescue team promptly.

42. **Replete** *(adj.)* — (*filled to capacity*) There is no peace in the family though the home is *replete* with every modern comfort.

43. **Rowdy** *(adj.)* — (*disorderly, disobedient*) On the eve of the visit of the Chief Minister, the *rowdy* elements in the city were rounded up by the police.

44. **Redundant** *(adj.)* — (*superfluous, surplus*) The use of computers in the government offices has made thousands of workers *redundant*.

45. **Rift** *(n.)* — (*opening, breach*) The *rift* between the two friends has become irreconcilable.

46. **Renunciation** *(n.)* — (*giving up, renouncing*) Life of *renunciation* contributes to both moral and physical health.

47. **Ruse** *(n.)* — (*trick, strategy*) Heavy shelling by Pakistan Army was a *ruse* to help the militants enter Indian territory.

48. **Rampant** *(adj.)* — (*unrestrained, growth beyond control*) Corruption is *rampant* in every section of Indian society.

49. **Replica** (n.) — (*a copy, miniature*) *Replicas* of world famous paintings are available these days.

50. **Rife** *(adj.)* — (*widespread*) The city is *rife* with rumours of communal riots.

51. **Redress** *(n.)* — (*remedy, compensation*) The victim of the police injustice sought legal *redress*.

52. **Retrieve** *(v.)* — (*recover, bring back*) The government is trying to *retrieve* the economy from recession.

53. **Redoubtable** *(adj.)* — (*formidable*) India needs *redoubtable* politicians to build India strong.

54. **Resume** *(n./v.)* — (*restart, summary*) She narrated the *resume* of the day's events.

55. **Reticence** *(n.)* — (*the quality of being reserved*) Her *reticence* makes her look mysterious.

1. **Slovenly** *(adj.)* — *(untidy, careless in work)* She is often reprimanded for her *slovenly* habits.
2. **Supple** *(adj.)* — *(flexible, pliant)* The *supple* limbs of the athletes impressed everybody.
3. **Sacrilegious** *(adj.)* — *(desecrating, profane)* The communal riots in the city broke out as a result of *sacrilegious* act of one community.
4. **Sangfroid** *(n.)* — *(coolness, courage)* The *sangfroid* of the Army Commander saved the check post from being recaptured by the enemy.
5. **Scourge** *(n.)* — *(severe punishment)* The Plague broke out in the province and people thought it to be a divine *scourge*.
6. **Salvage** *(v.)* — *(rescue from loss)* The army swung into action to *salvage* the havoc caused by the earthquake.
7. **Sultry** *(adj.)* — *(sweltering)* September and October are *sultry* months because of excessive humidity.
8. **Surmise** *(v.)* — *(guess)* I *surmised* that he would not succeed in his attempt to exploit his wife.
9. **Spurious** *(adj.)* — *(false, counterfeit, fake)* There is glut of *spurious* drugs in the market.
10. **Stamina** *(n.)* — *(strength)* She has a lot of *stamina* and works for hours together.
11. **Supersede** *(v.)* — *(take the place of)* When the Marketing Manager was *superseded* by his junior, the former resigned.
12. **Saga** *(n.)* — *(a traditional story of heroic deeds)* The *saga* of Indian soldiers on the war front is beyond description.
13. **Salutary** *(adj.)* — *(beneficial)* *Salutary* working conditions tend to improve the efficiency of the workers.
14. **Slander** *(n.)* — *(defamation)* The editor of the newspaper was charged with *slander*.
15. **Serenity** *(n.)* — *(calmness, tranquility)* The *serenity* of the valley in the evening overwhelmed the visitors.
16. **Sumptuous** *(adj.)* — *[lavish (feast)]* *Sumptuous* feast was served on the occasion of the wedding.
17. **Stagnant** *(adj.)* — *(motionless)* *Stagnant* water emits foul smell.
18. **Substantiate** *(v.)* — *(verify, support)* It is difficult to *substantiate* his statement for want of solid proof.
19. **Sedition** *(n.)* — *(rebellion)* The Prime Minister of the state was charged with *sedition* by the king and was executed.
20. **Stint** *(n.)* — *(assigned work)* Our servant performs his daily *stint* without grumbling.

21. **Span** *(n.)* (*distance* (*of time*) Within a short *span* of ten years he made remarkable progress in business.

22. **Supercilious** *(adj.)* (*haughty*) Everybody resents the *supercilious* treatment of the Manager.

23. **Savage** *(adj.)* (*uncivilised, primitive*) The *Sati* system is definitely a *savage* custom.

24. **Sporadic** *(adj.)* (*occuring irregularly*) *Sporadic* firing from across the borders continues throughout the year.

25. **Status quo** *(n.)* (*existing position*) India and Pakistan have agreed to maintain *status quo* in respect of Line of Control in Kashmir.

26. **Superannuated** *(v.)* (*retired on pension*) The *superannuated* army personnel are not satisfied with their pension grades.

27. **Sophistication** *(n.)* (*artificiality, refined*) *Sophistication* implies the loss of natural simplicity in a character.

28. **Scion** *(n.)* (*offspring*) A number of *scions* of the former rulers have joined politics to maintain their status.

29. **Sinister** *(adj.)* (*suggesting evil*) India has to be always vigilant to foil the *sinister* designs of Pakistan on Kashmir.

30. **Salient** *(adj.)* (*prominent*) The passive nature of the foreign policy of India has been its *salient* feature which has not paid dividends.

31. **Sagacious** *(adj.)* (*having insight*) My father is quite *sagacious* and is seldom taken in by the hypocrisy of his friends.

32. **Schism** *(n.)* (*split, division into two parts*) The *schism* in the party has led to polarisation of political forces on economic basis.

33. **Savour** *(v.)* (*have a distinct flavour, smell or quality*) The assurance of the opposition leaders to flood victims *savours* of sheer hypocrisy.

34. **Senility** *(n.)* (*old age, feeble mindedness of old age*) Because of *senility* he has lost hold over family business.

35. **Subsequent** *(adj.)* (*following, later*) The *subsequent* events have proved our apprehension about our business partner's treachery.

36. **Sartorial** *(adj.)* (*pertaining to dress*) In the modern era there are rapid changes in *sartorial* fashions.

37. **Scrupulous** *(adj.)* (*conscientious*) India is woefully lacking *scrupulous* politicians who are concerned with public welfare.

38. **Subsidy** *(n.)* (*financial aid*) Government is thinking of providing *subsidy* on import of edible oils.

39. **Subjugate** *(v.)* (*conquer*) The king was overthrown as he was unable to *subjugate* the traitors.

40. **Succour** *(n.)* (*aid, relief*) The government has provided ample *succour* to the farmers affected by flood in the form of financial subsidy.

41. **Sycophant** *(n.)* (*flatterer*) One must be wary of a *sycophant* who is just like a snake in the grass.

42. **Surruptitious** *(adj.)* (*secret*) The *surruptitious* visit of Henry Kissinger to China brought about revolutionary transformation in the relations between America and China.

43. **Solar** *(adj.)* (*of the sun*) *Solar* eclipse will be visible in India at 2 p.m. tomorrow.

44. **Stringent** *(adj.)* (*strict, severe*) *Stringent* laws to curb terrorism in India must be enforced.

45. **Scruple** *(n.)* (*sense of right and wrong*) He has no *scruple* in letting down his parents by his wanton behaviour.

46. **Shambles** *(n.)* (*scene of destruction*) The house where murder was committed was a *shambles*.

47. **Sacrosanct** *(adj.)* (*most sacred*) The President of India should not regard his privileges as *sacrosanct* and immune from public criticism.

48. **Spiteful** *(adj.)* (*contemptuous*) The *spiteful* behaviour of our neighbours is the result of their jealousy.

49. **Stigma** *(adj.)* (*mark of disgrace*) The *stigma* of having been sentenced to imprisonment always rankles in his mind.

50. **Succumb** *(v.)* (*die, yield*) The wounded soldier *succumbed* to his injuries later on.

51. **Sluggish** *(adj.)* (*slow*) The production activities in the factory have become *sluggish* on account of the apathy of the management.

52. **Sedentary** *(adj.)* (*requiring sitting*) Those engaged in *sedentary* jobs need physical exercise.

T

1. **Tantamount** *(adj.)* (*equal in effect*) To disown a pet is *tantamount* to cruelty.

2. **Tacit** *(adj.)* (*understood*) There seems to be a *tacit* understanding between China and Pakistan about destabilising India.

3. **Tirade** *(n.)* (*extended scolding*) It is a common practice of the opposition parties to indulge in *tirade* about the policies of the government.

4. **Tenacity** *(n.)* (*firmness, determination*) *Tenacity* of purpose alone can lead you to your goal of life.

5. **Tenure** *(n.)* (*duration, period*) The pension benefits are granted to an employee in proportion to the *tenure* of service.

6. **Tranquil** *(adj.)* (*calm, peaceful*) The *tranquil* atmosphere in the hills proves salutary to one's jaded spirits.

7. **Temporal** *(adj.)* — (*not lasting forever*) Everything in the world is *temporal* and mortal.

8. **Tyro** *(n.)* — (*beginner, novice*) Though he is just a *tyro* in business, he works like a veteran.

9. **Tepid** *(adj.)* — (*luke warm*) Please take the medicine with *tepid* water.

10. **Tortuous** *(adj.)* — (*winding, full of curves*) The journey on the *tortuous* roads in the valley was arduous.

11. **Tryst** *(n.)* — (*private meeting*) The villagers got wind of the *tryst* between the lovers and hacked them to death.

12. **Tentative** *(adj.)* — (*provisional, experimental*) Nothing is yet final, only *tentative* programme has been announced.

13. **Terminus** *(n.)* — (*last stop of rail, road*) Mumbai is the *terminus* of the Western Railways.

14. **Thwart** *(v.)* — (*baffle, frustrate*) The vigilant soldiers on the borders *thwarted* the intrusion of the militants into Kashmir.

15. **Trauma** *(n.)* — (*injury, shock*) The *trauma* of physical injury in war has made him suffer from neurosis.

16. **Travesty** *(n.)* — (*mockery, parody*) The trial of patriots like Bhagat Singh was a sheer *travesty* of justice.

17. **Throttle** *(v.)* — (*strangle*) The old woman was *throttled* to death by the dacoits.

18. **Trite** *(adj.)* — (*hackneyed, commonplace*) Such *trite* remarks as made by the opposition about Indian Army lowers the prestige of the country.

19. **Tempo** *(n.)* — (*speed of music*) The *tempo* of economic progress in India has been woefully slow resulting in unmanageable unemployment problem.

20. **Tenet** *(n.)* — (*doctrine, dogma*) The *tenets* of Buddhism emphasise the need of simple life.

21. **Tribulation** *(n.)* — (*sufferings*) She went through *tribulation* in life with fortitude.

22. **Taciturn** *(adj.)* — (*habitually, silent*) *Taciturn* persons don't commit themselves at random.

23. **Tenuous** *(adj.)* — (*fragile, delicate*) The constituents of the present government are held by *tenuous* ties.

24. **Terminology** *(n.)* — (*terms used in a subject*) Science *terminology* is Greek and Latin to a Sanskrit scholar.

25. **Terse** *(adj.)* — (*concise, pithy*) Dr. Johnson is admired for his *terse* style of writing.

26. **Travail** *(n.)* — (*painful labour, hard work*) He has gone through *travails* and sufferings in life manfully.

27. **Threshold** *(n.)* — (*entrance*) India is on the *threshold* of economic revolution.

28. **Tainted** *(adj.)* — (*infected, corrupt*) Ice cream sold by street hawkers is generally *tainted* and inedible.
29. **Talisman** *(n.)* — (*a magical object bringing good luck*) The mother made her son wear a *talisman* to ward off evil.
30. **Transcend** *(v.)* — (*surpass*) Peace of mind in one's life *transcends* all material achievements.

U

1. **Untenable** *(adj.)* — (*unsupportable*) Your arguments are *untenable* because they have no bearing on the subject.
2. **Unbridled** *(adj.)* — (*unchecked*) The city is torn with *unbridled* violence because of communal riots.
3. **Ubiquitous** *(adj.)* — (*present everywhere, omnipresent*) Dogs are *ubiquitous* in every Indian street.
4. **Upbraid** *(v.)* — (*scold, reproach*) She was *upbraided* for her impertinence.
5. **Uxorious** *(adj.)* — (*devoted to one's wife*) *Uxorious* husbands are not acceptable in the world of men.
6. **Utopia** *(n.)* — (*imaginary land*) Those who think of the world free from violence are living in *utopia*.
7. **Usurpation** *(n.)* — (*act of seizing power*) The military leader was charged with the *usurpation* of the throne.
8. **Umbrage** *(n.)* — (*resentment, anger*) She considered his remarks exceptionable and took *umbrage* at them.
9. **Ulterior** *(adj.)* — (*hidden, unstated*) She could not see through *ulterior* motives of her mother-in-law and came to grief.
10. **Unearth** *(v.)* — (*dig up*) The police were able to *unearth* the cause of murder only after sustained interrogation.
11. **Unkempt** *(adj.)* — (*dishevelled, untidy*) When he came out of the police station he looked shaken and *unkempt*.
12. **Unilateral** *(adj.)* — (*one sided*) He objected to the *unilateral* decision of his partner to enter into an agreement with a third party.
13. **Unequivocal** *(adj.)* — (*obvious, plain*) India has declared in *unequivocal* terms that she would not like third party mediation on the Kashmir issue.
14. **Unsavoury** *(adj.)* — (*nasty, disgusting*) Her *unsavoury* remarks about the host broke up the party suddenly.
15. **Unruly** *(adj.)* — (*unmanageable*) Her *unruly* behaviour in the class annoyed the teacher.

1. **Vivacious** *(adj.)* (*animated, gay*) *Vivacious* children are loved by everybody.
2. **Vacillation** *(n.)* (*fluctuation, wavering*) My friend's *vacillation* between fear and hope made all of us nervous.
3. **Vindicate** *(v.)* (*justify, clear of charge*) His innocence was *vindicated* and the judge acquitted him.
4. **Versatile** *(adj.)* (*having many talents*) India needs *versatile* players like Kapil Dev.
5. **Verity** *(n.)* (*truth, reality*) The *verity* of his statement has been vindicated by the subsequent events.
6. **Vociferous** *(adj.)* (*clamorous, noisy*) The traders had planned a peaceful march but the mob grew *vociferous* in excitement.
7. **Vie** *(v.)* (*contend, compete*) The middle class should not *vie* with the rich.
8. **Venerable** *(adj.)* (*deserving high respect*) *Venerable* persons are always respected in society.
9. **Vent** *(v.)* (*express, utter*) The writer seems to have *vented* his anger at the injustice done to him in his latest novel.
10. **Veer** *(v.)* (*change, turn*) When he was attacked he *veered* round and retaliated.
11. **Vehement** *(adj.)* (*with vigour, strong*) The teachers made *vehement* protest against the promotion policy of the University.
12. **Vagary** *(n.)* (*strange and sudden change*) The crop was destroyed because of the *vagary* of the nature.
13. **Vogue** *(n.)* (*popular fashion*) Jeans are in *vogue* these days.
14. **Vantage** *(n.)* (*position giving an advantage*) The militants occupied the position of *vantage* and started firing across the valley.
15. **Venal** *(adj.)* (*capable of being bribed*) The *venal* policemen did not take any action against the smuggler and set him free.
16. **Vitiate** *(v.)* (*spoil the effect of*) The reservation policy has *vitiated* Indian society giving rise to castist politics.
17. **Vendetta** *(n.)* (*family feud*) The abduction of Mr. Rastogi is attributed to *vendetta* between the two families.
18. **Viable** *(adj.)* (*able to exist*) Your argument is not *viable* because it has no bearing on the subject.
19. **Vilify** *(v.)* (*slander, malign*) Election is a period when politicians try to *vilify* the reputation of others.
20. **Vernal** *(adj.)* (*pertaining to spring*) *Vernal* rain in England is a common phenomenon.
21. **Vintage** *(n.)* (*rare, grape harvesting season*) A *vintage* car rally was held in India last year.

22. **Vindictive** *(adj.)* (*revengeful*) The elephant is *vindictive*.

23. **Vandalism** *(n.)* (*destruction of public property*) The unruly crowd was dispersed by the police when it indulged in *vandalism*.

24. **Vituperative** *(adj.)* (*disparaging*) It is a pity that modern politicians indulge in *vituperative* criticism in election campaigns.

1. **Waive** *(v.)* (*remove*) Government is thinking of *waiving* of import duty on life saving drugs.

2. **Wanton** *(adj.)* (*playful, immoral*) Her *wanton* conduct cost her loss of reputation in society.

3. **Withhold** *(v.)* (*keep back*) The university is forced to *withhold* the results of many students on account of non-receipt of answer-books from the teachers.

4. **Wreck** *(v.)* (*destroy*) The ship was *wrecked* when it collided with an invisible rock in the sea.

5. **Wont** *(n.)* (*habit*) Everybody was surprised at the manner of his behaviour because he acted differently from his *wont*.

6. **Wary** *(adj.)* (*chary, cautious*) You must be *wary* of strangers while travelling.

7. **Wean** *(v.)* (*separate*) The opposition is trying to woo the voters belonging to the minority by *weaning* them from the party in power.

8. **Warrant** *(v.)* (*justify*) His impudent behaviour towards the teacher was not at all *warranted*.

9. **Way-ward** *(adj.)* (*unruly, rowdy*) She is fickle minded and is accused of *way-ward* disposition by her friends.

10. **Wane** *(v.)* (*decline*) The popularity of the Congress party is certainly on the *wane*.

11. **Wilful** *(adj.)* (*obstinate*) The child is *wilful* and impervious to the advice of his parents.

12. **Wan** *(adj.)* (*pale looking, weak*) She looked *wan* and weak after long illness.

13. **Way-lay** *(v.)* (*rob*) The ladies were *way-laid* when they were returning from picnic.

14. **Wrath** *(n.)* (*anger*) The natural calamities are manifestation of divine *wrath* and scourge.

15. **Wilt** *(v.)* (*wither*) The plants *wilted* in the scorching heat of the sun.

16. **Wield** *(v.)* [*use (power)*] Dictators are accustomed to *wielding* power against their opponents ruthlessly.

17. **Wreak** *(v.)* (*give expression to*) Hamlet *wreaked* vengeance for the murder of his father.

18. **Wrest** *(v.)* (*take violently*) In elections every party tries to *wrest* initiative from opposite parties by hook or by crook.

19. **Whip** *(v./n.)* (*lash, flog*) The rapist was *whipped* publically by the residents.

20. **Wangle** *(v.)* (*manage by unfair means*) The employees always try to *wangle* extra benefits from their employers.

1. **Xenophobia** *(n.)* (*fear of foreigners, yellow peril*) The white races are obsessed with *xenophobia* and are afraid of losing hegemony.

1. **Yawn** *(v.)* (*deep breath with mouth open*) She *yawned* and fell asleep soon.

2. **Yearn** *(v.)* (*long for, keen desire*) She *yearns* to meet her daughter who is in the States.

3. **Yeoman** *(n.)* (*a working farmer on his own land*) Bal Gangadhar Tilak did *yeoman* service to the cause of Indian freedom.

4. **Yoke** *(n.)* (*used for oxen for pulling carts, a situation or experience that limits someone's freedom*) India was able to get rid of the *yoke* of the English after World War II.

5. **Yolk** *(n.)* (*yellow part of an egg*) The *yolk* of an egg is quite nutritious.

1. **Zest** *(n.)* (*enthusiasm, gusto*) She lost *zest* in life after the death of her only son.

2. **Zealot** *(n.)* (*fanatic*) The *zealots* are offensive to those who believe in humanitarian service.

3. **Zealous** *(adj.)* (*enthusiastic*) We must guard our freedom *zealously*.

4. **Zig-zag** *(n.)* (*winding with unequal bends*) The rash driving on *zig-zag* roads is quite dangerous.

5. **Zoom** *(n.)* (*rise, move upwards*) Prices of medicines *zoomed* when their imports were banned.

6. **Zenith** *(n.)* (*summit, peak*) Today he is at the *zenith* of his career.

Additional Words for Practice

	Word	Meaning
1.	**Annuity** *(n.)*	fixed income paid yearly
2.	**Arboreal** *(adj.)*	living or connected with trees
3.	**Asperity** *(n.)*	harshness
4.	**Aberration** *(n.)*	departure from usual/normal
5.	**Approbation** *(n.)*	approval
6.	**Amenable** *(adj.)*	responsive, willing to
7.	**Abstinence** *(n.)*	restraint in drinking or eating
8.	**Ambivalent** *(adj.)*	with conflicting emotions, wishes
9.	**Abector** *(n.)*	cattle thief
10.	**Apiarian** *(adj.)*	of bees (working habits)
11.	**Abash** *(v.)*	embarrass
12.	**Abdicate** *(v.)*	give up right to throne
13.	**Abortive** *(adj.)*	fruitless
14.	**Abstemious** *(adj.)*	moderate in eating and drinking
15.	**Aquiline** *(adj.)*	of eagle, curved, hooked
16.	**Agnostic** *(n.)*	sceptical about the existence of God
17.	**Adventitious** *(adj.)*	accidental
18.	**Accolade** *(n.)*	award
19.	**Abrogate** *(v.)*	annul, abolish
20.	**Amnesia** *(n.)*	loss of memory
21.	**Apex** *(n.)*	summit, peak
22.	**Awry** *(adj.)*	go wrong, distorted, haywire
23.	**Avuncular** *(adj.)*	of uncle
24.	**Axiomatic** *(adj.)*	needing no proof, evident
25.	**Anathema** *(n.)*	curse, dested thing
26.	**Accomplice** *(n.)*	partner in crime
27.	**Abettor** *(n.)*	one who incites, encourage
28.	**Aplomb** *(n.)*	poise
29.	**Annals** *(n.)*	historical records
30.	**Avid** *(adj.)*	voracious, enthusiastic
31.	**Apostate** *(n.)*	one who gives up religious/political faith
32.	**Ambience** *(n.)*	surrounding, environment
33.	**Avow** *(v.)*	declare
34.	**Asinine** *(adj.)*	extremly stupid or unreasonable
35.	**Austere** *(adj.)*	stern, severe

36.	**Assiduous** *(adj.)*	diligent
37.	**Auctorial** *(adj.)*	of author (Pen Power)
38.	**Arraign** *(v.)*	bring a criminal charge against a person
39.	**Animus** *(n.)*	hostile, intent
40.	**Apropos** *(adv.)*	properly, concerning
41.	**Abate** *(adv.)*	lessen intensity
42.	**Assimilate** *(v.)*	absorb
43.	**Apocalypse** *(n.)*	revelation about future
44.	**Apocryphal** *(adj.)*	of doubtful author
45.	**Archetype** *(n.)*	important example, ideal form
46.	**Abnegation** *(n.)*	self-sacrifice, repudiation
47.	**Abysmal** *(adj.)*	bottomless, dismal
48.	**Advent** *(n.)*	arrival
49.	**Advertent** *(adj.)*	intentional
50.	**Aegis** *(n.)*	sponsorship, patronage
51.	**Aphasia** *(n.)*	loss of speech
52.	**Abject** *(adj.)*	miserable, low
53.	**Ablution** *(n.)*	purification, cleansing
54.	**Acquiesce** *(v.)*	accept unwillingly
55.	**Ambush** (n./v.)	surprised attack
56.	**Artefacts** *(n.)*	objects of primitive culture
57.	**Augury** *(n.)*	prophecy, omen
58.	**Aver** *(v.)*	state confidently
60.	**Abeyance** *(adv.)*	in a suspended state
61.	**Appellation** *(n.)*	title
62.	**Accrue** *(n.)*	increase by addition
63.	**Arrant** *(adj.)*	thorough, sheer
64.	**Attrition** *(n.)*	gradual wearing down
65.	**Assail** *(v.)*	assault, criticise
66.	**Aspersion** *(n.)*	slanderous remarks
67.	**Acronym** *(n.)*	a word formed with the first letters
68.	**Alias** *(n.)*	assumed name
69.	**Asylum** *(n.)*	refuge, place for mentally ill
70.	**Ambit** *(n.)*	bound, extent of power
71.	**Affinity** *(n.)*	similarity, liking
72.	**Adumberate** *(n.)*	fore shadow
73.	**Apt** *(adj.)*	suitable, apt to (likely)
74.	**Auspices** *(n.)*	help, favour of somebody
75.	**Allegiance** *(n.)*	loyalty, faithfulness
76.	**Adaptation** *(n.)*	of something (play, novel)
77.	**Assailant** *(n.)*	one who violently attacks another person

78. **Auricular** *(adj.)* of ear, confession in ear
79. **Auspicious** *(adj.)* favourable, prosperous
80. **Augment** *(v.)* increase
81. **Alexia** *(n.)* word blindness (brain disorder)
82. **Asphyxia** *(n.)* suffocation caused by lack of air
83. **Albeit** *(conj.)* although, though
84. **Attenuate** *(v.)* make thin or weak
85. **Archaic** *(adj.)* old fashioned
86. **Avian** *(adj.)* concerning birds
87. **Aura** *(n.)* quality surrounding a person

B

1. **Besotted** *(adj.)* stupified with wine/drink, attract
2. **Beautitude** *(n.)* happiness, beautific state
3. **Bibulous** *(adj.)* fond of drinking
4. **Bergeon** *(v.)* grow forth, sprout
5. **Bonhomie** *(n.)* pleasantness of manners
6. **Bathos** *(n.)* anticlimax, (from sublime to foolish)
7. **Belabour** *(v.)* beat soundly
8. **Baroque** (adj./n.) florid, extravagance in architecture and art
9. **Beleaguer** *(v.)* surround, besiege
10. **Bucolic** *(adj.)* uncivilised, rustic
11. **Blithe** *(adj.)* gay, joyous
12. **Bare** *(adj.)* naked, scanty
13. **Bland** *(adj.)* mild, soothing
14. **Buttress** *(n.)* support with a prop
15. **Baleful** *(adj.)* threatening, harming
16. **Boisterous** *(adj.)* noisy, violent
17. **Bullwark** *(n.)* strong defence
18. **Bicameral** *(adj.)* having two chambers
19. **Blandishment** *(n.)* flattery to persuade
20. **Bountiful** *(adj.)* generous, liberal
21. **Bristle** *(v.)* rise like bristle, irritate
22. **Balmy** *(adj.)* fragrant, mild, soothing
23. **Benign** *(adj.)* kind, charitable
24. **Beholden** *(adj.)* obliged, indebted
25. **Balk** *(v.)* foil, frustrate
26. **Buxom** *(adj.)* fat, healthy looking
27. **Bludgeon** *(v.)* club with heavy weapon
28. **Brace** *(n.)* support to strengthen, pair, stimulating

29.	**Behest** *(n.)*	orders of somebody else
30.	**Barge** *(v.)*	rush into
31.	**Brook** *(v.)*	tolerate, *(n.)* a small stream
32.	**Belligerent** *(adj.)*	nation waging war, bellicose
33.	**Bilateral** *(adj.)*	between two parties
34.	**Brigand** *(n.)*	a robber (highway, forest)
35.	**Blaze** *(v.)*	burn with flames

C

1.	**Convivial** *(adj.)*	friendly
2.	**Connubial** *(adj.)*	of marriage (husband and wife)
3.	**Craven** *(adj.)*	cowardly, of crow
4.	**Cajole** *(v.)*	coax, wheedle
5.	**Callous** *(adj.)*	heartless, unfeeling
6.	**Conjugal** *(adj.)*	pertaining to marriage
7.	**Curtail** *(v.)*	cut down, reduce
8.	**Complicity** *(n.)*	involvement, participation
9.	**Connoisseur** *(n.)*	person with good judgement of taste and quality
10.	**Conspicuous** *(adj.)*	prominently visible
11.	**Credentials** *(n.)*	reliability, genuineness of testimonials
12.	**Candour** *(n.)*	frankness
13.	**Criterion** *(n.)*	standard of judging
14.	**Cursory** *(adj.)*	hasty, casual
15.	**Contiguous** *(adj.)*	adjacent to
16.	**Chequered/ Checkered** *(adj.)*	marked by ups and downs
17.	**Canard** *(n.)*	unfounded rumour
18.	**Carnal** *(adj.)*	relating to the physical feeling and wants of the body
19.	**Chicanery** *(n.)*	trickery, false argument
20.	**Circumvent** *(v.)*	baffle, outwit
21.	**Circumscribe** *(v.)*	confine, limit
22.	**Cessation** *(n.)*	stopping
23.	**Clairvoyant** *(n.)*	fortune teller
24.	**Circumspect** *(adj.)*	cautious, prudent
25.	**Confiscate** *(v.)*	seize, commandeer
26.	**Cognizance** *(n.)*	knowledge
27.	**Charade** *(n.)*	guessing the word from action (a game), pretence
28.	**Crazy** *(adj.)*	wildly excited, foolish
29.	**Chivalry** *(n.)*	courage marked with honour, courtesy
30.	**Charlatan** *(n.)*	fraud, quack

31. **Chubby** *(adj.)* round faced, plump
32. **Conjure** *(v.)* to make things happen by magic
33. **Choleric** *(adj.)* easily made angry
34. **Contravene** *(v.)* violate, conflict with
35. **Catchword** *(n.)* slogan
36. **Chimerical** *(adj.)* mythical, fanciful (bird, story, hope)
37. **Catalysm** *(n.)* sudden violent change
38. **Compassionate** *(adj.)* kind, benevolent
39. **Conjecture** *(n.)* guess
40. **Crux** *(n.)* central/cruical part of a problem
41. **Covet** *(v.)* desire eagerly
42. **Caveat** *(v.)* process to suspend proceedings (legal)
43. **Cupidity** *(n.)* greed for something
44. **Consort** *(n.)* the husband or the wife of the ruler
45. **Consanguine** *(adj.)* related by birth (same family)
46. **Congenital** *(adj.)* occuring since birth
47. **Crusade** *(n.)* a struggle or movement (religious)
48. **Coffers** *(n.)* treasury for valuables, money
49. **Castigate** *(v.)* punish, criticize severely
50. **Concoct** *(v.)* invent excuse, prepare by mixing
51. **Capitalise** *(v.)* use to one's advantage
52. **Culminate** *(v.)* reach the highest point
53. **Checkmate** *(n.)* obstruct, defeat
54. **Cordial** *(adj.)* warm, heartfelt
55. **Carousal** *(n.)* noisy revelry, feast
56. **Curb** *(v.)* check, control
57. **Cinderella** *(n.)* (a) something long neglected
    (b) a girl/woman whose merits have not been recognised
58. **Colossal** *(adj.)* huge, immense
59. **Cavalier** *(adj.)* without being serious, discourteous
60. **Convalescent** *(n.)* a person recovering from illness
61. **Celebrity** *(n.)* a famous person
62. **Coeval** *(adj.)* of the same origin/age
63. **Crunch** *(n.)* important and unpleasant situation, shortage

D

1. **Descry** *(v.)* seen from distance, dimly seen
2. **Delirium** *(n.)* violent excitement
3. **Disseminate** *(v.)* spread widely
4. **Duress** *(n.)* forcible restraint, threat

5.	**Decrepit** *(adj.)*	worn out by age
6.	**Desultory** *(adj.)*	aimless, jumping around
7.	**Devious** *(adj.)*	go astray, erratic
8.	**Diabolical** *(adj.)*	devilish
9.	**Debility** *(n.)*	weakness, feebleness
10.	**Debonair** *(adj.)*	friendly, pleasing
11.	**Derelict** *(adj.)*	abandoned (uncared for), negligent *(duty)*
12.	**Destitute** *(adj.)*	extremely poor
13.	**Dipsomaniac** *(n.)*	having strong craving for liquor
14.	**Debut** *(n.)*	first appearance
15.	**Debutant** *(n.)*	a person making first appearance
16.	**Discerning** *(adj.)*	having insight
17.	**Dissolute** *(adj.)*	loose in morals
18.	**Denigrate** *(v.)*	blacken, disparage
19.	**Doleful** *(adj.)*	sorrowful
20.	**Disconsolate** *(adj.)*	sad, grieving
21.	**Distraught** *(adj.)*	distracted by anxiety
22.	**Diatribe** *(n.)*	bitter scolding, invective
23.	**Discursive** *(adj.)*	rambling, tortuous
24.	**Delectable** *(adj.)*	delightful
25.	**Disparate** *(adj.)*	different, unrelated
26.	**Denizens** *(n.)*	inhabitants
27.	**Dispassionate** *(adj.)*	calm, impartial
28.	**Deviate** *(v.)*	go away from
29.	**Detente** *(n.)*	easing of strained relations
30.	**Doyen** *(n.)*	a person of repute in his field
31.	**Drudgery** *(n.)*	unpleasant work
32.	**Deteriorate** *(v.)*	worsen, become less in quality
33.	**Defalcation** *(n.)*	misappropriation, embezzlement
34.	**Dementia** *(n.)*	weakness (memory, mind)
35.	**Diaspora** *(n.)*	dispersal of the Jews (358 BC)
36.	**Diversion** *(n.)*	turning of road, amusement
37.	**Dilettante** *(n.)*	amateurs
38.	**Decamp** *(with)* *(v.)*	run away with
39.	**Decorum** *(n.)*	proper behaviour as desirable
40.	**Dispel** *(v.)*	remove doubt, fear
41.	**Disperse** *(v.)*	scatter here and there
42.	**Docile** *(adj.)*	easily manageable, flexible
43.	**Delinquent** *(n.)*	one who does misdeeds
44.	**Dismal** *(adj.)*	bleak, gloomy
45	**Disinter** *(v.)*	dig up from grave, exhume

46. **Discrepancy** *(n.)* mistake, difference
47. **Deviant** *(n.)* a person different from customary character
48. **Delirious** *(adj.)* excited with (joy)
49. **Diligent** *(adj.)* hard working

E

1. **Erratic** *(adj.)* irregular in behaviour, movement
2. **Elephantine** *(adj.)* like an elephant
3. **Excerpt** *(n.)* an extract from a book or writing
4. **Etiquette** *(n.)* polite manners and behaviour
5. **Elite** *(n.)* considered to be superior in knowledge, wealth
6. **Epitome** *(n.)* personification
7. **Escapade** *(n.)* reckless act causing trouble, daring
8. **Expedite** *(v.)* hasten, speed up
9. **Emeritus** *(adj.)* retired but retained in honorary capacity
10. **Extrovert** *(n.)* person interested in outward things, cheerful
11. **Enjoin** *(v.)* command, order
12. **Explicit** *(adj.)* definite, expressed
13. **Evince** *(v.)* show, exhibit clearly
14. **Epicure** *(n.)* one devoted to sensuous pleasures
15. **Exotic** *(adj.)* foreign, not native, strange
16. **Exuberant** *(adj.)* luxuriant, overflowing, spirited
17. **Exude** *(v.)* emit, ooze out
18. **Eerie** *(adj.)* causing feeling of fear and mystery
19. **Effete** *(adj.)* tired, worn out
20. **Egalitarian** *(n.)* person believing in equal rights and benefits
21. **Effervescent** *(adj.)* enthusiastic, bubbly
22. **Eulogy** *(n.)* praise
23. **Exasperate** *(v.)* vex, irritate
24. **Eclat** *(n.)* brilliant, applause
25. **Entail** *(v.)* make necessary, impose (expense)
26. **Ebb** *(v.)* flow back, grow weak
27. **Exigent** *(adj.)* urgent, pressing
28. **Espouse** *(v.)* support a cause
29. **Evolve** *(v.)* develop gradually
30. **Erstwhile** *(adj.)* former
31. **Exhort** *(v.)* advise earnestly
32. **Empathy** *(n.)* sharing and understanding
33. **Encore** *(Int.)* repeat (a song, poem), once more
34. **Exculpate** *(v.)* to free from charge

35. **Exhume** *(v.)* disinter, to dig up from grave
36. **Exacerbate** *(v.)* aggravate, worsen
37. **Exorcist** *(n.)* one who drives out evil spirits
38. **Elevate** *(n.)* to raise, promote
39. **Echelon** *(n.)* step like formation, hierarchy (of ranks)
40. **Empirical** *(adj.)* based on observation and experiment
41. **Ensconce** *(v.)* establish oneself safely
42. **Euphoria** *(v.)* state of well being, elation
43. **Esoteric** *(adj.)* group of small circle of disciples
44. **Euphemism** *(n.)* use mild and vague words for what is actual
45. **Euphemism** *(n.)* artificial and ornate style
46. **Eavesdrop** *(v.)* listen secretly
47. **Ebullient** *(adj.)* enthusiastic, energetic
48. **Exaggerate** *(v.)* describe beyond truth
49. **Enervated** *(adj.)* exhausted, feeling weak
50. **Enigma** *(n.)* puzzle, riddle

1. **Fumble** *(v.)* to grope, to find
2. **Flamboyant** *(adj.)* florid, showy, ostentatious
3. **Facetious** *(adj.)* amusingly mocking, teasing
4. **Flay** *(v.)* criticise, strip off skin
5. **Fritter** *(v.)* waste, squander, sap
6. **Fanfare** *(n.)* loud exciting (music)
7. **Flourish** *(v.)* prosper, wave about, thrive
8. **Fluke** *(n.)* stroke of luck, fortunate accident
9. **Fiasco** *(n.)* failure
10. **Forte** *(n.)* strong or special talent
11. **Foster** *(v.)* encourage, rear
12. **Factuous** *(adj.)* belonging to a faction
13. **Flinch** *(v.)* hesitate, shrink
14. **Frolicsome** *(adj.)* prankish, gay
15. **Fester** *(v.)* generate pus
16. **Fortuitous** *(adj.)* happening by lucky chance
17. **Felony** *(n.)* serious crime
18. **Frailities** *(n.)* fault, moral weakness
19. **Fissiparous** *(adj.)* dividing, splitting
20. **Fraudulent** *(adj.)* deceitful
21. **Fugitive** *(n.)* a person running from justice, forces
22. **Fulmination** *(n.)* loud protest

23.	**Flabbergasted** *(adj.)*	amazed, surprised
24.	**Fervid** *(adj.)*	fervent, earnest feeling
25.	**Flip** *(adj.)*	reverse, on the flip side
26.	**Fervour** *(n.)*	warmth of feeling
27.	**Fillip** *(n.)*	incentive, encouragement
28.	**Fetish** *(n.)*	obsession about something
29.	**Flippant** *(adj.)*	disrespectful
30.	**Furbish** *(v.)*	polish, improve
31.	**Fetter** *(n.)*	chain
32.	**Finesse** *(n.)*	delicate way of dealing with people
33.	**Forbearance** *(n.)*	patience, self-control
34.	**Forthright** *(adj.)*	outspoken, candid
35.	**Fraternity** *(n.)*	fraternal (brotherly) feeling
36.	**Furore** *(n.)*	general uproar
37.	**Feline** *(adj.)*	like cat
38.	**Facade** *(n.)*	false appearance
39.	**Fatuous** *(adj.)*	foolish, stupid
40.	**Foe** *(n.)*	enemy
41.	**Frisk** *(v.)*	search a person, gambol

G

1.	**Gastronomy** *(n.)*	science of preparing and serving food
2.	**Gamut** *(n.)*	entire range
3.	**Grudge** *(v.)*	unwilling to allow, resent
4.	**Gambol** *(v.)*	playful jumping
5.	**Gambit** *(n.)*	opening in chess, first step
6.	**Genial** *(adj.)*	kindly, sociable
7.	**Gullible** *(adj.)*	credulous, easily deceived
8.	**Garbled** *(adj.)*	mixed up
9.	**Generic** *(adj.)*	common feature of a class
10.	**Gruff** *(adj.)*	rough
11.	**Garrulous** *(adj.)*	talkative, loquacious
12.	**Gauche** *(adj.)*	clumsy, awkward
13.	**Gabble** *(v.)*	talk fast
14.	**Germane** *(adj.)*	pertinent, relevant
15.	**Gadfly** *(n.)*	a fly that stings horses/cattle
16.	**Gadget** *(n.)*	device, contrivance
17.	**Gaffe** *(n.)*	blunder, unwise act/remark
18.	**Galore** *(adj.)*	in plenty
19.	**Goof** *(n.)*	stupid, silly
20.	**Gorgeous** *(adj.)*	beautiful and attractive

21. **Gratuitous** *(adj.)* done without reason or purpose, unnecessary
22. **Gaunt** *(adj.)* lean and thin
23. **Grill** *(v.)* close, severe interrogation
24. **Gallows** *(n.)* site for hanging criminals
25. **Genesis** *(n.)* beginning, starting point
26. **Gloss** *(n.)* smooth, bright, gloss over (cover-up)
27. **Gory** *(adj.)* bloody violent (details, incidents)
28. **Grievous** *(adj.)* causing grief, pain

H

1. **Handy** *(adj.)* useful, available
2. **Husbandry** *(n.)* agriculture, frugality
3. **Hectic** *(adj.)* exciting, without rest
4. **Hiccup** *(n.)* sudden stopping of breath with cough
5. **Hibernation** *(n.)* torpid state in winter
6. **Hiatus** *(n.)* break in continuity
7. **Heresy** *(n.)* contrary to religious concept
8. **Hideous** *(adj.)* ugly, horrible
9. **Hunch** *(n.)* intuition, feeling (likely to happen)
10. **Hortative** *(n.)* exhorting, encouraging
11. **Hirsute** *(adj.)* hairy, shaggy
12. **Hagiology** *(n.)* literature about the lives of the saints
13. **Hallow** *(v.)* make holy, sanctify
14. **Hallmark** *(n.)* mark of quality, distinguishing feature
15. **Hanky-panky** *(n.)* underhand dealing
16. **Heirloom** *(n.)* something handed down for generations
17. **Hassle** *(v.)* wrangle, argue
18. **Headstrong** *(adj.)* obstinate, stubborn
19. **Haul** *(n.)* something gained with effort
20. **Hearse** *(n.)* carriage for coffin
21. **Hedonism** *(n.)* belief that pleasure is the chief good
22. **Hollow** *(adj.)* empty with a space inside
23. **Heist** *(n.)* a robbery
24. **Hierarchy** *(n.)* organisation with grades/ranks
25. **Hue** *(n.)* a shade of colour
26. **Horrendous** *(adj.)* horrid, terrible
27. **Haunt** *(v.)* visit, return to mind frequently
28. **Hobnob** *(v.)* to have social relations
29. **Hamper** *(n.)* gift-pack
30. **Hitchhike** *(v.)* travel on free ride
31. **Haywire** *(adj.)* go astray, out of control

I

1.	**Impair** *(v.)*	worsen, damage
2.	**Impetuous** *(adj.)*	hasty, thoughtless
3.	**Impetus** *(n.)*	moving force
4.	**Improvise** *(v.)*	compose at the nick of time
5.	**Impromptu** *(Adv.)*	without preparation, arranged hastily, extempore
6.	**Impunity** *(n.)*	freedom from punishment, risk
7.	**Impugn** *(v.)*	challenge, doubtful statement
8.	**Inhibition** *(n.)*	habitual shrinking from action/impulse
9.	**Imbecility** *(n.)*	weakness, feebleness of mind
10.	**Inadvertent** *(adj.)*	oversight, done not on purpose
11.	**Incriminate** *(v.)*	involve, accuse
12.	**Inculcate** *(v.)*	teach
13.	**Inured** *(adj.)*	hardened, accustomed
14.	**Invidious** *(adj.)*	trying to create ill-will
15.	**Insinuate** *(v.)*	hint, imply
16.	**Insomnia** *(n.)*	inability to sleep, wakefulness
17.	**Inarticulate** *(adj.)*	cannot be heard clearly
18.	**Internecine** *(adj.)*	mutually destructive
19.	**Infringe** *(v.)*	violate, encroach
20.	**Insidious** *(adj.)*	treacherous
21.	**Infer** *(v.)*	deduce, conclude
22.	**Iota** *(n.)*	small quantity
23.	**Ineffable** *(adj.)*	Indescribable
24.	**Implicit** *(adj.)*	implied, not expressed
25.	**Incantation** *(n.)*	words chanted in magic or spell
26.	**Innuendo** *(n.)*	unfavourable reference to a person
27.	**Inebriation** *(n.)*	state of being drunk
28.	**Ilk***(n.)*	of family, type
29.	**Idiosyncrasy** *(n.)*	peculiar thinking of a person, eccentricity
30.	**Iveigle** *(v.)*	to trick somebody into
31.	**Infidel** *(n.)*	unbelieving in religion
32.	**Incest** *(n.)*	immoral relations with near relations
33.	**Infernal** *(adj.)*	of hell, devilish
34.	**Inferno** *(n.)*	hell
35.	**Iriscible** *(adj.)*	easily irritable
36.	**Immolation** *(n.)*	to kill by burning

J

1. **Junket** *(n.)* — excursion, feast, sweet pudding
2. **Jacose** *(adj.)* — disposed to jesting
3. **Juxtapose** *(v.)* — place side by side
4. **Jurisdiction** *(n.)* — extent of authority
5. **Jocular** *(adj.)* — said in jest
6. **Jarring** *(adj.)* — causing disharmony
7. **Jaunty** *(adj.)* — showing self-confidence
8. **Jettison** *(v.)* — throw over board to lighten
9. **Jitters** *(n.)* — nervousness
10. **Jostle** *(v.)* — push against someone
11. **Juggernut** *(n.)* — a belief for which one sacrifices oneself, large vehicle
12. **Juggle** *(v.)* — to play tricks
13. **Jabber** *(v.)* — speak rapidly, chatter

1. **Kaleidoscope** *(n.)* — frequent changing pattern of bright scenes
2. **Ken** *(n.)* — range of knowledge
3. **Kinky** *(adj.)* — eccentric, perverted
4. **Knead** *(v.)* — make dough with flour
5. **Knuckle** *(n.)* — joint of a finger
6. **Kow tow** *(v.)* — be obsequious

1. **Lupine** *(adj.)* — of wolf
2. **Leonine** *(adj.)* — of lion
3. **Loquacious** *(adj.)* — talkative, garrulous
4. **Libellous** *(adj.)* — defamatory
5. **Legitimate** *(adj.)* — reasonable, lawful
6. **Lewd** *(adj.)* — lustful
7. **Licentious** *(adj.)* — wanton, dissolute
8. **Languid** *(adj.)* — listless, effortless
9. **Latent** *(adj.)* — dormant, hidden
10. **Legion** *(n.)* — numerous, numberless
11. **Largesse** *(n.)* — generous financial help
12. **Lackey** *(n.)* — one who obeys without question
13. **Lecherous** *(adj.)* — lustful
14. **Locale** *(n.)* — scene of an event

15. **Lustre** *(n.)* brightness
16. **Lusty** *(adj.)* healthy, strong
17. **Languish** *(v.)* suffer and become weak
18. **Leeway** *(n.)* freedom to act and change
19. **Live-wire** *(adj.)* a person full of energy

M

1. **Maltreat** *(v.)* ill-treat
2. **Mercurial** *(v.)* fickle, changing
3. **Mayhem** *(n.)* state of violent disorder, havoc
4. **Magnanimous** *(adj.)* generous, liberal
5. **Medley** *(n.)* mixture of things, persons of different sorts
6. **Mirage** *(n.)* unreal reflection
7. **Misapprehension** *(n.)* misunderstanding, error
8. **Mete** *(v.)* distribute, deal out
9. **Misgiving** *(n.)* distrust, suspicion
10. **Mendicant** *(n.)* beggar
11. **Moribund** *(adj.)* at the point of death
12. **Mortify** *(v.)* to be humiliated, ashamed
13. **Milieu** *(n.)* social surroundings, environment
14. **Moratoriun** *(n.)* deferment, delay
15. **Millennium** *(n.)* period of one thousand years
16. **Mealy mouthed** *(adj.)* insincere, evasive
17. **Muzzle** *(n.)* the nose and mouth of an animal
18. **Mutilate** *(v.)* cut off, disfigure (limb of a body)
19. **Munificent** *(adj.)* generous, liberal
20. **Multitude** *(n.)* large number of people, masses
21. **Muddle** *(v.)* confuse, perplex
22. **Motley** *(adj.)* of various colours
23. **Malaise** *(n.)* feeling of physical discomfort
24. **Malediction** *(n.)* curse, bane
25. **Manicure** *(n.)* care of hands and nails
26. **Manoeuvre** *(n.)* planned movement (armed forces) to deceive
27. **Maroon** *(v.)* deserted on uninhabited land
28. **Massacre** *(n.)* carnage, murder on large scale
29. **Materialise** *(v.)* bring about result
30. **Miniature** *(n.)* small-scale copy, model
31. **Misdemeanour** *(n.)* offence
32. **Metamorphosis** *(n.)* natural change in form
33. **Mellifluous** *(adj.)* sweet sounding

34. **Mongrel** *(n.)* mixed breed (of dog, plant, animal)
35. **Monarch** *(n.)* supreme ruler (king or queen)
36. **Maverick** *(n.)* dissenting, unorthodox
37. **Meliorist** *(n.)* one who believes in the betterment of mankind
38. **Matinee** *(n.)* afternoon show
39. **Maudlin** *(n.)* self pitying, sentimental
40. **Malice** *(n.)* ill-will

N

1. **Niggardly** *(adj.)* stingy, miserly
2. **Nuance** *(n.)* delicate difference in meaning
3. **Nostrum** *(n.)* not real but quack remedy
4. **Niche** *(n.)* suitable situation, recess in a wall
5. **Nee** *(adj.)* name used after the name of married woman and before her father's family name
6. **Nitty gritty** *(n.)* basic facts of a matter
7. **Naiveti** *(n.)* naivety, artlessness

O

1. **Olfactory** *(adj.)* relating to the sense of smell
2. **Obdurate** *(adj.)* stubborn, unpertinent
3. **Obeisance** *(n.)* respectful homage
4. **Onus** *(n.)* burden, responsibility
5. **Orifice** *(n.)* opening into cavity
6. **Obsolescent** *(adj.)* discarded, absolete
7. **Ominous** *(adj.)* of bad omen, threatening
8. **Obsequious** *(adj.)* servile, excessively respectful
9. **Opprobrious** *(adj.)* expressing scorn, abusive
10. **Officious** *(adj.)* meddlesome, trying to please
11. **Orgy** *(n.)* wild merry making, licentous, drunken
12. **Ocular** *(adj.)* of eye
13. **Obscene** *(adj.)* indecent, immoral, depraved
14. **Ombudsman** *(n.)* an authority to look into public grievances
15. **Onslaught** *(n.)* furious attack
16. **Ovation** *(n.)* enthusiastic welcome/approval
17. **Over-ride** *(v.)* prevail over decision

P

1.	**Porcine** *(adj.)*	relating to pig
2.	**Piscinine** *(adj.)*	relating to fish
3.	**Peristeronic** *(adj.)*	relating to pigeon
4.	**Pre-empt** *(v.)*	prevent before hand
5.	**Proselytize** *(v.)*	convert to a religion or belief
6.	**Panegyric** *(n.)*	a discourse in praise
7.	**Peculate** *(v.)*	embezzle, misappropriate
8.	**Permeable** *(adj.)*	through which substance can pass
9.	**Pontificate** *(v.)*	speak like a priest
10.	**Puissant** *(adj.)*	powerful
11.	**Precipitate** *(v.)*	hasten
12.	**Plausible** *(adj.)*	open to doubt but appearing to be truthful
13.	**Polemic** *(n.)*	controversy, argument in support
14.	**Paean** *(n.)*	song of praise
15.	**Platitude** *(n.)*	trite remark
16.	**Peevish** *(adj.)*	fretful
17.	**Periphery** *(n.)*	external boundary
18.	**Profligate** *(adj.)*	immortal
19.	**Prodigious** *(adj.)*	extremely great in ability, amount or strength
20.	**Pornography** *(n.)*	obscenity in writing/art
21.	**Probity** *(n.)*	honesty, uprightness
22.	**Presentiment** *(n.)*	premonition, foreboding
23.	**Progeny** *(n.)*	children, offspring
24.	**Propensity** *(n.)*	natural inclination
25.	**Procrastinate** *(v.)*	postpone, delay
26.	**Promiscuous** *(adj.)*	mix indiscriminately, immoral
27.	**Punctilious** *(adj.)*	stress on nicety of form/conduct
28.	**Plethora** *(n.)*	excess, abundance
29.	**Politic** *(adj.)*	prudent, expedient
30.	**Portent** *(n.)*	forewarning, omens
31.	**Precept** *(n.)*	practical rule guiding conduct
32.	**Punitive** *(adj.)*	punishing
33.	**Puny** *(adj.)*	insignificant, tiny
34.	**Palliate** *(v.)*	lessen the gravity
35.	**Prostrate** *(v.)*	stretch fully on ground
36.	**Parley** *(n.)*	conference
37.	**Proponent** *(n.)*	one who supports an idea
38.	**Perfidy** *(n.)*	violation of a trust
39.	**Parlance** *(n.)*	language, terminology
40.	**Pelf** *(n.)*	money, wealth

41. **Prefunctory** *(adj.)* not thorough, superficial
42. **Parry** *(v.)* ward off a blow
43. **Patent** *(adj.)* obvious, open
44. **Panorama** *(n.)* a comprehensive view
45. **Placebo** *(n.)* medicine given to soothe, not to cure
46. **Pilfer** *(v.)* steal in small quantity
47. **Pillion** *(n.)* seat behind a rider/driver
48. **Paranoid** *(adj.)* extremely worried about being harmed
49. **Profile** *(n.)* image, side view, brief biography
50. **Partisan** (n./adj.) a person uncritically devoted to a party or group
51. **Peremptory** *(adj.)* obligatory, mandatory
52. **Pejorative** *(adj.)* disparaging, belittling
53. **Petulant** *(adj.)* impatient, irritable
54. **Palpable** *(adj.)* obvious, that can be felt or touched
55. **Penultimate** *(adj.)* the one before the last
56. **Pretext** *(n.)* excuse, false reason
57. **Panache** *(n.)* confident manner
58. **Ploy** *(n.)* manoeuvre to take advantage
59. **Precincts** *(n.)* space enclosed by wall
60. **Paroxysm** *(n.)* sudden outburst of pain, anger
61. **Perpetrate** *(v.)* to commit crime
62. **Pedigree** *(n.)* the parents and other past family members of an animal or person
63. **Presage** *(n.)* presentiment, sign of impending event
64. **Passe** *(adj.)* obsolete, not in vogue
65. **Prowess** *(n.)* valour, bravery
66. **Pertain** *(v.)* belong as a part
67. **Peccadillo** *(n.)* small sin, fault
68. **Pedlar** *(n.)* peddler, one who travels about selling small things
69. **Plummet** *(v.)* fall, plunge steepily
70. **Prognosis** *(n.)* forecast of disease, trouble
71. **Profilerate** *(v.)* grow, multiply
72. **Prevaricate** *(v.)* to waver to tell the truth
73. **Petrify** *(v.)* to turn into stone, stun
74. **Parole** *(n.)* free a prisoner on undertaking not to escape
75. **Propitious** *(adj.)* favourable, good omen
76. **Postulate** *(v.)* to demand, taken for granted
77. **Paradigm** *(n.)* pattern, example
78. **Providence** *(n.)* working of divine, thrift
79. **Perseverance** *(n.)* constant, steadfast efforts
80. **Pandemic** *(n.)* a disease that spreads over a large area
81. **Propinquity** *(n.)* state of being near

Q

1. **Quagmire** *(n.)* soft, wet, marshy land
2. **Quail** *(v.)* show fear, tremble
3. **Quibble** *(v.)* avoid an answer, equivocate
4. **Quietus** *(v.)* final settlement of debt, the death of a person
5. **Quake** *(v.)* shake, tremble
6. **Quaint** *(adj.)* attractive (for being old-fashioned)
7. **Quantum** *(n.)* the smallest amount or unit of something
8. **Quaff** *(v.)* drink, enjoy drinking

R

1. **Reminiscence** *(n.)* recollection
2. **Revulsion** *(n.)* sudden change/reaction of feelings
3. **Renovate** *(n.)* renew, restore to new condition
4. **Retribution** *(n.)* vengeance, punishment
5. **Revelry** *(n.)* boisterous merry making
6. **Recourse** *(n.)* resort to as means
7. **Reimbursement** *(n.)* repayment of expenses
8. **Rejuvenate** *(v.)* make young and strong again
9. **Respite** *(n.)* interval of relief
10. **Revamp** *(v.)* construct, change
11. **Resurgent** *(adj.)* rising again after defeat
12. **Rote** *(n.)* repetition
13. **Rummage** *(v.)* ransack, search thoroughly
14. **Residue** *(n.)* remainder, balance
15. **Rabble** *(n.)* group of vulgar people
16. **Raillery** *(n.)* sarcasm, act of finding fault
17. **Recalcitrant** *(adj.)* stubborn, disobedient
18. **Resilient** *(adj.)* elastic buoyant nature
19. **Rabid** *(adj.)* furious, rabid dog
20. **Rendition** *(n.)* translation, artistic interpretation
21. **Resort** *(v.)* turn for help, frequently visit
    (n.) a place for pleasure making
22. **Resonant** *(adj.)* resounding, re-echo
23. **Rectitude** *(n.)* moral uprightness, righteousness
24. **Redolent** *(adj.)* reminiscent of past (smell, taste)
25. **Reconnaissance** *(n.)* act of surveying enemy positions
26. **Rumpus** *(n.)* uproar, noise
27. **Repast** *(n.)* meal, food

28.	**Relish** *(n.)*	liking, taste for food
29.	**Refute** *(v.)*	counter, prove wrong
30.	**Relentless** *(adj.)*	unyielding, pitiless
31.	**Recede** *(v.)*	to go back
32.	**Reprehensible** *(adj.)*	deserving condemnation
33.	**Refulgent** *(adj.)*	shining, brilliant
34.	**Resplendent** *(adj.)*	splendidly bright
35.	**Renege** *(on) (v.)*	fail to keep word
36.	**Resuscitate** *(v.)*	regain consciousness
37.	**Rigorous** *(adj.)*	severe, harsh
38.	**Ruckus** *(n.)*	exchange of angry words, protest
39.	**Ravenous** *(adj.)*	very hungry, greedy
40.	**Recipe** *(n.)*	direction, formula for preparing food
41.	**Recapitulate** *(v.)*	to repeat, go through again
42.	**Restitution** *(n.)*	restoring right, property
43.	**Retrench** *(v.)*	cut down expenses, staff
44.	**Resurrection** *(n.)*	coming to life again
45.	**Rigmarole** *(n.)*	wandering story, confusing procedure
46.	**Rue** *(v.)*	repent of, regret
47.	**Reciprocal** *(adj.)*	mutual
48.	**Rave** (about) *(v.)*	write enthusiastically
	(n.)	party (with drugs)

S

1.	**Simian** *(adj.)*	of monkey, ape
2.	**Serpentine** *(adj.)*	of serpent
3.	**Servile** (menial) *(adj.)*	of servant
4.	**Sacredotal** *(adj.)*	of priest
5.	**Salacious** *(adj.)*	anything obscene, indecent
6.	**Sardonic** *(adj.)*	disdainful, sarcastic
7.	**Scuttle** *(v.)*	subvert, sink
8.	**Sedate** *(adj.)*	calm, composed
9.	**Sojourn** *(n.)*	temporary stay
10.	**Sceptic** *(n.)*	one who doubts the truth, claim, theory
11.	**Seduce** *(v.)*	lure to do wrong, tempt
12.	**Scurrilous** *(adj.)*	taunting, abusive
13.	**Sundry** *(adj.)*	various, several
14.	**Sedition** *(n.)*	rebellion against government
15.	**Spate** *(n.)*	sudden flood, rise in business
16.	**Stalemate** *(n.)*	deadlock, impasse

17.	**Stalwart** *(n.)*	strong, steadfast
18.	**Secession** *(n.)*	act of seceding, withdrawal
19.	**Stoic** *(n.)*	one who is indifferent to pain or pleasure
20.	**Squalid** *(adj.)*	dirty, neglected condition
21.	**Solace** *(n.)*	comfort in trouble
22.	**Synchronise** *(v.)*	simultaneous with
23.	**Shirk** *(v.)*	avoid doing duty
24.	**Swelter** *(v.)*	oppressed with heat
25.	**Solicit** *(v.)*	ask for, request earnestly
26.	**Solicitous** *(adj.)*	concerned, worried about
27.	**Skullduggery** *(n.)*	cheating, deception
28.	**Savant**	a person of great learning
29.	**Savvy** *(n.)*	understanding, having common sense
30.	**Syndrome** *(n.)*	collective number of symptoms
31.	**Sleuth** *(n.)*	detective, a dog following a scent
32.	**Sanguine** *(adj.)*	cheerful, hopeful
33.	**Simulate** *(v.)*	pretend
34.	**Suave** *(adj.)*	smooth, gracious
35.	**Strident** *(n.)*	(of sound) shrill, harsh
36.	**Segregation** *(n.)*	isolate, separate
37.	**Sleazy** *(adj.)*	uncared for, dirty
38.	**Safari** *(n.)*	hunting expedition
39.	**Sabotage** *(v.)*	act of saboteur, to damage
40.	**Souvenir** *(n.)*	something as gift, taken in memory of
41.	**Shoddy** *(v.)*	rough, poor quality
42.	**Succinct** *(adj.)*	brief, terse but clear
43.	**Sabbatical** *(adj.)*	of sabbath, holiday (Sunday)
44.	**Sibling** *(adj.)*	having same parents, sister, brother
45.	**Spurt** *(v.)*	sudden outburst
46.	**Serenade** (music) *(n.)*	to sing to somebody
47.	**Serendipty** *(n.)*	fortunate, unexpected, discovery
48.	**Spree** *(n.)*	merrytime, lively
49.	**Spendthrift** *(n.)*	an extravagant person
50.	**Snub** *(v.)*	treat with contempt
51.	**Susceptible** *(adj.)*	easily influenced, affected
52.	**Snide** *(adj.)*	slyly critical, sneering
53.	**Snob** *(n.)*	one who is obsessed with social position
54.	**Squabble** *(n.)*	noisy petty quarrel
55.	**Squall** *(n.)*	sudden violent storm
56.	**Salubrious** *(adj.)*	salutary, healthful
57.	**Strand** *(v.)*	to be left without means of transport, money

58. **Sobriquet** *(n.)* nickname
59. **Sachet** *(n.)* a small packet
60. **Shibboleth** *(n.)* an old idea or custom, distinguishing
61. **Saturate** *(v.)* filled completely with no scope for addition

T

1. **Tonsorial** *(adj.)* of barber
2. **Tenable** *(adj.)* defensible by argument
3. **Transpire** *(v.)* become known, happen
4. **Tandem** *(n.)* one behind the other, in pair
5. **Tawdry** *(adj.)* showing, bright (in bad taste)
6. **Tentative** *(adj.)* done as a trial, experimental
7. **Tautological** *(adj.)* needless repetition
8. **Tamper** *(v.)* meddle with
9. **Tardy** *(adj.)* slow, sluggish
10. **Tarnish** *(v.)* make dull, spoil
11. **Temerity** *(adj.)* boldness, audacity
12. **Transulent** *(adj.)* transparent but partly
13. **Tantalise** *(v.)* raise hope but with obstacle
14. **Throes** *(n.)* violent pain (middle of activity)
15. **Tangible** *(adj.)* real, perceivable by touch
16. **Torpid** *(adj.)* lethargic, dormant
17. **Tantrum** *(n.)* fit of bad temper, petulance
18. **Transient** *(adj.)* short lived, fleeting
19. **Tendentious** *(adj.)* partial with a purpose
20. **Tenor** *(n.)* general routine
21. **Thespian** *(n.)* actor/actress
22. **Trenchant** *(adj.)* sharp, incisive
23. **Truculant** *(adj.)* savage, aggressive
24. **Trice** *(n.)* instant
25. **Turgid** *(adj.)* overflowing, swollen
26. **Truant** *(n.)* wandering, shirker, absence
27. **Tripartite** *(adj.)* of three parties
28. **Tyranny** *(n.)* unjust, cruel use of power
29. **Trove** *(n.)* treasure
30. **Twinge** *(n.)* a sudden sharp pain
31. **Tussle** *(n.)* struggle, conflict
32. **Turbid** *(adj.)* muddy, not clear
33. **Trounce** *(v.)* thrash, defeat
34. **Turbulent** *(adj.)* violent, uncontrolled

35. **Thrive** *(v.)* prosper, flourish
36. **Turmoil** *(n.)* trouble, violent agitation
37. **Turpitude** *(n.)* wickedness, depravity
38. **Tumult** *(n.)* uproar, disturbance
39. **Tumble** *(v.)* fall suddenly, collapse
40. **Trudge** *(v.)* walk wearily
41. **Temperance** *(n.)* moderation (eating and drinking)
42. **Temporise** *(v.)* delay in making a decision
43. **Thorough-bred** *(adj.)* thoroughly trained, of pure breed
44. **Tinsel** *(adj.)* glitter, superficial
45. **Topple** *(v.)* overturn
46. **Topsy turvy** *(adj.)* confusion, upside down
47. **Torrid** *(adj.)* hot, tropical
48. **Treason** *(n.)* betrayal of one's country
49. **Thesaurus** *(n.)* treasury of similar words, grouped together
50. **Tango** *(n.)* American dance with marked rhythm
51. **Traverse** *(v.)* travel across
52. **Termagant** *(n.)* a shrew, a quarrelsome woman

1. **Untoward** *(adj.)* unfortunate, unfavourable
2. **Usher** *(n.)* herald, announce
3. **Umpteen** *(adj.)* many times
4. **Unassuming** *(adj.)* shy, modest
5. **Unbecoming** *(adj.)* not suited to, not befitting
6. **Unctuous** *(adj.)* insincere, flattering
7. **Undaunted** *(adj.)* not daunted, fearless
8. **Under-hand** *(adj.)* sly, deceitful
9. **Undermine** *(v.)* weaken, lessen
10. **Underdog** *(n.)* poor and helpless
11. **Undertake** *(v.)* agree, start, promise
12. **Unerring** *(adj.)* accurate, faultless
13. **Unflagging** *(v.)* uninterrupted, untiring
14. **Unflinching** *(adj.)* fearless, resolute
15. **Unleash** *(v.)* release, set into action
16. **Unobtrusive** *(adj.)* not easily visible or noticeable
17. **Unravel** *(v.)* expose, clarify
18. **Unrelenting** *(adj.)* relentless, unyielding
19. **Unrequited** *(adj.)* unrewarded, not returned
20. **Unreservedly** *(adj.)* without restrictions/reservation

21.	**Unruffled** *(adj.)*	unperturbed, not upset
22.	**Unscathed** *(adj.)*	unharmed, unhurt
23.	**Unswerving** *(adj.)*	not changing
24.	**Unwieldy** *(adj.)*	awkward due to shape or size
25.	**Unwind** *(n.)*	relax after tension
26.	**Unsparing** *(adj.)*	liberal, not withholding
27.	**Unfazed** *(adj.)*	unperturbed
28.	**Uproar** *(n.)*	outburst of excitement, noise
29.	**Uprising** *(n.)*	rebellion, revolt
30.	**Upshot** *(n.)*	conclusion, outcome
31.	**Upheaval** *(n.)*	sudden change on a large scale
32.	**Unflappable** *(adj.)*	unperturbed, calm
33.	**Unmitigated** *(adj.)*	thorough, complete
34.	**Uncanny** *(adj.)*	mysterious, surpernatural
35.	**Upstage** (adv./adj.)	divert attention/direction
36.	**Urchin** *(n.)*	mischievous street boy
37.	**Urbane** *(adj.)*	polished, refined in manners

V

1.	**Vigilant** *(adj.)*	watchful, cautious
2.	**Vicissitude** *(n.)*	change of fortune, ups and downs
3.	**Valetudinarian** *(adj.)*	obsession about health
4.	**Vanquish** *(v.)*	defeat, subjugate
5.	**Valiant** *(adj.)*	brave, dauntless
6.	**Vainglorious** *(adj.)*	proud, conceited
7.	**Valour** *(n.)*	bravery, fortitude
8.	**Valedictory** *(adj.)*	of farewell
9.	**Vapid** *(adj.)*	dull, boring
10.	**Vicarious** *(adj.)*	feel pleasure from the acts of others
11.	**Vibes** *(n.)*	(vibrating) a mood or an atmosphere produced by a person or a thing
12.	**Variegated** *(adj.)*	multicoloured
13.	**Vanguard** *(n.)*	pioneer, forerunner
14.	**Vaunt** *(v.)*	boast, show off
15.	**Versimilitude** *(n.)*	resemblance of truth, appearing to be true
16.	**Veneer** *(n.)*	thin layer, outward appearance
17.	**Voluble** *(adj.)*	glib, fluent (speaker)
18.	**Voluptuous** *(adj.)*	sensual, of exciting senses
19.	**Volatile** *(adj.)*	of changing, unstable disposition
20.	**Vulpine** *(adj.)*	of fox, crafty

21.	**Vouchsafe** *(v.)*	guarantee, kind to give
22.	**Void** *(adj.)*	vacant, empty
23.	**Verve** *(n.)*	zest, spirit
24.	**Virile** *(adj.)*	of manly strength and energy
25.	**Verdant** *(adj.)*	green, fresh
26.	**Virtuoso** *(n.)*	highly skilled artist, musician
27.	**Veritable** *(adj.)*	real, rightly called
28.	**Virulent** *(adj.)*	bitter, poisonous
29.	**Version** *(n.)*	account of; interpretation of an event
30.	**Vis-a-vis** *(adv.)*	opposite, compared with
31.	**Virago** *(n.)*	shrew, ill-tempered woman
32.	**Vestige** *(n.)*	remains, traces
33.	**Visage** *(n.)*	appearance, face
34.	**Vertigo** *(n.)*	giddiness
35.	**Vituperative** *(adj.)*	abusive, scolding
36.	**Volition** *(n.)*	power of using of will, choice
37.	**Votary** *(n.)*	follower, devoted to a cause
38.	**Vista** *(n.)*	series of scenes, a view from distance
39.	**Vestal** *(adj.)*	pure, chaste, virginal
40.	**Valediction** *(n.)*	farewell, parting
41.	**Valentine** *(n.)*	letter/card sent to a sweetheart (anonymously)(St. Valentine Day-14th February)
42.	**Vignettes** *(n.)*	short sketch of a person, character, ornamental, design of title of the book
43.	**Vitriolic** *(adj.)*	biting, full of invective
44.	**Vibrant** *(adj.)*	thrilling, lively
45.	**Voyeuristic** *(adj.)*	pertaining to looking at lustful objects
46.	**Vigorous** *(n.)*	strong, full of vigour
47.	**Vamp** *(n.)*	female villain
48.	**Vicinity** *(adj.)*	neighbourhood, nearness in relations
49.	**Vague** *(adj.)*	not clearly expressed
50.	**Vandalism** *(n.)*	an act of destroying public property

W

1.	**Wheedle** *(v.)*	coax, cajole
2.	**Wade** *(v.)*	walk through water or mud
3.	**Wizard** *(n.)*	magician, one having amazing ability
4.	**Wager** *(v.)*	bet
5.	**Wily** *(adj.)*	cunning
6.	**Wanderlust** *(n.)*	having a strong desire to travel

7. **Weird** *(adj.)* unnatural, unearthly
8. **Wretched** *(adj.)* poor, miserable
9. **Whereabouts** *(n.)* place of residence, staying place
10. **Whittle** *(v.)* reduce, dwindle
11. **Whet** *(v.)* sharpen as knife
12. **Withstand** *(v.)* resist, hold out
13. **Wrangle** *(v.)* argue angrily
14. **Wince** *(v.)* show physical or mental pain
15. **Winsome** *(adj.)* attractive, pleasing
16. **Woo** *(v.)* court a woman, try to win
17. **Winnow** *(v.)* separate grain from husk
18. **Wistful** *(adj.)* sad and longing
19. **Wry** *(adj.)* forced, disappointed (smile)
20. **Woeful** *(adj.)* miserable, distressful
21. **Woebegone** *(adj.)* dismal, showing distress
22. **Wreath** *(n.)* garland of flowers
23. **Waif** *(n.)* homeless child
24. **Wherewithal** *(n.)* the money needed for a particular purpose
25. **Wholesome** *(adj.)* promoting good health
26. **Ware** *(n.)* manufactured goods

X

1. **X-Mas** *(n.)* observation of Christmas

Y

1. **Yokel** *(n.)* naive countryman
2. **Yearling** *(n.)* young animal

Z

1. **Zany** *(n.)* clown
2. **Zippy** *(adj.)* lively, brisk

4

Synonyms and Antonyms

Against each KEYWORD are given the lists of Synonyms and Antonyms separately. A student is required to study the words given in the list carefully. These words will add to the Theasurus comprising words and phrases that they have already learnt. If need be, they may look up a word in the dictionary for correct reference.

AWKWARD
Syn: clumsy, ungainly, ponderous, rough
Ant: clever, dexterous, apt, skilful

APPARENT
Syn: evident, obvious, perceptible, distinct
Ant: masked, obscure, indistinct, doubtful

ALLURE
Syn: entice, fascinate, tempt, seduce
Ant: repulse, repel, deter, distaste

ABORTIVE
Syn: vain, useless, fruitless, unproductive
Ant: effectual, productive, successful, progressive

ABOMINABLE
Syn: odious, detestable, repugnant, loathsome
Ant: likeable, pleasant, affectionate, enjoyable

ALLAY
Syn: pacify, soothe, lighten, assuage
Ant: aggravate, heighten, agitate, excite

AXIOM
Syn: maxim, saying, dictum, truth
Ant: absurdity, blunder, ridiculousness, irrelevant

ASSIDUOUS
Syn: constant, diligent, attentive, persevering
Ant: indifference, careless, indolent, lethargic

ABJURE
Syn: forsake, renounce, retract, revoke
Ant: approve, sanction, patronise, adopt

ABJECT
Syn: despicable, servile, base, contemptible
Ant: exalted, commendable, praiseworthy, imposing

AVERSION
Syn: dislike, hatred, indifferent, apathy
Ant: affection, fondness, niceness, liking

AUTHENTIC
Syn: genuine, reliable, valid, guaranteed
Ant: fictitious, counterfeit, unreal, false

AUDACITY
Syn: boldness, arrogance, insolence, haughtiness
Ant: mildness, humility, cowardice, submission

ASTUTE
Syn: clever, intelligent, wise, brilliant
Ant: dull, unintelligent, shallow, solid

ABETTOR
Syn: assistant, accomplice, colleague, associate
Ant: opponent, adversary, antagonist, rival

ABATE
Syn: moderate, mitigate, lessen, decrease
Ant: aggravate, intensify, augment, supplement

ARRAIGN
Syn: charge, blame, accuse, complain
Ant: exculpate, pardon, condone, exonerate

APATHY
Syn: unconcern, indifference, insensitivity, aloofness
Ant: concern, care, anxiety, eagerness

ALIEN
Syn: foreigner, outsider, stranger, emigrant
Ant: native, citizen, resident, occupant

ALACRITY
Syn: swiftness, briskness, promptness, speed
Ant: laziness, sluggishness, indolence, lethargy

AFFRONT
Syn: provoke, exasperate, indignity, irreverence
Ant: conciliate, appease, mollify, assuage

ADVERSITY
Syn: misfortune, calamity, misery, affliction
Ant: prosperity, fortune, assistance, favour

ANTIQUE
Syn: ancient, old fashioned, primitive, of past
Ant: modern, recent, novelty, vogue

ANTIPATHY
Syn: hostility, aversion, disillusion, dislike
Ant: admiration, approval, fascination, devotion

AMPLIFY
Syn: enlarge, extend, dilation, elevate
Ant: curtail, lessen, diminution, contraction

AMASS
Syn: gather, accumulate, store, collect
Ant: disperse, dissipate, spend, scatter

ALLEVIATE
Syn: abate, relieve, mitigate, lessen
Ant: intensify, augment, aggravate, enhance

ADMONISH
Syn: counsel, reprove, warn, chastise
Ant: approve, applaud, praise, flattery

ADJACENT
Syn: adjoining, beside, proximity, closeness
Ant: distant, separate, remoteness, aloofness

ADHERENT
Syn: follower, disciple, dependent, supporter
Ant: rival, adversary, opponent, antagonist

ACCOMPLISH
Syn: attain, succeed, triumph, exploit
Ant: forsake, deter, disappoint, collapse

ABSOLVE
Syn: pardon, forgive, reprieve, relent
Ant: compel, accuse, charge, bind

ACRIMONY
Syn: harshness, bitterness, inhumanity, enmity
Ant: sweetness, courtesy, humanity, benevolence

ACCUMULATION
Syn: store, amass, preservation, conservation
Ant: scattering, dissipation, separation, division

ACCORD
Syn: agreement, harmony, consonance, unison
Ant: disagreement, denial, controversy, discord

ABOUND
Syn: flourish, swell, teem, plentiful
Ant: deficient, destitute, want, scarce

ADAMANT
Syn: stubborn, obdurate, inflexible, rigid
Ant: flexible, soft, suppleness, tender

ABASH
Syn: discourage, confound, embarrass, discompose
Ant: encourage, uphold, embolden, hearten

ADJUNCT
Syn: appendage, complement, addition, joining
Ant: lessening, separation, subtraction, removal

ADROIT
Syn: proficient, expert, skilful, adept
Ant: inept, clumsy, unskilled, awkward

BUSTLE
Syn: haste, tumult, stir, flurry
Ant: slowness, sluggishness, quiet, inertness

BRITTLE
Syn: frail, fragile, delicate, breakable
Ant: tough, enduring, unbreakable, strong

BLEMISH
Syn: fault, smirch, stigma, stain
Ant: purity, impeccable, spotless, stainless

BLEAK
Syn: dismal, gloomy, chilly, dreary
Ant: bright, pleasant, balmy, cheerful

BLAME
Syn: reprove, upbraid, censure, reproach
Ant: commend, applaud, laud, praise

BENEVOLENCE
Syn: humanity, generosity, charity, liberality
Ant: malevolence, inhumanity, malignity, unkindness

BARBAROUS
Syn: uncivilized, savage, untamed, brutal
Ant: cultured, humane, refined, gentle

BAFFLE
Syn: confound, elude, frustrate, perplex
Ant: poise, composure, facilitate, co-operate

BEWITCHING
Syn: magical, fascinating, tantalising, spellbinding
Ant: repulsive, repugnant, nauseating, disgusting

CRITERION
Syn: measurement, test, standard, touchstone
Ant: fancy, probability, haphazard, conjecture

COVETOUS
Syn: cupidity, avarice, greed, voracity
Ant: liberality, benevolence, selfless, magnanimous

CORPULENT
Syn: obese, ugly, fat, awkward
Ant: thin, lean, slim, delicate

CONVERT
Syn: change, transform, transmute, proselytise
Ant: persist, maintain, enduring, perpetual

CONVENIENT
Syn: handy, suited, comfortable, advantageous
Ant: unsuitable, tedious, unpractical, fatiguing

CONTRARY
Syn: dissimilar, conflicting, contradictory, opposite
Ant: similar, alike, homogeneous, resembling

CONTRADICT
Syn: impugn, deny, oppose, confront
Ant: approve, confirm, sanction, endorse

CONTEMPT
Syn: scorn, disregard, disdain, despicable
Ant: regard, approval, praise, recommend

CONSTERNATION
Syn: fear, disappointment, dismay, hopelessness
Ant: peace, repose, calm, fearless

CONSPICUOUS
Syn: distinguished, prominent, obvious, visible
Ant: concealed, obscure, hidden, unapparent

CONSOLIDATE
Syn: combine, condense, compact, strong
Ant: separate, sever, weak, scattering

CONSEQUENCE
Syn: effect, outcome, repercussion, result
Ant: origin, start, beginning, incipient

CONSENT
Syn: agree, permit, accede, assent
Ant: object, disagree, dissent, differ

CONSCIOUS
Syn: aware, apprised, knowledge, informed
Ant: unaware, ignorant, unfeeling, faint

CONCEDE
Syn: yield, assent, permit, sanction
Ant: deny, reject, dissent, disallow

COMPRISE
Syn: include, contain, consist, compose
Ant: reject, lack, exclude, except

COMPASSION
Syn: kindness, sympathy, clemency, commiseration
Ant: cruelty, barbarity, persecution, apathy

CONCUR
Syn: approve, agree, consent, endorse
Ant: differ, disagree, dissent, oppose

COMMODIOUS
Syn: convenient, suitable, roomy, comfortable
Ant: inconvenient, unsuitable, uncomfortable, confined

COLLISION
Syn: encounter, clash, conflict, dissenting
Ant: agreement, harmony, compatible, union

CHERISH
Syn: nurture, treasure, foster, encourage
Ant: abandon, forsake, renounce, discard

CHASTISE
Syn: punish, admonish, scold, reprove
Ant: cheer, comfort, encourage, stimulate

CHASTE
Syn: virtuous, pure, honourable, immaculate
Ant: defiled, licentious, sullied, lustful

CESSATION
Syn: intermission, pause, discontinuity, hindrance
Ant: continuity, perpetuation, unceasing, prolongation

CATASTROPHE
Syn: disaster, calamity, misfortune, mishap
Ant: prosperity, blessing, restoration, resurgence

CARICATURE
Syn: exaggeration, imitation, ridicule, parody
Ant: exactness, precision, reality, truth

CARESS
Syn: fondle, embrace, hug, snuggle
Ant: repulse, spurn, displease, repel

CAPTIVITY
Syn: imprisonment, confinement, apprehend, restrain
Ant: freedom, liberty, liberation, release

CAPTIVATE
Syn: charm, fascinate, enchant, lure
Ant: disillusion, offend, scorn, despise

CAPTIOUS
Syn: irritate, fretful, critical, carping
Ant: appreciative, considerate, laudatory, thoughtful

CAPABLE
Syn: competent, suitable, qualified, able
Ant: incompetent, inefficient, imbecile, inept

CALUMNY
Syn: defamation, aspersion, accusation, libel
Ant: commendation, praise, vindication, goodwill

CALLOUS
Syn: obdurate, unfeeling, heartless, indifferent
Ant: compassionate, tender, kind, sympathetic

CALCULATE
Syn: enumerate, estimate, evaluate, consider
Ant: miscalculate, blunder, predetermine, misconceive

CALAMITY
Syn: adversity, misfortune, misery, mishap
Ant: happiness, benefit, prosperity, fortune

CAVITY
Syn: depth, depression, hole, aperture
Ant: elevation, projection, mound, height

CEASE
Syn: terminate, pause, desist, discontinue
Ant: commence, continue, initiate, originate

CIRCUMLOCUTION
Syn: redundancy, verbosity, tediousness, verbiage
Ant: terseness, compression, directness, brevity

COMMOTION
Syn: turmoil, disturbance, agitation, excitement
Ant: tranquility, stillness, quietness, calm

DISASTER
Syn: misfortune, calamity, mishap, catastrophe
Ant: prosperity, boon, happiness, auspicious

DESPICABLE
Syn: contemptible, worthless, shameless, base
Ant: worthy, decent, honourable, respectable

DISDAIN
Syn: detest, despise, loathe, scorn
Ant: approve, praise, love, laud

DERIDE
Syn: mock, taunt, ridicule, jeer
Ant: inspire, encourage, stimulate, comfort

DEPRIVE
Syn: despoil, divest, dispossess, disinherit
Ant: restore, renew, invest, endow

DEPLORE
Syn: lament, bemoan, complain, regret
Ant: rejoice, cheer, applaud, celebrate

DENOUNCE
Syn: indict, condemn, censure, reprimand
Ant: praise, commend, vindicate, laud

DEMOLISH
Syn: ruin, devastate, dismantle, raze
Ant: repair, construct, create, erect

DELUSION
Syn: deception, hallucination, illusion, fallacy
Ant: reality, certainty, veracity, fact

DELICIOUS
Syn: palatable, tasteful, appetising, dainty
Ant: distasteful, unsavoury, tolerable, inedible

DELIBERATE
Syn: ponder, intentional, meditate, consider
Ant: rash, sudden, indifferent, random

DEGRADATION
Syn: disgrace, dishonour, humiliation, debase
Ant: exaltation, praise, triumphant, honour

DEFRAY
Syn: meet, bear, spend, pay
Ant: declaim, decline, refuse, abjure

DEFILE
Syn: contaminate, pollute, profane, desecrate
Ant: purify, sanctity, cleanse, disinfect

DEFICIENT
Syn: scanty, inadequate, lacking, wanting
Ant: adequate, ample, sufficient, abundant

DEFER
Syn: prolong, suspend, postpone, delay
Ant: accelerate, expedite, stimulate, hasten

DEFAULT
Syn: failure, omission, negligence, lapse
Ant: perfection, vigilance, attentive, observance

DEDICATE
Syn: devote, consecrate, loyal, surrender
Ant: refuse, negate, prohibit, reject

DECIPHER
Syn: interpret, reveal, decode, transcribe
Ant: misinterpret, distort, confuse, pervert

DECEIT
Syn: deception, artifice, treachery, duplicity
Ant: veracity, sincerity, truth, honesty

DECAY
Syn: collapse, decomposition, deteriorate, putrefaction
Ant: flourish, progress, growth, development

DAUNT
Syn: discourage, frighten, agitate, intimidate
Ant: encourage, animate, embolden, inspire

DAINTY
Syn: elegant, delicate, refined, exquisite
Ant: clumsy, coarse, unpleasant, insipid

EXULT
Syn: brag, rejoice, applaud, triumph
Ant: deplore, lament, bemoan, grieve

EXPLICIT
Syn: definite, intelligible, obvious, apparent
Ant: hidden, vague, doubtful, implicit

EXEMPT
Syn: release, excuse, exclude, absolve
Ant: confine, hold, retard, enforce

EXALT
Syn: extol, dignify, glorify, elevate
Ant: dishonour, disgrace, degrade, denounce

EVIDENT
Syn: obvious, apparent, distinct, conspicuous
Ant: obscure, concealed, hidden, invisible

EVADE
Syn: avoid, elude, dodge, shun
Ant: acknowledge, confront, verify, confirm

ETERNAL
Syn: perpetual, endless, imperishable, immortal
Ant: temporary, momentary, transient, fleeting

ESTEEM
Syn: respect, regards, honour, reverence
Ant: ridicule, spurn, despise, humilitate

ERADICATE
Syn: destroy, exterminate, abolish, remove
Ant: secure, plant, restore, revive

EQUIVOCAL
Syn: uncertain, hazy, ambiguous, vague
Ant: obvious, lucid, clear, plain

EPITOME
Syn: precise, example, miniature, summary
Ant: increment, expansion, lengthen, enlargement

ENORMOUS
Syn: colossal, mammoth, immense, spacious
Ant: insignificant, diminutive, trivial, negligible

ENLIGHTEN
Syn: elucidate, educate, illumine, inculcate
Ant: ignorance, distortion, delude, obscure

ENJOIN
Syn: direct, counsel, exhort, command
Ant: prohibit, forbid, revolt, dissuade

ENDURANCE
Syn: submission, forbearance, tolerance, patience
Ant: break down, despair, volatile, agitating

ENDOWMENT
Syn: grant, benefit, bequest, gift
Ant: drawback, damage, loss, disinherit

ENDEAVOUR
Syn: undertake, aspire, venture, struggle
Ant: cease, quit, shun, idle

ENCUMBRANCE
Syn: hindrance, obstacle, burden, impediment
Ant: incentive, stimulant, patronize, vantage

ENCROACH
Syn: infringe, intrude, tresspass, violate
Ant: avoid, evade, shun, abide

EMBRACE
Syn: cling, hug, adopt, caress
Ant: reject, neglect, shun, slight

EMBEZZLE
Syn: forge, swindle, defraud, peculate
Ant: redeem, restitute, reimburse, compensate

ELUCIDATE
Syn: enlighten, clarify, expound, illustrate
Ant: equivocate, confuse, distort, confound

ELOQUENCE
Syn: expression, fluency, peroration, oration
Ant: halting, stammering, indistinct, inarticulate

ELIMINATE
Syn: expel, oust, exclude, remove
Ant: restore, accept, retain, include

ELEVATE
Syn: dignify, heighten, promote, raise
Ant: deprecate, denounce, lower, decline

ELEGANT
Syn: graceful, distinguished, refined, polished
Ant: obnoxious, unrefined, ridiculous, coarse

ELATION
Syn: joy, exaltation, delight, enthusiasm
Ant: gloom, despair, depression, melancholy

EFFACE
Syn: destroy, obliterate, annihilate, abolish
Ant: retain, maintain, regenerate, resurrect

ECSTASY
Syn: delight, exultation, overjoy, rapture
Ant: despair, calamity, doldrums, depression

ECCENTRIC
Syn: strange, abnormal, cranky, odd
Ant: natural, conventional, uniform, methodical

EARNEST
Syn: ardent, sincere, resolute, determined
Ant: unheeding, frivolous, negligent, careless

EVASION
Syn: prevaricate, avoid, neglect, pretext
Ant: response, defence, compliance, action

FABRICATE
Syn: construct, produce, manipulate, build
Ant: destroy, dismantle, wreck, demolish

FRUGALITY
Syn: economical, providence, thrift, parsimony
Ant: lavishness, extravagance, prodigality, improvidence

FRIVOLOUS
Syn: petty, worthless, capricious, volatile
Ant: solemn, significant, essential, pertinent

FRANTIC
Syn: violent, agitated, frenzied, wild
Ant: subdued, gentle, lucid, coherent

FRANCHISE
Syn: suffrage, right, privilege, patronise
Ant: bondage, oppression, serfdom, irresolute

FRAGMENTS
Syn: scraps, residue, segment, section
Ant: total, entire, gross, aggregate

FRAGILE
Syn: weak, infirm, brittle, frail
Ant: enduring, tough, robust, tenacious

FORSAKE
Syn: desert, renounce, relinquish, disown
Ant: hold, maintain, retain, claim

FORMIDABLE
Syn: dangerous, invincible, redoubtable, dreadful
Ant: harmless, insignificant, weak, feeble

FORERUNNER
Syn: precursor, predecessor, ancestor, pioneer
Ant: descendant, follower, heir, successor

FOE
Syn: opponent, antagonist, adversary, contender
Ant: comrade, helper, friend, fellow

FLUENT
Syn: fast, smooth, voluble, glib
Ant: hesitant, slow, sluggish, halting

FLUCTUATE
Syn: deflect, vacillate, vary, deviate
Ant: stable, resolute, constant, inalterable

FLOURISH
Syn: prosper, triumph, thrive, blossom
Ant: decay, collapse, wither, deteriorate

FLIMSY
Syn: trifling, transparent, brittle, unsubstantial
Ant: firm, tenacious, durable, retentive

FLEETING
Syn: transient, temporary, ephemeral, transitory
Ant: enduring, eternal, perpetual, unceasing

FIDELITY
Syn: loyalty, trustworthiness, obedience, devotion
Ant: treachery, unfaithfulness, chicanery, defiance

FICKLE
Syn: wavering, unreliable, unsteady, volatile
Ant: resolute, determined, inalterable, invariable

FEUD
Syn: strife, quarrel, row, contention
Ant: fraternity, harmony, reconciliation, recompose

FEROCIOUS
Syn: untamed, barbarous, fierce, dangerous
Ant: gentle, innocent, benevolent, symapthetic

FEEBLE
Syn: weak, frail, impotent, defenceless
Ant: strong, robust, vigorous, resolute

FATIGUE
Syn: weariness, exhaustion, exertion, tiredness
Ant: vigour, liveliness, vivacity, briskness

FANTASY
Syn: imagination, vision, image, visualization
Ant: reality, substantiality, actuality, existence

FANTASTIC
Syn: fanciful, uncommon, imaginary, marvellous
Ant: ordinary, normal, customary, common

FANATICAL
Syn: narrow-minded, stubborn, orthodox, biased
Ant: liberal, tolerant, unprejudiced, generous

FALTER
Syn: fluctuate, demur, dither, waver
Ant: persist, endure, stable, unerring

FALLACY
Syn: delusion, mistake, deception, illusion
Ant: veracity, truth, honesty, certainty

FACSIMILE
Syn: miniature, reproduction, copy, replica
Ant: distinction, dissimilarity, novelty, originality

FABULOUS
Syn: legendry, amazing, remarkable, marvellous
Ant: historical, common, medicore, substantial

FACILE
Syn: dexterous, quick, skilful, effortless
Ant: clumsy, slow, laborious, arduous

GUILE
Syn: cunning, deceit, duplicity, chicanery
Ant: honesty, frankness, sincerity, integrity

GRUDGE
Syn: hatred, aversion, unwilling, objection
Ant: benevolence, affection, goodwill, kindness

GRISLY
Syn: disgusting, atrocious, monstrous, loathsome
Ant: pleasing, attractive, beautiful, alluring

GRACIOUS
Syn: courteous, beneficent, magnificent, dignified
Ant: rude, unforgiving, discourteous, uncourtly

GORGEOUS
Syn: magnificient, dazzling, brilliant, grand
Ant: dull, unpretentious, modest, plain

GLUT
Syn: stuff, satiate, overflow, cram
Ant: reduce, abstain, moderate, restrain

GLOOM
Syn: obscurity, darkness, dejection, disillusion
Ant: delight, mirth, joviality, bright

GIGANTIC
Syn: huge, enormous, immense, monstrous
Ant: small, diminutive, miniature, slight

GENUINE
Syn: real, authentic, creative, original
Ant: deceptive, spurious, imitative, derivative

GENIAL
Syn: cheerful, pleasant, joyful, affable
Ant: sullen, dismal, morose, melancholy

GENEROUS
Syn: liberal, unselfish, benevolent, hospitable
Ant: miserly, stingy, covetous, greedy

GARRULOUS
Syn: loquacious, talkative, communicative, informative
Ant: reserved, quiet, taciturn, reticent

GALLANT
Syn: heroic, intrepid, valorous, chivalrous
Ant: coward, timid, craven, base

GAUDY
Syn: garish, brilliant, glittering, tawdry
Ant: faded, dull, sobre, solemn

HUSTLE
Syn: hurry, haste, bustle, activity
Ant: lull, quiet, idle, motionless

HYPOCRISY
Syn: deception, affectation, trickery, illusion
Ant: sincerity, integrity, honesty, ingenuousness

HIDEOUS
Syn: frightful, shocking, abominable, monstrous
Ant: attractive, alluring, splendid, appealing

HERETIC
Syn: nonconformist, secularist, dissident, offender
Ant: conformable, adaptable, religious, believer

HAZARD
Syn: presumption, danger, peril, risk, presume
Ant: conviction, security, assurance, certainty

HAUGHTY
Syn: arrogant, pompous, obstinate, imperious
Ant: humble, submissive, modest, inoffensive

HARASS
Syn: irritable, molest, suppress, tyranny
Ant: assist, comfort, tolerant, connive

HAPLESS
Syn: unfortunate, ill-fated, hostile, doomed
Ant: fortunate, lucky, favoured, satisfied

HAPHAZARD
Syn: random, sudden, unsorted, reckless
Ant: deliberate, considered, thoughtful, discerning

HAMPER
Syn: retard, prevent, hinder, obstruct
Ant: promote, facilitate, foster, assist

HAGGARD
Syn: exhausted, lean, emaciated, gaunt
Ant: exuberant, active, lively, robust

HOMELY
Syn: plain, coarse, unadorned, simple
Ant: sauve, polished, dignified, refined

HAIL
Syn: greet, welcome, acclaim, honour
Ant: disregard, belittle, avoid, despise

HEINOUS
Syn: outrageous, vile, awful, wicked
Ant: righteous, pleasing, exquisite, appealing

IRREPRESSIBLE
Syn: irresistible, unconfined, unhindered, unshackled
Ant: composed, hesitant, submissive, grave

INVINCIBLE
Syn: unconquerable, impregnable, unsubdued, unbeatable
Ant: effeminate, languid, crippled, fragile

INTIMIDATE
Syn: frighten, dictate, hopeless, irresolute
Ant: console, encourage, appease, hearten

INTREPID
Syn: brave, courageous, valorous, chivalrous
Ant: scared, frightened, timid, cowardly

INTRICATE
Syn: tangled, complicated, formidable, arduous
Ant: regulated, orderly, manageable, ductile

INTRIGUE
Syn: scheme, conspiracy, manipulation, counterplot
Ant: candour, sincerity, bluntness, honesty

INTRINSIC
Syn: genuine, fundamental, inherent, congenital
Ant: extraneous, incidental, extrinsic, derived

INVECTIVE
Syn: accusation, censure, malediction, denunciation
Ant: approval, acclamation, admiration, approbation

INSTIL
Syn: inculcate, inject, infuse, implant
Ant: eradicate, extract, eliminate, expel

INSOLVENT
Syn: indigent, destitute, bankrupt, defaulter
Ant: wealthy, solvent, affluent, substantial

INSIPID
Syn: tasteless, vapid, savourless, unflavoured
Ant: delicious, luscious, pungent, piquant

INSINUATE
Syn: communicate, allude, hint, suggest
Ant: conceal, camouflage, suppress, mask

INQUISITIVE
Syn: inquiring, curious, searching, studious
Ant: distracted, negligent, indifferent, impassive

INNOCUOUS
Syn: salutary, wholesome, innocent, harmless
Ant: deleterious, baneful, insanitary, injurious

INGENUOUS
Syn: undisguised, naive, candid, guileless
Ant: wily, crafty, perfidious, treacherous

INFRINGE
Syn: violate, encroach, transgress, tresspass
Ant: comply, concur, conform, observe

INEVITABLE
Syn: unavoidable, ascertained, imminent, substantial
Ant: unlikely, doubtful, indefinite, uncertain

INGENIOUS
Syn: deft, proficient, dexterous, adroit
Ant: unskilled, incompetent, immature, unqualified

INDULGE
Syn: gratify, pamper, comfort, satisfy
Ant: annoy, trouble, torment, displease

INDOLENT
Syn: lazy, listless, languid, sluggish
Ant: energetic, vivacious, prompt, agile

INDISPENSABLE
Syn: essential, expedient, requisite, unavoidable
Ant: superfluous, redundant, needless, tranquility

INDIGNATION
Syn: resentment, ire, wrath, rage
Ant: modesty, tranquility, forbearance, equanimity

INDIGENCE
Syn: privation, destitution, insolvency, penury
Ant: affluence, abundance, opulence, luxury

INCONGRUOUS
Syn: inappropriate, absurd, ridiculous, awkward
Ant: compatible, harmonious, homogeneous, consistent

INCOMPETENT
Syn: inefficient, unskilled, immature, unqualified
Ant: dexterous, skilled, ingenious, competent

INCLINATION
Syn: disposition, affection, proneness, propensity
Ant: neutrality, indifference, apathy, unresponsive

INCITE
Syn: instigate, provoke, motivate, arouse
Ant: deter, discourage, restrain, dissuade

INCENTIVE
Syn: motivation, allurement, inducement, spur
Ant: dissuasion, reluctance, deterrent, discouragement

IMPUTE
Syn: attribute, ascribe, charge, indict
Ant: exculpate, support, vindicate, excuse

IMPUDENCE
Syn: sauciness, impertinence, insolence, arrogance
Ant: submissiveness, modesty, humility, meekness

IMPIOUS
Syn: irreligious, unholy, irreverent, hypocritical
Ant: pious, devout, spiritual, venerate

IMPETUOUS
Syn: violent, impulsive, imprudence, indiscretion
Ant: considerate, composed, discretion, prudence

IMPEDIMENT
Syn: hurdle, obstruction, hindrance, retardation
Ant: assistance, concurrence, deliverance, aid

IMPARTIAL
Syn: just, unbiased, equitable, evenhanded
Ant: prejudiced, biased, unjust, inequitable

IMPART
Syn: divulge, bestow, inform, convey
Ant: withhold, conceal, suppress, deny

IMPAIR
Syn: diminish, deteriorate, decompose, worsen
Ant: restore, revive, resurrect, repair

IMMUNITY
Syn: prerogative, privilege, exemption, non-liability
Ant: blame, censure, prescription, interdiction

IMMINENT
Syn: impending, brewing, overhanging, approaching
Ant: distant, receding, retreating, withdrawing

IMMERSE
Syn: submerge, involve, descend, drown
Ant: emerge, uncover, restore, recover

IMMENSE
Syn: huge, enormous, gigantic, colossal
Ant: puny, insignificant, paltry, trifling

IMMACULATE
Syn: unsullied, spotless, untarnished, untainted
Ant: defiled, tarnished, obscene, profane

IMBECILE
Syn: weak, senile, feeble, unsound
Ant: sane, sagacious, astute, wise

IMAGINARY
Syn: illusory, visionary, insubstantial, subjective
Ant: factual, tangible, genuine, evident

IGNORANCE
Syn: illiteracy, darkness, unawareness, unconsciousness
Ant: knowledge, enlightenment, apprehension, recognition

IGNOMINIOUS
Syn: disgraceful, shameful, dishonourable, scandulous
Ant: dignified, distinguished, creditable, stately

JUVENILE
Syn: young, tender, youthful, adolescent
Ant: dotage, antiquated, senile, old

JUSTIFY
Syn: defend, exculpate, warrant, vindicate
Ant: impute, arraigned, accuse, incriminate

JUST
Syn: honest, impartial, righteous, upright
Ant: unequal, unfair, discriminatory, unseasonable

JUDICIOUS
Syn: thoughtful, prudent, discerning, discriminating
Ant: irrational, foolish, misconception, fatuous

JUBILANT
Syn: rejoicing, triumphant, gay, cheerful
Ant: melancholy, depressing, gloomy, despondent

JOVIAL
Syn: frolicsome, cheerful, merry, exultant
Ant: solemn, morose, malcontent, sad

JADED
Syn: tired, exhausted, fatigued, languish
Ant: renewal, recreation, restorative, refreshed

JEJUNE
Syn: dull, boring, uninteresting, monotonous
Ant: interesting, exciting, piquant, thrilling

KINDRED
Syn: relation, species, relative, affinity
Ant: unrelated, dissimilar, hetrogeneous, disparate

KEEN
Syn: sharp, poignant, eager, acute
Ant: vapid, insipid, blunt, undesiring

KNAVE
Syn: dishonest, scoundrel, vagabond, rogue
Ant: paragon, innocent, benefactor, idealist

KNELL
Syn: death knell, last blow, demolish, suppress
Ant: reconstruction, rediscovery, procreation, resurrection

KNOTTY
Syn: complicated, difficult, arduous, onerous
Ant: simple, manageable, tractable, flexible

LUXURIANT
Syn: profuse, abundant, dense, plentiful
Ant: scanty, meagre, inadequate, deficient

LUSCIOUS
Syn: palatable, delicious, delectable, delightful
Ant: unsavoury, tart, sharp, sour

LURE
Syn: attract, entice, tempt, induce
Ant: repel, dissuade, confute, threaten

LUNACY
Syn: delusion, insanity, madness, imbecility
Ant: normalcy, sanity, sagacity, shrewdness

LUDICROUS
Syn: absurd, bizarre, preposterous, grotesque
Ant: balanced, congruous, consistent, solemn

LUCID
Syn: sound, rational, coherent, sane
Ant: obscure, hidden, incomprehensible, unintelligible

LISTLESS
Syn: lazy, inattentive, spiritless, incurious
Ant: brisk, attentive, diligent, agile

LINGER
Syn: loiter, prolong, hesitate, delay
Ant: hasten, quicken, dart, hurry

LIBERATE
Syn: emancipate, rescue, unshackle, absolve
Ant: suppress, menacle, obstruct, detain

LIBERAL
Syn: magnanimous, hospitality, generous, benevolence
Ant: stingy, niggardly, malevolent, malicious

LIABLE
Syn: accountable, bound, responsible, likely
Ant: unaccountable, apt to, irresponsible, exempt

LENIENT
Syn: compassionate, merciful, moderate, tolerant
Ant: cruel, severe, violent, vehement

LAX
Syn: slack, careless, negligence, indifferent
Ant: firm, reliable, meticulous, scrupulous

LAVISH
Syn: abundant, excessive, profuse, extravagant
Ant: scarce, deficient, frugal, conserve

LASSITUDE
Syn: languor, tiredness, weariness, lethargy
Ant: vivacity, agility, animate, lively

LAUDABLE
Syn: deserving, honourable, praiseworthy, acceptable
Ant: vicious, blame worthy, venomous, condemnable

LANGUID
Syn: pensive, lethargic, exhausted, fatigued
Ant: lively, animated, refreshed, restored

LAMENT
Syn: grieve, deplore, regret, bemoan
Ant: amuse, entertain, enliven, solace

LAG
Syn: retard, falter, linger, dawdle
Ant: quicken, accelerate, expedite, spurt

LACONIC
Syn: brief, condensed, concise, compact
Ant: dilated, profused, diffuse, wordy

MUTUAL
Syn: joint, identical, correlative, reciprocal
Ant: separate, distinct, divergent, individual

MUTINOUS
Syn: recalcitrant, insurgent, unruly, revolutionary
Ant: submissive, faithful, compliant, loyal

MURKY
Syn: dusky, dreary, dismal, bleak
Ant: bright, shining, luminous, radiant

MUNIFICENT
Syn: liberal, hospitable, benevolent, kind
Ant: frugal, penurious, moderate, economical

MULTITUDE
Syn: crowd, throng, mass, swarm
Ant: minority, handful, paucity, scarcity

MOROSE
Syn: surly, sulky, sullen, depressed
Ant: sprightly, animated, buoyant, blithe

MONOTONOUS
Syn: irksome, tedious, humdrum, insipid
Ant: varied, pleasant, appealing, captivating

MOMENTOUS
Syn: notable, eventful, consequential, stirring
Ant: trivial, insignificant, commonplace, immaterial

MOLLIFY
Syn: appease, assuage, relieve, mitigate
Ant: irritate, infuriate, aggravate, exasperate

MOLEST
Syn: pester, harass, vex, misbehave
Ant: console, soothe, comfort, cheer

MODEST
Syn: reserved, unpretentious, humble, courteous
Ant: audacious, arrogant, pompous, vain

MODERATE
Syn: limited, reasonable, lenient, temperate
Ant: excessive, extravagant, violent, vehement

MITIGATE
Syn: alleviate, relieve, lessen, assuage
Ant: augment, enhance, intensify, aggravate

MIRACULOUS
Syn: marvellous, extraordinary, astounding, amazing
Ant: ordinary, trivial, familiar, natural

MINUTE
Syn: diminutive, miniature, small, microscopic
Ant: large, colossal, stupendous, immense

METTLE
Syn: courage, determination, stamina, spirit
Ant: timidity, fear, cowardice, diffident

MERITORIOUS
Syn: commendable, admirable, deserving, praiseworthy
Ant: unworthy, infamous, disreputable, culpable

MERCURIAL
Syn: variable, changeable, unstable, erratic
Ant: stable, constant, steady, steadfast

MENDACITY
Syn: falsehood, deception, perjury, perfidious
Ant: probity, honesty, veracity, candour

MELODIOUS
Syn: dulcet, musical, harmonious, sweet
Ant: grating, dissonant, discordant, rancour

NUMEROUS
Syn: profuse, various, multitude, plenteous
Ant: scarce, deficient, paucity, sparse

NULLIFY
Syn: cancel, annul, obliterate, invalidate
Ant: confirm, uphold, empower, endorse

NOXIOUS
Syn: baneful, injurious, pernicious, disastrous
Ant: healing, profitable, innocuous, salubrious

NOVICE
Syn: tyro, beginner, debutant, apprentice
Ant: veteran, ingenious, experienced, mentor

NOURISH
Syn: sustain, nurture, tend, foster
Ant: exhaust, starve, weaken, enervate

NONCHALANT
Syn: indifferent, negligent, uncaring, heedless
Ant: attentive, considerate, vigilant, scrupulous

NIMBLE
Syn: prompt, brisk, lively, agile
Ant: sluggish, languid, weary, tardy

NIGGARDLY
Syn: miserly, covetous, inadequacy, deficiency
Ant: generous, profuse, redundant, excessive

NEGLIGENT
Syn: inattentive, careless, heedless, perfunctory
Ant: vigilant, careful, considerate, alert

NEFARIOUS
Syn: detestable, atrocious, heinous, unlawful
Ant: commendable, worthy, upright, inoffensive

NAUSEOUS
Syn: unsavoury, loathsome, abominable, repellent
Ant: commendable, worthy, benevolent, inoffensive

NATIVE
Syn: original, vernacular, indigenous, aboriginal
Ant: alien, extraneous, exotic, foreign

NASTY
Syn: offensive, defiled, malevolent, malignant
Ant: pleasing, gratifying, benevolent, attractive

NOMINAL
Syn: trifling, insubstantial, bare, negligible
Ant: substantial, considerable, excessive, exorbitant

OVERWROUGHT
Syn: excited, agitated, fervent, intense
Ant: quiet, tranquil, composed, cool

OVERWHELM
Syn: triumph, subjugate, overpower, vanquish
Ant: flounder, falter, restore, impotent

OVERSIGHT
Syn: omission, error, fault, slip
Ant: precision, observance, circumspection, caution

OVERBEARING
Syn: oppressive, domineering, intimidating, despotic
Ant: submissive, humble, lenient, forbearing

OUTRAGE
Syn: offence, maltreatment, assault, irreverent
Ant: praise, favour, esteem, reverence

OUTBREAK
Syn: eruption, insurrection, explosion, outburst
Ant: compliance, subjection, passivity, harmony

OSTENTATION
Syn: display, pretension, vaunt, pomposity
Ant: modesty, constraint, diffidence, economy

OSTENSIBLE
Syn: apparent, evident, obvious, overt
Ant: concealed, covert, obscure, vague

ORNAMENTAL
Syn: decorative, adorned, glamorous, picturesque
Ant: unseemly, plain, blemished, disfigured

ORDAIN
Syn: order, impose, prescribe, proclaim
Ant: revoke, abolish, violate, abrogate

ORACULAR
Syn: cryptic, vague, enigmatic, profound
Ant: lucid, distinct, intelligible, unambiguous

OPAQUE
Syn: filmy, dim, obscure, shady
Ant: transparent, bright, translucent, revealing

ONEROUS
Syn: arduous, troublesome, inconvenient, formidable
Ant: facile, agreeable, uncomplicated, flexible

OMINOUS
Syn: threatening, inauspicious, forebode, menacing
Ant: consoling, auspicious, propitious, comforting

OFFSPRING
Syn: descendants, siblings, posterity, progeny
Ant: ancestors, forefathers, pedigree, progenitors

OFFENSIVE
Syn: abhorrent, arrogant, insolent, impudent
Ant: docile, compliant, courteous, captivating

ODIOUS
Syn: abhorrent, obnoxious, prejudice, malevolent
Ant: engaging, fascinating, endearing, captivating

OCCULT
Syn: latent, ambiguous, esoteric, elusive
Ant: intelligible, transparent, fathomable, scrutable

OBVIOUS
Syn: evident, apparent, distinct, conspicuous
Ant: obscure, ambiguous, indiscernible, confusing

OBSTRUCT
Syn: impede, prevent, restrain, retard
Ant: hasten, encourage, expedite, promote

OBSTINATE
Syn: stubborn, resolute, unyielding, obdurate
Ant: submissive, obedient, amenable, pliable

OBSOLETE
Syn: outworn, archaic, antiquated, obsolescent
Ant: modern, novel, vogue, contemporary

OBSEQUIOUS
Syn: slavish, servile, sycophantic, subservient
Ant: insolent, arrogant, defiant, assertive

OBNOXIOUS
Syn: pernicious, detestable, abhorrent, offensive
Ant: attractive, gratifying, beneficial, desirable

OBJECTIVE
Syn: goal, purpose, intention, resolve
Ant: origin, inception, deviating, subjective

PUNGENT
Syn: acute, penetrating, sharp, strong
Ant: mild, soothing, pleasant, palatable

PUERILE
Syn: shallow, immature, childish, trivial
Ant: wise, farsighted, profound, sensible

PRUDENT
Syn: cautious, discreet, judicious, circumspect
Ant: impetuous, unwise, reckless, rash

PROVOKE
Syn: inflame, incite, agitate, aggravate
Ant: pacify, comfort, dissuade, placate

PROTRACT
Syn: prolong, delay, stretch, procrastinate
Ant: abbreviate, curtail, abridge, compress

PROSCRIBE
Syn: prohibit, exclude, ban, forbid
Ant: solicit, include, permit, sanction

PROPITIATE
Syn: appease, soothe, pacify, placate
Ant: aggravate, annoy, scorn, displease

PROMULGATE
Syn: declare, proclaim, notify, announce
Ant: reserve, suppress, disguise, withhold

PROMISCUOUS
Syn: confused, indiscriminate, casual, random
Ant: regular, discriminate, orderly, select

PROFUSE
Syn: lavish, abundant, generous, plentiful
Ant: scarce, scanty, meagre, paucity

PROFLIGATE
Syn: dissolute, degenerate, immoral, flagitious
Ant: virtuous, upright, moral, ethical

PRODIGY
Syn: miracle, marvel, wonder, extraordinary
Ant: normal, average, mediocre, common

PRODIGIOUS
Syn: vast, enormous, immense, huge
Ant: unimpressive, diminutive, slight, puny

PRESUMPTUOUS
Syn: presuming, arrogant, affected, insolent
Ant: unassuming, modest, bashful, unobtrusive

PREMATURE
Syn: precocious, untimely, mistimed, inopportune
Ant: belated, opportune, timely, mellow

PREDICAMENT
Syn: plight, dilemma, fix, quandary
Ant: resolution, confidence, firmness, certainty

PRECARIOUS
Syn: doubtful, insecure, unreliable, uncertain
Ant: assured, undeniable, reliable, substantial

POMPOUS
Syn: haughty, arrogant, flamboyant, florid
Ant: unpretentious, humble, coy, modest

POISE
Syn: equanimity, composure, equilibrium, patience
Ant: excitement, vehemence, frenzy, outburst

PLIGHT
Syn: predicament, perplexity, adversity, difficulty
Ant: facility, confidence, certainty, assurance

PLIANT
Syn: docile, amenable, pliable, submissive
Ant: defiant, adamant, rigid, obdurate

PIQUE
Syn: offence, resentment, indignation, displeasure
Ant: joy, rejoice, gratification, pleasure

PIQUANT
Syn: interesting, charming, tasteful, exciting
Ant: insipid, nauseating, unpalatable, unsavoury

PILLAGE
Syn: ransack, ravage, despoil, plunder
Ant: recompense, recover, redeem, restoration

PERVERSE
Syn: petulant, obstinate, stubborn, unyielding
Ant: complacent, docile, willing, consenting

PERTNESS
Syn: flippancy, impudence, impertinence, petulance
Ant: modesty, diffidence, subservient, obedient

PERSPICUITY
Syn: transparency, discernment, lucidity, intelligiblity
Ant: perplexity, intricacy, obscurity, vagueness

PERSEVERANCE
Syn: persistence, endurance, tenacity, steadfastness
Ant: indolence, lethargy, stupor, sloth

PERSECUTE
Syn: torment, harass, intimidate, domineer
Ant: recompense, redress, comfort, console

PERPLEX
Syn: puzzle, confound, frustrate, baffle
Ant: convince, ascertain, confident, assure

PERPETUAL
Syn: uninterrupted, lasting, perennial, incessant
Ant: passing, transient, ephemeral, fleeting

PERIL
Syn: hazard, danger, jeopardy, compulsory
Ant: caution, security, safety, assurance

PEREMPTORY
Syn: overbearing, absolute, arbitrary, compulsory
Ant: tolerant, indecisive, optional, indulgent

PENETRATE
Syn: pierce, perforate, insert, infiltrate
Ant: discharge, leak, seep, emerge

PEEVISH
Syn: perverse, sullen, irritable, fretful
Ant: suave, amiable, polite, pleasant

PEERLESS
Syn: matchless, unrivalled, unique, surpassing
Ant: mediocre, commonplace, inferior, imperfect

PARAMOUNT
Syn: foremost, eminent, supreme, unrivalled
Ant: trivial, inferior, subsidiary, ordinary

PANIC
Syn: apprehension, dismay, alarm, dread
Ant: calm, confidence, security, tranquility

PAMPER
Syn: spoil, indulge, flatter, please
Ant: chasten, correct, deny, disparage

PALPABLE
Syn: distinct, prominent, plain, concrete
Ant: concealed, obscure, intangible, covert

PALLIATE
Syn: extenuate, moderate, alleviate, soften
Ant: denounce, condemn, reproach, reprehend

PLACID
Syn: tranquil, calm, compose, unruffled
Ant: turbulent, hostile, agitated, volatile

QUESTIONABLE
Syn: uncertain, disputable, dubious, unverifiable
Ant: positive, authentic, reliable, substantial

QUELL
Syn: subdue, reduce, supress, extinguish
Ant: exacerbate, agitate, foment, instigate

QUAINT
Syn: queer, strange, **odd, ridiculous**
Ant: familiar, usual, common, normal

QUACK
Syn: impostor, deceiver, dissembler, knave
Ant: upright, unfeigned, trained, genuine

QUIBBLE
Syn: equivocate, prevaricate, evade, dissemble
Ant: unfeign, plain, scrupulous, conscientious

QUASH
Syn: abrogate, annul, cancel, revoke
Ant: uphold, empower, authorise, permit

QUARANTINE
Syn: isolate, separate, seclude, screened
Ant: gregarious, amiable, sociable, companionable

RUTHLESS
Syn: remorseless, inhuman, savage, unrelenting
Ant: compassionate, lenient, benevolent, humanitarian

RUSTIC
Syn: pastoral, bucolic, rural, uncivilised
Ant: cultured, refined, urban, urbane

ROUT
Syn: defeat, overthrow, vanquish, subjugate
Ant: succumb, withdraw, retreat, consolidate

RIGHTEOUS
Syn: virtuous, honest, upright, just
Ant: unjust, immortal, unprincipled, unfair

REVERENCE
Syn: respect, esteem, regards, veneration
Ant: disrespect, dishonour, affront, offence

REVEAL
Syn: disclose, expose, unfold, divulge
Ant: hide, conceal, confine, cover

RETRACT
Syn: recant, repudiate, revoke, withdraw
Ant: confirm, assert, declare, affirm

REMOTE
Syn: inaccessible, farther, distant, slight
Ant: adjoining, adjacent, proximate, contiguous

REMORSE
Syn: regret, penitence, deplore, lament
Ant: ruthless, obduracy, pitiless, relentless

RESENTMENT
Syn: displeasure, wrath, ire, bitterness
Ant: content, cheer, pleasure, agreement

RESCIND
Syn: annul, abrogate, revoke, repeal
Ant: delegate, permit, authorize, propose

REPULSIVE
Syn: repellent, forbidding, hideous, detestable
Ant: agreeable, enticing, attractive, alluring

REPUGNANT
Syn: hostile, offensive, disagreeable, distasteful
Ant: agreeable, pleasant, friendly, tasteful

REMONSTRATE
Syn: censure, protest, argue, expostulate
Ant: agree, laud, endorse, commend

REMNANT
Syn: residue, piece, part, remainder
Ant: entire, whole, complete, unbroken

RELINQUISH
Syn: forsake, abandon, surrender, abdicate
Ant: persist, continue, occupy, hold

REDRESS
Syn: relief, restoration, remedy, repair
Ant: retribution, forfeiture, harm, degenerate

REDEEM
Syn: recover, liberate, fulfil, rescue
Ant: lose, barter, neglect, conserve

RAZE
Syn: demolish, destroy, annihilate, dismantle
Ant: restore, construct, repair, build

RAVISH
Syn: captivate, enchant, seize, charm
Ant: disgust, annoy, displease, oppress

RAVAGE
Syn: devastate, destroy, ruin, despoil
Ant: restore, organize, reconstruct, renovate

RATIFY
Syn: consent, approve, endorse, corroborate
Ant: deny, contradict, dissent, oppose

RAPTURE
Syn: bliss, delight, pleasure, ecstasy
Ant: melancholy, distress, sorrow, agonize

RAPID
Syn: swift, fast, speedy, accelerate
Ant: sluggish, lethargic, languid, listless

RANCOUR
Syn: hatred, malice, resentment, bitterness
Ant: love, regards, respect, friendliness

RADIANCE
Syn: glow, brilliance, splendour, gleaming
Ant: dullness, shady, overcast, dusky

SYCOPHANT
Syn: parasite, flatterer, cringing, servile
Ant: devoted, loyal, truthful, faithful

SWAY
Syn: influence, control, command, power
Ant: impotence, futility, disability, incapacity

SUPERFLUOUS
Syn: excessive, surplus, redundant, unnecessary
Ant: scanty, inadequate, dearth, scarce

SUPERFICIAL
Syn: partial, shallow, cursory, flimsy
Ant: profound, discerning, substantial, deep

SUBVERT
Syn: overthrow, suppress, demolish, sabotage
Ant: accomplish, sustain, generate, organise

SUBSTANTIAL
Syn: durable, lasting, concrete, tangible
Ant: tenuous, abstract, fragile, immaterial

SUBSEQUENT
Syn: consequent, following, later, afterwards
Ant: preceding, previous, prior, earlier

STUPOR
Syn: lethargy, insensibility, unconsciousness, coma
Ant: consciousness, sensibility, sensitive, feeling

STERN
Syn: harsh, severe, austere, rigorous
Ant: lenient, considerate, benevolent, generous

STAIN
Syn: blemish, tarnish, disgrace, stigma
Ant: honour, purify, virtuous, noble

STABLE
Syn: abiding, lasting, steadfast, constant
Ant: erratic, wavering, unsteady, restless

SQUALID
Syn: dirty, soiled, filthy, odious
Ant: attractive, tidy, polished, spruce

SPURIOUS
Syn: counterfeit, adulterated, fake, fraudulent
Ant: genuine, positive, original, sincere

SPORADIC
Syn: intermittent, scattered, isolated, infrequent
Ant: incessant, frequent, constant, regular

SPONTANEOUS
Syn: unforced, instinctive, sudden, unintentional
Ant: intended, devised, premeditated, intentional

SOLICIT
Syn: entreat, implore, approach, accost
Ant: protest, oppose, prohibit, disapprove

SNEER
Syn: mock, scorn, despise, spurn
Ant: flatter, praise, encourage, laud

SLANDER
Syn: defame, malign, detract, despise
Ant: applaud, approve, commend, exalt

SINISTER
Syn: woeful, disastrous, evil, ruinous
Ant: auspicious, fortunate, propitious, harmless

SHREWD
Syn: running, observant, crafty, artful
Ant: thoughtless, rash, simple, imbecile

SHALLOW
Syn: trivial, slight, superficial, insubstantial
Ant: profound, wise, substantial, deep

SHABBY
Syn: miserable, impoverished, deteriorated, impaired
Ant: prosperous, thriving, restoring, flourishing

SCANTY
Syn: scarce, insufficient, paucity, sparseness
Ant: lavish, luxuriant, multitude, several

SCANDAL
Syn: disgrace, disrepute, indignity, defamation
Ant: praise, admiration, flattery, adulation

SAUCY
Syn: impudent, insolent, brazen, impertinent
Ant: modest, humble, esteem, meek

SARCASTIC
Syn: derisive, ironical, sardonic, invective
Ant: courteous, complaisant, gracious, polite

SANGUINE
Syn: hopeful, optimistic, buoyant, confident
Ant: despondent, pessimistic, depressed, despairing

SALUTARY
Syn: wholesome, salubrious, healthful, beneficial
Ant: harmful, deleterious, pernicious, ruinous

TYRO
Syn: beginner, learner, novice, debutant
Ant: proficient, veteran, adept, connoisseur

TUMULTUOUS
Syn: uproarious, violent, disorderly, riotous
Ant: peaceful, passive, orderly, harmonious

TRIVIAL
Syn: trifling, insignificant, frivolous, worthless
Ant: significant, important, consequential, essential

TRITE
Syn: ordinary, commonplace, stale, hackneyed
Ant: interesting, extraordinary, becoming, proper

TRENCHANT
Syn: assertive, forceful, sharp, spirited
Ant: feeble, ambiguous, shallow, vacillating

TREACHEROUS
Syn: faithless, deceitful, disloyal, unreliable
Ant: faithful, reliable, dependable, trustworthy

TRANSIENT
Syn: temporal, transitory, fleeting, passing
Ant: lasting, enduring, perpetual, immortal

TRANQUIL
Syn: peaceful, composed, calm, placid
Ant: violent, furious, restless, distracting

TORTURE
Syn: torment, agony, pang, oppress
Ant: comfort, consolation, pleasure, delight

TIMID
Syn: modest, humble, diffident, apprehensive
Ant: bold, intrepid, undaunted, courageous

THRONG
Syn: assembly, gathering, congregation, crowd
Ant: dispersion, scattering, handful, sparsity

TENACIOUS
Syn: resolved, resolute, determined, dogged
Ant: vacillating, timid, wavering, unstable

TEMPERATE
Syn: cool, moderate, reasonable, lenient
Ant: boisterous, vehement, violent, excessive

TEMERITY
Syn: boldness, audacity, imprudence, indiscretion
Ant: discretion, prudence, caution, wisdom

TEDIOUS
Syn: wearisome, irksome, tiring, monotonous
Ant: exhilarating, lively, delightful, diverting

TAINTED
Syn: contaminated, corrupt, vitiated, polluted
Ant: unblemished, wholesome, restorative, pure

TACITURN
Syn: reserved, uncommunicative, silent, reticent
Ant: talkative, loquacious, garrulous, extrovert

TABOO
Syn: prohibit, prevent, forbid, ban
Ant: permit, sanction, consent, license

UTTERLY
Syn: completely, entirely, extremely, wholly
Ant: deficient, incomplete, insufficient, partial

USURP
Syn: seize, wrest, encroach, coup
Ant: restore, compensate, grant, reinstate

UNSEEMLY
Syn: undesirable, inappropriate, uncouth, awkward
Ant: becoming, acceptable, decorous, admirable

UNGAINLY
Syn: clumsy, unskilled, immature, slovenly
Ant: active, expert, skilful, dexterous

UNCOUTH
Syn: awkward, ungraceful, inelegant, vulgar
Ant: elegant, graceful, distinguished, shapely

UMBRAGE
Syn: resentment, bitterness, dissatisfaction, offence
Ant: sympathy, goodwill, amity, esteem

VULGAR
Syn: inelegant, offensive, nasty, ungraceful
Ant: refined, graceful, elegant, civil

VOUCH
Syn: confirm, consent, approve, endorse
Ant: repudiate, prohibit, recant, retract

VOLATILE
Syn: light, changing, transient, temporal
Ant: heavy, ponderous, perpetual, stable

VIGILANT
Syn: cautious, alert, wary, circumspect
Ant: careless, negligent, inattentive, casual

VICIOUS
Syn: corrupt, obnoxious, degraded, demoralized
Ant: noble, virtuous, innocent, underfiled

VIBRATE
Syn: swing, oscillate, fluctuate, undulate
Ant: cease, pause, rest, discontinue

VENOM
Syn: poison, resentment, malevolence, rancour
Ant: antidote, remedy, benevolent, sympathetic

VENERABLE
Syn: esteemed, honoured, respectable, worthy
Ant: unworthy, immature, degrade, degenerate

VANITY
Syn: conceit, pretension, immodesty, pride
Ant: modesty, humility, meek, bashful

VALOUR
Syn: bravery, prowess, heroism, chivalry
Ant: fear, cowardice, unmanliness

VALID
Syn: sound, authentic, genuine, reliable
Ant: fallacious, deceptive, dubious, uncertain

VALIANT
Syn: brave, gallant, courageous, chivalrous
Ant: fearful, afraid, coward, dastardly

VAGRANT
Syn: idle, roaming, wanderer, roving
Ant: steady, settled, stationary, stable

WAIVE
Syn: relinquish, remove, abjure, renounce
Ant: impose, clamp, grasp, retain

WARY
Syn: cautious, circumspect, prudent, chary
Ant: heedless, negligent, impulsive, reckless

WICKED
Syn: immoral, dissolute, vicious, nefarious
Ant: virtuous, ethical, innocent, noble

WITHHOLD
Syn: reserve, restrain, hamper, retard
Ant: emancipate, liberate, dispense, release

WANE
Syn: decline, dwindle, decrease, deteriorate
Ant: ameliorate, rise, revive, wax

WAYWARD
Syn: volatile, capricious, unstable, inconstant
Ant: stable, determined, resolute, straight

WILT
Syn: wither, perish, deteriorate, smother
Ant: revive, bloom, refresh, restore

WIELD
Syn: use, exercise, exert, employ
Ant: abstain, avoid, forbear, forgo

WAN
Syn: pale, fade, discolour, feeble
Ant: bright, healthy, colourful, gaudy

WILFUL
Syn: stubborn, obstinate, obdurate, inexorable
Ant: amenable, irresolute, pliable, yielding

YOKE
Syn: connect, harness, hitch, shackle
Ant: liberate, release, detach, disconnect

YIELD
Syn: surrender, abdicate, succumb, consent
Ant: resist, protest, prohibit, forbid

YELL
Syn: shout, shriek, exclaim, gesticulate
Ant: suppress, whisper, muffled, muted

YEARN
Syn: languish, crave, require, pine
Ant: content, unwanted, satisfied, gratified

YAWN
Syn: gape, sleepy, slumber, doze
Ant: close, active, brisk, wakeful

ZIGZAG
Syn: oblique, crooked, winding, wayward
Ant: straight, even, direct, unbent

ZEST
Syn: delight, enthusiasm, various, energetic
Ant: disgust, passive, detriment, languid

ZENITH
Syn: summit, apex, maximum, pinnacle
Ant: nadir, base, bottom, floor

ZEALOT
Syn: fanatic, partisan, bigot, chauvinist
Ant: tolerant, liberal, blasphemy, impious

ZEAL
Syn: eagerness, fervour, enthusiasm, ardour
Ant: apathy, lethargy, indifference, reluctant

Revision Exercises

(Based on Synonyms)

Exercise A

Directions *In the following sentences, a word or phrase is written in bold. For each* **bold** *part four words/phrases are listed below each sentence. Choose the word nearest in meaning to bold part.*

1. The inspector was a **vigilant** young man.
(*a*) smart (*b*) watchful
(*c*) ambitious (*d*) intelligent

2. Few teachers have been spared the problem of an **obstreperous** pupil in the class.
(*a*) awkward (*b*) lazy
(*c*) unruly (*d*) sullen

3. Ritu asked Rashmi not to **meddle** in her affairs.
(*a*) intercede (*b*) impose
(*c*) cross (*d*) interfere

4. **Incensed** by his rude behaviour the manager suspended the work.
(*a*) enthused (*b*) enraged
(*c*) inflamed (*d*) excited

5. The Collector has yet not **relinquished** his charge.
(*a*) give up (*b*) abdicate
(*c*) leave (*d*) renounce

6. Her views are not in **consonance** with her husband's.
(*a*) in disagreement (*b*) in conflict
(*c*) in agreement (*d*) contradictory

7. The maidservant left the police station **contrite.**
(*a*) penitent (*b*) sore
(*c*) angry (*d*) remorseless

8. Being a sociable bird she was **conspicuous** by her absence in the club last evening.
(*a*) important (*b*) prominent
(*c*) ignorant (*d*) apparent

9. The communal politics has done **imponderable** loss to the unity of India.
(*a*) incalculable
(*b*) invaluable
(*c*) irreparable
(*d*) invulnerable

10. **Furtive** glances were exchanged between the lovers at the feast.
(*a*) unknown (*b*) secret
(*c*) unsuspecting (*d*) clandestine

Exercise B

Directions *In the following sentences, a word or phrase is written in bold. For each* **bold** *part four words/phrases are listed below each sentence. Choose the word nearest in meaning to bold part.*

1. The newspapers are **clamouring** against the injustice to the landless labourers.
   (a) protesting (b) noising
   (c) complaining (d) demonstrating
2. Honest officers find it difficult to **attune** themselves to corrupt bureaucracy.
   (a) tune (b) adapt
   (c) harmony (d) accusation
3. The five day week in Government Offices is bound to benefit the **jaded** office goers.
   (a) refreshed (b) routined
   (c) fatigued (d) vigorous
4. The resignation of the Chief Minister is **intriguing.**
   (a) curious (b) interesting
   (c) secret (d) diplomatic
5. There was no **ostensible** reason for her being angry at her husband's remarks.
   (a) hidden (b) covert
   (c) apparent (d) secret
6. She **upbraided** the little girl who got frightened.
   (a) make tails (b) make up
   (c) scolded (d) handed
7. She is not seen even smiling these days; she is rather **pensive**.
   (a) sad (b) thoughtful
   (c) gloomy (d) black
8. What meaning have you **drawn** from her tongue in cheek remarks.
   (a) deduced (b) induced
   (c) conduced (d) deduct
9. There is a **tacit** agreement between the super powers not to engage themselves in armed conflict.
   (a) unspoken (b) speechless
   (c) silent (d) introvert
10. Mohinder Amarnath had **penchant** for hook shots.
   (a) art (b) inclination
   (c) strength (d) desire

Exercise C

Directions *In the following sentences, a word or phrase is written in bold. For each* **bold** *part four words/phrases are listed below each sentence. Choose the word nearest in meaning to bold part.*

1. The flat has been **refurbished** recently.
   (a) white-washed (b) painted (c) renovated (d) repaired

2. Even the most careful researcher cannot predict the possible future **ramifications** of his findings.
(a) uses (b) developments (c) consequences (d) conclusions

3. Graduation day is a **momentous** day for most students.
(a) memorable (b) melancholy (c) important (d) hectic

4. **Forthrightness** in speech may not always be a desirable quality.
(a) outspokenness (b) obliqueness
(c) mendacity (d) equivocation

5. Such conduct deserves **reprimand**.
(a) praise (b) punishment
(c) rebuke (d) reward

6. She is very **discreet.**
(a) mannered (b) mild
(c) proud (d) prudent

7. After he came back from his evening walk, he felt **famished.**
(a) exhausted (b) hungry
(c) peevish (d) relaxed

8. She purchased **gimcrack** ornaments from the market.
(a) expensive (b) worthless
(c) rare (d) smuggled

9. He is a good looking but an **insipid** young man.
(a) arrogant (b) unscrupulous
(c) sick (d) lacking in spirit

10. He had **insidiously** wormed his way into her affections.
(a) in a polite manner (b) in a secret manner
(c) in ugly way (d) in a forceful manner

11. The **acerbic** remarks of the manager were unwarranted.
(a) bitter (b) furious
(c) arrogant (d) childish

12. It was an **astute** move to sell the property at that stage.
(a) shrewd (b) unwise
(c) dishonest (d) inexplicable

13. The five experiments gave **disparate** results.
(a) similar (b) encouraging
(c) strange (d) different

14. The chairman conducted the meeting with **aplomb.**
(a) arrogance (b) annoyance
(c) poise (d) authority

15. The early monsoon have brought **respite** to the people.
(a) despite (b) interval of relief
(c) inspite of (d) rest

Exercise ⓓ

Directions *In the following sentences, a word or phrase is written in bold. For each* **bold** *part four words/phrases are listed below each sentence. Choose the word nearest in meaning to bold part.*

1. The coach followed a **devious** course to its destination.
   (a) difficult (b) short-cut
   (c) straight (d) winding
2. It would be **impertinent** to suggest that he was generally wrong.
   (a) fair (b) correct
   (c) rude (d) impartial
3. Our fates seemed **intertwined**.
   (a) complicated (b) destined
   (c) complex (d) linked
4. He displayed a distinct tendency to **long-winded** speeches when asked how he was.
   (a) boring (b) reasonable
   (c) circumlocutory (d) hyperbolic
5. This library was built with donations from the **munificent** citizens of the city.
   (a) well-to-do (b) generous
   (c) respectable (d) learned
6. Some satirists are knwon for their **trenchant** style.
   (a) sharp (b) critical
   (c) aggressive (d) incisive
7. The navy gave **tactical** support to the marines.
   (a) sensitive (b) strategic
   (c) expedient (d) expert
8. Businessmen who lack **acumen** cannot be expected to be very successful.
   (a) smartness (b) sharpness
   (c) keenness (d) cleverness
9. We are happy that the two countries are trying to find an **amicable** solution to their disputes.
   (a) a just (b) an appropriate
   (c) a durable (d) a friendly
10. It is **exasperating** to listen to the suggestions of the minister about the educational reforms of which he knows nothing.
    (a) irritating (b) amusing
    (c) disappointing (d) boring
11. The **disgruntled** members of a party are a constant source of tension to the party leader.
    (a) disloyal (b) dishonest
    (c) discontented (d) dispirited
12. He is so **garrulous** that all sober persons avoid his company.
    (a) quarrelsome (b) talkative
    (c) domineering (d) foolish
13. **Temperance** in eating is conductive to health.
    (a) discipline (b) caution
    (c) moderation (d) care

14. We have had a **virtuoso** performance from him today.
(*a*) futuristic (*b*) stubborn
(*c*) prompt (*d*) exceptionally skilled

15. The air of the room was **fetid** with stale tobacco smoke.
(*a*) comical (*b*) ornament
(*c*) stinking (*d*) regular

Exercise E

Directions *In the following sentences, a word or phrase is written in bold. For each* ***bold*** *part four words/phrases are listed below each sentence. Choose the word nearest in meaning to bold part.*

1. He could rise to this stature because of his **invincible** courage.
(*a*) inviolable (*b*) unmanageable
(*c*) unbeatable (*d*) immeasurable

2. Though he is a teacher, his speech lacks **distinctness.**
(*a*) clarity (*b*) precision
(*c*) distinction (*d*) fluency

3. He tried to **alleviate** the sufferings of his neighbours.
(*a*) swell (*b*) dissipate
(*c*) remove (*d*) relieve

4. Her evidence totally **refuted** the charges.
(*a*) refused (*b*) denied
(*c*) disproved (*d*) repelled

5. One's **remonstration** against social ills has to be consistent to be fruitful.
(*a*) outrage (*b*) demonstration
(*c*) protest (*d*) criticism

Exercise F

Directions *Each of the following questions containing main word followed by four words. Select the word that is* ***most similar in meaning.***

1. Solitude
(*a*) musical composition (*b*) aloofness
(*c*) true statement (*d*) single mindedness

2. Propitious
(*a*) favourable (*b*) clean
(*c*) nearby (*d*) patriotic

3. Rectitude
(*a*) duplication (*b*) integrity
(*c*) rectification (*d*) recovery

4. Commiseration
(*a*) commission (*b*) vastness
(*c*) sympathy (*d*) commendation

5. Slipshod
(*a*) vulgar (*b*) careless
(*c*) common place (*d*) retaliatory

6. Masquerade
(*a*) to provide support
(*b*) to go in disguise
(*c*) to mesmerise
(*d*) marathon race

7. Preposterous
(*a*) careful
(*b*) casual
(*c*) absurd
(*d*) deterrent

8. Parsimonious
(*a*) thrifty
(*b*) cunning
(*c*) extravagant
(*d*) upright

9. Conundrum
(*a*) riddle
(*b*) dampness
(*c*) impudence
(*d*) servility

10. Prosaic
(*a*) uninspiring
(*b*) poetic
(*c*) exotic
(*d*) imaginative

11. Surmount
(*a*) overcome
(*b*) discount
(*c*) surround
(*d*) capture

12. Itinerant
(*a*) frequent use of 'it'
(*b*) anything involving repetition
(*c*) plan for proposed journey
(*d*) travelling from place to place

13. Ostentatious
(*a*) showy
(*b*) pretence
(*c*) abundance
(*d*) plenty

14. Flutter
(*a*) soar
(*b*) agitate
(*c*) change
(*d*) float

15. Estranged
(*a*) jealous
(*b*) angry
(*c*) separated
(*d*) suspicious

16. Restive
(*a*) rested
(*b*) restless
(*c*) limited
(*d*) limitless

17. Premonition
(*a*) insight
(*b*) uncertainty
(*c*) forewarning
(*d*) scope

18. Derogatory
(*a*) infurious
(*b*) shattering
(*c*) disparaging
(*d*) destructive

19. Decrepitude
(*a*) disease
(*b*) coolness
(*c*) crowd
(*d*) feebleness

20. Craven
(*a*) greedy
(*b*) cowardly
(*c*) flattering
(*d*) restless

Exercise G

Directions *In these questions, choose the word similar in meaning to the word given.*

1. Scorn
   (a) concise (b) despise
   (c) bias (d) fierce
2. Cantankerous
   (a) noisy (b) quarrelsome
   (c) rash (d) disrespectful
3. Aberration
   (a) justification (b) intensification
   (c) deviation (d) rationality
4. Admonition
   (a) reason (b) warning
   (c) admission (d) hindrance
5. Onus
   (a) inclination (b) responsibility
   (c) prudence (d) antipathy
6. Relish
   (a) realise (b) taste
   (c) enjoy (d) reveal
7. Poignant
   (a) showy (b) sad
   (c) silly (d) snobbish
8. Reverie
   (a) determination (b) daydream
   (c) reality (d) realisation
9. Prognosis
   (a) diagnosis (b) forecast
   (c) preface (d) identity
10. Repartee
    (a) refuse (b) celebrate
    (c) response (d) question
11. Exhort
    (a) recommend (b) coax
    (c) pressure (d) splendid
12. Vindictive
    (a) imaginative (b) accusative
    (c) spiteful (d) aggressive
13. Inclement
    (a) selfish (b) active
    (c) unfavourable (d) inactive
14. Enigma
    (a) truth (b) fear
    (c) difficulty (d) puzzle

15. Foreboding
(*a*) alarm (*b*) forecast
(*c*) failure (*d*) foresight

16. Emulate
(*a*) echo (*b*) mimic
(*c*) reiterate (*d*) simulate

17. Sordid
(*a*) sore (*b*) unpleasant
(*c*) splendid (*d*) dissatisfied

18. Mellow
(*a*) melodious (*b*) dramatic
(*c*) genial (*d*) fruity

19. Atrocity
(*a*) envy (*b*) violence
(*c*) jealousy (*d*) absurdity

20. Vacillate
(*a*) waver (*b*) never
(*c*) quiver (*d*) queer

Exercise H

Directions (Q.Nos. 1-3) *Choose the word which is most nearly the same in meaning of the given word.*

1. Indict
(*a*) implicate (*b*) elude (*c*) charge (*d*) manifest

2. Deluge
(*a*) confusion (*b*) deception
(*c*) flood (*d*) weapon

3. Preponderance
(*a*) pre-eminence (*b*) remnant
(*c*) domineering (*d*) preoccupation

Directions (Q.Nos. 4-6) *Out of the four alternatives, choose the one which best expresses the meaning of the given word.*

4. Intrepid
(*a*) hesitant (*b*) extrovert (*c*) fearless (*d*) rash

5. Prodigal
(*a*) exclusive (*b*) productive (*c*) lavish (*d*) carefree

6. Perspicuous
(*a*) relevant (*b*) precise
(*c*) brief (*d*) clear

Directions (Q.Nos. 7-14) *Each of following sentences is followed by four words or groups of words. Select the synonym of the word (occurring in the sentence in **bold** letters) as per the context.*

7. The song had **a soporific** effect on the child.
(*a*) soothing (*b*) terrific
(*c*) supreme (*d*) sleep-inducing

8. His **allegiance** to the party was suspect from the very beginning.
(*a*) servility (*b*) obedience
(*c*) loyalty (*d*) passivity

9. Sympathetic criticism has a **salutary** effect.
(*a*) premature (*b*) terrible
(*c*) disastrous (*d*) beneficial

10. His bad behaviour **evoked** punishment.
(*a*) escaped (*b*) called for
(*c*) produced (*d*) summoned

11. He was the court appointed lawyer for fifty-six **indigent** defendants.
(*a*) Indian men (*b*) poor
(*c*) guilty (*d*) untried .

12. The boy said that pain had **abated**.
(*a*) reduced (*b*) vanished
(*c*) increased (*d*) stabilised

13. He became known as an **implacable** for of fundamentalism.
(*a*) relentless (*b*) pleasing
(*c*) dangerous (*d*) couragesous

14. The queen was aware of the **insolent** behaviour of the lords.
(*a*) violent (*b*) polite
(*c*) insulting (*d*) frivolous

Directions (Q.Nos. 15-23) *Each question in this section consists of a word followed by four words or groups of words. Select the word or groups of words that is* ***most similar in meaning .***

15. Crass
(*a*) casual (*b*) coarse
(*c*) stupid (*d*) sterile

16. Cursory
(*a*) little (*b*) quick
(*c*) eager (*d*) tender

17. Envisaged
(*a*) ensured (*b*) idealised
(*c*) contemplated (*d*) created

18. Fickle
(*a*) awkward (*b*) inconsistent
(*c*) silly (*d*) ugly

19. Resentment
(*a*) annoyance (*b*) anger
(*c*) disagreement (*d*) dismissal

20. Obdurate
(*a*) angry (*b*) calm
(*b*) obessed (*d*) adamant

21. Ostracise
(*a*) censure (*b*) sentence
(*c*) banish (*d*) berate

22. Imbecility
(*a*) stupidity (*b*) rusticity (*c*) verbosity (*d*) incoherence

23. Collusion
(*a*) a conflict (*b*) a secret agreement
(*c*) a consultation (*d*) a misunderstanding

Directions (Q.Nos. 24-30) *Each question in this section consists of a word or a group of words followed by four words or groups of words. Select the word or group of words that is* ***most similar in meaning****.*

24. Contradict
(*a*) request politely (*b*) deny emphatically
(*c*) talk abusively (*d*) contempt

25. Eradicate
(*a*) put up (*b*) remove
(*c*) soften (*d*) suppress

26. Adhere
(*a*) act reluctantly (*b*) give allegiance
(*c*) waver frequently (*d*) read promptly

27. Infer
(*a*) conclude (*b*) calculate
(*c*) debate (*d*) suggest

28. Explicit
(*a*) immediate (*b*) plainly stated
(*c*) marked (*d*) revealing the secret

29. Repress
(*a*) express (*b*) impress (*c*) curb (*d*) confuse

30. Vindictive
(*a*) cruel (*b*) harsh
(*c*) revengeful (*d*) rude

Directions (Q.Nos. 31-35) *Each of the following sentences is followed by four words or groups of words. Select the synonym of the word or words (occurring in the sentence in* ***bold*** *letters) as per the context.*

31. **Momentous** changes are taking place in the social and economic life of India.
(*a*) notorious (*b*) momentary
(*c*) offical (*d*) enormous

32. She is a pretty **insipid** young lady.
(*a*) clever (*b*) lazy
(*c*) dull (*d*) lean

33. She thought that **running into** her old friend was a stroke of fate.
(*a*) meeting by chance (*b*) colliding
(*c*) travelling with (*d*) quarrelling with

34. He was a **charismatic** leader.
(*a*) exceptionally fascinating (*b*) particularly popular
(*c*) compulsively pleasant (*d*) strangely haunting

35. He is an **indefatigable** worker.
(*a*) tired (*b*) tireless (*c*) brave (*d*) skilful

Directions (Q.Nos. 36-39) *In these questions, out of the four alternatives choose the one which best expresses the meaning of the given word.*

36. Camouflage
(a) disguise *(b)* cover *(c)* demonstrate *(d)* fabric

37. Yearn
(a) deny *(b)* confront *(c)* cajole *(d)* crave

38. Pensive
(a) reluctant *(b)* unhappy *(c)* contemplative *(d)* precise

39. Narcissism
(a) unpleasant behaviour *(b)* self-condemnation
(c) self-admiration *(d)* rude behaviour

Directions (Q.Nos. 40-44) *In this section, select the word or group of words that is* ***most similar in meaning*** *to the bold word or group of words in the given sentence.*

40. The two **executioners** approached the tree with a red mark on its side.
(a) executive engineers *(b)* explorers
(c) experimenters *(d)* those who inflict capital punishment

41. He is very intelligent, but **ill-favoured** by nature.
(a) unlucky *(b)* weak in health
(c) short-tempered *(d)* ugly

42. People thronged to pay **homage** to the departed leader.
(a) humility *(b)* tribute
(c) obedience *(d)* allegiance

43. For better health we must **refrain** from smoking.
(a) dissuade *(b)* desist
(c) prevent *(d)* curb

44. The article was so well written that it **merited** careful study.
(a) deserved *(b)* encouraged *(c)* prompted *(d)* supported

Directions (Q.Nos. 45-48) *In these questions, out of the four alternatives choose the one which best expresses the meaning of the given word.*

45. Gaol
(a) destination *(b)* garden
(c) jail *(d)* bird

46. Loathing
(a) warmth *(b)* affectation
(c) hatred *(d)* affection

47. Notion
(a) thought *(b)* fact
(c) truth *(d)* hypothesis

48. Vivacious
(a) poisonous *(b)* energetic
(c) tricky *(d)* slow

Directions (Q.Nos. 49-53) *In these questions, out of the four alternatives choose the one which best expresses the meaning of the given word .*

49. Forbearance
(*a*) relevance (*b*) deliverance
(*c*) patience (*d*) extravagance

50. Bequeath
(*a*) surround (*b*) give
(*c*) disclose (*d*) scold

51. Nonchalant
(*a*) formal (*b*) imaginary
(*c*) casual (*d*) neutral

52. Annexure
(*a*) development (*b*) retirement
(*c*) commencement (*d*) attachment

53. Errand
(*a*) blunder (*b*) energy
(*c*) task (*d*) mistake

Directions (Q.Nos. 54-58) *Each of the following sentences are followed by four words or groups of words. Select the synonym of the word or words (occurring in the sentence in* **bold** *letters) as per the context.*

54. The convict's **ingenuous** explanation brought tears in every eye.
(*a*) candid (*b*) secret
(*c*) insincere (*d*) consisten

55. The **enormity** of the population problem is irksome.
(*a*) intensity (*b*) vastness
(*c*) cruelty (*d*) fragility

56. He **induces** human being to want things they don't want.
(*a*) influences (*b*) dictates
(*c*) persuades (*d*) appreciates

57. He is not **cut out** to be a teacher.
(*a*) trained (*b*) suited (*c*) selected (*d*) guided

58. The Chief Minister **reprimanded** the officers for their methods of handling the public.
(*a*) adulated (*b*) scolded severely
(*c*) disapproved of (*d*) suspended

Directions (Q.Nos. 59-71) *Each of the following questions consists of a word followed by four words or groups of words. Select the word or group of words that is most similar in meaning.*

59. Painstaking
(*a*) feeling panic (*b*) thorough and rigorous
(*c*) taking risk (*d*) painful and sorrowful

60. Substantial
(*a*) delicate (*b*) graceful
(*c*) sensational (*d*) significant

61. Indolent
(*a*) cautious (*b*) lazy
(*c*) unintelligent (*d*) stubborn

62. Vehemently
(a) devoutly (b) serenely
(c) hysterically (d) forcefully

63. Feigned
(a) pretended (b) played
(c) developed (d) failed

64. Penury
(a) poverty (b) petty
(c) phony (d) pathetic

65. Affectation
(a) adoration (b) artificiality
(c) appreciation (d) proficiency

66. Stifle
(a) starve (b) smother
(c) stumble (d) stagger

67. Stalemate
(a) degeneration (b) exhaustion
(c) deadlock (d) settlement

68. Forthright
(a) honest and outspoken (b) serious and stubborn
(c) strong and brave (d) willing and determined

69. Discreet
(a) mature (b) clever
(c) intelligent (d) prudent

70. Portend
(a) profess (b) portray (c) think (d) foreshadow

71. Odium
(a) illness (b) hatred (c) oddity (d) devious

Directions (Q.Nos. 72-76) *Each of the following sentences are followed by four words or groups of words. Select the synonym of the word (occurring in the sentence in **bold** letters) as per the context.*

72. A wise man puts past **rancour** behind and moves ahead
(a) dislike (b) hatred
(c) division (d) criticism

73. We saw a **scintillating** fireworks display.
(a) fascinating (b) unforgettable
(c) beautiful (d) sparkling

74. The **pact** has been in effect for twenty years.
(a) treaty (b) monarchy
(c) lease (d) trend

75. He had a reputation of being a **prudent** businessman.
(a) skilful (b) wealthy
(c) careful (d) dishonest

76. The violence erupted because of the **zealot**.
(a) enthusiastic (b) brave
(c) timid (d) fanatic

Directions (Q.Nos. 77-81) *Each of the following sentences are followed by four words or groups of words. Select the synonym of the word (occurring in the sentence in* ***bold*** *letters) as per the context.*

77. Europe, America and Japan have taken to the field of science with **singular** vigour and activity.
(*a*) peculiar (*b*) outstanding
(*c*) familiar (*d*) single

78. As I look around I see the crumbling ruins of a proud civilization strewn like a vast heap of **futility.**
(*a*) irrelevance (*b*) absurdity
(*c*) pointlessness (*d*) downtrodden

79. Mark Antony's **eulogy** of Caesar is finely recorded by Shakespeare in his play.
(*a*) prayer (*b*) honour
(*c*) praise (*d*) denunciation

80. Your **intervention** was required.
(*a*) interference (*b*) interruption
(*c*) disturbance (*d*) connection

81. It is difficult to **discern** the sample on the slide without adjusting the microscope.
(*a*) discard (*b*) arrange
(*c*) determine (*d*) debate

Directions (Q.Nos. 82 and 83) *In the following questions, out of the four alternatives, choose the one which best expresses the meaning of the given word.*

82. Tribulation
(*a*) palpitation (*b*) suffering
(*c*) weakness (*d*) stimulation

83. The Prime Minister goes on the **ramparts** of the Red Fort to hoist the National flag.
(*a*) rompway (*b*) staircase
(*c*) parapet (*d*) scaffold

Directions (Q.Nos. 84-89) *In the following questions, you find a number of sentences, parts of which are bold . For each bold part, four words/phrases are listed below. Choose the word/phrase nearest in meaning to the bold part.*

84. She is a woman of **sterling** qualities.
(*a*) interesting (*b*) genuine (*c*) irritating (*d*) exciting

85. Although the boys in his class were naughty, he never resorted to **corporal** punishment.
(*a*) harsh (*b*) physical (*c*) unjust (*d*) general

86. She adjusted quite well with her husband's **idiosyncrasies**.
(*a*) peculiar habits (*b*) bad habits
(*c*) weaknesses (*d*) stupid manners

87. Deputy Inspector General made a **perfunctory** inspection of the police station.
(*a*) thorough and complete
(*b*) superficial
(*c*) done as a routine but without interest
(*d*) intensive

88. A scientist generally carries out his investigations **empirically**.
(*a*) by intuitively (*b*) by verbally
(*c*) by through written communication (*d*) by observation and experiment

89. I cannot believe in the **veracity** of his statement.
(*a*) truth (*b*) usefulness
(*c*) sincerity (*d*) falsity

Directions (Q.Nos. 90-100) *In each of these sentences, a word or a phrase has been bold followed by words or phrases listed (a), (b), (c) and (d). Choose the most appropriate word/phrase closest in meaning to the bold word or phrase.*

90. He **disdained** to notice the insult.
(*a*) was very proud (*b*) refused
(*c*) was unhappy (*d*) was too reluctant

91. He gave an **evocative** rendering of his recent poems.
(*a*) thrilling (*b*) enchanting
(*c*) emotional (*d*) incantatory

92. **Expeditious** steps should be taken to complete the work in two weeks.
(*a*) unmerciful and punitive (*b*) strict and forceful
(*c*) disciplinary (*d*) prompt and efficient

93. Why did you make that **flippant** remark?
(*a*) highly critical (*b*) not showing deserved respect
(*c*) casual (*d*) indifferent

94. That is not an occasion to make an **impromptu** speech.
(*a*) without preparation (*b*) thoughtless
(*c*) improper (*d*) long and boring

95. There is not a single word that is **redundant** in the report.
(*a*) unimportant (*b*) not needed
(*c*) bombastic (*d*) flowery

96. The country's economy is beginning to **look up** now.
(*a*) look clear (*b*) go down
(*c*) remain static (*d*) improve

97. It needs an expert to **decipher** the secret message sent to the Army Officers during war time.
(*a*) swindle (*b*) decode
(*c*) make up (*d*) defy

98. Bana in Sanskrit, Lyly in English and Prasad in Hindi are celebrated for their **florid** style.
(*a*) ornate (*b*) rich
(*c*) refined (*d*) rambling

99. The eyewitness testimony was **incontrovertible**.
(*a*) disputable (*b*) debatable
(*c*) unacceptable (*d*) unquestionable

100. On account of the **paucity** of the funds, plan remained incomplete.
(*a*) lack (*b*) surplus
(*c*) abundance (*d*) excess

Revision Exercises

(Based on Antonyms)

Exercise A

Directions *The following sentences consist of a word or a phrase which is written in* **bold** *letters. Each of them is followed by four words or phrases. Select the word or the phrase which is closest to the opposite in meaning of the* **bold** *word or phrase.*

1. He was charged with **abetting** the murder of an innocent child.
(a) baffle (b) instigate
(c) promote (d) support

2. The visit of the Vice Chancellor has been **deferred** indefinitely.
(a) expedited (b) dissolved
(c) postponed (d) put off

3. How dare you **desecrate** an idol of this temple.
(a) defile (b) pollute
(c) deify (d) impious

4. There exists **rancour** between the two brothers.
(a) animosity (b) harmony
(c) devotion (d) enmity

5. Born in **squalid** surroundings of the slums, she rose to stardom overnight.
(a) dirty (b) clean
(c) disorderly (d) mean

6. Mrs Nisha made a **fervent** appeal to the members of the club to maintain unity.
(a) active (b) impassive
(c) cold (d) passionate

Exercise B

Directions *The following sentences consist of a word or a phrase which is written in* **bold** *letters. Each of them is followed by four words or phrases. Select the word or the phrase which is closest to the opposite in meaning of the* **bold** *word or phrase.*

1. You are advised to show **clemency** to the defeated enemy.
(a) callousness (b) mercy
(c) leniency (d) kindness

2. The Board of Directors showered **encomium** on the Chairman for his liberal policies.
(a) denunciation (b) generosity
(c) tribute (d) praise

3. A lady of a few words she is given to **laconic** answers.
(a) copious (b) lingering
(c) terse (d) brief

4. A character without a **blemish** is a virtue of a leader.
(a) stigma (b) adornment
(c) strength (d) blot

5. There was **dismal** atmosphere in the dressing room of the defeated team.
   (a) cheerful (b) dreadful
   (c) gloomy (d) jovial

6. **Modesty** is a virtue but it must not be allowed to be exploited.
   (a) reserve (b) boldness
   (c) mildness (d) humility

7. At his success in the examination he felt **elated.**
   (a) exultant (b) dejected
   (c) resting (d) jubilant

8. The minister was accused of indulging in **nepotism.**
   (a) impartiality (b) hatred
   (c) condemnation (d) indifference

Exercise C

Directions *The following sentences consist of a word or a phrase which is written in **bold** letters. Each of them is followed by four words or phrases. Select the word or the phrase which is closest to the opposite in meaning of the **bold** word or phrase.*

1. The facts of the case were **obscured** by the speech of the defence counsel.
   (a) reflected (b) illustrated
   (c) clarified (d) exhibited

2. He glanced through the letter **perfunctorily.**
   (a) nicely (b) ceremoniously
   (c) carefully (d) particularly

3. It is not difficult to take note of his **immaculate** style of writing.
   (a) stained (b) uneven
   (c) impure (d) flawed

4. The research showed that the drug has **pernicious** effect on the health of patients.
   (a) fair (b) advantageous
   (c) beneficial (d) satisfactory

5. I am in a rather **precarious** position in my place of work.
   (a) comfortable (b) senior
   (c) privileged (d) secure

6. There are no permanent **adversaries** in politics.
   (a) associates (b) allies
   (c) collaborators (d) partners

7. He produced **cogent** reasons for the change of policy.
   (a) flimsy (b) unconvincing
   (c) improper (d) simple

8. The Prime Minister's radio broadcast **glavanised** the people's spirit.
   (a) frightened (b) pacified
   (c) dampened (d) distracted

Exercise D

Directions *The following sentences consist of a word or a phrase which is written in **bold** letters. Each of them is followed by four words or phrases. Select the word or the phrase which is closest to the opposite in meaning of the **bold** word or phrase.*

1. The young business executive was very **perspicacious.**
   (*a*) banal (*b*) clever (*c*) humble (*d*) unreliable
2. There are many anecdotes about his sister who is an **imperious** personality.
   (*a*) characterless (*b*) pious (*c*) arrogant (*d*) submissive
3. Though aware of his crimes, he remained **impenitent** throughout.
   (*a*) repentant (*b*) sorrowful (*c*) hot-headed (*d*) pertinent
4. In facing adverse situations, he was very **stoical**.
   (*a*) tactless (*b*) flinching (*c*) awkward (*d*) assured
5. They made a **profligate** use of scarce resources.
   (*a*) proper (*b*) extravagant (*c*) effective (*d*) thrifty
6. The consultant analysed the proposal carefully before he decided to **jettison** it.
   (*a*) abandon (*b*) strengthen
   (*c*) accept (*d*) modify
7. The politician was **flummoxed** by the questions put to him.
   (*a*) comfortable (*b*) annoyed
   (*c*) delighted (*d*) disconcerted
8. Throughout the evening, Rahul looked very **doleful.**
   (*a*) aggressive (*b*) cheerful
   (*c*) tired (*d*) involved
9. He is showing signs of **senility**.
   (*a*) virility (*b*) laziness
   (*c*) maturity (*d*) exhaustion
10. There is not a trace of **vanity** in her behaviour.
    (*a*) proudness (*b*) selflessness
    (*c*) modesty (*d*) dignity
11. They approached the stranger **warily.**
    (*a*) suspiciously (*b*) cautiously
    (*c*) carefully (*d*) carelessly
12. The forwards of their football team made **sporadic** raids into the opponent's territory.
    (*a*) rare (*b*) frequent
    (*c*) sharp (*d*) co-ordinated
13. She was **overstrung** before the performance.
    (*a*) excited (*b*) calm
    (*c*) enthusiastic (*d*) cheerful
14. The booking-clerk looked very **grumpy.**
    (*a*) surly (*b*) pleasant
    (*c*) efficient (*d*) honest
15. She paid special attention to those women who had **succumbed** to adversity.
    (*a*) surrendered (*b*) given up
    (*c*) overcome (*d*) demanded

Exercise E

Directions *The following sentences consist of a word or a phrase which is written in **bold** letters. Each of them is followed by four words or phrases. Select the word or the phrase which is closest to the opposite in meaning of the **bold** word or phrase.*

1. Her dress was too **slovenly** for that kind of interview.
   (a) gaudy (b) tidy
   (c) formal (d) old fashioned
2. I was deeply affected by his **urbane** behaviour.
   (a) rural (b) indifferent
   (c) rude (d) unsympathetic
3. The judge thought that the offence was **deliberate.**
   (a) negligible (b) casual
   (c) unintentional (d) legitimate
4. The state government for its part can identify **vulnerable** villages where these forces can be stationed.
   (a) important (b) famous
   (c) remote (d) invincible
5. Some of the needs of a modern man are surely **dispensable.**
   (a) desirable (b) acceptable
   (c) relevant (d) essential
6. Some democratic countries believe in racial **segregation.**
   (a) subordination (b) integration
   (c) inferiority (d) domination
7. The task assigned to him was **arduous.**
   (a) absorbing (b) good
   (c) plain (d) easy
8. His **magnanimous** gesture came to his employees as a surprise.
   (a) small (b) cruel
   (c) thoughtless (d) mean

Exercise F

Directions *Each of the following main words are followed by four words. Select the word that is furthest (opposite) in meaning to the main word.*

1. Forbearance
   (a) patience (b) self-control
   (c) intolerance (d) preference
2. Paltry
   (a) obsolete (b) cautious
   (c) random (d) plentiful
3. Propensity
   (a) disinclination (b) forecast
   (c) stagnation (d) restlessness
4. Encomium
   (a) meagre (b) unethical
   (c) diffidence (d) hypercriticism

5. Chimerical
(a) fearful (b) breathtaking
(c) serene (d) practical idea

6. Petulant
(a) fearless (b) scrupulous
(c) industrious (d) calm

7. Laconic
(a) uncivilised (b) talkative
(c) erudite (d) livid

8. Exodus
(a) influx (b) return
(c) home coming (d) restoration

9. Affluence
(a) poverty (b) misery
(c) stagnation (d) neglect

10. Agony
(a) pleasure (b) anger
(c) irritation (d) rage

11. Mournful
(a) playful (b) joyous
(c) laughable (d) humorous

12. Timorous
(a) trembling (b) cowardly
(c) bright (d) bold

13. Sublime
(a) amusing (b) ludicrous
(c) hilarious (d) mean

14. Demented
(a) sensible (b) sensitive
(c) sensual (d) inordinate

15. Cumbersome
(a) heavy (b) convenient
(c) smooth (d) automatic

16. Arid
(a) cloudy (b) juicy
(c) marshy (d) wet

17. Senile
(a) suspicious (b) mentally alert
(c) corrupt (d) affluent

18. Blithesome
(a) graceful (b) sullen
(c) adventurous (d) mammoth

19. Consanguine
(a) of different kind (b) invisible
(c) urbane (d) untenanted

20. Redoubtable
(*a*) truthful (*b*) crafty
(*c*) widely travelled (*d*) ordinary

Exercise G

Directions (Q. Nos. 1-7) *Choose the word opposite in meaning to the word given.*

1. Subservient
(*a*) eligible (*b*) inferior
(*c*) superior (*d*) powerful

2. Redundant
(*a*) repentant (*b*) surplus
(*c*) singular (*d*) required

3. Boisterous
(*a*) serenity (*b*) calm
(*c*) cheerful (*d*) courageous

4. Substantial
(*a*) flimsy (*b*) hefty
(*c*) actual (*d*) excess

5. Dwindle
(*a*) decrease (*b*) diminish
(*c*) shrink (*d*) increase

6. Relinquish
(*a*) vanish (*b*) quench
(*c*) relish (*d*) continue

7. Insipid
(*a*) colourless (*b*) dull
(*c*) tasty (*d*) colourful

Directions (Q. Nos. 8-14) *Choose the word opposite in meaning to the word given.*

8. Foment
(*a*) repulse (*b*) cease
(*c*) control (*d*) quell

9. Tardy
(*a*) prompt (*b*) gradual
(*c*) late (*d*) quick

10. Susceptible
(*a*) incredible (*b*) immune
(*c*) predictable (*d*) unpredictable

11. Cessation
(*a*) commencement (*b*) renewal
(*c*) ongoing (*d*) interruption

12. Procrastinate
(*a*) experiment (*b*) expedite
(*c*) exclude (*d*) propagate

13. Insolent
(*a*) submissive (*b*) arrogant
(*c*) overbearing (*d*) disdainful

14. Rancid
(*a*) putrified (*b*) delicious
(*c*) fresh (*d*) stale

Directions (Q. Nos. 15-17) *Choose the word opposite in meaning to the word given.*

15. Impetuous
(*a*) agitated (*b*) impulsive
(*c*) cautious (*d*) reckless

16. Culmination
(*a*) completion (*b*) climax
(*c*) conclusion (*d*) beginning

17. Curb
(*a*) help (*b*) allow
(*c*) restrain (*d*) remove

Directions (Q. Nos. 18-20) *Choose the word opposite in meaning to the word given.*

18. Chivalrous
(*a*) gallant (*b*) dastardly
(*c*) amorous (*d*) defiant

19. Erudite
(*a*) barbarous (*b*) crude
(*c*) boring (*d*) ignorant

20. Concur
(*a*) disagree (*b*) disappear
(*c*) disarrange (*d*) discourage

Exercise H

Directions (Q. Nos. 1 and 2) *Choose the word which is most opposite in meaning of the word.*

1. Feasible
(*a*) unattended (*b*) physical
(*c*) practical (*d*) unviable
(*e*) wasteful

2. Indifference
(*a*) interest (*b*) difference
(*c*) ignorance (*d*) rule-bound
(*e*) insignificance

Directions (Q.Nos. 3-8) *Each of the following sentences are followed by four words or group of words. Select the antonym of the word (occurring in the sentence in* **bold** *letters) as per the context.*

3. His assignments have taken him to many **exotic** locations around the world.
(*a*) wonderful (*b*) cosmopolitan
(*c*) irrelevant (*d*) common

4. He has given up his **vicious** habits.
(a) godly (b) virtuous
(c) sublime (d) friendly

5. The issue was raised **tangentially** in the negotiations.
(a) partly (b) forcefully
(c) candidly (d) fitfully

6. **Escalating** prices are causing hardship to the poor.
(a) fixed (b) fluctuating
(c) falling (d) reasonable

7. I have **malice** towards none.
(a) sympathy (b) goodwill
(c) friendship (d) attraction

8. The boy comes of an **affluent** family.
(a) poor (b) ordinary
(c) infamous (d) backward

Directions (Q. Nos. 9-29) *Each question in this section consists of a word followed by four words or groups of words. Select the word or groups of words that is most nearly opposite in meaning to the word given.*

9. Probity
(a) dishonesty (b) timidity
(c) treachery (d) insincerity

10. Sporadic
(a) surviving (b) sweeping
(c) restrained (d) persistent

11. Implication
(a) consideration (b) exoneration
(c) conclusion (d) interpretation

12. Apposite
(a) intemperate (b) inappropriate
(c) indecent (d) incriminatory

13. Gregarious
(a) indecent (b) unsociable
(c) above reproach (d) unlovable

14. Chivalry
(a) dishonesty (b) discourtesy
(c) disobedience (d) disaffection

15. Dismal
(a) bright (b) indifferent
(c) fast (d) energetic

16. Sanguine temper
(a) despairing nature (b) peaceful temperament
(c) rude behaviour (d) selfish nature

17. Imperil
(a) safeguard (b) construct
(c) create (d) brighten

18. Ostensibly
(a) elaborately (b) really
(c) vaguely (d) sensibly

19. Consolidated
(a) disjointed (b) broken
(c) weakened (d) lost

20. Chronic
(a) pathetic (b) characteristic
(c) temporary (d) mild

21. Callous
(a) considerate (b) indifferent
(c) indulgent (d) generous

22. Vituperative
(a) joyous (b) congratulatory
(c) critical (d) virtuous

23. Smug
(a) satisfied (b) dissatisfied
(c) serious (d) delighted

24. Oppressive
(a) gentle (b) kindly
(c) smooth (d) orderly

25. Obscure
(a) inconspicuous (b) veiled
(c) clear (d) distinct

26. Clinch
(a) lose (b) clasp
(c) deal (d) seal

27. Enervate
(a) decelerate (b) strengthen
(c) push forward (d) aggravate

28. To put up with
(a) to stay together (b) to talk politely
(c) to dislike (d) to move along with

29. Established
(a) small (b) new
(c) orthodox (d) modern
(e) remaining

Directions (Q. Nos. 30-36) *Each question in this section consists of a word followed by four words or groups of words. Select the word or group of words that is most opposite in meaning to the word given.*

30. Urbane
(a) elegant (b) slow
(c) crude (d) foolish

31. Spurious
(a) genuine (b) authentic
(c) real (d) artificial

32. Barren
(a) wet (b) rich
(c) fertile (d) exception

33. Conceal
(a) reveal (b) show off
(c) describe (d) explain

34. Graceful
(a) awkward (b) ignorant
(c) slow (d) disloyal

35. Provoke
(a) attract (b) convince
(c) gratify (d) pacify

36. Vague
(a) clear (b) pleasant
(c) profound (d) sufficient

Directions (Q. Nos. 37-44) *In the following questions, each of the following sentences are followed by four words or groups of words. Select the antonym of the word or words (occurring in the sentence in* ***bold*** *letters) as per the context.*

37. A small **altercation** between the children started off a riot.
(a) quarrel (b) friendly discussion
(c) contest (d) race

38. He agreed reluctantly to sign the form but looked **at ease.**
(a) embarrassed (b) comfortable
(c) welcome (d) easy

39. My mother has been working hard for the last two weeks and she feels **run down.**
(a) energetic (b) cold
(c) emotional (d) morbid

40. The three states signed a pact to have **collective** economy.
(a) distributive (b) disintegrative
(c) individual (d) divided

41. He was deeply hurt by her **curt** reply.
(a) abrupt (b) short
(c) expansive (d) rude

42. He was asked to **accelerate** the pace of work.
(a) slacken (b) control
(c) stiffen (d) supervise

43. The child was **abducted** when he was going to school.
(a) seized (b) set free
(c) kidnapped (d) ransomed

44. The baby has a very **delicate** body.
(a) crude (b) strong
(c) hard (d) bony

Directions (Q. Nos. 45-49) *In these questions, choose the word opposite in meaning to the given word.*

45. Augment
(*a*) increase (*b*) defend
(*c*) supplement (*d*) decrease

46. Amateurish
(*a*) seasoned (*b*) trained
(*c*) skilled (*d*) professional

47. Ignominious
(*a*) valuable (*b*) desirable
(*c*) honourable (*d*) clever

48. Disparage
(*a*) compliment (*b*) convince
(*c*) comfort (*d*) connect

49. Garrulous
(*a*) quiet (*b*) exaggerated
(*c*) gruesome (*d*) creative

Directions (Q. Nos. 50-61) *In this section, select the word or group of words that is most opposite in meaning to the* **bold** *word or group of words in the given sentence.*

50. Poisonous gases emitted from factories **contaminate** the air we breathe in.
(*a*) sanctify (*b*) invigorate
(*c*) taint (*d*) purify

51. **Reckless** driving causes accidents.
(*a*) careful (*b*) slow (*c*) good (*d*) correct

52. Some of their customs are **barbarous**.
(*a*) civilised (*b*) modem
(*c*) polite (*d*) praiseworthy

53. They are going to **embark upon** a mountaineering expedition.
(*a*) launch (*b*) analyse
(*c*) break off (*d*) conclude

54. There has been a gradual **falling off** in the quality of articles manufactured locally.
(*a*) shrinkage (*b*) erosion
(*c*) improvement (*d*) descent

55. Though he had lost the battle, he decided not to **yield to** the enemy.
(*a*) submit to (*b*) persuade
(*c*) resist (*d*) seek terms with

56. It was a baseless rumour that **triggered** riots and arson at an unprecedented scale throughout the country.
(*a*) choked (*b*) tapered off
(*c*) diluted (*d*) ignited

57. The old man **manifested** his greed at the sight of a huge amount of money.
(*a*) displayed (*b*) concealed
(*c*) suppressed (*d*) marked

58. The fallen trees **blocked** our passage freedom from the wood.
(*a*) facilitated (*b*) started (*c*) checked (*d*) promoted

59. He **fell foul of me** when I asked him to apologise to his teacher.
(a) quarrelled with me (b) attacked me
(c) made friends with me (d) showed appreciation for me

60. He wanted to **inaugurate** the project right on schedule.
(a) terminate (b) inculcate
(c) facilitate (d) ameliorate

61. They decided to **embellish** the dress with imported ribbons.
(a) dishonour (b) demolish
(c) spoil (d) suffice

Directions (Q. Nos. 62-64) *In these questions, choose the word opposite in meaning to the given word.*

62. Forthright
(a) blunt (b) tricky
(c) candid (d) plainspoken

63. Antagonism
(a) cordiality (b) animosity
(c) hostility (d) enmity

64. Vanity
(a) humanity (b) humility
(c) pretension (d) arrogance

Directions (Q. Nos. 65-68) *In these questions, choose the word opposite in meaning to the given word.*

65. Niggardly
(a) miserly (b) avaricious
(c) extravagant (d) generous

66. Amenable
(a) unwilling (b) acquiescent
(c) distrustful (d) inattentive

67. Reproof
(a) appropriation (b) approbation
(c) apposition (d) condemnation

68. Conspicuous
(a) obscure (b) blatant
(c) definite (d) obvious

Directions (Q. Nos. 69-71) *Choose the word which is most opposite in meaning to the given word.*

69. Myriad
(a) trivial (b) difficult
(c) few (d) effortless

70. Tepid
(a) moderate (b) high
(c) whole hearted (d) irregular

71. Myth
(a) reality (b) belief
(c) contrast (d) idealism

Directions (Q. Nos. 72-76) *Each of the following sentences are followed by four words. Select the antonym of the word (occurring in the sentence in **bold** letters) as per the context.*

72. A large number of designer clothes are **revolting.**
(*a*) inviting (*b*) beautiful
(*c*) fashionable (*d*) delightful.

73. **Recession** is a major cause of unemployment.
(*a*) education (*b*) boom
(*c*) poverty (*d*) computerisation

74. He finally **conceded** that he was involved in smuggling.
(*a*) admitted (*b*) accepted
(*c*) denied (*d*) concealed

75. The accused emphatically **denied** the charge in the court.
(*a*) accepted (*b*) agreed
(*c*) asserted (*d*) affirmed

76. This cloth is a **coarse** to touch.
(*a*) delicate (*b*) rough (*c*) painful (*d*) harsh

Directions (Q. Nos. 77-91) *Each of the following questions consists of a word followed by four words or groups of words. Select the word or group of words that is farthest in meaning to the word given.*

77. Laudatory
(*a*) laughable (*b*) derogatory
(*c*) abusive (*d*) detriment

78. Pertinent
(*a*) eloquent (*b*) distant
(*c*) relevant (*d*) irrelevant

79. Colossal
(*a*) fragile (*b*) small
(*c*) colourful (*d*) impressive

80. Indispensable
(*a*) tolerable (*b*) superfluous
(*c*) expensive (*d*) hostile

81. Vindictive
(*a*) forgiving (*b*) humane
(*c*) polite (*d*) liberal

82. Frivolous
(*a*) amusing (*b*) serious
(*c*) confusing (*d*) teasing

83. Slacken
(*a*) weaken (*b*) grow (*c*) quicken (*d*) provoke

84. Defile
(*a*) purify (*b*) pollute (*c*) disturb (*d*) glorify

85. Fortuitous
(*a*) unfortunate (*b*) accidental (*c*) planned (*d*) ludicrous

86. Aversion
(*a*) promotion (*b*) attraction (*c*) hatred (*d*) passion

87. Imperious
(a) characterless
(b) impermanent
(c) imperfect
(d) submissive

88. Vexation
(a) comfort
(b) slyness
(c) fright
(d) nervousness

89. Doleful
(a) aggressive
(b) cheerful
(c) tired
(d) involved

90. Senility
(a) virility
(b) laziness
(c) maturity
(d) exhaustion

91. Ungainly
(a) quick
(b) short
(c) awkward
(d) graceful

Directions (Q. Nos. 92-97) *Each of the following sentences are followed by four words or groups of words. Select the antonym of the word (occurring in the sentence in* ***bold*** *letters) as per the context.*

92. His **candid** remarks impressed the authorities.
(a) blunt
(b) guarded
(c) sincere
(d) unconventional

93. The guilty appealed to the jury to **condone** his punishment.
(a) accept
(b) forgive
(c) condemn
(d) criticise

94. His family **severed** ties with him for marrying inter-caste.
(a) joined
(b) included
(c) detached
(d) disrupted

95. It is easy to understand his **fuzzy** thoughts.
(a) misty
(b) vague
(c) clear
(d) useful

96. He drove his car through **slimy** road to reach your office.
(a) ugly
(b) clean
(c) beautiful
(d) slippery

97. His **eloquent** speech helped him bag the award.
(a) lucid
(b) vivid
(c) short
(d) inarticulate

Directions (Q. Nos. 98-100) *Each of the following sentences are followed by four words. Select the antonym of the word (occurring in the sentence in* ***bold*** *letters) as per the context.*

98. Her illness **enervated** the whole family.
(a) enhanced
(b) exhausted
(c) weakened
(d) energized

99. The teacher **inserted** another picture to illustrate the point.
(a) deducted (b) added (c) removed (d) reclined

100. The committee rejected his **ludicrous** proposal.
(a) absurd (b) reasonable (c) farcical (d) stupid

Exam Practice

Exercise A

Directions (Q. Nos. 1-3) *In the following questions, out of the four alternatives, choose the one which best expresses the meaning of the given word.* **SSC CGL 2015**

1. Predilection
(a) favour (b) preference (c) whim (d) prejudice

2. Devout
(a) dedicated (b) solemn (c) futile (d) traitor

3. Ire
(a) brutal (b) wrath (c) surprise (d) prohibit

Directions (Q. Nos. 4-6) *Out of the four alternatives, choose the one which best expresses the meaning of the given word.* **SSC CGL 2015**

4. Ingenuous
(a) careless (b) crafty (c) candid (d) creative

5. Damp
(a) complicated (b) clear (c) light (d) wet

6. Resurgence
(a) repletion (b) reluctance (c) renewal (d) relocation

Directions (Q. Nos. 7 and 8) *Choose the word, which is most similar in meaning to the given words.* **SSC CGL 2016**

7. Dishevelled
(a) tidy (b) clean
(c) neat (d) untidy

8. Venerate
(a) despise (b) disobey
(c) disregard (d) revere

Directions (Q. Nos. 9 and 10) *Choose the word/group of words which is most similar in meaning to the word/group of words printed in* ***bold*** *as used in the passage.* **IBPS PO/MT 2016**

9. **SURVEILLANCE**
(a) spying (b) cameras (c) security (d) observation
(e) alertness

10. **PREREQUISITE**
(a) result (b) association (c) necessity (d) factor
(e) mystery

Directions (Q. Nos. 11 and 12) *In the following questions, out of the four alternatives, select the word similar in meaning to the given words.* **SSC CGL 2017**

11. Fossilise
(a) amalgamate (b) dissolve (c) flex (d) liquefy

12. Depict
(a) conceal (b) distort (c) characterise (d) suppress

Directions (Q. Nos. 13 and 14) *Pick out the nearest correct meaning or synonyms of the words given below.* **IBPS PO 2017**

13. Abstinence
(a) synchronic (b) torrential (c) restraint (d) gluttony
(e) indulgence

14. Taciturnity
(a) dumbness (b) changeableness (c) hesitation
(d) reserved (e) talkative

Directions (Q. Nos. 15-18) *Select the most appropriate synonym of given words.*

15. PERPLEX **SSC CGL 2018**
(a) surprise (b) bewilder (c) complex (d) deceive

16. ENDEAVOUR **SSC CGL 2018**
(a) attempt (b) achievement (c) result (d) success

17. OBSTACLE **SSC CGL 2018**
(a) benefit (b) clearance (c) accessory (d) barrier

18. DEFER
(a) dread (b) despair (c) dictate (d) delay

Directions (Q. Nos. 19 and 20) *Select the synonym of the given words.*

19. PATHETIC **SSC CGL 2020**
(a) pitiful (b) curious (c) insignificant (d) dull

20. PENITENCE **SSC CGL 2020**
(a) admiration (b) misery (c) patience (d) repentance

Directions (Q. Nos. 21-25) *In the following questions, choose the word opposite in meaning to the given word.* **SSC CGL 2015**

21. Tremulous
(a) steady (b) healthy (c) young (d) obese

22. Fake
(a) wrong (b) fanciful (c) ideal (d) real

23. Disconsolate
(a) thankful (b) prominent (c) joyous (d) unprejudiced

24. Eccentric
(a) carefree (b) peculiar (c) unusual (d) normal

25. Zenith
(a) nadir (b) shallow (c) low (d) bottom

Directions (Q. Nos. 26 and 27) *Choose the word, which is most opposite in meaning to the given words.* **SSC CGL 2016**

26. Congenial
(a) accord (b) snug (c) engaging (d) unpleasant

27. Abjure
(a) renounce (b) relinquish (c) abnegate (d) acquire

Directions (Q. Nos. 28-32) *In the questions given below, five words are given in which four of them have a similar meaning and one word is the antonym for the other four words. Choose the word opposite in meaning to the other four as your answer.* **SSC CGL 2017**

28. (a) Incommensurate (b) Inordinate (c) Unsymmetrical (d) Proportionate
(e) Lopsided

29. (a) Dissipate (b) Lavish (c) Splurge (d) Squander
(e) Retrieve

30. (a) Fractious (b) Affable (c) Grouchy (d) Bad-tempered
(e) Shrewish

31. (a) Conciseness (b) Eloquence (c) Rhetoric (d) Magniloquence
(e) Blarney

32. (a) Eradicate (b) Exterminate (c) Abolish (d) Ratify
(e) Squash

Directions (Q. Nos. 33 and 34) *Pick out the opposite meaning or antonym of the words given below.* **IBPS PO 2017**

33. Perigee
(a) apogee (b) hybrid (c) descent (d) night
(e) sky

34. Boisterous
(a) serenity (b) calm (c) cheerful (d) courageous
(e) noisy

Directions (Q. Nos. 35-38) *Select the most appropriate antonym of the given words.*

35. WEAKNESS **SSC CGL 2018**
(a) illness (b) strength (c) disability (d) bravery

36. MEAGRE **SSC CGL 2018**
(a) plentiful (b) inadequate (c) scanty (d) premium

37. TYRANT **SSC CGL 2018**
(a) rival (b) benefactor (c) patron (d) champion

38. VICIOUS **SSC CGL 2018**
(a) unfortunate (b) virtuous (c) sinful (d) baneful

Directions (Q. Nos. 39-43) *In the questions given below, four words are given of which two are either most nearly same or opposite in meaning. Find the two words which are most nearly same or opposite in meaning and indicate your answer by marking the option which represents the correct letter combination.* **SBI PO 2016**

39. A. Tranquility B. Loyalty C. Calamity D. Uproar
(a) A -C (b) B - D (c) B - C (d) C - D
(e) None of these

40. A. Vilification B. Nullification C. Denigration D. Falsification
(a) A - B (b) B - C (c) A - C (d) B - D
(e) None of these

41. A. Census B. Censure C. Reprimand D. Universe
(a) A - B (b) A - D (c) A - C (d) B - C
(e) C - D

42. A. Exorbitant B. Expeditious C. Quick D. Quest
(a) C - D (b) A - B (c) A - D (d) C - B
(e) None of these

43. A. Opaque B. Transparent C. Transverse D. Transvestite
(a) A - D (b) B - D (c) C - A (d) B - A
(e) None of these

Directions (Q. Nos. 44-48) *In each of the question given below, there is a word given in bold which is followed by the five options. In each of the option, a pair of words is given which is either the pair of synonyms or antonyms or synonyms and antonyms of the word given in bold. Choose that pair as your answer.* **IBPS Clerk 2019**

44. BESMIRCH
(a) Smear : loss
(b) Commemorate : smatter
(c) Slander : praise
(d) Lamentable : grandiose
(e) Temperament : transient

45. STIGMATIZE
(a) Inject : reject
(b) Inaugurate : inculcate
(c) Repulsive : attractive
(d) Condemn : denounce
(e) Chide : charlatan

46. SCANDALIZE
(a) Repel : attract
(b) Nauseate : impress
(c) Indignant : merry-making
(d) Awe-inspiring : freeze
(e) Countable : limitless

47. ASPERSION
(a) Slandering : reimbursing
(b) Radiating : shimmering
(c) Aversion : conversion
(d) Analysing : overlooking
(e) Vituperation : Derogation

48. AVERSION
(a) Odium : inclination
(b) Inversion : reversion
(c) Insulting : concocting
(d) Commendable : contumacy
(e) Rationalisation : reasoning

Exercise B

Directions (Q. Nos. 1 and 2) *Each sentence in this section consists of an underlined word or words followed by four words or groups of words. Select the word on groups of words that is most* ***similar*** *in meaning to the underlined word.* **NDA 2016**

1. Hospitality is a virtue for which the natives of the East in general are highly admired.
(a) Duty of a doctor
(b) Generosity shown to guests
(c) Cleanliness in hospitals
(d) Kindness

2. House rent in cities like Mumbai or Delhi has risen to astronomical figures beyond the reach of even high-salaried people.
(a) Exorbitant
(b) Commercial
(c) Planetary
(d) Illogical

Directions (Q. Nos. 3-7) *Each question in this section consists of a sentence with an underlined word/words followed by four words. Select the option that is nearest in meaning to the underlined word/words and mark your response in your answer sheet accordingly.* **NDA 2018**

3. I do not want you to lead a life of sycophancy as you did during the foreign rule.
(a) admiration (b) love (c) appreciation (d) flattery

4. In India, it has become easy to attack cultural artefacts these days.
(a) beckon (b) assault (c) belch (d) appreciate

5. He is always anxious. **NDA 2019**
(a) worried (b) dispassionate (c) sluggish (d) torpid

6. The poems of Kabir are ecstatic in nature.
(a) efficacious (b) eerie (c) rapturous (d) reverential

7. Ravi loves seclusion. Therefore, he lives in the mountains.
(a) nature (b) scripture (c) seafaring (d) solitariness

Directions (Q. Nos. 8-10) *Each question in this section consists of a sentence with an underlined word/words followed by four words. Select the option that is nearest in meaning to the underlined word and mark your response accordingly.* **NDA 2020**

8. She got the divorce within no time.
(a) detachment (b) breaking down (c) annulment (d) punishment

9. He was known for his gentle disposition.
(a) harmful (b) amiable (c) cunning (d) adjusting

10. The harder we kick, the better the ball bounces back.
(a) recoils (b) deflates (c) inflates (d) ascends

Directions (Q. Nos. 11-20) *Each question in this section consists of a sentence with an underlined word/words followed by four words. Select the option that is nearest in meaning to the underlined word/words and mark your response.*

11. A truly respectable old man is a ripe person. **CDS 2018**
(a) senior (b) mature (c) perfect (d) seasoned

12. The soldiers repulsed the enemy. **CDS 2018**
(a) defeated (b) destroyed (c) rejected (d) repelled

13. The differences include increase in mean temperature and heavy precipitation in several regions. **CDS 2019**
(a) drought (b) oasis (c) rainfall (d) snowing

14. The portal will help victims and complainants to anonymously report cyber crime. **CDS 2019**
(a) Incognito (b) directly (c) unfailingly (d) in situ

15. He is suffering from a terminal disease. **CDS 2019**
(a) sublunary (b) terrific (c) chronic (d) incurable

16. Doctors are reluctant to take rural postings despite big salary offers. **CDS 2019**
(a) disinclined (b) eager (c) fervent (d) unrepentant

17. The captain produced yet another stellar show to make her team enter the semi-finals. **CDS 2020**
(a) extraordinary (b) eclipse (c) poor (d) not a great

18. He is such a leader that his actions are contagious. **CDS 2020**
(a) complicated (b) transmittable (c) effective (d) unthinkable

19. The budget incorporated a number of tax reforms which included higher taxes for the very rich. **CDS 2020**
(a) excluded (b) integrated (c) laid down (d) removed

20. His thesis makes all generic statements which have already been proved. **CDS 2020**
(a) specific (b) crude (c) broad (d) non-standard

Directions (Q. Nos. 21-25) *In the given sentences, one word is given in **bold**. Below the sentence five words are suggested, one of which can replace the word given in bold without changing the meaning of the sentence. Find out the appropriate word in the given sentence.*
IBPS PO/MT 2015

21. The content of this passage **relates** to the Mughal period.
(a) depicts (b) shows (c) seems (d) happens
(e) pertains

22. Nilima's husband **compelled** her to give up her job.
(a) cautioned (b) forced (c) protected (d) restricted
(e) continued

23. Rahul played well to third **rank** in the competition.
(a) finish (b) find (c) number (d) establish
(e) get

24. It was **evident** that the gold ring was stolen by the domestic servant.
(a) unknown (b) reveal (c) agreed (d) clear
(e) proof

25. The sad tale narrated by the distressed woman **affected** everyone.
(a) contacted (b) realised (c) touched (d) surprised
(e) cautioned

Directions (Q. Nos. 26-30) *In the following sentence, one word has been printed in **bold**. Below the sentence five words are suggested, one of which can replace the word given in **bold** without changing the meaning of the sentence. Find out that word.* **IBPS PO/MT 2016**

26. He is good looking but **insipid** young man.
(a) arrogant (b) unscrupulous (c) spiritless (d) sick
(e) shrewd

27. The manager conducted the meeting with **aplomb**.
(a) Poise (b) annoyance (c) authority (d) sluggish
(e) aggression

28. She is so **garrulous** that all sober persons avoid his company.
(a) quarrelsome (b) foolish (c) domineering (d) talkative
(e) boring

29. He is known to be a **prolific** writer.
(a) great (b) versatile (c) powerful (d) civilized
(e) productive

30. They offered us an excellent **repast**.
(a) entertainment (b) fate (c) meal (d) pass time
(e) drug

Directions (Q. Nos. 31-40) *In this section, each sentence consists of an underlined word and is followed by four words. Select the word that is most opposite in meaning to the underlined word.*

31. My first lecture in the classroom was a fiasco. **NDA 2017**
(a) success (b) joy (c) fun (d) disaster

32. It was indeed arduous to cross streets in New York. **NDA 2017**
(a) pleasant (b) effortless (c) interesting (d) risky

33. Unlike his brother, he is affable. **NDA 2017**
(a) reserved (b) gullible (c) irritable (d) lovable

34. The country's economy must be geared to wartime requirements. **NDA 2018**
(a) subordinated to (b) related to (c) adjusted to (d) unlinked to

35. Why does fire attract insects? **NDA 2018**
(a) discharge (b) destroy (c) repel (d) remove

36. The party was excellent, and I would like to thank all the people concerned. **NDA 2018**
(a) cared (b) attentive (c) dependable (d) uninvolved

37. The bill received a vehement resistance from the opposition party in the Parliament. **NDA 2019**
(a) animated (b) apathetic (c) fervent (d) vigorous

38. He has been obstinate since his childhood. **NDA 2019**
(a) stubborn (b) dogged (c) amenable (d) rigid

39. For important medical decisions, even finding a doctor you trust is not enough. **NDA 2020**
(a) significant (b) trivial (c) basic (d) probable

40. Planets move in their orbits. **NDA 2020**
(a) push (b) rotate (c) stall (d) flow

Directions (Q. Nos. 41-50) *Each question in this section consists of a sentence with an underlined word followed by four words. Select the word that is opposite in meaning to the underlined word and mark your response in your answer sheet accordingly.*

41. Whether the rewards are in commensurate with the efforts or not, a society will always have workaholics and the shirk work groups. **CDS 2017**
(a) disproportionate (b) equal to (d) matched (d) unparalleled

42. Wars leave behind a large number of emaciated soldiers in the camps of both the victorious and the vanquished. **CDS 2017**
(a) hefty (b) thin (c) disillusioned (d) determined

43. It was a mystery as to where the young girl had acquired such a naive belief. **CDS 2018**
(a) credulous (b) childlike (c) wise (d) innocent

44. It's the only treatment suitable for cancer. **CDS 2018**
(a) insufficient (b) impertinent (c) befitting (d) congenial

45. Some of the criticisms which they had to put up were very unfair. **CDS 2018**
(a) scold (b) scorn (c) appreciation (d) censure

46. According to GB Shaw, men have become inert. Therefore, life force has chosen women to perform its functions. **CDS 2019**
(a) lively (b) quiescent (c) dormant (d) apathetic

47. Some of the men are highly misanthropic. **CDS 2019**
(a) anti-social (b) philosophic (c) atrophic (d) philanthropic

48. Everyone has to fight the inertia in the system. **CDS 2020**
(a) sluggishness (b) indolence (c) activity (d) torpor

49. There is a need to promote philanthropy in education. **CDS 2020**
(a) charity (b) benevolence (c) nastiness (d) likeliness

50. What we lack in the current times is compassion. **CDS 2020**
(a) empathy (b) carefulness (c) indifference (d) hardship

Answers

Revision Exercises (Based on Synonyms)

Exercise A

1. (b)	**2.** (c)	**3.** (d)	**4.** (b)	**5.** (a)	**6.** (c)	**7.** (a)
8. (b)	**9.** (a)	**10.** (b)	**11.** (c)			

Exercise B

1. (a)	**2.** (b)	**3.** (c)	**4.** (a)	**5.** (c)	**6.** (c)	**7.** (b)
8. (a)	**9.** (a)	**10.** (b)	**11.** (b)			

Exercise C

1. (c)	**2.** (c)	**3.** (c)	**4.** (a)	**5.** (c)	**6.** (d)	**7.** (b)
8. (b)	**9.** (d)	**10.** (b)	**11.** (a)	**12.** (a)	**13.** (d)	**14.** (c)
15. (b)						

Exercise D

1. (d)	**2.** (c)	**3.** (d)	**4.** (c)	**5.** (b)	**6.** (d)	**7.** (b)
8. (b)	**9.** (d)	**10.** (a)	**11.** (c)	**12.** (b)	**13.** (c)	**14.** (d)
15. (c)						

Exercise E

1. (c)	**2.** (a)	**3.** (d)	**4.** (c)	**5.** (c)

Exercise F

1. (b)	**2.** (a)	**3.** (b)	**4.** (c)	**5.** (b)	**6.** (b)	**7.** (c)
8. (a)	**9.** (a)	**10.** (a)	**11.** (a)	**12.** (d)	**13.** (a)	**14.** (b)
15. (c)	**16.** (b)	**17.** (c)	**18.** (c)	**19.** (d)	**20.** (b)	

Exercise G

1. (b)	**2.** (b)	**3.** (c)	**4.** (b)	**5.** (b)	**6.** (c)	**7.** (b)
8. (b)	**9.** (b)	**10.** (c)	**11.** (b)	**12.** (c)	**13.** (c)	**14.** (d)
15. (a)	**16.** (b)	**17.** (b)	**18.** (c)	**19.** (b)	**20.** (a)	

Exercise H

1. (d)	**2.** (a)	**3.** (c)	**4.** (c)	**5.** (c)	**6.** (b)	**7.** (d)
8. (c)	**9.** (d)	**10.** (b)	**11.** (b)	**12.** (a)	**13.** (a)	**14.** (c)
15. (c)	**16.** (b)	**17.** (c)	**18.** (b)	**19.** (b)	**20.** (d)	**21.** (c)
22. (a)	**23.** (b)	**24.** (b)	**25.** (b)	**26.** (b)	**27.** (a)	**28.** (b)
29. (c)	**30.** (c)	**31.** (d)	**32.** (c)	**33.** (a)	**34.** (a)	**35.** (b)
36. (a)	**37.** (d)	**38.** (c)	**39.** (c)	**40.** (d)	**41.** (d)	**42.** (b)
43. (b)	**44.** (a)	**45.** (c)	**46.** (c)	**47.** (a)	**48.** (b)	**49.** (c)
50. (b)	**51.** (c)	**52.** (d)	**53.** (c)	**54.** (a)	**55.** (b)	**56.** (c)
57. (b)	**58.** (b)	**59.** (d)	**60.** (d)	**61.** (b)	**62.** (d)	**63.** (a)

64. (a)	**65.** (c)	**66.** (b)	**67.** (c)	**68.** (a)	**69.** (d)	**70.** (d)
71. (b)	**72.** (b)	**73.** (d)	**74.** (a)	**75.** (c)	**76.** (d)	**77.** (b)
78. (c)	**79.** (c)	**80.** (a)	**81.** (c)	**82.** (b)	**83.** (c)	**84.** (b)
85. (b)	**86.** (a)	**87.** (b)	**88.** (d)	**89.** (a)	**90.** (b)	**91.** (c)
92. (d)	**93.** (b)	**94.** (a)	**95.** (b)	**96.** (d)	**97.** (b)	**98.** (a)
99. (d)	**100.** (a)					

Revision Exercises (Based on Antonyms)

Exercise A

1. (a) **2.** (a) **3.** (c) **4.** (b) **5.** (b) **6.** (b)

Exercise B

1. (a) **2.** (a) **3.** (a) **4.** (b) **5.** (a) **6.** (b) **7.** (b)
8. (a)

Exercise C

1. (c) **2.** (c) **3.** (d) **4.** (c) **5.** (d) **6.** (b) **7.** (b)
8. (c)

Exercise D

1. (d) **2.** (d) **3.** (a) **4.** (b) **5.** (d) **6.** (c) **7.** (a)
8. (b) **9.** (a) **10.** (c) **11.** (d) **12.** (b) **13.** (b) **14.** (b)
15. (c)

Exercise E

1. (b) **2.** (c) **3.** (c) **4.** (d) **5.** (d) **6.** (b) **7.** (d)
8. (d)

Exercise F

1. (c) **2.** (d) **3.** (a) **4.** (d) **5.** (d) **6.** (d) **7.** (b)
8. (a) **9.** (a) **10.** (a) **11.** (b) **12.** (d) **13.** (b) **14.** (a)
15. (b) **16.** (d) **17.** (b) **18.** (b) **19.** (a) **20.** (d)

Exercise G

1. (c) **2.** (d) **3.** (b) **4.** (a) **5.** (d) **6.** (d) **7.** (c)
8. (d) **9.** (a) **10.** (b) **11.** (a) **12.** (b) **13.** (a) **14.** (c)
15. (c) **16.** (d) **17.** (b) **18.** (d) **19.** (d) **20.** (a)

Exercise H

1. (d)	**2.** (a)	**3.** (d)	**4.** (b)	**5.** (b)	**6.** (c)	**7.** (b)
8. (a)	**9.** (a)	**10.** (d)	**11.** (b)	**12.** (b)	**13.** (b)	**14.** (b)
15. (a)	**16.** (a)	**17.** (a)	**18.** (b)	**19.** (a)	**20.** (c)	**21.** (a)
22. (b)	**23.** (b)	**24.** (a)	**25.** (c)	**26.** (a)	**27.** (b)	**28.** (c)
29. (b)	**30.** (c)	**31.** (a)	**32.** (c)	**33.** (a)	**34.** (a)	**35.** (d)
36. (a)	**37.** (b)	**38.** (b)	**39.** (a)	**40.** (c)	**41.** (c)	**42.** (a)
43. (b)	**44.** (b)	**45.** (d)	**46.** (d)	**47.** (c)	**48.** (a)	**49.** (a)
50. (d)	**51.** (a)	**52.** (a)	**53.** (d)	**54.** (c)	**55.** (c)	**56.** (b)
57. (b)	**58.** (a)	**59.** (c)	**60.** (a)	**61.** (c)	**62.** (b)	**63.** (a)
64. (b)	**65.** (c)	**66.** (a)	**67.** (b)	**68.** (a)	**69.** (c)	**70.** (c)
71. (a)	**72.** (a)	**73.** (b)	**74.** (c)	**75.** (a)	**76.** (a)	**77.** (b)
78. (d)	**79.** (b)	**80.** (b)	**81.** (a)	**82.** (b)	**83.** (c)	**84.** (a)
85. (c)	**86.** (b)	**87.** (d)	**88.** (a)	**89.** (b)	**90.** (a)	**91.** (d)
92. (b)	**93.** (c)	**94.** (a)	**95.** (c)	**96.** (b)	**97.** (d)	**98.** (d)
99. (b)	**100.** (b)					

Exam Practice

Exercise A

1. (b)	**2.** (a)	**3.** (b)	**4.** (c)	**5.** (d)	**6.** (c)	**7.** (d)
8. (d)	**9.** (d)	**10.** (c)	**11.** (a)	**12.** (c)	**13.** (c)	**14.** (d)
15. (b)	**16.** (a)	**17.** (d)	**18.** (d)	**19.** (a)	**20.** (d)	**21.** (a)
22. (d)	**23.** (c)	**24.** (d)	**25.** (a)	**26.** (d)	**27.** (d)	**28.** (d)
29. (e)	**30.** (b)	**31.** (a)	**32.** (d)	**33.** (a)	**34.** (b)	**35.** (b)
36. (a)	**37.** (c)	**38.** (b)	**39.** (e)	**40.** (c)	**41.** (d)	**42.** (d)
43. (d)	**44.** (c)	**45.** (d)	**46.** (a)	**47.** (e)	**48.** (a)	

Exercise B

1. (b)	**2.** (a)	**3.** (d)	**4.** (b)	**5.** (a)	**6.** (c)	**7.** (d)
8. (c)	**9.** (b)	**10.** (a)	**11.** (b)	**12.** (d)	**13.** (c)	**14.** (a)
15. (d)	**16.** (a)	**17.** (a)	**18.** (b)	**19.** (b)	**20.** (c)	**21.** (e)
22. (b)	**23.** (c)	**24.** (d)	**25.** (c)	**26.** (c)	**27.** (a)	**28.** (d)
29. (e)	**30.** (c)	**31.** (a)	**32.** (b)	**33.** (a)	**34.** (d)	**35.** (c)
36. (d)	**37.** (b)	**38.** (c)	**39.** (b)	**40.** (c)	**41.** (a)	**42.** (a)
43. (c)	**44.** (b)	**45.** (c)	**46.** (a)	**47.** (d)	**48.** (c)	**49.** (c)
50. (c)						

5

Foreign Words and Expressions

(Often Used in English)

1.	a' la mode	in the fashion, in vogue.
2.	albeit	although.
3.	avant garde	a pioneer in movement of art/literature.
4.	ab initio	from the very beginning.
5.	ad hoc	arranged for special purpose.
6.	au revoir	until we meet again.
7.	ad interim	meanwhile.
8.	alma mater	mother institution that a person had attended.
9.	ad valorem	according to value.
10.	annus mirabilis	a wonderful year in which great events take place.
11.	a'propos	to the point, with reference to.
12.	alibi	false plea of absence.
13.	ad nauseam	to offensive limit.
14.	alter ego	a bosom friend, one's other self.
15.	alumni	ex students of an institution (alumnus–singular)
16.	ante meridiem	time between midnight and moon (a.m.).
17.	animus	bad intention.
18.	a priori	deductive, to infer fact from cause
19.	amicus curiae	friend of the court in any judicial proceeding
20.	ad infinitum	for indefinite period, forever.
21.	alpha and omega	from beginning to end.
22.	alias	otherwise, nick name.
23.	amour propre	self love, vanity
24.	Anno Domini	in the Christian era (AD) after the death of.

25.	agent provocateur	a secret agent employed to find suspected criminals.
26.	blitzkreig	lightning attack.
27.	bona fide	in a good faith, sincere, real, not false.
28.	bon voyage	pleasant journey to you.
29.	bourgeoisie	middle class.
30.	bete noire	an object of dislike.
31.	bonhomie	pleasantness of manners.
32.	carte blanche	full freedom of action.
33.	communique	official intimation or note.
34.	casus belli	act/event leading to war.
35.	coup d' etat	violent or unconstitutional change in government.
36.	circa	about (born circa 150 BC).
37.	chaperon	a person (usually an elderly lady) who accompanies a young girl.
38.	commune bonum	the common good.
39.	coiffeur	hairdresser.
40.	charge d' affairs	one who acts as an ambassador.
41.	coup de grace	the final blow.
42.	coiffure	style of hairdressing.
43.	couturier	someone who designs and makes very expensive clothes.
45.	canard	a rumour, a hoax.
46.	cuisine	a particular style of cooking food, especially the style of a particular country or region.
47.	cause celebre	a very notable trial.
48.	detenu	a prisoner.
49.	de tour	indirect way.
50.	de novo	afresh.
51.	debut	first appearance on stage or in any event.
52.	debutant	one making first appearance (male).
53.	debutante	one making first appearance (female).
54.	detente	easing of strained relations.
55.	de jure	according to the law, by right.
56.	de facto	in fact, real.
57.	demarche	a political step/presentation.
58.	deja vu	a feeling that something has happened before.
59.	denouement	final conclusion in a play.
60.	dramatis personae	characters in a play.
61.	emeritus	retired but retaining honorary title on merit.
62.	elite	select, choice.
63.	en bloc	in a group, collectively.

64.	entrenous	between ourselves.
65.	en masse	in a mass.
66.	ex gratia	as a matter of grace, favour.
67.	ex post facto	by subsequent act.
68.	en route	on the way to.
69.	esprit de corps	spirit of belonging to one organisation.
70.	ex officio	by virtue of one's post.
71.	ennui	boredom.
72.	ex parte	done not in the presence of other.
73.	elan	energy, style and enthusiasm.
74.	et al	and other people.
75.	exempli gratia	*e.g.,* for example.
76.	enfant terrible	one who is a source of trouble.
77.	entente	understanding between the two states.
78.	entourage	a person's subordinates.
79.	forte	a person's special talent.
80.	fait accompli	something that has already happened or been done and cannot be changed.
81.	fiance	a man to whom one is engaged to marry.
82.	fiancee	a woman to whom one is engaged to marry.
83.	gratis	free of charge.
84.	genre	a particular style used in cinema, writing or art, which can be recognised by certain features.
85.	hauteur	haughtiness.
86.	hors de combat	out of combat, disabled.
87.	homo sapiens	men as thinking people.
88.	ipso facto	really, by that very fact.
89.	ibid	in the same book/chapter.
90.	impasse	deadlock.
91.	id est	*i.e.,* (that is to say).
92.	infra dig	below one's dignity.
93.	inter alia	among other things.
94.	in camera	not open to public.
95.	instant	of this month.
96.	joie de vivre	joy of living.
97.	laissez faire	free from government control/interference.
98.	locus standi	right to be heard, to interfere.
99.	lingua franca	common language spoken by people.
100.	literatur	a literary person.
101.	literati	literary persons.
102.	lacuna	an absent part, especially in a book or other piece of writing.
103.	leitmolif	a recurring theme.

104.	melange	mixture, blending, medley.
105.	mutatis mutandis	with necessary changes.
106.	menage	the members of a household.
107.	mala fide	illegal or dishonest
108.	modus vivandi	way of living.
109.	modus operandi	method of dealing with work.
110.	magnum opus	a great book, a work of art.
111.	melee	mixed fight, stampede.
112.	matinee	a film shown or play performed during the day, especially in the afternoon.
113.	nouveau riche	people who are newly rich.
114.	nota bene	take note or observe carefully.
115.	nom de plume	pen name, assumed name.
116.	nexus	bond, link, connection.
117.	non pareil	incomparable, unparallel.
118.	nee	name used after the name of married woman to indicate father's family name.
119.	outre	extremely unusual and strange.
120.	obiter dictum	a passing remark.
121.	persona non grata	a person not acceptable.
122.	persona grata	a person acceptable.
123.	pro rata	in proportion.
124.	per se	by itself.
125.	par excellence	excellent, superb.
126.	potpourri	a mixture of unusual or interesting things.
127.	post meridiem	afternoon (p.m.).
128.	prima facie	based on the first impression.
129.	proletarian	a member of the poor class.
130.	pari passu	at an equal rate/pace.
131.	parole	prisoner's word of honour.
132.	protege	one who is patronised by others.
133.	quid pro quo	something given or returned as an equivalent of something (tit for tat).
134.	raison d'etre	reason for existence, real purpose.
135.	rendezvous	private meeting place.
136.	reposte	repartee, retort.
137.	R.S.V.P.	repondez s'ilvous plait (reply, if you please).
138.	religio loci	the religious feeling of a place.
139.	resume	a summary, an abstract.
140.	sangfroid	the ability to stay calm in a difficult or dangerous situation
141.	status quo	the present position.
142.	sine die	for an indefinite period.

143.	sub judice	under consideration.
144.	sobriquet	pseudonym.
145.	summum bonum	chief good.
146.	sans	without, deprived of.
147.	sine qua non	indispensable condition to achieve something.
148.	sanctum sanctorum	the holy of holies
149.	son et lumiere	a historical play staged with sound and light.
150.	suo moto	on one's own.
151.	tour de force	a feat of strength or skill.
152.	tete-a-tete	a private conversation between two people.
153.	ultra vires	beyond one's authority.
154.	via	through.
155.	versus	against.
156.	viva voce	an oral test.
157.	viz	namely, that is to say.
158.	vice versa	in opposite ways.
159.	vide	see, refer.
160.	via media	middle course.
161.	vox populi, vòx dei	voice of the people is the voice of God.
162.	vox populi	voice of the people.
163.	vendetta	family feud.
164.	vis-a-vis	in relation to
165.	volte-face	a complete turn about, reversal of policy.
166.	xerox	a photocopy.
167.	zeitgeist	the general set of ideas, beliefs, feelings, etc. that is typical of a particular period in history.

6

The Sentence Completion

Sentence Completion questions are designed to test the comprehension ability as well as the knowledge of the meaning of the words required to be filled in. The candidate is asked to select the best of the alternatives given below a sentence.

A word of caution may be put in here for the benefit of the students. Before attempting this section they must go through the preceding chapters in this book that contain plethora of words to guide them in choice of selecting the best of the alternatives.

Revision Exercises

Exercise A

Directions *Four alternatives a, b, c and d are given under each sentence, you are required to select the most suitable alternative to fill in the blank/blanks in the sentence to make it meaningful.*

1. The salt spray has gradually ..... the bridge.
(a) spoilt (b) ravaged (c) demolished (d) eroded

2. The volcanic ..... was the cause of great devastation.
(a) outburst (b) eruption (c) erosion (d) movement

3. It was impossible to recover the victims' bodies as the place of the accident was ..... .
(a) inaccessible (b) marshy (c) distant (d) rocky

4. In order to maintain good health one should eat a ..... diet.
(a) rich (b) spicy (c) balanced (d) salty

5. As a result of ..... many unsuitable candidates were selected for the posts.
(a) tolerence (b) favouritism (c) humility (d) weakness

6. There are several ways of ..... the price at which a product can be marketed.
(a) arriving (b) thinking (c) determining (d) noticing

7. Although they are not rich, they always wear ..... clothes.
(a) respectful (b) respective (c) respectable (d) respected

8. After a recent mild paralytic attack his movements are ..... restricted, otherwise he is still very active.
(a) entirely (b) nowhere (c) not (d) slightly

9. The prisoner was released on ..... for good behaviour.
(a) probation (b) bail (c) parole (d) guarantee

10. Rajeev is too ..... as far as his food habits are concerned.
(a) enjoyable (b) fastidious (c) curious (d) interesting

11. My father keeps all his ..... papers in a lock and key.
(a) required (b) necessary (c) useful (d) confidential

12. I ..... you to keep quiet.
(a) beg of (b) beg from (c) beg (d) beg for

13. The splendour of the Himalayas ..... .
(a) beggars its description (b) needs no description
(c) is so charming (d) inspires awe

14. Every candidate has to poll a minimum number of votes in order to avoid ..... of his security.
(a) penalty (b) cancellation (c) forefeiture (d) loss

15. He stood ..... as a rock and faced the challenge.
(a) quiet (b) strong (c) solid (d) firm

Exercise B

1. My mother upset the kettle of boiling water and ..... her right hand badly.
(a) wounded (b) sizzled (c) scorched (d) scalded

2. Please do not ..... an offer made by the Chairman.
(a) refrain (b) refute (c) refuse (d) refuge

3. The government is confident that the standard of living will begin to ..... again soon.
(a) revive (b) lift (c) flourish (d) rise

4. Sharing heavy responsibilities with colleagues does not involve loss of prestige or ..... of the authority of an institute's Head.
(a) deterioration (b) decrease (c) diminution (d) loss

5. The problem of proliferation of nuclear arms is never going to be solved unless the two super powers agree to ..... .
(a) a solution (b) understand each other
(c) sit together (d) meet half-way

6. Your case is so unique that I am not getting any ..... to support it.
(a) reason (b) help (c) happening (d) precedent

7. Take possession of the records immediately lest they should be ..... with.
(a) tampered (b) destroyed (c) manhandled (d) mishandled

8. Let us take him upon his word. I see no room for any ..... in the matter.
(a) duplicity (b) deviation (c) cynicism (d) difference

9. The ..... arguments put forth for not disclosing the facts did not impress anybody.
(a) intemperate (b) spurious (c) specious (d) convincing

10. Director, he said, would ..... the matter at once.
(a) invigilate (b) explore (c) investigate (d) survey

11. Everyone was ..... by surprise when she announced her plan to marry that boy.
(a) moved (b) shaken (c) taken (d) prevailed

12. On second reading his poems strike us as singularly ..... of sublime emotions.
(a) attributive (b) significative (c) symptomatic (d) evocative

13. It is becoming more and more ..... that the Principal is losing the confidence of his staff.
(a) prominent (b) conspicuous (c) manifest (d) apparent

14. Health is too important to be ..... .
(a) neglected (b) detested (c) despised (d) discarded

15. Even a ..... glance will reveal the mystery.
(a) crude (b) cursory (c) critical (d) curious

Exercise C

1. The pilot was ..... injured, he died within half an hour.
(a) seriously (b) fatally (c) fatefully (d) vitally

2. His ..... directions misled us; we did not know which road to take.
(a) complex (b) obscure (d) mingled (d) vague

3. He was very friendly with the press and it really ..... him even for what he did not achieve.
(a) praised (b) lionised (c) appreciated (d) highlighted

4. The police ..... the mob.
(a) scattered (b) disbanded (c) drove (d) dispersed

5. I cannot ..... to know much about it.
(a) imagine (b) conceive (c) pretend (d) contemplate

6. We ..... trouble on our borders.
(a) comprehend (b) supplement (c) complement (d) apprehend

7. If you drink too much, it will ..... your judgement.
(a) impede (b) impair (c) impose (d) impel

8. The punch made the boxer ..... with pain.
(a) wince (b) gap (c) grumble (d) fumble

9. These essays are intellectually ..... and represent various levels of complexity.
(a) revealing (b) modern (c) superior (d) demanding

10. The soldiers were instructed to ..... restraint and handle the situation peacefully.
(a) exercise (b) control (c) prevent (d) enforce

11. Since one cannot read every book, one should be content with making a ..... selection.
(a) normal (b) standard (c) moderate (d) judicious

12. He is too ..... to be deceived easily.
(a) strong (b) modern (c) intelligent (d) kind

13. There has been a ..... lack of efficiency in all the crucial areas of the working of Public Sector Undertakings.
(a) positive (b) surprising (c) conspicuous (d) stimulative

14. The shepherd was looking after the ..... of sheep.
(a) crew (b) gang (c) fleet (d) flock

15. The Managing Director treated the employees to a ..... lunch at an expensive hotel.
(a) precious (b) thriving (c) stupendous (d) sumptuous

Exercise D

1. A politician's speech must be read ..... the lines, it may have a double ..... .
(a) behind; edge (b) between; meaning
(c) among; ends (d) beyond; face

2. Those who live in ..... houses should not throw ..... at others.
(a) big; abuse (b) own; challenges
(c) stone; bricks (d) glass; stones

3. I write a letter to you ..... tentatively the dates of the programme.
(a) involving (b) urging (c) guiding (d) indicating

4. Contemporary economic development differs ..... from the Industrial Revolution of the 19th century.
(a) naturally (b) usually (c) literally (d) markedly

5. Ravi had to drop his plan of going to picnic as he had certain ..... to meet during that period.
(a) preparations (b) observations
(c) urgencies (d) commitments

6. It was ..... hot that day and the cable suffered the brunt of the heat.
(a) treacherously (b) acceptably
(c) unfailingly (d) unbelievably

7. ..... eye-witness, the news reporter gave a graphic description of how fire broke out.
(a) Reporting (b) Observing (c) Seeing (d) Quoting

8. ..... my knowledge, Mr Ashok has a prejudice ..... foreigners.
(a) In; for (b) As; towards (c) For; at (d) To; against

9. He gave me an additional ..... of ₹100 a month by the ..... of the commissioner.
(a) allowance; permission (b) pay; allowance
(c) payment; agreement (d) salary; admittance

10. There is no glory in war ..... the blood it ..... .
(a) considering; sheds (b) comparing; spills
(c) worth; costs (d) thinking; demands

11. The Director has ..... me to ..... a speech for him.
(a) notified; do (b) demanded; prepare
(c) entrusted; write (d) commissioned; draft

12. I will come tomorrow ..... I hear to the ..... .
(a) unless; contrary (b) until; contradictory
(c) except; oppose (d) despite; otherwise

13. The children are so ..... , their parents are thinking of sending them to a ..... school.
(a) small; high (b) naughty; neighbouring
(c) misruled; lodging (d) unruly; boarding

14. Only ..... people are ..... after death.
(a) vicious; condemned (b) virile; forgotten
(c) virtuous; remembered (d) virulent; glorified

15. The Secretary ..... the society's funds, ... he was dismissed.
(a) robbed; thus (b) pirated; therefore
(c) misplaced; and (d) embezzled; therefore

Exercise E

1. In one election after another, officers have been guilty of serious ..... of duty.
   (a) dereliction (b) carelessness (c) lapses (d) abandoning
2. Being extremely ..... he examines every detail of the case before forming his opinion.
   (a) cautious (b) meticulous (c) eccentric (d) suspicious
3. It is very unfortunate that the two communities which were so friendly till recently are now ..... .
   (a) unfriendly (b) at daggers drawn (c) hostile (d) unhappy
4. ..... by repeated failures he presisted with his research and finally succeeded in isolating the mosquito responsible for carrying malaria.
   (a) Unaffected (b) Unmoved (c) Uninfluenced (d) Undaunted
5. Because of the bitter experiences of the past he ..... everywhere.
   (a) disbelieves (b) smells a rat (c) sees a danger (d) suspects foul
6. On seeing the police approach, the miscreants ..... .
   (a) cooled their heels (b) wore at their heels
   (c) took to their heels (d) took upon their heels
7. The committee's appeal to the people for money ..... little response.
   (a) evoked (b) provoked (c) gained (d) provided
8. Colgate has also got an ambitious aim of ..... an eight per cent value share of the toothpaste market by the end of the first year.
   (a) keeping (b) distributing (c) cornering (d) soliciting
9. He is very ..... on meeting foreigners and befriending them.
   (a) anxious (b) find (c) insistent (d) keen
10. If a speech is full of pompous words, it is ..... .
    (a) verbose (b) bombastic (c) grandiose (d) grandiloquent
11. We don't know what ..... him to commit this crime.
    (a) excited (b) roused (c) prompted (d) attracted
12. He is like a body without a soul, an eye without light or a flower without ..... .
    (a) smell (b) fragrance (c) petal (d) odour
13. This is the ..... chosen for the hospital complex to be built next year.
    (a) area (b) locality (c) site (d) sight
14. The photographs in the papers bore no ..... at all to the original.
    (a) nearness (b) comparison (c) identity (d) resemblance
15. Oh! such a pretty girl. Whom has she ..... ?
    (a) taken after (b) took after (c) taken by (d) took by

Exercise F

1. The Deputy Manager ..... to resign because all his proposals were ..... down by his superiors.
   (a) offered; thrown (b) gave; held
   (c) began; kept (d) threatened; turned
2. The counter clerk was very busy and ..... not pay ..... to Sameer's request.
   (a) can; help (b) could; respect (c) had; cash (d) did; attention

3. He was initially ..... at the suggestion but was soon ..... it himself.
(a) frowning; rejecting (b) shocked; advocating
(c) impressed; negating (d) thrilled; propagating

4. Shalini was not ..... by the criticism and paid no ..... even when her best friend talked against her.
(a) bothered; attention (b) troubled; mind
(c) threatened; warning (d) deterred; heed

5. She was ..... because all her plan had gone ..... .
(a) elated; wild (b) dejected; splendidly
(c) distraught; awry (d) frustrated; magnificently

6. He preaches liberal views but in practice, he is not ..... and is ..... narrow-minded than almost any other person.
(a) hard; openly (b) tolerant; more
(c) ambitious; hardly (d) acceptable; genuinely

7. Shakti is a ..... and he always does what is ..... and fruitful.
(a) optimist; hopeful (b) pragmatist; practical
(c) erudite; educative (d) idealist; theoretical

8. The birth of a daughter is no more a/an ..... occasion because education has ..... the people.
(a) magnificent; liberalised (b) benign; esteemed
(c) ominous; enlightened (d) propitous; blinded

9. He is always ..... to his uncle because he considers him a ..... fellow.
(a) disrespectful; venerable (b) respectful; dishonourable
(c) respectful; venerable (d) impudent; respectable

10. When she explained truthfully all that had happened my ..... were ..... .
(a) story; true (b) doubts; dispelled
(c) doubts; discouraged (d) suspicion; arouse

11. The police was at last able to ..... the ..... of her disappearance from her husband's home.
(a) reveal; secret (b) expose; mystery
(c) confirm; doubt (d) solve; mystery

12. The relations between two friends are ever so ..... that a slight misunderstanding can ..... them.
(a) tenuous; embitter (b) fragile; cement
(c) tanacious; break (d) strong; sweeten

13. Ravi ..... a bit ..... he was not invited by his friend to attend the party.
(a) took; before (b) angered; since
(c) expressed; than (d) grumbled; when

14. He is ..... to ..... any kind of work with due sincerity.
(a) fond; perform (b) reluctant; entrust
(c) determined; undertake (d) eager; avoid

15. Children are more ..... than adults, it is ..... their quickness in learning a new language.
(a) intelligent; disproved by (b) adaptable; reflected in
(c) conservative; seen in (d) susceptible; demonstrated in

Exercise G

1. ..... politicians alone can survive in politics where ..... rules the roost.
(a) Clever; practical (b) Wily; treacherous
(c) Wily; treachery (d) Ideal; prestigious

2. I am not ..... about your success because your ..... approach to study is disappointing.
(a) despaired; irresolute (b) hopeful; regular
(c) optimistic; perfunctory (d) happy; reckless

3. Prabha's ..... in athetics yielded rich ..... as she got a scholarship.
(a) performance; money (b) defeat; results
(c) behaviour; appreciation (d) excellence; dividends

4. The police ..... any attempt of arson by ..... at the trouble spot quite in time.
(a) squashed; surrounding (b) made; encircling
(c) pre-empted; arriving (d) thwarted; presenting

5. The war ..... immediately after the cease-fire proposal was ..... bilaterally.
(a) receded; exchanged (b) started; prepared
(c) ended; accepted (d) extended; mitigated

6. The ..... imposed for non-payment was too ..... for it to bring in improvement in collection.
(a) fine; severe (b) toll; simple
(c) penalty; low (d) damage; cruel

7. Somesh ..... me coming to his table, he smiled and ..... me a chair.
(a) found; signalled (b) met; sat
(c) looked; gave (d) saw; offered

8. The leaders were ..... needed by those to ..... they addressed.
(a) angrily; who (b) readily; which
(c) scarcely; whom (d) rarely; where

9. Neena's plea for ..... fell on deaf ears as her husband was not ..... enough to overlook her minor omission.
(a) clemency; gracious (b) mercy; unkind
(c) forgiveness; pardonable (d) apology; forgivable

10. The attempt of the robbers was ..... because the travellers showed enough .....
(a) foiled; fortitude (b) encouraged; cowardice
(c) averted; farsight (d) checked; foresight

11. Nowadays progress in life depends more on ..... rather than on ..... .
(a) favouritism; ability (b) consideration; capability
(c) utility; sincerity (d) pragmatism; ideal

12. The reasons why syllabi are ..... in India because UGC has failed to live upto the ..... of the people.
(a) outdated; expectations (b) outmoded; ambition
(c) practical; hopes (d) obsolete; desires

13. The Indian Railways have yet to ..... an effective mechanism to avert a series of ..... leading to horrifying tragedy.
(a) evolve; lapses (b) develop; mistake
(c) improve; omissions (d) contrive; errors

14. I am not ..... to sell you my house unless you offer a more ..... price.
(a) conform; true (b) prepared; realistic
(c) ready; correct (d) having; actual

15. Due to ..... rainfall this year, there will be ..... cut in water supply.
(a) enough; substantial (b) meagre; least
(c) sufficient; no (d) surplus; abundant

Exercise H

1. She is ..... and simple in looks though her husband is ..... .
(a) plain; flamboyant (b) garrulous; talkative
(c) taciturn; silent (d) credulous; gullible

2. To ..... yourself from ..... wear warm clothes.
(a) prohibit; heat (b) protect; cold
(c) save; heat (d) suffer; cold

3. We ..... him with many promises, but nothing would ..... him.
(a) tempted; influence (b) provoked; move
(c) attracted; fascinate (d) gave; deprive

4. In his ....., he followed the ..... course.
(a) agony; funny (b) ignorance; wrong
(c) hurry; diversified (d) predicament; proper

5. The construction of the hall has been ..... because of the ..... of cement in the market.
(a) held; non-availability (b) denied; restrictions
(c) hampered; shortage (d) prevented; supply

6. Only when ..... failed, the police restored to ..... .
(a) efforts; power (b) arrests; imprisonment
(c) persuasions; force (d) power; punishment

7. The partners broke off as they found each other .....: of ..... breach of promise.
(a) faulty; severe (b) responsible; serious
(c) guilty; flagrant (d) accused; rigid

8. They wanted to ..... all these books, but they could not find ..... time to do so.
(a) cover; almost (b) pursue; necessary
(c) dispose; some (d) read; sufficient

9. Though he is reputed for his technical ....., his books were sadly ..... of the work of others and he lacked originality.
(a) advice; unconscious (b) skill; independent
(c) knowledge; ignorant (d) expertise; derivative

10. He had managed to ..... several times, but was finally ..... by the police.
(a) deceive; cheated (b) defend; acquitted
(c) escape; arrested (d) cheat; robbed

11. The candidate's ..... at the polls was ..... as he won with a striking margin.
(a) claim; unrealistic (b) victory; overwhelming
(c) image; real (d) strategy; unsuccessful

12. In ..... of international matters, there is always an element of risk in ..... one might do.
(a) view; whichever (b) many; doing
(c) defence; wrong (d) case; whatever

13. We must prevent endangered wild animal species from becoming ..... in order that our future generation may ..... the great diversity of animal life.
(a) rare; escape (b) outdated; know
(c) extinct; enjoy (d) powerful; protect

14. We cannot ..... such a/an ..... act of violence.
(a) tolerate; insipid
(b) consider; important
(c) commit; magnificent
(d) pardon; egregious

15. The secretary ..... the society's funds, ... he was dismissed.
(a) misplaced; soon
(b) rolled; thus
(c) pirated; therefore
(d) misappropriated; so

Exercise 1

1. It is ..... for every tax payer to ..... the tax returns to the Income Tax Department.
(a) necessary; lodge
(b) binding; pay
(c) obligatory; submit
(d) possible; remlt

2. The ..... of glory lead but to the ..... .
(a) ways; happiness
(b) acts; prosperity
(c) paths; grave
(d) achievements; suffering

3. Cholestrol has long been identified as a silent killer because the patient has no ..... of the danger freely ..... his system.
(a) idea; infecting
(b) thought; attacks
(c) information; invading
(d) inkling; traversing

4. Synthetic milk ..... real milk in all ..... except taste and nutritional qualities.
(a) resembles; respects
(b) exempted; respect
(c) copies; manners
(d) marks; qualities

5. If we do not take ..... care in our industry, we will have to ..... a grave problem.
(a) normal; experience
(b) proper; face
(c) adequate; catch
(d) intensive; aggravate

6. He shifted to his late parents' house not because of the ..... it provided but for purely ..... reasons.
(a) convenience; sentimental
(b) grace; aesthetic
(c) value; monetary
(d) comforts; personal

7. Some people have the ..... for learning foreign languages but they have no ..... in speaking.
(a) mania; urge
(b) aptitude; interest
(c) stamina; fondness
(d) capacity; ability

8. The increasing revival of dramatic classics is, to one critic, ...; it seems to him a sign of the ..... of the modern theatre.
(a) auspicious; resurgence
(b) deplorable; anaemia
(c) incomprehensible; paradox
(d) astounding; vitality

9. We must explore ..... sources of energy as our supply of fossil fuel has been ..... .
(a) alternate; depleted
(b) guaranteed; over
(c) natural; exhausted
(d) sufficient; increased

10. This partly explains how the Mehra family has been able to ..... its lavish life-style in recent times, despite the fact that all its assets have been ..... .
(a) keep up; destroyed
(b) develop; attacked
(c) afford; liquidated
(d) keep; removed

Exercise J

1. He was so convinced that people were driven by ..... motives that he believed there was no such thing as a purely ..... act.
   (a) personal; anti-social (b) personal; eternal
   (c) altruistic; praiseworthy (d) ulterior; selfless

2. Any system is likely to ..... for ..... of support from the public.
   (a) survive; lack (b) succeed; reason
   (c) fail; want (d) finish; failure

3. Since we ..... read every book, we ..... only the famous ones.
   (a) have; sold (b) should; buy
   (c) cannot; select (d) can; purchase

4. The education minister emphasised the need to discover and ..... each student's ..... talents.
   (a) enlarge; dormant (b) belittle; concealed
   (c) develop; intrinsic (d) flourish; hidden

5. The mill workers were not ..... with their low wages and non-payment of wages for last three months ..... fuel to the flames.
   (a) good; put (b) satisfied; added
   (c) joyful; poured (d) pleased; directed

6. He is usually ....., but today he appears rather ..... .
   (a) strict; unwell (b) tense; restless
   (c) calm; disturbed (d) happy; humorous

7. The changes made in the system were so ..... that they did'nt require any ..... .
   (a) big; time (b) genuine; intelligence
   (c) obvious; modifications (d) certain; expertise

8. He was ..... of playing ..... and loose with the sentiments of his dearest friends.
   (a) complained; thick (b) accused; tight
   (c) innocent; false (d) guilty; fast

9. He granted the request because he was ..... to ..... his friend.
   (a) bound; hurt (b) destined; agonise
   (c) reluctant; disappoint (d) unwilling; please

10. I would like to ..... your attention to the second paragraph of my letter ..... to the terms of sale of the machinery.
    (a) invite; according (b) withdraw; regarding
    (c) react; mainly (d) draw; pertaining

Exam Practice

Directions *(Q. Nos 1-3) In this section, each of the following sentences has blank space and four words given after the sentence. Select whichever word you consider most appropriate for the blank space.* **NDA 2016**

1. When the bus was at full speed, its brakes failed and an accident was ....
 (a) inevitable (b) underniable (c) fatal (d) miserable

2. To explain his design to his visitors, the architect .... a simple plan on the blackboard.
 (a) built (b) finalised (c) sketched (d) arranged

3. Through Bonsai, a well known art form, originated in China, it was .... by the Japanese.
 (a) cultivated (b) finished (c) perfected (d) enlarged

Directions *(Q. Nos. 4-7) Each of the following sentences in this section has a blank space and four words or groups of words given after the sentence. Select whichever word or group you consider most appropriate for the blank space.* **NDA 2017**

4. I .... you to be at the party this evening.
 (a) look forward to (b) hope (c) expect (d) think

5. When I met John yesterday, it was the first time I .... him since Christmas.
 (a) saw (b) have seen (c) had seen (d) have been seeing

6. He .... to listen to my arguments and walked away.
 (a) denied (b) disliked (c) prevented (d) refused

7. The flow of blood was so .... that the patient died.
 (a) intense (b) adequate (c) profuse (d) extensive

Directions *(Q. Nos. 8-19) Each of the following sentences in this section has a blank space and four words or group of words given after the sentence. Select the word or group of words you consider most appropriate for the blank space and indicate your response on the Answer Sheet accordingly.*

8. The tired traveller .... on in the hope of finding some resting place. **NDA 2018**
 (a) strolled (b) scurried (c) paraded (d) plodded

9. The car was damaged beyond repair in the .... accident. **NDA 2018**
 (a) outrageous (b) ghastly (c) nasty (d) heinous

10. Crores of villagers are .... a sit-in protest against the construction of a new underpass. **NDA 2019**
 (a) performing (b) sitting (c) staging (d) standing

11. It is common for patients to stop .... medicine as soon as they start feeling better. **NDA 2019**
 (a) earing (b) gulping (c) swallowing (d) taking

12. A four-year-old girl got a new lease of life after doctors at a hospital .... a cancerous tumour from one of her kidneys. **CDS 2019**
 (a) rejuvenated (b) removed (c) displaced (d) replaced

13. In this University, there is no .... for awarding scholarships on the basis of merit in examination alone. **CDS 2017**
 (a) precedent (b) opportunity (c) chance (d) possibility

14. Can you pay .... all these articles? **CDS 2017**

(a) out (b) of (c) for (d) off

15. Ravi has the habit of .... a headache. **CDS 2018**

(a) complaining (b) complain (c) complaining to (d) complaining of

16. I always want to go alone for a ride, but my mother .... going with my brother. **CDS 2018**

(a) insists (b) insists on (c) insists in (d) insisted

17. How we .... to ageing is a choice we must make wisely? **CDS 2019**

(a) respond (b) absolve (c) discharge (d) overlook

18. Complementary medicine .... fewer risks; since it is used alongwith standard remedies, often to lessen side effects and enhance the feeling of well-being. **CDS 2019**

(a) reacts (b) releases (c) ejects (d) carries

19. Stress may .... fertility in man and women. **CDS 2019**

(a) engage (b) reduce (c) inject (d) deduce

Directions (Q. Nos. 20-24) *In the following questions, the sentences given with blank are to be filled in with an appropriate word. Select the correct alternative out of the four and indicate it by selecting the appropriate option.* **SSC CGL 2017**

20. The psychopath gets a .... sense of enjoyment from torturing animals. **SSC CGL 2017**

(a) perverse (b) agreeable
(c) happy (d) reasonable

21. When Jaspal got angry, he started to .... his feelings with his hands. **SSC CGL 2017**

(a) participate (b) immolate
(c) intoxicate (d) gesticulate

22. The committee reached .... decision regarding the apointment of the chairman. **SSC CGL 2018**

(a) a compatible (b) a unanimous
(c) an exemplary (d) an agreeable

23. It is hard to conceive of a more .... route than the one that this determined traveller chose to follow. **SSC CGL 2018**

(a) stimulating (b) dashing
(c) daunting (d) provoking

24. She got a lucrative job of a translator because she was .... in Franch. **SSC CGL 2018**

(a) sufficient (b) efficient
(c) deficient (d) proficient

Directions (Q. Nos. 25-30) *In each of the questions given blow, a sentence is given with one blank. Below each sentence four words are given out of which two can fit the sentence. Five options are given with various combinations of these words. You have to choose the combination with the correct set of words which can fit in the given sentences.* **IBPS Clerk 2017**

25. Would you like to have .... coffee?

A. much B. more C. some D. many

(a) A-B (b) A-D (c) B-C (d) C-D
(e) A-C

26. The Dysart Unified School District says they are investigating threats made .... the district and Dysart High School.
A. towards B. against C. for D. after
(a) A-B (b) A-D (c) B-C (d) C-D
(e) A-C

27. I was going .... to say hellow when I realised that I couldn't remember his name.
A. beyond B. over C. through D. across
(a) A-B (b) A-D (c) B-C (d) C-D
(e) B-D

28. In 1997, the sales tax was lowered to 4%, then in 2001 it was abolished ....
A. together B. laterally C. completely D. altogether
(a) A-B (b) A-D (c) B-C (d) B-C
(e) B-D

29. Children .... their parents' authority far more nowadays than they did in the past.
A. dispute B. question
C. confront D. challenge
(a) A-B (b) A-D (c) B-C (d) C-D
(e) B-D

30. The United Nations has .... its authority to restore peace in the area.
A. used B. blown C. exercised D. refused
(a) A-C (b) A-D (c) B-C (d) C-D
(e) B-D

Directions (Q. Nos. 31-34) *Each question below has one blank, which is incidating that something has been omitted. Find out which option(s) can be used to fill up the blank in the sentence in the same sequence to make it meaningfully complete.* **IBPS Clerk 2019**

31. Maharashtra has been .... into a new party system over the past few years, with the BJP trying hard to replace the Congress as the dominant party in the State.
(i) investigated (ii) transitioning
(iii) framing
(a) Only (i) (b) Only (ii) (c) Both (i) and (iii) (d) Both (i) and (ii)
(e) None of these

32. The theme song of downton Abbey along with a panoramic shot of the imposing monarchic structure is enough to .... memories.
(i) evoke (ii) recall (iii) sent
(a) Only (i) (b) Only (ii) (c) Both (ii) and (iii) (d) Both (i) and (ii)
(e) None of these

33. With tomato and onion prices continuing to sour, the Centre is considering a .... to increase cultivation of these staple vegetables in the North Indian region.
(i) proposal (ii) role (iii) novel
(a) Only (i) (b) Only (ii) (c) Both (ii) and (iii) (d) Both (i) and (ii)
(e) None of these

34. The Railways will speed up trains to reduce running time and maximise .... of infrastructure across its network.
(i) collecting (ii) effectiveness (iii) utilisation
(a) Only (i) (b) Only (ii) (c) Both (ii) and (iii) (d) Both (i) and (ii)
(e) None of these

Directions (Q. Nos. 35-39) *In each question below, two sentences I and II are given. Each sentence I and II has a blank in it. Against the question, five options are suggested. Out of these, only one fits at both places in the context of each sentence. Mark that option as your answer.* **SBI Cleak 2016**

35. (i) I didn't to .... my heart out to you, but I guess I had to talk to someone.
(ii) She went to the kitchen to .... herself a big glass of orange juice.
(a) make (b) prepare (c) share (d) cry
(e) pour

36. (i) As Sheela's motives were found to be harmless, no disciplinary .... will be taken against her.
(ii) I imitated his .... even wearing his spectacles, thinking they might help solve the mystery.
(a) trick (b) sentence (c) motion (d) dead
(e) action

37. (i) The plush residential complex will fulfil your wish of living in a .... location.
(ii) Both the .... Minister and our Ambassador in Vienna knew him and valued his contribution.
(a) home (b) posh (c) finance (d) prime
(e) aloof

38. (i) If you are trying to make a .... impression on your audience, you cannot do so by being ambiguous.
(ii) The crane is a large and .... bird.
(a) intense (b) strong (c) small (d) broken
(e) agile

39. (i) Police searched her father's bag against his................ .
(ii) My father excluded my siblings from his................. .
(a) will (b) property (c) wish (d) list
(e) consent

Directions (Q. Nos. 40-44) *There are two different sentences with a blank space in each sentence. Choose the word from the given options which fits appropriately in both the blanks adding a proper and logical meaning to the sentences.* **IBPS Clerk 2019**

40. (i) The .... furniture designer is known for turning unusual objects into tables and chairs.
(ii) There were .... recluse plans to convert the entire building into a private summer residence. **IBPS Clerk 2019**
(a) eccentric (b) apathetic
(c) lethargic (d) insipid
(e) vapid

41. (i) Soft soap is used by dermatologists in the treatment of .... eczema and opodeldoc is a domestic remedy for stiffness and sprains.
(ii) There is no easy short-term solution to Britain's .... economic malaise. **IBPS Clerk 2019**
(a) alternate (b) impulsive
(c) chronic (d) aberrant
(e) exclusive

42. (i) Regulations are changed on a whim, resulting in .... results that distort long-established competitive values.
(ii) When the astronomer looked into the telescope, he was shocked by the sight of a star moving in an .... path. **IBPS Clerk 2019**

(a) flourishing (b) auspicious (c) thriving (d) aberrant
(e) groomed

43. (i) The absent-minded couple acted .... to the mess their child made in the restaurant.
(ii) In his druken stupor, Fred was .... to the fact he was driving in the wrong lane. **IBPS Clerk 2019**

(a) religious (b) oblivious (c) astute (d) facile
(e) adroit

44. (i) Jefferson was an expert violinist, a good singer and dancer, ... in outdoor sports and an excellent horseman.
(ii) With practice people can become .... at recognising and turning off the tension with in the body for themselves without drugs. **IBPS Clerk 2019**

(a) naive (b) candid (c) genuine (d) scrupulous
(e) proficient

Directions (Q. Nos. 45-49) *In each of the questions given below, a paragraph is given which has some blanks and those blanks have to be filled with the same word out of five words igven below it. You have to choose that same as your answer and fill up the blanks with that appropriate answer.* **SBI Clerk 2018**

45. Can we make such a .... disqualifying persons against whom charges of heinous crimes have been framed by courts of .... or should we tell the parliament that by not laying down such a ...., you are really giving criminals encouragement and hope?

(a) norms (b) authority (c) law (d) ideas
(e) basics

46. Currently, the .... has powers to seek call data records as part of its probes, but the committee is of the view that the .... needs more powers to assist in its .... responsibilities.

(a) State (b) rurler-rule
(c) dictator (d) regulator/regulatory
(e) party

47. The bilingual channel (Hindi and English) will offer scheduled programming as well as video-on-demand facility. According to the India .... website, it will cover the "entire landscape" of .... and technology including engineering, health and medicine, natural ...., environment and wildlife, agriculture among others.

It will have documentaries, discussion, demonstrations/experiment shows and quizzes.

(a) science (b) biological
(c) physical (d) atmosphere
(e) technical

48. Till Wednesday night, revenue authorities were expecting only a limited release of .... through a single shutter, resulting in rise in .... level of Periyar by around only one metre. But with all four shutters being opened, there is, as yet, no clear idea about the expected rise in .... levels in the Periyar.

(a) grants (b) funds (c) assistance (d) support
(e) water

49. The main idea of a .... is the point of the pasage, minus all the details. It is the main point or concept that the author wants to communicate to the readers about the topic. Hence, in a .... when the main idea is stated directly, it is expressed in what is called the topic sentence. It gives the overarching idea of what the paragraph is about and is supported by the details in the ....

(a) comprehensive
(b) paragraph
(c) story
(d) event
(e) scenario

Directions (Q. Nos. 50-54) *Each sentence below has two blanks, each blank indicating that something has been omitted. Choose the set of words for each blank that best fits the meaning of the sentence as a whole.*

SBI PO 2016

50. Biological clocks are of .... adaptive value to animals since it .... nervous and physiological functions of the body.

(a) immense, assumes
(b) great, regulates
(c) ultimate, created
(d) high, engulfs
(e) no, governs

51. Each occupation has its own ...., bankers, lawyers and computer professionals, for example all use among themselves .... that outsiders find difficult to follow.

(a) merits, incidents
(b) disadvantages, methods
(c) rewards, endearment
(d) jargon, language
(e) problems, fundamentals

52. The two artists.......... markedly in their temperaments, one was reserved and courteous the other .... and boastful.

(a) changed, irritable
(b) similar, jovial
(c) differed, rude
(d) appeared, funny
(e) addressed, ill-tempered

53. Many people believed that spices help .... food; however nutritionists found that most spices were .... of having any effect on growth of microbes present in the food.

(a) preserve, incapable
(b) produce, impossible
(c) save, preventive
(d) spoil, probable
(e) protect, deprived

54. Despite a growing .... that a lot needs to be done to help those without clean water, a .... says that more than 34 million people die every year of water borne diseases.

(a) interest, reason
(b) recognition, report
(c) fantasy, review
(d) authority, legend
(e) turbulence, logic

Directions (Q. Nos. 55-59) *Each question below has two blanks, each blank indicating that something has been omitted. Choose the set of words for each blank which best fits the meaning of the sentence as a whole.*

IBPS PO 2018

55. What goes into making a marriage can only be .... by trail and error and couples are best left to .... out what what works.

(a) discovered, translate
(b) regulated, find
(c) learnt, figure
(d) seen, thrash
(e) experienced, judge

56. The producer is known to .... with new stars and fresh talent and thought there have been a few hits and misses, this film maker totally .... for the new breed.

(a) try, demands
(b) experiment, vouches
(c) sign, goes
(d) produce, promises
(e) work, supports

57. The Government stated that it had the .... right to use as much force as was necessary to regain control of areas .... by terrorists.

(a) free, marked
(b) practical, left
(c) fundamental, infest
(d) basic, undertaken
(e) legitimate, dominated

58. Obesity and alcohol .... together to .... the risk of liver disease in both men and women.

(a) act, increase
(b) result, aggravate
(c) taken, arrest
(d) put, heighten
(e) mix, lower

59. There weer screams, chills and thrills .... at the discotheque the other night as the director along with the producers hosted a party to .... the success of their latest horror flick.

(a) combined, downplay
(b) alike, mourn
(c) experiences, mark
(d) galore, celebrate
(e) risen, generate

Directions (Q. Nos. 60-63) *In the questions given below a sentence is given with two blanks in each. Corresponding to each question, two columns are given with three words in each column. Which combination of words from the two columns will perfectly fit into the blanks to make the sentence contextually correct and meaningful.* **IBPS Clerk 2018**

60. Mutual political suspicion and a lack of .... of the complexities of the international situation have brought about a confrontation. The Chief Minister may have even made .... and tactical misjudgements.

	Column I		Column II
A.	Appreciation	D.	Acceptable
B.	Acknowledgement	E.	Diplomatic
C.	Plethora	F.	Strategic

(a) C-E
(b) A-F
(c) B-F and A-E
(d) B-D
(e) C-D

61. The investigation also .... that another pilot flying as Staff On Duty entered the cockpit after pressing the cockpit buzzer several times. The pilot in command .... that he allowed the SOD inside the cockpit because the buzzer was distracting.

	Column I		Column II
A.	Divulged	D.	Advanced
B.	Rejected	E.	Submitted
C.	Communicated	F.	Recommended

(a) C-D
(b) B-F
(c) A-E
(d) A-F
(e) B-E

62. A committee, chaired by Union Environment Minister Harsh Vardhan, has .... wildlife clearance to the Mumbai-Ahmedabad high speed train corridor that .... upon a flamingo sanctuary and the Sanjay Gandhi National Park, home to leopards, in Mumbai.

Column I	Column II
A. Alienated	D. Encroaches
B. Estranged	E. Repelled
C. Accorded	F. Admonish

(a) A-F *(b)* B-D and A-E *(c)* C-F *(d)* C-D *(e)* B-E

63. The CBI says there was no proper response to the earlier .... it sent to the Police Commissioner and alleges that he could have destroyed evidence that was initially gathered by the Special Investigation Team that he had .... in the initial stage of the probe.

Column I	Column II
A. Declaration	D. Supervised
B. Summonses	E. Govern
C. Command	F. Administered

(a) A-D *(b)* C-E *(c)* B-E *(d)* B-F and C-E
(e) B-F and B-D

Answers

Revision Exercises

Exercise A

1. (d) **2.** (b) **3.** (a) **4.** (c) **5.** (b) **6.** (c) **7.** (c)
8. (d) **9.** (c) **10.** (b) **11.** (d) **12.** (a) **13.** (a) **14.** (c)
15. (d)

Exercise B

1. (d) **2.** (c) **3.** (d) **4.** (c) **5.** (d) **6.** (d) **7.** (a)
8. (a) **9.** (c) **10.** (c) **11.** (c) **12.** (d) **13.** (d) **14.** (a)
15. (b)

Exercise C

1. (b) **2.** (d) **3.** (b) **4.** (d) **5.** (c) **6.** (d) **7.** (b)
8. (a) **9.** (c) **10.** (a) **11.** (d) **12.** (c) **13.** (c) **14.** (d)
15. (d)

Exercise D

1. (b) **2.** (d) **3.** (d) **4.** (d) **5.** (d) **6.** (d) **7.** (d)
8. (d) **9.** (a) **10.** (a) **11.** (d) **12.** (a) **13.** (d) **14.** (c)
15. (d)

Exercise E

1. (a) **2.** (b) **3.** (b) **4.** (d) **5.** (b) **6.** (c) **7.** (a)
8. (c) **9.** (d) **10.** (d) **11.** (c) **12.** (b) **13.** (c) **14.** (d)
15. (a)

Exercise F

1. (d) 2. (d) 3. (b) 4. (a) 5. (c) 6. (b) 7. (b)
8. (c) 9. (c) 10. (b) 11. (d) 12. (a) 13. (d) 14. (c)
15. (b)

Exercise G

1. (c) 2. (c) 3. (d) 4. (c) 5. (c) 6. (c) 7. (d)
8. (c) 9. (a) 10. (a) 11. (a) 12. (a) 13. (a) 14. (b)
15. (c)

Exercise H

1. (a) 2. (b) 3. (a) 4. (b) 5. (c) 6. (c) 7. (c)
8. (d) 9. (d) 10. (c) 11. (b) 12. (d) 13. (c) 14. (d)
15. (d)

Exercise I

1. (c) 2. (c) 3. (c) 4. (a) 5. (b) 6. (a) 7. (b)
8. (a) 9. (a) 10. (c)

Exercise J

1. (d) 2. (c) 3. (c) 4. (c) 5. (b) 6. (c) 7. (c)
8. (d) 9. (c) 10. (d)

Exam Practice

1. (a) 2. (c) 3. (c) 4. (c) 5. (c) 6. (d) 7. (c)
8. (d) 9. (b) 10. (c) 11. (d) 12. (b) 13. (a) 14. (c)
15. (d) 16. (b) 17. (a) 18. (d) 19. (b) 20. (a) 21. (d)
22. (b) 23. (c) 24. (d) 25. (c) 26. (a) 27. (e) 28. (d)
29. (e) 30. (a) 31. (b) 32. (a) 33. (a) 34. (c) 35. (e)
36. (e) 37. (d) 38. (b) 39. (a) 40. (a) 41. (c) 42. (d)
43. (b) 44. (e) 45. (c) 46. (a) 47. (a) 48. (e) 49. (b)
50. (b) 51. (d) 52. (c) 53. (a) 54. (b) 55. (c) 56. (b)
57. (d) 58. (a) 59. (d) 60. (c) 61. (c) 62. (d) 63. (e)

7

Cloze Test

Cloze Test is primarily meant to test a candidate's knowledge of comprehension with regard to grammar, usage and vocabulary. The examinees are required to make a choice from multiple alternatives for each word to be filled in the blank, not in a sentence, but in a passage. The blanks are numbered which are to be filled in with the most suitable alternative.

Work Book Exercise

Directions *In the following passages, there are blanks each of which has been numbered. The suitable word for the blank has been mentioned against the number below every passage. A student is required to fill the blank choosing the appropriate word in the context of the whole passage.*

Passage 1

The ...... 1...... to marriage in urban India is turning turtle. The financial imperatives of modern, urban living demand that both ......2...... should have a career. The crunch comes when the career woman demands an entity distinct from her husband and a measure of financial independence.

The woman's ......3...... is that the man as the bread-winner should be ......4...... the household expenses, while what she earns is the jam over the bread and butter. And she gets to choose the brand of jam.

Mrinalini Singh, a manager in a high ......5...... company, says, "My husband earns enough to keep the home ......6...... burning. When I take on the responsibility of home as well as office, it is not just to sink in all the money. I earn into the home kitty. I definitely want a ......7...... in where my money goes. As a high profile executive, I need to keep up a certain ......8...... personally as well as of my husband and children. I also need to ......9...... the image of my home because of the people who visit me. Where ......10...... would the money for all this come from ?"

1. *(a)* demands *(b)* economics *(c)* attitude
2. *(a)* partners *(b)* pairs *(c)* couples
3. *(a)* example *(b)* idea *(c)* stance
4. *(a)* shouldering *(b)* bearing *(c)* sharing
5. *(a)* powered *(b)* profile *(c)* income

6. (a) cooking (b) stove (c) fire
7. (a) say (b) answer (c) statement
8. (a) reputation (b) image (c) face
9. (a) keep up (b) keep on (c) keep for
10. (a) from (b) else (c) for

Passage 2

Broadcasting of which we have begun to ......1...... so much nowadays is an invention of recent ......2...... and development. Half a century ago no one could ever ......3...... how important it would become in the life of the people of the twentieth century. Nowadays its value in the sphere of education, entertainment and state administration is ......4...... recognised and accepted.

To Marconi falls the credit for the ......5...... of the wireless. He is the Edison of the wireless world. It was in 1896 that Marconi first took out a patent for it. He soon succeeded in sending messages ......6...... the Atlantic ocean to America.

From Marconi's first ......7...... to broadcasting as we know it is a long road. But scientists travelled along it ......8...... by difficulties and obstacles on the way.

Wireless service was ......9...... between India and England in 1927. Later, a broadcasting service was maintained by the Indian Broadcasting Company. The company failed and the Government of India stepped into the ......10....... .

1. (a) hear (b) listen (c) admire
2. (a) period (b) age (c) origin
3. (a) imagine (b) know (c) think
4. (a) well (b) universally (c) rightly
5. (a) invention (b) finding (c) discovery
6. (a) to (b) across (c) over
7. (a) step (b) achievement (c) success
8. (a) unafraid (b) undeterred (c) unchecked
9. (a) introduced (b) originated (c) started
10. (a) feet (b) shoes (c) foot prints

Passage 3

One of the major causes of the failure of ......1...... countries on economic front is their ......2...... to evolve a judicious mixture of ......3...... substitution and export promotion. Zambia which ......4...... on imports after its independence 20 years ......5...... has depleted 50% of its national ......6......, whereas South Korea, which started its ......7...... development from a war ravaged status ......8...... the fifties by equalising high exports ......9...... high imports, is one of the ......10...... nations today.

1. (a) developed (b) developing
   (c) advanced (d) advancing
2. (a) inability (b) disadvantage
   (c) incapacity (d) handicap

3. (a) scientific (b) invention
(c) export (d) import
4. (a) expected (b) traded
(c) banked (d) carried
5. (a) later (b) ago
(c) earlier (d) since
6. (a) capital (b) deposit
(c) income (d) credit
7. (a) financial (b) fiscal
(c) economic (d) economical
8. (a) upto (b) over
(c) on (d) in
9. (a) over (b) with
(c) and (d) into
10. (a) richest (b) innovative
(c) prolific (d) advancing

Passage 4

Come October and you are burnt by the mid-day Sun. The storm and the sizzle is particularly ......1...... as it comes after the relatively cool monsoon months. Though it is hot and muggy, that does not ......2...... people from coming out on the streets to ......3...... the traditional festivals. And it must be shopping time also, colourfully decorated showrooms are ......4...... the passerby to let his hair down, splurge and take a ......5...... of gifts home for the family. After all, the New year's just ......6...... the corner.

1. (a) traumatic (b) sultry
(c) pleasant (d) fantastic
2. (a) oppose (b) deny
(c) prevent (d) reject
3. (a) boycott (b) moot
(c) herald (d) invite
4. (a) drawing (b) fascinating
(c) pursuing (d) exhorting
5. (a) token (b) list
(c) bagful (d) placement
6. (a) round (b) at
(c) near (d) along

Passage 5

The ......1...... of today is a huge financial undertaking with the same outlook as any other limited company. The ......2...... staff have to make circulation and if they do not, they will soon be ......3...... by those who can. Their independence, therefore, suffers a grave limitation. It is further ......4...... by the fact that a newspaper is as much an advertising medium as a vehicle for ......5....... It is said that the ......6...... which the public pays for its newspaper covers no more than a third of the ......7...... of production, the other two-thirds is accounted ......8...... by advertisement revenue.

1. (a) newspaper (b) hospital
   (c) school (d) theatre
   (e) library
2. (a) medical (b) performing
   (c) teaching (d) editorial
   (e) company
3. (a) sustained (b) treated
   (c) cured (d) covered
   (e) supplanted
4. (a) destroyed (b) deepened
   (c) curtailed (d) failed
   (e) aggravated
5. (a) news (b) epidemics
   (c) training (d) business
   (e) patients
6. (a) value (b) tax
   (c) price (d) cost
   (e) fee
7. (a) expenses (b) sale
   (c) amount (d) price
   (e) cost
8. (a) into (b) in
   (c) from (d) for
   (e) with

Passage 6

Democracy has its dangers, the greatest of which is that it may be the rule of ignorance. Citizens who are not ......1...... intelligent and educated are ......2...... to commit errors of judgement in the casting of votes. The best men may thus ......3...... to get elected. Elections are usually a ......4...... of propaganda. Another criticism of democracy is that it is wanting ......5...... efficiency. For prompt and effective action, unity of action is ......6....... . In a multitude of minds, much ......7...... discussion takes place, whereas unity of control is needed for vigorous national life. This criticism, however, is not very ......8...... because in times of war the British Prime Minister usually ......9...... the power of a dictator. Another criticism of democracy in times of war is that secrecy in military affairs becomes difficult, if not ......10......, and that the opposition usually lowers the morale of the people by its condemnation of the actions of the cabinet.

1. (a) barely (b) sufficiently
   (c) highly (d) perfectly
2. (a) sure (b) deliberately
   (c) unlikely (d) likely
3. (a) fail (b) succeed
   (c) try (d) desire
4. (a) kind (b) process
   (c) matter (d) result

5. (a) of (b) for
(c) at (d) in
6. (a) enough (b) dispensable
(c) essential (d) superfluous
7. (a) profitable (b) unprofitable
(c) detailed (d) exhaustive
8. (a) unfair (b) absurd
(c) strong (d) convincing
9. (a) gains (b) wields
(c) demands (d) misuses
10. (a) easy (b) probable
(c) impossible (d) obscure

Passage 7

For generations man has ......1...... against the wilds to create a world where only he ......2...... whether animals and plants survive or are ......3...... out. Earlier we accepted as self-evident that any ......4...... in our environment brought about by science and technology must be improvements ......5...... the world of our ......6...... However, many people all over the world have begun to feel that ......7...... are going too far and that we should try to ......8...... some of the world's original life before we find it ......9...... too late. The same science which had led us away from nature is now ......10...... the miracle of creation.

1. (a) faced (b) stood
(c) struggled (d) challenged
2. (a) decides (b) thinks
(c) advises (d) observes
3. (a) taken (b) wiped
(c) put (d) thrown
4. (a) differences (b) increments
(c) changes (d) replacements
5. (a) in (b) at
(c) over (d) for
6. (a) aborigins (b) ancients
(c) successors (d) ancestors
7. (a) ourselves (b) we
(c) us (d) some
8. (a) demolish (b) cherish
(c) save (d) renovate
9. (a) occurs (b) sounds
(c) seems (d) gets
10. (a) unfolding (b) discussing
(c) arguing (d) narrating

Passage 8

We are citizens of no mean country and we are ......1...... of the land of our birth, of our people, our culture and our ......2....... .That pride should not be for a romanticised past to which we have to ......3......, nor should it encourage exclusiveness or a want of ......4...... of other ways than our own. It must never allow us to ......5...... our many weaknesses and failing or ......6...... our longing to be rid of them. We have a long way to go and much leeway to make ......7...... before we take our proper ......8...... with others in the van of human civilization and progress. And we have to ......9...... for the time at our disposal is ......10...... .

1. *(a)* aware *(b)* proud *(c)* reminded *(d)* fond
2. *(a)* customs *(b)* ceremonies *(c)* traditions *(d)* festivals
3. *(a)* return *(b)* glorify *(c)* sing *(d)* cling
4. *(a)* appreciation *(b)* enthusiasm *(c)* criticism *(d)* condemnation
5. *(a)* reject *(b)* forget *(c)* avoid *(d)* remember
6. *(a)* blunt *(b)* demolish *(c)* disappear *(d)* spur
7. *(a)* out *(b)* for *(c)* up *(d)* of
8. *(a)* role *(b)* site *(c)* equation *(d)* station
9. *(a)* tarry *(b)* hurry *(c)* ponder *(d)* debate
10. *(a)* scarce *(b)* sufficient *(c)* plenty *(d)* limited

Passage 9

Something has happened in the last twenty years that surely must ......1...... anything that has happened before. Some historians are already saying that thrust ......2...... space represents a vital turning point in history. Moon flights are considered ......3...... less than steps in human evolution ......4...... to the time when life on earth emerged from the sea and established itself on land. Of course, not everyone ......5...... enraptured by space. Critics have often said that space flight has been an ......6...... use of resources that should have ......7...... to feeding, clothing and housing people. There is, however, no proof that if we had ......8...... been working on space we would have done anything of great human value. In fact, research and exploration have ......9...... spin-offs, quite apart from the fact that they demonstrate that ......10...... is alive and insatiably curious.

1. (a) terminate (b) transcend
   (c) precede (d) recede
2. (a) on (b) upon
   (c) in (d) into
3. (a) nothing (b) certainly
   (c) sufficiently (d) probably
4. (a) exceeding (b) contrasting
   (c) comparable (d) matching
5. (a) was (b) has been
   (c) had been (d) being
6. (a) economical (b) extravagant
   (c) appropriate (d) benevolent
7. (a) devoted (b) allotted
   (c) reserved (d) gone
8. (a) not (b) occasionally
   (c) seldom (d) possibly
9. (a) renowned (b) renounced
   (c) remarkable (d) relevant
10. (a) one (b) man
    (c) human (d) individual

Passage 10

Tea prices in the domestic ......1...... continue to rule high in the ......2...... year despite the expectation of a ......3...... production as compared to the previous year. According to a preliminary assessment ......4...... on the weather ......5...... in recent months, tea output in 1990 may reach 740 million kg. as......6.......700 million kg. last year. During the past three months, tea prices have generally shown an ......7....... Unlike last year, when tea prices rose dramatically, this year, prices seem to have ......8...... at a rather high level. In the subsequent four months, the ......9...... average price showed a downtrend but in September the prices have ......10...... hardened to a considerable extent.

1. (a) sector (b) production
   (c) area (d) market
2. (a) current (b) first
   (c) second (d) last
3. (a) large (b) maximum
   (c) optimum (d) higher
4. (a) conducted (b) based
   (c) shared (d) strategy
5. (a) outbursts (b) outbreak
   (c) conditions (d) forecast

6. (a) above (b) per
(c) to (d) against

7. (a) downtrend (b) increment
(c) reduction (d) uptrend

8. (a) increased (b) surfaced
(c) synchronised (d) stabilised

9. (a) monthly (b) weekly
(c) daily (d) annual

10. (a) then
(b) never
(c) again
(d) since

Passage 11

Our scientific spirit must be shocked not only by the ......1...... of fabulous ......2...... and ......3...... poverty, but also by those of intense holiness and ......4...... superstition. In our relations with one another, we have ......5...... to apply scientific and social wisdom. The failure is ......6...... large ......7...... our society. Some social ......8...... like untouchability are ......9...... simply because the spirit in us is oppressed by the force of ......10....... .These are practised by ......11...... kindly persons, who have ceased to feel and whose understanding is ......12...... by tradition. There are millions in our country today who use scientific ......13...... and yet ......14...... superstition as mystical revelation and adhere to absurd social customs ......15...... the name of tradition.

1. (a) phenomenon (b) contrasts
(c) existence (d) comparison

2. (a) property (b) prosperity
(c) resources (d) wealth

3. (a) common (b) rampant
(c) grovelling (d) growing

4. (a) religious (b) blind
(c) popular (d) prevailing

5. (a) attempted (b) refused
(c) succeeded (d) failed

6. (a) writ (b) written
(c) wrought (d) wrapped

7. (a) in (b) on
(c) among (d) for

8. (a) abuses (b) ceremonies
(c) function (d) obligations

9. (a) allowed (b) approved
(c) tolerated (d) resisted

10. (a) opinion (b) habit
(c) society (d) custom
11. (a) fairly (b) very
(c) otherwise (d) somewhat
12. (a) stupefied (b) sanctified
(c) subsidised (b) substantiated
13. (a) discoveries (b) devices
(c) apparatus (d) machines
14. (a) consider (b) decry
(c) declare (d) revere
15. (a) on (b) for
(c) in (d) with

Passage 12

Directions *In the following passages, some of the words have been left. Try to understand what it is about. Then fill in the blanks with the help of the alternatives given.*

When I go into stranger's library I ...1... round the bookshelves. This is to know the type of person he is and I feel that I know the ...2... to his mind.

A house without books is a ...3... house, no matter how rich the carpets are. These only tell you whether he ...4... a lot of money, but the books tell you whether he has a mind as well. It is not a ...5... of money that we do not buy books.

1. (a) wonder (b) run
(c) look (d) wander
2. (a) secret (b) mystery
(c) key (d) solution
3. (a) characterless (b) bleak
(c) unlucky (d) bad
4. (a) had (b) has
(c) have (d) has had
5. (a) reason (b) question
(c) issue (d) cause

Passage 13

Any regular viewer of programmes on the television will certainly have some reservations about commercials. When television shows are ......1... good, the commercials that ...2... them are a disgrace. One of the many bad ...3... of commercials is their loudness. They seem to be ...4... as loud as the programme and the viewer is almost ...5... when they come on. Any attempt ...6... conversation during commercials is futile. Commercials also take up too much time and ...7... too often.

The impression one ...8... gets is that the shows are sandwiched in ....9... long periods of advertising all of it the same. Often commercials ....10.... a show at a particularly in appropriate time.

1. (a) reasonably (b) rationally
   (c) unreasonably (d) irrationally
2. (a) join (b) accommodate
   (c) accompany (d) admit
3. (a) features (b) feature
   (c) property (d) mark
4. (a) two (b) pair
   (c) twice (d) double
5. (a) deafening (b) blind
   (c) deafened (d) deaf
6. (a) on (b) in
   (c) to (d) at
7. (a) repeat (b) is repeated
   (c) repeated (d) are repeated
8. (a) usually (b) usual
   (c) use to (d) used to
9. (a) after (b) before
   (c) between (d) during
10. (a) involve (b) integrate
    (c) invert (d) interrupt

Passage 14

There is an enemy beneath our ...1... He recognises no national boundaries, no ...2...... parties. Everyone in the world is ......3...... by him. The enemy is the Earth itself. The ......4...... of a quake is greater than ......5...... man himself can produce. But ......6...... scientists are directing more of their ......7...... into finding some way of ......8...... earthquakes and it is possible that at ......9...... time in the near future, ...10...... will have discovered a means of protecting itself from it.

1. (a) shelter (b) feet
   (c) land (d) surface
2. (a) economical (b) historical
   (c) geographical (d) political
3. (a) threatened (b) feared
   (c) effected (d) dominated
4. (a) strength (b) power
   (c) force (d) ability
5. (a) everything (b) nothing
   (c) something (d) anything
6. (a) this day (b) today
   (c) lately (d) at present
7. (a) efforts (b) strength
   (c) capacity (d) tasks
8. (a) watching (b) directing
   (c) opposing (d) combating

9. (a) any (b) some
   (c) every (d) all
10. (a) scientists (b) humanity
   (c) people (d) mankind

Passage 15

'Quit India' came not from the lips, but the **aching hearts** of millions. In this open rebellion, the Indian ......1...... reached its climax. The British were not only ......2...... by it, but also were obliged to quit unilaterally. The importance of Quit India can be ......3...... from Lord Linlithgow's statement, 'I am engaged here in meeting by far the most ......4...... rebellion since, that of 1857, the gravity and extent of which we have so far ......5...... from the world for reasons of military security.' Still more significant was Churchill's gloomy disclosure to the King Emperor that, 'the idea of ......6...... of power had become an admitted ......7...... in the minds of British party leaders, although his public statements were diametrically opposite.

The ......8...... created by Quit India made the British ......9...... that they could no longer keep India in ......10...... .

1. (a) freedom (b) patriotism
   (c) liberation (d) revolution
2. (a) threatened (b) inspired
   (c) attacked (d) impressed
3. (a) diffused (b) gauged
   (c) established (d) determined
4. (a) trivial (b) magnificent
   (c) serious (d) auspicious
5. (a) excluded (b) elicited
   (c) prevented (d) concealed
6. (a) transfer (b) seizure
   (c) grabbing (d) retainment
7. (a) tactics (b) fantasy
   (c) inevitability (d) occurrence
8. (a) violence (b) taboos
   (c) vengeance (d) anarchy
9. (a) imagine (b) pretend
   (c) realise (d) anxious
10. (a) power (b) bondage
   (c) exile (d) suspense

Revision Exercise

Directions *In the following passages, there are blanks each of which has been numbered. The suitable word for the blank has been mentioned against the number below every passage. A student is required to fill the blank choosing the appropriate word in the context of the whole passage.*

Passage 1

No communication has ever provided so many people with as ......1...... a range of new ......2...... as television has. Without ......3...... their homes, people can watch Government Officials ......4...... important functions and see how people in ......5...... lands look and live. Television takes its ......6...... to deserts, jungles and even the sea floor. Television gives us a ......7...... of real life tragedy as when it comes to the ......8...... of war, natural disasters and poverty. It also ......9...... moments of great triumph, such as when the astronaut just ......10...... foot on the Moon.

1. (a) large (b) wide (c) many (d) broad
2. (a) experiences (b) incidents (c) happenings (d) anecdotes
3. (a) parting (b) moving (c) departing (d) leaving
4. (a) perform (b) accomplish (c) pursue (d) achieve
5. (a) far out (b) far off (c) by far (d) far and wide
6. (a) watchers (b) audience (c) viewers (d) spectators
7. (a) glimpse (b) glance (c) look (d) sight
8. (a) wounded (b) army (c) victims (d) soldiers
9. (a) ceases (b) captures (c) seizes (d) catches
10. (a) set (b) put (c) kept (d) placed

Passage 2

An archaeologist studies the ......1...... and from the ......2...... he finds, he is able to ......3...... the daily lives of men and women, who lived thousands of years ago. He makes a......4...... study of those things which those men and women left ......5...... them.

From the ......6...... he judges the size of the animals their owners could kill, from their tools he learns what ......7...... they had mastered and from their pots, needles and combs, he ......8...... the domestic skills of their ......9...... Thus, it has been possible to write a generally ......10...... account of human evolution going back some half a million years.

1. (a) rocks (b) history
(c) past (d) future
2. (a) witness (b) evidence
(c) knowledge (d) matters
3. (a) create (b) build-up
(c) rebuild (d) reconstruct
4. (a) scientific (b) historic
(c) realistic (d) research
5. (a) with (b) behind
(c) under (d) below
6. (a) weapons (b) bullets
(c) guns (d) targets
7. (a) industries (b) products
(c) crafts (d) knowledge
8. (a) values (b) assesses
(c) judges (d) criticises
9. (a) friends (b) animals
(c) women-folk (d) neighbours
10. (a) reliable (b) unmistakable
(c) perfect (d) dependable

Passage 3

The last decade has been ......1...... for management education and development. When the economies of most Western countries were ......2...... in the early 1980's there were ......3...... cuts both in corporate training and in higher education. During the boom years of the mid 1980's there were some ......4...... in both areas. In the early 1990's industrialised countries were in the ......5...... of another severe recession and a ......6...... retrenchment was to be reasonably ......7...... throughout the training world.

But this has not been the case so far. Many leading companies are ......8...... their belief in training as the key to future competitiveness and governments are ......9...... an era of rapid ......10...... in higher education.

1. (a) dogmatic (b) paradoxical
(c) praiseworthy (d) outstanding
2. (a) galvanised (b) developing
(c) faltering (d) privatised
3. (a) judicious (b) marginal
(c) proportionate (d) severe
4. (a) reactivity (b) slashing
(c) pro-activity (d) curiosity
5. (a) area (b) grip
(c) context (d) mood
6. (a) critical (b) profound
(c) slight (d) tough

7. (a) fabricated (b) advocated
(c) projected (d) expected

8. (a) asserting (b) rejecting
(c) managing (d) criticising

9. (a) establishing (b) encouraging
(c) circulating (d) preaching

10. (a) degradation (b) communication
(c) exhibition (d) expansion

Passage 4

The word 'ticket' is ......1...... to every language in India. ......2...... those who are actively ......3...... in the political process ......4...... a ticket as permission to ......5...... an election as candidate ......6...... a political party. The ......7...... if elected, sits in the ......8...... assembly or any other ......9...... for which he/she contests, as ......10...... of that party.

1. (a) general (b) peculiar
(c) common (d) familiar

2. (a) So (b) But
(c) And (d) Since

3. (a) involved (b) scene
(c) leading (d) attracted

4. (a) look (b) interpret
(c) interfere (d) interrupt

5. (a) stand in (b) campaign
(c) vote (d) contest

6. (a) inside (b) of
(c) for (d) to

7. (a) leader (b) party
(c) candidate (d) ticket

8. (a) legislative (b) legal
(c) political (d) electoral

9. (a) body (b) election
(c) party (d) institute

10. (a) candidate (b) participant
(c) representative (d) interpreter

Passage 5

I am delighted to see here the dignitaries representing their great countries. Their presence among us is a symbol of ......1...... in our efforts towards creating a sense of brotherhood among man. Our primary objective is promoting love and ......2...... We have to work towards ......3...... fear and mistrust. It is an admitted fact that violence is not ......4...... in the present world. Peace and love are major ......5...... of life. They are ......6...... upon each other. Each is ......7...... without the other. Peace cannot possibly be achieved without ......8...... in man, the subtle feelings of real love for his fellow human being. And this is not possible unless man becomes ......9...... of his own place in the universe. Human self is a highly important ......10...... of human nature.

1. *(a)* commonality *(b)* community
   (c) solidarity *(d)* sympathy
2. *(a)* harmony *(b)* balance
   (c) correspondence *(d)* agreement
3. *(a)* stamping *(b)* eradicating
   (c) terminating *(d)* abolishing
4. *(a)* maintainable *(b)* workable
   (c) sustainable *(d)* supportable
5. *(a)* portion *(b)* fixing
   (c) section *(d)* ingredients
6. *(a)* coexistent *(b)* interdependent
   (c) reliable *(d)* symbiotic
7. *(a)* impartial *(b)* undone
   (c) unfinished *(d)* incomplete
8. *(a)* awakening *(b)* realising
   (c) emerging *(d)* arising
9. (a) known (b) familiar
   (c) aware (d) acquainted
10. *(a)* parcel *(b)* aspect
    (c) characterisation *(d)* view

Passage 6

India and 25 other countries agreed to the Copenhagen Accord even as other developing countries accepted it as an irreversible decision later. The accord came out of ......1...... bargaining lasting almost 20 hours among ......2...... of governments of some of the most ......3...... countries of the world.

At the ......4...... of the day on Saturday, India ......5...... to have given ground on some ......6......, but blocked intrusion on other red lines. It had become ......7...... within the first week of the ......8...... that the best four emerging and ......9...... economies of the developing world were going to do was to defend the ......10...... economic resource sharing regimes.

1. *(a)* difficult *(b)* hard
   (c) easy *(d)* early
2. *(a)* rulers *(b)* kings
   (c) heads *(d)* chiefs
3. *(a)* influential *(b)* corrupted
   (c) useless *(d)* beautiful
4. *(a)* middle *(b)* evening
   (c) night *(d)* end
5. *(a)* proved *(b)* appeared
   (c) viewed *(d)* cleared

6. (a) materials (b) thoughts
(c) issues (d) discussions
7. (a) evident (b) ambiguous
(c) vague (d) indecisive
8. (a) accord (b) talks
(c) issues (d) thoughtial
9. (a) economic (b) political
(c) powerful (d) praiseworthy
10. (a) expected (b) existing
(c) resultant (d) consequential

Passage 7

Martin Luther King, Jr was born Michael Luther King Jr, ...1...... his grandfather had his name ......2...... to Martin. Martin Luther attended segregated public schools in Georgia, ...3...... from high school at the age of fifteen; he received the BA degree in 1948 ......4...... Morehouse college, a distinguished Negro institution of Atlanta from which both his father and grandfather had graduated. After three years of ......5...... study at Crozer Theological Seminary in Pennsylvania where he was elected President of a ......6...... white senior class, he was awarded the B D in 1951. ......7...... a fellowship won at Ebenezer he enrolled in graduate studies at Boston University, completing his residence ......8...... the doctorate in 1953 and receiving the degree in 1955. In Boston he ......9...... and married Coretta Scott, a young woman of ......10...... intellectual and artistic attainments.

1. (a) and (b) so
(c) since (d) but
2. (a) given (b) changed
(c) become (d) made
3. (a) graduating (b) finishing
(c) graduated (d) finished
4. (a) in (b) from
(c) by (d) with
5. (a) theological (b) intellectual
(c) educational (d) psychological
6. (a) predetermined (b) predominantly
(c) significations (d) somewhat
7. (a) From (b) By
(c) With (d) Through
8. (a) for (b) of
(c) about (d) to
9. (a) saw (b) eloped
(c) met (d) watched
10. (a) common (b) particular
(c) uncommon (d) general

Passage 8

Almost every full Moon night, the officials in Andaman and Nicobar islands take part in a cautious ritual. The tribesmen watch from a safe distance as the officials ......1...... the island in a boat ......2...... gifts for them. The islanders come ......3...... hesitantly only after the officials ......4...... dumped the coconuts brought ......5...... them onto the beach and begin ......6...... away from their small island. On some nights the tribals even ......7...... up enough courage to swim upto a few feet ......8...... from the boat. The officials mention that they do ......9...... want to interfere with the way of life of the tribals. The island ......10...... heavily on the mainland for most foods.

1. (a) approach (b) depart
   (c) present (d) absent
2. (a) coming (b) leaving
   (c) carrying (d) relieving
3. (a) forward (b) backward
   (c) sides (d) upward
4. (a) has (b) have
   (c) had (d) be
5. (a) by (b) to
   (c) in (d) for
6. (a) watching (b) seeing
   (c) sailing (d) stopping
7. (a) leave (b) muster
   (c) come (d) present
8. (a) correctly (b) distantly
   (c) near (d) away
9. (a) no (b) neither
   (c) not (d) nor
10. (a) spy (b) rely
    (c) occupy (d) reply

Directions *In the following passages there are blanks, each of which has been numbered. These numbers are printed below the passage and against each, five words are suggested, one of which fits the blank appropriately. Find out the appropriate word in each case.*

Passage 9

As the country embarks on planning.......1....... the 12th Plan (2012-17) period, a key question mark ....2...... hangs over the process is on the energy requirements. Growth is energy hungry and the aspirations of growing at 9-10% will ......3..... huge demands on the energy resources of the country. In this energy jigsaw, renewable energy will.........4....... like never before in the 12th Plan and......5.......

By the rule of the thumb India will......6....... about 100 gigawatts (Gw) -100000 megawatts of capacity addition in the next five years. Encouraging trends on energy efficiency and sustained....7.......by some parts of the government-the Bureau of Energy Efficiency in particular needs to be complimented for this-have led to substantially lesser energy intensity of economic growth. However, even the tempered demand numbers are.......8....... to be below 80 Gw. As against this need the coal supply from domestic sources is unlikely to support more than 25 Gw equivalent capacity. Imported coal can add some more, but at a much.......9....... cost. Gas-based electricity generation is unlikely to contribute anything substantial in view of the unprecedented gas supply challenges. Nuclear will be.........10....... in the foreseeable future. Between imported coal, gas, large hydro and nuclear, no more than 15-20Gw equivalent can be.......11......... to be added in the five-year time block.

.......12........13..........this, capacity addition in the renewable energy based power generation has touched about 3Gw a year. In the coming five years, the overall capacity addition in the electricity grid........14......... renewable energy is likely to range between 20Gw and 25Gw. Additionally, over and above the grid-based capacity, off-grid electricity applications are reaching remote places and.......15...... lives where grid-based electricity supply has miserably failed.

1. *(a)* on *(b)* against
(c) for *(d)* onwards
(e) at

2. *(a)* where *(b)* that
(c) inside *(d)* always
(e) who

3. *(a)* replace *(b)* forward
(c) subject *(d)* place
(e) demand

4. *(a)* light *(b)* pass
(c) publish *(d)* feature
(e) find

5. *(a)* earlier *(b)* likewise
(c) publicity *(d)* next
(e) after

6. *(a)* consumed *(b)* waste
(c) require *(d)* highlight
(e) generate

7. *(a)* developmental *(b)* structures
(c) efforts *(d)* projections
(e) practices

8. *(a)* likely *(b)* sure
(c) unsure *(d)* unexpected
(e) unlikely

9. *(a)* expected *(b)* nominal
(c) excelled *(d)* higher
(e) lower

10. *(a)* marginal *(b)* failure
(c) success *(d)* dangerous
(e) maximum

11. *(a)* sure *(b)* certain
(c) linked *(d)* remarked
(e) expected

12. (a) As (b) When
(c) But (d) However
(e) If

13. (a) against (b) for
(c) with (d) is
(e) ever

14. (a) capacity (b) through
(c) project (d) versus
(e) against

15. (a) generating (b) lightening
(c) making (d) touching

Directions *In the following passages there are blanks, each of which has been numbered. These numbers are printed below the passage and against each, five words/phrases are suggested, one of which fits the blank appropriately. Find out the appropriate word/phrase in each case.*

Passage 10

Greenhouse gases are only.......1........ of the story when it comes to global warming. Changes to one part of the climate system can.........2......... additional changes to the way the planet absorbs or reflects energy. These secondary changes are........3........ climate feedbacks and they could more than double the amount of warming caused by carbon dioxide alone. The primary feedbacks are........4........to snow and ice, water vapour, clouds and the carbon cycle.

Perhaps the most well......5....... feedback comes from melting snow and ice in the Northern Hemisphere. Warming temperatures are already........6.........a growing percentage of Arctic sea ice, exposing dark ocean water during the.........7......... sunlight of summer. Snow cover on land is also.........8.......... in many areas. In the.......9......... of snow and ice, these areas go from having bright, sunlight-reflecting surfaces that cool the planet to having dark, sunlight-absorbing surfaces that.......10........ more energy into the Earth system and cause more warming.

1. (a) whole (b) part
(c) material (d) issue
(e) most

2. (a) raise (b) brings
(c) refer (d) stop
(e) cause

3. (a) sensed (b) called
(c) nothing (d) but
(e) term

4. (a) due (b) results
(c) reason (d) those
(e) because

5. (a) done (b) known
(c) ruled (d) bestowed
(e) said

6. *(a)* mastering *(b)* sending
   (c) melting *(d)* calming
   (e) increasing
7. *(a)* make-shift *(b)* ceasing
   (c) troubled *(d)* perpetual
   (e) absent
8. *(a)* dwindling *(b)* manufactured
   (c) descending *(d)* generating
   (e) supplied
9. *(a)* progress *(b)* reduced
   (c) existence *(d)* midst
   (e) absence
10. *(a)* repel *(b)* waft
    (c) monitor *(d)* bring
    (e) access

Passage 11

Traditional bank architecture is based on bank branches. These branches ensure the physical......1........ of a customer's savings. A customer may go there to deposit and withdraw money.......2.......... loans and in other financial transactions. In the past two decades banking architecture has ....3........ Automated Teller Machine (ATM) has been a big.........4.......... and credit and debit cards have created new financial spaces.........5........the bank branch has remained the bedrock of the banking system after all a person needs a bank account in a branch before he can operate a debit or ATM card. This may be about to change as technocrats now ......6........cell phones as the new architecture of virtual banks. This has the potential to make branches......7.......... Cell phone banking looks especially relevant for India, since it can penetrate the countryside cheaply and......8......The world over cell phones are spreading at a.........9........ rate and in India alone new cell phone connection are growing at the rate of six million a month a rate of customer.........10......... that no bank can dream of.

1. *(a)* knowledge *(b)* security
   (c) presence *(d)* confidentiality
   (e) guarantee
2. *(a)* negotiate *(b)* advance
   (c) credit *(d)* disburse
   (e) sanction
3. *(a)* pursue *(b)* interact
   (c) changed *(d)* enable
   (e) engage
4. *(a)* drawback *(b)* hurdle
   (c) consequence *(d)* luxury
   (e) innovation
5. *(a)* Despite *(b)* Although
   (c) Even *(d)* Yet
   (e) Until

6. (*a*) view (*b*) realise
(*c*) display (*d*) engineer
(*e*)assess

7. (*a*) essenial (*b*) obsolete
(*c*) extant (*d*) retreat
(*e*) expired

8. (*a*) moderately (*b*) occasionally
(*c*) compulsorily (*d*) indiscriminately
(*e*) effectively

9. (*a*) phenomenal (*b*) gradual
(*c*) proportionate (*d*) competitive
(*e*) projected

10. (*a*) discount (*b*) base
(*c*) expansion (*d*) satisfaction
(*e*) relationship

Directions *In the following passages at certain points you are given a choice of three words in brackets, one of which fits the meaning of the passage. Choose the word which best fits the meaning of the passage and mark the corresponding letter on your answer sheet.*

Passage 12

One of the most interesting new books published recently is 'Spaceship' by Prof E C Walker. Our Earth he says **1.** *(a) is* like a spaceship and all the 400 million people
(b) have been
(c) will be

2. *(a) over* Earth are passengers on it. And we are heading **3.** *(a) about* a disaster
(b) on *(b) to*
(c) upon *(c) towards*

The levels of atmospheric pollution **4.** *(a) increasing* in the cities and industrial areas of
(b) arriving
(c) coming

the world could in no time change the weather patterns of the Earth, raising the temperature. **5.** *(a) in* the whole of planet. If this rose a few **6.** *(a) degrees,* the deserts
(b) of *(b) steps*
(c) for *(c) miles*

of the world would expand to double their size. The polar ice caps would start melting. If the polar ice caps melted, the **7.** *(a) water* level all over the world would rise
(b) ice
(c) sea

8. *(a) in* about 60 m. Prof Walker's **9.** *(a) idea* is not at all about gloom and doom.
(b) by *(b) thought*
(c) to *(c) book*

He admits that the **10.** *(a) ideas* he describes could take thousands of years.
(b) solutions
(c) changes

Passage 13

Sometimes the messages are sent with **1.** (a) *many* accompanying words and we
(b) few
(c) no

speak in **2.** *(a) body* language alone. But, what gestures make **3.** *(a) with*
(b) signal *(b) up*
(c) foreign *(c) into*

body language? Most of us are **4.** *(a) easy* with the common hand gestures. Some
(b) familiar
(c) efficient

5. *(a) students* cannot talk without using their hands. **6.** *(a) We* reach out as they
(b) people *(b) Arms*
(c) officers *(c) They*

explain almost **7.** *(a) exacting* their words, emphasising and exaggerating and
(b) shaping
(c) changing

8. *(a) teaching* with their hands. Other people hardly **9.** *(a) adjust* their hands at
(b) holding *(b) use*
(c) punctuating *(c) wave*

all when they **10.** *(a) lecture*
(b) unite
(c) talk

Passage 14

A young man riding a motor-cycle approached a policeman in a market place and sought his assistance in reaching a particular locality. The policeman gave him. some **1.** *(a) instructions* and the motor-cyclist left. He **2.** *(a) reached* back after some time
(b) directions *(b) came*
(c) advice *(c) went*

and **3.** *(a) asked* the policeman that he could not **4.** *(a) find* the place. The policeman
(b) convinced *(b) hit*
(c) told *(c) see*

got the **5.** *(a) idea* to help him and agreed to **6.** *(a) start* with the motor-cyclist. On
(b) inclination *(b) go*
(c) urge *(c) proceed*

reaching the **7.** *(a) station* the motor-cyclist left in a hurry leaving the policeman
(b) destination
(c) spot

on the road. The policeman was surprised and returned to his spot. A little later, a senior police officer reached the place and took the policeman to task for dereliction of duty.

Exam Practice

Passage 1

Directions (Q. Nos. 1-10) *In the following passage, at certain points you are given a choice of four words marked (a), (b), (c) and (d), one of which fits the meaning of the passage. Choose the best word out of the four. Mark the letter relating to this word.* **NDA 2017**

After this incident I went to Nainital and returned after nearly a month, I had.........1.......... taken.........2.......... my clothes when I saw Gangu standing ....3.......... a new baby. He was.........4.......... with joy. Even Nanda.........5.......... not have.........6.......... such joy.........7.......... getting Krishna. His face had the same.........8.......... that.........9.......... on face of a.........10.......... man after a full meal.

1. *(a)* hardly *(b)* barely *(c)* merely *(d)* rarely taken

2. *(a)* out *(b)* away *(c)* off *(d)* on

3. *(a)* by *(b)* near *(c)* with *(d)* at

4. *(a)* jumping *(b)* bursting *(c)* dancing *(d)* singing

5. *(a)* could *(b)* would *(c)* should *(d)* ought

6. *(a)* experimented *(b)* shown *(c)* felt *(d)* heard

7. *(a)* at *(b)* in *(c)* on *(d)* into

8. *(a)* light *(b)* glow *(c)* sense *(d)* hope

9. *(a)* comes *(b)* appears *(c)* rices *(d)* shows

10. *(a)* starved *(b)* starving *(c)* hungry *(d)* satisfied

Passage 2

CDS 2016

Many of us believe that science is something modern,
1. *(a) if* *(b) though* *(c) unless* the truth is that **2.** *(a) men* *(b) people* *(c) man* has been using science for

3. *(a) the* *(b) a* *(c) that* very long time. However, it has **4.** *(a) has* *(b) have* *(c) had* a greater effect on human lives in

the last 25 **5.** *(a) and* *(b) or* *(c) either* 30 years than in the hundreds of years **6.** *(a) from* *(b) for* *(c) since* the invention of

the plough. The

7. *(a) marvellous* gifts of science have made modern life **8.** *(a) dull* and comfortable.
(b) costly *(b) exciting*
(c) inexpensive *(c) aimless*

But science has

9. *(a) at* the same time created new problems. One of these which may become
(b) in
(c) within

10. *(a) bad* in the years to come, is **11.** *(a) those* of 'jet-lag'. With the coming of
(b) worse *(b) this*
(c) good *(c) that*

modern jets, flying at more than 900 km an hour, the world **12.** *(a) can* become very small
(b) become
(c) has become

indeed. Today if you **13**. *(a) leave* New Delhi at 4.00 in the morning, you
(b) will leave
(c) would leave

14. *(a) will* eat an early breakfast in the sky **15.** *(a) at* Kabul, and be in London by
(b) can *(b) on*
(c) must *(c) over*

about 1.00 p.m.

Passage 3

CDS 2018

So the ______ **1.** *(a) difficulty* is that in the present social structure, discipline
(b) difficult
(c) difference
(d) different

has become an important factor because we want large numbers of children ______ **2.** *(a) educated* together and ______ **3.** *(a)* as quick as possible.
(b) to be educated *(b)* as quickly as possible.
(c) to be educating *(c)* as possible as.
(d) to educate *(d)* quickly.

Educated to be what? To be bank clerks or super salesmen, capitalists or commissars. When you are a superman ______ **4.** *(a)* of some kind, as/or a super
(b) of same kind,
(c) of some,
(d) of same,

governor or a subtle parliamentary debater, what have you done? You are probably very clever, full of facts, Anybody can pick up facts; but we are human beings, not factual machines, not ______ **5.** *(a)* beast routine automatons. But again, sirs, you are
(b) bear
(c) beastly
(d) bare

not interested. You are listening to me and ______ **6.** *(a)* smiling for
(b) smiling to
(c) smiling with
(d) smiling at

each other, you are not going to do a thing about radically changing the education system; so it will drag on ______ **7.** *(a)* until there are a monstrous revolution, which
(b) still there is
(c) till there was
(d) till there is

will merely be another substitution–there will be much more control because the totalitarian government knows how to shape the minds and hearts of the people, they ______ **8.** *(a)* had learnt the trick.
(b) learnt
(c) have learnt
(d) had been learnt

Passage 4

CDS 2018

This cultural form ______ **1.** *(a)* originating from Japan has a name which means
(b) originates
(c) originated
(d) organising

'whimsical or impromptu pictures'. It ______ **2.** *(a)* had been in existence since
(b) has been
(c) was
(d) is

the 12th century when the first ______ **3.** *(a)* instance for this art form was seen.
(b) incident
(c) accident
(d) events

Since the language itself is read from right of left, the books with ______ **4.** *(a)* that
(b) this
(c) these
(d) which

art form follows the same pattern. ______ **5.** *(a)* For when English translations
(b) Beginning
(c) During
(d) Initially

were made, they flipped the pictures and published it. This ______ **6.** *(a)* enrage
(b) enlarged
(c) engraved
(d) enraged

the purists as it showed left-handed samurai, who did not exist in the original book. Hence, nowadays even English translations follow ______ **7.** *(a)* the right to left format.
(b) a
(c) some
(d) same

The name of this art form is Manga.

Passage 5

CDS 2019

The Nobel Prize for Chemistry this year is a tribute to the power of ....

1. (a) evolution
   (b) devolution.
   (c) revolution.
   (d) involution.

The laureates harnessed evolution and used it in the .... 2. (a) microscope
(b) field
(c) market
(d) laboratory

with amazing results. Frances H Arnold, an American who was given one-half of the prize, used 'directed evolution' to .... 3. (a) inhibit
(b) synthesise
(c) hamper
(d) hold back

variants of naturally occurring enzymes that could be used to ....

4. (a) constitute
   (b) sink
   (c) manufacture
   (d) resolve

biofuels and pharmaceuticals. The other half went to George P Smith, also of the US and Sir Gregory P Winter, from the UK, who evolved antibodies to ....

5. (a) combat
   (b) support
   (c) observe
   (d) invite

autoimmune diseases and even metastatic cancer through a process called phage display.

Passage 6

Directions (Q. Nos. 1-5) *In the following passage, there are blanks, each of which has been numbered. Against each, five words are suggested, one of which fits the blank appropriately. Find out the appropriate word in each case.* **SBI Clerk 2016**

The night fell heavy in the heights of the mountains and one could not see anything. All was black and the moon and the stars were covered by clouds.

As Tom was climbing only a few feet away from the top of the mountain, he **(1)** and fell in to the air, falling at great speed. He could only see black spots as he went down. He kept failing, when all of a **(2)** he felt the rope tied to his waist pull at him very hard. His body was hanging in the air. Only the rope was holding him and in that moment of stillness, he had no other **(3)** but to scream, 'Help me God'. All of a sudden a deep voice coming from the sky answered.

'What did you want me to do?' 'Save me God,' said Tom. 'Do you really think I can save you?' asked the voice. 'Of course you can,' **(4)** Tom. 'Then cut the rope tied to your waist,' said the voice. There was a moment of silence as Tom decided to hold on to the rope with 'all his **(5)**. The rescue team said that the next day a climber was found dead and frozen, his body hanging from a rope, only one foot away from the ground.

1. (a) stumbled (b) talked (c) tried (d) slapped (e) caused
2. (a) time (b) instant (c) sudden (d) shock (e) moment
3. (a) option (b) person (c) want (d) limitation (e) body
4. (a) asked (b) questioned (c) replied (d) denied (e) doubted
5. (a) strength (b) feet (c) family (d) reason (e) portions

Passage 7

Directions *(Q. Nos. 1-6) In the passage given below, there are blanks which are to be filled with the options given below. Find out the appropriate pair of words in each case which can most suitably complete the sentence without altering meaning of the statement.* **IBPS PO 2017**

While the Padmavati issue rages on, it is instructive to observe how little by way of a/an ...... (1) reaction by the government has been forthcoming. In the face of public .... (2) made in the full glare of national media, by those protesting against the film as well leaders of its own party, the government has offered no substantive comment.

Instead, several states have acted by banning the film, without having seen it. At a time when a comment on social media can get young people into jail, the people making the very gruesome threats against some well-liked public figures have faced no ...... (3) whatsoever. This has already invited much criticism on social media, but what is ...... (4) is how easy it is for the state to ignore the critics and go about its business unaffected.

Democracy works by creating several ......(5) of oversight, each acting in a specific way. The opposition, the legislative, the judiciary, the bureaucracy, the media including social media and finally, the electorate are some of the mechanisms by which a regime becomes ...... (6). Together, these institutions work to guide, shape challenge, amplify, audit and limit any regime's actions.

1. (a) Canonical/Fitting (b) Customary/Bonafide (c) Firm/Stout (d) Authoritative/Official (e) Crucial/Paramount
2. (a) Demands/Appeal (b) Presages/Threats (c) Rampart/Staves (d) Abutment/Backing (e) Controversy/Affairs

3. (a) Backlash/Reverberation (b) Repercussion/Support
(c) Alacrity/Hoopla (c) Lining/Stanchion
(e) Negation/Action

4. (a) Striking/Startling (b) Noticeable/Evident
(c) Chronic/Inveterate (c) Moot/Dubious
(e) Contrasting/Unusual

5. (a) Platoons/Cartels (b) Assemblages/Groups
(c) Stages/Notches (c) Strata/Layers
(e) Phases/Division

6. (a) Efficient/Competent (b) Accountable/Liable
(c) Systematic/Virtuous (c) Gratifying/Prolific
(e) Resilient/Tractable

Passage 8

Directions (Q. Nos. 1-5) *In the following passage some words have been deleted. Fill in the blanks with the help of the alternatives given. Select the most appropriate option for each blank.*

SSC CGL 2018

Leaving his car with the valet, he (1) .... the hotel and joined the large crowd milling (2) .... He found a badge waiting for him (3) .... the receptionist's table and took his (4) .... in the rear of the hall. When the place was (5) .... the moderator welcomed the crowd.

1. Select the most appropriate option to fill in blank No. 1.
(a) accessed (b) entered
(c) admitted (d) invaded

2. Select the most appropriate option to fill in blank No. 2.
(a) about (b) aside
(c) into (d) out

3. Select the most appropriate option to fill in the blank No. 3.
(a) over (b) at
(c) in (d) by

4. Select the most appropriate option to fill in blank No. 4.
(a) stand (b) lounge
(c) couch (d) seat

5. Select the most appropriate option to fill in the blank No. 5.
(a) filled (b) completed
(c) stuffed (d) empty

Passage 9

Directions (Q. Nos. 1-6) *In the following passage there are blanks, each of which has been numbered. These numbers are printed below the passage and against each, five options are given. Find out the appropriate word which fits the blank appropriately to make a grammatically and contextually correct sentence.*

Two decades have passed since the mid-day meal became a part of the daily routine in government schools nationwide. In this long passage of time, procedures have (1) but accidents continue to occur.

IBPS Clerk 2019

Funds from the Centre flow smoothly though procurement of food items faces hurdles of different kinds. The latest **(2)** in mid-meal stories concerns milk. Government norms entitle every child to receive 150 ml of milk as part of the mid-day meal. However, a video revealed recently how one litre of milk was mixed in a bucketful of water so that it would **(3)** for the more than 80 children present that day in a school in rural Uttar Pradesh (UP).

This was somewhat similar to the one reported from Uttar Pradesh a couple of months ago. In the earlier incident, a video showed plain chapatis being served with salt. The two videos made it to the national media; they also proved useful for the officers who **(4)** the mid-day meal scheme since they also depend on unauthorised video graphers to learn about the reality in schools.

Each such revelation leads to the same **(5)** official statement: punish the guilty, locate the video-maker and deal with him/her. In the latest mid-meal story narrated above, authorities in Uttar Pradesh have reportedly done the **(6)** needful, i.e. they have fired the apparent culprit who is a para-teacher.

1. *(a)* balances *(b)* stabilised *(c)* persistent *(d)* stabilising *(e)* None of these

2. (a) stained *(b)* retaliate *(c)* accusations *(d)* blunder *(e)* None of these

3. (a) suffice *(b)* assent *(c)* patriotism *(d)* benefit *(e)* None of these

4. *(a)* react *(b)* negate *(c)* supervise *(d)* unify *(e)* None of these

5. (a) amalgamate *(b)* reflexive *(c)* applicable *(d)* unlikely *(e)* None of these

6. *(a)* permit *(b)* annihilate *(c)* customary *(d)* stride *(e)* None of these

Passage 10

Directions (Q. Nos. 1-5) *In the following passage, some words have deleted. Fill in the blanks with the help of the alternatives given. Select the most appropriate option for each blank.*

Machines were made to be man's servants. Yet-man has grown so **(1)** on them that they are in a fair way to become his **(2)**. Already men spend most of their lives looking after and waiting **(3)** machines. Machines are very stern bosses. They must be fed with coal and **(4)** petrol to drink and oil to wash with and must be kept at an **(5)** temperature. **SSC CGL 2020**

Select the most appropriate option for blank no. 1.
(a) dependent *(b)* helpless
(c) inferior *(d)* subordinate

Select the most appropriate option for blank no. 2.
(a) masters *(b)* victims
(c) slaves *(d)* administrators

Select the most appropriate option for blank no. 3.
(a) under (b) from
(c) upon (d) into

Select the most appropriate option for blank no. 4.
(a) gave (b) give
(c) given (d) gives

Select the most appropriate option for blank no. 5.
(a) optimum (b) optional
(c) optimist (d) outdated

Passage 11

Directions (Q. Nos. 1-10) *In the given passage, there are blanks, each of which has been numbered. Against each number, five words are suggested, one of which fits the blank appropriately. Find out the appropriate word in each case.* **IBPS PO/MT 2015**

Schools all over India **(1)** 'Children's Day' on 14th November every year. It was on this day that our **(2)** first Prime Minister was **(3)**. His **(4)** had come down from Kashmir to rich plains below. Kaul had been his **(5)** name. This changed to Kaul Nehru, and in **(6)** years Kaul was **(7)** and he became simply Nehru. Jawaharlal Nehru was the **(8)** son of his prosperous parents. And so he grew up and spent his early years as a **(9)** child with no **(10)** of his age.

1. (a) consider (b) regard (c) celebrate
(d) enjoy (e) respect

2. (a) great (b) only (c) formerly
(d) importantly (e) arrogant

3. (a) chose (b) rejected (c) decided
(d) selected (e) born

4. (a) descendant (b) ancestors (c) following
(d) colleague (e) off-spring

5. (a) false (b) nick (c) family
(d) oldest (e) first

6. (a) many (b) after (c) later
(d) starting (e) subsequently

7. (a) forgot (b) dropped (c) overlook
(d) special (e) fallen

8. (a) only (b) spoil (c) old
(d) troubling (e) famous

9. (a) feared (b) protective (c) lovely
(d) lonely (e) pamper

10. (a) competitions (b) associating (c) play
(d) partnership (e) companion

Passage 12

Directions (Q. Nos. 1-10) *In the following passage, there are blanks each of which has been numbered. These numbers are printed below the passage and against each five words are suggested, one of which fits the blank appropriately. Find out the appropriate word in each case.*

SBI PO 2015

I used to look....**(1)**....to the holidays. I was usually....**(2)**....to my uncle's house where I....**(3)**....his children. I did not get paid a salary for....**(4)**.... What I received in return, however, was far more....**(5)**.... My uncle was an avid reader. During the time I spent with his family I had an....**(6)**....to read the vast amount of books and magazines that he possessed. This improved my English to some....**(7)**.... Reading became my new....**(8)**.... ....**(9)**....spending my pocket money on a ticket to the cinema I began to....**(10)**....books. This has benefited me greatly.

1. (*a*) forward (*b*) towards (*c*) backward (*d*) up (*e*) around

2. (*a*) went (*b*) sent (*c*) visited (*d*) travelled (*e*) gone

3. (*a*) cared (*b*) occupy (*c*) guarded (*d*) taught (*e*) played

4. (*a*) them (*b*) whom (*c*) this (*d*) now (*e*) which

5. (*a*) expensive (*b*) deserving (*c*) helping (*d*) demanding (*e*) valuable

6. (*a*) opportunity (*b*) ability (*c*) use (*d*) encouragement (*e*) achievement

7. (*a*) distance (*b*) extent (*c*) time (*d*) limits (*e*) degrees

8. (*a*) activity (*b*) hope (*c*) hobby (*d*) duty (*e*) worship

9. (*a*) Despite (*b*) Though (*c*) By (*d*) Instead of (*e*) While

10. (*a*) sell (*b*) read (*c*) exchange (*d*) invest (*e*) buy

Passage 13

Directions (Q. Nos. 1-10) *In the following passage, there are blanks each of which has been numbered. These numbers are printed below the passage and against each five words are suggested,one of which fits the blank appropriately. Find out the appropriate word in each case.*

IBPS Clerk 2015

The dwarf honey bee, *Apis florea*, is the smallest of the honeybees. Its small nest **(1)** 1 to 8 m above the ground, anchored to a slender branch of a tree or shrub. Sometimes it nests **(2)** caves, the honeycomb being suspended **(3)** the roof. Compared to the honeycombs of the bigger species, the dwarf's yields very **(4)** honey, barely a few hundred grams, but even this small amount **(5)** plunderers, both human and animal, **(6)** driven away either through deception or attack. Deceptions involves clinging to each other and forming a thick blanker of bees to **(7)** cover the nest. If an intruder approaches, the tiny bees raise **(8)** abdomens and shake them from side to side,in unison and produce a hissing sound. This is enough to confuse and frighten **(9)** many animals. If the intrusion persists the bees leave the nest and attack.

The blanket of bees is made up of almost three-quarters of the worker bee population and besides its defensive nature also serves to regulate the internal temperature of the nest.

Dwarf bees are found in Oman, Iran, Pakistan, India, Sri Lanka and some **(10)** of South-East Asia.

1. *(a)* hangs *(b)* depends *(c)* looks *(d)* benefits *(e)*attracts

2. *(a)* with *(b)* in *(c)* to *(d)* into *(e)* after

3. *(a)* with *(b)* to *(c)* into *(d)* after *(e)* from

4. *(a)* big *(b)* small *(c)* little *(d)* gignatic *(e)* large

5. *(a)* depends *(b)* look *(c)* goes *(d)* attracts *(e)* behind

6. *(a)* is *(b)* has *(c)* had *(d)* are *(e)* had been

7. *(a)* completely *(b)* generalry *(c)* independantly *(d)* together with *(e)* accordingly

8. *(a)* its *(b)* their *(c)* his *(d)* her *(e)* them

9. *(a)* up *(b)* down *(c)* to *(d)* into *(e)* away

10. *(a)* lands *(b)* countries *(c)* grounds *(d)* places *(e)* locations

Passage 14

Directions (Q. Nos. 1-10) *In the following passage, there are blanks, each of which has been numbered. These numbers are printed below the passage and against each, five words are suggested, one of which fits the blank appropriately. Find out the appropriate word in each case.*

The World Diabetes Congress has determined that India has the largest number of diabetics in the world. Apart from the loss of productivity, the **(1)** burden is alarming-$2.8 billion annually. Sedentary jobs, **(2)** of electronic entertainment, changing diet patterns and **(3)** dependence on automobiles have driven the activity **(4)** of Indians' lives especially in cities.

The **(5)** is, therefore, to make people physically **(6)** and requires interventions which impact a large **(7)** of the population. Admittedly, physical activity is a **(8)** of choice and is strongly driven by **(9)** preferences. But policymaking needs to shift to **(10)** moderate levels of physical activity in the daily lives of people. One way to accomplish this is to create walkable communities that give residents a variety of destinations within walking distance. **IBPS PO/MT 2016**

1. *(a)* economic *(b)* finance *(c)* subsidy *(d)* physical *(e)* health

2. *(a)* broadcast *(b)* spread *(c)* prevalent *(d)* expand *(e)* widespread

3. *(a)* totally *(b)* entirely *(c)* grown *(d)* mutual *(e)* increasing

4. *(a)* most *(b)* out *(c)* from *(d)* through *(d)* outside

5. *(a)* ultimatum *(b)* hazard *(c)* sensitivity *(d)* challenge *(d)* dispute

6. *(a)* equip *(b)* built *(c)* active *(d)* trained *(e)* qualified

7. *(a)* section *(b)* scale *(c)* degree *(d)* percent *(e)* piece

8. *(a)* want *(b)* matter *(c)* scarcity *(d)* right *(e)* lack

9. *(a)* showing *(b)* given *(c)* special *(d)* personal *(d)* individually

10. *(a)* pursuit *(b)* indulge *(c)* introduce *(d)* insist *(e)* attract

Answers

Work Book Exercise

Passage 1

1. (a)	**2.** (a)	**3.** (b)	**4.** (b)	**5.** (b)	**6.** (c)	**7.** (a)
8. (b)	**9.** (a)	**10.** (b)				

Passage 2

1. (a)	**2.** (b)	**3.** (a)	**4.** (b)	**5.** (a)	**6.** (b)	**7.** (a)
8. (b)	**9.** (c)	**10.** (b)				

Passage 3

1. (b)	**2.** (a)	**3.** (d)	**4.** (c)	**5.** (b)	**6.** (a)	**7.** (c)
8. (d)	**9.** (b)	**10.** (a)				

Passage 4

1. (b)	**2.** (c)	**3.** (c)	**4.** (d)	**5.** (c)	**6.** (a)

Passage 5

1. (a)	**2.** (d)	**3.** (e)	**4.** (c)	**5.** (a)	**6.** (c)	**7.** (e)
8. (d)						

Passage 6

1. (b)	**2.** (d)	**3.** (a)	**4.** (c)	**5.** (d)	**6.** (c)	**7.** (b)
8. (d)	**9.** (b)	**10.** (c)				

Passage 7

1. (c) 2. (a) 3. (b) 4. (c) 5. (a) 6. (d) 7. (b)
8. (c) 9. (d) 10. (a)

Passage 8

1. (b) 2. (c) 3. (d) 4. (a) 5. (b) 6. (a) 7. (c)
8. (d) 9. (b) 10. (d)

Passage 9

1. (b) 2. (b) 3. (a) 4. (c) 5. (a) 6. (b) 7. (d)
8. (a) 9. (c) 10. (b)

Passage 10

1. (d) 2. (a) 3. (d) 4. (b) 5. (c) 6. (d) 7. (d)
8. (d) 9. (a) 10. (c)

Passage 11

1. (c) 2. (c) 3. (d) 4. (a) 5. (d) 6. (a) 7. (b)
8. (a) 9. (c) 10. (b) 11. (a) 12. (a) 13. (b) 14. (a)
15. (c)

Passage 12

1. (d) 2. (c) 3. (a) 4. (b) 5. (b)

Passage 13

1. (a) 2. (c) 3. (a) 4. (c) 5. (c) 6. (d) 7. (d)
8. (a) 9. (c) 10. (d)

Passage 14

1. (b) 2. (d) 3. (a) 4. (a) 5. (d) 6. (b) 7. (a)
8. (d) 9. (b) 10. (a)

Passage 15

1. (b) 2. (a) 3. (b) 4. (c) 5. (d) 6. (a) 7. (c)
8. (d) 9. (c) 10. (b)

Revision Exercise

Passage 1

1. (c) 2. (a) 3. (d) 4. (a) 5. (b) 6. (c) 7. (a)
8. (c) 9. (b) 10. (a)

Passage 2

1. (c) 2. (b) 3. (d) 4. (a) 5. (b) 6. (a) 7. (c)
8. (b) 9. (c) 10. (a)

Passage 3

1. (d) 2. (c) 3. (b) 4. (a) 5. (b) 6. (c) 7. (d)
8. (a) 9. (b) 10. (d)

Passage 4

1. (c) 2. (b) 3. (a) 4. (b) 5. (d) 6. (b) 7. (c)
8. (a) 9. (a) 10. (c)

Passage 5

1. (c) 2. (a) 3. (b) 4. (c) 5. (d) 6. (b) 7. (d)
8. (a) 9. (c) 10. (b)

Passage 6

1. (b) **2.** (c) **3.** (a) **4.** (d) **5.** (b) **6.** (c) **7.** (a)
8. (b) **9.** (c) **10.** (b)

Passage 7

1. (d) **2.** (b) **3.** (a) **4.** (b) **5.** (a) **6.** (b) **7.** (d)
8. (a) **9.** (c) **10.** (c)

Passage 8

1. (a) **2.** (c) **3.** (a) **4.** (b) **5.** (d) **6.** (c) **7.** (b)
8. (d) **9.** (c) **10.** (b)

Passage 9

1. (c) **2.** (b) **3.** (d) **4.** (d) **5.** (e) **6.** (c) **7.** (c)
8. (e) **9.** (d) **10.** (a) **11.** (e) **12.** (a) **13.** (a) **14.** (b)
15. (b)

Passage 10

1. (b) **2.** (e) **3.** (b) **4.** (a) **5.** (b) **6.** (c) **7.** (d)
8. (a) **9.** (e) **10.** (e)

Passage 11

1. (b) **2.** (d) **3.** (c) **4.** (e) **5.** (c) **6.** (a) **7.** (b)
8. (e) **9.** (a) **10.** (c)

Passage 12

1. (a) **2.** (b) **3.** (c) **4.** (a) **5.** (b) **6.** (a) **7.** (c)
8. (b) **9.** (b) **10.** (c)

Passage 13

1. (c) **2.** (a) **3.** (b) **4.** (b) **5.** (b) **6.** (c) **7.** (b)
8. (c) **9.** (b) **10.** (c)

Passage 14

1. (b) **2.** (b) **3.** (c) **4.** (a) **5.** (a) **6.** (b) **7.** (b)

Exam Practice

Passage 1

1. (b) **2.** (c) **3.** (c) **4.** (b) **5.** (a) **6.** (c) **7.** (c)
8. (b) **9.** (b) **10.** (b)

Passage 2

1. (b) **2.** (c) **3.** (b) **4.** (c) **5.** (b) **6.** (c) **7.** (a)
8. (b) **9.** (a) **10.** (b) **11.** (c) **12.** (c) **13.** (a) **14.** (b)
15. (a)

Passage 3

1. (a) **2.** (b) **3.** (b) **4.** (a) **5.** (c) **6.** (d) **7.** (d)
8. (c)

Passage 4

1. (a) **2.** (b) **3.** (a) **4.** (b) **5.** (d) **6.** (d) **7.** (a)

Passage 5

1. (a) **2.** (d) **3.** (b) **4.** (c) **5.** (a)

Passage 6

1. (a) **2.** (c) **3.** (a) **4.** (c) **5.** (a)

Passage 7

1. (d) **2.** (b) **3.** (e) **4.** (a) **5.** (d) **6.** (b)

Passage 8

1. (b) **2.** (a) **3.** (b) **4.** (d) **5.** (a)

Passage 9

1. (b) **2.** (c) **3.** (a) **4.** (c) **5.** (b) **6.** (c)

Passage 10

1. (a) **2.** (a) **3.** (c) **4.** (c) **5.** (a)

Passage 11

1. (c) **2.** (a) **3.** (e) **4.** (b) **5.** (c) **6.** (c) **7.** (b)
8. (a) **9.** (d) **10.** (e)

Passage 12

1. (a) **2.** (b) **3.** (d) **4.** (c) **5.** (e) **6.** (a) **7.** (b)
8. (c) **9.** (d) **10.** (e)

Passage 13

1. (a) **2.** (b) **3.** (e) **4.** (c) **5.** (d) **6.** (d) **7.** (a)
8. (b) **9.** (e) **10.** (d)

Passage 14

1. (a) **2.** (b) **3.** (e) **4.** (b) **5.** (d) **6.** (c) **7.** (a)
8. (b) **9.** (d) **10.** (c)

PART C

1

Sequence of Sentences

Sequence of Sentences and Paragraphs

One of the questions set in the objective test in English relates to Sequence of Sentences. A student is required to rearrange the parts of a sentence into a meaningful paragraph. Infact there are no hard and fast rules for this kind of test.

Only sound knowledge of English language and constant practice may enable a student to grasp the meaning of the rearranged sentences or reconstructed paragraphs. This section of the book in your hand equips the students with the essentials of this kind of test.

Type I : Reconstruction of a Sentence

In this type of rearrangement of sentences six parts of a **sentence** are given. The positions of sentences 1 and 6 are fixed. The rest of the four parts are numbered as PQRS which are jumbled. A student is expected to arrange these four parts in a meaningful sequence and mark the correct order from among the alternatives provided. *For example*

1 : It is well-known that
P : youngesters in the cities and the villages
Q : the effect
R : of the cinema
S : on the school and college going
6 : is very bad

(*a*) Q S P R (*b*) Q R S P
(*c*) R S P Q (*d*) R Q P S

The correct sequence is (*b*) Q R S P.

Type II : Reconstruction of a Paragraph

In this type of questions six sentences are given. The first and the sixth sentences of the paragraph are labelled as S_1 and S_6 respectively. The middle four sentences are jumbled up. A candidate is required to find the proper order for the four sentences to make a meaningful paragraph. Consider S_1 as the first sentence and S_6 as the last one. *For example*

(a) S_1 : But how does a new word get into the dictionary?

S_6 : He sorts them according to their grammatical function and carefully writes a definition.

P : When a new dictionary is being edited, a lexicographer collects all the alphabetically arranged citation slips for a particular word.

Q : The dictonary makes a note of it on a citation slip.

R : The moment a new word is coined, it usually enters the spoken language.

S : The word then passes from the realm of hearing to the realm of writing.

(a) P Q R S *(b)* P R Q S
(c) R Q P S *(d)* R S Q P

The correct sequence is *(d)* R S Q P.

(b) Sometimes the jumbled up sentences are given with Roman Numbers *For example*

I : He tried the door

II : The room was neat and clean

III : Then he stepped into the room

IV : he waited for a minute or two

V : it opened easily and he peaked in

(a) IV, I, III, II, V *(b)* I, V, II, IV, III
(c) II, III, V, I, IV *(d)* I, V, III, II, IV

The correct sequence is *(b)* I, V, II, IV, III.

Type III

In this type of reconstruction of paragraph, a paragraph comprising five or six sentences in a jumbled order is given to a candidate so as to arrange the given sentences to form a meaningful paragraph. Then the student is asked to answer the questions based on the sequence so formed. *For example*

A. Absence of other parental figures in the family has worsened the situation.
B. Drug abuse among youngsters seems to be on the increase.
C. The need for many mothers to work has put an additional claim on the time available for the children.
D. Breakdown of the extended family has put a lot of burden on the parents.
E. Psychologists attribute this to the growing alienation of the new generation from their parents.

1. Which sentence should come first in the paragraph?

(a) D *(b)* E
(c) B *(d)* A
(e) C

The correct answer is *(c)*.

2. Which sentence should come last in the paragraph?

(a) C *(b)* B
(c) D *(d)* A
(e) E

The correct answer is *(d)*.

3. Which sentence should come third in the paragraph?
(a) E (b) D
(c) B (d) C
(e) A
The correct answer is (b).

4. Which sentence should come second in the paragraph?
(a) B (b) E
(c) D (d) A
(e) C
The correct answer is (b).

5. Which sentence should come fourth in the paragraph?
(a) A (b) D
(c) E (d) B
(e) C
The correct answer is (e).

Work Book Exercise A

(Jumbled Parts of a Sentence)

Directions *In the following questions, the first and the last parts of the sentence are numbered as 1 and 6. The rest of the sentence is split into four parts and are named as P, Q, R and S. These four parts are not given in their proper order. Read the jumbled parts of the sentence and find out which of the four combinations is correct. Then find the correct answer.*

1. 1 : India has been a land
P : but in the sense that learning has always been very highly valued
Q : not indeed in the sense that education has been universal
R : and the learned man has been held in higher esteem
S : of learning throughout the ages
6 : than the warrior or the administrator.
(a) P Q S R (b) R Q P S
(c) R S Q P (d) S Q P R

2. 1 : Religion has been used
P : both as a weapon of isolation
Q : to dull awareness
R : about real problems
S : and as morphia
6 : like education, health and employment.
(a) P Q R S (b) P S Q R
(c) Q P S R (d) R P Q S

3. 1 : Inspite of an unprecedented boom in the market
P : and had to remain content
Q : the paper-dealer could not
R : push up his sales
S : with a volume of sale lower than
6 : what he had sold the previous year.
(a) Q R P S (b) S P R Q
(c) P R Q S (d) R P S Q

4. S_1 : For some people patriotism
S_6 : as much as to any one country.
P : today man belongs to the whole world
Q : it should be condemned because
R : type of patriotism is an evil and
S : means hatred for other countries, but this
(a) S R Q P (b) P Q S R
(c) R S P Q (d) Q P S R

5. S_1 : A connection had long been suspected
S_6 : of this connection had not been understood.
P : since both were at their worst in the
Q : same regions and seasons, but the nature
R : between the abundance of mosquitoes
S : and the occurrence of malaria
(a) Q S P R (b) R S P Q
(c) P S Q R (d) S P R Q

6. S_1 : Science does not merely add new truths
S_6 : men's thinking and their lives.
P : destroy some old truths and
Q : discovers new truths that
R : thereby upsets the way of
S : to old ones, it also
(a) Q S R P (b) R P S Q
(c) P S R Q (d) S Q P R

7. S_1 : An outstanding feature of this century has been
S_6 : has meant greater political power.
P : living conditions of the
Q : the improvement of the income and
R : greater security and education which
S : working man leading to
(a) P S Q R (b) R S P Q
(c) Q P S R (d) S R Q P

8. S_1 : Hobbies can fill our spare
S_6 : do not hinder our regular work.
P : physical fatigue and
Q : moments with enjoyment
R : and pleasure, they also relieve
S : mental tiredness and
(a) R Q P S (b) Q R S P
(c) S Q P R (d) P Q S R

9. S_1 : Moisture is continuously lost
S_6 : lifeless complexion.
P : and as result of the stresses
Q : as part of a natural process
R : and strains of daily life
S : leading to a dull, dry and
(a) S Q P R (b) P R S Q
(c) R S Q P (d) Q P R S

Work Book Exercise B

Directions (Q. Nos. 1-16) *In the following questions, some parts of the sentence have been jumbled up. You are required to re-arrange these parts which are labelled as P, Q, R and S to produce the correct sentence. Choose the proper sequence.*

1. So, now India can lose out at first base because it's too busy chasing an ephemeral dream (P) either put aside its hopes of getting the veto power and (Q) first concentrate on ensuring that (R) the Security Council is enlarged or (S)

   Which one of the following sequences is correct?
   (a) Q P S R (b) S R Q P
   (c) Q R S P (d) S P Q R

2. But Nelson Mandela modern country in a modern way (P) and could run a new, (Q) shifted the beliefs of the people (R) so they could heal the racial confict (S)

   Which one of the following sequences is correct?
   (a) R S Q P (b) Q P R S
   (c) R S P Q (d) Q S R P

3. But, Kuala Lumpur where modern Malay executives (P) but will never miss Friday prayers (Q) might have a cellular phone in hand, (R) is a city firmly rooted in tradition (S)

   Which one of the following sequences is correct?
   (a) R Q S P (b) S P R Q
   (c) R P S Q (d) S Q R P

4. If farming life is not to collapse, there is need for (P) as a profession and as a way of (Q) attention today to farmers' needs in the areas (R) of water, credit, technology, market and land and agrarian reforms (S)

   Which one of the following sequences is correct?
   (a) Q P R S (b) R S Q P
   (c) Q S R P (d) R P Q S

5. Having achieved success to ride the next big outsourcing wave (P) in software exports and information technology areas, (Q) –this time in manufacturing from the U.S. (R) Indian manufacturers-exporters are well equipped (S)

Which one of the following sequences is correct?
(a) P S Q R (b) Q R P S
(c) P R Q S (d) Q S P R

6. It shows it is also conscious of its (P) India means business; (Q)
sovereignty and elements that threaten it (R)
while it is for transparent and open ties (S)

Which one of the following sequences is correct?
(a) Q S P R (b) P R Q S
(c) Q R P S (d) P S Q R

7. Travel to where you don't know the local language (P) and see how your (Q)
a foreign country, even a region of India (R) hands and expressions do the talking (S)

Which one of the following sequences is correct?
(a) S Q P R (b) R P Q S
(c) S P Q R (d) R Q P S

8. If fair play fair trade and the protection of the planet, (P) is going to encompass (Q)
in sport's many codes of conduct (R) these should be enshrined (S)

Which one of the following sequences is correct?
(a) Q S P R (b) R P S Q
(c) Q P S R (d) R S P Q

9. While the recent century show that the June rainfall is (P)
of a drought, India's rainfall data for over a (Q) rain may have soothed concerns (R)
no predictor of the monsoon's outcome (S)

Which one of the following sequences is correct?
(a) P S R Q (b) R Q P S
(c) P Q R S (d) R S P Q

10. On the contrary, in countries like China and the other Pacific countries, (P)
permission for shooting but also (Q) film-makers not only obtain quick (R)
get subsidies to undertake the job (S)

Which one of the following sequences is correct?
(a) P R Q S (b) Q S P R
(c) P S Q R (d) Q R P S

11. There are <u>from different walks of life as human rights</u> (P) <u>so much is written by so many persons</u> (Q) <u>very few subjects in</u> (R) <u>contemporary times on which</u> (S)

Which one of the following sequences is correct?

(a) Q S R P
(b) R P Q S
(c) Q P R S
(d) R S Q P

12. Scientists carrying <u>glacier feeding the Ganga may melt before the end of the 21st century</u> (P) <u>because of climatic changes</u> (Q) <u>caused by man-made carbon dioxide emissions</u> (R) <u>out a study have warned that an ancient</u> (S)

Which one of the following sequences is correct?

(a) S R Q P
(b) Q P S R
(c) S P Q R
(d) Q R S P

13. It is <u>stressful or joyful</u> (P) <u>with the belief in the evanescence of life itself</u> (Q) <u>necessary to rise above the situations</u> (R) <u>and in the philosophical quest of the purpose of life</u> (S)

Which one of the following sequences is correct?

(a) R P Q S
(b) Q S R P
(c) R S Q P
(d) Q P R S

14. The difference <u>and development on the other affects</u> (P) <u>in the relationship between death and birth-rates on the one hand</u> (Q) <u>but the age structure of the population</u> (R) <u>not just the rate of population growth</u> (S)

Which one of the following sequences is correct?

(a) S R Q P
(b) Q P S R
(c) S P Q R
(d) Q R S P

15. As a <u>maestro appeared to be enjoying every bit of it</u> (P) <u>and followed every composition the</u> (Q) <u>thunderous applause from</u> (R) <u>an appreciative audience preceded</u> (S)

Which one of the following sequences is correct?

(a) P Q S R
(b) R S Q P
(c) P S Q R
(d) R Q S P

16. Keeping farmers to smoke their fields during

P

in view the prevailing weather conditions agricultural experts have advised

Q R

the night to protect vegetables from cold.

S

Which one of the following sequences is correct?

(a) S R P Q
(b) Q P R S
(c) S P R Q
(d) Q R P S

Directions (Q. Nos. 17-23) *Each of the following questions in this section consists of a sentence, the parts of which have been jumbled. These parts have been labelled P, Q, R and S. Given below each sentence there are four sequences namely (a), (b), (c) and (d). You are required to re-arrange the jumbled parts of the sentence and select the proper sequence.*

17. As the situation has changed, since we last discussed this matter

P

it was best to contact-you it appeared to me without losing time

Q R S

The proper sequence should be

(a) P Q R S
(b) P R S Q
(c) P R Q S
(d) S P R Q

18. The management having agreed the workers called off the strike

P Q

to increase their wages and returned to work

R S

The proper sequence should be

(a) P Q R S
(b) P S R Q
(c) P R Q S
(d) S P Q R

19. All religions are to advance the cause of peace in a holy partnership

P Q

justice and freedom bound together

R S

The proper sequence should be

(a) P Q R S
(b) P R Q S
(c) S P Q R
(d) S Q P R

20. The natives of Caribbean regarded the papaya because of its ability

P Q

as a magic tree to keep them healthy

R S

The proper sequence should be

(a) P R S Q
(b) P R Q S
(c) R P Q S
(d) R P S Q

21. The Indian woman wants in a male dominated society (P) as an equal partner (Q) and it is not too much to demand (R) her rightful place (S)

The proper sequence should be

(a) S R P Q *(b)* R S Q P
(c) S Q P R *(d)* Q P S R

22. This is a letter by a young lady (P) who was lately wounded in a duel (Q) written passionately (R) wherein she laments the misfortune of a gentleman (S)

The proper sequence should be

(a) S R P Q *(b)* R S Q P
(c) R P S Q *(d)* Q P S R

23. It is a wonder that migratory birds (P) without ever getting lost (Q) always manage to find their home (R) flying thousands of kilometres (S)

The proper sequence should be

(a) P Q R S *(b)* S P Q R
(c) S Q R P *(d)* P S R Q

Work Book Exercise C

(Ordering of Sentences)

Directions (Q. Nos. 1-18) *In the following items, each passage consists of six sentences. The first and the sixth sentences are given in the beginning and labelled as S_1 and S_6 respectively. The middle four sentences in each have been removed and jumbled up. These are labelled as P, Q, R and S. You are required to find the proper order for the four sentences and mark accordingly.*

1. S_1 : The lion used to be very widely distributed in Africa and Asia.
S_6 : No hunting is permitted in such reserved areas.
P : There are special forest zones set aside for wildlife in various countries.
Q : Indiscriminate killing by hunters has been the cause of this drastic fall in their numbers.
R : Today they are a relatively rare species.
S : If the species survives at all it will be only in national parks.

Which one of the following sequences is correct?

(a) Q S P R *(b)* R S P Q
(c) S R P Q *(d)* R Q S P

2. S_1 : Yes, a mirage can be photographed.
S_6 : That kind of mirage obviously cannot be photographed.
P : That is hallucination.
Q : Anything reflected by the lens of the human eye will naturally be picked up by the photographic lens.
R : Sometimes, however, a person imagines he is seeing something but actually he is not.
S : The image, of course, will be hazy and simmering because of refraction of light.

Which one of the following sequences is correct?

(a) S P R Q (b) Q R P S
(c) P S Q R (d) Q S R P

3. S_1 : One of the greatest curses of the world is the belief in the necessity of poverty.
S_6 : We have been poor in the very midst of abundance, simply because of our own blighting limiting thought.
P : There need not be a poor person on the planet.
Q : But there was no poverty, no want, no lack, in the creator's plan for man.
R : Most people have a strong conviction that some must necessarily be poor, that they were made to be poor.
S : The Earth is full of resources which we have scarcely yet touched.

Which one of the following sequences is correct?

(a) S P Q R (b) R S P Q
(c) R Q P S (d) P Q S R

4. S_1 : There is nothing strange in the fact that so many foreign students should wish to learn English.
S_6 : This key will open to him whatever is valuable in the literature of the world.
P : If any valuable book is written in another language an English translation of it is sure to be speedily published.
Q : Anyone who masters the English tongue acquires a key.
R : Most books found to be generally useful are written in English.
S : The English speaking want no monopoly of knowledge.

Which one of the following sequences is correct?

(a) P S Q R (b) S Q R P
(c) R P S Q (d) P Q S R

5. S_1 : Much of our adult behaviour and our attitudes are determined by our upbringing.
S_6 : Psychologists have studied these forces in depth.
P : But the process does not stop here.
Q : In particular by the effects of that small part of society which is our family.
R : As we grow we are constantly and increasingly affected by new forces such as the social pressure of our friends and the largest world of society.
S : The family and our early life have profound effect on our later life.

Which one of the following sequences is correct?

(a) S R P Q (b) P R S Q
(c) Q P S R (d) Q S P R

6. S_1 : Chanakya, by his foresight and strength of character, built up the Mauryan Empire.
S_6 : It is not true as some people said that Sardar Patel was not particular about the means as long as he achieved his end.
P : They were men of iron.
Q : Therefore, they were impervious to criticism and had implicit confidence in themselves.
R : Both of them were guided by stern realism and would tolerate no deviations from the objectives which they pursued relentlessly.
S : Similarly, Patel refashioned a compact India out of the fragments left by the British.

Which one of the following sequences is correct?

(a) S Q R P (b) S R Q P
(c) S R P Q (d) P Q S R

7. S_1 : The spiritual training of the boys was a much more difficult training.

S_6 : And I held that this was an essential part of the training of the young and that all training without culture of the spirit was of no use and might be even harmful.

P : I had realised that the training of the spirit was a thing in itself.

Q : Of course, I believed that every student should be acquainted with the elements of his own religion and have a general knowledge of his own scriptures.

R : I relied little on religious books for spiritual training.

S : To develop the spirit is to build character and to enable one to work towards a knowledge of God and self-realisation.

Which one of the following sequences is correct?

(a) P Q S R
(b) R Q S P
(c) R P Q S
(d) P R S Q

8. S_1 : The word 'victory' generally reminds us of wars and conquerors like Alexander and Napoleon.

S_6 : The victories of peace are more lasting and useful to humanity than the victories of war.

P : Thousands of people are killed and hundreds of towns and cities are destroyed.

Q : But the victory associated with a war comes after so much of destrcution

R : In this category we may include the achievements of scientists and scholars, statesmen and social reformers and the like.

S : However, there is another type of victory which is creative and constructive.

Which one of the following sequences is correct?

(a) P R Q S
(b) S P Q R
(c) Q P S R
(d) R P Q S

9. S_1 : Europeans are not used to the serpentine queues we encounter in the Indian subcontinent.

S_6 : That the European youth was willing to go through these hardships to pay tribute to a spiritual head was unthinkable.

P : We line up even for our filthy public toilets and to pay the electricity bills.

Q : We wait eternally at railway crossings, ration shops and bank counters.

R : Particularly so in Europe where it is claimed that God is dead and religion defunct.

S : Hence, the fact that millions, and mostly the youth, made it to the funeral of Pope John Paul II, braving long journeys and queuing for hours on end, is truly remarkable.

Which one of the following sequence is correct?

(a) S P Q R
(b) Q R S P
(c) S R Q P
(d) Q P S R

10. S_1 : If India is hot right now, its thanks to a host of random developments.

S_6 : The SARS outbreak in 2002-03 bypassed India and the tsunami affected countries like Thailand more than it impacted India.

P : Nature helped too.

Q : Arguably, it all began with the IT boom, which coupled with the unceasing tide of outsourcing, made India a global buzz.

R : And, as the saying goes, today's business travellers are tomorrow's leisure travellers.

S : That put in the global consciousness and led to a surge in business travellers.

Which one of the following sequences is correct?

(a) Q S R P
(b) R P Q S
(c) Q P R S
(d) R S Q P

11. S_1 : Sleep is the only natural elixir that repairs the body.
S_6 : Sleep and upward mobility make for incompatible bedfellows.
P : The incessant ringing of mobile phones, the clamour of multiple TV sets, late night parties and the Internet are all par for the course in average urban households.
Q : At work, the manic race against time means we are working longer hours.
R : At home, our lives are no less hectic.
S : But in today's fast-paced world, sleep is the one aspect that is compromised the most.
Which one of the following sequences is correct?
(a) P R Q S *(b)* S Q R P
(c) P Q R S *(d)* S R Q P

12. S_1 : The pleasure of being able to communicate with people from another culture and to understand their society is a valuable experience.
S_6 : They employ linguistic experts to teach their employees the required language and to interact with employees on the client site.
P : Because of the level of interactions with foreign experts, translators are mandatory in many companies.
Q : Many Indian MNCs with global footprints need linguists to help them in foreign lands.
R : But learning a foreign language is fast becoming a necessary job skill in its own right.
S : As the global market-place expands, the need for personnel who can communicate in foreign languages will increase.
Which one of the following sequences is correct?
(a) P Q R S *(b)* R S P Q
(c) P S R Q *(d)* R Q P S

13. S_1 : What gives a place its distinct identity?
S_6 : So, what memories will you bring home?
P : And that's what best captures Singapore—a dynamic, cosmopolitan city-state where different cultures, ethnic groups and religions have blended over centuries to bridge the East-West divide.
Q : Apart from its geographical location, people and landscape, it's the passage of time.
R : With its friendly, welcoming people, state-of-the art infrastructure and something new happening every day, Singapore is easy to appreciate.
S : Singapore is a city where age-old traditions and cutting-edge innovations are celebrated simultaneously.
Which one of the following sequences is correct?
(a) R P S Q *(b)* Q S P R
(c) R S P Q *(d)* Q P S R

14. S_1 : The fact is that good writing is a craft which can be acquired like any other craft.
S_6 : In short, he has to become a wordsmith.
P : Much the same is the case with the one who aspires to become a good craftsman of English.
Q : Let's take examples.
R : A young man, who wants to become a goldsmith or a silversmith, becomes an apprentice with a seasoned man in that craft.
S : After a few years of apprenticeship, he learns the ins and outs of it and becomes a skilful craftsman.

Which one of the following sequences is correct?

(a) S P Q R *(b)* Q R S P
(c) S R Q P *(d)* Q P S R

15. S_1 : Yet, things are not that bad.
S_6 : Fortune, after all, favours the brave, not the complainers.
P : Some of the successful people started out with more handicaps than us.
Q : It is time we stopped feeling sorry for ourselves and got over our doubts and fears to face the world.
R : If we look around ourselves, we find people who had less than us but went on to make their fortunes.
S : Perhaps we can replicate what they did for themselves.

Which one of the following sequences is correct?

(a) R Q S P *(b)* S P R Q
(c) R P S Q *(d)* S Q R P

16. S_1 : Any discussion on human rights is incomplete without reference to the security and terrorist threats facing the country.
S_6 : It is necessary to underline that it will be wrong to treat all such violent movements as pure law and order problems.
P : The Police as also the armed forces are facing an uphill task in containing these violent activities and maintaining peace and order.
Q : It must be appreciated that there is an imperative need for such special legislations as the normal laws are not adequate to deal with the situation.
R : An important issue which has come up in this context relates to the need for special legislation to cope with the situation.
S : Several parts of the country have been rocked by violence, terrorism, secessionist movement and insurgency.

Which one of the following sequences is correct?

(a) S P Q R *(b)* P S Q R
(c) S P R Q *(d)* P S R Q

17. S_1 : What are the outstanding features of the Indian Freedom Struggle?
S_6 : It not only permitted but encouraged free expression of opinion within the party and the movement.
P : The movement popularized democratic ideas and institutions in India.
Q : The Indian National Congress was organized on a democratic basis and in the form of a parliament.
R : The nationalists fought for the introduction of a representative government.
S : A major aspect is the value and modern ideals on which the movement itself was based and the broad socio-economic and political vision of its leadership.

Which one of the following sequences is correct?

(a) P S R Q *(b)* S P R Q
(c) P S Q R *(d)* S P Q R

18. S_1 : Indian media still has not matured as far as election coverage goes.
S_6 : There is nothing wrong in the demand for unbiased, non-casteist and non-communal reporting.
P : Today, it is common for public relation's firms to cultivate journalists and planting stories.
Q : At the same time, nobody has addressed to the menace of corruption in the media itself.

R : In such a scenario, the reader feels shortchanged as unbiased election coverage is not available.

S : Press conferences are used openly for giving gifts and bribes to journalists.

Which one of the following sequences is correct?

(a) P Q S R (b) Q P R S
(c) P Q R S (d) Q P S R

Directions (Q. Nos. 19-22) *In these questions, the 1st and the last sentences of the passage are numbered as S_1 and S_6. The rest of the passage is split into four parts and named P, Q, R and S. These four parts are not given in their proper order, read the sentence and find out, which of the four combinations is correct. Then find the correct answer.*

19. S_1 : Fires in the steppes or bushes scared humans earlier.

P : Gradually, they learnt to appreciate the power of fire.

Q : It gave them light and warmth and kept away wild animals.

R : About 700000 years ago, humans, started fire accidentally by lightning.

S : They could harden the tips of wooden spears and cook meat in it.

S_6 : Soon they learnt to produce fire by striking flintstone and pyrite with each other or by rubbing lumbers.

The proper sequence should be

(a) P Q R S (b) Q R S P
(c) Q S P R (d) P Q S R

20. S_1 : There are a lot of ways to communicate : speaking, singing, clapping, hooting.

P : Even animals communicate with one another.

Q : Only humans can express their thoughts and feelings in words because of our superior brain.

R : Both humans and animals also communicate through body language.

S : But their ways differ from the humans.

S_6 : Sometimes we don't use words, but make gestures (like traffic signs) or simple movements of the hand in order to communicate.

The proper sequence should be

(a) P Q R S (b) P S Q R
(c) P R S Q (d) Q P R S

21. S_1 : Egotism is the most common fault of mankind.

P : However, with time it becomes an exaggerated form of self display.

Q : It is the product of a perfectly natural desire to display oneself.

R : This is necessary as it impairs the personality and frustrates all efforts at self improvement.

S : Beyond any shadow of doubt, it is a defect that ought to be constantly hunted down and scotched.

S_6 : One should always be on guard not to give into egotism.

The proper sequence should be

(a) P Q S R (b) Q P S R
(c) Q P R S (d) P R Q S

22. S_1 : The lion used to be very widely distributed in Africa and Asia.

P : There are special forest zones set aside for wild-life in various countries.

Q : Indiscriminate killing has caused the number to fall.

R : Today they are a relatively rare species.

S : If the species survives at all, it will be only in national parks.

S_6 : No hunting is permitted in such reserved areas.

The proper sequence should be

(a) R S P Q (b) Q S P R
(c) R Q S P (d) S R P Q

Directions (Q. Nos. 23-26) *In these questions, the 1st and the last sentences of the passage are numbered as S_1 and S_6. The rest of the passage is split into four parts and named P, Q, R and S. These four parts are not given in their proper order, read the sentence and find out, which of the four combinations is correct. Then find the correct answer.*

23. S_1 : Plato's 'Republic' has exercised tremendous influence
P : he states that statesmen should
Q : on human thought and intelligence
R : integrity because he felt that, only such men
S : be men of supreme intelligence and impeccable
S_6 : could enlighten the darker side of human nature into a positive one.

The proper sequence should be

(a) R S Q P (b) Q P S R
(c) R P S Q (d) S Q P R

24. S_1 : India has a vibrant space science programme
P : the Indian space science programme has been working
Q : formulating an industrial participation policy to
R : covering astronomy, astrophysics and space science.
S : with cooperative Indian industries and has been
S_6 : aid the growth of space industry in India.

The proper sequence should be

(a) S Q P R (b) P Q R S
(c) Q P R S (d) R P S Q

25. S_1 : Delhi's Indira Gandhi International Airport is the only one in the country to have runways equipped with a CAT HIB instrument Landing System.
P : This technology guides pilots to land even when visibility is cut to 50 metres
Q : This is because
R : Finding an explanation for such failure won't be easy
S : However, it fails to operate often
S_6 : the issue involves multiple stake-holders and a web of unclear briefs.

The proper sequence should be

(a) P Q R S (b) P R S Q
(c) P S R Q (d) P Q S R

26. S_1 : Ram has an important examination to sit for in a few weeks time
P : But he could not concentrate
Q : What he saw was not very nice he was very pale
R : He sat down to prepare for it
S : After a while he looked at himself in the mirror
S_6 : He said to himself, "What I need is fresh air."

The proper sequence should be

(a) P Q R S (b) R P S Q
(c) Q S P R (d) S Q R P

Directions (Q. Nos. 27-29) *In these questions, the 1st and the last sentences of the passage are numbered as S_1 and S_6. The rest of the passage is split into four parts and named P, Q, R and S. These four parts are not given in their proper order, read the sentence and find out, which of the four combinations is correct. Then find the correct answer.*

27. S_1 : After an entire generation of parents and teachers
P : the level of depression
Q : children's self-esteem, an indicator of good mental health
R : has worked hard to improve its
S : in young people has skyrocketed.
S_6 : It is how we feel about our selves,
The proper sequence should be
(a) P Q R S
(b) Q S R P
(c) R Q S P
(d) S P R Q

28. S_1 : The vegetable bin of my refrigerator contained an assortment of weird looking items.
P : The carrots dropped into U shapes as I picked them up with the tips of my fingers.
Q : To the right of the oranges was a bunch of carrots that had begun to sprout points, spikes and tendrils.
R : Near the carrots was a net bag of onions.
S : Next to a shriveled, white-coated lemon were two oranges covered with blue fuzz.
S_6 : Each onion had sent curling shoots through the net until the whole thing resembled a mass of green spaghetti.
The proper sequence should be
(a) S Q P R
(b) Q S R P
(c) P R S Q
(d) R S Q R

29. S_1 : Helen Keller has an ageless qualily about her in keeping with her amazing life story.
P : Although warned by this human reaction, she has no wish to be set aside from the rest of mankind.
Q : She is an inspiration to both blind and who can see everywhere.
R : When she visited Japan after World War II, boys and girls from remote villages ran to her, crying, 'Helen Keller'.
S : Blind, deaf and mute from early childhood, she rose above her triple handicap to become one of the best known characters in the modern world.
S_6 : She believes the blind should live and work with their fellows, with full responsibility.
The proper sequence should be
(a) Q P S R
(b) P Q S R
(c) R S Q P
(d) S Q R P

Directions (Q. Nos. 30-38) *In these questions, the 1st and the last sentences of the passage are numbered as S_1 and S_6. The rest of the passage is split into four parts and named P, Q, R and S. These four parts are not given in their proper order, read the sentence and find out, which of the four combinations is correct. Then find the correct answer.*

30. S_1 : A lot of people simply dump their rubbish in open
P : All sorts of diseases are carried by the flies.
Q : Then they come into the house and infect uncovered food.
R : In this rubbish the flies breed and multiply.
S : Such carelessness invites flies to the rubbish.
S_6 : Consumption of such food can only bring disease and sickness.
The proper sequence should be
(a) S P Q R
(b) R Q P S
(c) R P Q S
(d) S R Q P

31. S_1 : Six year old Prabodh aimed his toy gun at his sister while playing.
P : "You may aim at the pole or at the wall or at the tree, where no one can get hurt."
Q : Mother got up immediately saying, "No one shoots a human being and calmly removed the gun from Prabodh.
R : Still Prabodh aimed his gun at the kid.
S : When his mother saw this she said "No Prabodh! Not at the body!"
S_6 : With such a firm action on his mother's part, Prabodh realised where the gun should not be aimed.
The proper sequence should be
(a) P R S Q (b) Q S P R
(c) S P R Q (d) S R Q P

32. S_1 : Proud Little Astronomer sees a huge dragon in the Moon.
P : Big Astronomer calls him and shows him the fly.
Q : He runs to the Big Astronomer and calls him home.
R : He is very excited and remembers his rival Big Astronomer.
S : Big Astronomer agrees and later discovers a fly in the telescope lens.
S_6 : Little Astronomer is shamefaced and becomes humble.
The proper sequence should be
(a) R Q S P (b) P Q R S
(c) R S P Q (d) Q P S R

33. S_1 : Plants need carbon for building the tissue of their bodies.
S_6 : Thus through a complex process called photosynthesis, plants receive their requirements from the soil and Sun.
P : The breaking up of carbon dioxide into its components requires energy, which they derive from the Sun.
Q : Plant's other needs of nutrients are derived from the soil and water through their roots.
R : They derive this carbon from the carbon dioxide in the air.
S : They break up the carbon dioxide, absorb the carbon and discharge oxygen into the air for animals to breathe.
The proper sequence should be
(a) Q S P R (b) R S P Q
(c) S Q R P (d) P R Q S

34. S_1 : I searched for my friend all day.
S_6 : When I woke up the Sun was already above the horizon.
P : Although I was weary and hungry, I was not discouraged.
Q : I crept in and lay on the ground with my bag for a pillow.
R : When midnight came I felt that I could not walk much further.
S : At last I came to a place where the pavement was raised and had a hollow underneath.
The proper sequence should be
(a) P R S Q (b) P S Q R
(c) R P S Q (d) S R Q P

35. S_1 : While on a fishing trip last summer, I watched an elderly man fishing off the edge of a dock.
S_6 : Cheerfully, the old man replied, 'Small frying pan'.
P : "Why didn't you keep the other big ones?" I asked.
Q : He caught an enormous trout, but apparently not satisfied with its size, he threw it back into the water.

R : He finally caught a small pike, threw it into his pail and smiling happily prepared to leave.

S : Amazed, I watched him repeat this performance.

The proper sequence should be

(a) P S Q R (b) Q S R P
(c) P Q S R (d) Q P S R

36. S_1 : The essence of democracy is the active participation of the people in government affairs.

S_6 : By and large it is the actual practice of our way of life.

P : When the people are active watchmen and participants, we have that fertile soil in which democracy flourishes.

Q : Our democracy is founded upon a faith in the overall judgement of the people as a whole.

R : When the people do not participate, the spirit of democracy dies.

S : When the people are honestly and clearly informed, their commonsense can be relied upon to carry the nation safely through any crisis.

The proper sequence should be

(a) R P S Q (b) P R S Q
(c) S P Q R (d) P S R Q

37. S_1 : Always remember that regular and frequent practice is essential if you are to learn to write well.

S_6 : If you keep your eyes and ears open, you will find plenty of things to write about.

P : Even with the most famous writers, inspiration is rare.

Q : Writing is ninety nine per cent hard work and one per cent inspiration, so the sooner you get into the habit of writing, the better.

R : It is no good waiting until you have an inspiration before you write.

S : You learn to write by writing.

The proper sequence should be

(a) S R P Q (b) R P S Q
(c) S P R Q (d) Q P S R

38. S_1 : Human ways of life have steadily changed.

S_6 : During the last few years change has been even more rapid than usual.

P : From that time to this, civilisation has always been changing.

Q : About ten thousand years ago, man lived entirely by hunting.

R : Ancient Egypt-Greece-the Roman Empire-the Dark Ages and the Middle Ages-the Renaissance-the age of modern science and of modern nations-one has succeeded the other and history has never stood still.

S : A settled civilised life began only when agriculture was discovered.

The proper sequence should be

(a) Q S R P (b) Q S P R
(c) R S Q P (d) S P R Q

Directions (Q. Nos. 39-42) *In the following items, each passage consists of six sentences. The first sentence S_1 and the final sentence S_6 are given in the beginning. The middle four sentences in each have been removed and jumbled up. These are labelled P, Q, R and S. You are required to find out the proper sequence of the four sentences.*

39. S_1 : Her sisters recognised her at once.
S_6 : As for the young prince, he found her more lovely and lovable than ever and insisted upon marrying her immediately.
P : She embraced them, telling them she forgave them with all her heart.
Q : Then she departed with the herald to the King's palace.
R : They were not in the least surprised, for everybody believed in fairies and everybody longed to have a fairy godmother.
S : She told her whole story to his Majesty and the royal family.
The proper sequence should be
(a) R S Q P *(b)* Q P S R
(c) P Q S R *(d)* P S Q R

40. S_1 : The wise men laughed at Galileo for presuming to differ from the great Aristotle.
S_6 : Both struck the ground together, as he had asserted that they would.
P : He then climbed to the top, carrying with him a ten pound shot and a one pound shot.
Q : So one morning he took some students and teachers to the base of the famous Leaning Tower.
R : Balancing them on the edge of the tower, he let them fall together.
S : But Galileo said he could prove his statement.
The proper sequence should be
(a) S Q P R *(b)* Q P S R
(c) P R S Q *(d)* R S Q P

41. S_1 : The Earth was initially very hot and without an atmosphere.
S_6 : But it contained a lot of other gases that are poisonous to us.
P : The atmosphere came from the emission of gases from the rocks.
Q : Because it contained no oxygen.
R : In the course of time it cooled and acquired an atmosphere.
S : This early atmosphere was not one in which we could have survived.
The proper sequence should be
(a) R P S Q *(b)* P S R Q
(c) S P Q R *(d)* Q R P S

42. S_1 : The train was running fast and the next station was nearly an hour ahead.
S_6 : She bought four cups of ice cream and all of them became busy with eating.
P : The children were pestering their aunt with embarrassing questions.
Q : The occupants of the first carriage among others were a tall girl, a little girl and a little boy.
R : Luckily an ice cream vendor came to the rescue of the aunt.
S : Their aunt was occupying a corner seat.
The proper sequence should be
(a) P Q R S *(b)* Q S P R
(c) R P Q S *(d)* S R Q P

Work Book Exercise D

Directions *In each of the questions below a number of sentences are given which are denoted by I, II, III and IV. By using all the sentences you have to frame a meaningful paragraph. The correct order of the sentences is your answer. Choose from the five alternatives and the one having the correct order is your answer.*

1. I. Now under liberated economy they are learning to compete domestically and globally.
II. In India corporations until, recently achieved success by avoiding competition using protected and regulated domestic markets.
III. The trend is irreversible.
IV. Business leaders are preparing themselves to meet competitive challenges and to avoid being swept away.
Which one of the following sequences is correct?
(a) I, II, IV, III *(b)* II, IV, III, I
(c) II, IV, I, III *(d)* IIi, IV, II, I
(e) II, I, IV, III

2. I. Recovery was given inadequate attention and consequently some bank branches regularly incurred heavy losses and their parent bodies had to bale them out.
II. As a result banks indulged in extensive lending to borrowers who had little or no potential to make repayments.
III. To fulfil the social objectives laid down by the masters of nationalisation banks were asked to lend to identify priority sectors.
IV. 1992-93 results showed that the loss making branches of public sector's banks increased from 10,000 to 13,000 and the quantum of losses showed at 3,369 crore.
Which one of the following sequences is correct?
(a) II, I, III, IV *(b)* IV, I, II, III
(c) III, II, I, IV *(d)* III, II, I, IV
(e) IV, III, II, I

3. I. However different rulers and government dealt with the different groups in a compartmentalised manner.
II. Various situational political changes have taken place over the past three and half-centuries.
III. This tendency resulted in deeply embedded fragmented South-African society which became even more prominent in the period 1948 until the commencement of the new constitution on May 10, 1994.
IV. South Africa is a racially divided society since the first European settlers arrived in 1652.
Which one of the following sequences is correct?
(a) II, IV, I, III *(b)* IV, II, I, III *(c)* III, I, II, IV *(d)* I, III, IV, II
(e) II, I, III, IV

4. I. Such a system will help identify and groom executives for positions of strategists.
II. Evaluation of performance is more often than not done for the purpose of reward or punishment for past performance.
III. They must become an integral part of the executive evaluation system.
IV. Even where the evaluation system is for one's promotion to assume higher responsibilities it rarely includes items that are a key for playing the role of strategists effectivity e.g. the skills for playing the role of change agent and creative problem solving.
Which one of the following sequences is correct?
(a) IV, II, I, III *(b)* IV, III, II, I *(c)* I, II, III, IV *(d)* II, IV, III, I
(e) III, IV, II, I

5. I. But categorisation schemes are not always helpful in determining what one can do with or about organisational culture.

II. Much of the literature on organisational culture is focussed on categorising types of cultures.

III. It has taken the understanding of corporate culture for beyond what use to be called 'the informal organisation'.

IV. This literature is both 'interesting and informative'.

Which one of the following sequences is correct?

(a) II, IV, I, III (b) II, I, IV, III (c) II, III, IV, I (d) IV, I, II, III (e) IV, II, I, III

6. I. Much of the argument that goes on around the alternative solution occurs because people hold different perceptions of the problem.

II. One of the reasons that Japanese managers are preceived as making superior decisions compared to Western managers is that they spend a great deal of effort and time determining that the problem is correctly defined.

III. Unfortunately, too often in the West, managers assume that the initial definition of the situation is correct.

IV. Up to half the time in meetings is spent in asking 'Is this the real problem?'

Which one of the following sequences is correct?

(a) II, IV, III, I (b) II, III, IV, I (c) III, II, IV, I (d) I, III, IV, II (e) I, II, III, IV

Work Book Exercise E

(Based on Type III)

Directions *Rearrange the following sentences A, B, C, D and E in the proper sequence so as to form a meaningful paragraph; then answer the questions given below.*

I. A. He borrowed some money from his neighbour for me.
B. However, he promised to get the money I needed.
C. Since I had no money with me, I decided to borrow from my friend
D. The electricity bill had to be paid immediately.
E. But, he had no money with him to lend me.

1. Which of the following sentences should come third in the paragraph?
(a) A (b) B (c) C (d) D (e) E

2. Which of the following sentences should come first in the paragraph?
(a) A (b) B (c) C (d) D (e) E

3. Which of the following sentences should come fifth in the paragraph?
(a) A (b) B (c) C (d) D (e) E

4. Which of the following sentences should come second in the paragraph?
(a) A (b) B (c) C (d) D (e) E

5. Which of the following sentences should come fourth in the paragraph?
(a) A (b) B (c) C (d) D (e) E

II. A. When I turned around, I saw none other than Rajesh.
B. It was then that someone loudly called out my name.
C. I started looking around for Rajesh.
D. The train had already arrived by the time I reached the station.
E. Not finding him, I decided to return home.

1. Which sentence should come second in the paragraph?
(a) A (b) B (c) C (d) D (e) E
2. Which sentence should come third in the paragraph?
(a) A (b) B (c) C (d) D (e) E
3. Which sentence should come first in the paragraph?
(a) A (b) B (c) C (d) D (e) E
4. Which sentence should come last in the paragraph?
(a) A (b) B (c) C (d) D (e) E
5. Which sentence should come fourth in the paragraph?
(a) A (b) B (c) C (d) D (e) E

Directions *Rearrange the given five sentences A, B, C, D and E in the proper sequence so as to form a meaningful paragraph and then answer the given questions.*

III. A. With so many products and opportunities available in the market, it is very easy to get this planning wrong.
B. Planning, therefore, is imperative and should begin as early as possible.
C. What amount will we need and when will we need it?
D. Most of us would put our children's education above any other priority in life including our own retirement.
E. So, let's try to find the best solution by asking two important question.

1. Which of the following should be the second sentence after rearrangement?
(a) D (b) B (c) C (d) E (e) A
2. Which of the following should be the fifth sentence after rearrangement?
(a) A (b) B (c) C (d) E (e) D
3. Which of the following should be the first sentence after rearrangement?
(a) A (b) B (c) E (d) C (e) D
4. Which of the following should be the third sentence after rearrangement?
(a) D (b) B (c) C (d) E (e) A
5. Which of the following should be the fourth sentence after rearrangement?
(a) A (b) B (c) E (d) D (e) C

Directions *Rearrange the following sentences A, B, C, (D), E and F into a meaningful paragraph and then answer the questions given below it.*

IV. A. Moreover salaries in public sector enterprises are not as competitive as those offered by private or foreign corporates.
B. This trend should be a wake up call for stakeholders to examine why employees are seeking better opportunities with private companies in India and abroad.
C. Public Sector Enterprises (PSEs) have been experiencing severe challenges in attracting motivating and retaining their key staff.
D. Having identified these as the reasons employees leave PSEs it is important empower stakeholders to find ways to remedy the situation.
E. One reason is that young employees lured away to private firms are more willing to undertake professional risks.
F. Employees" in specialist roles especially have become increasingly difficult to retain.

1. Which of the following should be the first sentence after rearrangement?
(a) A (b) B (c) C (d) D (e) E

2. Which of the following should be the second sentence after rearrangement?
(a) A (b) B (c) C (d) D (e) F

3. Which of the following should be the third sentence after rearrangement?
(a) A (b) B (c) C (d) D (e) E

4. Which of the following should be fifth sentence after rearrangement?
(a) A (b) B (c) C (d) D (e) E

5. Which of the following should be the last (sixth) sentence after rearrangement?
(a) A (b) B (c) C (d) D (e) E

Directions *Rearrange the following six sentences A, B, C, D, E and F in the proper sequence to form a meaningful paragraph; then answer the questions given below them.*

V. A. If China is the world's factory, India has become the world's outsourcing centre-keeping in line with this image.

B. But, India's future depends crucially on its ability to compete fully in the creative economy-not just in tech and software, but across design and entrepreneurship; arts, culture and entertainment and the knowledge-based professions of medicine, finance and law. .

C. While its creative assets outstrip those of other emerging competitors, India must address several challenges to increase its international competitiveness as the world is in the midst of a sweeping transformation.

D. This transformation is evident in the fact that the world is moving from an industrial economy to a creative economy that generates wealth by harnessing intellectual labour, intangible goods and human creative capabilities.

E. Its software industry is the world's second-largest, its tech outsourcing accounts for more than half of the $ 300 billion global industry, according to a technology expert.

F. If the meeting of world leaders at Davos is any indication, India is rapidly becoming an economic 'rock star'.

1. Which of the following should be the sixth (Last) sentence after the rearrangement?
(a) A (b) B (c) C (d) D (e) E

2. Which of the following should be the third sentence after the rearrangement?
(a) A (b) B (c) C (d) D (e) E

3. Which of the following should be the fifth sentence after the rearrangement?
(a) A (b) B (c) C (d) F (e) E

4. Which of the following should be the first sentence after the rearrangement?
(a) F (b) B (c) C (d) A (e) E

5. Which of the following should be the second sentence after the rearrangement?
(a) A (b) B (c) C (d) D (e) F

Directions *Rearrange the following seven sentences A, B, C, D, E, F and G in the proper sequence to form a meaningful paragraph; then answer the questions given below them.*

VI. A. To elaborate briefly on these characteristics and dimensions that the author is talking about -NRMs are general tests intended to be used to classify students by percentile for measuring either or proficiency for admissions into or placement within a program.

B. Contrastingly, the CRM, such at; a locally produced achievement test, measures absolute performance that is compared only with the learning objective, hence a perfect score is theoretically obtainable by all students who have a mastery of the pre-specified material or conversely, all students may fail the test.

C. In most of these books the authors classify a measurement strategy as either norm-referenced (NRM) or criterion-referenced (CRM).

D. Another author points out how the type of interpretation that an NRM offers is the relative performance of the students compared with that of all the others resulting in, ideally, a bell curve distribution.

E. Numerous books on constructing and using language tests have been written by various authors.

F. CRMs, on the other hand, are more specific, achievement or diagnostic tests intended to be used for motivating students by measuring to what percent they have achieved mastery of the taught or learned material.

G. One of the authors clearly delineates the differences of these two types by focusing on the categories of "test characteristics" and "logistical dimensions."

1. Which of the following should be the first sentence after rearrangement?
(*a*) G (*b*) C (*c*) C (*d*) D (*e*) E

2. Which of the following should be the seventh (Last) sentence after rearrangement?
(*a*) A (*b*) B (*c*) C (*d*) D (*e*) E

3. Which of the following should be the fifth sentence after rearrangement?
(*a*) A (*b*) B (*c*) C (*d*) F (*e*) G

4. Which of the following should be the second sentence after rearrangement?
(*a*) A (*b*) B (*c*) C (*d*) D (*e*) E

5. Which of the following should be the third sentence after rearrangement?
(*a*) A (*b*) B (*c*) G (*d*) D (*e*) E

Exam Practice

Exercise A

Directions (Q. Nos. 1-4) *Each of the following questions in this section consists of a sentence, the parts of which have been jumbled. Thease parts have been labelled P, Q, R and S. Given below each sentence has four sequences, namely (a), (b), (c) and (d). You are required to rearrange the jumbled parts of the sentence and mark your response accordingly.* **NDA 2016**

1. The statement (P) therefore you must listen carefully (Q) what the speaker has said (R) in order to understand (S) will be made just once.
The proper sequence should be
(a) SPRQ (b) SRQP (c) RSPQ (d) SPQR

2. The small boy who (P) climbed the wall (Q) fell down and (R) broke his leg (S).
The proper sequence should be
(a) PSRQ (b) PQRS (c) QSRP (d) SPRQ

3. According to an engineer might hit the (P) market next year (Q) a newly developed air-cooler system (R) that employed in conventional room coolers (S), which is based on a principle radicaly different from.
The proper sequence should be
(a) SQRP (b) RSQP (c) QSRP (d) PQRS

4. The clerk on the desk (P) left the money (Q) in the safe (R) which he should have locked up (S)
The proper sequence should be
(a) PQRS (b) PQSR (c) QRPS (d) RPQS

Directions (Q.Nos. 5-7) *Each of the following questions in this section consists of a sentence, the parts of which have been jumbled. (d) These parts have been labelled P, Q, R and S. Given below each sentence has four sequence namely (a), (b), (c) and (d). You are required to rearrange the jumbled parts of the sentence and mark your response accordingly.* **NDA 2017**

5. The spirit of man has slowly and painfully surmounted (P) and his growing intelligence (Q) all the obstacles that have come in his way (R) has faced all kinds of dangers (S)

(a) QPSR (b) SQPR (c) RPQS (d) PRQS

6. After our school boys had won a well-contested hockey match so that they might communicate the (P) news of their victory to the headmaster who is a keen sportsman (Q) they came to school in high spirits (R) and takes a very lively interest in school games (S)

(a) QPSR (b) SQPR (c) RPQS (d) PRQS

7. Even a leisurely game like cricket demanding grace rather than strength (P) and over the rough tactics of the Australian team that visited England in 1921 (Q) as we saw in the controversy over body line bowling (R) can cause much ill-will (S)

(a) PSRQ (b) RSPQ (c) SRQP (d) QPRS

Directions (Q.Nos. 8-12) *Each of the following items in this section consists of a sentence, the parts of which have been jumbled. These parts have been labelled P, Q, R and S. Given below each sentece has four sequences namely (a), (b), (c) and (d). You are required to rearrange the jumbled parts of the sentence.* **NDA 2018**

8. Domestic fires in Indian villages
P. as the heat is dispersed
Q. in unhealthy smoke accumulates in unventilated houses
R. are wasteful
S. lit in Chulhas

The correct sequence should be

(a) PQSR (b) PQRS (c) SPQR (d) SRPQ

9. Bold rocks near at hand
P. makes a fine forest for the imagination
Q. than distant Alps
R. are more inspiring
S. and the thick fern upon a health

The correct sequence should be

(a) QRSP (b) RSQP (c) RQSP (d) SRQP

10. Newton discovered that

P. due to the gravitational pull
Q. of the earth
R. the apple falls
S. on the ground

The correct sequence should be

(a) QPRS (b) RSPQ (c) QSPR (d) SQRP

11. The knocking

P. were still in the house
Q. for some time
R. although the echoes of it
S. ceased

The correct sequence should be

(a) SRPQ (b) SQRP (c) PQSR (d) RSPQ

12. The history of mankind is

P. and steady progress
Q. continuos change
R. the history of
S. from barbarism to refinement

The correct sequence should be

(a) PQRS (b) RQPS (c) QSPR (d) SQRP

Directions (Q. Nos. 13-15) *Each of the following questions in this section consists of a sentence, the parts of which have been jumbled. These parts have been labelled P, Q, R and S. Given below each sentence has four sequences namely (a), (b), (c) and (d). You are required to rearrange the jumbled parts of the sentence and mark your response accordingly.* **NDA 2019**

13. the urban local body elections (P) unidentified gunmen (Q) and injured another during (R) shot dead two workers (S)

(a) QSRP (b) PQSR (c) SPRQ (d) RPSQ

14. both intense political and (P) this state has a history of (Q) of syncretic accomplishments (R) religious contestation and (S)

(a) SQPR (b) PQSR (c) SQRP (d) QPSR

15. the father also (P) in his quest for justice (Q) by the system (R) feels let down (S)

(a) SQPR (b) PSRQ (c) SQRP (d) PQRS

Directions (Q.Nos. 16-20) *Each of the following question in this section consists of a sentence(s), the parts of which have been jumbled. These parts have been labelled as P, Q, R and S. Given below each sentence has four sequences namely (a), (b), (c) and (d). You are required to rearrange the jumbled part of the sentence and mark your response accordingly.* **NDA 2020**

16. several years ago. (P) course on climate change at Texas (Q) A & M university Professor Andrew Dessler created an introductory (R) for freshman and sophomores (S)

(a) PRQS (b) QRPS (c) SQRP (d) PQRS

17. I realize that solving the climate change problem (P) than solving (Q) will be much harder (R) the ozone depletion problem (S)

(a) PRQS (b) QRPS (c) SQRP (d) PQRS

18. although the temperature of this layer of the (P) when directly comparing the satellite (Q) measurements of temperature (R) atmosphere should generally track the surface temperature, we must be careful (S)

(a) PRQS (b) PSQR (c) SQRP (d) PQRS

19. the element heats up, (P) eventually reaching high temperatures (Q) glowing like a dark orange that radiates (R) the visible range (S)

(a) PQSR (b) QPSR (c) SQRP (d) PRSQ

20. two people argue about why Venus is so much warmer (P) to the Sun, so it absorbs more solar energy. The second argues (Q) that it's because Venus has a thick, greenhouse gas rich atmosphere (R) than the Earth. The first argues that it's because Venus is closer (S)

(a) PSQR (b) QRPS (c) SQRP (d) PQRS

Directions (Q.Nos. 21-23) *Each of the following questions in this section consists of a sentence, the parts of which have been jumbled. These parts have been labelled P, Q, R and S. Given below each sentence has four sequences namely (a), (b), (c) and (d). You are required to rearrange the jumbled parts of the sentence and mark your response accordingly.* **CDS 2016**

21. Georgian loyalists and rebel forcesafter a week of fighting (P) agreed to (Q) a ceasefire today in (R) which 51 people were killed (S)

The correct sequence should be

(a) PQRS (b) QRSP (c) QPSR (d) QRPS

22. The ultimate hope will force the nations (P) that the destructive nature of (Q) weapons to give up war (R) has not been fulfilled (S)

The correct sequence should be

(a) PSQR (b) PQRS
(c) QPRS (d) PRQS

23. The leader of the opposition, in the mannr he had planned to convince them, (P) on realising that he had failed to (Q) convince the assembly, who had a (R) reputation for speech making, was very much disappointed (S)

The correct sequence should be

(a) PSRQ (b) QSRP (c) RSQP (d) SPRQ

Directions (Q.Nos. 24-31) *In each of the questions in this section, there is a sentence of which some parts have been jumbled up. You are required to rearrange these parts, which are labelled P, Q, R and S to produce the correct sentence. Choose the proper sequence and mark accordingly.*

24. he/(P) almost/(Q) planned the entire strategy of operation/(R) single-handed/(S).

The correct sequence should be **CDS 2017**

(a) RSPQ (b) PRQS (c) SQRP (d) QPSR

25. It is a fact that rice is one of the most prolific/(P) than almost any other crop/(Q) yielding a greater return per acre/(R) of food crops/(S).

The correct sequence should be

(a) SRQP (b) RPSQ (c) QRSP (d) PSRQ

26. up to the end of the eighteenth century, not only because it was often fatal/(P) smallpox was a particularly dreaded disease/(Q) but also because those who recovered/(R) were permanently disfigured/(S).

The correct sequence should be **CDS 2017**

(a) PQRS (b) QRSP (c) PRSQ (d) QPRS

27. a person bitten by a rabid dog/(P) would be seized by violent symptoms/(Q) after an incubation period of a month/(R) or two and die an agonizing death/(S)

The correct sequence should be **CDS 2017**

(a) PRSQ (b) SRQP (c) PRQS (d) PQRS

28. to accept any of the important (P)/disillusionment (Q)/ demands of the nationalists produced (R)/the failure of the British Government. (S)

The correct sequence should be **CDS 2018**

(a) SPRQ (b) PQRS (c) SRQP (d) QRPS

29. showed that a backward (P)/the rise of (Q)/ modern Japan after 1868 (R) Asian country could develop itself without Western control. (S)

The correct sequence should be **CDS 2018**

(a) PQRS (b) SRQP (c) PRQS (d) QRPS

30. and the current Hindu emphasis (P)/and urged the people to imbibe the spirit of free-thinking (Q)/ on rituals, ceremonies and superstitions. (R)/ Vivekananda condemned the caste system. (S)

The correct sequence should be

(a) PQRS (b) SPRQ (c) SPQR (d) RPSQ

31. Mr. John
who was hardly six months old (P)/ Charles (Q)/as his son (R)/ adopted. (S)

The correct sequence should be **CDS 2018**

(a) SQRP (b) PSQR (c) RSPQ (d) PRSQ

Directions (Q.Nos. 32-34) *Each of the following questions in this section consists of a sentence, the parts of which have been jumbled. These parts have been labelled as P, Q, R and S. Given below each sentence has four sequences namely (a), (b), (c) and (d). You are required to rearrange the jumbled parts of the sentence and mark your response accordingly.* **CDS 2019**

32. the company are often asked (P) the formal or informal interviews (Q) employees who are leaving (R) for their opinions during (S)

The correct sequence should be

(a) RPSQ (b) RQPS (c) PSQR (d) PQSR

33. a hailstorm activity in the evenings (P) there is a possiblity of (Q) while there could be (R) heavy rain towards the weekend (S)

The correct sequence should be

(a) SQPR (b) QSRP (c) QRPS (d) SPRQ

34. has been below normal since last week (P) the minimum temperature (Q) in some part of the city (R) when rain and hailstorm activity recorded (S)

The correct sequence should be

(a) RSPQ (b) SPRQ (c) QPSR (d) PSQR

Directions (Q.Nos. 35-39) *Each of the following items in this section consists of a sentence, the parts of which have been jumbled. These parts have been labelled as P, Q, R and S. Given below each sentence has four sequences namely (a), (b), (c) and (d). You are required to rearrange the jumbled parts of the sentence and mark your response accordingly.* **CDS 2020**

35. for long and (P) the backbone of India (Q) will continue to be the same (R) agriculture has been (S)

(a) SPQR (b) SQPR (c) QRSP (d) QSRP

36. the cry of general public (P) agenda in any country (Q) public policy making (R) is generally driven by (S)

(a) RQSP (b) RPSQ (c) PSRQ (d) QRSP

37. before it starts (P) of the government is (Q) the essential power (R) the power to manage conflict (S)

(a) RSPQ (b) SQRP (c) RQSP (d) QRSP

38. a majority of the vote (P) the party that received (Q) of the government (R) must take control (S)

(a) QPSR (b) PSRQ (c) RSPQ (d) SQPR

39. can express a view on (P) in which the electorate (Q) a particular issue of public policy (R) a referendum is a vote (S)

(a) SQPR (b) RPQS (c) QRSP (d) PQRS

Directions (Q.Nos. 40 and 41) *Each of these questions below consists of a set of labelled sentences. Out of the four options given, select the most logical order of the sentences to form a coherent paragraph.*
SSC CGL 2017

40. Evidently it was too
X-of a deadly-looking cobra or
Y-two we saw no reptiles
Z-dry for game, and with the exception

(a) YZX (b) YXZ (c) XZY (d) ZXY

41. Some of these
X-height of more than
Y-2000 feet above the sea
Z-rocks rise to the

(a) YZX (b) ZXY (c) YXZ (d) XZY

42. Given below are four jumbled sentencess. Select the option that gives their correct order.
SSC CGL 2017

A. Only natural dyes are used in Kalamkari and it involves several steps.
B. There are two distinctive styles of Kalamkari in India.
C. They are the Sri Kalahasti style and the Machilipatnam style.
D. Kalamkari is a type of hand-painted or block-printed cotton textile, produced in the Indian States of Andhra Pradesh and telangana.

(a) ACBD (b) CBDA (c) DABC (d) DCBA

43. Given below are four jumbled sentences. Select the option that gives their correct order.
SSC CGL 2018

A. The brain is active too during sleep, sending messages for the heart to beat regularly.
B. However, the body utilizes the sleeping time effectively.
C. We spend about one third of our time sleeping.
D. It produces energy and releases hormones for repair and growth during the night.

(a) CBDA (b) BADC (c) ABDC (d) CABD

44. Given below are four jumbled sentences. Select the option that gives their correct order.
SSC CGL 2018

A. Its value is linked to what it is being used for.
B. Such questions often baffle you.
C. How emotional should one get about money and its value?
D. Money on its own has no value, until you have some use for it.

(a) DBAC (b) CBDA (c) CABD (d) ACDB

45. Given below are four jumbled sentences. Select the option that gives their correct order.
SSC CGL 2018

A. But they faced grave danger if they tried to criticize these decisions.
B. The nationalists now began to openly criticize the policies of the British.
C. The freedom movement changed this situation.

D. Under colonial rule, the people had lived in fear of the British government and did not agree with many of the decisions that they took.
(a) CBAD (b) DBAC (c) BADC (d) DACB

46. Given below are four jumbled sentences. Out of the given options pick the one that gives their correct order. **SSC CGL 2020**
A. Nevertheless, sound health, economic security and mental satisfaction are desired by all
B. A change that is conducive to happiness may be termed as progress.
C. But different people find happiness in different things.
D. So, if a change contributes to the growth of these factors, it is progress.
(a) BCAD (b) BDCA (c) ABCD (d) DBCA

47. Given below are four jumbled sentences. Out of the given options pick the one that gives their correct order. **SSC CGL 2020**
A. Can I borrow your camera?
B. I will give it back to you next week.
C. I am going to jungle safari tomorrow.
D. My friend told me that jungle is beautiful in these days.
(a) BACD (b) CADB (c) CDAB (d) ADBC

Directions (Q.Nos. 48-52) *in each question below some sentences are given which are divided into five parts. The first part of the sentence (1) is correct and is given in followed by four parts named A, B, C and D. Rearrange the four parts of the sentence to make a coherent paragraph. The rearranged sequence of the parts will be your answer. If the given sentence is correct as it is then choose option (e).* **CBI Clerk 2018**

48. **Crashes in the early days** (1)/to be caused by technical faults, (A)/of commercial jets tended (B)/such as metal fatigue (C)/in the airframe or engines (D)
(a) DCAB (b) ABCD (c) BACD (d) CABD
(e) No arrangement required

49. **There have been a lot of (1)**/drivers not obeying (A)/complaints recently about (B)/in downtown boston (C)/the speed limits (D)/
(a) BADC (b) ABCD (c) BCAD (d) CABD
(e) No arrangement required

50. **Chinese officials say (1)**/ dropped to a three-year (A)/low because of (B)/economic growth has (C)/the world economy (D)
(a) BADC (b) CABD (c) BCAD (d) CADB
(e) No arrangement required

51. **I think its a shame that (1)**/some foreign language teachers (A)/studied with a native speaker (B)/college without ever having (C)/were able to graduate from (D)
(a) BADC (b) CABD (c) BCAD (d) ADCB
(e) No arrangement required

52. **The Gita is a spiritual philosophy(1)**/ addressed to all and we know that (A)/there are all kinds of people, (B)/each kind differing (C)/ quite significantly from the other (D)
(a) BADC (b) CABD (c) BCAD (d) ADCB
(e) No arrangement required

Directions (Q.Nos. 53-57) *In the following questions, a grammatically correct and meaningful sentence is given which is divided into five parts, (A), (B), (C) and (D). Part (E) is fixed and highlighted in BOLD. You have to arragne the other four parts to make a contextually and grammatically meaningul sentence (the meaning can be different from the one given in the question). If no such rearrangement is possible mark (E) as your answer i.e. 'No rearrangement' is possible.* **IBPS Clerk 2018**

53. Of formal and informal rules, assure (A)/according to some norms that enable as well as (B)/ institutions, as the embodiment (C)/citizens that the government exercises power (D) **regulate state capacity** (E).

(a) ACBDE (b) CADBE (c) DABCE (d) BACDE
(e) No rearrangement is possible

54. British rule, secularism was an article of faith across (A)/ the ideological spectrum, though only in a limited definition as (B)/ the community-based template of political competition introduced under (C)/ in the aftermath of Partition, seen as the outcome of (D)/ **a seamless sense of national identity** (E).

(a) BADCE (b) CBDAE (c) ACBDE (d) DCABE
(e) No rearrangement is possible

55. The exclusion was not based on gender or sex, but on religious (A)/ by veteran lawyer K. Parasaran, sought a (B)/the Nair Service Society, represented (C)/review of the verdict on the ground that (D)/ **faith in and character of the deity** (E).

(a) DACBE (b) ABDCE (c) CBDAE (d) BCDAE
(e) No rearrangement is possible

56. Represented by solicitor general tushar metha. (A)/ while Mr. Venugopal said he did not (B)/ on Mr. Bhushan, the government, (C)/ want the court to impose any punishment (D)/ **was of the opposite opinion** (E).

(a) DABCE (b) BDCAE (c) CDABE (d) ABCDE
(e) No rearrangement is possible

57. Deposit-taking activities altogether, by making them an offence (A)/ the principle is that the bill would ban unregulated (B)/framework that only comes into effect (C)/ex-ante rather than the existing legislative-cum-regulatory (D)/ **ex-post with considerable time lags** (E).

(a) ADCBE (b) BACDE (c) CDBAE (d) BADCE
(e) No rearrangement is possible

Exercise B

Directions *In this section each item consists of six sentences of a passage. The first and the sixth sentences are given in the beginning as S1 and S6. The middle four sentences in each have been jumbled up and labelled as P, Q, R and S. You are required to find out the proper sequence of the four sentences and mark your response accordingly on Answer Sheet.*

1. S1 : The ruin of India handicrafts was reflected in the ruin of the towns and cities which were famous for their manufactures. **NDA 2018**

S6: Centres were developed and laid waste.
P : Dacca, Surat, Murshidabad and many other rising industrial
Q : ravages of war and plunder, failed to
R : survive British conquest
S : Cities which had withstood the

The proper sequence should be

(a) PQRS (b) SQRP (c) SRPQ (d) QRSP

2. S1 : The Subsidiary Alliance system was extremely advantageous to the British.
S6: They controlled the defence and the foreign relations of the protected ally.
P : They could now maintain a large army at the cost of Indian states.
Q : if many war occurred in the territories
R : either of the British ally or of the Britishers
S : This enabled them to fight wars far away from their own territories
The proper sequence should be
(a) PQRS (b) PSQR (c) QRPS (d) SRPQ

3. S1 : The Indian Civil Service gradually developed into one of the most efficient and powerful civil services in the world. **NDA 2018**
S6 : though these qualities obviously served. British, and not Indian interests.
P : and often participated in the making of policy
Q : independence, integrity and hard work
R : They developed certain traditions of
S : Its members exercised vast power
The proper sequence should be
(a) PQRS (b) QRSP (c) RSQP (d) SPRQ

4. S1: We do not know what to do with our knowledge.
S6 : In the course of time they may rule over us altogether.
P : for example, we are unable to manage our machines.
Q : We already find it difficult to do without machines.
R. : Machines should be fed properly and waited upon attentively; otherwise they refuse to work or cause destruction.
S. : Science has given us superhuman powers, which we do not use properly.
The proper sequence should be
(a) SPRQ (b) PSQR (c) QRPS (d) SRPQ

5. S1: The British rule in India has brought about moral, material, cultural and spiritual ruination of this great country. **NDA 2019**
S6: We are not to kill anybody but it is our *dharma* to see that the curse of this Government is blotted out.
P : I regard this rule as a curse.
Q : Sedition had become my religion.
R : Ourse is a non-violent battle.
S : I am out to destroy this system of Government.
The proper sequence should be
(a) SPRQ (b) PSQR (c) QRPS (d) SRPQ

6. S1 : Iguanodon was one of the first dinosaurs to be scientifically described.
S6 : This quardrupedal dinosaur lived about 70 million years ago and its fossils are dound in many parts of England, Europe, Asia and North Africa.
P : These teeth formed a dental battery in which replacing teeth were constantly growing.
Q : The forelimbs were slightly larger than other members of its group known as *Ornithischia*.
R : It had numerous teeth in the sides of the jaws, arranged in rows.
S : It was about 40 feet in length.
The proper sequence should be
(a) QSRP (b) SRPQ (c) RQPS (d) PQSR

7. S1 : A single device can heat fluids without requiring an electrical element.

S6 : Because there is no electrical element, there is no risk of fire, so the system is suitable for dangerous environments.

P : A heat exchanger transfers heat from the central cavity to an air heater, a water heater or an industrial processor.

Q : It has a container like the crank case of a car's engine, which contains the fluid to be heated.

R : Compression and friction at the nozzles heat the fluid, so that the temperature in the central cavity rises steadily.

S : A motor and pulley inside the container turn a rotor wheel, which in turn forces the fluid again and again through narrow nozzles into a central cavity.

The proper sequence should be

(a) RPSQ (b) SPQR (c) QSRP (d) SRPQ

8. S1 : People's fear of snakes seems to be based on a series of misconceptions. **CDS 2017**

S6 : Yet people will insist that they cannot touch a snake because of its sliminess.

P : The most common one is the conviction that all these creatures are poisonous.

Q : Another very popular idea is that these reptiles are slimy to touch.

R : Snakes are really dry and cold; not slimy like a wet cake of soap, but rather like a crocodile-skin handbag to the touch.

S : In fact, the non-poisonous ones outnumber the poisonous ones by about ten to one.

The proper sequence should be

(a) RQPS (b) RPQS (c) PSQR (d) RQSP

9. S1 : The first great discovery that man probably made was that of fire.

S6 : The animals were not clever enough to learn anything from this. **CDS 2017**

P : Fires sometimes occur by themselves in the forests perhaps by rubbing together of flints or something else.

Q : We light a fire now by a match.

R : In olden times fires were made by striking two flints against each other till a spark came for setting fire to a dry thing.

S : But matches are quite recent things.

The proper sequence should be

(a) PRSQ (b) QSPR (c) PQSR (d) RPQS

10. S1 : At 4 O' clock this morning, Hitler attacked and invaded Russia

S6 : Under its clock of false confidence, the German armies drew up in immense strength along a line which stretches from the White Sea to the Black Sea **CDS 2018**

P : No complaint had been made by Germany of its non-fulfilment.

Q : All his usual formalities of perfidy were observed with scrupulous technique.

R : No one could have expected that Hitler would do it.

S : A non-aggression treaty had been solemnly signed and was in force between the two countries.

The correct sequence should be

(a) RQSP (b) RSQP (c) PSQR (d) QPSR

11. S1 : Roderick Usher has always been a quiet person who talked little of himself. **CDS 2018**

S6 : In the part of the country where he lived, the 'House of Usher' had come to mean both the family and its ancestral mansion.

P : Many of his ancestors had been famous for their artistic and musical abilities.

Q : Others were known for their exceptional generosity and charity.

R : Yet I did know that his family was an old one.

S : So, I did not know too much about him.

The correct sequence should be

(a) PQRS (b) SRQP (c) SPRQ (d) SRPQ

12. S1 : The weak have no place here, in this life or in any other life. Weakness leads to slavery. **CDS 2019**

S6 : This is the great fact : strength is life weakness is death. Strength is felicity, life eternal; immortal; weakness is constant strain and misery; weakness is death.

P : They dare not approach us, they have no power to get a hold on us, until the mind is weakened.

Q : Weakness leads to all kinds of misery, physical and mental. Weakness is death.

R : But they cannot harm us unless we become weak, until the body is ready and predisposed to receive them.

S : There are hundreds of thousands of microbes surrounding us.

The correct sequence should be

(a) PQRS (b) PRQS (c) QRSP (d) QSRP

13. S1 : The Nobel Prize for Economics in 2018 was awarded to Paul Romer and William Nordhaus for their work in two separate areas : economic growth and environmental economics respectively. **CDS 2019**

S6: Among recent winners of Nobel Prize in Economics, it's hard to think of one issue which is more topical and relevant to India.

P : But there is a common thread in the work.

Q : In economic jargon it's termed as externality.

R : Productive activity often has spillovers, meaning that is can impact an unrelated party.

S : Romer and Nordhaus both studied the impact of externalities and came up with profound insights and economic models.

The correct sequence should be

(a) PQRS (b) PRQS (c) QSPR (d) QSRP

14. S1 : Few scientists manage to break down the walls of the so-called ivory tower of academia and touch and inspire people who may not otherwise be interested in science. **CDS 2019**

S6: Not many would have survived this, let alone excelled in the manner he did.

P : Stephen Hawking was one of these few.

Q : Around this time he was diagnosed with amyotrophic Lateral Sclerosis, an incurable motor neuron disease and given two years to live.

R : Judging by the odds he faced as a young graduated student of physics at Cambridge University, nothing could have been a more remote possibility.

S : When he was about 20 years old, he got the shattering news that he could not work with the great Fred Hoyle for his PhD, as he had aspired to.

The correct sequence should be

(a) PQSR (b) PRQS (c) SRPQ (d) PRSQ

15. S1 : Biology is the study of life in its entirety. **CDS 2020**

S6: Classical descriptive and clueless biology found a theoretical framework in the evolutionary theory of Darwin.

P : In later years, the focus was physiology and internal morphology or anatomy.

Q : Darwinian ideas of evolution by natural selection changed the perception completely.

R : The growth of biology as a natural science during the last 1000 years is interesting from many points of view.

S : One feature of this growth is changing emphasis from mere description of life forms to identification and classification of all recorded living forms.

The correct sequence should be

(a) RSPQ (b) SPRQ (c) QRPS (d) PQRS

16. S1 : Biology is the youngest of the formalized disciplines of natural science. **CDS 2020**

S6 : Life expectancy of human beings has dramatically changed over the years.

P : However, the twentieth century and certainly the twenty-first century has demonstrated the utility of biological knowledge in furthering human welfare, be it in health sector or agriculture.

Q : The discovery of antibotics and synthetic plant-derived drugs, anaesthetics have changed medical practice on one hand and human health on the other hand.

R : Applications of physics and chemistry in our daily life also have a higher visibility than those of biology.

S : Progress in physics and chemistry proceeded much faster than in biology.

The correct sequence should be

(a) QPRS (b) PRQS (c) RPQS (d) SRPQ

17. S1 : People in society need many goods and services in their everyday life including food, clothing, shelter, transport, etc. **CDS 2020**

S6 : The teacher in the local school has the skills required to impart education to the students.

P : A weaver may have some yarn, some cotton and other instruments required for weaving cloth.

Q : A family farm may own a plot of land, some grains, farming implements, may be a pair of bullocks and also the labour services of the family members.

R : Every individual has some amount of the goods and services that one would like to use.

S : In fact, the list of goods and services that any individual needs is so large that no individual in society, to begin with, has all the things one needs.

The correct sequence should be

(a) PQRS (b) RSPQ
(c) QPSR (d) SRQP

Directions (Q.Nos. 18-22) *Rearrange the given six sentences/group of sentences A, B, C, D, E and F in a proper sequence so as to form a meaningful paragraph and then answer the given questions.* **SBI Clerk 2015**

A. Beena grew by the day and was charming and polite but as the goddess predicted she had to have new outfit everyday and for a while the king and queen were happy to let their way but soon realised that this had to stop.

B. They longed for the child and prayed and prayed till finally one day their prayers were answered but the goddess warned, "you will soon have a little girl and though she will be a loving child, she will love new clothes too much and will be cursed if she covert another's clothes."

C. They tried to get mend her ways but in vin and one day when Beena saw a beautiful girl simply dressed in a cotton saree and noticed how people were admiring the simply dressed girl she demanded the dress.

D. The kingdom was at peace, subjects wer happy and there was a bumper crop but the King and Queen were very sad.

E. As foretold, Beena turned into an onion. A plant with many layers to symbolise the many dresses she had.

F. The king and Queen were ready to accept this and when the Queen gave birth to a baby girl the entire kingdom rejoiced.

18. Which of the following should be **FIFTH** sentence after rearrangement?
(a) A (b) C (c) D (d) E
(e) F

19. Which of the following should be **SIXTH** (Last) sentence after rearrangement?
(a) A (b) B (c) C (d) D
(e) E

20. Which of the following should be **FIRST** sentence after rearrangement?
(a) A (b) B (c) C (d) D
(e) F

21. Which of the following should be **SECOND** sentence after rearrangement?
(a) A (b) B (c) C (d) D
(e) F

22. Which of the following should be **THIRD** sentence after rearrangement?
(a) A (b) B (c) D (d) E
(e) F

Directions (Q.Nos. 23-27) *Rearrange the given six sentences/group of sentences A, B, C, D, E and F in a proper sequence so as to form a meaningful paragraph and then answer the given questions.* **SBI Clerk 2016**

A. The next day Shiva appeared at Raghu's house and spotted a metal chest on the rooftop which had all the money and ornaments that Raghu owned.

B. When Raghu arrived at Shiva's house, Shiva asked him to guess what fruit it was, saying that if Raghu failed he (Shiva) would carry one thing out of Raghu's house and if Raghu guessed correctly then Raghu could carry one thing out of Shiva's house.

C. Seeing him Raghu thanked him saying, Thank you for sparing my wealth and carrying out only the ladder!

D. One day Shiva hatched a plan to outwit Raghu. He plucked a mango and wrapped it well in a piece of cloth.

E. 'Oh ho!' You thought that you'd hide all your wealth from me said Shiva going into Raghu's house and bringing out a ladder began to climb up onto the roof.

F. ButRaghu's guesses were incorrect.

23. Which of the following should be the FIFTH sentence after rearrangement?
(a) A (b) B (c) D (d) E
(e) F

24. Which of the following should be the SECOND sentence after rearrangement?
(a) A (b) B (c) C (d) E
(e) F

25. Which of the following should be the THIRD sentence after rearrangement?
(a) A (b) B (c) C (d) D
(e) F

26. Which of the following should be the SIXTH (LAST) sentence after rearrangement?
(a) A (b) B (c) C (d) D
(e) E

27. Which of the following should be the FIRST sentence after rearrangement?
(a) A (b) C (c) D (d) E
(e) F

Directions (Q.Nos. 28-32) *Rearrange the following six sentences A, B, C, D,E and F in a proper sequence to form a meaningful paragraph and then answer the given questions.* **SBI Clerk 2016**

A. The full extent and impact of the forest fires in Uttarakhand can be assessed only after they have abated with better weather conditions, but the furious blaze that has swept the hill State drives home, the truth that governments are yet to find scientific ways to tackle the phenomenon.

B. Some of the studies reported by organisations affiliated to the Union Environment Ministry point to the effective intervention of community-led 'Van Panchayats' forest councils in preventing fires.

C. Progress can be made also by providing environmental education to local residents and officials.

D. Significantly, the use of biomass alternatives, including cooking gas, has had a beneficial impact on fire risk and this must be expanded.

E. The Uttarakhand government should learm from the severity of the experience, and involve its large rural communities in preparing for the future.

F. It is pssible that the changing patterns of climate may be exacerbating the problem, more research is required to conclude whether the El Nino that set in last year, marked by a lack of pre-monsoon showers, also played a part in intensifying the fires.

28. Which of the following will be the FOURTH sentence after rearrangement?
(a) E (b) B (c) F (d) A (e) C

29. Which of the following will be the THIRD sentence after rearrangement?
(a) E (b) B (c) F (d) A (e) C

30. Which of the following will be the FIRST sentence after rearrangement?
(a) D (b) E (c) A (d) B (e) F

31. Which of the following will be the SIXTH (LAST) sentence after rearrangement?
(a) E (b) D (c) B (d) A (e) C

32. Which of the following will be the FIFTH sentence after rearrangement?
(a) E (b) C (c) D (d) A (e) B

Directions (Q.Nos. 33-37) *Rearrange the following six sentences A, B, C, D,E and F in a proper sequence to form a meaningful paragraph and then answer the question given below.* **SBI Clerk 2016**

A. Anything that you touch will turn into gold. The king was delighted with his good fortune.

B. Even thugh he was very rich he always craved for more and more.

C. Everything he touched turned into gold. He turned trees, grass, tables, chairs, flowers, and vases into gold.

D. One day, he called his court magician and commanded, find me a spell that can get me more treasures than I already have.

E. King Midas was a very greedy king.

F. The magician said, Your majesty, I can give you a power that no one else in this world has.

33. Which of the following should be the FIRST sentence after rearrangement?
(a) F (b) E (c) B (d) A (e) C

34. Which of the following should be the SECOND sentence after rearrangement?
(a) A (b) B (c) C (d) E (e) D

35. Which of the following should be the THIRD sentence after rearrangement?
(a) E (b) F (c) D (d) C (e) B

36. Which of the following should be the FOURTH sentence after rearrangement?
(a) A (b) B (c) F (d) E (e) C

37. Which of the following should be the LAST (SIXTH) sentence after rearrangement?
(a) C (b) A (c) B (d) D (e) F

Answers

Work Book Exercise A

1. (d) **2.** (b) **3.** (a) **4.** (a) **5.** (b) **6.** (d) **7.** (c)
8. (b) **9.** (d)

Work Book Exercise B

1. (c) **2.** (a) **3.** (b) **4.** (a) **5.** (d) **6.** (a) **7.** (b)
8. (c) **9.** (b) **10.** (a) **11.** (d) **12.** (c) **13.** (c) **14.** (b)
15. (b) **16.** (d) **17.** (b) **18.** (c) **19.** (d) **20.** (b) **21.** (c)
22. (c) **23.** (d)

Work Book Exercise C

1. (d) **2.** (d) **3.** (c) **4.** (c) **5.** (d) **6.** (c) **7.** (c)
8. (c) **9.** (c) **10.** (a) **11.** (b) **12.** (a) **13.** (d) **14.** (b)
15. (c) **16.** (d) **17.** (b) **18.** (a) **19.** (a) **20.** (b) **21.** (c)
22. (c) **23.** (b) **24.** (d) **25.** (c) **26.** (b) **27.** (c) **28.** (a)
29. (d) **30.** (d) **31.** (c) **32.** (a) **33.** (b) **34.** (a) **35.** (b)
36. (b) **37.** (a) **38.** (b) **39.** (c) **40.** (a) **41.** (a) **42.** (b)

Work Book Exercise D

1. (e) **2.** (c) **3.** (d) **4.** (d) **5.** (c) **6.** (a)

Work Book Exercise E

I. 1. (e) **2.** (d) **3.** (a) **4.** (c) **5.** (b)
II. 1. (c) **2.** (e) **3.** (d) **4.** (a) **5.** (b)
III. 1. (b) **2.** (c) **3.** (e) **4.** (e) **5.** (c)
IV. 1. (c) **2.** (e) **3.** (e) **4.** (b) **5.** (d)
V. 1. (d) **2.** (e) **3.** (c) **4.** (d) **5.** (e)
VI. 1. (e) **2.** (b) **3.** (d) **4.** (c) **5.** (c)

Exam Practice

Exercise A

1. (a) **2.** (b) **3.** (c) **4.** (b) **5.** (b) **6.** (c) **7.** (a)
8. (d) **9.** (c) **10.** (b) **11.** (b) **12.** (b) **13.** (a) **14.** (d)
15. (b) **16.** (a) **17.** (a) **18.** (b) **19.** (d) **20.** (a) **21.** (d)
22. (c) **23.** (c) **24.** (b) **25.** (d) **26.** (d) **27.** (d) **28.** (a)
29. (d) **30.** (b) **31.** (a) **32.** (a) **33.** (b) **34.** (c) **35.** (b)
36. (a) **37.** (c) **38.** (a) **39.** (a) **40.** (d) **41.** (b) **42.** (c)
43. (a) **44.** (b) **45.** (d) **46.** (a) **47.** (c) **48.** (c) **49.** (a)
50. (b) **51.** (d) **52.** (e) **53.** (b) **54.** (d) **55.** (c) **56.** (b)
57. (d)

Exercise B

1. (b) **2.** (b) **3.** (d) **4.** (a) **5.** (b) **6.** (b) **7.** (c)
8. (c) **9.** (d) **10.** (a) **11.** (d) **12.** (d) **13.** (b) **14.** (d)
15. (a) **16.** (d) **17.** (d) **18.** (b) **19.** (e) **20.** (d) **21.** (b)
22. (e) **23.** (d) **24.** (b) **25.** (e) **26.** (c) **27.** (c) **28.** (b)
29. (a) **30.** (c) **31.** (b) **32.** (b) **33.** (b) **34.** (b) **35.** (c)
36. (c) **37.** (a)

2

Objective Comprehension

Objective Comprehension of a given passage or a number of passages is an integral part of any examination test in English. The objective English tests of competitive examination are designed to assess examinees through questions the verbal ability, language skills, the knowledge of grammar, vocabulary and comprehension of written English. Therefore, a student is required to read the passage carefully and choose a correct answer out of the alternatives given under the question. However, the questions are challenging and they all require an appreciation of more than just the superficial understanding of the passage. Therefore, it is very important that due attention should be paid to comprehension exercises.

The important points to be noted in this field are given as under :

(a) It is pertinent to note that sense of language and fund of words should be ample enough so that students may not feel disadvantaged on that account.

(b) The questions are based on what is stated or implied in each passage.

(c) Invariably the inference is based on the logical consequence of the information in the passage. Therefore, the answers must be based on and supported by the information given in the passage under reference.

(d) In some competitive examinations the students are also required to answer questions on synonyms and antonyms given in the passage. It is very important to note that the meaning of the word should be chosen from the alternatives in the context of the theme of the passage. One must not take into account only the literal meaning of the word.

Passage 1

Directions *Read the following passages carefully and answer the questions that follow.*

The forces that generate conditions conducive to crime and riots are stronger in urban communities than in rural areas. Urban living is more anonymous living. It often releases the individual from community restraints more common in tradition-oriented societies. But more freedom from constraints and controls also provides greater freedom to deviate. And living in the more impersonalized, formally controlled Urban society means that regulatory orders of conduct are often directed by distant bureaucrats. The police are strangers executing these prescriptions on an anonymous set of subjects. Minor offences in small town or village are often handled without resort to official police action. As disputable as such action may seem to be, it results in fewer recorded violations of the law compared to the big cities. Although perhaps causing some decision-difficulties for the police in small town, formal and objective law enforcement is not always acceptable to villagers.

Urban areas with mass population, greater wealth, more commercial establishments and more products of our technology also provide more frequent opportunities for theft. Victims are impersonalized, property is insured, consumer goods in more abundance are vividly displayed and are more portable. The crime-rate increases despite fromal moral education given in schools.

1. According to the passage, all the following contribute to higher crime-rates in urban areas except
(a) vivid display of consumer goods
(b) higher standard of living
(c) urban impersonalized living
(d) increasing population
(e) inadequate police force

2. Which of the following is a characteristic of an urban setting?
(a) Unreported minor crimes
(b) Deviation from freedom
(c) Less forceful social control
(d) Minimal opportunities of crime due to better law enforcement
(e) Fewer recorded violations of the law

3. The author's view of 'Traditional Societies' is best expressed by which of the following?
(a) They provide less freedom for the individual in many circumstances
(b) They have lower crime-rates because of the moral teachings in schools
(c) They provide inadequate freedom for personal movements and travel
(d) They do not have adequate modern technology
(e) They are ruled and controlled by distant bureaucrats

4. People live under more social control in
(a) formally controlled urban societies
(b) the presence of the police authorities
(c) an anonymous form of living
(d) non-traditional societies
(e) None of the above

5. It can be inferred from the passage that urban crime can be controlled by
(a) greater emphasis on moral education
(b) enforcement of law by distant bureaucrats
(c) vivid display of expensive consumer goods
(d) making the expensive consumer goods less portable
(e) None of the above

6. Which of the following statements is true in the context of the passage?
(a) The display of consumer goods is the main cause of crime
(b) Lack of personal contacts increases crimes in Urban areas
(c) Small communities have more minor crimes than in urban centres
(d) Urban crime areas cannot be prevented
(e) Police in urban areas settle minor disputes without official action

7. Which of the following statements is not true in the context of the passage?
(a) Moral education imparted in schools is ineffective in checking crime-rate
(b) There is less freedom in the present society than in a traditional society
(c) Urban areas are thickly populated and commercialized
(d) Anonymous living in urban areas may lead to a freedom to deviate from rules
(e) Urban areas provide more opportunities for crime than rural areas do

8. According to the passage, the crime in small towns
(a) is less frequently reported or dealt with officially
(b) is brought well under control by distant bureaucrats
(c) leads to an impersonalized style of living
(d) is often dealt with objective law enforcement
(e) always causes difficulties for the police authorities

Passage 2

A close look at the facts relating to political interference in administration shows that it is not a one-way process. There is often a nexus between power-hungry and corrupt politicians and civil servants with convenient principles. Many civil servants are only too anxious to oblige the politicians, and then cash the obligation when they need some special favour. So the attitude of self-righteousness adopted by the civil service is sometimes only a way of covering their own flaws by blaming others.

Every now and then some retired civil servants come out with his memoirs, painting a glorious picture of the heights of administrative efficiency reached during his reign. There is often the suggestion that had there not been so much political interference, things would have been even more fantastic. It is not unusual for the self-styled hero to blame not only interfering politicians but also fellow civil servants who were idiots or crooks, for his failures. This attitude of smug self-satisfaction is, unfortunately, developed during the years of service. Self-preservation rather than service is encouraged by our whole system of rules and procedures.

The remedy has to be drastic and quickly effective. The over-protection now granted to civil servants must end. Today to remove an erring civil servant is just not possible. And the only thing that the highest authority in the Govenment, both in the State and at the Centre, can do is to transfer an official from one job to another.

The rules for taking disciplinary action are so complicated that, in the end, the defaulting civil servant gets away, and gets his full emoluments even for the period of the disciplinary proceedings, thus making it a paid holiday for him.

The result is that the administration has become rule-oriented and not result-oriented. Action is possible against the official who takes some interest in his work, but no action is ever taken against a person who does not deliver the goods. If the country is to adopt a result-oriented approach, it is necessary to link job performance with job retention.

1. The facts relating to the problem of political interference indicate that
(a) honest bureaucrats are always being troubled by politicians
(b) politicians are often misled and trapped by civil servants
(c) politicians and civil servants co-operate to gain mutual advantages
(d) politicians and civil servants use interference as an excuse for victimizing the common man

2. The attitude of self-righteousness adopted by the civil service, according to the writer
(a) is not welcomed and supported by politicians
(b) is dishonest and conceals the facts
(c) is very difficult to maintain because of opposition
(d) does not really help the public get fair treatment

3. Civil servants who write their memoirs after retiring
(a) claim that they would have achieved outstanding success if interference had not come in the way
(b) prove that constant political interference made it impossible for them to do anything properly
(c) complain that the credit for their achievements goes to dishonest politicians
(d) prove that people of inferior quality in the civil service bring about interference

4. The existing system of administration seems to encourage civil servants
(a) to become self-styled heroes and boss over others
(b) to present a glorious picture of the administration
(c) to become self-centred and concerned mainly about their own gain
(d) to become self-righteous and fight back against corrupt politicians

5. The problem with the present set-up needing urgent action is
(a) a lack of accountability on the part of civil servants
(b) a lack of control over the power of politicians
(c) a neglect of the ideals of self-righteousness
(d) complicated rules and procedures that greatly reduce efficiency

6. The main principle of the remedy proposed by the writer is, that
(a) the politicians should be made accountable for all their decisions
(b) the high level of protection enjoyed by civil servants should be reduced
(c) the common man's right to efficient and fair administration must be protected
(d) rules should be simplified so that there is less scope for misuse

7. According to existing procedures, if a civil servant is found to be unsuitable or dishonest,
(a) he can appeal to an authority like the Supreme Court
(b) politicians with whom he has special links will interfere to help him
(c) transferring him to another post is the usual action taken
(d) a conflict between Central Government and State Government interests can arise

8. The writer refers to 'a paid holiday' to support his argument that
(a) civil servants get a lot of extra benefits
(b) disciplinary action is generally not quick or effective
(c) lazy and inefficient bureaucrats seem to be on holiday even when on duty
(d) special postings that 'favoured' civil servants are unnecessary and wasteful

9. The expression 'linking job performance with job retention' refers to a policy in which
(a) selection to civil service jobs is on the basis of rigorous performance tests
(b) selection to civil service jobs is on the basis of rigorous performance and not a minister's opinions is the basis of transfer or promotion
(c) retention of good Government servants by discouraging their going to private companies
(d) continuation in service will depend on satisfactory performance

10. The expression 'deliver the goods' means
(a) show good job performance
(b) accept bribes or other illegal favours
(c) make payments of black money as bribes
(d) successfully defend oneself against a charge, in a disciplinary inquiry

Passage 3

True, it is the function of the army to maintain law and order in abnormal times. But in normal times there is another force that compels citizens to obey the laws and to act with due regard to the rights of others. The force also protects the lives and the properties of law abiding men. Laws are made to secure the personal safety of its subjects and to prevent murder and crimes of violence. They are made to secure the property of the citizens against theft and damage to protect the rights of communities and castes to carry out their customs and ceremonies, so long as they do not conflict with the rights of others.

Now the good citizen, of his own free will obey these laws and he takes care that everything he does is done with due regard to the rights and well-being of others. But the bad citizen is only restrained from breaking these laws by fear of the consequence of his actions. And the necessary steps to compel the bad citizen to act as a good citizen are taken by this force. The supreme control of law and order in a State is in the hands of a Minister who is responsible to the State Assembly and acts through the Inspector General of Police.

1. The expression 'customs and ceremonies' means
- *(a)* fairs and festivals
- *(b)* habits and traditions
- *(c)* usual practices and religious rites
- *(d)* superstitions and formalities

2. A suitable title for the passage would be
- *(a)* the function of the army
- *(b)* laws and the people's rights
- *(c)* the fear of the law and citizen's security
- *(d)* the functions of the police

3. Which of the following is not implied in the passage?
- *(a)* Law protects those who respect it
- *(b)* Law ensures people's religious and social rights absolutely and unconditionally
- *(c)* A criminal is deterred from committing crimes only for fear of the law
- *(d)* The forces of law help to transform irresponsible citizens into responsible ones

4. According to the writer, which one of the following is not the responsibility of the police?
- *(a)* To protect the privileges of all citizens
- *(b)* To check violent activities of citizens
- *(c)* To ensure peace among citizens by safeguarding individual rights
- *(d)* To maintain peace during extraordinary circumstances

5. Which of the following reflects the main thrust of the passage?
- *(a)* It deals with the importance of the army in maintaining law and order
- *(b)* It highlights role of the police as superior to that of the army
- *(c)* It discusses the roles of the army and the police in different circumstances
- *(d)* It points to the responsibility of the Minister and the Inspector General of Police

6. "They are made to secure the property of citizens against theft and damage", means that the law
- *(a)* helps in recovering the stolen property of the citizens
- *(b)* assist the citizens whose property has been stolen or destroyed
- *(c)* initiate process against offenders of law
- *(d)* safeguard people's possessions against being stolen or lost

7. Out of the following which one has the opposite meaning to the word 'restrained' in the passage?
(a) Promoted *(b)* Accelerated
(c) Intruded *(d)* Inhibited

8. Which one of the following statement is implied in the passage?
(a) Peaceful citizens seldom violate the law, but bad citizens have to be restrained by the police
(b) Criminals, who flout the law, are seldom brought to book
(c) The police hardly succeeds in converting bad citizens into good citizens
(d) The police check the citizens, whether they are good or bad, from violating the law

9. Which of the following statements expresses most accurately the idea contained in the first sentence?
(a) It is the job of the army to ensure internal peace at all times
(b) It is the police that should always enforce law and order in the country
(c) Army and the police ensure people's security through combined operations
(d) It is in exceptional circumstances that the army has to ensure peace in the country

10. The last sentence of the passage implies that
(a) The Inspector General of Police is the sole authority in matters of law and order
(b) In every State, maintenance of public peace is under the overall control of the responsible Minister
(c) A Minister and a responsible State Assembly exercises direct authority in matters pertaining to law and order
(d) The Inspector General of Police is responsible to the State Assembly for maintaining law and order

Passage 4

The first step is for us to realise that a city need not be a frustrater of life; it can be among other things, a mechanism for enhancing life, for producing possibilities of living which are not to be realized except through cities. But, for that to happen, deliberate and drastic planning is needed. Towns as much as animals, must have their systems of organs–those for transport and circulation are an obvious example.

What we need now are organ systems for recreation, leisure, culture, community expression. This means abundance of open space, easy access to unspoilt Nature, beauty in parks and in fine buildings, gymnasia and swimming baths and recreation grounds in plenty, central spaces for celebrations and demonstrations, halls for citizens' meetings, concert halls and theatres and cinemas that belong to the city.

And the buildings must not be built anyhow or dumped down anywhere; both they and their groupings should mean something important to the people of the place.

1. Cities can be made to provide full facilities for life, only if
(a) these can be mechanically developed
(b) proper transport system is introduced
(c) cinemas, theatres and concert halls are established there
(d) these are thoughtfully and vigorously designed to serve people's needs

2. A suitable title for the passage would be
(a) Towns versus Animals
(b) The Need for Planned Cities
(c) Transport and Communication System in a City
(d) The Need for Entertainment Centres in a City

3. "A city need not be a frustrater of life" means that
(*a*) one does not expect fulfilment of all life's requirements from a city
(*b*) city life provides all the essential needs of life
(*c*) a city does not necessarily lift man's standard of living
(*d*) a city should not defeat the fulfilment of life's aspirations and aims

4. Which one of the following has the opposite meaning to the word 'frustrater' in the passage?
(*a*) Promoter (*b*) Applauder
(*c*) Approver (*d*) Executer

5. "The building must not be built anyhow or dumped down anywhere"....the statement implies that building
(*a*) should be built with suitable material
(*b*) should be constructed, according to some suitable design, not indiscriminately
(*c*) should be scattered to provide for more of open space
(*d*) should be built to enable citizens to enjoy nature

6. The word 'drastic' in the passage means
(*a*) orderly. (*b*) powerful.
(*c*) consistent. (*d*) determined.

7. The author talks about 'Unspoilt Nature'. In what way can Nature remain unspoilt?
(*a*) If Nature is not allowed to interfere with people's day-to-day life
(*b*) By building cities with the system of organs like those of animals
(*c*) By allowing free access to parks and open spaces
(*d*) By allowing Nature to retain its primitive, undomesticated character

8. According to the author, the function of a city is to
(*a*) provide adequate community expression
(*b*) make available centres of recreation and public gatherings
(*c*) facilitate traffic and communication
(*d*) raise the tone of life and make it more meaningful

9. The opening sentence of the passage implies that
(*a*) the possibilities of living a decent life cannot be found in a city
(*b*) only a city can provide the means to lead a full life
(*c*) among other places, a city can also help man to lead a successful life
(*d*) a city provides better opportunities for good living than a village

Passage 5

A pioneering scheme has been started recently in Southampton on England's south coast to educate motorists who have been convicted of drunken driving.

The penalty for drunken driving might be the loss of a driving licence and a heavy fine. But under the new scheme, convicted drivers do not pay the fine. Instead they have to attend eight training sessions—one a week organized by the local authority probation service.

Designed to demonstrate the damage alcohol can do, the scheme was devised by senior probation officer John Cook. He said about a quarter of the people who came to him had a drink problem, but had not realized how much they were drinking.

One way of getting the message across was to make the drivers pour out their usual ration of alcohol and then measure it. Almost everyone pours out not a single measure but a double at least an example of how easy it is to have more than just one drink and to encourage other people to do the same.

The instructors on the course are giving clinical evidence of the effects of alcohol on the body and brain. The sober truth is that drinking badly affects driving skills, although the drinker might like to believe otherwise.

1. The Southampton scheme requires convicted drivers
- *(a)* to pay a heavy fine
- *(b)* to attend eight driving sessions once a week
- *(c)* to undergo a probation service
- *(d)* to surrender their driving licence

2. John Cook devised the scheme
- *(a)* as a demonstration technique for driving
- *(b)* to demonstrate the harmful effects of alcohol
- *(c)* to show that Southampton was concerned about drivers
- *(d)* to prove that alcohol does influence driving

3. The problem with a quarter of the people who went to John Cook was that they
- *(a)* did not want to stop drinking
- *(b)* were unaware of the fact that they could get drunk
- *(c)* would not admit that they had a drinking problem
- *(d)* did not know how much they were drinking

4. Most drivers start off with at least
- *(a)* a double measure
- *(b)* a single measure
- *(c)* a little less than a single measure
- *(d)* two doubles

5. The truth is that alcohol
- *(a)* does not affect the body but only the brain
- *(b)* affects only the brain
- *(c)* affects the body and the brain
- *(d)* has no effect on the body or the brain

Passage 6

The reformer must know that what moves people is the authentic life, not mere writing. The newspaper and journals that Lokmanya Tilak and other reformers ran, the books they wrote, sold little, but had enormous effect. Their writing was known to reflect and be just an extension of, their exemplary lives. It was the authenticity of their lives which lent weight to their message, to their example. All knew that their lives were an integral whole-they were not moral in public life and lax in private, nor vice versa. They were not full of pious thoughts and sacred resolutions within the walls of a temple.

A writer who is merely entertaining his readers, even one who is merely informing them, can do what he wants with the rest of his life. But the writer, who sets out to use his pen to reform public life, cannot afford such dualities. Here is the testimony of one great man-about the influence of another, Lokmanya Tilak.

"I believe that an editor who has anything worth saying and who commands a clientele cannot be easily hushed. He delivered his finished message as soon as he is put under duress. The Lokmanya spoke more eloquently from the Mandalay fortress than through columns of the printed Kesari.

His influence was multiplied thousand fold by his imprisonment and his speech and his pen had acquired much greater power after he was discharged than before his imprisonment. By his death we have been editing his paper without pen and speech through the sacred resolution of the people to realize his life's dream.

He could possibly have done more if he were today in the flesh preaching his view. Critics like me would perhaps be still finding fault in the expression of his or that. Today his message rules millions of hearts which are determined to raise a permanent living memorial by the fulfilment of his ambition in their lives."

1. Lokmanya Tilak's messages were most effective
(a) when he delivered them through his editorials
(b) after his death
(c) before his imprisonment
(d) when he delivered speeches
(e) None of the above

2. Which of the following is the result of Lokmanya Tilak's exemplary life?
(a) The newspapers edited by him did not incur monetary loss
(b) The books written by him were useful
(c) People resolved to fulfil his life's dream
(d) Critics still find fault with his views
(e) He was put in jail at Mandalay

3. Which of the following is the general tendency of critics according to the passage?
(a) To find fault with one or the other expression of a writer
(b) To praise only those writers whom they like
(c) To condemn one and all the reformer writers
(d) To suggest new ideas to the public
(e) To justify their criticism

4. In the context of the passage, a reformer becomes effective if
(a) he is a journalist with an objective viewpoint
(b) he is an author with an excellent style of writing
(c) he is an effective political leader of the masses
(d) he is a person with consistency in his writing and lifestyle
(e) he is good critic of social practices

5. In the context of the passage, which of the following statements about Lokmanya Tilak and the reformers is true?
(a) They were moral in private life but lax in public life
(b) Their influence on people was negligible
(c) Very few people used to read the newspapers edited by them
(d) They were allowed to edit their newspapers even from inside the jail
(e) Their influence was multiplied a thousand fold by their imprisonment

6. Which of the following types of writers can be moral in their personal life and lax in public life?
(a) Those who want to reform people
(b) Those who want to entertain people
(c) Those who have a large number of followers who wish to emulate them
(d) Those who lead an authentic life
(e) Those whose writing is an extension of their exemplary lives

Passage 7

A person who takes the trouble to form his own opinions and beliefs, will feel that he owes no responsibility to the majority for his conclusions. If he is a genuine lover of truth, if he is inspired by a passion for seeing things as they are and an abhorrence of holding ideas which do not conform to facts, he will be wholly independent of the assent of those around him. When he proceeds to apply his beliefs in the practical conduct of life, the position is different. There are then good reasons why his attitude should be less inflexible. The society in which he is placed is an ancient and composite growth. The people from whom he dissents have not come by their opinions, customs and by a process of mere haphazard.

These opinions and customs all had their origin in a certain real supposed fitness. They have certain depth of root in the lives of a proportion of the existing generation. Their congruity with one another may have come to an end. That is only one side of the truth. The most zealous propagandism cannot penetrate to them. In common language, we speak of a generation as something possessed of a kind of exact unity, with all its parts and members homogenous. Yet, plainly it is not this. It is a whole but a whole in a state of constant flux its factors and elements are eternally shifting. It is not one but many generations.

Each of the seven ages of man is neighbour to all the rest. The column of the veterans is already sinking into the last abyss, while the column of the newest recruits is forming to each its tradition, its tendency and its possibilities. Only a proportion of each can have nerve enough to grasp the banner of a new truth and endurance to bear it along rugged and untrodden ways. Thus we must remember the stuff of which life is made.

We must consider what an overwhelming preponderence of the most tenacious energies and most concentrated interests of a society must be absorbed between material cares and the solitude of the affections.

It is obviously unreasonable to lose patience and quarrel with one's time because it is tardy in throwing off its institutions and beliefs and slow to achieve the transformation which is the problem in front of it. Men and women have to live.

The task for most of us is arduous enough to make us well pleased with even such imperfect shelter as we find in daily use and wont.

To insist on whole community being made at once to submit to the reign of new practices and ideas that have just begun to commend themselves to the most advanced speculative intelligence of the time, this even if it were a possible process, would do hurry on social dissolution.

1. What is the hard task the author is referring to in the paragraph?
(a) To earn a living
(b) To live normal life
(c) To change the society
(d) To change according to times
(e) To find shelter

2. According to the passage, customs and traditions originate from?
(a) Beliefs
(b) Conflicts of life
(c) Social utility
(d) Contemporary leadership
(e) Ignorance

3. According to the author, the attitude of self-opinionated person in the practical social life should be

(*a*) rigid (*b*) flexible
(*c*) generous (*d*) optimistic
(*e*) revolutionary

4. According to the author, a generation is a whole but it is always

(*a*) homogeneous (*b*) unified in values
(*c*) growing (*d*) constant
(*e*) heterogeneous

5. What does the author mean by describing 'apply his beliefs in the practical conduct of life' in line six of the passage?

(*a*) To practise what he believes (*b*) To preach what he believes
(*c*) To indoctrinate what he believes (*d*) To adhere to what he believes
(*e*) To denounce what he believes

6. According to the author, why overnight change in social setting is not desirable?

(*a*) It will invigorate our life (*b*) It is difficult to bring about
(*c*) It will lead to social disintegration (*d*) It will retard progress of the society
(*e*) None of these

7. The author's attitude towards the problem he discusses is

(*a*) opportunistic (*b*) realistic
(*c*) pessimistic (*d*) intransient
(*e*) doctrinaire

Passage 8

The capitalist system of society does not foster healthy relations among human beings. A few people own all the means of production and others–though nominally few have to sell their labour under conditions imposed upon them. The emphasis of capitalism being on the supreme importance of material wealth the intensity of its appeal is to the acquisitive intensity. It promotes worship of economic power with little regard to the means employed for its acquisition and the end that it serves. By its exploitation of human beings to the limits of endurance its concentration is on the largest profit rather than maximum production.

Thus the division of human family is done on the basis of economic circumstance. All this is injurious to division of human dignity. And when the harrowed poor turn to the founders of religion for succour, they rather offer a subtle defence of the established order. They promise future happiness for their present suffering and conjure up visions of paradise to redress the balance to soothe the suffering and the revolt of the tortured men. The system imposes injustice, the religion justifies it.

1. The passage indicates that the capitalist system is

(*a*) fair (*b*) ambitious
(*c*) prosperous (*d*) dehumanising

2. The established order is supported by religion to

(*a*) alleviate the suffering of the poor in the capitalist system
(*b*) perpetuate the injustice imposed by the capitalist system
(*c*) balance the suffering of the poor with hopes of future rewards
(*d*) help the tortured men to seek redress

3. In a capitalist system
(*a*) the means justify the ends
(*b*) the ends justify the means
(*c*) the means endorsed by religion are strictly followed
(*d*) means which lead to exploitation are strictly prohibited

4. Capitalism is injurious to human relations because it divides society into two groups, *i.e.*
(*a*) working and non-working
(*b*) exploiters and exploited
(*c*) religious and irreligious
(*d*) buyers and sellers

5. In a capitalistic system of society each man wishes
(*a*) to acquire maximum wealth
(*b*) to produce maximum wealth
(*c*) to have visions of paradise
(*d*) to soothe the sufferings of other

Passage 9

If I had been asked in my early youth whether I preferred to have dealings only with men or only with books, my answer would certainly have been in favour of books. In later years this has become less and less. Not that I have had so much better experiences with men than with books, on the contrary delightful books even now come my way more often than purely delightful men. But the many bad experiences with men have nourished the meadow of my life as the noblest book could not do.

1. The author says that in later years his love of books diminished because
(*a*) he did not get many delightful books to read
(*b*) he had better experiences with men than with books
(*c*) he had given up the habit of reading books
(*d*) even the bad experiences he had with men were more valuable than what the noblest books could give

2. Which one of the following statements best reflects the main arguments of the passage?
(*a*) Books are always better than men
(*b*) There are more purely delightful men than purely delightful books
(*c*) It is the experience with other human beings that nourishes one's life and not necessarily books
(*d*) Neither men nor books give any worth while experience

3. Which one of the pairs of phrases best helps to bring out the metaphorical meaning of 'the meadow of my life'?
(*a*) Pure and healthy life
(*b*) Vast and rich life
(*c*) Well nourished but dull life
(*d*) Poor but simple life

4. In his early youth, the author
(*a*) liked to have more dealings with books than with men
(*b*) preferred to have dealings only with books
(*c*) liked to have more dealings with men than with books
(*d*) liked to have equal dealings with men and books

Passage 10

The stock-taking done at the first national convection on Consumer Protection served to highlight the areas that called for special attention to sustain the momentum of the movement as genuine forum for safeguarding the people's interests. Spreading awareness about the rights of the consumers and the relief open to them in case they did not get their money's worth of goods and services has rightly been identified as the first priority.

While this may not be a difficult task in urban areas, where the movement is concentrated at present, taking it to the vast rural hinterland calls for a multi-media approach in which radio and television have a crucial role to play. The involvement of the 500-odd consumer organizations in the country in publicising the concept of fair trade practices and the remedies available against their violation will prove rewarding, if the message is conveyed through village bodies. Government efforts remain confined at best to setting up the infrastructure after the formal launch of the movement with the enactment of the Consumer Protection Act. The mounting backlog of cases in consumer courts, points to the need for toning up the district level redressal machinery.

The main objective of the movement is the creation of a culture that denies place in the market for products that are not consumer friendly. This is possible only if consumer bodies take over the watch-dog role performed by the Government till now and exercise social control over the market to see that the benefits of liberalization are not reaped by traders alone. But the plea to industry to exercise self-regulation and maintain minimum standards of quality and devise appropriate pricing is bound to go unheeded unless strict measures are taken to ensure compliance.

1. The first national convention on Consumer Protection has

(a) highlighed the areas for special attention
(b) spread awareness about consumer rights
(c) specified in relief open to the consumer
(d) given it a momentum

2. Consumer Protection Act proposes to give the Consumer Protection against

(a) highly priced substandard goods
(b) cheating by selling substandard goods
(c) non-consumer friendly products
(d) denial of relief if the product is not upto the mark

3. Government contributed to the Consumer Protection Movement by

(a) toning up a district level redressal machinery
(b) clearing the backlog cases in the consumer court
(c) setting up infrastructure
(d) enactment of the Consumer Protection Act

4. Spreading Consumer Protection Movement to the rural areas needs

(a) official patronage
(b) a multi-media approach
(c) consumer organization to canvass this
(d) message to be conveyed by village bodies

5. Role of consumer bodies is
   (a) to maintain minimum standards of quality
   (b) to function as a watch-dog
   (c) to make a plea to industry to exercise self-control
   (d) to exercise social control over the market

Passage 11

Though the U.S. prides itself on being a leader in the world community, a recent report shows that it lags far behind other industrialized countries in meeting the needs of its youngest and most vulnerable citizens. The U.S. has a higher infant mortality-rate, a higher proportion of low birth-weight babies, a smaller proportion of babies immunized against childhood diseases and a much higher rate of adolescent pregnancies.

These findings, described as a 'quiet crisis' requiring immediate and far-reaching action, appeared in a report prepared by a task force of educators, doctors, politicians and business people. According to the report, a fourth of the nation's 12 million infants and toddlers live in poverty. As many as half confront risk factors that could harm their ability to develop intellectually, physically and socially. Child immunizations are too low, more children are born into poverty, more are in substandard care while their parents work and more are being raised by single parents. When taken together, these and other risk factors can lead to educational and health problems that are much harder and more costly to reverse.

The crisis begins in the womb with unplanned parenthood. Women with unplanned pregnancies are less likely to seek pre-natal care. In the U.S. 80% of teenage pregnancies and 56% of all pregnancies are unplanned. The problems continue after birth where unplanned pregnancies and unstable partnerships often go hand in hand. Since 1950, the number of single parent families has nearly tripled. More than 25 per cent of all births today are to unmarried mothers. As the number of single parent families grow and more women enter the work force, infants and toddlers are increasingly in the care of people other than their parents.

Most disturbingly, recent statistics show that American parents are increasingly neglecting or abusing their children. In only four years from 1987-1991, the number of children in foster care increased by over 50 per cent. Babies under the age of one are the fastest growing category of children entering foster care. The crisis affects children under the age of three most severely, the report says. Yet, it is this period-from infancy through pre-school years–that sets the stage for a child's future.

1. The main focus of the passage is on the plight of
   (a) orphaned children
   (b) teenage mothers
   (c) low birthweight babies
   (d) unwed mothers
   (e) None of these

2. Children falling in which age-group are most severely affected by the 'quiet crisis'?
   (a) Below one year
   (b) Below three years
   (c) Between two and three years
   (d) Between one and three years
   (e) None of these

3. Which of the following does not constitute the 'quiet crisis' in the U.S. as per the task force report?

(a) Lower proportion of new born babies with normal weight
(b) Higher incidence of adolecent girls becoming mothers
(c) Lower rate of babies surviving childhood diseases
(d) Larger proportion of babies who are deprived of immunization
(e) Increasing cases of teenage couples getting divorced

4. Which of the following statements is not true in the context of the passage?

(a) The number of single parent families today is approximately three times more than four decades ago
(b) The number of children in the U.S. entering foster care has decreased after 1991
(c) In the U.S., the number of infants living in poverty is about 3 million
(d) Only 20 per cent of all the pregnancies in the U.S. are planned
(e) About 6 million infants in the U.S. are likely to develop educational and health problems

5. The number of children born to married mothers in the U.S. is approximately how many times the number of children born to unwed mothers?

(a) 1.5 times *(b)* 2 times
(c) 3 times *(d)* 3.5 times
(e) Not mentioned in the passage

6. Children born out of unplanned pregnancies are highly vulnerable because

(a) they are raised by single parents
(b) their parents are mostly poor
(c) they are mostly malnourished
(d) they are less likely to receive prenatal care
(e) their parents are emotionally immature

7. Decide which of the following factors is/are responsible for the physical, intellectual and social under-development of infants in the U.S.?

A. Illiteracy of parents B. Lack of parental care C. Poverty

(a) Only A *(b)* Only B
(c) Only C *(d)* Both A and C
(e) Both B and C

8. An increasing number of infants in the U.S. are in foster care on account of

(a) an increasing number of single parent families with the female member working.
(b) an increasing number of women maintaining the status of unwed motherhood and becoming economically independent.
(c) an increasing number of employed couples who are required to stay apart.
(d) an increasing number of women getting divorced and abandoning their babies.
(e) an increasing number of parents who lack awareness about baby-care.

9. The task force report seems to be based on the data pertaining to the period

(a) 1987-91. *(b)* 1950 onwards till date
(c) 1987 onwards till date *(d)* 1950-91
(e) 1991 onwards till date

Directions *Choose the word which is most nearly the same in meaning as the given word as used in the passage.*

10. Confront

(a) face *(b)* tolerate
(c) succumb *(d)* eliminate
(e) oppose

11. Vulnerable

(a) insecure
(b) indispensable
(c) risky
(d) promising
(e) delicate

12. Abusing

(a) cursing
(b) beating
(c) Ill treating
(d) accusing
(e) oppressing

Directions *Choose the word which is most opposite in meaning to the given word as used in the passage.*

13. Severely

(a) drastically
(b) intensely
(c) minutely
(d) normally
(e) slightly

14. Unstable

(a) changing
(b) steady
(c) stagnant
(d) confined
(e) constant

15. Substandard

(a) impoverished
(b) compassionate
(c) excellent
(d) beneficial
(e) valuable

Passage 12

Street theatre in India is a well established ancient art form despite the proliferation of modern means of entertainment and communication, steet theatre continues to flourish in India. Street theatre as a channel of communication has for centuries been propagating reforms by highlighting social, economic and political issues present in the society.

Unlike in the olden days, its performance is no longer restricted to villages or small localities of the city. Today small groups of performers including students, would stage performances to mobilise public opinion or to help create or raise awareness over a particular public importance.

Themes on substance abuse, AIDS awarencess and domestic villages are some of the areas highlighted by contemporary street theatre troupe. Unlike regular drama, street drama employs very little props and images. the human body becomes the main tool in which choreography, mime, dialogues, songs and slogans are extensively used.

Street theatre is one of the most intimate media. Its appeal is to the emotions leading to quick psychological impact on audiences. By being local and live they also are able to establish not only direct contact with the audience, but by being cost-effective and flexible they are popular among all age groups.

1. Modern means of entertainment and communication ... street theatre.

(a) does affect
(b) does not affect
(c) helps pupularise
(d) help establish

2. In the olden days street theatre ... to villages or small localities of the city.
(a) was restricted (b) was not restricted
(c) was opened (d) was entertained

3. Street theatre usually...with issues of public importance.
(a) is distanced (b) is performed
(c) deals (d) does not deal

4. Street theatre is ... than stage.
(a) nothing (b) costly
(c) reasonable (d) affordable

5. Street theatre creates an/a ... impact on audiences.
(a) intimate (b) emotional
(c) mystical (d) physical

Passage 13

Self-directed learning, in its broadest meaning, describes a process in which individuals take the initiative with or without the help of others, in diagnosing their learning needs, formulation of learning goals, identifying resources for learning, choosing and implementing learning strategies and evaluating learning, outcomes. Thus, it is important to attain new knowledge easily and skillfully for the rest of his or her life.

What is the need for self-directed learning? One reason is that there is convincing evidence that people, who take the initiative in learning, learn more things and learn better than people waiting to be taught. the second reason is that self-directed learning is more in tune with our natural processes of psychological development; an essential aspect of maturing is developing the ability to take increasing responsibility of our own lives to become increasingly self-directed. The third reason is that many of the new development in education put a heavy responsibility on the learners to take a good deal of initiative in their own learning. To meet the challenges in today's instructive environment, self-directed learning is most essential.

1. In self-directed learning, an individual
(a) takes initiative with or without the help of others
(b) is passive and waits for directions
(c) is helpless and dependent
(d) takes initiative, without an objective

2. There is need for self-directed learning because
(a) it is less challenging
(b) it helps people to learn more things and learn better
(c) it is more cost-effective method
(d) it is a modern method of learning

3. Which word best describes self-directed learning?
(a) Active learning (b) Passive learning
(c) Compulsory learning (d) Repulsive learning

4. The modern environment according to the author is
(a) restrictive (b) instructive
(c) less developed (d) impracticable

5. The synonym of the word 'diagnosing' is
(a) searching
(b) examining
(c) identifying
(d) complying

Passage 14

The stunning Baltimore Oriole is a common summer visitor to Eastern and mid Western deciduous woodlands, neighbourhoods and gardens. Baltimore Orioles winter in the tropics. About 7 inches in length, the male Baltimore Oriole has a black head, throat, back and wings. Its breast, stomach and rump are bright orange. It also has an orange patch on the top of each wing and white wing bars. The tail is mostly black with orange fringes. The female is dull orange throughout.

Baltimore Orioles range throughout the Eastern and mid Western United States and can be found as far West as the Dakotas. At the Western edge of their range, Baltimore Orioles may breed with the Bullock's Oriole (They were once considered the same species under the name Northern Oriole). Baltimore Orioles build unusual pouch like nests that hang down from branches.

They usually nest high in the trees, but often come down to lower heights, flashing bright orange and black feathers to delighted observers. Active and acrobatic by nature, Baltimore Orioles may even feed upside down at times. Baltimore Orioles eat insects and berries. They can easily be attracted to gardens by nailing orange wedges to tree branches. Baltimore Orioles are also known to feed at hummingbird feeders and sapsucker wells.

1. The Baltimore Oriole spend winters in the
(a) dakotas
(b) carolinas
(c) tropics
(d) deserts

2. What is the colour of the female Baltimore Oriole?
(a) Bright orange
(b) Light orange
(c) Dull orange
(d) White

3. Which of the following does not attract the Baltimore Oriole?
(a) Oranges
(b) Hummingbird feeders
(c) Sapsucker wells
(d) Sunflower seeds

4. The Baltimore Oriole can be found as far West as
(a) North and South Dakota
(b) The Carolina
(c) California
(d) Baltimore

5. Which of the following is incorrect about the Baltimore Oriole?
(a) They feed upside down sometimes
(b) They may breed with the Bullock's Oriole
(c) The Baltimore Oriole is uncommon in the US
(d) The Baltimore Oriole has a black throat

6. Where would I probably not find a Baltimore Oriole?
(a) High in the trees
(b) In gardens and neighbourhoods
(c) Deciduous woodlands
(d) The Sahara desert

7. The nest of the Baltimore Oriole
(a) is in a tree cavity
(b) stands upon a branch of a tree
(c) hangs from a branch of a tree
(d) is usually low in the branches

8. The other name of Baltimore Oriole was

(a) Bullock's Oriole
(b) Baltimore's Oriole
(c) Northern Oriole
(d) Southern Oriole

9. Which of these colours is not found on a Baltimore Oriole?

(a) Purple
(b) Orange
(c) White
(d) Black

10. Which of the following is the closest in size to a Baltimore Oriole?

(a) The size of a half-scale
(b) A little more than a half-scale
(c) A-little less than a half-scale
(c) A foot ruler

Passage 15

As the rulers of the planet, humans like to think that it is the large creatures who will emerge victorious from the struggle for survival. However, nature teaches us the opposite it is often the smallest species which are the toughest and most adaptable. A perfect example is the hummingbird, which is found in the Americas. One species of hummingbird is known as the bee hummingbird ranks as the world's smallest and lightest bird and it is barely visible when it is in flight.

Humming birds are the only birds that can fly backwards. They feed mainly on the nectar of flowers, a liquid that is rich in energy. Nectar is an ideal food source, for hummingbirds need an incredible amount of energy to sustain their body metabolism. A hummingbird's wings flap at a rate of about 80 times per second and its tiny heart beats more then 1000 times per minute. This is why they must consume relatively large quantities of food. In the course of a day, a hummingbird consumes about half its body weight in nectar.

1. Nature has made man realise the fact that

(a) the large creatures emerge victorious from the struggle for survival
(b) the smallest creatures are the toughest and most adaptable
(c) humans who rule the planet are the most powerful beings on Earth
(d) the largest and the smallest species are equally tough and strong

2. Which of the following statements about the bee hummingbird is true?

(a) It is obviously visible when it flies
(b) It escapes our sight when it is in flight
(c) It could fly hight beyond the clouds
(d) It cannot be seen when it is in flight

3. Hummingbirds need a lot of energy in order to

(a) maintain their body metabolism
(b) flap their wings and fly backwards
(c) sustain a steady rhythm of heart-beat
(d) win in the struggle for survival

4. The hummingbirds are exclusive in the sense that

(a) they subsist only on nectar
(b) their pulse rate is more than 1000 per minute
(c) they consume half their body weight everyday
(d) they can fly backwards

5. The word, 'incredible' in the passage mean

(a) tremendous
(b) inexhaustible
(c) unbelievable
(d) phenomenal

Revision Exercise

Passage 1

John had never thought much about the origin of wealth or inequalities in life. It was his firm belief that if this world was not good, the next would be good and this faith sustained him. He was not like some others whom he knew, who would sell their souls to the devil.

He always thought of God before doing anything. He lived the life of an honest man. He had not married, but did not desire another man's wife. He believed that women weakened men as was described in the story of Samson and Delilah.

1. "To sell one's soul to the devil" means
(a) suppressing one's conscience
(b) giving up goodness in exchange for evil
(c) giving up one's honesty for the sake of monetary benefits
(d) to sell oneself to earn livelihood

2. John thought that women weakened men because
(a) he thought that women were evil
(b) he believed that a woman was a fancy devil
(c) he thought that a woman would spoil his life
(d) he was convinced that what the story of Samson and Delilah illustrates is correct

3. It was John's belief that
(a) one can be happy only by remaining a bachelor
(b) the world is a happy place
(c) there is no other world
(d) one must lead an honest life

4. By not desiring another man's wife John showed that
(a) he wanted to get married
(b) he was a man of principles
(c) he felt sorry for other men
(d) he had no desire for another's wealth

5. From the above passage we understand that John was
(a) not highly educated
(b) a man of simple faith
(c) a deeply pessimistic man
(d) a scholar of scriptures

Passage 2

Stammering is a habit disorder linked with lack of self-confidence. Basically, for a child to understand a language, there are four stages. The first is learning to understand the spoken language and the second is speaking. Both of these usually develop around the age of two.

The third stage is speaking complex sentences, which develops at around 3rd and the 4th is when the child recognises the written alphabet. In 80% of children while the 3rd and 4th stage are at play, the first two get disturbed because something new is being incorporated in the mind.

This is absolutely normal. But what over cautious mothers do is fret a lot and the child develops a fear which later manifests itself as stammering. In fact, most text books on stammering state in bold that "Had there not been any over cautious mothers, hardly any one would have suffered from stammering." Fluency can be incorporated in the speech of such patients through hypnosis.

1. Stammering is caused because of
(*a*) physical disorder
(*b*) hindered growth
(*c*) lack of self-confidence
(*d*) lack of understanding

2. The second stage of a child's understanding the language is
(*a*) speaking
(*b*) writing
(*c*) listening
(*d*) reading

3. .... are basically the reason for developing a fear in the child's mind.
(*a*) Parents
(*b*) Over cautious mothers
(*c*) Fathers
(*d*) Uncles

4. Fluency in such patients can be incorporated in the speech of such patients through
(*a*) hypnosis
(*b*) slap
(*c*) punishment
(*d*) symbiosis

5. By the time the child becomes two years old he/she can
(*a*) speak complex sentences
(*b*) only understand spoken language
(*c*) understand and speak simple language
(*d*) write the alphabets

Passage 3

The e-waste (Management and Handling) Rules, 2011, notified by the Ministry of Environment and Forests, have the **potential to turn** a growing problem into a developmental opportunity. With almost half-a-year to go before the rules take **effect**, there is enough time to create the necessary infrastructure for collection, dismantling, and recycling of electronic waste. The focus must be on sincere and efficient implementation. Only decisive action can reduce the pollution and health costs associated with India's hazardous waste recycling industry. If India can achieve a transformation, it will be creating a whole new employment sector that provides good wages and working conditions for tens of thousands.

The legacy response of the states to even the basic law on urban waste, the Municipal Solid Wastes (Management and Handling) Rules, has been one of **indifference**, many cities continue to simply burn the garbage or dump it in lakes. With the emphasis now on segregation of waste at source and recovery of materials, it should be **feasible** to implement **both sets of rules** efficiently, A welcome feature of the new e-waste rules is the emphasis on extended producer responsibility. In other words, producers must take responsibility for the disposal of end-of-life products. For this provision to work, they must ensure that consumers who sell scrap get some form of financial incentive.

The e-waste rules, which derive from those pertaining to hazardous waste, are scheduled to come into force on 1st May, 2012. Sound as they are, the task of scientifically disposing a few hundred thousand tonnes of trash electronics annually depends heavily on a system of oversight by State Pollution Control Boards (PCBs). Unfortunately, most PCBs remain unaccountable and often lack the resources for active enforcement.

It must be pointed out that, although agencies handling e-waste must obtain environmental **clearances** and be authorised and registered by the PCBs even under the Hazardous Wastes (Management, Handling and Transboundary Movement) Rules, 2008, there has been little practical impact. Over 95% of electronic waste is collected and recycled by the informal sector. The way forward is for the , PCBs to be made accountable for enforcement of the e-waste rules and the levy of penalties under environmental laws. Clearly, the first order priority is to create a system that will absorb the 80000-strong workforce in the informal sector into the proposed scheme for scientific recycling. Facilities must be created to upgrade the skills of these workers through training and their occupational health must be ensured.

Recycling of e-waste is one of the biggest challenges today. In such a time, when globalization and information technology are growing at a pace **which could only be imagined few years back**, e-waste and its hazards have become more prominent over a period of time and should be given immediate attention.

1. What according to the passage is important now for e-waste management?
(a) Making rules
(b) Reviewing rules
(c) Implementing rules
(d) Notifying rules
(e) Amending rules

2. Which of the following can be one of the by-products of effective e-waste management?
(a) India can guide other countries in doing so
(b) It will promote international understanding
(c) It will promote national integration
(d) It will create a new employment sector
(e) It will further empower judiciary

3. Which of the following rules has not been indicated in the passage?
(a) e-waste Rules, 2011
(b) Pollution Check Rules
(c) Hazardous Wastes Rules, 2008
(d) Municipal Solid Wastes Rules
(e) All of these have been indicated

4. **"both sets of rules"** is being refered to which of the following?
(a) Solid wastes and Hazardous wastes
(b) e-waste and Hazardous waste
(c) Solid waste and e-waste
(d) e-waste and e-production
(e) Solid waste and recycling waste

5. e-waste rules have been derived from those pertaining to
(a) Hazardous waste
(b) PC waste
(c) Computer waste
(d) Municipal solid waste
(e) National waste

6. Which of the following will help implement "both sets of rules"?
(a) Employment opportunities
(b) International collaboration
(c) Financial incentive
(d) Segregation of waste at source
(e) Health costs

7. e-waste Rules came/come into force from
(a) 2008
(b) 2009
(c) 2010
(d) 2011
(e) 2012

8. Which of the following best explains the meaning of the phrase "**which could only be imagined few years back**", as used in the passage ?
(a) It was doomed
(b) It took us few years
(c) It took us back by few years
(d) Imagination is better than IT
(e) None of these

9. Which of the following is true in the context of the passage ?

(a) No city dumps its waste in lakes
(b) Some cities burn garbage
(c) PCBs have adequate resources for active enforcement
(d) e-waste was a much bigger challenge in the past
(e) None of the above

10. Which of the following is not true in the context of the passage?

(a) Some form of financial incentive is recommended for the producers
(b) Some financial incentive is recommended for the consumers
(c) e-waste will be a few hundred thousand tonnes
(d) The agencies handling e-waste have to obtain environmental clearances
(e) Those involved in e-waste management would need to upgrade their skills

Passage 4

Organized retail has **fuelled** new growth categories-like liquid hand wash, breakfast cereals and pet food in the consumer goods industry, accounting for almost 50% of their sales, said data from market search firm Nielsen. The figures showed some of these new categories got more than 40% of their business from modern retail outlets. The data also suggests how products in these categories reach the neighbourhood kirana stores after they have established themselves in modern trade.

While grocers continue to be an important channel, for the new and evolving categories we saw an increased presence of high-end products in modern trade. e.g., **premium** products in laundry detergents, dishwashing, car air fresheners and surface care increased in availability through this format as these products are aimed at **affluent** consumers who are more likely to shop in supermarket/hypermarket outlets and who are willing to pay more for specialized products.

Some other categories that have grown exceptionally and now account for bulk of the sales from modern retail are frozen and ready-to-eat foods, pet food, diapers, pre- and post-wash products, hair conditioners and high-end shaving products, besides others. "With the evolution of modern trade, our growth in this channel has been healthy as it is for several other categories. Modern retail is an important part of our business" said managing director, Kellogg India.

What modern retail offers to companies experimenting with new categories is the chance to educate customers which was not the case with a general trade store. "Category creation and market development starts with modern trade but as more consumers start consuming this category, they **penetrate into other channels**, said President, food & FMCG category, Future Group the country's largest retailer which operates stores like Big Bazaar.

But a point to note here is that modern retailers themselves push their own private brands in these very categories and can emerge as a big threat for the consumers goods and foods companies. For instance, Big Bazaar's private label Clean Mate is hugely popular and sells more than a brand like Harpic in its own stores. "So, there is a certain amount of conflict and competition that will play out over the next few years which the FMCG companies will have to **watch out for**", said KPMG's executive director (retail).

In the past, there have been instances of retailers boycotting products from big FMCG players on the issue of margins, but as modern retail becomes increasingly significant for **pushing** new categories, experts say we could see more partnerships being forged between retailers and FMCG companies. "Market development for new categories takes time so brand wars for leadership and consumer franchise will be fought on the modern retail platform. A new brand can overnight compete with **established** companies by tying up with few retailers in these categories", President of Future Group added.

1. Which of the following is being referred to as new growth category?
(a) Soap cake
(b) Fresh fruits
(c) Fresh vegetables
(d) Liquid Hand-wash
(e) Usual groceries

2. Which of the following is being referred to as modern retail outlet?
(a) Kirana Store
(b) On-line Store
(c) Door-to-door Selling
(d) Road-side Hawkers
(e) Supermarket

3. Which of the following best conveys the meaning of the phrase, "**watch out for**" as used in the passage ?
(a) Demand justice
(b) Avoid conflict
(c) Be on the alert
(d) Passively accept
(e) Open for competition

4. Which of the following is being referred to as 'certain amount of conflict'?
(a) Retailers selling their own products with products of companies
(b) Retailers selling similar products of different consumer companies
(c) Offering differential rate of margin for different products
(d) New products killing the old products
(e) Different retailers selling same category of products

5. The new growth category products
(a) reach first the neighbourhood Kirana shop and then the modern retail outlets
(b) account for less than 20% of sales in organized retail
(c) reach all the outlets almost at the same time
(d) first become popular in modern trade outlets before reaching Kirana shops
(e) are aimed at the poor section of the society

6. Which of the following is not true in the context of the passage?
(a) Clean Mate is a product of an organized retailer
(b) Some retailers don't keep some products if the profit margin is not good
(c) A new brand can never quickly displace an established brand
(d) Kirana store still remains an important channel
(e) In future there will be more partnerships between retailers and FMCG Companies

7. Which of the following categories has become very popular through sales from modern retail outlets?
(a) Frozen foods
(b) Computers
(c) Cell phones
(d) Fresh fruits
(e) Soft-drinks

8. Which class/section of people are more likely to shop in Hypermarket outlets?
(a) Senior citizens
(b) Younger generation
(c) Rich consumers
(d) Poor section
(e) Women

9. Which of the following advantages do modern retail outlets provide for new categories of products as compared to general trade stores?

(a) Higher profit margins
(b) Experimenting with new products
(c) Competition with similar products
(d) Better packing of the product
(e) Products at much lower-price

10. " ...... penetrate into other Channels." Which of the following is being referred to as Channels?

(a) Products
(b) Companies
(c) New products
(d) Existing products
(e) None of these

Passage 5

In a reversal of the norm elsewhere, in India policymakers and economists have become optimists while bosses do the worrying. The country's Central Bank has predicted that the country's economy is likely to grow at a double digit rate during the next 20-30 years. India has the capability with its vast labour and lauded entrepreneurial spirit. But the private sector which is supposed to do the heavy lifting that turns India from the world's tenth largest economy to its third largest by 2030 has become fed up. Business people often carp about India's problems but their irritation this time has a nervous edge.

In the first quarter of 2011, GDP grew at an annual rate of 7.8%; in 2005-07 it managed 9-10%. The economy may be slowing naturally as the low interest rates and public spending that got India through the global crisis are belatedly withdrawn. At the same time the surge in inflation caused by exorbitant food prices has spread more widely, casting doubt over whether India can grow at 8-10 per cent in the medium term without overheating.

In India, as in many fast growing nations, the confidence to invest depends on the conviction that the long term trajectory is intact and it is that which is in doubt. Big Indian firms too sometimes seem happier to invest abroad than at home, in deals that are often hailed as symbols of the country's growing **clout** but sometimes speak to its weaknesses-purchases of natural resources that India has in abundance but struggles to get out of the ground. In fact a further dip in investment could be self-fulfilling: if fewer roads, ports and factories are built, this will hurt both short term growth figures and reduce the economy's long term capacity.

There is a view that because a fair amount of growth is assured the government need not try very hard, The liberalisation reforms that began in 1991 freed markets for products and gave rise to vibrant competition, at the same time what economists call factor markets, those for basic inputs like land, power, labour etc. remain unreformed and largely under state control, which creates difficulties. Clearances today can take three to four years and many employers are keen to replace workers with machines despite an abundance of labour force.

This can be attributed to labour laws which are inimical to employee creation and an education system that means finding quality manpower a major problem. In fact the Planning Commission, concluded that even achieving 9% growth will need **marked** policy action in unreformed sectors. Twenty years ago it was said that the yardstick against which India should be measured was its potential and it is clear that there remains much to do.

1. Which of the following can be said about the Indian economy at present?
(a) It can comfortably achieve double digit growth rate at present
(b) High food prices have fed to overheating of the economy
(c) Citizens are affluent owing to laxity in regulation
(d) Private sector confidence in India's growth potential is high
(e) Unreformed sectors are a drag on economic growth

2. Why are employers reluctant to hire Indian labour force?
(A) India's labour force is overqualified for the employment opportunities available.
(B) High attrition rate among employees stemming from their entrepreneurial spirit.
(C) Labour laws are not conducive to generating employment.
(a) Only C
(b) All of these
(c) Both A and C
(d) Both A and B
(e) None of these

3. What is the state of India's basic input sectors at present?
(a) These sectors attract Foreign Direct Investment because of their vast potential
(b) These sectors are lagging as projects are usually awarded to foreign companies
(c) These sectors are stagnating and badly in need of reforms
(d) These sectors are well regulated as these are governed by the State
(e) None of the above

4. What is the author's main objective in writing the passage?
(a) Showcasing the potential of India's growth potential to entice foreign investors
(b) Exhorting India to implement measures to live up to its potential
(c) Recommending India's model of development to other developing countries
(d) Berating the private sector for not bidding for infrastructure development projects
(e) Criticising the measures taken by India during the global economic crisis

5. What impact has the GDP growth of 7.8% had?
(A) Indian Industry is anxious about India's economic growth.
(B) India has achieved status as the world's third largest economy at present.
(C) Foreign investment in India has drastically increased.
(a) Only A
(b) All of these
(c) Both A and C
(d) Both A and B
(e) None of these

6. Which of the following is most similar in meaning to the word **Clout** given in bold as used in the passage?
(a) Strike
(b) Standing
(c) Force
(d) Launch
(e) Achieve

7. Which of the following is most opposite in meaning to the word **Marked** given in bold as used in the passage?
(a) Decreased
(b) Ignored
(c) Clear
(d) Assessed
(e) Imperceptible

8. What measures do experts suggest be taken to ensure targeted economic growth?
(a) Lowering of interest rates to help industries hit by recession
(b) Prolonged financial support for basic input industries
(c) Incentives to Indian companies to invest in infrastructure
(d) Formulation of policies and their implementation in factor markets
(e) Stringent implementation of licensing system

Passage 6

In many countries, a combustible mixture of authoritarianism, unemployment and youth has given rise to disaffection with strongmen rulers which has in turn spilled over into uprisings. Young people in these countries are far better educated than their parents were. In 1990 the average Egyptian had 4.4 years of schooling; by 2010 the figure had risen to 7.1 years. Could it be that education, by making people less willing to put up with restrictions on freedom and more willing to question authority, **promotes** democratization. Ideas about the links between education, income and democracy are at the heart of what social scientists have long studied.

Since then plenty of economists and political scientists have looked for statistical evidence of a causal link between education and democratization. Many have pointed to the strong correlation that exists between levels of education and measures like the pluralism of party politics and the existence of civil liberties. The patterns are similar when income and democracy are considered. There are outliers, of course - until recently, many Arab countries managed to combine energy-based wealth and decent education with undemocratic political systems. But some deduce from the overall picture that as China and other authoritarian states get more educated and richer, their people will agitate for greater political freedom, culminating in a shift to a more democratic form of government.

This apparently reasonable intuition is shakier than it seems. Critics of the hypothesis point out that correlation is hardly causation. The general trend over the past half-century may have been towards rising living standards, a wider spread of basic education and more democracy, but it is entirely possible that this is being driven by another variable. Even if the correlation were not spurious, it would be difficult to know which way causation ran.

Does more education lead to greater democracy? Or are more democratic countries better at educating their citizens? A recent NBER paper compared a group of Kenyan girls in 69 primary schools whose students were randomly selected to receive a scholarship with similar students in schools which received no such financial aid. Previous studies had shown that the scholarship programme led to higher test scores and increased the likelihood that girls enrolled in secondary school.

Overall, it significantly increased the amount of education obtained. For the new study the authors tried to see how the extra schooling had affected the political and social attitudes of the women in question. Findings suggested that education may make people more interested in improving their own lives but they may not necessarily see democracy as the way to do it.

Even in established democracies, more education does not always mean either more active political participation or greater faith in democracy. Poorer and less educated people often vote in larger numbers than their more educated compatriots, who often express disdain for the **messiness of democracy** yearning for the kind of government that would deal strongly with the corrupt and build highways, railway lines and bridges at a dizzying pace of authoritarian China.

1. Which of the following most aptly describes the central theme of the passage?
   (a) Democratic nations are richer and have a better track record of educating their citizens
   (b) Education does not necessarily lead to greater enthusiasm for a democratic form of government
   (c) Educated societies with autocratic form of government enjoy a better quality of life than democracies
   (d) Citizens can fulfill their personal aspirations only under a democratic form of government
   (e) Democracy makes citizens more intolerant as it does not restrict personal freedoms

2. Which of the following is most similar in meaning to the word **Promotes** given in bold as used in the passage?
   (a) Upgrades　　*(b)* Prefers
   (c) Recommends　　*(d)* Advocates
   (e) Publicises

3. What conclusion can be drawn from the statistics, cited about Egypt's education system?
   (a) Job prospects have been on the rise in Egypt in recent times
   (b) Authoritarian leaders have played a vital role in reforming Egypt's education system
   (c) Egypt has one of the youngest and best educated demographies in the world
   (d) Egypt is likely to be successful vibrant democracy
   (e) There has been a rise in education levels in Egypt in recent times

4. In the context of the passage which of the following characterise(s) democracies?
   (A) Active participation of majority of educated citizens in electoral process.
   (B) Fast paced economic growth and accountability of those in power,
   (C) Better standards of living and access to higher education.
   (a) All of these　　*(b)* Both B and C
   (c) Only C　　*(d)* Both A and B
   (e) None of these

5. What according to the author has led to uprisings in authoritarian countries?
   (a) Lack of access to education
   (b) Vast numbers of uneducated and unemployable youth
   (c) Frustration with the existing system of governance
   (d) Unavailability of natural energy resources like coal and oil
   (e) Government's overambitious plans for development

6. Which of the following is/are true about China in the context of the passage?
   (A) China's citizens are in favour of a more representative form of government.
   (B) China has made huge strides in infrastructure developments.
   (C) China is in the midst of a political revolution.
   (a) None of these　　*(b)* Only A
   (c) Both A and C　　*(d)* Only B
   (e) All of these

7. What does the phrase **"messiness of democracy"** convey in the context of the passage?
   (a) Democratic nations are chaotic on account of individual freedoms
   (b) Most democratic countries frequently have violent revolts among their citizens
   (c) The divide between the poor and educated is growing wider in democracies
   (d) High levels of pollution on account of frentic pace of infrastructure development
   (e) Resigned acceptance of intrinsic corruption in the education system

Passage 7

When times are hard, doomsayers are aplenty. The problem is that if you listen to them too carefully, you tend to overlook the most obvious signs of change. 2011 was a bad year, Can 2012 be any worse ? Doomsday forecasts are the easiest to make these days, So, let's try a contrarian's forecast instead. Let's start with the global economy. We have soon a steady flow of good news from the US. The employment situation seems to be improving rapidly and consumer sentiment, reflected in retail expenditures on discretionary items like electronics and clothes, has picked up.

If these trends sustain, the US might post better growth numbers for 2012 than the 1.5-1.8% being forecast currently. Japan is likely to pull out of a recession in 2012, as post-earthquake reconstruction efforts gather momentum and the fiscal stimulus announced in 2011 begins to pay off. The consensus estimate for growth in Japan is a respectable 2% for 2012. The "hard-landing" scenario for China remains and will remain a **myth**. Growth might decelerate further from the 9% that it expected to clock in 2011, but is unlikely to drop below 8-8.5 % in 2012.

Europe is certainly in a spot of trouble. It is perhaps already in recession and for 2012, it is likely to post mildly negative growth. The risk of implosion has dwindled over the last few months -peripheral economies like Greece, Italy and Spain have new governments in place and have made progress towards genuine economic reform.

Even with some of these positive factors in place, we have to accept the fact that global growth in 2012 will be **tepid**. But there is a flipside to this. Softer growth means lower demand for commodities and this is likely to drive a correction in commodity prices. Lower commodity inflation will enable emerging market and central banks to reverse their monetary stance. China, for instance, has already reversed its stance and has pared its reserve ratio twice. The RBI also seems poised for a reversal in its rate cycle as headline inflation seems well on its way to its target of 7% for March, 2012.

That said, oil might be an exception to the general trend in commodities. Rising geopolitical tensions, particularly the continuing face-off between Iran and the US, might lead to a spurt in prices. It might make sense for our oil companies to hedge this risk instead of buying oil in the spot market. As inflation fears **abate** and emerging market and central banks begin to cut rates, two things could happen. Lower commodity inflation would mean lower interest rates and better credit availability. This could set a floor to growth and slowly reverse the business cycle within these economies.

Second, as the fear of untamed, runaway inflation in these economies abates, the global investor's comfort levels with their markets will increase. Which of the **emerging** markets will outperform and who will get left behind? In an environment in which global growth is likely to be weak, economies like India, that have a powerful domestic consumption, should lead; those dependent on exports should, prima facia, fall behind. Specifically for India, a fall in the exchange rate could not have come at a better time. It will help Indian exporters gain market share even if global trade remains depressed. More importantly, it could lead to massive import substitution that favours domestic producers. Let's now focus on India and start with a caveat.

It is important not to confuse a short-run cyclical dip with a permanent do-rating of its long-term structural potential. The arithmetic is simple. Our growth rate can be in the range of 7-10% depending on policy action. 10%, if we get everything right, 7% if we get it all-wrong. Which policies and reforms are critical to taking us to our 10% potential ? In judging this, let's again be careful. Let's not go by the laundry list of reforms that FIIs like to wave increase in foreign equity limits in foreign shareholding, greater voting rights for institutional shareholders in banks, FDI in retail, etc. These can have an impact only at the margin. We need not bend over backwards to appease the FIIs through these reforms- they will invest in our markets when momentum picks up and will be the first to exit when the momentum flags, reforms or not.

The reforms that we need are the ones that can actually raise our sustainable long-term growth rate. These have to come in areas like better targeting of subsidies, making projects in infrastructure viable so that they **draw** capital, raising the productivity of agriculture improving healthcare and education, bringing the parallel economy under the tax net, implementing fundamental reforms in taxation like GST and the direct tax code and finally easing the **myriad** rules and regulations that make doing business in India such a nightmare. A number of these things do not require new legislation and can be done through executive order.

1. Which of the following is not true according to the passage?
(a) China's economic growth may decline in the year 2012, as compared to the year 2011
(b) The European Economy is not doing very well
(c) Greece is on the verge of bringing about economic reforms
(d) In the year 2012, Japan may post a positive growth and thus pull out of recession
(e) All of the above are true

2. Which of the following will possibly be a result of softer growth estimated for the year 2012 ?
(A) Prices of oil will not increase. (B) Credit availability would be lesser.
(C) Commodity inflation would be lesser.

Which of the statements given above is/are correct?
(a) Only B *(b)* Both A and B
(c) Both A and C *(d)* Only C
(e) All of these

3. Which of the following can be said about the present status of the US Economy?
(a) There is not much improvement in the economic scenario of the country from the year 2011
(b) The growth in the economy of the country, in the year 2012, would definitely be lesser than 1.8%
(c) The expenditure on clothes and electronic commodities, by in consumers, is lesser than that in the year 2011
(d) There is a chance that in 2012, the economy would do better than what has been forecasted
(e) The pace of change in the employment scenario of the country is very slow

4. Which of the following is possibly the most appropriate title for the passage?
(a) The Economic Disorder
(b) Indian Economy Versus the European Economy
(c) Global Trade
(d) The Current Economic Scenario
(e) Characteristics of the Indian Economy

5. According to the author, which of the following would characterise Indian growth scenario in 2012?

(A) Domestic producers will take a hit because of depressed global trade scenario

(B) On account of its high domestic consumption. India will lead

(C) Indian exporters will have a hard time in gaining market share

Which of the statements given above is/are correct?

(a) Only A
(b) Both A and B
(c) Both B and C
(d) Only A
(e) All of these

6. Why does the author not recommend taking up the reforms suggested by FIIs?

(a) These will bring about only minor growth

(b) The reforms suggested will have no effect on the economy of our country, whereas will benefit the FIIs significantly

(c) The previous such recommendations had backfired

(d) These reforms will be the sole reason for our country's economic downfall

(e) The reforms suggested by them are not to be trusted as they will not bring about any positive growth in India

7. Which of the following is true as per the scenario presented in the passage?

(a) The highest growth rate that India can expect is 7%

(b) The fall in the exchange rate will prove beneficial to India

(c) Increased FDI in retail as suggested by FIIs would benefit , India tremendously

(d) The reforms suggested by the author require new legislation in India

(e) None of the above is true

8. According to the author, which of the following reform/s is/are needed to ensure long term growth in India?

(A) Improving healthcare and educational facilities.

(B) Bringing about reforms in taxation.

(C) Improving agricultural productivity.

Which of the statements given above is/are correct?

(a) Only B
(b) Both A and B
(c) Both B and C
(d) Only A
(e) All of these

Passage 8

A majority of Indians prefer to use the internet for accessing banking and other financial services than shopping online, shows a new survey.

Almost 57% of Indian respondents using the internet prefer to bank online and use other financial services due to **hassle-free** access and time saving feature of online banking according to the survey.

Checking information on products and services online comes a close second at 53% while 50% shop for products online. The fourth on the list-around 42% of respondents in India surfed online to look for jobs, the survey said. Online banking has made things much easier for the people and it saves a lot of time.

It has **eliminated** the problems associated with traditional way of banking where one had to stand in a queue and fill up several forms. Most of the banks in India have introduced customer-friendly online banking facility with advanced security features to protect customers against cybercrime.

The easy registration process for net banking has improved customers' access to several banking products increased customer loyalty, facilitated money transfer to any bank across India and has helped banks-attract new customers. The Indian results closely track the global trends as well conducted among 19216 people from 24 countries, the survey showed that banking and keeping track of finances and searching for jobs are the main tasks of internet users around the globe.

Overall, 60% of people surveyed used the web to check their bank account and other financial assets in the past 90 days, making it the most popular use of the internet globally, Shopping was not too far behind at 48%, the survey showed and 41% went online in search of a job in terms of country preferences, almost 90% of respondents in Sweden use e-banking.

Online banking has also caught on in a big way in nations like France, Canada, Australia, Poland, South Africa and Belgium, the survey showed. The Germans and British come on top for using online shopping with 74% of respondents in both countries having bought something online in the past three months. They are followed by 68% of respondents in Sweden, 65% in US and 62% in South Korea.

1. If the given sentences were to be arranged in their order of their popularity (from most popular to least popular), which one of the following would represent the correct sequences as given in the passage?

A. Use internet to gain information about products and services.
B. Use internet to search for jobs.
C. Use internet for online banking.

(*a*) B, A, C
(*b*) C, B, A
(*c*) C, A, B
(*d*) A, B, C
(*e*) A, C, B

2. Which of the following is not true in the context of the passage?

(*a*) Internet users across the globe are mainly interested in looking for jobs and keeping track of finances
(*b*) Germany and Great Britain are the top countries where online shopping is quite popular
(*c*) Many people in Sweden use e-banking to maintain their finances
(*d*) A majority of Indians prefer shopping online as compared to other online activities
(*e*) All the given statements are true

3. According to the passage, banks are successful in attracting more customers due to

A. better training to sales staff
B. opening more branches at various locations
C. easy registration process for net banking

(*a*) Only B
(*b*) Both B and C
(*c*) Both A and B
(*d*) Both A and C
(*e*) Only C

4. How many of the Indians using the internet shop online?

(*a*) Between 40% and 50%
(*b*) One-fourth of them
(*c*) One-third of them
(*d*) Half of them
(*e*) All of them

5. Which of the following is most nearly the same in meaning as the word **hassle-free** used in the passage?

(*a*) unskilled
(*b*) Not annoying
(*c*) Subtle
(*d*) Unsaddle
(*e*) Notable

6. Based on the passage, what can be said about the internet is a nutshell?
(a) It has increased the number of cybercrimes
(b) It is useful only for the rich
(c) It has been hyped for no reason
(d) It is more popular for online shopping than anything else
(e) It has made lives easier than before

7. Which of the following can be an appropriate title for the passage?
(a) The growing utility of the internet
(b) Internet and its drawbacks
(c) The traditional versus modern ways of shopping
(d) Use of the internet in different countries
(e) Internet-The Curse

8. Which of the following is/are true in the context of the passage?
A. More than 50% Indians using internet prefer online banking.
B. Many banks in India have introduced facilities to suit the needs of customers (customer-friendly).
C. More people shop online in South Korea as compared to those in Sweden.
(a) Only B
(b) Both B and C
(c) Both A and B
(d) Both A and C
(e) Only C

9. Which of the following is most nearly the same in meaning as the word 'eliminated' as used in the passage?
(a) taken
(b) introduced
(c) begun
(d) removed
(e) cancelled

10. According to the passage, globally, the most popular use of internet is
(a) looking for a job
(b) checking bank accounts and maintaining financial assets
(c) finding out information about various products
(d) shopping online
(e) blogging and tweeting every update in one's personal life

Exam Practice

Passage 1

Directions *In this section, you have a passage. After the passage you will find some questions. First, read the passage and answer the questions based on it. You are required to select your answers based on the contents of the passage and opinion of the author only.* **NDA 2018**

"Now, ladies and gentlemen,' said the conjuror, 'having shown you that the cloth is absolutely empty. I will proceed to take from it a bowl of goldfish. Presto!"

All around the hall people were saying, "Oh, how wonderful! How does he do it?"

But the Quick Man on the front seat said in a big whisper to the people near him, "He had itup his slccvc."

Then the people nodded brightly at the Quick Man and said, 'Oh, of course'; and everybody whispered round the hall, "He had it up his sleeve."

"My next trick," said the conjuror, "is the famous Hindostanee rings. You will notice that the rings are apparently separate, at a blow they all join (clang, clang, clang)–Presto!"

There was a general buzz of stupefaction till the Quick Man was heard to whisper, "He must have had another lot up his sleeve".

Again everybody nodded and whispered, "The rings were up his sleeve."

The brow of the conjuror was clouded with a gathering frown.

"I will now," he continued, "show you a most amusing trick by which I am enabled to take any number of eggs from a hat. Will some gentleman kindly lend me his hat?' Ah, thank you–Presto!"

He extracted seventeen eggs and for thirty-five seconds the audience began to think that he was wonderful. Then the Quick Man whispered along the front bench, "He has a hen up his sleeve," and all the people whispered it on. "He has a lot of hens up his sleeve".

The egg trick was ruined.

It went on like that all through. It transpired from the whispers of the Quick man that the conjuror must have concealed up his sleeve, in addition to the rings, hens and fish, several packs of cards, a loaf of bread, a doll's Cradle, a live guinea pig, a fifty-cent piece and a rocking chair.

1. "The brow of the conjuror was clouded with a gathering frown." The sentence means that the conjuror

(a) was very pleased
(b) was very sad
(c) was rather angry
(d) was very afraid

2. "The egg trick was ruined". This means that

(a) eggs were all broken
(b) people were unconvinced
(c) conjuror was disappointed
(d) the trick could not be performed

3. According to the Quick Man, the conjuror

(a) had everything bought for production
(b) produced things with the magic he knew
(c) had things in the large sleeves of his coat
(d) created an illusion of things with his magic

4. The author believes that the Quick Man was really
(a) foolish *(b)* clever *(c)* wrong *(d)* right

5. The conjuror extracted seventeen eggs from the hat of
(a) the Quick Man
(b) his own
(c) one gentleman from the audience
(d) None of the above

Passage 2

My most interesting visitor comes at night, when the lights are still burning—a tiny bat who prefers to fly in through the open door, and will use the window only if there is no alternative. His object in entering the house is to snap up the moths that cluster around the lamps. All the bats I have seen fly fairly high, keeping near the ceiling; but this particular bat flies in low, like a dive-bomber, zooming in and out of chair legs and under tables. Once, he passed straight between my legs. Has his radar gone wrong, I wondered, or is he just plain crazy? **NDA 2018**

1. Consider the following statements
1. The tiny bat flew in low like a dive bomber.
2. The tiny bat like all bats keeps near the ceiling.
3. It has lost direction because its radar has gone wrong.
4. It wants to entertain the author with its skill in flying.

Which of the above statements may be assumed to be true from the information given in the passage?
(a) 1 only *(b)* 1 and 3 *(c)* 2 and 4 *(d)* 3 and 4

2. The bat entered the room
(a) because there was no alternative
(b) to eat the moths round the lamps
(c) as it had gone mad
(d) as it preferred to fly in through the open door

3. After comparing the habits of the tiny bat with those of other bats, the author was
(a) sure that this bat had lost its direction
(b) not sure of its preferences
(c) surprised to find that it was an expert flier
(d) unable to give the correct explanation for its behaviour

4. The author calls the tiny bat an "interesting visitor". This means
(a) the bat visits him at night
(b) the bat is interested in the moths
(c) this bat has peculiar qualities
(d) this bat surprised him by zooming in and out like a drive-bomber

5. What, according to you, can be the most suitable title for the passage?
(a) Someone visits me
(b) Night of Mysteries
(c) My Nocturnal Visitor
(d) A Funny Visitor

Passage 3

I do not wish yo suggest that because we were one nation, we had no differences, but it is submitted that our leading men travelled throughout India either on foot or in bullockcarts. They learned one another languages and there was no aloofness amongst them. What do you think could have been the intention of those farseeing ancestors of ours who established Setubandha (Rameshwar) in the South, Jagannath in the East and Haridwar in the North as places of pilgrimage? You will admit they were no fools. They knew that worship of God could have been performed just as well at home. They taught us that those whose hearts were aglow with righteousness had the Ganges in their own homes. But they saw that India was one undivided land so made by nature. They, therefore, argued that it must be one nation.

Arguing thus, they established holy places in various parts of India and fired the people with an idea of nationality in a manner unknown in other parts of the world. And we Indians are one as no two Englishmen are. Only you and I and others who consider ourselves civilised and superior persons imagine that we are many nations. It was after the advent of railways that we began to believe in distinctions and you are at liberty now to say that it is through the railways that we are beginning to abolish those distinctions.

An opium-eater may argue the advantage of opium-eating from the fact that he began to understand the evil of the opium habit after having eaten it. I would ask you to consider well what I had said on the railways. **NDA 2019**

1. According to the author, India
(a) has never been one nation
(b) has been an aggregate of several nations
(c) has always been one nation along with differences
(d) became a nation after the British came

2. Why did the great sages of India establish pilgrimages in the different corners of the country?
(a) Because they wanted to push people to travel to different places.
(b) Because they could observe the underlying unity of the country as made by nature.
(c) Because they themselves had travelled to these places
(d) Because they wanted people to be religious everywhere

3. In the passage, the author's attitude towards the railways is
(a) critical (b) sympathetic
(c) indifferent (d) apathetic

4. What does the author mean when he says that "Whose hearts were aglow with righteousness had the Ganges in their own homes"?
(a) One need not visit the Ganges to take holy bath
(b) The Ganges had been polluted, so one should bath at home
(c) One should take a holy dip in the Ganges to purify one's heart
(d) The purity of heart is superior to observance of any ritual

5. The passage is written in a
(a) dialogic style (b) prescriptive style
(c) descriptive style (d) analytical style

Passage 4

Directions (Q. Nos. 1-5) *In this section you have a short passage. After the passage, you will find some questions based on the passage. First read the passage and then answer the questions based on it. You are required to select your answers based on the contents of the passage and opinion of the author only.*

NDA 2019

Studies serve for delight, for ornament, and for ability. Their chief use for delight, is in privateness and retiring; for ornament, is in discourse; and for ability, is in the judgment, and disposition of business. For expert men can execute, and perhaps judge of particulars, one by one; but the general counsels, and the plots and marshalling of affairs, come best from those that are learned. To spend too much time in studies is sloth; to use them too much for ornament, is affectation; to make judgment wholly by their rules, is the humor of a scholar. They perfect nature, and are perfected by experience: for natural abilities are like natural plants, that need pruning, by study, and studies themselves do give forth directions too much at large, except they be bounded in by experience. Crafty men condemn studies, simple men admire them, and wise men use them; for they teach not their own use; but that is a wisdom without them, and above them, won by observation. Read not to contradict and confute; nor to believe and take for granted; nor to find talk and discourse but to weigh and consider.

1. According to the author, why should one study?
(*a*) To gather information about the world
(*b*) To pass the time in a creative way
(*c*) For pleasure, enhanced capability and holistic growth
(*d*) To become only worldly wise

2. Why does the author not recommed too much of studies?
(*a*) Because it reflects idleness
(*b*) Because it requires too much money
(*c*) Because it is dangerous for the health of the mind
(*d*) Because it makes men crafty

3. According to the author, how can studies be perfected?
(*a*) By reflection
(*b*) By application
(*c*) By conversation
(*d*) By experience

4. Which kind of human beings denounce studies?
(*a*) Innocent
(*b*) Cunning
(*c*) Stupid
(*d*) Wise

5. According to the author, one should read to
(*a*) only argue
(*b*) only believe
(*c*) evaluate and understand
(*d*) preach and believe

Passage 5

Direction (Q. Nos. 1-4) *Read the passage and answer the questions based on it. You are required to select your answers based on the content of the passage and opinion of the author only.*

One of the most important things to notice about the power of art is the way in which great works continue to exert their influence through the ages. Scientific discoveries, which are of major importance at the time, when they are made, are superseded.

Thus, Newton's theory of gravitation has been superseded by Einstein's theory of relativity. Hence, the work of great scientists has value in stages on the way to a goal, which supersedes them.

Broadly speaking, the achievements of generals, politicians, and statesmen have an importance only in their own time. Hence, these people and their acts, great as they may have been are like milestones which mankind passes on its way to something else.

But with works of art it is not so.

The place which they occupy in the estimation of succeeding ages and the power, which they exercise over men's spirits are as great as they were in the age, which produced them; indeed, their power tends to increase with time, as they came to be better understood. **CDS 2016**

1. The power of art can be judged through
(a) its influence on a few individuals
(b) its influence on the people over the years
(c) the greatness of great artists
(d) the opinions of great thinkers

2. The statement "Newton's theory of gravitation has been superseded by Einstein's theory of relativity" suggests that
(a) the theory of relativity has nothing to do with the theory of gravitation
(b) the theory of relativity is new in comparison to the theory of gravitation
(c) the theory of relativity is an improvement over the theory of gravitation
(d) the theory of relativity has suppressed the theory of gravitation

3. The achievements of generals, politicians and statesmen have been compared to milestones by the author because
(a) they are inscribed on the milestones
(b) they have contemporary relevance
(c) they have topical and historical interest
(d) they are strong and lasting stones

4. How is a work of art different from the work of a scientist?
(a) A work of art is permanent as the work of a scientist
(b) The influence of a work of art increases from age to age unlike the work of a scientist which diminishes in course of time.
(c) A work of art has no material value like the work of a scientist
(d) A work of art is an expression of creative power while the work of a scientist is not

Passage 6

I must say a word about the Eiffel Tower. I do not know what purpose it serves today. But I then heard it greatly disparaged as well as praised. I remember that Tolstoy was the chief among those who disparaged it. He said that the Eiffel Tower was a monument of man's folly, not of his wisdom. Tobacco, he argued, was the worst of all intoxicants, in as much as a man addicted to it was tempted to commit crimes, which a drunkard never dared to do; liquor made a man mad, but tobacco clouded his intellect and made him build castles in the air. The Eiffel Tower was one of the creations of a man under such influence. There is no art about the Eiffel Tower. In no way can it be said to have contributed to the real beauty of the Exhibition. Men flocked to see it and ascended it as it was a novelty and of unique dimensions. It was the toy of the Exhibition. So long as we are children, we are attracted by toys, and the

Tower was a good demonstration of the fact that we are children attracted by trinkets. That may be claimed to be the purpose served by the Eiffel Tower. **CDS 2017**

1. Why did Tolstoy disparage Eiffel Tower?
1. Man was foolish to build it.
2. Huge man-made structures did not appeal to him.
3. Men hocked to see it.

Which of the statements given above is/are correct?
(a) Only 1 (b) 1 and 2
(c) 1 and 3 (d) 2 and 3

2. Why did Tolstoy believe that tobacco was the worst of all intoxicants?
(a) Man lost his intellectual abilities under the influence of tobacco
(b) Tobacco kept man in a state of inebriation.
(c) People who commit crimes are invariably addicted to tobacco.
(d) Statements (a) and (b) above are correct in this context?

3. Why did men flock to the Eiffel Tower?
(a) Men were attracted to the castles built in the air.
(b) Men lost their wisdom under the influence of intoxicants.
(c) Men were attracted to childish things.
(d) Men were attracted to things of no value.

Passage 7

To eat and not be eaten—that's the imperative of a caterpillar's existence. The leaf roller reduces its risks of being picked off by predators by silking together a temporary shelter in which to feed and rest. Adopting a different line of defense, the jelly slug extrudes a sticky translucent coating that may foul the mouth-parts of marauding ants. For its part, the aquatic larva, by its watery element, fashions a portable hideout from fragments of aquatic leaves. Cutting a serpentine trail as it feeds on tender young leaves, the minute citrus leaf miner spends its entire larval life inside its host plant, thus keeping its appetising body safely under wraps. **CDS 2018**

1. Which varieties of caterpillars 'build' shelters to protect themselves?
(a) Leaf roller and aquatic larva (b) Leaf roller and jelly slug
(c) Jelly slug and aquatic larva (d) Jelly slug and citrus leaf miner

2. Which one of the following caterpillars produces a sticky covering?
(a) Leaf roller (b) Jelly slug
(c) Aquatic larva (d) Citrus leaf miner

3. Which one of the following pairs of words in the passage describes enemies of the caterpillar?
(a) Serpentine and host (b) Predator and marauding ants
(c) Serpentine and marauding (d) Predator and host

4. Which one of the following makes itself unpalatable?
(a) Leaf roller (b) Jelly slug
(c) Aquatic larva (d) Leaf miner

5. The main idea of the passage is that caterpillars
(a) like to eat a lot (b) have to protect themselves while feeding
(c) are good to eat (d) are not good to eat

Passage 8

Much has been said of the common ground of religious unity. I am not going just now to venture my own theory. But if anyone here hopes that this unity will come by the triumph of anyone of the religions and the destruction of the others, to him I say, "Brother, yours' is an impossible hope." Do I wish that the Christian would become Hindu? God forbid. Do I wish that the Hindu or Buddhist would become Christian? God forbid.

The seed it put in the ground and earth and air and water are placed around it. Does the seed become the earth, or the air, or the water? No. It becomes a plant.

It develops after the law of its own growth,, assimilates the air, the earth and the water, converts them into plant substance and grows into a plant. Similar is the case with religion. The Christian is not to become a Hindu or a Buddhist, nor a Hindu or a Buddhist to become a Christian. But each must assimilate the sprit of the others and yet preserve his individuality and grow according to his own law of growth.

If the Parliament of Religions has shown anything to the world, it is this: it has proved to the world that holiness, purity and charity are not the exclusive possessions of any church in the world and that every system has produced men and women of the most exalted character.

In the face of this evidence, if anybody dreams of the exclusive survival of his own religion and the destruction of the others, I pity him from the bottom of my heart and point out to him that upon the banner of every religion will soon be written in spite of resistance: 'Help and not fight,' 'Assimilation and not Destruction,' 'harmony and Peace and not Dissension.'

CDS 2019

1. According to the author of the passage, people should
(a) change their religions
(b) follow their religions and persuade others to follow it
(c) follow their own religions and respect other religions
(d) disrespect other religions

2. The Parliament of Religions is
(a) a Christian organisation
(b) a Buddhist organisation
(c) a Hindu organisation
(d) a platform for discussion about every religion of the world

3. What does the author think about those who dream about the exclusive survival of their own religions and the destruction of the others?
(a) He hates them
(b) He desires to imprison them
(c) He pities them
(d) He praises them

4. According to the passage, what is 'impossible hope'?
(a) One day all the people of the world will follow only one religion
(b) One day, there will be no religion
(c) Purity and charity are the exclusive possessions
(d) Banner of every religion will soon be written

Passage 9

Directions (Q. Nos. 1-5) *Read the passage and answer the items based on it. You are required to select your answers based on the contents of the passage and opinion of the author only.*

Not all agricultural societies become civilizations, but no civilisation can become one without passing through the stage of agriculture. This is because at some stage in the development of agriculture, as productivity improves, not all people would need to be engaged in producing or procuring food. A significant number of people could be freed up to pursue outer activities such as building walls or monuments for new cities; making new tools, weapons and jewellery; organising long-distance trade; creating new artistic masterpieces; coming up with new inventions; keeping accounts; and perhaps constructing new public infrastructure such as irrigation canals that further improve the productivity of agriculture, thus realizing even more people to do new things.

This can happen, of course, only if a society that has transitioned to high-productivity agriculture has also, at some stage in its evolution, found a way to channel the bonanza of free time into other work fruitfully. In the ancient world, this often involved creating new ideologies and new hierarchies or power structures to coerce or otherwise convince large groups of people to devote their time to the new tasks for very little reward. **CDS 2020**

1. Which one of the following statements is true according to the author?

(*a*) Agriculture has always been part of all civilisations.

(*b*) Not all civilisations have undergone the processes of agriculture.

(*c*) Agriculture gave birth to new civilisations.

(*d*) Communities discontinued agriculture to become civilisations.

2. A significant number of people were sent to carry out other work from agriculture because.

(*a*) there were insufficient agricultural products.

(*b*) people were needed to build monuments, weapons, jewellery, etc.

(*c*) there were sufficient agricultural products.

(*d*) this enabled the development of civilisations.

3. What kind of agriculture based societies would emerge as civilisations?

(*a*) Societies which achieved high productivity in agriculture had the opportunity to find time for other work.

(*b*) Societies which depended on agriculture completely moved to other fruitful work so as to move to many places.

(*c*) Societies which transitioned from one stage of agriculture to another.

(*d*) Societies which could not do agriculture for lack of resorces moved to other work.

4. People as groups were convinced to do new work through

(*a*) reward, force and community persuasions.

(*b*) ideologies, hierarchies and power structures.

(*c*) excessive agricultural products.

(*d*) very high rewards.

5. Which word in the passage means 'changeover'?

(*a*) Transitioned

(*b*) Channel

(*c*) Coerce

(*d*) Hierarchies

Passage 10

When we pick up a newspaper, a book, or an article, we come to our task with certain preconceptions and predispositions. We expect to find a specific piece of information or be presented with an argument or an analysis of something, say, the likelihood of recession in the next six months or the reasons why children can't read. We probably know a little about the book or article we are reading even before we start. There was, after all, some reason why we chose to read one peice of writing rather than another.

Our expectations and predispositions may, however, blind us to what the article and its author is actually saying. If, for example, we are used to disagreeing with the author, we may see only what we expect to see and not what is actually there. Day after day in our routine pattern of life we expose ourselves to the same newspaper, the same magazine, even book by authors with the same perspectives. In order to reflect on our reading habits and improve our skills we need to break out of this routine, step back and look at what we are doing when we read. **CDS 2020**

1. According tothe author, which one of the following statements is not true?
(a) Reader's preconceptions influence their reading.
(b) Readers have expectations when they read an article or a book.
(c) Readers look for specific information in any of their readings.
(d) Readers asume that everything they read will have new information.

2. Our expectations and predispositions may, however, blind us because
(a) we may not get the actual ideas of the author.
(b) we will get the actual ideas of the author.
(c) we may disagree with the author.
(d) we will agree with all the ideas of the author.

3. One of the ways to improve our reading habits is to
(a) break the routine by changing the time of reading.
(b) change the types of topics we read.
(c) break the routine of reading the same newspaper.
(d) stop reading for some time and then restart reading.

4. Which quality does the author here advocate, to be a good reader?
(a) Being objective to the ideas of the author
(b) Having preconceptions and predispositions
(c) Having continuous routines
(d) Disagreeing with the author

5. Which word in the passage means 'viewpoints'?
(a) Preconceptions (b) Predispositions
(c) Pattern (d) Perspectives

Passage 11

Directions (Q. Nos. 1-5) *You have a passage with 5 questions following. Read the passage carefully and choose the best answer to each question out of the four alternatives.*

In September 2011, The Hindustan Times did a study in Delhi and reported that the number of malaria (and dengue) cases at the time were actually thrice as many as revealed by the city authorities. Earlier, in Mumbai, a municipal claim that 145 people died due to malaria in 2010 was exposed a lie after Praja, a city NGO, extracted figures from the municipality itself. Following an RTI petition, Praja revealed 1190 deaths. This seems to be a habit.

A paper in the leading UK medical journal. The Lancet, published following nationwide interviews undertaken by an international team, reveals that the number of malarial deaths all over India every year may be as high as 205000, which is many times the world Health Organization's figure of about 15000, of the National Vector Borne Disease Control Programme's figure of just around 1000. While the Lancet paper has been disputed, it is clear that there must be gross under-reporting of malarial deaths. Wouldn't that be one of the big reasons why malaria, which is easily cured if properly treated after timely diagnosis, continues to kill, so many Indians?

SSC CGL 2015

1. The findings of the Lancet were published after
(a) nationwide interviews were carried out
(b) international reviews of the findings were done
(c) proper verifications of the findings were done
(d) the international team left India

2. One of the big reasons for malarial death is
(a) untimely diagnosis
(b) under-reporting of malarial deaths
(c) over-reporting of malarial deaths
(d) lack of proper treatment

3. The Hindustan Times found that the number of malaria cases in 2011 was
(a) exactly as the numbers revealed by the authorities
(b) three times the numbers revealed by the authorities
(c) half the numbers revealed by the authorities
(d) twice than the numbers revealed by the authorities

4. What is "the habit" mentioned in the passage?
(a) Filing RTIs
(b) Hiding the real figures of malaria cases
(c) Conducting studies and surveys in towns and cities
(d) Exposing the authority's incompetence

5. The Lancet is a
(a) journal *(b)* magazine
(c) newspaper *(d)* medical book

Passage 12

Directions (Q. Nos. 1-5) *Read the passage carefully and choose the best answer to each question out of the four alternatives.*

The crowd surged forward through the narrow streets of Paris. There was a clatter of shutters being closed hastily by trembling hands-the citizens of Paris knew that once the fury of the people was excited there was no telling what they might do. They came to an old house which had a workshop on the ground floor. A head popped out of the door to see what it was all about. "Get him! Get Thimonier! Smash his devilish machines!" yelled the crowd.

They found the workshop without its owner. M. Thimonier had escaped by the back door. Now the fury of the demonstrators turned against the machines that were standing in the shop, ready to be delivered to buyers. They were systematically broken up and destroyed –dozens of them. Only when the last wheel and spindle had been trampled under foot did the infuriated crowd recover their senses.

"That is the end of M'Sieur Thimonier and his sewing machines," they said to one another and went home satisfied. Perhaps now they would find work, for they were all unemployed tailors and seamstresses who believed that their livelihood was threatened by that new invention. **SSC CGL 2015**

1. Shutters were being closed because the shopkeepers
(a) wanted to attack the crowd
(b) wanted to protect Thimonier
(c) feared their shops would be destroyed
(d) wanted to support the crowd

2. The aim of the crowd was to
(a) humiliate Thimonier
(b) destroy the sewing machines
(c) kill Thimonier
(d) drive Thimonier away

3. The passage throws light on
(a) what mischief an inventor can do to ordinary people
(b) how dangerous an invention can be
(c) why inventions should be avoided
(d) how a well-meant invention can be misunderstood

4. The people thought that
(a) they would be deprived of their livelihood
(b) Thimoner was mad
(c) the sewing machine was dangerous
(d) their lives were in danger

5. The crowd was protesting against
(a) the newly invented sewing machine
(b) the misdoings of Thimonier
(c) Thimonier for keeping the invention a secret
(d) the closings of workshop

Passage 13

Directions (Q. Nos. 1-5) *Read the passage carefully and choose the best answer to each question out of the four alternatives.*

The instinctive, natural way to express anger is to respond aggressively. Anger is a natural, adaptive response to threats, it inspires powerful, often aggressive, feelings and behaviours, which allow us to fight and to defend ourselves when we are attacked. On the other hand, we can't physically lash out at every person or object that irritates or annoys us, laws, social norms and common sense place limits on how our anger can take us. People use a variety of both conscious and unconscious processes to deal with their angry feelings. The three main approaches are expressing, suppressing and calming. Expressing your angry feelings in an assertive-not aggressive-manner is the healthiest way to express anger. Being assertive doesn't mean being pushy or demanding, it means being respectful of yourself and others. Anger can be suppressed and then converted or redirected. This happens when you hold in your anger, stop thinking about it and focus on something positive. **SSC CGL 2015**

1. According to the author, how should people deal with their anger?
(a) Expressing consciously
(b) Express aggressively
(c) Expressing unconsciously
(d) Express assertively

2. How, according to the author, can one suppress anger?
(a) By redirecting anger
(b) By converting anger
(c) By thinking about one's anger
(d) By holding one's anger

3. How does a person naturally express anger?
(a) By defending oneself
(b) By responding aggressively
(c) By inspiring powerful feelings
(d) By adapting strong behaviour

4. Which one of the following places limits on how far we can take our anger?
(a) Feelings
(b) Instinct
(c) Behaviour
(d) Law

5. What does the author mean by being assertive?
(a) Being calm
(b) Being demanding
(c) Being pushy
(d) Being respectful

Passage 14

Directions (Q. Nos. 1-4) *Read the following passage carefully and answer the questions given below in the context of the passage.*

Every profession or trade, every art and every science has its technical vocabulary, the function of which is partly to designate things or processes which have no names in ordinary English and partly to secure greater exactness in nomenclature. Such special dialects or jargons renecessary in technical discussion of any kind. Being universally understood by the devotees of the particular science or art, they have the precision of a mathematical formula. Besides, they save time, for it is much more economical to name a process than to describe it. Thousands of these technical terms are very properly included in every large dictionary, yet, as a whole, they are rather on the outskirts of the English language than actually within its borders.

Different occupations, however, differ widely in the character of their special vocabularies. In trades and handicrafts and other vacations like farming and fishing that have occupied great numbers of men from remote times, the technical vocabulary is very old. An average man now uses these in his own vocabulary. The special dialects of law, medicine divinity and philosophy have become familier to cultivated persons. **SSC CGL 2016**

1. Special words used in technical discussion
(a) may become part of common speech
(b) never last long
(c) should resemble mathematical formula
(d) should be confined to scientific fields

2. The writer of this article is
(a) a scientist
(b) a politician
(c) a linguist
(d) a businessman

3. This passage is primarily concerned with
(a) various occupations and professions
(b) technical terminology
(c) scientific undertakings
(d) a new language

4. It is true that
(a) various occupations and professions often interchange words.
(b) there is always a non-technical word that maybe substituted for the technical word.
(c) the average man often uses in his own vocabulary what was once technical language not meant for him.
(d) everyone is interested in scientific findings.

Passage 15

Direction (Q. Nos. 1-5) *A passage is given with five questions following it. Read the passage carefully and choose the best answer to each question out of the four alternatives.*

There's more than the 101-seater dining table at the Falaknuma palace that is awe inspiring. The library done in rosewood and mahogany is a place that will force anyone to pause, if only to admire the fine original polish, the furniture and the walnut carved high roof. The last is supposedly an imitation of the one at Windsor Castle.

The library is almost the size of a large banquet hall and acts as the passage to other parts of the palace including the dining area. For years, the palace had no librarian because they couldn't find the right person to do justice to the treasure trove of books collected by the Nizam's family over several decades. That is until they found Asif Husain Arastu, who belongs to the family that owned the famous AA Husain book store in Abids. So, when his friend and historian Anuradha Naik pointed out the palace's requirement at the library, Husain was delighted. On his very first day as the librarian at the magnificent Taj Falaknuma place, Asif Husain found a reference book on 'How to paint grass' by Alfred East. **SSC CGL 2016**

1. Which of the following is false about Arastu?
(a) He was a descendent of the Nizam's family
(b) He was the librarian at the Falaknuma Palace
(c) He owned a book store
(d) He was a friend of Anuradha Naik

2. The roof of the library has carvings made of..........wood.
(a) Rosewood (b) Mahogany (c) Sandalwood (d) Walnut

3. Name the author of the book that Husain found on his first day as the librarian?
(a) Alfred East (b) Anuradha Naik (c) Mark Twain (d) Charles Dickens

4. The books at the library were collected by.........
(a) Hyderabad University (b) Anuradha Naik
(c) The Nizam's Family (d) Asif Husain Arastu

5. Which part of the palace is an imitation of the Windsor Palace?
(a) 101-seater dinning table (b) The library's roof
(c) The banquet hall (d) The library's furniture

Passage 16

Directions (Q. Nos. 1-8) *Read the passage carefully and answer the questions given below it. Certain words/ phrases have been given in* ***bold*** *to help you locate them while answering some of the questions.* **SBI Clerk 2016**

Some time ago, there lived a King. The King should have been contented with his life, given all the riches and luxuries he had. However, this was not the case, the King always found himself wondering why he just never seemed contented with his life.

Sure, he had the attention of everyone wherever he went, attended fancy dinners and parties, but somehow, he still felt something was lacking and he couldn't put his finger on it. One day, the King had woken up earlier than usual to **stroll** around his palace. He entered his huge living room and came to a stop when he heard someone happily singing away. Following this singing, he saw that one of the servants was singing and had a very contented look on his face.

This **fascinated** the King and he summoned this man to his chambers. The man entered the King's chambers as ordered. The King asked why he was so happy. to this the man replied, "Your Majesty, I an nothing but a servant, but I make enough of a living to keep my wife and children happy. We don't need too much, a roof over our heads and warm food to fill our tummy. My wife and children are inspiration; the are content with whatever little I bring home. I am happy because my family is happy." Hearing this, he King dismissed the servant and summoned his Personal Assistant to his chambers.

The King related his personal anguish about this feelings and then related the story of the servant to his Personal assistant, hoping that somehow, he will be able to come up with some reasoning that here was a King, who could have anything he wished for at a snap of his fingers and yet was not contented, whereas his servant, having so little, was extremely contented. Personal Assistant listened attentively and come to a conclusion. He said, "Your Majesty, I believe that the servant has not been made part of The 99 Club." "The 99 Club? And what exactly is that?" the King inquired.

To which the Assistant replied, "Your Majesty, to truly know what The 99 club is, you will have to do the following: Place 99 gold coins in a bag and leave it at the servant's doorstep. You will then understand what the 99 club is." That very same evening, the King arranged for 99 gold coins to be placed in a bag at the servant's doorstep. Although, he was slightly hesitant and he thought he should have put 100 gold coins into the bag, yet since his assistant had advised him to put 99, that is what he did.

The servant was just stepping out of his house, when he saw a bag at his doorstep. wondering about its contents, he took it into his house and opened the bag. When he opened the bag, he let out a great big shout of joy, "Gold coins. so many of them." He could hardly believe it. He called his wife to show her the coins.

He then took the bag to a table and emptied it out and began to count the coins. Doing so, he realised that there were 99 coins and he thought it was an odd number, so he counted again and again only to come to the same conclusion-99 gold coins.

He began to wonder, what could have happened to that last one coin? for no one would leave 99 coins. He began to search his entire house, looked around his backyard for houses, not wanting to lose out that one coin. Finally, exhausted, he decided that he would work harder than ever to make up for that one gold coin to make his entire collection an even 100 gold coins.

He got up the next morning in an extremely horrible mood, shouting at the children and his wife for his delay, not realising that he had spent most of the night conjuring ways of working hard, so that the had enough money to buy himself that gold coin. He went to work as usual–but not in his usual best mood, singing happily - as he grumpily did his dally errands.

Seeing the man's attitude change so **drastically**, the king was puzzled. He promptly summoned his Assistant to his chambers. The King related his thoughts about the servant and once again, his Assistant listened. The King could not believe that the servant who until yesterday had been singing away and was happy and contented with his life had taken a sudden change of attitude, even though he should have been happier after receiving the gold coins.

To this the Assistant replied, "Ah! But your Majesty, the servant has now officially joined the 99 Club." He explained: "The 99 club is just a name given to those people, who have everything but yet are never contented, therefore they are always working hard and striving of that extra one to round it out to 100.

We have so mush to be thankful for and we can live with very little in our lives, but the minute we are given something bigger and better, we want even more! We are not the happy contented person we used to be. We want more and more and by wanting more and more we don't realise the price we pay for it. We lose our sleep, our happiness; we hurt the people around us just as a price to pay for our growing needs and desires. That is what joining. The 99 club is all about." Hearing this, the King decided that from that day onwards, he was going to start appreciating all the little things in life.

Striving for more is always good, but let's not strive so hard and for so much that we lose all those near and dear to out hearts. We shouldn't compromise our happiness for moments of luxuries.

1. Why did the king summon the servant?
  (a) Because the servant was singing a sad song.
  (b) Because he was fascinated by the happiness of the servant
  (c) Because the servant had shown disrespect to him.
  (d) Because the servant was also assigned the job of a spy.
  (e) Other than those given as options.

2. What was/were the reason for he servant's happiness?
  A. He was not a part of The 99 Club.
  B. He was too poor to look after his family.
  C. His family was happy.
  (a) A and B *(b)* B and C *(c)* A and C *(d)* all of these
  (e) Only B

3. What was not the effect of placing the bag containing 99 gold coins at the servant's doorstep?
  (a) The servant become overjoyed to find the bag containing gold coins.
  (b) He counted the gold coins again and again to confirm whether they were just ninety nine or a hundred.
  (c) He began to search the last one coin in and around his house.
  (d) Finally, he could find the last one coin in his backyard.
  (e) Other than those given as options.

4. What happened to the servant, when he became part of the 99 Club?
  (a) He got up the next morning in a horrible mood.
  (b) He rebuked the members of his family.
  (c) He went to work in a depressed mood.
  (d) He did his work grumpily.
  (e) All of the above

5. In the context of the passage, what do you mean by the 99 Club?
  (a) The 99 Club is a group of rich people. *(b)* It is the club of dissatisfied people.
  (c) It is a club of minster of the royal court. *(d)* It is the club of people.
  (e) Other than those given as options.

6. Choose the word, which is most similar in meaning to the word 'Fascinated' given in bold as used in the passage.

(a) Bored
(b) Attracted
(c) Repulsed
(d) Exhausted
(e) Irritated

7. choose the word which is most opposite in meaning to the word 'Stroll' given in bold as used in the passage.

(a) Excursion
(b) Lazy walk
(c) Survey
(d) Breath
(e) Run

8. Choose the word, which is most similar in meaning to the word 'Drastically' given in bold as used in the passage?

(a) Vehemently
(b) Effectively
(c) Firmly
(d) Compulsively
(e) Emphatically

Passage 17

Directions (Q. Nos. 1-10) *Read the following story carefully and answer the questions given. Certain words/phrases have been given in to help you locate them while answering some of the questions.*

Once there was a king who had been trying really hard to capture an elephant, but that prize had proved elusive. All the hunters in the kingdom had tried but their efforts were 'in vain'. So the king announced that anyone who could capture the elephant would get half his kingdom.

The tortoise heard about this and went to the king to accept the challenge. The king was very amused. 'All my hunters have failed to capture the elephant and you think you can succeed?' asked the king. The tortoise insisted that he was up to the task and promised to deliver that elephant to the king within forty eight hours. The tortoise then dug a big hole, big enough to hold the elephant along a path leading to the village. Then he covered the hole with sticks and leaves so that it was not visible unless inspected closely. When this was done, the tortoise went in search of the elephant.

When the tortoise met the elephant, he told him, 'You know you are the largest animal in the forest and you should be a king?' The elephant had never considered this before but he thought it was not a bad idea. The tortoise told the elephant that the villagers had decided to make the largest animal their king and were all expecting the elephant to come to the village and be crowned as their king. The more the elephant heard, the more excited he became.

The tortoise **adorned** the elephant with colourful beads and beating a gong, he sang songs praising the elephant while he led the way to the village. soon they approached the trap and the tortoise being lighter and smaller walked over the trap. The elephant who was following him fell through the sticks and leaves into the deep hole and this helped the tortoise in achieving his goal well within the time limit. **SBI Clerk 2016**

1. As mentioned in the story, despite the king doubting his ability, the tortoise accepted the challenge.
   A. he was forced to do so by the villagers.
   B. to prove to the king that only a tortoise and his family could complete the challenge.
   C. he wanted the entire kingdom to himself.
   (a) Only A *(b)* A and B *(c)* Only B *(d)* Only C
   (e) None of these
2. Which of the following correctly explains the meaning of the phrase, **'in vain'** as used in the story?
   (a) Were painful *(b)* Were unsuccessful *(c)* Were in order *(d)* Were untruthful
   (e) Were simple
3. Which of the following could be a suitable title to the story?
   (a) The Elephant who Became the Most Popular King
   (b) The Wise King
   (c) The Clever Tortoise
   (d) The Villagers and their Love for the Elephant
   (e) The Selfish Villagers
4. Which of the following is most nearly the **opposite** in meaning as the word 'Excited' as used in the story?
   (a) Bored *(b)* Interested *(c)* Affected *(d)* Feeling
   (e) Merciless
5. Which of the following statements is true in the context of the story?
   (a) The king refused to share his kingdom with the tortoise.
   (b) The tortoise kept his word by providing the king with what he desired.
   (c) It was the king's idea that helped the tortoise achieve his target.
   (d) The elephant was popular for his beautiful skin.
   (e) None of the given statements is true.
6. As mentioned in the story, the elephant followed tortoise's advice because
   A. for him, the tortoise was the wisest animal in the village
   B. he really believed that the villagers wanted him as the king
   C. he had always wanted to become rich and powerful
   (a) Only A *(b)* A and C *(c)* A and B *(d)* Only B
   (e) all of these
7. Which of the following is most nearly the **same** in meaning as the word 'Insisted' as used in the story?
   (a) Requested *(b)* Revived *(c)* Repeated *(d)* Invited
   (e) Showed
8. Which of the following is most nearly the **opposite** in meaning as the word 'Praising' as used in the story?
   (a) Insulting *(b)* Concealing *(c)* Hiding *(d)* Refusing
   (e) Removing
9. As mentioned int he story, which of the following can be said about the elephant?
   (a) He had a good sense of humour. *(b)* He was foolish.
   (c) He was balanced. *(d)* He was logical.
   (e) He was short tempered.
10. Which of the following is most nearly the **same** in meaning as the word 'Adorned' as used in the story?
    (a) Touched *(b)* Adored *(c)* Charmed *(d)* Decorated
    (e) Stuffed

Passage 18

Directions (Q. Nos. 1-7) *Read the following passage carefully and answer the questions given below them. Certain words/phrases have been printed in bold to help you locate them while answering some of the questions.*

Life is messy. If we want our best and brightest in the workforce, we need to accept that they have complex lives. We need to be flexible when it comes to the realities of balancing career and family. Being flexible at work does not just benefit people trying to balance their outside lives with work. An extensive body of research demonstrates the business benefits of flexible working. Yet despite this overwhelming evidence, access to fixable work and careers is not widespread. Flexible work is still regarded as an add-on, something we do for mothers for a few months when they are back from parental leave. But in the face of rapid changes to the way we work, organisations need to move beyond just having policies for flexible working or making ad-hoc adjustments for certain individuals. Companies need to fundamentally rethink the way they design work and jobs.

The World Economic Forum predicts that we are on the cusp of a fourth industrial revolution. Technological, socio-economic and demographic shifts are transforming the way we work, demanding flexibility in the way individuals, teams and organisations work. We all have different things happening in our lives at different times. Not just caring for young kids, but other family members, community roles, study and volunteering. And all of these parts of our identities bring with them different skill sets. in today's workforce, fewer people identify with the stereotype of the ideal worker- a full-time, fully committed employee without personal or family commitments that impact on availability.

There are a few factors driving the demand for increased flexibility. Globalisation is one. The development of a 24/7 marketplace and the rapid expansion of the services economy are also having a transformational effect on the workplace, requiring organisations to think creatively about how they can best organise jobs and work to respond to an increasingly diverse and demanding customer base. Similarly technology is driving-and enabling-greater flexibility. It is dramatically reshaping our workplaces, blurring the boundaries between work and home and diversifying where, when and how employees work. Advances in mobile, intranet and cloud technologies, the rapid development of computing power and the digital connection between multiple objects have all driven workplace innovations such as remote working, telecommuting, co-working spaces video/teleconferencing and virtual teams and collaboration.

So the future of work demands new approaches to work design-but have workplaces risen to the challenge? The evidence suggests we have yet to grasp this opportunity to be more innovative.

While some employers are making flexible work more available, there is still a high prevalence of bolted-on **temporary** arrangements. these arrangements are seen as the exception to the rule, with the full-time, 'face-time', long hours, ideal worker still the model to which everyone is expected to adhere.

Many people make assumptions about flexible workers, including that they're not interested in training and development, aren't committed to the organisation or don't have any career aspirations. We need to explore and challenge these biases.

There are good international examples of successful work redesign that have involved the input of a team of employees. For example, a UK bakery sat down with their bakers and came up with a flexible system of two to three baking shifts a day to maintain a steady supply of fresh bread. The team agreed to rotate their hours each week so no team member permanently worked a shift that did not suit. After the change was made, bakery sales increased by more than 65% in the first year and employee satisfaction in the bakery has risen 10% since the change to 93%. So work redesign is not only doable, it can deliver business benefits, although it does require a completely new approach. By changing our thinking and focusing on the team and the organisation as a whole, rather than the individual, we have the opportunity to create more adaptable and sustainable workplace.

1. According to the author, how is flexible working still regarded as?

(a) The way of designing work and jobs.
(b) The way to identify the stereotype of an ideal worker.
(c) An add-on, something we do for mothers for a few months when they are back from parental leave.
(d) Advances in mobile, internet and cloud technologies and the rapid development of computing power.
(e) None of the above

2. According to the passage, in today's workforce, which among the following is/are the stereotype(s) of an ideal worker?

I. A full time worker
II. an employee who is fully committed to work
III. The employee has no personal or family commitments that impact his availability

(a) Only II (b) Only III (c) II and III (d) I and III
(e) All of these

3. According to the passage, how is technology driving and enabling greater flexibility?

(a) It is identifying the stereotype of an ideal worker.
(b) It is dramatically reshaping our workplaces, blurring the boundaries between work and home and diversifying where, when and how employees work.
(c) It is training the workers on how to transform the ways in which flexibility can be introduced
(d) It is one of the factors that is contributing in declining the demand for flexibility at the workplace worldwide.
(e) None of the above

4. Which of the following were the steps taken by the UK Bakery with regards to the working time of their bakers?

I. The UK Bakery came up with a flexible system of two to three baking shifts a day to maintain a steady supply of fresh bread.
II. The Bakery team agreed to rotate their hours each week so no team member permanently worked a shift that did not suit.
III. The bakery sales increased by more than 65% in the first year and employee satisfaction in the bakery has risen 10% since the change to 93%.

(a) Only III (b) I and III (c) II and III (d) I and II
(e) All of these

5. The most appropriate title of the passage is
   (a) Complex lives of the Workforce
   (b) Role of Technology in Increasing Flexibility of Workers
   (c) The Brightest Workforce Requires more Flexible work
   (d) How a UK Bakery Increased their Sales
   (e) Importance of globalisation in Increasing Workforce
6. Choose the word which most nearly the **Same** in meaning as the word printed in **bold** as used in he passage.
   Predict
   (a) Ignore (b) Forecast
   (c) Misunderstand (d) Recount
   (e) Narrate
7. Choose the word which is most nearly the **Opposite** in meaning as the word printed in **bold** as used in the passage.
   Temporary
   (a) Substitute (b) Alternate
   (c) Expedient (d) Provisional
   (e) Permanent

Passage 19

Directions (Q. Nos. 1-8) *Read the following passage and answer the following questions based on the given passage. Some of the words are highlighted which would help you to answer some of the questions given.*

For years, world-wide organisations have become increasingly excited about the prospect of a cloud-based future. As the dream becomes an ever closer reality for many kinds of business and Forecaster predicted that enterprise spending on cloud services is set to surge. IDC also predicted that global spending on public cloud services and infrastructure would reach 210 bn in 2019, an increase of 24% from 2018. But one obstacle stands create friction and introduce risk; the process of migration.

As all indications point to a **massive** shift in data deployments to the cloud, it is more important than ever that the transition from on-premises to cloud is as risk free as possible. In today's climate any loss or disruption to data can have a huge business impact. It's a complex process, is frequently underestimated and many organisations have found there's a lot that can go wrong that can impact the business.

Organisations across the globe have found the cloud to be an ideal place to run modern data applications due to big data's elastic resource requirements.

Furthermore, with the lack of data talent on ever-looming issue for most companies today they have been determined to **adopt** a cloud-first strategy to ensure business operations are accessible for a range of employees.

The cloud offers great promise for developers especially, as it can increase the speed at which they develop software features and increase the resilience of applications once they are deployed-along with enhanced security through the use of multiple server locations. with all this considered, it is no surprise that 42% of UK businesses leverage some kind of cloud service, according to Eurostat.

However, all the perceived benefits of leveraging the cloud are redundant if organisations come up against barriers to accessing cloud services. Cloud-based data pipelines still suffer from complexity challenges at the moment, along with the lack of visibility into cost and resource usage at the application and user level.

the anser to this is automation fueled by Robust Machine Learning Traning Models and Artificial Intelligence. These concepts and the tools that enable them can determine the prerequisites of cloud infrastructure, application dependencies, the appropriate target cloud instance profiles and provide troubleshooting in real-time.

To summarise, the promise of the cloud had created a sense of excitement amongst enterprises, however, they have proceeded to **go full steam** ahead into adopting a cloud service, without sufficient data to **ensure** performance Service Level Agreements (SLAs). **SBI Clerk 2019**

1. How can we tackle the risks associated with the process of migrations?

(a) By ensuring that organisations only migrate the apps to the cloud that will thrive in the cloud.
(b) The surge in the investment in the cloud technology.
(c) The use of predictive power of Artificial Intelligence.
(d) The transition from on-premises to cloud
(e) None of the above

2. Why the promise of the cloud has created a sense of excitement amongst enterprises?

(a) As it ensures that business operations are accessible for a range of employees.
(b) As the enterprise spending on cloud services is surging.
(c) Reduction in the cost of operation it may entail.
(d) The secure platform it provides to the data it stores.
(e) None of the above

3. How the process of migration stands as an obstacle to the cloud technology?

(a) The expensive cost of providing safety to the data.
(b) The lack of sound technology in Artificial Intelligence.
(c) Complexities of the data migrated to the cloud
(d) It exposes the companies to the risk of losing important information.
(e) None of the above

4. Which of the following statement (s) is/are correct in context of the passage?

1. The cloud technology can help in increasing the speed at which the software features are developed.
2. There is no risk associated with the cloud technology.
3. Cloud technology is not a very complex process.

Codes

(a) Only 2 *(b)* Both I and 2
(c) Only 3 *(d)* Only 1
(e) All are correct

5. What is the meaning of the phrase 'Full steam ahead'?

(a) Interrupting and activity *(b)* Acting cautiously
(c) Great increase *(d)* Progressing quickly
(e) Prudent progression

6. Which of the following words is most similar to the word Adopt as given in the passage?

(a) Mold *(b)* Deduce
(c) Embrace *(d)* Creative
(e) Fluster

7. Which of the following words is most similar to the word Ensure as given in the passage?
   (a) Confirm (b) Paced (c) Redundant (d) Weaken
   (e) Reject
8. Which of the following words is most opposite to the word massive of given in the passage?
   (a) Prominent (b) Insignificant (c) Enlarged (d) Eilthy
   (e) Vouch

Passage 20

Directions (Q. Nos. 1-5) *Read the following passage carefully and answer the questions given below it.*

When Hurricane Harvey loomed off the coast of my home State of Texas, it seemed to fill the entire Gulf of Mexico. When it roared on land, it pummelled the towns of Rockport and Port Aransas, whose tawny beaches I' ve walked with my kids, pointing out the indigo sails of Portuguese man O war jellyfish. Harvey's eye took direct aim at the University of Texas' Marine Science Institute, flattening not just the facility itself, but priceless samples awaiting analysis. After Harvey left Post Aransas, it spun back into the Gulf of Mexico over record sea temperatures as great as 4° above normal. Thermodynamic laws require that warmer an holds more water vapour. The heat armed the storm with a mighty arsenal of water vapour. Then Harvey returned to land, dumping a catastrophic amount of rain on Houston. My Facebook feed filled with pleas for rescue from the rising waters. Friends' houses flooded houses that had always been on dry land before. A chemical plant blew up, twice. Toxic chemicals oozed from superfund sites. Dozens died in the deluge, mostly by drowning. And all the while, alongside the heartbreak and horror, I kept thinking about a strange harbinger: jellyfish.

Play video diaphanous in form yet menacing in sting, jellyfish have a powerful capacity to capture our imagination. They undulate in a primal rhythm, blinking open and closed like eyes that can peer into the soul of the sea. And what they are seeing are changes produced by us here on land. Because we burn fossil fuels, which release greenhouse gases, not just the atmosphere, but ocean waters are warming.

At the same time, our ship traffic transports animals to new places, and sometimes these exotics find home-like conditions where in the past those conditions would have been unsuitable. That's what happened in the eastern Mediterranean, where a jellyfish from the tropical Indian Ocean has found warm, homey waters and now forms huge aggregations called blooms that stretch for tens of miles every summer. The fierce stings of these animals chase beach goers out of the water. Their gooey bodies clog machinery at power plants, halting operations.

Rampant coastal development provides new habitat for a jellyfish stage called a polyp that looks like a sea anemone. When it finds a hard surface like a dock or a jetty to grow on, a single polyp can proliferate into a dozen or even more medusae. And fields of polyps grow on those hard structures. That's likely what happened off the coast of Italy, where gas platforms are thought to be the home for a new invasion of jellyfish.

In the twentieth century in the Adriatic sea, moon jellies, pinkish with their characteristic four-leafed clover on top, were a rarity. Now they are ubiquitous. And as we wash pollution into our waters, we create low-oxygen environments. some jellyfish, with their low metabolic rate due to their a-cellular jelly insides, can survive more easily there than fish, with their oxygen guzzling muscled tissues.

That is part of what happened in the Yellow sea, where pollution is unchecked. it is the birthplace of a maroon jellyfish that reaches a weight of 500 pounds. Blooms of the creature were a once-a-generation event before 2000 the kind of thing fishermen mentioned to their sons. But jellyzillas swept from China in the Tsushima Current, have plagued Japan's coast almost every year of the 21st century. In 2009, a fishing boat caught so many that their weight capsized the vessel. (Fortunately, the crewmembers were rescued). And our lack of oversight of the fishing industry, which has removed more than 90% of the large fish from the seas, has depleted the predators of jellyfish as well as their competitors.

Jellyfish are eaten by some fish, and jellyfish eat the same small zooplankton that fish do. the ecological vacuum left by unrestrained fishing can allow jellyfish to expand their influence in marine ecosystems. that's what happened off the coast of Namibia, once one of the world. **IBPS Clerk 2017**

1. How is jellyfish able to survive in polluted water more than the other fishes?
   1. Jellyfish has oxygen guzzling muzzled tissues.
   2. Due to low metabolic rate.
   3. Jellyfish eat small zooplankton to survive.

   (a) Only 1 (b) Only 2 (c) 1 and 2 (d) 2 and 3
   (e) All are correct

2. How Hurricane Harvey can be termed as devastating with reference to the passage?
   (a) Many people died by drowning.
   (b) Hurricane blew up the Chemical plants.
   (c) Toxic chemicals got exuded from superfund sites.
   (d) Hurricane flooded many houses.
   (e) All of the above

3. What is the author's main idea regarding the passage?
   (a) How to ameliorate ecological imbalance.
   (b) The author gave his opinion regarding jellyfish that what they know humans don't
   (c) Water pollution creating a low oxygen environment affecting aquatic life.
   (d) Hurricane Harvey destroyed many lives.
   (e) Endangered condition of Jellyfish.

4. Which of the following statements is/are true in context of the given passage?
   (a) Maroon jellyfish is found in Yellow sea where pollution is unchecked.
   (b) Hurricane Harvey with strong winds battered the entire Gulf of Mexico.
   (c) Jellyzillah sweeping from China have afflicted Japan's coast
   (d) Jellyfish survive more than other fishes in low oxygen environment.
   (e) All of the above

5. Which of the following statements regarding jellyfish is/are related to the country Namibia?
   (a) The attenuation in the number of jellyfish is due to the low oxygen environment.
   (b) The predators of jellyfish are depleting because of uncontrolled fishing.
   (c) Jellyfish can proliferate their population in the situation of ecological imbalance.
   (d) Both (a) and (b)
   (e) All of the above

Passage 21

Directions (Q. Nos.1-8) *Read the following passage carefully and answer the questions given below them.*

Animal of all sorts live together in various ecosystems. Within these natural communities, the animals eat specific diets that connect them together in a food chain. The three diets of animals include creatures that eat only plants, those that eat only meat and animals that eat both plants and meat. Animals that eat plants exclusively are herbivores, and animals that eat only meat are carnivores.

When animals eat both plants and meat, they are called omnivores. The **balance** of an ecosystem depends on the presence of every type of animal. if one type of animal becomes too numerous or scarce, the entire balance of the ecosystem will change.

Carnivores will feed on herbivores, omnivores and other carnivores in an ecosystem. A natural community depends on the presence of carnivores to control the populations of other animals. Large carnivores include wolves and mountain lions. A large carnivore might hunt down large herbivores such as elk and deer.

Medium-sized carnivores include hawks and snakes and these animals typically feed on rodents, birds, eggs, frogs and insects. Example of small carnivores include some smaller birds and toads. These carnivores may eat insects and worms. Carnivorous animals have strong jaws and sharp teeth to enable them to tear and rip prey. These animals often have long, sharp claws that they also use to tear prey. Carnivores depend on **sufficient** prey in the food chain to given them the food they need. If the herbivore population or the population of other carnivores declines in an ecosystem, carnivores may not survive.

With a diet comprised of only plants, herbivores can be surprisingly large animals. Examples of large herbivore include cows, elk and buffalo. These animals eat grass, tree bark, aquatic vegetation and shrubby growth. Herbivores can also be medium-sized animals such as sheep and goats, which eat shrubby vegetation and grasses.

Small herbivores include rabbits, chipmunks, squirrels and mice. These animals eat grass, shrubs, seeds and nuts. An ecosystem must provide (1) plants to sustain herbivores and many of them spend the majority of their lives eating to stay alive. If plant availability declines, herbivores may not have enough to eat.

This could cause a decline in herbivore numbers, which would also impact carnivores. Herbivores usually have special biological system to digest a variety of different plants. Their teeth also have special designs that enable them to rip off the plants and then grind them up with flat molars.

Omnivores have an advantage in an ecosystem because their diet is the most diverse. These animals can vary their diet depending on the food that is most plentiful, sometimes eating plants and other times eating meat. Herbivores have different digestive systems than omnivores, so omnivores usually cannot eat all of the plants that an herbivore can.

Generally, omnivores eat fruits and vegetables freely, but they can't eat grasses and some grains due to digestive limitations. Omnivores will also hunt both carnivores and herbivores for meat, including small mammals, reptiles and insects.

Large omnivores include bears and humans. Examples of medium sized omnivores include raccoons and pigs. Small omnivores include some fish and insects such as flies. Omnivore teeth often resemble carnivore teeth because of the need for tearing meat. Omnivores also have flat molars for grinding up food. **IBPS Clerk 2019**

1. Why the balance of the ecosystem depends one each kind of animal?
(a) Scarcity or abundant of a single kind can cause disturbance in the ecosystem balance.
(b) Carnivores and Omnivorous should be less in number than herbivorous.
(c) Specific diets of each kind of animals bring food chain in sync.
(d) Both (b) and (c)
(e) None of the above

2. How natural community depends upon Carnivores?
(a) They feed on grass eating, plant and meat eating animals.
(b) They feed on other carnivores.
(c) They control populations of other animals.
(d) All of the above
(e) None of the above

3. What is the threat to survival of carnivores?
(a) Insufficient number of preys in the food chain.
(b) Decline in population of herbivores and other carnivores
(c) Both (a) and (b)
(d) Only (b)
(e) None of the above

4. Which of the following statement(s) is/are true about herbivores?
(a) Their diet include only vegetation
(b) Their survival depends upon abundant plants
(c) A major part of herbivores' life is spent on eating
(d) They have a digestive system suitable to digest diverse kind of plants
(e) All of the above

5. Why Omnivores are said to have an advantage?
(a) Diverse diet
(b) Both (a) and (c)
(c) Diet depends upon food which is available in plentiful amount.
(d) Only (a)
(e) Only (c)

6. Which is the following can fill the blank (1) as given in the passage, to make the sentence grammatically and contextually correct?
(a) Largely
(b) Abundant
(c) Diversity
(d) Quite
(e) None of the above

7. Which of the following words is most **similar** in meaning as 'Balance' highlighted in the given passage?
(a) Affecting
(b) Poignant
(c) Equilibrium
(d) Considerate
(e) None of these

8. Which of the following words is most **opposite** in meaning with 'Sufficient', highlighted in the given passage?
(a) Inadequate
(b) Ample
(c) Plenty
(d) Enough
(e) None of these

Passage 22

Directions (Q. Nos. 1-10) *Read the following passage and answer the given questions. Certain words/phrases are given in* **bold** *to help you locate them while answering some of the questions.*

There is a market failure in cyber security. Solutions being suggested or tried include increasing transparency about data losses, helping consumers and firms to make more informed decisions about cybe-security; shedding more light on how Internet-Service Providers (ISPs) tackle malware infections, they spot on customers' computer; and using liability laws to force software companies to produce safer code. On transparency. America has led the way . Almost all American States now have data-breach laws that require firms to reveal any loss of sensitive customer information. In Europe, telecom firms have been obliged to notify customers of breaches for some time now, and there are plans to extend reporting to a wider range of industries.

Breach laws have encouraged insurance companies to offer coverage against potential losses. This is helpful because they are in a position to gather and share information about best practice across a wide range of companies. A cyber-insurer advises companies on defensive tactics, and also on how to minimise the damage if something goes wrong. The american government should create a Syber-equivalent of the National Transportation Safety Board, which investigates **serious** accidents and shares information about them.

Such a body could look into all breaches that cost over, $50m and make sure the lessons are shared widely. But insurers are likely to remain wary of taking on broader risks because the costs associated with a serious cyber-incident could be astronomic. Insurers can deal with acts of God, but not acts of Anonymous (hacking groups or acts of state sponsored hacking). This explains why the overall cyber-insurance market is still small. Governments are weighing in, too, not least by supporting private-sector efforts to clean up 'botnets, or networks of compromised computers controlled by hackers. These networks, which are prevalent in countries, such as America and China, can be used to launch attacks and spread malware.

In Germany, an initiative called Bot-Frei, which helps people clean up their infected computer, received government support to get started, though it is now self-financing. The American government has also worked closely with private firms to bring down large botnets. Another strategy involves issuing standards to encourage improved security. America's National Institute of Standards and Technology published as set of voluntary guidelines for companies in critical-infrastructure sectors, such as energy and transport. Britain has also launched a scheme called cyber-essentials' under which firms can apply for a certificate showing they comply with certain minium security standards. Applicants undergo an external audit and, if successful, are awarded a badge which they can use on marketing materials. Whether governments are best placed to set minimum standards is debatable, but they have certainly raised awareness of cyber-security as an issue that needs attention.

They could also help to get more information into the public domain. Researchers have argued persuasively that collecting and publishing data about the quantity of spam and other bad traffic handled by ISPs could encourage the worst performers to do more to tackle the problem, thus improving overall security. Another debate has revolved around getting software companies to produce code with fewer flaws in it. One idea is to make them liable for damage caused when, say, hackers exploit a weakness in a software program.

Most software companies currently insist costumers accept end-user licensing agreements that specifically protect firms from legal claims unless local laws prohibit such exclusions. The snag is that imposing blanket liability could have a **chilling** effect on innovation. Companies that are selling millions of copies of programmes might take fright at the potential exposure and leave the business. Strict liability be applied only to firms which produce software that cannot be patched if a security flaw is found. There is quite a lot of that sort of code around. **SBI PO 2017**

1. Which of the following is the **same** in meaning as the word 'Broader' as used in the passage?
(a) Spacious *(b)* subtle *(c)* Weaker *(d)* Comprehensive
(e) Approximate

2. Which of the following is/are the argument(s) in favour of cyber-essentials?
A. It boosts transparency and promotion of firms.
B. The certification is given by hackers which makes it authentic.
C. Firms benefit from paying attention to cyber-security and so do users.
(a) Only A *(b)* Only B *(c)* A and C *(d)* B and C
(e) All of these

3. Which of the following is the **same** in meaning as the word 'Tried' as used in the passage?
(a) Convicted *(b)* Accused *(c)* Attempted *(d)* Exasperated
(e) None of these

4. Which of the following is the **opposite** of the word 'Serious' as used in the passage?
(a) genuine *(b)* witty
(c) noisy *(d)* insignificant
(e) irresistible

5. Which of the following is the opposite of the word 'Chilling' as used in the passage?
(a) Promoting *(b)* Reassuring
(c) Encouraging *(d)* Fostering
(e) All of these

6. Which of the following best describes the author's view of liability laws?
(a) These will act as incentives for computer firms to produce more secure software.
(b) These are pointless as they cannot be uniformly or strictly implemented.
(c) These will not greatly impact computer firms as the financial profits from software are huge.
(d) These are not an appropriate approach to cyber security.
(e) None of the given options

7. Which of the following can be said about government efforts with regard to cyber security?
A. Government efforts have been coupled with private sector cooperation.
B. Government efforts have been focused on destroying botnet infrastructure.
C. These are not worthwhile and too small in magnitude.
(a) Only A *(b)* Only B *(c)* Only C *(d)* B and C
(e) A and B

8. Why has the author mentioned the National Transportation Security Board in the passage?

A. To urge America to set-up a body to share data in cyber-related instances.

B. To monitor cyber security episodes whose losses are over a certain sum.

C. To publish and enforce standards for cyber-security for sectors like energy.

(a) Only A *(b)* A and B *(c)* Only B *(d)* B and C
(e) All of these

9. Which of the following is/are a theme(s) of the passage?

(a) Holding cyber firms accountable for flaws in their products.
(b) Cyber-crime infrastructure in certain countries.
(c) Ways to secure cyber-space.
(d) Limits of cyber-insurance.
(e) All the given options are themes.

10. Which of the following is/are true in the context of the passage?

(a) Breach laws can be helpful for organisations.
(b) America is leading the way in terms of laws for disclosure of cyber-breaches.
(c) Pressure is increasing on software companies to produce safer products.
(d) Varied efforts are being made to create a market which values cyber-security.
(e) All the given options are true in the context of the passage

Passage 23

Directions (1-8) *Read the following passage carefully and answer the questions given below it. Certain parts are given in bold to anser some of the questions based on the passage.*

We all are aware of the fact that nothing is permanent in this world, neither products nor technology. As day by day, improvements and updations are made in technology, leading to new inventions and innovations in every sphere of life. Invention refers to the creation of a brand new product or device. Conversely, innovation is an act of making changes to the existing product or the process by introducing new ways or ideas. At first sight, the two terms sound alike, but if you dig deeper, you will find that there is a fine line of difference between invention and innovation that lies in their connotations. While invention is all about creating or designing something, innovation is the process of turning a creative idea into reality. **[A] There is often a fine line between genius and insanity.** Innovation is not only important on the individual level, but can make or break a business as well.

Innovative businesses create dynamic products, adjust existing service, and/or implement new ideas. **[B] They are not afraid to color outside the lines and try something new, even if it is risky.** If a business is not innovative, they risk losing work to competitors. Lack of innovation also has indirect results such as losing staff and decreasing engagement. Therefore, innovation cannot be an afterthought, but rather a crucial element that is included in part of your strategy. It should be a cultural outlook that impacts thinking and improves problem solving. Many successful companies attribute their success to their innovative practices. That said, inventing and innovation are not one in the same. Invention focuses on creating new items or new ways to produce existing items. Very often, invention is a result of innovation, but it is not a requirement. Although invention can be beneficial to a business, the level of importance and necessity can vary according to the industry.

[C] The era of invention is not over, but they have definitely been pushed aside for an era of innovation.

While many people are still out there trying to come up with the next "big invention" that is going to improve humanity, businesses have discovered that innovation seems to not only trump invention in furthering a company's brand and profitability, but it can be far cheaper when all the framework is already completed. This can be seen from many major businesses that choose to innovate rather than invent, such as Apply and Sony, first, we must distinguish the difference between invention and innovation. Invention is the creation of a product or introduction of a new process, for example the Alternating Current induction motor is an invention created in 1888. An innovations occurs when someone improves on or makes a significant contribution to an item or process that has already been invented; the Apple iPhone is an innovation of the cell phone. It seems that great inventors are smaller in number– perhaps business models are leaning towards enabling innovation.

Sony's influence in the technology market started with the invention of the first tape recorder, and through years of creativity and perseverance, became innovators of a variety of categories, from computing and electronics to entertainment. Sony shows corporations that for a business to thrive in today's market, a company cannot stay stagnant with on particular item – innovations are essential.

Innovation drives economic growth. Five combination patterns are what create innovation. These are, the production of a new good, a new method of production, a new market, acquiring a new source of raw minerals and the emergence of a new organisation. **[D] A company does not need to invent to have a competitive edge in the market, but need to innovate and create a product that is based on the needs and desires of the consumer.** **SBI PO 2018**

1. With what example has the author described 'innovation' as a change that can even prove to be economically lucrative?

(a) Since innovation is coming up with a fresh idea, it leads to research and development department of the organisation
(b) Innovation is a result of invention and hence is economically feasible too
(c) It focuses on creating new items or new ways to produce existing items
(d) Innovation can make or break a business as well
(e) Innovation results in boosting up of economy as an idea for a product or process that has never been made before is highlighted

2. How is innovation a crucial element that its absence impacts business strategy?

(a) As the companies are destined to fail in its absence because of the stagnant growth
(b) Competitors could avail benefits over not so innovative businesses
(c) The lack of innovation has secondary impacts such as losing staff and decreasing engagement
(d) Both *(a)* and (b)
(e) Both *(b)* and (c)

3. Which of the following statement/s infers that an era of invention has not been dissipated but instead pushed aside by that of innovation?

(a) Innovation outclasses invention in enhancing a company's brand's name and profit.
(b) Innovation is far cheaper than invention when all the framework is completed
(c) As business models are leading towards enabling new inventions which require scientific skills.
(d) Both *(a)* and (b)
(e) Both *(b)* and (c)

4. "Sony chose to innovate rather than invent". How has this helped its business to grow?
   (a) Sony made a significant contribution to the item by inventing products according to the needs of the consumer.
   (b) Sony needs to invent to have a competitive edge in the market.
   (c) Innovation helped Sony against staying stagnant with one item.
   (d) Business models like Sony are leaning towards enabling invention which has helped businesses to grow.
   (e) All of the above
5. What can be illustrated from statement [A] "There is often a fine line between genius and insanity."
   (a) One should be careful while innovating as a successful innovation can build a business while a failure can destabilise the business.
   (b) Genius and insane innovations cannot be separated through a thin line of difference.
   (c) Genius innovations can turn into insane outcomes if they fall within the line.
   (d) Insane innovations provide a line to develop genius innovations.
   (e) None of the above
6. What can be inferred from statement [B] "They are not afraid to color outside the lines and try something new, even if it is risky"?
   (a) Businessmen innovate every colorful product even though it is risky for their enterprise.
   (b) Businessmen do not analyse the pros and cons while developing the new innovation.
   (c) Businessmen are ready to think or act in way that does not conform to set rules even though it is quite risky for the business.
   (d) Businessmen set their minds to break the rules required to introduce a new innovation.
   (e) None of the above
7. **Statement [C]** "The era of invention is not over, but they have definitely been pushed aside for an era of innovation" in the passage may not be grammatically or contextually correct. Choose the most suitable alternative that will replace the statement to adhere to the grammatical syntax of the paragraph.
   (a) The era of invention is not over, but is has definitely been pushed aside to an era of innovation.
   (b) The era of invention is not over, but it has definitely been pushed aside for an era of innovation.
   (c) The eras of invention is not over, but they have definitely been pushed aside for an eras of innovation.
   (d) The era of invention is not over, but they had definitely been pushed aside for an era of innovation.
   (e) None of the above
8. According to the author, in reference with the statement [D] "A company does not need to invent to have a competitive edge in the market, but need to innovate and create a product that is based on the needs and desires of the consumer", what should be the criteria for innovation?
   (a) Profits
   (b) Market trends
   (c) Competition
   (d) Customer satisfaction
   (e) None of the above

Passage 24

Directions (Q. Nos. 1-4) *Read the following passage and answer the questions as directed.*

Paragraph 1 One of the easiest ways to establish a savings habit is to participate in your employer's 401(k) plan. Funds are withheld from each paycheck and deposited into your account. If your employer matches part of your contribution – and many do! – your will accumulate **yet** more. A second way to consistently save is with an automatic savings transfer programma with your financial institution. You decide how much and when you want funds transferred from your checking account into a savings account. You can also use a payroll deduction plan from your employer and get the same results.

Paragraph 2 Along with how much and how often you save, what you earn on your funds will determine how fast your money grows. You cannot control what happens with interest rates or the stock market, but you can consider different types of savings vehicles that provide different returns. The simplest savings vehicle to consider is buying Certificates of Deposits (CDs) instead of leaving funds in a savings account. CDs usually offer higher interest rates, but they are time deposits and have .... for early withdrawal. If you can accept not having immediate access to your funds, CDs can be an attractive savings vehicle. **IBPS PO 2018**

1. Which of the following can be inferred as the theme of the passage?
(a) Certificate of deposits is the best way to establish saving habit.
(b) Establishing a consistent saving habit and also smart saving with CDs.
(c) Employer's 401(k) plan provides a convenient way for consistent and smart savings.
(d) Your savings decide how well you flourish and grow.
(e) None of the above

2. Which of the following can replace the word given in bold in the passage?
(a) though (b) even (c) quitely (d) accrue
(e) more

3. What is the tone of writing in the passage?
(a) Satirical (b) Critical (c) Didactic (d) Sarcastic
(e) Nostalgic

4. Which of the following words can fill in the blank to make it meaningful?
(a) gifts (b) lucrative (c) casualties (d) penalties
(e) None of these

Passage 25

Directions (Q. Nos.1-3) *Read the following paragraph and answer the question as directed.*

Budgeting is an important tool for saving. First, you need to segregate all your income and expenses. Now, categorise your expenses as least important, important and very important to prioritise them while settling them through your income, which is limited. Try to figure out ways in which you can **increase** expenses. *Ensure that your income exceeds the expenses with as wider a margin as possible.* The surplus fund after meeting all the expenses would be your saving. It is only after you have assured savings that you can thinking about investment. **IBPS PO/MT 2018**

1. Which of the following is the correct chronology of steps as can be inferred from the passage?
(a) Saving-Budgeting-Investment
(b) Investment-Budgeting-Saving
(c) Budgeting-Saving-Investment
(d) Budgeting-Investment-Saving
(e) None of the above

2. Which of the following words, opposite of the word given in bold, should replace the word given in bold in the passage?
(a) Enhance
(b) Curtail
(c) Damage
(d) Lengthen
(e) Leverage

3. Which of the following is the best way of writing the line given in italics in the paragraph, without changing its intended meaning?
(a) Surely, the income will exceed the expenses by a wider margin.
(b) The income will be greater than the expenses is not a possibility.
(c) Make sure that the income is greater than the expenses by a margin as wide as possible.
(d) If the income does not exceed the expenses by a wider margin, it will be useless.
(e) None of the above

Passage 26

Directions (Q. Nos. 1-5) *Read the following passage and answer the questions below.*

IBPS PO/MT 2019

Wayanad, Congress President Rahul Gandhi's choice as his second constituency, is arguably the safest seat for the Congress in South India and among the safest in the entire country. Mr Gandhi's main rival will be PP Suneer of the CPI. The BJP has a marginal presence in the constituency.

The Congress chief had been undecided over contesting from Wayanad, considering the multiple battles of perception that it brings. First, while he has been pointedly trying to define the 2019 election as a fight to save India from advancing Hindutva, he will end up facing-off with the Left, an adversary in Kerala but an ally nationally. Second, he will be accused of running away from Amethi.

Third, the more fundamental question: whether contesting two seats will be seen as a sign of weakness. After weighing the pros and cons, on which he received divergent opinions, the decision was taken. Congress sources close to Mr Gandhi are emphatic that they sense no challenge in Amethi.

But the volatility in Uttar Pradesh, despite the formation of the SP-BSP alliance and its declaration of support for Mr. Gandhi in Amethi, is palpable. The battle lines in the critical State have not been defined yet, and Prime Minister Narendra Modi's campaign blitz has only begun.

That said, the reason for national leaders contesting' a second seat is less because of any insecurity in one seat and more for expanding their personal imprint to critical territories, as Mr Modi himself did in 2014 by contesting from Vadodara in Gujarat and Varanasi in UP.

1. Which State according to the passage is the safest seat for Congress in South India?
(a) Kannur
(b) Wayanad
(c) Kozhikode
(d) Pathanamthitta
(e) Vadodara

2. Which word in is closest to the meaning of the word 'Emphatic'?
(a) Hesitant
(b) Tentative
(c) Ambiguous
(d) Lethargic
(e) Decisive

3. What is the reason for national leaders less contesting for a second seat?
(a) Over insecurity in one State
(b) Expanding their personal imprint to critical territories
(c) Both *(a)* and (b)
(d) Because of election lines not being defined properly
(e) None of the above

4. Why is Congress President undecided in contesting from Wayanad?
(a) Battle with the left
(b) Accused of running away from Amethi
(c) Sign of weakness
(d) All the three
(e) None of the above

5. Which word is in closest to the word 'divergent'?
(a) Correspondent
(b) Homogenous
(c) Similar
(d) Uniform
(e) Diverse

Answers

Passage 1

1. (e) **2.** (c) **3.** (a) **4.** (e) **5.** (e) **6.** (b) **7.** (b) **8.** (a)

Passage 2

1. (c) **2.** (b) **3.** (a) **4.** (c) **5.** (a) **6.** (b) **7.** (c) **8.** (b) **9.** (d) **10.** (a)

Passage 3

1. (c) **2.** (d) **3.** (b) **4.** (d) **5.** (c) **6.** (d) **7.** (b) **8.** (d) **9.** (d) **10.** (b)

Passage 4

1. (d) **2.** (b) **3.** (d) **4.** (a) **5.** (b) **6.** (b) **7.** (d) **8.** (d) **9.** (b)

Passage 5

1. (b) **2.** (b) **3.** (d) **4.** (a) **5.** (c)

Passage 6

1. (d) **2.** (c) **3.** (a) **4.** (d) **5.** (c) **6.** (b)

Passage 7

1. (d) **2.** (c) **3.** (b) **4.** (c) **5.** (a) **6.** (c) **7.** (b)

Passage 8

1. (d) **2.** (c) **3.** (b) **4.** (b) **5.** (a)

Passage 9

1. (d) **2.** (c) **3.** (b) **4.** (a)

Passage 10

1. (a) **2.** (c) **3.** (c) **4.** (b) **5.** (b)

Passage 11

1. (e) 2. (b) 3. (e) 4. (b) 5. (c) 6. (d) 7. (e)
8. (a) 9. (d) 10. (a) 11. (e) 12. (c) 13. (e) 14. (b)
15. (d)

Passage 12

1. (b) 2. (a) 3. (c) 4. (d) 5. (b)

Passage 13

1. (a) 2. (b) 3. (a) 4. (b) 5. (c)

Passage 14

1. (c) 2. (c) 3. (d) 4. (a) 5. (c) 6. (d) 7. (c)
8. (c) 9. (a) 10. (b)

Passage 15

1. (b) 2. (b) 3. (a) 4. (d) 5. (c)

Revision Exercise

Passage 1

1. (c) 2. (d) 3. (d) 4. (b) 5. (b)

Passage 2

1. (c) 2. (a) 3. (b) 4. (a) 5. (c)

Passage 3

1. (c) 2. (d) 3. (e) 4. (c) 5. (a) 6. (d) 7. (e)
8. (e) 9. (b) 10. (a)

Passage 4

1. (d) 2. (e) 3. (c) 4. (a) 5. (d) 6. (c) 7. (a)
8. (c) 9. (b) 10. (e)

Passage 5

1. (e) 2. (a) 3. (c) 4. (b) 5. (a) 6. (b) 7. (e)
8. (d)

Passage 6

1. (b) 2. (d) 3. (e) 4. (c) 5. (c) 6. (d) 7. (a)

Passage 7

1. (e) 2. (d) 3. (d) 4. (d) 5. (a) 6. (a) 7. (b)
8. (e)

Passage 8

1. (c) 2. (d) 3. (e) 4. (d) 5. (b) 6. (e) 7. (a)
8. (c) 9. (d) 10. (b)

Exam Practice

Passage 1

1. (c) 2. (b) 3. (c) 4. (a) 5. (c)

Passage 2

1. (a) 2. (b) 3. (d) 4. (c) 5. (c)

Passage 3

1. (c) 2. (b) 3. (b) 4. (c) 5. (c)

Passage 4

1. (c) 2. (a) 3. (d) 4. (b) 5. (c)

Passage 5

1. (b) 2. (d) 3. (b) 4. (b)

Passage 6

1. (a) 2. (a) 3. (c)

Passage 7

1. (a) 2. (b) 3. (b) 4. (b) 5. (b)

Passage 8

1. (c) 2. (d) 3. (c) 4. (a)

Passage 9

1. (a) 2. (c) 3. (a) 4. (b) 5. (a)

Passage 10

1. (d) 2. (a) 3. (c) 4. (a) 5. (d)

Passage 11

1. (a) 2. (b) 3. (b) 4. (b) 5. (a)

Passage 12

1. (c) 2. (b) 3. (d) 4. (a) 5. (a)

Passage 13

1. (d) 2. (d) 3. (b) 4. (d) 5. (d)

Passage 14

1. (a) 2. (c) 3. (b) 4. (c)

Passage 15

1. (a) 2. (d) 3. (a) 4. (c) 5. (b)

Passage 16

1. (b) 2. (c) 3. (d) 4. (e) 5. (b) 6. (b) 7. (e)
8. (a)

Passage 17

1. (e) 2. (b) 3. (c) 4. (a) 5. (b) 6. (d) 7. (c)
8. (a) 9. (b) 10. (d)

Passage 18

1. (c) 2. (e) 3. (b) 4. (e) 5. (e) 6. (b) 7. (e)

Passage 19

1. (c) 2. (a) 3. (d) 4. (d) 5. (d) 6. (c) 7. (a)
8. (b)

Passage 20

1. (e) 2. (e) 3. (b) 4. (b) 5. (a) 6. (d)

Passage 21

1. (a) 2. (d) 3. (c) 4. (e) 5. (b) 6. (b) 7. (c)
8. (a)

Passage 22

1. (d) 2. (c) 3. (c) 4. (d) 5. (d) 6. (b) 7. (a)
8. (b) 9. (d) 10. (d)

Passage 23

1. (d) 2. (e) 3. (d) 4. (c) 5. (a) 6. (c) 7. (b)
8. (d)

Passage 24

1. (b) 2. (b) 3. (c) 4. (d)

Passage 25

1. (c) 2. (b) 3. (c)

Passage 26

1. (b) 2. (e) 3. (c) 4. (d) 5. (e)

PART D
(Practical Grammar)

Narration

(a) **Direct Narration** Direct narration is a kind of speech which is reported by another person exactly in the words spoken by the speaker. This speech is placed within inverted commas.

(i) She said to him, "I shall give you money." *(Direct Narration)*

(b) **Indirect Narration** Indirect narration is a speech which is reported by another without quoting the speaker. This is done by using certain conjunctions in place of commas and making necessary changes in the verbs and the pronouns of the reported speech.

(i) She told him that she would give him money. *(Indirect Narration)*

For the purpose of changing narration, sentences are divided as follows.

1. Assertive/Declarative Sentences

Sentences denoting affirmative or negative statements or opinions.

- You are playing.
- She was not sleeping.
- He did this work.
- They will not write to us.

2. Interrogative Sentences

(a) Sentences beginning with auxiliary verbs. (Yes or No answer type questions)

- Are you playing?
- Was she sleeping?
- Did he do this work?
- Will they write to us?

(b) Sentences beginning with question words such as .... when, where, why, who, which, what etc.

- When are you playing?
- Where was she sleeping?
- Why did he do this work?
- What will they write to us?

3. Imperative Sentences

Sentences denoting command, request and advice.

- Soldiers, turn to the right.
- Please give me something to eat.
- Do not waste time.
- Let me stay here.

4. **Exclamatory Sentences**

Sentence expressing great emotions such as excitement, surprise, happiness, anger, etc.

- How nice of him!
- What a pretty girl she is!
- Ah! It is beautiful locket.
- Alas! All is over.

5. **Optative Sentences**

Sentences expressing wish, prager, curse, etc.

- May you live long!
- Happy Diwali, children!
- Good bye, my daughters!
- Fie, what an ughy sight!

Change in Narration

Assertive Sentences

1. **Assertive Sentences** Assertive sentences are changed in indirect narration as follows

(A) **Reporting Verb** Verb is changed into 'tell' or 'told' with an object otherwise 'say' and 'said' are retained.

'Think/wonder to oneself' can also be used.

(i) He says, "I am a doctor". *(Direct)*
He says that he is a doctor. *(Indirect)*

(ii) She said, "I am a doctor."
She said that she was a doctor.

(iii) She says to me, "I am a doctor."
She tells me that she is a doctor.

(iv) She thought, "She will not go out with him."
She thought to herself that she would not go out with him.

(B) **Inverted Commas** 'That' is used in place of inverted commas.

She said to me, "I am a doctor."
She told me that she was a doctor.

(C) **Tense**

(a) **If the Reporting verb is in the Present or Future tense or the Reported speech is a universal truth, the tense of Reported speech does not change.**

(i) She says, "I shall go to Delhi."
She says that she will go to Delhi.

(ii) I say to her, "I shall give her money."
I tell her that I shall give her money.

(iii) Teacher said to the students, "The sun rises in the East."
Teacher told the students that the sun rises in the East.

(b) **If the Reporting verb is in the past tense, the tense of the Reported speech changes into past as follows** *(i)* **Present tense changes into past tense**

Present Indefinite	Past Indefinite
Present Continuous	Past Continuous
Present Perfect	Past Perfect
Present Perfect Continuous	Past Perfect Continuous

(ii) **Past tense changes as follows**

Past Indefinite	Past Perfect
Past Continuous	Past Perfect Continuous
Past Perfect	No change
Past Perfect Continuous	No change

(iii) **Future tense**

Will/Shall change into Would/Should

(iv) **Modals are changed as follows**

May	Might
Can	Could
Have to	Had to
Had to	Had had to
Should	No change
Must	No change

Some Hints on Exceptions Change of Tenses

1. Need not, used to, would rather, would better, had rather, had better, should, must, subjunctive mood do not change.
2. **Past Continuous**
   (a) Past continuous changes when it refers to a **complete action.**
   (i) She said to me, "I was thinking of helping him but changed my mind later on".
   (ii) She told me that she had been thinking of helping him but changed her mind later on. (*Complete action*)
3. **Past continuous does not change when it is used in time clause.**
   (i) He said to me, "While I was singing, she was dancing."
   (ii) He told me that while he was singing, she was dancing.
4. **Past indefinite does not change in the following cases**
   (a) When it is used in time clause.
   (i) She said to me, "When I met him, he was playing."
   She told me that when she met him he was playing.
   (ii) She said to her mother, "Father had left before/when she reached home."
   She told her mother that father had left before/when she reached home.
   (b) When it expresses two simultaneous actions.
   (i) She said, "I cooked vegetables and he fried rice."
   She said that she cooked vegetables and he fried rice.
   (c) When it expresses historical Past.
   (i) He said, "Netaji was born in Kolkata."
   He said that Netaji was born in Kolkata.

Change of 'Will'

'Will' change into 'Should' when the speaker seeks advice or request.

(i) The mother said, "What will I do with so much money, My son!"
The mother asked her son what she should do with so much money.

Change of 'Need'

(i) She said, "Need I write a letter?"
She asked if she had to write a letter.

(ii) She said, "If I am selected, I needn't study further."
She said that if she was selected she would not have to study further.

Change of 'Could'

Could is changed in cases of Permission

(i) She said to me, "When I was a student I could not go out alone."
She told me that when she was a student she was not allowed to go alone.

Change of 'Must'

(a) 'Must' normally does not change when it refers to duty or laws of nature.

(i) Rahul said to her, "You must obey your parents."
Rahul said to her that she must obey her parents.

(ii) She said, "We must all die."
She said that we must all die.

(b) 'Must' changes in the following cases

(i) She said, "I must leave at once."
She said that she had to leave at once.

(ii) Natasha said, "I must get up early tomorrow."
Natasha said that she would have to get up early the next day.

(iii) Lekha said, "Mansi, You must be silent."
Lekha ordered Mansi to be silent.

Changes of Pronouns in the Reported Speech

1. **First Person** (I, we) in the reported speech change into the subject of the Reporting verb.

(i) She said to me, "I am unwell."
She told me that she was unwell.

(ii) Rohan said to her, "I shall leave Jaipur soon."
Rohan told her that he would leave Jaipur soon.

(iii) The Captain said, "We have won at last."
The captain told his teammates that they had won at last.

NOTE 'We' does not change in the following cases.

(a) When 'we' is used in general sense.
 (i) The saint said, "We are mortals."
 The saint said that we are mortals.

(b) When object 'me' is included in the subject.
 (i) She said to me, "We are to leave for temple early."
 She told me that we were to leave for temple early.

(c) But 'We' changes into 'It' when used by a newspaper or an organisation.
 (i) The Pioneer said, "We are not responsible for any error."
 The Pioneer said that it was not responsible for any error.

2. Second Person You in the Reported speech changes into the object of the Reporting verb.

(i) He said to his mother, "Will you give me money."
He asked his mother if she would give him some money.

(ii) The teacher said to the students, "You are not to leave the class without permission."
The teacher advised the student that they were not to leave the class without permission.

3. Third Person (He, She, They, It) in the Reported speech does not change.

(i) I said to her, "He will not come."
I told her that he would not come.

(ii) The boy said to his father, "They have not returned the book."
The boy told to his father that they had not returned the book.

5. Adverbials of time, place and demonstrative.

***(i)* Adverbial of Time**

Now	changes into	then
Ago	,,	before
Today	,,	That day
Tomorrow	,,	The next day
Yesterday	,,	The previous day/The day before
Last night	,,	The previous night/The night before
Next month	,,	The following month
The day before yesterday	,,	Two days before
The day after tomorrow	,,	In two days time

NOTE **Today, Tomorrow, Tonight** do not change when the speech is reported the same day.

(a) This morning he said, "I shall leave Chennai tomorrow."
 This morning he said that he would leave Chennai tomorrow.

(b) Esha said today, "I am leaving Pune tonight."
 Esha said today that she was leaving Pune tonight.

(ii) **Adverbs of Place**

Change of 'Here' 'Here' Changes into 'there'.

'Here' changes' to 'there' only when there is reference to place.

He said, "I live here." *(Direct)*

He told me he lived here. (*Indirect*)

(iii) **Change of Demonstratives**

Change of This, These

(i) Used with time .... changes into 'that' 'those'.

This week	That week
These months	Those months

(ii) Used as adjective ....changes into 'the'.

This book	The book
These books	The books

(iii) Used as Pronoun .... changes into 'it'.

I shall do this tomorrow.	I shall do it tomorrow.

(iv) Used as subject .... does not change.

'This', 'these', give the sense of the object being near.

This is my book.	These are my books.

Examples

Some examples are worked out as follows

(a) **Direct** Rahul says, "The teacher is ill."
Indirect Rahul says that the teacher is ill.

(b) **Direct** She said, "The sun rises in the East."
Indirect She said that the sun rises in the East.

(c) **Direct** Shashi said, "I have completed my work."
Indirect Shashi said that she had completed her work.

(d) **Direct** They said, "We won the match."
Indirect They said that they had won the match.

(e) **Direct** You said to her, "I have called my friends."
Indirect You told her that you had called your friends.

(f) **Direct** I said, "I shall leave Chennai soon."
Indirect I said that I should leave Chennai soon.

(g) **Direct** Jatin said, "I had to leave my village because of poverty."
Indirect Jatin said that he had had to leave his village because of poverty.

(h) **Direct** He said, "I shall leave tomorrow."
Indirect He said that he would leave the next day.

(i) **Direct** He said to her, "I want to see you now."
Indirect He told her that he wanted to see her then.

(j) **Direct** She said, "well, I shall accompany you."
Indirect She told me that she would accompany me.

(k) **Direct** She said, "you see, you cannot meet the boss."
Indirect She told me that I could not meet the boss.

NOTE When the words such as well, you see, okay, you know, therefore, so yet, but, etc., are used in the reported speech, they do not change.

Interrogative Sentences

1. **Reporting Verb** Verb is changed into ask/asked, inquire/ inquired, want /wanted to know, demand/demanded or wonder/wondered depending on the context of the question.
   (i) Mother said to daughter, "Have you completed your home work?"
   Mother asked daughter if she had completed her homework.
2. **Inverted Commas**
   (a) In 'yes' or 'no' Answer type questions, 'if' or 'whether' is used in place of inverted commas.
   (i) Father said to me, "Do you know the residence of the doctor?"
   Father asked me if I knew the residence of the doctor.
   (b) In the sentences beginning with Question words, inverted commas are replaced by question word itself (who, when, what, etc.)
   (i) The teacher said to Rohan, "Why are you late?"
   The teacher asked Rohan why he was late.
   (c) In yes or no answer type question and questions starting with interrogative pronouns, 'that' is used before the question word.
   (i) She said to me, "When she will come is not certain?"
   She told me that when she would come was not certain.
   (ii) I said to him, "whether she will pass is not certain?"
   I told him that whether she would pass was not certain.

(d) **Tense**	The changes in these parts
(e) **Pronouns**	of the reported speech
(f) **Adverbs of time and place**	are same as in the case of assertive sentences.

NOTE Students are required to change interrogative sentences into Assertive sentences before changing the Narration. *For example*

Direct She said to her mother, "Will you take me to temple"?
Indirect She asked her mother whether/if she would take her to temple.

Examples

Some examples are worked out as follows

(a) **Direct** Tina said to Rohan, "Will you help me today?"
Indirect Tina asked Rohan if he would help her that day.

(b) **Direct** He said to me, "What are you doing?"
Indirect He asked me what I was doing.

(c) **Direct** Anil said to me, "Why did you do it?"
Indirect Anil inquired of me why I had done it.

(d) **Direct** Pearl said to Riya, "Do you know Rohit?"
Indirect Pearl asked Riya if she knew Rohit.

(e) **Direct** The teacher said to the boy, "Have you done your home work?"
Indirect The teacher asked the boy if he had done his home work.

(f) **Direct** She said, "How can I do such a foolish work?"
Indirect She thought/wondered how she could do such a foolish work.

(g) **Direct** Sonia said to her brother, "When my husband will return tonight is uncertain."
Indirect Sonia told her brother that when her husband would return that night was uncertain.

(h) **Direct** Nisha said, "Whether (if) you have qualified, the test cannot be confirmed."
Indirect Nisha told her sister that whether (if) she would qualify the test could not be confirmed.

(i) **Direct** Rahul said to Ritesh, "What you are doing is immoral."
Indirect Rahul told Ritesh that what he was doing was immoral.

(j) **Direct** She said to her companions, "Why not stay overnight here?"
Indirect She suggested to her companions that they should stay overnight there.

(k) **Direct** Manu said to his friend, "Why help him now?"
Indirect Manu told his friend that it was no use helping him then.

NOTE **Could, would would like** used as polite request in interrogative sentences are reported as follows

Request, Advice + Object + to (Refer to Models)

She said to her friend, "Could/would you please lend me some money?"
She requested her friend to lend her some money.
The captain said to the lady, "Would you like to have dinner with me?"
The captain requested/invited the lady to have dinner with him.

Imperative Sentences

(a) **Reporting Verb** The verb changes into **command/order, beg, request, advise, forbid, suggest, propose, assure, ask, remind, warn, agree, refuse, promise, etc.**

(i) She said, "Mohan, please bring me that book."
She requested Mohan to bring her that book.

(ii) Mother said to me, "Take the umbrella with you when you go out".
Mother advised me to take the umbrella with me when I went out.

(iii) I said to my friend, "Don't go out in dark."
I forbade my friend to go out in dark.

(iv) The captain said, "Soldiers, March on till it is dark.
The captain commanded the soldiers to march on till it was dark.

(v) The lady said, "Thanks, I shall never forget this kindness, Arnav."
The lady thanked Arnav and assured him that she would never forget his kindness.

(vi) Richa said, "Congratulations my son, you have won."
Richa congratulated her son telling him that he had won.

(b) **Inverted Commas** 'To/not to' is used in place of inverted commas.

(i) She said to the Postman, "Either go or wait."
She asked the Postman to either go or wait.

(ii) The lady said to the soldier, "Please do come sometime."
The lady requested the soldier to come sometime.

(iii) Richa said to her friend, "If I were you, I would not care for such a man".
Richa advised her friend not to care for such a man.

(iv) The manager ordered the clerk, "Run to the next office and bring some stationery.
The manager ordered the clerk to run to the next office and bring some stationery.

(v) She said to the stranger, "You must leave my room at once."
She ordered the stranger to leave her room at once.

(vi) The teacher said to Suhani, "Will you stop talking now?"
The teacher ordered Suhani to stop talking then.

(vii) I said to her, "Would/Could you please help me"?
I requested her to help me.

(c) **Tense**
(d) **Pronouns**
(e) **Adverbs of time and place**

The change in these parts of reported speech are same as in the case of assertive sentences.

NOTE It should be noted that when 'to' is used in place of inverted commas, the form of the verb does not change.
to + 1st form of the verb –'to go'.

Change of 'Let'

(a) **Let as a proposal/suggestion.**

(i) He said, "Let us go to the movie."
He proposed that they should go to the movie.

(ii) I said to Deepa, "Let us buy a new house."
I suggested to Deepa that we should buy a new house.

(iii) Reena said to me, "Let us celebrate X-Mas."
I said, "No, let us not."
Reena proposed to me that we should celebrate X-Mas. But I did not agree to her proposal.

(b) **'Let' as a request.**

(i) Ravi said to the manager, "Let me go home."
Ravi requested the manager to let him go home.

(ii) The girls said to the gatekeeper, "Let us enter the school".
The girls requested the gatekeeper to let them enter the school.

(c) **Let as an order.**

(i) The manager said to his assistant, "Let the customers in."
The manager ordered his assistant to let the customers in.

(d) **Let as 'did not care'.**

(i) Sawant said, "Let it rain, I have to go."
Sawant persisted that he did not care for the rain and he had to go.

Some examples are worked out as follows

1. Pearl said to her friend, "Let us go on a long drive."
Pearl suggested to her friends that they should go on a long drive.

2. She said, "Let it rain, I have to go."
She persisted that she did not care for the rain and she had to go.

3. She said to the postman, "Either go or wait."
She asked the postman to either go or wait.

4. The lady said to her, "Please do come some time."
The lady requested her to come sometime.

5. The Mother said to her daughter, "Shut the door, will you"?
The mother asked her daughter to shut the door.

6. She said, "You are playing, are not you?"
She asked me if I was not playing

7. The mother asked Arnav, "You did not meet Sonia, did you"?
The mother asked Arnav if he had met Sonia.

8. Payal said to Rohan, "I did not go to the movie, did you"?
Payal told Rohan that she had not gone to the movie and asked him if he had gone.

9. "Well spoken," The audience cried.
The audience applauded/appreciated his speech that he had spoken well.

10. "Beware, there is a danger," The captain warned.
The captain warned the soldiers to beware of the danger.

11. "Be sure, I am always with you," said the mother.
The mother assured her daughter that she was always with her.

12. "Father", said the son, The teacher said to me, "you are a naughty boy."
The son told his father that the teacher had told him that he was a naughty boy.

13. "When I shall learn swimming," said a small girl, "is not certain."
A small girl told me that when she would learn swimming was not certain.

Exclamatory Sentences

(a) **Reporting Verb** Verb is changed into 'Exclaimed with sorrow,' 'Exclaimed with surprise', 'Exclaimed with joy', 'Cry out', etc.

(i) Portia said, "Good Heavens, I am ruined".
Portia exclaimed with sorrow that she was ruined.

(ii) The director said, "What a good dance, Suhani! you have won the contest."
The director applauded that Suhani had danced well and declared that she had won the contest.

(iii) Mona said, "Hello Sameer, Good Morning!"
Mona greeted Sameer and wished (bade) him good morning.

(iv) The king said, "How foolish of me!"
The king confessed with regret that he was very foolish.

(b) **Inverted Commas** 'That' is used in place of inverted commas.

(i) Tarun said, "How clever I am!"
Tarun exclaimed that he was very clever.

(ii) Deepa said, "What a pity! you have not succeeded.
Deepa exclaimed that it was a pity that he had not succeeded.

(iii) "So help me Heaven!" He cried, "I shall never cheat anyone.
He called upon heaven to witness his resolve that he would never cheat any one.

(iv) "Be Sure, I am always with you," said the mother.
The mother assured her daughter that she was always with her.

(c) **Tense** The change in these parts of
(d) **Pronoun** reported speech are same as
(e) **Adverb of time and place** in the case of assertive sentences

Take care of the following changes

(i) What, Oh, Ah, Good Heavens, Hurrah	Joy, Sorrow, Surprise
(ii) Bravo	Applause, Appreciation
(iii) Hark	Listen
(iv) Fie/Phooh	Contempt

NOTE Before changing the narration, exclamatory sentences are first transformed into assertive sentences.

Optative Sentences (Prayer & Wish)

(a) **Reporting Verb** Verb is changed into 'wish' and 'pray'.

(i) The old man said to his son, "May God bless you!"
The old man wished his son that God might bless him.

(ii) They said, "May God save our country."
They prayed that God might save their country.

(b) **Inverted Commas** 'That' is used in place of inverted commas.

(i) He said, "May God pardon my sins!"
He prayed that God might pardon his sins.

(ii) The beggar said, "May you live long".
The beggar prayed that she might live long.

(iii) The old woman said to the child, "God helps you!"
The old woman prayed that God might help the child.

(c) **Tense**
(d) **Pronouns**
(e) **Adverb of time and place**

The change in these parts of Reported speech are same as in the case of assertive sentences.

NOTE Before changing the Narration, optative sentences are first converted to assertive sentences.

Practice Exercise 1

1. The clerk said to me, "I will not attend the office tomorrow."
2. Hari said to them, "Mohan did not sleep here yesterday."
3. Gita said to Rita, "Will you help me in this work?"
4. Sadhna said to me, "Can you go with me to the station?"
5. I said to him, "Don't you know that I am your friend?"
6. Ram said to me, "Why do you not go home?"
7. He said to her, "Go away from here at once."
8. The teacher said to the boys, "work hard."
9. The doctor said to the patient, "Do not eat much to escape from the disease."
10. The servant said to him, "Sir, grant me leave for two days."
11. He said, "Let us wait for our friends."
12. The spectators said, "Bravo! well done."
13. The captain said, "Hurrah! we have won the match."
14. The doctor said, "Alas! The poor man is no more."
15. The teacher said to me, "What a pity you did not follow my advice."
16. She said, "How beautiful the rose is!"
17. Ram said to his friend, "May you succeed in the examination."
18. The teacher said to the boy, "I shall report the matter to the Principal if you misbehave again."
19. I said, "When it gets dark, light the lamp."
20. 'Doctor', cried the patient, "Please tell me how much time I have."

Practice Exercise 2

1. He said to me, "She left Ahemdabad after I had gone."
2. She said to him, "But you are a fool. You do not understand me."
3. My friend told Rita, "I am going out. Will you go along with me?"
4. The teacher said, "Boys, If you want to pass, you should work hard."
5. "Will you give me lodging for one night?" asked the weary traveller, "Yes", said my father, "you are very welcome."
6. The Governor of the town asked the slave, "How has this hungry lion forgotten his nature?" The slave replied, "This very lion which is standing before you was my friend in the woods."
7. Seema said to Arnav, "Will you go to hospital today?" Arnav said, "No." "Why?" asked seema, "Because I am feeling better." replied Arnav.
8. The teacher said to Rita, "Did you finish your work yesterday?" Rita said, "No, Sir, my mother was ill."
9. "Go down to the bazar. Bring me some oil and lump of ice," ordered his master.
10. Rameshwar said to his teacher, "Sir, I did not do my work as I was ill."
11. Father said to Mohit, "Dear, why are you sad today?"
12. Father said to Mohit, "Bring me a glass of water."
13. He said, "O! Son, my daughter will marry the strongest and greatest person. There is no one stronger and greater than you. Will you accept her as your wife?"
14. A farmer took his sons to the field and said, "There is a treasure hidden here in the earth. If you find it, share it amongst you."
15. The student said, "May I come in, Sir? I am late today." The teacher said, "Yes, you may but this is not your first chance of getting late."
16. The woman said, "All travellers are welcome for the sake of one."
17. Ram said to me, "Thank you for all your help. I could not have finished the work without your help."
18. He said to the shopkeeper, "You are a fool. You have done the opposite of what I desired you to do. Instead of changing the perfume you have changed the shaving cream."
19. "I am a dead man, Hardy," said Nelson, "I am going fast, it will be all over with me soon. Let my dear lady have my hair and other things belonging to me."
20. A young prince once asked a lady, "How is it that you are so fascinating?" The lady felt shy and left the room saying, "Beauty lies in the eyes of a beholder."
21. He said, "Yes, I have broken the slate."
22. The candidate said to the boss, "I assure you of my best service."
23. The doctor said to the patient, "I hope you are better now."
24. "Since it is fine, let us go swimming, "Juliet said to Arnav."
25. "How steep the hill is!" They said, "We are tired."
26. "Why have you come to disturb me," said the master, "Go away."
27. Said Shaurya to Sameer, "Be up. It is no use wasting time." "But I have no work to do today." replied Sameer.
28. "Ladies are," said the Chaueffer, "waiting outside. They are getting impatient, Sir."
29. "Mohan made this mess. Let him clear it up," said his father.
30. I said, "Let Mohan do his worst, he cannot harm me."

Practice Exercise 3

Directions (Q. Nos. 1 and 2) *In the following questions has been given in direct/indirect speech. Out of the four alternatives suggested select the one, which best expresses the same sentence in indirect/direct speech.*

1. Moti asked Gangu whether the latter was in his senses.
(a) "Hey Gangu, are you in your senses now?" asked Moti.
(b) "Gangu, have you lost your senses?" asked Moti.
(c) "Gangu, are you in your senses''? asked Moti.
(d) " Are you senseless, Gangu?" asked Moti.

2. "Who now," they had asked, "will listen to our troubles and protect us from the crocodiles?"
(a) They had wanted to know who would listen to their troubles and protect them from the crocodiles.
(b) They had wanted to know who then would listen to their troubles and protect them from the crocodiles.
(c) They had wanted to know who will now listen to their troubles and protect them from the crocodiles.
(d) They wanted to know who will listen to their troubles and protect them from the crocodiles.

Directions (Q. Nos. 3-8) *In the following questions has been given in direct/indirect speech. Out of the four alternatives suggested select the one, which best expresses the same sentence in indirect/direct speech.*

3. Suresh asked Prasad whether he had watched the cricket match on television the previous night.
(a) Suresh asked Prasad, "Have you watched the cricket match on television last night?"
(b) Suresh said to Prasad, "Did you watch the cricket match on television last night?"
(c) Suresh asked to Prasad, "Did you watch the cricket match on television last night?"
(d) Suresh asked Prasad, "Did you watch the cricket match on television previous night?"

4. He said, "Garima wants to take up a job while her husband wants her to look after the family."
(a) He said that Garima wanted to take up a job while her husband wanted her to look after the family.
(b) He said that Garima wants to take up a job while her husband wanted her to look after the family.
(c) He told that Garima wanted to take up a job while her husband wants her to look after the family.
(d) He said to Garima that though she wanted to take up a job while her husband wanted her to look after the family.

5. She said, "When I was a child, I wasn't afraid of ghosts."
(a) She said that when she was a child she wasn't not afraid of ghosts.
(b) She said that when she was a child she hadn't been afraid of ghosts.
(c) She said that when she was a child she wasn't afraid of ghosts.
(d) She said that when she had been a child she wasn't afraid of ghosts.

6. He said,"Let Hari come with us, mother. I'll take care of him."
(a) He requested his mother to let Hari come with them as he will take care of him.
(b) He informed his mother to let Hari come with them as he would take care of him.
(c) He told his mother to let Hari come of with them as he would take care of him.
(d) He told to his mother let Hari come with us as he would take care of him.

7. "No," said the child, "I won't kneel for if I do, I shall spoil my new pair of trousers.

(a) The child said that he would not kneel for if he did so he will spoil his new pair of trousers.
(b) The child said that he will not kneel for if he kneels he will spoil his trousers.
(c) The child said that he would not kneel for if he did so he would spoil his new pair of trousers.
(d) The child said that i will not kneel for if he should spoil his new pair of trousers.

8. He said, "I do not wish to see any of you, go away."

(a) He said that he had not wished to see any of them and ordered them to go away.
(b) He said that he did not wish to see any of them and ordered them to go away.
(c) He told that he did not wish to see any of them and ordered them to go away.
(d) He said that he does not wish to see any of us and ordered us to go away.

Directions (Q. Nos. 9-11) *In the following questions has been given in direct/indirect speech. Out of the four alternatives suggested select the one, which best expresses the same sentence in indirect/direct speech.*

9. The lady said to the servant, "If you don't wash the clothes properly, I will dismiss you".

(a) The lady warned the servant that she would dismiss her if she didn't wash the clothes properly.
(b) The lady told the servant that she would dismiss her on the event of bad work.
(c) The lady cautioned the servant that she must wash the clothes properly.
(d) The lady advised the servant to wash the clothes properly.

10. "There are ceremonies going on", he said to me.

(a) He told me that there were ceremonies going on.
(b) He told that there had been ceremonies going on.
(c) He told that there had been ceremonies going on.
(d) He told that there are ceremonies going on.

11. "Would you mind taking off your shoes before entering the house?" He said to the foreigner.

(a) He requested the foreigner to take off his shoes before entering the house.
(b) He told the foreigner that the must take off his shoes before entered the house.
(c) He said the foreigner that to take off his shoes before entered the house.
(d) Before entering the house he said that shoes must be taken off.

Directions (Q. Nos. 12-22) *In the following questions has been given in direct/indirect speech. Out of the four alternatives suggested select the one, which best expresses the same sentence in indirect/direct speech.*

12. Kiran asked, "Did you see the cricket match on television last night?"

(a) Kiran asked me whether I saw the cricket match on television the earlier night.
(b) Kiran asked me whether I had seen the cricket match on television the earlier night.
(c) Kiran asked me did I see the cricket match on television last night.
(d) Kiran asked me whether I had seen the cricket match on television last night.

13. He said to her, "What a cold day!"

(a) He told her that it was a cold day.
(b) He exclaimed that it was a cold day.
(c) He exclaimed sorrowfully that it was a cold day.
(d) He exclaimed that it was a very cold day.

14. The tailor said to him, "Will you have the suit ready by tomorrow evening?"

(a) The tailor asked him that he will have the suit ready by the next evening.
(b) The tailor asked him that he would had the suit ready by the next evening.
(c) The tailor asked him if he would have the suit ready by the next evening.
(d) The tailor asked him if he will like to have the suit ready by the next evening.

15. He said to the interviewer, "Could you please repeat the question?"
(a) He requested the interviewer if he could please repeat the question.
(b) He requested the interviewer to please repeat the question.
(c) He requested the interviewer to repeat the question.
(d) He requested the interviewer if he could repeat the question.

16. He said, "Be quiet and listen to my words."
(a) He urged them to be quiet and listen to his words.
(b) He urged them and said be quiet and listen to words.
(c) He said they should be quiet and listen to his words.
(d) He said you should be quiet and listen to my words.

17. The teacher said to Mahesh, "Congratulations! Wish you success in life."
(a) The teacher congratulated Mahesh and said wish you success in life.
(b) The teacher wished congratulations and success in life to Mahesh.
(c) The teacher said congratulations to Mahesh and wished him success in life.
(d) The teacher congratulated Mahesh and wished him success in life.

18. The poor examinee said, "O God take pity on me."
(a) The poor examinee prayed God to take pity on him.
(b) The poor examinee, invoking God, implored him to take pity on him.
(c) The poor examinee exclaimed that God take pity on him.
(d) The poor examinee asked God to take pity on him.

19. "Where will you be tomorrow," I said, "in case I have to ring you?"
(a) I asked where you will be the next day in case I will ring him.
(b) I asked where he would be the next day in case I had to ring him.
(c) I said to him where he will be in case I have to ring him.
(d) I enquired about his whereabouts the next day in case I would have to ring up.

20. The father warned his son that he should beware of him.
(a) The father warned his son, "Beware of him!"
(b) The father warned his son, "Watch that chap!"
(c) The father warned his son, "Be careful about him"
(d) The father warned his son, "Don't fall into the trap"

21. "What about going for a swim," he said, "It's quite fine now."
(a) He asked me what about going for a swim as it was quite fine then.
(b) He proposed going for a swim as it was quite fine.
(c) He suggested going for a swim as it was quite fine.
(d) He advised me to go for a swim as it was quite fine.

22. "You can't bathe in this sea, " he said to me, "it's very rough''.
(a) He said that you can't bathe in this sea because it's rough.
(b) He said that I couldn't bathe in that sea if it was very rough.
(c) He said that I couldn't bathe in that sea as it was very rough.
(d) He said that you can't bathe in this sea since it was very rough.

Revision Exercise

Directions (Q. Nos. 1-12) *In the following question, a sentence has been given in Direct / Indirect speech. Out of the four alternatives suggested, select the one, which best expresses the same sentence in Indirect / Direct speech.*

1. Manoj said, "I must go now."
(a) Manoj said that he must go then.
(b) Manoj said that he must go than.
(c) manuol said he has to go then.
(d) Manoj said that he should be going than.

2. Do you have anything to say on behalf of the accused ?' said the judge finally.
(a) The judge finally asked that if he had anything to say on behalf of the accused.
(b) The judge finally ask that whether he had anything to sayan behalf of the accused.
(c) The judge finally asked that if he has anything to say on behalf of the accused
(d) The judge finally asked that if he has had anything to say on behalf of the accused.

3. The coach said, "Don't move, boys."
(a) The coach told to the boys don't move.
(b) The coach said to the boys not to be moving.
(c) The coach asked the boys not to move.
(d) The coach told to them, don't move boys.

4. "Alas I have broken my grandfather's watch" said Amit.
(a) Amit was sorrowful that he broke his grandfather's watch.
(b) Amit exclaimed sorrowfully that he has broken his grandfather's watch.
(c) Amit was sorrowful that he had broken his grandfather's watch.
(d) Amit exclaimed sorrowfully that he had broken his grandfather's watch.

5. Mother said, "Lie down, Arjun."
(a) Mother told lie down Arjun.
(b) Mother asked Arjun to lie down.
(b) Mother told Arjun for lying down.
(d) Mother asked Arjun to be lied down.

6. Sita said to her mother, "Do you always get up early?"
(a) Sita asked her mother that, whether she always got up early.
(b) Sita asked her mother that, whether she has been always getting up early.
(c) Sita asked her mother that, if she has been always getting up early.
(d) Sita asked her mother if she always got up early.

7. Rita said, "Alas! I am undorle."
(a) Rita said that she was undone.
(b) Rita told me that she was undone.
(c) Rita exclaimed sadly that she was undone.
(d) Rita said that alas, she was undone.

8. Raju wrote, "He will be going to Mumbai the next weekend."
(a) Raju wrote that he will be going to Mumbai the next weekend.
(b) Raju wrote that he would be going to Mumbai the last weekend.
(c) Raju wrote that he would be going to Mumbai the next weekend.
(d) Raju wrote that he should be gone to Mumbai the next weekend.

9. The principal said, "I want to meet her parents."
(a) The principal wanted to meet her parents.
(b) The principal said that he wants to meet her parents.
(c) The principal said that he wanted to meet her parents.
(d) The principal asked if he could meet her parents.

10. Mr. Pattinson said, "I brought a chocolate for you."
(a) Mr. Pattinson brought a chocolate for me.
(b) Mr. Pattinson said that he had brought a chocolate for me.
(c) A chocolate was brought by Mr. Pattinson for me.
(d) Mr. Pattinson said he brought a chocolate for me.

11. Sita said, "Will he listen to such a man?"
(a) Sita said would we listen to such a man.
(b) Sita ask if he would listen to such a man.
(c) Sita said would I listen to such a man.
(d) Sita asked whether he would listen to such a man.

12. "German is easy to teach," she said.
(a) She says German is easy.
(b) She told us that German was easy to teach.
(c) She informed German was easy to teach.
(d) She said that German was easy to teach.

Directions (Q. Nos. 13-20) *Select the correct indirect form of the given sentence.*

13. The boss said to his employee, "I will be happy if you finish this project by evening."
(a) The boss told his employee that he would be happy If he will finish this project by evening.
(b) The boss told his employee he will be happy if he finished this project by evening.
(c) The boss told his employee that he would be happy if he finishes that project by evening.
(d) The boss told his employee that he would be happy if he finished that project by evening.

14. Mahesh said to the interviewer, "Sir, I was in charge of the production unit at my previous office."
(a) Mahesh told the Interviewer I was in charge of the production unit at his previous office.
(b) Mahesh told the interviewer that he had been incharge of the production unit at his previous office.
(c) Mahesh told the interviewer that Sir was in charge of the production unit at my previous office.
(d) Mahesh told the interviewer you were in charge of the production unit at my previous office.

15. Mr. Puri said to me, "Why are you taking down this fence?"
(a) Mr. Puri asked me why was I taking down this fence.
(b) Mr. Puri said to me why you were taking down that fence.
(c) Mr. Puri asked me why I was taking down that fence.
(d) Mr. Puri said to me that why are you taking down this fence.

16. The interviewer asked Ashok, "Why did you leave that job last month?"
(a) The interviewer asked Ashok why he had left that job the previous month.
(b) The interviewer asked ashok that why did he leave that job the previous month.
(c) The interviewer asked Ashok that why he leave that job the last month.
(d) The interviewer asked Ashok why you have left that job the previous month.

17. The doctor told his patient, "Continue the same course of medicines for the next week."
(a) The doctor told his patient that he may continue the same course of medicines in the following week.
(b) The doctor told his patient to continued the same course of medicines in the next week.
(c) The doctor told his patient for continuing the same course of medicines for the next week.
(d) The doctor told his patient to continue the same course of medicines for the following week.

18. Uma asked me, "How's your brother?"
(a) Uma asked me how your brother was. (b) Uma asked me how is my brother.
(c) Uma asked me how my brother was. (d) Uma asked me how was my brother.

19. The shopkeeper asked me, "Where is your car"?
(a) The shopkeeper asked me where was my car.
(b) The shopkeeper asked me where is your car.
(c) The shopkeeper asked me where my car is.
(d) The shopkeeper asked me where my car was.

20. The interviewer asked Ramesh, "Do you have any idea about our products?"
(a) The interviewer asked Ramesh that if he had any idea about the products.
(b) The interviewer asked Ramesh if he had any idea about their products.
(c) The interviewer asked Ramesh if he have any idea about their products.
(d) The interviewer asked Ramesh if they had any idea about his products.

Exam Practice

Directions (Q Nos. 1-6) *Each question in this section has a direct statement followed by its reported form in indirect speech. Select the correct statement in indirect speech and mark it in the Answer Sheet accordingly.*

1. The captain said to his soldiers, "Move forward and face the target now." **CDS 2018**
(a) The captain ordered his soldiers to move forward and face the target.
(b) The captain informed his soldiers that they should move forward and face the target now.
(c) The captain asked his soldiers to move forward and face the target then.
(d) The capitain told his soldiers that they move forward and face the target immediately.

2. Vivek said to his friend, "Could you please turn off the switch?" **CDS 2018**
(a) Vivek told his friend to turn off the switch.
(b) Vivek asked his friend to please turn off the switch.
(c) Vivek requested his friend to turn off the switch.
(d) Vivek told his friend that he should turn off the switch.

3. The manager said to his colleagues, "We have received a serious threat to our business now and we need to act to face it." **CDS 2018**
(a) The manager told his colleagues that they had received a serious threat to our business then and they needed to act to face it.
(b) The manager told his colleagues that they received a serious threat to their business then and they needed to act to face it.
(c) The manager said his colleagues that they had received a serious threat to our business then and they needed to act to face it
(d) The manager told his colleagues that they had received a serious threat to their business at that time and they needed to act to face it.

4. Romila said to Rahim, "Where were your ideas when we faced the troubles last week?" **CDS 2018**
(a) Romila asked Rahim where his ideas had been when they had faced the trouble the week before.
(b) Romila asked Rahim where his ideas had been when they faced the trouble the last week.

(c) Romila requested Rahim where his ideas had been when they faced the trouble the week before.
(d) Romila told Rahim where his ideas were when they faced the trouble the week before.

5. Jhe actor said to his co-star, Sarita, “Will you go with me for a cup of tea in the evening today?” **CDS 2018**
(a) The actor said to his co-star if she would go for a cup of tea with him in evening today .
(b) The actor told his co-star Sarita if she would go with him for a cup of tea in evening that day.
(c) The actor requests his co-star, Sarita if she would go with him for a cup of tea in that evening that day.
(d) The actor asked his co-star Sarita if she would go with him for a cup of tea in the evening that day.

6. The preacher said to the crowd, “The Sun rises everyday for all of us without any expectations in return.” **CDS 2018**
(a) The preacher told the crowd that the Sun rose everyday for all of them without any expectations in return.
(b) The preacher told the crowd that the Sun rises everyday for all of us without any expectations in return.
(c) The preacher told the crowd that the Sun has risen everyday for all of them without any expectations in return.
(d) The preacher told the crowd that the Sun rises everyday for all of them without any expectations in return.

Directions (Q. Nos. 7-16) *In this section direct speech sentences are given and you are required to find the correct indirect speech sentence of the same. Choose the correct response (a), (b), (c) or (d) and indicate on the Answer Sheet accordingly.*

7. Rahul said to his teacher, “Madam, what is the way to solve the question?” **CDS 2020**
(a) Rahul asked his teacher what the way to solve the question was.
(b) Rahul told his teacher what was the way to solve the question.
(c) Rahul asked to his teacher what the way was to solve the question.
(d) Rahul told his teacher what the way was to solve the question.

8. He Said to his friend, “Could you please close the door?”
(a) He requested his friend to close the door.
(b) He requested his friend to please close the door.
(c) He ordered his friend to close the door.
(d) He wanted his friend to close the door for him.

9. Raj said to Sheela, “The Sun rises in the east.”
(a) Raj told Sheela that the Sun rose in the east.
(b) Raj told Sheela that the Sun rises in the east.
(c) Raj asked Sheela that the Sun rises in the east.
(d) Raj said to Sheela that the Sun has arisen in the east.

10. Navanitha said to her friends, "What a scintillating beauty it is!"
(a) Navanitha told to her friends that it was a scintillating beauty.
(b) Navanitha exclaimed to her friends what a scintillating beauty it was.
(c) Navanitha asked her friends whether it was a scintillating beauty.
(d) uty. rvanitha exclaimed to her friends that it was a scintillating beauty.

11. The Captain said to the soldiers, "March forward and aim atthe peak of the hill today." **CDS 2020**
(a) The Captain requested the soldiers to march forward and aim at the peak of the hill that day.

(b) The Captain ordered the soldiers to march forward and aim at the peak of the hill today.
(c) The Captain ordered the soldiers to march forward and aim at the peak of the hill that day.
(d) he Captain told the soldiers that they should march forward and aim at the peak of the hill that day.

12. "Where were you last evening?" said the lady to her maid.
(a) The lady asked her maid where she had been the previous evening.
(b) The lady asked her maid where she had been in the last evening.
(c) The lady asked her maid where had she been the evening before.
(d) The lady told her maid where she had been to the last evening.

13. "Those who sowed the seeds last season will reap the harvest this season," said the leader to her followers. **CDS 2020**
(a) The leader said to her followers that those who sowed the seeds the previous season would reap the harvest that season.
(b) The leader addressed her followers that those who have sown the seeds the previous season would reap the harvest this season.
(c) The leader addressed her followers that those who had sown the seeds the previous season would reap the harvest that season.
(d) The leader advised her followers that those who sow the seeds the previous season would reap the harvest this season.

14. He said to his manager, "Could you please pass the bill this week?" **CDS 2020**
(a) He told his manager that bill to be passed.
(b) He requested his manager to pass the bill that week.
(c) He ordered his manager to pass the bill that week.
(d) He requested his manager to pass the bill this week.

15. The village chief said to the villagers, "All of us need to adopt new regulations. We will protect our Earth forever." **CDS 2020**
(a) The village chief ordered the villagers that all of them needed to adopt new regulations and they would protect their Earth forever.
(b) The village chief told the villagers that all of them need to adopt new regulations and they will protect their Earth forever.
(c) The village chief wanted the villagers needed to adopt new regulations and they would protect their Earth forever.
(d) The village chief told the villagers that all of them needed to adopt new regulations and they would protect their Earth forever.

16. The grandfather said to the baby, "May you live long with all good things of life."
(a) The grandfather blessed to the baby with long life and all good things of life. **CDS 2020**
(b) The grandfather asked the baby that she would live long with all good things of life.
(c) The grandfather wanted the baby to live long with all good things of life.
(d) The grandfather blessed the baby that she would live long with all good things of life.

Directions (Q. Nos 17 and 18) *In the following question, a sentence has been given in Direct/indirect speech. Out of the four alternatives suggested, select the one which best expresses the same sentence in Indirect/Direct speech.*

17. The watchman said, thief! "thief! catch him"?
(a) The watchman shouted to the crowd to catch the thief.
(b) The watchman shouted to the crowd, thief, thief, catch him.
(c) The watchman shouted to the crowd, catch the thief.
(d) The watchman shouted to the crowd catch him.

18. He said to me, 'What are you doing?'

(a) He asked me what I was doing.
(b) He asked me that what was I doing.
(c) He said what I had been doing.
(d) He said that what I was doing.

Answers

Practice Exercise 1

1. The clerk told me that he would not attend the office the next day.
2. Hari told them that Mohan had not slept there the previous day.
3. Gita asked Rita if she would help her in the work.
4. Sadhna asked me if I could go with her to the station.
5. I asked him if he did not know that I was his friend.
6. Ram asked me why I did not go home.
7. He ordered her to go away from there at once.
8. The teacher advised the boys to work hard.
9. The doctor advised the patient not to eat much to escape from the disease.
10. The servant requested him to grant him leave for two days.
11. He said that they should wait for their friends.

    Or

    Pie told me that we should wait tor our friends.
12. The spectators applauded them saying that they had done well.
13. The captain exclaimed with joy that they had won the match.
14. The doctor exclaimed with sorrow htat the poor man was no more.
15. The teacher expressed regret that ii was a great pity that I had not followed his advice.
16. She exclaimed with wonder that the rose was very beautiful.
17. Ram wished that his friend might succeed in the examination.
18. The teacher threatened/warned the boy to report the matter to the Principal if he misbehaved again.
19. I told her to light the lamp when it got dark.

    Or

    I told her that when it got dark she should light the lamp.
20. The patient pleaded with the doctor to tell her how much time she had.

Practice Exercise 2

1. He told me that she left Ahmedabad after he had gone.
2. But she told him that he was a fool because he did not understand her.
3. MY friend told Rita that she was going out and asked her if she would go along with her.
4. The teacher told the boys that if they wanted to pass, they should work hard.
5. The weary traveller asked my father if he would give him lodging for one night. My father replied that he would and added that he was very welcome.
6. The governor of the town asked the slave how the hungry lion had forgotten his nature. To this the slave replied that very lion which was standing before him had been his friend in the woods.
7. Seerna asked Arnay if he would go to hospital that day. Arnav replied that he would not. Then Seema asked him why he would not. Arnav replied that he would not go because he was feeling better
8. I'he teacher asked Rita if she had finished her work the previous day. Rita replied respectfully that she had not because her mother had been ill.

9. His master ordered the servant to go down to the bazar and bring him some oil and lump of Ice.
10. Rameshwar told his teacher respectfully that he had not done his work as he had been ill.
11. Father asked Mohit lovingly why he was sad that day.
12. Father asked Mohit to bring him a glass of water.
13. Addressing him as his son he told him that his daughter would marry the strongest and greatest person and there was no one stronger and greater than he. So he asked him if he would accept her as his wife.
14. A farmer took his sons to the field and told them that there was a treasure hidden there in the earth. He advised them to share to amongst them, if they found it.
15. The student asked the teacher respectfully if he might come in although he was late that day. The teacher replied that he might but reminded him that that was not his first chance of getting late.
16. The woman told that all travellers were welcome for the sake of one.
17. Ram thanked me for all my help and said that he could not have finished the work without my help.
18. He reprimanded the shopkeeper saying that he was a fool because he had done the opposite of what he had desired him to do. He informed him that instead of changing the perfume he had changed the shaving cream.
19. Nelson called Hardy near him and told hlrn that he was a dead man and he was going fast because it would be all over with him soon. So he requested Hardy to let his dear lady had his hair and other things belonging to him.
20. A young prince-once as1.edajady how it was that she was so fascinting. She felt Shy and left the room saying that beauty lay in eyes ala beholder.
21. He admitted-that he had broken the slate.
22. The candidate assured the boss of his best services.
23. The doctor hoped that the patient was better then,
24. Juliet suggested to Arnav that they should go swimrninq since at was fine.
25. They exclaimed that the hill was very steep and they were tired.
26. The master scolded his servant for disturbing him and ordered him to go away.
27. Shaurya asked Sameer to be up as it was no use wasting time. But Sameer replied that he had no work to do that day.
28. The chauffer told his master repectfully that the ladies were waiting outside and they were getting impatient.
29. Mohan's father said that Mohan had made that mess and that he was to clear it.
30. I declared that Mohan might do his worst, he could not harm me.

Practice Exercise 3

1. (c)	2. (a)	3. (b)	4. (a)	5. (c)	6. (c)	7. (c)
8. (b)	9. (a)	10. (a)	11. (a)	12. (b)	13. (d)	14. (c)
15. (c)	16. (a)	17. (d)	18. (a)	19. (b)	20. (a)	21. (a)
22. (c)						

Revision Exercise

1. (a)	2. (a)	3. (c)	4. (d)	5. (c)	6. (d)	7. (c)
8. (c)	9. (c)	10. (b)	11. (d)	12. (d)	13. (d)	14. (b)
15. (c)	16. (a)	17. (d)	18. (c)	19. (d)	20. (b)	

Exam Practice

1. (c)	2. (c)	3. (b)	4. (a)	5. (d)	6. (d)	7. (a)
8. (a)	9. (b)	10. (d)	11. (c)	12. (a)	13. (c)	14. (b)
15. (d)	16. (d)	17. (a)	18. (a)			

Synthesis

Definition *Synthesis means the combination of two or more simple sentences into one simple, complex or compound sentence.*

Part I

Combining two or more simple sentences into one Complex sentence with the help of subordinate conjunctions to make.

(a) Noun Clause
(b) Adjective Clause
(c) Adverb Clause

Part II

Combining two or more simple sentences into one simple sentence as follows

(a) By using Infinitive
(b) By using Participle
(c) By using Nominative Absolute
(d) By using Gerund and Noun with Preposition before it.
(e) By using Noun or Phrase in Apposition.
(f) By using Adjective
(g) By using Conjunction 'And'
(h) By using Adverb or Adverbial Phrase

NOTE All these combinations are related to Subordinate Clause (Noun, Adjective and Adverb).

Part III

Combining two or more simple sentences into one compound sentence by using Co-ordinating conjunctions to make a Co-ordinate Clause.

Part I

Complex Sentence

A complex sentence is formed by joining two or more simple sentences with the help of subordinate conjunctions.

As stated earlier a complex sentence consists of more than one clause. Besides a principal clause, one or more subordinate clauses form a complex sentence. There are three kinds of subordinate clauses joined by their respective subordinating conjunctions. *For example*

(i) I know **that** he is a good boy. (Noun clause)
(ii) I know the man **who** was here yesterday. (Adjective clause)
(iii) I shall give you money **when** you do this work. (Adverb clause)

These sentences contain three kinds of subordinate clauses.

(a) Noun clause. (b) Adjective clause.
(c) Adverb Clause.

(A) Noun Clause

I know that he is a good boy.

In the above sentence 'I know' is a principal clause. 'that he is a good boy' is a noun clause as it does the work of a noun. A Noun clause answers the verb or noun in the principal or any other subordinate clause.

Subordinate conjunctions of a Noun clause are–**that, if, whether, when, where, how, why, what, who, whose, whom, which, whatever.**

A set of simple sentences may be combined in the following manner by making a noun clause.

(a) **Object to a Transitive Verb**

(i) I say it. He is a good man.
I say that he is a good man.

(ii) I said it. He was a good man.
I said that he was a good man.

(iii) I cannot say. Will he come tomorrow?
I cannot say if/whether he will come tomorrow.

(iv) I don't know. What is he doing?
I don't know what he is doing.

(b) **Object of Infinitive, Gerund and Participle**

(i) Everybody was pleased to know. She was absent.
Everybody was pleased to know that she was absent.

(ii) She kept on asking. When will her mother return?
She kept on asking when her mother would return.

(c) **Object to Preposition**

(i) I don't believe. She said something.
I don't believe in what she said.

(ii) Please listen. Your teacher is telling something.
Please listen to what your teacher is telling.

(d) **Complement of a Verb**

(i) The hope is. She will return tomorrow.
The hope is that she will return tomorrow.

(ii) The fact is. Nisha has not qualified the test.
The fact is that Nisha has not qualified the test.

NOTE Noun clause following the verbs –'to be, become, seem, appear, grow, taste, smell, prove, look, make' etc. –perform the function of a complement of these verbs (in place of a predicate).

(e) **The Case in Apposition to a Noun**

(i) She never believed in his statement. His father is a doctor.
She never believed in his statement that his father was a doctor.

(ii) No one heard the news. The prime minister is coming tomorrow.
No one heard the news that the prime minister was coming the next day.

(f) **The Case in Apposition to a Pronoun**

(i) It is true. My brother has left for America.
It is true that my brother has left for America.

(ii) It was not known. What is she doing in Indore?
It was not known what she was doing in Indore.

(g) **The Subject of a Verb**

(i) It is true. What he knows.
(a) It is true what he knows.
(b) What he knows is true. (subject of a verb)

(ii) It is not known. When will she come?
(a) It is not known when she will come.
(b) When she will come is not known. (subject of a verb)

Noun clause as a subject may be used in place of pronouns. 'It, this, that,' Noun clause works as a subject in this type of sentences.

Examples worked out for the students.

1. I say. She is a good woman.
I say that she is a good woman.

2. I said. He is an honest man.
I said that he was an honest man.

3. I cannot say. She will come.
I cannot say whether/if she will come.

4. I did not know. Will he come?
I did not know if he would come.

5. I doubt. Can he do it?
I doubt if he can do it.

6. I am certain. She has got through the examination.
I am certain that she has got through the examination.

7. I don't know. He said something.
I don't know what he said.

8. What you say. I shall not do.
I shall not do what you say.

9. It is not clear. What he says.
(a) It is not clear what he says.
(b) What he says is not clear.

10. It is true. She will succeed.
(a) That she will succeed is true.
(b) It is true that she will succeed.

11. She came sometime in the morning. It is a mystery.
(a) When she came in the morning is a mystery.
(b) It is a mystery when she came in the morning.

12. I wonder. How can she pass?
I wonder how she can pass.

13. He denied. He has committed theft.
He denied that he had committed theft.

14. The fact is. He is a hard-working fellow.
The fact is that he is a hard working fellow.

15. The fact is well known. He is an honest person.
The fact that he is an honest person is well known.

16. She came from somewhere in 1970. It is not revealed.
(a) It is not revealed where she came from in 1970.
(b) Where she came from in 1970 is not revealed.

17. Someone misguided him. His parents don't know.
His parents don't know who misguided him.

18. A certain number of students were admitted. The Principal does not know this number.
The Principal does not know how many students were admitted.

19. Everybody wants to know the reason. The two friends quarrelled yesterday.
Everybody wants to know why the two friends quarrelled yesterday.

20. Do you know the time? The train will arrive at a certain time.
Do you know when the train will arrive?

Practice Exercise 1

Combine the following sentences into complex sentences.

1. I don't know. He will come.
2. He is going somewhere. I cannot say.
3. He was not guilty. That was the verdict of the bench.
4. There is no doubt in it. He will do it.
5. He is correct. I am sure of it.
6. You gave him stolen money. That was his statement.
7. He may be guilty. I am not certain.
8. Some one arrived late at night. I do not know.
9. I don't believe it. He said something to me.
10. Nobody informed me. My mother went to temple sometime in the evening.
11. Everybody doubts it. He will pass.
12. This is my belief. He will cheat you.
13. My father will come here. I do not know the time.
14. Where have you put my purse? Please tell me.
15. Are you listening? I am saying something.
16. He came late. I cannot tell the reason.
17. The news is wrong. He died last night.
18. He confessed. He had committed murder.
19. It was expected. He will arrive soon.
20. It is believed. Netaji died in aircrash.
21. I cannot say, She may be a doctor.
22. What is your attitude to life? All depends on this.
23. My son is anxious to learn. How can one travel to space?
24. The fact is. He is a coward.
25. She declared her intention. She will not marry next year.
26. He wasted a certain amount of money. His wife cannot tell.
27. I cannot rely on it. She has promised me something.
28. The police are trying to inquire. When did she leave the party?
29. She told me the fact. Her father will not allow her to go abroad.
30. Our expectation was. We will succeed.
31. The news is not correct. She has returned from Chennai.
32. She confessed. She went to Delhi last night.
33. My sister kept on asking. When shall I come back from Indore?
34. The verdict of the judges has been challenged. He is guilty.
35. I can not tell. She came sometime in the morning.
36. The rumour is baseless. He died last night.
37. She completed this work in a strange manner. Everyone wonders.
38. It is certain. She will arrive today.
39. I heard him telling his mother. He is leaving for America very soon.
40. It cannot be confirmed. Has he married?

(B) **Adjective Clause**

I know the man who was here yesterday.

In the above sentence 'I know the man' is a principal clause. 'Who was here yesterday' is an Adjective clause. It does the work of an Adjective qualifying the noun 'the man'. Adjective clause qualifies noun or pronoun as the case may be.

Subordinate conjunctions of Adjective clause are **"Who, whose, whom, which, of which, that, as, why, when, where."**

Examples worked out for the students.

1. I know the man. He is a doctor.
I know the man who is a doctor.

2. This is my pen. It is very costly.
This is my pen which is very costly.

3. I don't know any of the men. They live here.
I don't know any of the men that live here.

4. I have met all the boys. They are studying in the college.
I have met all the boys that are studying in the college.

5. The Sanskrit language is not difficult to learn. It is taught in our school.
The Sanskrit language that is taught in our school is not difficult to learn.

6. The monster was proud of his power. He was defeated by Hercules.
The monster who was proud of his power was defeated by Hercules.

7. He settled in the town. He retired there from service.
He settled in the town where he retired from service.

8. It was midnight. The trains collided then.
It was midnight when the trains collided.

9. I had many friends in prosperity. All of them have deserted me now.
In prosperity I had many friends who all have deserted me now.

10. He has become suddenly rich. I can tell you the reason.
I can tell you the reason why he has become suddenly rich.

11. Shalini bought only one of the flats? These were built by AWHO.
Shalini bought only one of the flats that was built by AWHO.

12. I have invited Mohan. Everybody likes him.
I have invited Mohan whom everybody likes.

13. He bought a new book. Its price is very cheap.
He bought a new book the price of which is very cheap.

14. The book has been found. I lost it yesterday.
The book which I lost yesterday has been found.

15. He settled in Nagpur. He was born there.
He settled in Nagpur where he was born.

Practice Exercise 2

Combine the following simple sentences into complex sentences.

1. Shakespeare was a great dramatist. He is the author of a number of plays.
2. You have put my purse somewhere. Please show me the place.
3. This is the college. I studied here.
4. It was 10 o'clock. My father left for office then.
5. Can you tell me the reason? You are wasting time.
6. The boy was present there. The teacher gave him a prize.
7. I bought a pen. I shall give you the same pen.
8. I was the first man. I heard his name on the radio.
9. They were sitting under a tree. Its shade was very cool.
10. I shall go by the Taj Express. It goes to Agra direct.
11. They are reading a book. It is very rare.
12. The news is true. He gave it yesterday.
13. Yesterday I bought a book. It is very cheap.
14. They committed a mistake. It was quite serious.
15. You can not believe such a person. The person is dishonest.
16. We undertook a journey to Gwalior. It was tiring.
17. A soldier was lying in the field. He was wounded.
18. The dog felled the candle. It was burning.
19. They are healthy. The healthy do not need a doctor.
20. The man died last night. He was wounded in an accident.
21. The magic ball was eaten by the jester. It was meant for king.
22. Seema was the last person. She left for home.
23. This is a class room. It is not the place to play.
24. He has a large family. He has to educate them.
25. He has some bills. He must pay them in cash.
26. I have no friend. I cannot talk to him.
27. Childhood is a time. One can teach good habits to children.
28. I know the reason. He could not succeed.
29. The time is not certain. He will come tomorrow.
30. Nobody appreciated the way. She behaved at the party.
31. I was informed of the place. He was living there.
32. I remember very well the year. He retired then.
33. You can have anything. Whatever you like.
34. The students are very hard working. They hail from Bihar.
35. The girl is a cousin of my wife. The girl has long hair.
36. I never visit any of my uncles. They reside in Manekshaw Enclave.
37. The news is true. The Voice of America broadcast it.
38. The players were present at the function. The President awarded them cash prize.
39. Good deeds live after men. They do them in their lives.
40. Kabir was a famous poet. He wrote spiritual poetry.

(C) Adverb Clause

When you do this work, I shall give you money.

In the above sentence, 'I shall give you money' is a principal clause. 'When you do this work' is an adverb clause. It does the work of an Adverb. It is required to modify some verb, Adverb or Adjective in some other clause.

Adverb clause may be classified as follows.

Examples worked out for the students.

Time Clause Conjunctions : When, as, while, as soon as, before, after, by the time, until, till whenever, small, as long as.

1. He saw the police departing. He immediately got into his car.
   As he saw the police departing, he immediately got into his car.
2. I will get money for you. Don't go till then.
   Don't go until I get money for you.
3. I left office. My wife arrived afterwards.
   My wife arrived after I had left office.
4. He was going to school. He was caught in the rain.
   While he was going to school, he was caught in the rain.
5. His father retired last year. He has been idle from that time.
   Since his father retired last year he has been idle.

Condition Clause

Conjunctions : If, unless, suppose, in case, on condition that, provided, I wish, I would, would that, if only.

1. Work hard. You will fail.
   If you do not work hard, you will fail.
2. We may go tomorrow. It depends on the weather.
   We may go tomorrow if weather permits.
3. Do it well. You will be rewarded.
   If you do it well, you will be rewarded.
4. Work hard. You will fail otherwise.
   If you do not work hard, you will fail.
5. She had laboured. Otherwise she would not have succeeded.
   If she had not laboured, She would not have succeeded.

Purpose

Conjunctions : So that, lest, in order that, that

1. He went to Delhi. He wanted to meet his mother.
   He went to Delhi so that he might meet his mother.
2. He is afraid of getting late. He will go by his own car.
   He will go by his own car lest he should get late.

Place

Conjunctions : Where, wherever

1. I shall go. He works there in a factory.
   I shall go where he works in a factory.
2. You can stay. You can stay anywhere.
   You can stay wherever you like.

Result

Conjunctions : 'That' (followed by 'such', 'so')

1. He grew weaker and weaker. He was admitted to hospital.
   He grew so weak that he was admitted to hospital.
2. He drove very fast. He soon overtook us.
   He drove so fast that he soon overtook us.

Reason

Conjunctions : Because, since, as, that, now that.

1. The students disobeyed the teacher. He was annoyed.
   The teacher was annoyed because the students disobeyed him.
2. You are disturbing me. I can not work.
   I cannot work as you are disturbing me.
3. He came late. He was punished.
   He was punished because he came late.
4. It was dark outside. I did not go out.
   Since it was dark outside, I did not go out.

Concession or Contrast

Conjunctions : Although, though, as, even if, however, whether, even though, no matter what, no matter that, notwithstanding that, much as, whatever.

1. He is very old. He can still run very fast.
   Although he is very old, he can run very fast.
2. He has succeeded in life. He is still humble.
   Though he has succeeded in life, he is still humble.
3. He is lucky. he will not win this match.
   However lucky he may be, he will not win this match.
4. She is rich. She is not kind.
   Rich as she is, she is not kind.

Manner

Conjunctions : As, as if, as though

1. I advised him. He acted accordingly.
   He acted as I advised him.
2. He is not educated. He speaks like an educated person.
   He speaks as if he were an educated person.

Comparison

Conjunctions : Than, as

1. The tiger is larger. The cat is smaller.
   The tiger is larger than the cat.
2. Her mother is wise. Richa is equally wise.
   Richa is as wise as her mother is.

Practice Exercise 3

Combine the following simple sentences into complex sentences.

1. He ran very quickly. He overtook everybody.
2. You always disturb me. I cannot work.
3. I had left office. My boss called me.
4. The members of the committee arrived. The conference started.
5. You must hurry. Otherwise you will miss the train.
6. It was very sultry noon. I could not go out.
7. I left office. The rain started that very moment.
8. He will not leave at night. He cannot bear the idea of being robbed.
9. He came to me. He wanted my help.
10. He found out his mistake. Then he repented very much.
11. Do not sleep out side. You will be ill.
12. I reached the station. The train had left.
13. You left India. You have not written any letter since.
14. The old man walks fast. He walks like a young person.
15. He is rich. He is unhappy.
16. Help others. God will help you.
17. They were playing in the garden. It started raining.
18. No money was given to me. The work was stopped.
19. The patient grew weaker and weaker. He died last night.
20. His brother died. He has been very poor from that time.
21. Everybody will admire him. His being hard-working is a condition.
22. Go out. You will catch cold.
23. He was sick. Even then he went out.
24. He was cremated in the village. He settled there after his retirement.
25. He is admired by everybody. He is still not proud.
26. He was sitting on the grass. A snake bit him.
27. She waited for her friend. She waited till her arrival.
28. She came late. Else she would have enjoyed music.
29. Do you want to go to Malabar Hills? Then bring money with you.
30. I shall go. My cousin works there.
31. Water is very cold. No one can drink it.
32. He employed a watchman. He wanted to be safe.

33. They helped me. Otherwise I would not have got success.
34. I would have been glad. I could have given you money.
35. He did not stop working. He achieved success.
36. The signal was given. The train started immediately.
37. You can stay here. It is your wish.
38. She is beautiful. No other member in her family is so beautiful.
39. Let us wait. The train stops.
40. I make a promise. I stick to it.
41. He is working hard. His aim is to join Army.
42. He fled. He wanted to escape being caught.
43. I will get money for you. Please do not go till then.
44. Everybody will admire you. Your honesty is the condition.
45. He did not receive help in time. He would not have died from burns.
46. He gets more. Then he works more.
47. Do not get into the train. The train must stop.
48. It may rain. The schools may be closed.
49. We shall leave for Shimla. It depends on weather.
50. I should be glad. I could help your husband.
51. He worked hard. He would have failed.
52. I shall be glad. I can help you in getting a job.
53. She treated me in a certain manner. I shall treat her so.
54. My younger sister behaves with me. She behaves like an elder sister.
55. She wrote an essay. She wrote to the best of her ability.
56. She speaks well. She writes better.
57. She is wise. She is kinder.
58. He is not rich. He spends like a rich person.
59. The candidates stayed in the hall. They stayed till the departure of the supervisor.
60. She is wise. Her mother is equally wise.
61. I advised him. He did the work accordingly.
62. He will go by his own car. He is afraid of getting late.

Part II : Synthesis (Simple Sentences)

Simple Sentences

Examples worked out for the students.

The following are the usual ways of combining a set of simple sentences into one simple sentence.

(A) **By using Infinitive**

(i) He bought a pen. He wanted to give it to me.
He bought a pen to give it to me.

(ii) The work was very easy for her. She could do it.
The work was very easy (easy enough) for her to do.

(iii) She is very weak. She cannot understand a single word of the letter.
She is too weak to understand a single word of the letter.

(iv) I went to the station. My object was to receive my uncle.
I went to the station to receive my uncle.

(v) I have a lot of money. I would spend it tonight.
I have a lot of money to spend tonight.

(vi) She admitted. She met him last evening.
She admitted to have met him last evening.

(vii) It appears. She is improving in her studies.
She appears to be improving in her studies.

(viii) It is expected. She will come tomorrow.
She is expected to come tomorrow.

(ix) I advised her. She acted accordingly.
She acted according to my advice.

(B) **By using Participle** (Present, Past, Perfect)

1. Present Participle

(i) She entered the mall. She was very happy.
Entering the mall she was very happy.

(ii) I was hungry. I took my food.
Being hungry I took my food.

(iii) I reached college. I went direct to my classroom.
Reaching college I went direct to my classroom.

2. Past Participle

(i) She was disappointed. She left her study.
Being disappointed she left her study.

(ii) I gave him a candle. It was burnt.
I gave him a burnt candle.

(iii) I found my pen. It was lost.
I found my lost pen.

3. Perfect Participle

(i) I took food. I went to college.
Having taken food I went to college.

(ii) He picked my pocket. He fled.
Having picked my pocket he fled.

(C) **By using Nominative Absolute**

(i) The police arrived. The pickpocket fled.
The police having arrived, the pickpocket fled.

(ii) The picture ended. The audience left.
The picture having ended, the audience left.

(D) **By using Preposition before Gerund or Noun**

(i) She insisted. She would go with me.
She insisted on going with me.

(ii) Suhani persisted. She wanted to live in Hyderabad.
Suhani persisted in living in Hyderabad.

(iii) My brother bought a new house. He bought it for his wife.
My brother bought a new house for his wife.

(E) **Noun or Phrase in Apposition**

In such kind of sentences a Noun or a Phrase is placed within commas after the Nouns referred to.

(i) My brother went to Shimla. Shimla is a beautiful hill station in Himachal.
My brother went to Shimla, a beautiful hill station in Himachal.

(ii) Kapil Dev was the best bowler. He was the Captain of the Indian Cricket team.
Kapil Dev, the Captain of the Indian Cricket team, was the best bowler.

(F) **By using Adjective**

(i) I came across a girl in the garden. She was beautiful.
I came across a beautiful girl in the garden.

(ii) They laughed at a small boy. He was hungry.
They laughed at a small hungry boy.

(G) **By using Conjunction 'and'**

(i) I saw a cow. I saw a calf also.
I saw a cow and a calf.

(ii) He bought new books. He bought also old books.
He bought new and old books.

(iii) Nisha went to the movie. Her husband also went with her.
Nisha and her husband went to the movie.

(H) **By using Adverbs or Adverbial Phrases**

(i) She went to parlour. She went frequently.
She went to parlour frequently.

(ii) He was running. His speed was slow.
He was running slowly.

(iii) I am sure. She will go to the movie.
I am sure that she will go to the movie.

Practice Exercise 1

Combine the following set of simple sentences into simple sentences.

(A) **By using Infinitive**

1. He is very weak. He can not run.
2. I want a knife. I shall peel the vegetables.
3. He had a large family. He had to support them.
4. She has no pen. She cannot write a cheque.
5. He heard of my success. He was glad of it.
6. It is believed. He died from heart attack.
7. I expect. I shall pass next year.
8. It is reported. She has married lately.

(B) **By using Participle**

1. He drew the sword. He attacked the enemy.
2. He could not eat nuts. He had no teeth.
3. I was returning home. I saw a black dog.
4. He resolved firmly. He never smoked.
5. She completed the letter. She posted it.
6. He was disappointed. He gave up the job.
7. Turn to the right. You will find my house.
8. She was tired of riding. She went to bed.
9. We heard no answer. We rang the bell again.
10. Ceaser was stabbed. He died from the wounds.

(C) **By using Nominative Absolute**

1. The sun rose. Fog disappeared.
2. Archana was late. The teacher punished her.
3. The letter was written. I posted it soon.
4. The time was over. We handed our the note books.
5. It was cloudy. We went on picnic.
6. The rain is scanty this year. Sugar is dear in the market.
7. His uncle died. He inherited the property.
8. Rashmi's father was rich. She was not proud of this.
9. The Ganga is our sacred river. We should keep it clean.

(D) **By using Preposition before Gerund or Noun**

1. He killed his enemy. He was justified in this.
2. She wanted to go to market. She insisted on this.
3. He won praise. He saved the life of the prince.
4. The teacher was absent. We were informed of this.
5. The girl has long hair. The girl is the cousin of my wife.
6. He has stolen my book. There is no doubt about this.
7. He is reading comics. He is fond of them.
8. He was wounded. I heard of this.
9. All returned safe. We all were happy at this.
10. I bought a new house. I paid huge amount for it.

(E) **By using Noun or Phrase in Apposition**

1. Suniti is the daughter of a doctor. She stood first in the college.
2. Mr. Sinha is an engineer. He works in the Hydel department.
3. Harsh is a famous poet. He writes love poetry.
4. Nanda is a great builder. He has built a number of apartments.
5. He bought a very costly picture. It is a work by a most famous artist of India.

(F) **By using Adverbs or Adverbial Phrase**

1. He replied back. This took him no time.
2. He saved money. This was wise of him.
3. I escaped from the den of gangster. This was lucky.
4. I got help from my friends. This was not expected.
5. I shall return tonight. It will not be long.
6. I shall get through the examination. There is no doubt about this.
7. She went to college. She was in a hurry.
8. She will go to the States next year. It is certain.

(G) **By using 'Adjective' or 'And'**

1. I am buying a house next week. It is very costly.
2. A girl entered the room. She was young.
3. She was kind. She was generous.
4. Why are you nervous? Why are you sad?

(A) **Noun Clause** (Simple Sentence)

Some examples worked out

1. There is no doubt in it. He will do it.
   Undoubtedly, he will do it.
2. He is correct. I am sure of it.
   I am sure of his being correct.
3. Nobody informed me. My father went sometime in the evening.
   Nobody informed me of the time of my father's departure in the evening.

4. It is alleged. He committed a murder.
He is alleged to have committed a murder.

5. It is understood. He is honest.
He is understood to be honest.

6. The news is wrong. That he died.
The news of his death is wrong.

7. They did not inform me. Their mother was ill.
They did not inform me of their mother illness.

8. He confessed. He had committed the murder.
He confessed to have committed the murder.

9. He hoped. He will succeed.
He hoped to succeed.

10. I told you something. You must believe.
You must believe in my statement.

11. We believe. The news is true.
We believe in the truthfulness of the news.

12. It is high time. You should start working hard.
It is high time for you to start working hard.

13. I wish. You should be quiet.
I wish you to be quiet.

14. You saved money. It was prudent.
It was prudent of you to save money.

15. He will marry her. He is not afraid of it.
He is not afraid of marrying her.

16. I expect. I will meet you tomorrow.
I expect to meet you tomorrow.

17. I expect. He will pass with credit.
(a) I expect him to pass with credit.
(b) He is expected to pass with credit.

18. It appears. He is rich.
He appears to be rich.

19. It is believed. He is honest.
He is believed to be honest.

20. It is reported. He is doing well in business.
He is reported to be doing well in business.

21. It appears. He has been cheated.
He appears to have been cheated.

22. He denies. He met her yesterday.
He denies to have met her yesterday.

23. He insisted. He will join college.
He insisted on joining college.

24. He will succeed. It is certain.
(a) He is certain to succeed.
(b) He will certainly succeed.

25. I do not know. How did he travel to Delhi?
I do not know the manner of his travelling to Delhi.

26. I cannot tell the reason. Why did he leave his sister.
I cannot tell the reason of his leaving his sister.

27. He left yesterday. No body informed me.
No body informed me about his leaving yesterday.

28. He declared. He was innocent.
He declared his innocence.

29. How long will the war last? It is uncertain.
The duration of the war is uncertain.

30. The king ordered. The murderer should be hanged.
The king ordered the murderer to be hanged.

Practice Exercise 2

Combine the following sentences into complex, compound or one simple sentence

1. The student admitted. He was absent.
2. I am not aware. What is he?
3. I don't know. What is his name?
4. I cannot recall. Where does he live?
5. I have no faith in his promise. She promissed to help me.
6. It is certain. She will succeed.
7. My faith is firm. He will succeed.
8. That makes the offence worse. You were absent.
9. She is sure. She will secure high marks.
10. She persisted. She will continue her study.
11. My father insisted. I should join army.
12. We do not know the reason. She left the party suddenly.
13. The soldiers were told. How could they climb the hill?
14. I expect. He is honest.
15. We hope. We will be invited.
16. He denied. He sold spurious drugs to the customers.
17. It is certain. She has two sons.
18. It is expected. She will qualify Entrance Examination.
19. It appears. She is honest.
20. It is believed. Netaji died in air crash.

21. It is alleged. He stole his brother's jewellery.
22. It is likely. She may come late.
23. It is certain. He will be punished tomorrow.
24. He is sure. He wil succeed.
25. It is beyond doubt. She will recover from illness.

(B) Adjective Clause to Simple Sentence

Examples worked out

***Combine two simple sentences into one simple sentence** (Relating to Adjective clause)*

(i) He gave me money. He gave it to spend.
He gave me money to spend.

(ii) He has a lot of money. He will spend it on books.
He has a lot of money to spend on books.

(iii) In the park we saw children. They were playing baseball.
In the park we saw children playing baseball.

(iv) I will board a train. It connects Udaipur.
I will board a train connecting Udaipur.

(v) They are watching match. It is very interesting.
They are watching a very interesting match.

(vi) The magic ball was eaten by the jester. It was meant for the king.
The magic ball meant for the king was eaten by the jester.

(vii) The soldier lay in the battle field. He was wounded.
The wounded soldier lay in the battle field.

(viii) He visited the Taj. It is an artistic building.
He visited the Taj, an artistic building.

(ix) The book is very costly. I purchased it yesterday.
The book purchased by me yesterday is very costly.

(x) Rathore is our captain. He scored five runs.
Rathore, our captain, scored five runs.

(xi) The girl is cousin of my wife. She has long hair.
The girl with long hair is the cousin of my wife.

Practice Exercise 3

Combine the following simple sentences into one simple sentence.

1. She has arrived earlier. Do you know the reason?
2. Kabir was a famous poet. He was a weaver.
3. I bought a house last year. It is quite large.
4. We came across a soldier. He was in trouble.
5. He invented a machine. It is used for stitching.
6. Mr Verma is our teacher. Everybody loves him.

7. This is a class room. It is not the place to play.
8. We committed a mistake. It is quite serious.
9. Do you know the time? Your father left in the morning.
10. The boys are honest. They live near my house.
11. The man could not do work well. The man was tired.
12. We undertook a journey. The journey was tiring.
13. I was the first man. I heard his name on the radio.
14. He has a large family. He has to educate them.
15. He has some bills. He must pay them.
16. They admitted the offence. They committed last night.
17. You cannot believe such a person. The person is dishonest.
18. We undertook a journey to Gwalior. The journey was tiring.
19. In the street we saw a beggar. He was begging from door to door.
20. The man died last night. He was wounded in an accident.
21. The police discovered the weapon. It was used to kill the victim.
22. Air is the first necessity of life. It is the cheapest thing in the world.
23. Childhood is a time. One can learn good habits during this time.
24. I know the reason. He could not succeed.
25. The time has been announced. He will come tomorrow.
26. I remember very well the year. He retired then ?
27. These students are very hard working. They hail from Bihar.
28. The offence is unpardonable. She committed it intentionally.
29. The good deeds live after men. They do them in life.
30. Malini repaid the debt. Her father had incurred it.

(C) Adverb Clause to Simple Sentence

Examples worked out

(i) She is very poor. She cannot carry on her study.
She is too poor to carry on her study.

(ii) He employs a watchman. He wants to be safe.
He employs a watchman to be safe.

(iii) He heard the news. He fainted.
On hearing the news he fainted.

(iv) He was sitting on a tree. A snake bit him.
Sitting on a tree he was bitten by a snake.

(v) The police arrived. The rioters fled.
The police having arrived the rioters fled.

(vi) She was late. she was punished.
Being late, she was punished.

(vii) She came late. She was not punished.
Inspite of being late, she was not punished.

(viii) Work hard. You will succeed.
By working hard you will succeed.

(ix) Work hard. You will fail otherwise.
Without working hard you will fail.

(x) She had laboured hard otherwise. She would not have succeeded.
But for hard labour she would not have succeeded.

Practice Exercise 4

Combine the following simple sentences into one simple sentence

1. I had passed high school examination. I got a job.
2. He takes dinner early. He is afraid of getting ill.
3. The thief saw the police. He fled immediately.
4. He was sitting on the grass. A snake bit him.
5. He was late. He was punished.
6. The weather was unpleasant. We did not go out.
7. She was insulted. She left the room.
8. He was overpowered by the enemy. The enemy stabbed him.
9. He posseses huge wealth. He is not happy.
10. Go out. You will catch cold.
11. Work hard. You will fail.
12. Examine the paper carefully. You can not give your opinion.
13. He is very lazy. He is not fit to be a player.
14. We may go tomorrow. It depends on the weather.
15. Every Sunday he goes to Delhi. He goes to see his sick brother.
16. He is so weak. He cannot even walk.
17. I advised him. He did the work accordingly.
18. He is working hard. His aim is to join Army.
19. He is very kind. He helps everybody.
20. Permit me. I shall leave the room.
21. The work was done. I was present then.
22. He is very honest. He will not deceive you.
23. Turn to right. You will see a tall building.
24. He was going to school. He was caught in the rain.
25. His father retired last year. He has been idle from that time.
26. He drove very fast. He soon overtook us.
27. He succeeded in life. He is still humble.
28. He is very clever. He can see through your tricks.
29. Your sorrow is too deep. It cannot be expressed in tears.
30. This house is too small. It cannot serve my purpose.

Practice Exercise 5

(Based on Noun, Adjective and Adverb Clauses)

Combine the following set of sentences into simple sentences

1. The lady entered the Mall. She went straight to the manager.
2. Archana lost her purse. It was very costly. It contained a lot of cash.
3. He came late. He was punished for this.
4. Small families are not an advantage. It is certain now.
5. Some people drink. This is injurious to health.
6. He has some new clothes. They are in the box.
7. He told a lie. He was not afraid of it.
8. We reached Shimla. We went to our hotel.
9. Yesterday my brother went to Chandigarh. Rohan went also.
10. She was clever. I could notice it.
11. It was very hot. I did not go out.
12. The train was late. We reached home late.
13. My father did not sell the house. This was wise.
14. They were walking in the garden. They enjoyed themselves.
15. Rohit had no money. He succeeded in his aim.
16. Work hard. You will pass.
17. The speech ended. We went to dinner.
18. He had no house. He could not sell.
19. He fired at his friend. He was arrested for this.
20. She earns a lot of money. She runs a beauty parlour.
21. Ashok was a great emperor. He became compassionate. It happened after the battle of Kalinga.
22. He was walking in the street. He saw a beggar. The beggar was not able to walk.
23. He arrived at the party. He was pleased. He met all of his friends.
24. We come to the Institute. We come to study. We study English.
25. Deepa was driving. She heard Reema's voice. She was humming a song.
26. I am threatened. I will speak the truth. I am not afraid of it.
27. It was dark. He fired at his enemy. He wanted to kill him.
28. He was successful. I was told. I was glad of it.
29. The child had broken window pane. It was tinted. He was playing cricket. He was punished for this.
30. We were delighted. We saw him. He was buying fruit. He was buying mangoes.

Part III : Compound Sentence

We have already studied that a compound sentence contains a co-ordinate clause or more than one main clause. They are joined by co-ordinating conjunctions.

Some Examples worked out

Co-ordinating conjunctions are given as follows

(A) Illative conjunction are used when one statement is concluded from the other. They express reason.

They are – so, therefore, for

(a) She came late. She was punished.
She came late, so she was punished.

(b) I cannot go out. It is very cold outside.
(i) I cannot go out for it is very cold outside.
(ii) It is very cold outside, therefore, I cannot go out.

(B) Adversative conjunctions add two statements to make a compound sentence. They express a contrast. They are **"still, nevertheless, but, yet, whereas, while, however"** They express contrast.

(a) She is intelligent. She is dishonest.
She is intelligent but dishonest.

(b) She was ill. She came.
She was ill yet she came.

(C) Alternative conjunctions express a choice between alternatives. They are **"or, nor, otherwise, else, or else"**. They express condition.

(a) Work hard. you will fail.
Work hard or you will fail.

(b) Do not be angry. Do not be rash.
Be neither angry nor rash.

(D) Cumulative (Copulative) Conjunction add one statement to the other. They are **both-and, not only-but also, as well as, and neither-nor, either-or.**

(a) He is a fool. He is dishonest also.
He is not only fool but also dishonest.

(b) He is handsome. He is smart also.
He is not only handsome but also smart.

Practice Exercise 1

Combine the simple sentences into compound sentences

1. He is intelligent. He is careless.
2. He can succeed. He will not work hard.
3. Morning walk is a good exercise. Everybody should walk.
4. He came late. He would have enjoyed music.
5. Walk fast. You will catch bus.
6. Wait here. He will not meet you.

7. The bus was slow. He reached late.
8. You are a liar. Your brother is a liar.
9. She is smart. She is honest too.
10. Do not be a borrower. Do not be a lender.
11. You may be correct. You may be wrong.
12. She is often late. She comes on foot.
13. Stand outside. Come in.
14. Weather was not fair. We went on picnic.
15. She came. She consoled me.

Practice Exercise 2

1. She came late. She was punished.
2. I can not go out. It is very cold outside.
3. She is intelligent. She is dishonest.
4. She was ill. She came.
5. Work hard. You will fail.
6. Do not be angry. Do not be rash.
7. He is a fool. He is dishonest also.
8. He is handsome. He is smart.
9. He is intelligent. He is careless.
10. He can succeed. He will not work hard.
11. Morning walk is a good exercise. Everybody should walk.
12. He came late. He would have got the bus.
13. Walk fast. You will catch bus.
14. Wait here. He will not meet you.
15. The bus was slow. He reached late.
16. You play piano. Your brother plays piano.
17. She is obedient. She is polite also.
18. Do not be a borrower. Do not be a lender.
19. Richa cannot sing. Esha cannot sing.
20. Everything decays. Truth Survives.
21. I doubt it. He will pass.
22. I went to Indore. I spent a few days there.
23. I requested her to lend me some money. She refused.
24. You come by car. We shall take you to temple.
25. He took bath. He put on new clothes.
26. He fell off the stairs. He died from injuries.
27. Say one word. I shall kill you.
28. Write to father. Otherwise I would do so.
29. He is working hard. He wants to pass.
30. Sona cannot sing. Her husband cannot sing.

Exam Practice

Directions *In this section two sentence are given and you are required to find the correct sentence which combines both the sentences. Choose the correct response (a), (b), (c) an5d (d) and indicate on the Answer Sheet accordingly.* **CDS 2020**

1. Which is the correct combination of the given two sentences?
The officer will return from China on Monday. You can meet him.
(a) You can meet the officer when he returned from China on Monday.
(b) You can meet the officer when he will return from China on Monday.
(c) You can meet the officer when he returns from China on Monday.
(d) The officer will meet you when you return from China on Monday.

2. Which is the correct combination of the given two sentences?
He is hard-working. He is honest too.
(a) He is not only hard-working, but also honest.
(b) He is only hard-working and honest.
(c) He is hard-working but honest too.
(d) He is not hard-working but also honest.

3. Which is the correct combination of the given two sentences?
Parents have been waiting since morning. They want to meet the counsellor.
(a) the counsellor has been waiting to meet the parents since morning.
(b) Parents had been waiting to meet the counsellor since the morning.
(c) Parents are waiting to meet the counsellor in the morning.
(d) Parents have been waiting since morning to meet the counsellor.

4. Which is the correct combination of the given two simple sentences using 'If' clause?
Minchi should have worked hard. She would have cleared the test.
(a) If Minchi had worked hard, she would have cleared the test.
(b) Had not Minchi worked hard, she could not have cleared the test.
(c) If Minchi has worked hard, she would have cleared the test.
(d) If Minchi had worked hard, she will have cleared the test.

5. Which one of the following is the correct statement combining the two statements using 'though'?
He has been trying his level best to win. He could not succeed.
(a) Though he is trying his level best to win, he could not succeed.
(b) He is trying his level best to win, though he could not succeed.
(c) Though he has been trying his level best to win, he could not succeed.
(d) Though the had been trying his level best to win, he could not succeed.

6. Which is the correct combination of the given two sentences using 'relative clause'?
Gandhiji preached peace. He is an apostle of peace.
(a) Gandhiji who preached peace is an apostle of peace.
(b) Gandhiji preached peace because he is an apostle of peace.
(c) GAndhiji who preached peace is called an apostle of peace.
(d) Gandhiji is an apostle of peace because he preached peace.

7. Which is the correct combination of the given two sentences?
Priya reached the station. The bus left before her.
(a) When Priya reached the station, the bus had already left.
(b) When Priya had reached the station, the bus already left.
(c) Priya reached the station, when the bus already left.
(d) When Priya had reached the station, the bus had already left.

8. Which is the correct combination of the given two sentences?
He is too tired. He could not stand.
(a) He is so tired that he could scarcely stand.
(b) He is too tired and cannot stand.
(c) He will not stand and he is very tired.
(d) He is so tired that he could not be standing.

9. Which is the correct combination of the given two sentences?
The teacher entered the classroom. All students stropped talking.
(a) No sooner did the teacher enter the classroom than the students stopped talking.
(b) As soon as the teacher entered the classroom all students were asked to stop talking.
(c) All students stopped talking as the teacher enters the classroom.
(d) No sooner did the students stop talking than the teacher entered the classroom.

10. Which one of the following is the correct statement of the combination of the two sentences given below using 'whereas'?
Kavya is interested in reading books. Her sister shows interest in outdoor games.
(a) Kavya is interested in reading books whereas her sister's interest is outdoor games.
(b) kavya is interested in reading books whereas her sister is not interested in it.
(c) Kavya is interested in reading whereas her sister's interest is outdoor games.
(d) Kavya is interested in reading books whereas her sister's interest is to play outside.

Answers

Part I

Practice Exercise 1

1. I do not know whether he will come.
2. I cannot say where he is going.
3. The verdict of the bench was that he was not guilty.
4. There is no doubt that he will do it.
5. I am sure that he is correct.
6. (a) His statement was that you gave him stolen money./
(b) That you gave him stolen money was his statement.
7. I am not certain if he is guilty.
8. I do not know who arrived late at night.
9. I do not believe in what he said to me.
10. Nobody informed me when my mother went to temple in the evening.
11. Everybody doubts if he will pass.
12. (a) This is my belief that he will cheat you.
(b) That he will cheat you is my belief.
13. I do not know when my father will come here.
14. Please tell me where you have put my purse.
15. Are you listening to what I am saying.
16. I cannot tell why he came late.
17. The news that he died last night is wrong.
18. He confessed that he had committed murder.

19. It was expected that he would arrive soon.
20. It is believed that Netaji died in air crash.
21. I cannot say whether/if she is a doctor.
22. All depends on what your attitude to life is.
23. My son is anxious to learn how one can travel to space.
24. The fact is that he is a coward.
25. She declared her intention that she would not marry the following year.
26. His wife cannot tell how much money he wasted.
27. I cannot rely on what she has promised to me.
28. The police are trying to inquire when she left the party.
29. She told me the fact that her father would not allow her to go abroad.
30. Our expectation was that we would succeed.
31. The news that she has returned from Chennai is not correct.
32. She confessed that she had gone to Delhi the previous night.
33. My sister kept on asking when I would come back from Indore.
34. The verdict of the Judges that he is guilty has been challenged.
35. I can not tell when she came in the morning.
36. The rumour that he died last night is baseless.
37. Everyone wonders how she completed this work.
38. It is certain that she will arrive today.
39. I heard him telling his mother that he was leaving for America very soon.
40. (a) It cannot be confirmed whether he has married.
    (b) Whether he has married cannot be confirmed.

Practice Exercise 2

1. Shakespeare who was a great dramatist is the author of a number of plays.
2. Please show me the place where you have put my purse.
3. This is the college where I studied.
4. It was ten o'clock when my father left for office.
5. Can you tell me the reason why you are wasting time?
6. The boy whom the teacher gave a prize was present there.
7. I shall give you the same pen that I bought.
8. I was the first man who heard his name on the radio.
9. They were sitting under a tree the shade of which was very cool.
10. I shall go by the Taj express which goes to Agra direct.
11. They are reading a book which is very rare.
12. The news that he gave yesterday is true.
13. Yesterday I bought a book which is very cheap.
14. They committed a mistake which was quite serious.
15. You cannot believe such a person as is dishonest.
16. We undertook a journey to Gwalior which was tiring.
17. A soldier who was wounded was lying in the field.
18. The dog felled the candle which was burning.
19. Those who are healthy do not need a doctor.

20. The man who was wounded in accident died last night.
21. The magic ball which was meant for the king was eaten by the jester.
22. Seema was the last person who left for home.
23. This is a class room which is not the place to play.
24. He has a large family whom he has to educate.
25. He has some bills which he must pay in cash.
26. I have no friend whom I can talk to.
27. Childhood is a time when one can teach good habits to children.
28. I know the reason why he could not succeed.
29. The time when he will came tomorrow is not certain.
30. Nobody appreciated the way in which she behaved at the party.
31. I was informed of the place where he was living.
32. I remember very well the year when he retired.
33. You can have anything that you like.
34. The students who hail from Bihar are very hard working.
35. The girl who has long hair is a cousin of my wife.
36. I never visit any of my uncles that reside in Manekshaw Enclave.
37. The news which the voice of America broadcast is true.
38. The players whom the president awarded cash prize were present at the function.
39. The good deeds which men do in their lives live after them.
40. Kabir who was a famous poet wrote spiritual poetry.

Practice Exercise 3

1. He ran so quickly that he overtook everybody.
2. As you always disturb me, I cannot work.
3. When I had left office, my boss called me.
4. When the members of the committee arrived, the conference started.
5. You must hurry lest you should miss the train.
6. I could not go out because it was very sultry noon.
7. As soon as I left office, the rain started.
8. He will not leave at night, lest he should be robbed.
9. He came to me so that I might help him.
10. When he found out his mistake, he repented very much.
11. If you sleep outside, you will be ill.
12. When I reached the station, the train had left.
13. Since you left India, you have not written any letter.
14. The old man walks as fast as a young person.
15. (a) Rich as he is, he is unhappy.
    (b) Though he is rich, he is unhappy.
16. If you help others, God will help you.
17. While they were playing in the garden, it started raining.
18. The work was stopped because no money was given to me.
19. The patient grew so weak that he died last night.
20. Since his brother died, he has been very poor.

21. Everybody will admire him if he is hard-working.
22. If you go out, you will catch cold.
23. Although he was sick yet he went out.
24. He was cremated where he settled after his retirement.
25. Though he is admired by everybody, he is not proud.
26. While he was sitting on the grass, a snake bit him.
27. She waited for her friend till she arrived.
28. If she had not come late, she would have enjoyed music.
29. If you want to go to Malabar Hills, bring money with you.
30. I shall go where my cousin works.
31. Water is so cold that no one can drink it.
32. He employed a watchman so that he might be safe.
33. If they had not helped me, I would not have got success.
34. If I had given you money, I would have been glad.
35. He did not stop working until he achieved success.
36. As soon as the signal was given, the train started.
37. You can stay here if you wish.
38. No other member in her family is as beautiful as she is.
39. Let us wait till the train stops.
40. If I make a promise, I stick to it.
41. He is working hard so that he may join Army.
42. He fled lest he should be caught.
43. Please do not go until I get money for you.
44. Everybody will admire you on condition that you are honest.
45. If he had received help in time, he would not have died from burns.
46. The more he gets, the more he works.
47. Do not get into the train until it stops.
48. If it rains, the schools may be closed.
49. We shall leave for Shimla if weather permits.
50. I should be glad if I could help your husband.
51. If he had not worked hard, he would have failed.
52. I shall be glad if I can help you in getting a job.
53. I shall treat her as she treated me.
54. My younger sister behaves as if she were an elder sister.
55. She wrote an essay as well as she could.
56. She writes better than she speaks.
57. She is more kind than wise.
58. He spends as if he were a rich person.
59. The candidates stayed in the hall till the supervisor departed.
60. She is as wise as her mother is.
61. He did the work as I advised him.
62. He will go by his own car lest he should get late.

Part II

Practice Exercise 1

(A) By using Infinitive

1. He is too weak to run.
2. I want a knife to peel the vegetables.
3. He had a large family to support.
4. She has no pen to write a cheque.
5. He was glad to hear of my success.
6. He is believed to have died from heart attack.
7. I expect to pass next year.
8. She is reported to have married lately.

(B) By using Participle

1. Drawing the sword he attacked the enemy.
2. Having no teeth he could not eat nuts.
3. Returning home I saw a black dog.
4. Having resolved firmly he never smoked.
5. Having completed the letter she posted it.
6. Disappointed he gave up the job.
7. Turning to the right you will find my house.
8. Tired of riding she went to bed.
9. Hearing no answer we rang the bell again.
10. Having been stabbed Ceaser died from the wounds.

(C) By using Nominative Absolute

1. The sun having risen, fog disappeared.
2. Archna being late, the teacher punished her.
3. The letter having been written, I posted it soon.
4. The time being over, we handed over the note books.
5. It being cloudly, we went on picnic.
6. The rain being scanty this year, sugar is dear in the market.
7. His uncle having died, he inherited the property.
8. Despite his father being rich, she was not proud.
9. The Ganga being our sacred river, we should keep it clean.

(D) By using Preposition before Gerund or Noun

1. He was justified in killing his enemy.
2. She insisted on going to the market.
3. He won praise for saving the life of the prince.
4. We were informed of the absence of the teacher.
5. The girl with long hair is the cousin of my wife.
6. There is no doubt about his stealing my book.
7. He is fond of reading comics.
8. I heard of his being wounded.
9. We all were happy at the safe return of all.
10. I paid huge amount for a new house.

(E) By using Noun or Phrase in Apposition

1. Suniti, the daughter of a doctor, stood first in the college.
2. Mr. Sinha, an engineer, works in the Hydel department.

3. Harsh, a famous poet, writes love poetry.
4. Nanda, a great bulider, has built a number of apartments.
5. He bought a very costly picture, a work by a most famous artist of India.

(F) **By use of Adverbs or Adverbial phrase**

1. He replied back in no time.
2. He saved money wisely.
3. I escaped from the den of the gangsters luckily.
4. I got help from my friends unexpectedly.
5. I shall return tonight before long.
6. Undoubtely, I shall get through the examination.
7. She went to college hurriedly.
8. She will certainly go to the states next year.

(G) **By using 'Adjective' or 'And'**

1. I am buying a very costly house next week.
2. A young girl entered the room.
3. She was kind and generous.
4. Why are you nervous and sad?

Practice Exercise 2

1. (a) The student admitted to have been absent.
   (b) The student admitted his absence.
2. I am not aware of his profession.
3. I don't know his name.
4. I cannot recall his residence.
5. I have no faith in her promise to help me.
6. (a) Her success is certain.
   (b) She will certainly succeed.
7. My faith in his success is firm.
8. Your absence makes the offence worse.
9. She is sure of securing high marks.
10. She persisted in countinuing her study.
11. My father insisted on my joining army.
12. We do not know the reason of her leaving the party suddenly.
13. The soldiers were told the manner of climbing the hill.
14. I expect him to be honest.
15. We hope to be invited.
16. He denied to have sold spurious drugs to the customers.
17. She has certainly two sons.
18. She is expected to qualify Entrance Examination.
19. She appears to be honest.
20. Netaji is believed to have died in air crash.
21. He is alleged to have stolen his brother's jewellery.
22. She is likely to come late.
23. He will certainly be punished tomorrow.
24. He is sure to succeed.
25. Undoubtedly, she will recover from illness.

Practice Exercise 3

1. Do you know the reason of her arrival earlier?
2. Kabir, a famous poet, was a weaver.
3. I bought a quite large house last year.
4. We came across a soldier in trouble.
5. (a) He invented a stitching machine.
   (b) He invented a machine used for stitching.
6. Mr. Verma, our teacher, is loved by everybody.
7. The class room is not a place to play.
8. We committed a quite serious mistake.
9. Do you know the time of your father's departure in the morning?
10. The boys, living near my house, are honest.
11. The tired man could not do work well.
12. We undertook a tiring journey.
13. I was the first man to hear his name on the radio.
14. He has a large family to educate.
15. He has some bills to pay.
16. They admitted the offence committed by them last night.
17. You cannot believe a dishonest person.
18. We undertook a tiring journey to Gwalior.
19. In the street we saw a beggar begging from door to door.
20. The man wounded in an accident died last night.
21. The police discovered the weapon used to kill the victim.
22. Air, the cheapest thing in the world, is the first thing in life.
23. Childhood is the time to learn good habits.
24. I know the reason of his failure.
25. The time of his arrival has been announced.
26. I remember very well the year of his retirement.
27. These students hailing from Bihar are very hard working.
28. The offence she committed intentionally is unpardonable.
29. The good deeds done by men in life live after them.
30. Malini repaid the debt incurred by her father.

Practice Exercise 4

1. After having passed high school examination, I got a job.
2. (a) He takes dinner early to avoid sickness.
   (b) He takes dinner early so as not to get sick.
3. Seeing the police, the thief fled immediately.
4. While sitting on the grass, he was bitten by a snake.
5. Being late, he was punished.
6. The weather being unpleasant, we did not go out.
7. Being insulted, she left the room.
8. Being over powered by the enemy, he was stabbed.
9. Inspite of possessing huge wealth, he is not happy.

10. By going out, you will catch cold.
11. Without working hard you will fail.
12. Without examining the paper carefully, you can not give your opinion.
13. He is too lazy to be a player.
14. Depending on the weather, we may go tomorrow.
15. Every Sunday he goes to Delhi to see his sick brother.
16. He is too weak to walk.
17. He did the work in accordance with my advice.
18. He is working hard to join the army.
19. He is kind enough to help everybody.
20. I shall leave the room with your permission.
21. The work was done in my presence.
22. He is honest enough not to deceive you.
23. Turning to right you will see a tall building.
24. While going to school, he was caught in the rain.
25. Since retirement, his father has been idle.
26. He drove fast enough to overtake us.
27. Inspite of success in life he is humble.
28. He is too clever not to see through your tricks.
29. Your sorrow is too deep for tears.
30. This house is so small for me.

Practice Exercise 5

1. Entering the Mall, she went straight to the manager.
2. Archana lost her very costly purse containing a lot of cash.
3. He was punished for coming late.
4. Small families are certainly not an advantage now.
5. Drinking is injurious to health.
6. He has some new clothes in the box.
7. He was not afraid of telling a lie.
8. Reaching Shimla, we went to our hotel.
9. Yesterday my brother and Rohan went to Chandigarh.
10. I could notice her cleverness.
11. It being very hot, I did not go out.
12. The train being late, I reached home late.
13. My father did not wisely sell the house.
14. While walking in the garden, they enjoyed themselves.
15. Inspite of having no money, Rohit succeeded in his aim.
16. You will pass by working hard.
17. The speech having ended, we went for dinner.
18. He had no house to sell.
19. He was arrested for firing at his friend.
20. She earns a lot of money by running a beauty parlour.
21. Ashoka a great emperor became compassionate after the battle of Kalinga.

22. Walking in the street, he saw a beggar unable to walk.
23. Arriving at the party, he was pleased to meet all of his friends.
24. We come to the institute to study English.
25. Driving Deepa heard Reena humming a song.
26. Inspite of being threatened, I am not afraid of speaking the truth.
27. He fired at his enemy in dark to kill him.
28. I was glad to be told that he was successful.
29. The child was punished for breaking the tinted pane while playing cricket.
30. We were delighted to see him buying mangoes.

Part III

Practice Exercise 1

1. He is intelligent but careless.
2. He can succeed but he will not work hard.
3. Morning walk is a good exercise, therefore, everybody should walk.
4. He came late otherwise, he would have enjoyed music.
5. Walk fast and you will catch bus.
6. Wait here otherwise, he will not meet you.
7. The bus was slow, so he reached late.
8. You are a liar and so is your brother.
9. She is both smart and honest.
10. Neither be a borrower nor be a lender.
11. You may be either correct or wrong.
12. She comes on foot so she is often late.
13. Stand outside or come in.
14. Weather was not fair yet we went on picnic.
15. She came and consoled me.

Practice Exercise 2

1. She came late, so she was punished.
2. It is very cold outside, therefore I cannot go.
3. She is intelligent but dishonest.
4. She was ill yet she came.
5. Work hard or you will fail.
6. Be neither angry nor rash.
7. Besides being dishonest he is a fool.
8. (a) He is handsome as well as smart.
(b) He is handsome and smart too.
9. He is intelligent but careless.
10. He can succeed but he will not work hard.
11. Morning walk is good exercise, therefore everybody should walk.
12. He came late otherwise, he would have got the bus.
13. Walk fast and you will catch bus.
14. Wait here otherwise, he will not meet you.
15. The bus was slow, so he reached late.
16. You play piano and so does your brother.
17. She is not only obedient but also polite.

18. Be neither a borrower nor a lender
19. Richa cannot sing nor can Esha.
20. Everything decays but truth survives.
21. He will pass and I doubt it.
22. I went to Indore and there I spent a few days.
23. I requested her to lend me some money but she refused.
24. Come by car and we shall take you to temple.
25. He took bath and he put on new clothes.
26. He fell off the stairs and so he died from injuries.
27. One word more and I shall kill you.
28. Either you write or I must write to father.
29. He wants to pass and so he is working hard.
30. (a) Neither Sona nor her husband can sing.
    (b) Sona cannot sing and her husband cannot sing either.
    (c) Sona cannot sing and neither can her husband.

Exam Practice

1. (c) **2.** (a) **3.** (d) **4.** (a) **5.** (d) **6.** (c) **7.** (a)
8. (a) **9.** (a) **10.** (a)

3

Transformation

Transformation is a process of changing sentences into various forms given below.

Part I (Simple Sentences)

Change of a simple sentence to a complex sentence is made by expanding a phrase or words into a subordinate clause.

(a) Noun phrase/Noun to Noun clause.
(b) Adjective phrase/Adjective to Adjective clause.
(c) Adverb phrase/Adverb to Adverb clause.

Part II (Complex Sentences)

Change of a complex sentence to a simple sentence is made by replacing a subordinate clause into a word or phrase as follows.

(a) Noun clause to Noun phrase, Noun, Infinitive, Gerund case in apposition, etc.
(b) Adjective clause to Adjective phrase/Adjective, Participle, Infinitive case in apposition etc.
(c) Adverb clause to Adverbial phrase/Adverb, Participle, Infinitive etc.

Part III (Compound Sentences)

(a) Change of a simple sentence to a compound sentence.
(b) Change of a complex sentence to a compound sentence.

NOTE Students are again reminded of the instructions that all sentences simple, complex and compound have bearing on Inter-relationship of the clauses.

This fact has been explained variously in chapters on

1. Clauses **2.** Clause Analysis, **3.** Synthesis **4.** Transformation

Part IV (Miscellaneous Sentences)

(a) Interchange of degree of comparison.
(b) Interchange of affirmative and negative sentences.
(c) Interchange of assertive and interrogative sentences.

(d) Interchange of exclamatory and assertive sentences.
(e) Sentences expressing condition.
(f) Sentences expressing contrast.
(g) Removal of adverb 'too'.
(h) Interchange of Parts of Speech
(i) Interchange of voice.
(j) Change of Narration

(Refer to chapters on Voice and Narration in the book.)

Part I

Simple to Complex

A simple sentence can be changed to a complex sentence by expanding a phrase or a group of words into a subordinate clause as explained below

(a) Noun phrase/Noun to Noun clause.
(b) Adjective phrase/Adjective to Adjective clause.
(c) Adverb phrase/Adverb to Adverb clause.

(A) **Noun phrase is a group of words that do the work of a noun (explanation).**

Study the following examples

(i) He hopes to succeed. *(object to verb)*
(ii) Truth cannot perish. *(subject to verb)*
(iii) Pay attention to his words. *(object to preposition)*
(iv) My faith about his success is firm. *(case in apposition to Noun)*
(v) It is unfortunate to be cheated by friends. *(case in apposition to a pronoun 'it')*
(vi) My wish is to do something useful. *(complement of a verb 'is')*

Change of Noun Phrase/Noun to a Noun Clause

(i) He hopes that he will succeed.
(ii) What is true cannot perish.
(iii) Pay attention to what he says.
(iv) My faith that he will succeed is firm.
(v) It is unfortunate that one is cheated by friends.
(vi) My wish is that I should do something useful.

(B) **Adjective phrase is a group of words that do the work of an Adjective** (qualification).

Study the following examples.

(i) He is a student of great promise.
(ii) I met my friend living in Mumbai.
(iii) They found a dead body covered with a white sheet.
(iv) He is a man of few words.
(v) Mohan with a lot of wealth is a miser.

Change of Adjective Phrase/Adjective to an Adjective Clause.

(i) He is a student who holds a great promise.
(ii) I met my friend who is living in Mumbai.
(iii) They found a dead body which was covered with white sheet.
(iv) He is a man who speaks a few words.
(v) Mohan who has a lot of wealth is a miser.

(C) **Adverb phrase is a group of words that does the work of Adverb** (modification).

(i) I shall do it in your presence.
(ii) Do not go till my return.
(iii) He went there to buy books.
(iv) He was blamed for telling a lie.
(v) For all his wealth he is unhappy.

Change the Adverbial Phrase/Adverb into Adverb Clause

(i) I shall do it when you are present.
(ii) Do not go until I return.
(iii) He went there so that he might buy books.
(iv) He was blamed as he told a lie.
(v) Although he is wealthy, he is unhappy.

NOTE Subordinate clauses can be introduced by subordinating conjunctions as given in chapter on Clauses.

Practice Exercise 1 (a)

Simple to Noun Clause

Change the following simple sentences into complex sentences by using Noun clause.

1. He confessed his guilt.
2. All depends on his future.
3. His age is not known.
4. Speak the truth.
5. His silence proved his complicity in the crime.
6. He appears to be running temperature.
7. He denied to have murdered.
8. He is believed to be honest.
9. She informed me of her arrival.
10. The news of his death is wrong.
11. Subhash Chandra Bose is believed to have died in Japan.
12. I have already heard his statement.
13. He is sure to have been punished.
14. He is expected to give me money.

15. Mohit may do anything.
16. I wish you to be successful in life.
17. He wishes to be a very rich person.
18. There is no truth in his remarks.
19. The place of his hiding is likely to be discovered very soon.
20. We believe the news to be true.
21. Your innocence is beyond any doubt.
22. I have long doubted his honesty.
23. I have long suspected his guilt.
24. His father is likely to give him punishment.
25. It is high time to leave India.
26. His resignation is out of the question.

Practice Exercise 1 (b)

Change the following complex sentences into simple ones by using Noun clause.

1. I have long suspected him to be a thief.
2. The news of his arrival has not been intimated.
3. Her remarks about my failure were disgusting.
4. Truth is eternal.
5. She is expected to learn good manners.
6. Pay heed to my instructions.
7. She has a desire to learn swimming.
8. Her wish is to do social work in future.
9. He is reported to have lost his reputation.
10. I kept on wondering about her success.
11. Everybody is responsible for his deeds.
12. His fall is certain.
13. She did not inform me of his profession.
14. Nobody knows his whereabouts.
15. She jumped at my offer.

Practice Exercise 2 (a)

Simple to Adjective Clause

Change the following simple sentences into complex sentences by using Adjective clause.

1. I bought a very cheap pen yesterday.
2. I saw a beggar begging from door to door.
3. This is my native village.
4. Do you know the reason of his failure?
5. The value of exercise is great.
6. His offence is unpardonable.

7. They came across the students smoking by the roadside.
8. A tired man cannot do work well.
9. This is not the manner to please your boss.
10. He gave me money to spend.
11. The pen given by him is very cheap.
12. I have no friend to talk to.
13. He was the last to arrive at the party.
14. He gave me a fake news.
15. How can you believe a dishonest person?

Practice Exercise 2 (b)

Change the following simple sentences to complex sentences by using Adjective clause.

1. We committed a quite serious mistake.
2. They found a rare piece of diamond.
3. We undertook quite a tiring journey.
4. The tired man could not do work well.
5. The dog felled the burning candle.
6. The murder committed by him ruined his life.
7. He invented a machine for stitching.
8. He saw a brightly burning candle in the corner.
9. A classroom is not the place to play.
10. He has a large family to educate.
11. He was the last man to attend the funeral.
12. Do you know the time of your father's departure?
13. Do you know the reason of her arrival earlier?
14. Nobody appreciated her behaviour at the party.
15. I was informed of his residence.
16. Kabir, a weaver, was a famous poet.
17. Everybody loves Mr. Verma, our teacher.
18. The boys living near my house are honest.
19. The place of the cremation of the leader was thronged with people.
20. She told me the reason of her being late.
21. Shakespear, a great dramatist, wrote a number of plays.
22. The girl with long hair is a cousin of my wife.
23. They live just near the bypass on the outskirts of the city.
24. The players awarded cash prize by the President were present at the function.
25. The offence committed by them intentionally is unpardonable.
26. I paid the debt incurred by my father.

Practice Exercise 3

Simple to Adverb Clause

Change the following simple sentences into complex sentences by using Adverb clause.

1. For all his experience he is still not efficient.
2. He can not succeed without hard work.
3. On being scolded he left the room.
4. The signal having been given the train started.
5. I shall be very glad to help him.
6. He is too simple to win the game.
7. He was punished on account of his mischief.
8. The work was done in my presence.
9. Despite his wealth he is not respected.
10. You must wait here till the arrival of your father.
11. Notwithstanding his poverty, he is honest.
12. Do it to the best of your ability.
13. Nobody must expect to become rich without hard work.
14. My heart is too full for words.
15. With a view of continuing his higher study he borrowed money from the bank.
16. Being very fat she is undergoing slimming treatment.
17. In comparison with the tiger the cat is swifter.
18. I am thankful to you for helping my brother.
19. But for the timely help he would have died from burns.
20. She is kind enough to help everybody.
21. He did not stop working before his success.
22. They were afraid of being caught in the shower.
23. You must act in accordance with the rules.
24. Considering his capability he was promoted.
25. Weather permitting we shall leave for Shimla.
26. Water is too hot to drink.
27. All being well I shall meet her parents today.
28. I shall be glad to be invited.
29. I would be glad to be there.
30. I would have been glad to have been there.
31. Your behaviour was too much for the guests.
32. She is too good for me.
33. He was quick enough to overtake me.
34. It being a junk food we did not taste it.
35. But for our poverty we would have been a happy family.

Part II

Complex to Simple

A complex sentence can be changed to simple sentence by contracting a subordinate clause into a phrase or a word.

(a) Noun clause to Noun phrase/Noun, Infinitive, Participle, Gerund, Case in apposition etc.

(b) Adjective clause to Adjective phrase/Adjective (Infinitive/Participle, Case in apposition etc.

(c) Adverb clause to Adverb phrase/Adverb, Participle, Infinitive etc.

NOTE We have already studied the examples in the foregoing explanation.

Practice Exercise 1 (a)

Change the following complex sentences to simple sentences by replacing Noun clause.

1. It is much regretted that she is dishonest.
2. He admitted that his enemy was generous.
3. I know where your brother lives.
4. Pay heed to what your officers say.
5. Never say what is wrong.
6. We believe that God exists.
7. I expect that he will pass.
8. It is unfortunate that he died young.
9. He asked me why I gave money to his brother.
10. He confessed that he had met her last evening.
11. I agreed that I would teach him.
12. I informed him that she had gone.
13. It appears that he has been scolded by his father.
14. I ordered him that he should leave the room at once.
15. People are certain that he is honest.

Practice Exercise 1 (b)

Change the following complex sentences into simple ones by replacing Noun clause.

1. He confessed that he was guilty.
2. I do not care for what she has remarked.
3. Mohit may do what he likes.
4. I have long doubted if he is honest.
5. The rumour that he has died is baseless.
6. How old he is, is not known.
7. What she said is disgusting.

8. The fact that he was silent proved his complicity in the crime.
9. He denied that he had murdered.
10. It appears that she is absent today.
11. It was alleged that she had abused him.
12. She wanted to know what his name was.
13. My hope is that I should earn a lot of money.
14. It is sure that he has been punished.
15. It is expected that he will give me money.
16. All depend on what his future is.
17. I don't believe in what she said.
18. I agreed to what he proposed.

Practice Exercise 2 (a)

Change the following complex sentences to simple sentences by replacing Adjective clause.

1. He is not such a man as can be trusted.
2. A student who is careless cannot succeed.
3. He is not a man who will cheat anyone.
4. He has a large house in which he lives.
5. The statement they made is false.
6. You can have anything that you like.
7. Dogs that bark seldom bite.
8. I know the reason why he could not succeed.
9. Milton who was a famous poet, wrote 'Paradise Lost'.
10. The train that connects New Delhi is late.
11. Childhood is a time when good habits can be learnt.
12. The man who was wounded died last night.
13. Those who are healthy do not need a doctor.
14. The good deeds that man does live after him.
15. The place where the leader was cremated was thronged with people.

Practice Exercise 2 (b)

Change the following sentences to simple ones by replacing Adjective clause.

1. Yesterday I bought a book which is very cheap.
2. You cannot believe a person who is dishonest.
3. Those who are hard working succeed in life.
4. A soldier who was wounded was lying in the field.
5. The players who were tired could not perform well.
6. The monster who was proud of his power was defeated by Hercules.
7. In the street we saw a beggar who was begging from door to door.
8. The man who was wounded in the accident died last night.

9. The police discovered the weapon which was used to kill the victim.
10. The magic ball which was meant for the king was eaten by the jester.
11. Seema was the last person who left for home.
12. My uncle was the first man who heard her name on the radio.
13. He has some bills which he must pay in cash.
14. I have no friend whom I can talk to.
15. Childhood is a time when one can teach good habits to children.
16. The time when he will come tomorrow is not certain.
17. All of us were told the reason why he had become rich suddenly.
18. I remember very well the year when he retired.
19. The people who reside in our colony were shouting for justice.
20. Rathore who is our captain scored fifty runs.
21. Edison, who was a great scientist invented electricity.
22. We visited the Taj which is a unique building.
23. I shall travel by the Taj Express which goes to Agra direct.
24. The students who hail from Bihar are very hard-working.
25. Tomorrow I will board a train which connects Udaipur.
26. The news which the Voice of America broadcast is true.
27. I met a poet whom I had already known.
28. Mr. Gupta will buy the house which I built only last year.
29. The book which I had lost has been found out.
30. Those who live in glass houses should not throw stones at others.

Practice Exercise 3

Change the following complex sentences into simple sentences by replacing Adverb clause.

1. He did as I wished.
2. We get up when it is morning.
3. When we had finished work, we went home.
4. As he saw me, he ran away.
5. While she was walking in the garden, a stranger addressed her.
6. He is so kind that he helps everybody.
7. We went home after the teacher had arrived.
8. He wrote as fast as he could.
9. He will not return money unless he is threatened.
10. I succeeded better than I expected.
11. When the thief was found out, he was arrested.
12. Although she was punished, she was not ashamed.
13. You can talk as much as you like.
14. Poor as he is, he is honest.
15. Notwithstanding that he is honest, he is not hard working.
16. If they had not helped me, I would not have gained success.

17. He ran fast so that he might catch taxi.
18. As she ran fast, the teacher declared her first.
19. As he is poor, we will help him.
20. If God wills, you will succeed.
21. If I make a promise, I will stick to it.
22. Everybody complimented him because he had succeeded.
23. He has come to Chandigarh so that capable doctors may treat him.
24. As it was fine, we left for picnic.
25. While they were watching T.V. their friends visited them.
26. While she was crossing the road, a scooter knocked her down.
27. Sania is so slow that she cannot be a good tennis player.
28. She is too clever not to see through your tricks.
29. Her sorrow is so deep that it cannot be expressed in tears.
30. He will stick to his job lest he should starve.
31. When the signal was given, the train started.
32. Since I arrived in Chennai, I have not had any rest.
33. The project was not launched because no money was given to me.
34. This house is so small that I cannot live in it.
35. Since the weather was very pleasant, we went on a long drive.

Part III

Simple and complex sentences to compound sentences.

(a) Change of simple sentences to compound sentences.
(b) Change of complex sentences to compound sentences.

(A) Simple sentence can be converted to compound sentence by changing phrase and a co-ordinating clause:

(i) Noun phrase/Noun to co-ordinate clause.
(ii) Adjective phrase/Adjective to co-ordinate clause.
(iii) Adverb phrase/Adverb to co-ordinate clause.

(B) Complex sentence can be converted to compound sentences by changing subordinate clause to co-ordinating clause :

(i) Noun clause to co-ordinate clause.
(ii) Adjective clause to co-ordinate clause.
(iii) Adverb clause to co-ordinate clause.

NOTE

(a) Co-ordinate clause is also called Independent clause.

(b) We have already studied co-ordinating conjunctions in chapter on Clauses and Synthesis.
They are : **and, but, yet, still, neverthless, whereas, while, or, otherwise, else, or else, nor, as well as.**

(A) Change of Simple Sentences into Compound Sentences

Examples worked out for the students

1. Climbing up the stairs he fell down.
   He was climbing up the stairs and he fell down.
2. Being disappointed he left the job.
   He was disappointed, so he left the job.
3. Having taken bath, he put on new clothes.
   He had taken bath and put on new clothes.
4. Inspite of being rich, he is not happy.
   He is rich but he is not happy.
5. By running very fast, you can catch the bus.
   Run very fast and catch the bus.
6. It being very hot we left for Nainital.
   (a) We left for Nainital for it was very hot.
   (b) It was very hot so we left for Nainital.
7. Arriving at home she found her son missing.
   She arrived at home and she found her son missing.
8. Without respecting others you will not be respected.
   Respect others otherwise you will not be respected.
9. For all his knowledge he could not earn money.
   He had knowledge but he could not earn money.
10. Being stabbed fatally he died.
    He was stabbed fatally, so he died.

Practice Exercise 1

Change the following simple sentences into compound sentences

1. I shall leave the room with your permission.
2. For all his knowledge he is a fool.
3. He was punished on account of his fault.
4. Despite his wealth, he is not respected.
5. He worked hard to secure high percentage of marks.
6. On his return we asked him many questions.
7. In addition to mathematics he also teaches Hindi.
8. I am thankful to you for sending me money.
9. Besides being rich he is learned also.
10. Notwithstanding my request he left Jhansi.
11. He was sitting in the drawing room watching T.V.
12. With all his contacts he never used unfair means.
13. He must admit his fault on pain of punishment.
14. He must work hard to secure high percentage of marks.
15. He was dismissed for embezzlement.

16. The weather being very fine, we left for swimming.
17. In the event of his death his son will inherit the property.
18. He did not follow the rules out of ignorance.
19. To my surprise he could not qualify examination.
20. Only the rich can afford such a costly treatment.
21. Do this to escape suffering.
22. He went by car fearing rain.
23. Without being invited I shall not go.
24. Neither of the statements is correct.
25. Do not desire without deserving.

(B) **Change of Complex Sentences Into Compound**

Examples worked out for the students

1. When she arrived at home, she found her son missing.
   She arrived at home and she found her son missing.
2. While he was climbing up, the stairs, he fell down.
   He was climbing up the stairs and fell down.
3. As he was disappointed, he left the job.
   He was disappointed so he left the job.
4. When he had taken bath, he put on new clothes.
   He had taken bath and put on new clothes.
5. Although he is rich, he is not happy.
   He is rich but he is not happy.
6. If you run very fast, you can catch the bus.
   Run very fast and catch the bus.
7. As it was very hot, we left for Nainital.
   (a) We left for Nainital for it was very hot.
   (b) It was very hot so we left for Nainital.
8. If you do not respect others, you will not be respected.
   Respect others otherwise you will not be respected.
9. Although he had knowledge he could not earn money.
   He had knowledge but he could not earn money.
10. As he was stabbed fatally, he died.
    He was stabbed fatally, so he died.

Practice Exercise 2

Change the following complex sentences into compound sentences replacing subordinate clause.

1. Although she is sick, she will come.
2. If you come by car, we will take you to the temple.
3. As it was cold, we did not go out.
4. When the thief was found out, he was arrested.
5. When she arrived, everybody welcomed her.
6. If you do not stop smoking, you will suffer from lung disease.
7. I shall not go, unless I am invited.
8. If you listen seriously, I will tell you all.
9. I am glad that he has recovered from illness.
10. I have found the pen that I had lost.
11. He had a dog that was very faithful.
12. Unlucky as he is, he is never disappointed.
13. (a) Do this lest you should suffer.
    (b) If you do not do this, you will suffer.
14. However, intelligent he may be, he can not succeed.
15. If he had not given me money, I would not have started business.
16. If he were at home, I would meet him.
17. If he is at home, I shall give him money.
18. In case he dies, his son will inherit his property.
19. He must work hard so that he may pass.
20. He could afford to spend something but he spent more.

Part IV

Interchange of following sentences

(a) Interchange of Degree
(b) Interchange of Affirmative and Negative Sentence
(c) Interchange of Assertive and Interrogative Sentence
(d) Interchange of Exclamatory and Assertive Sentence
(e) Sentences Expressing Condition
(f) Sentences Expressing Contrast
(g) Removal of Adverb 'too'
(h) Interchange of Parts of Speech

(a) Interchange of Degrees without Changing the Meaning

Rule I

1. **Comparative** She is more intelligent than her brother is.
   Positive Her brother is not so intelligent as she is.
2. **Comparative** She is not more intelligent than her brother is.
   Positive Her brother is as intelligent as she is.
3. **Positive** She is not so intelligent as he.
   Comparative He is more intelligent than she.

Rule II

4. **Positive** Very few writers in India are as famous as R.K. Narayan.
   Comparative R.K. Narayan is more famous than most of the Indian writers.
   Superlative R.K. Narayan is one of the most famous Indian writers.

Rule III

5. **Positive** No other writer in India is so famous as R.K. Narayan.
   Comparative R.K. Narayan is more famous than any other writer in India.
   Superlative R.K. Narayan is the most famous of all the writers in India.
6. **Positive** No other bowler in India is so famous as Kapil Dev.
   Comparative Kapil Dev is more famous than any other bowler in India.
   Superlative Kapil Dev is the most famous of all the bowlers in India.

Rule IV

7. **Superlative** Varanasi is not the oldest of all the cities in U.P.
   Comparative Varanasi is not older than some other cities in U.P.
   Positive Some other cities in U.P. are at least as old as Varanasi.

More Solved Examples

1. **Positive** Rustam was as powerful as his brother.
   Comparative Rustam's brother was not more powerful than Rustam.
2. **Superlative** Shivaji was one of the greatest warriors of India.
   Comparative Shivaji was greater than most of the warriors in India.
3. **Positive** Very few countries are as rich in heritage as India.
   Comparative India is richer in heritage than most of the countries.
4. **Comparative** Eagle flies higher than any other bird.
   Positive No other bird flies as high as eagle.
   Superlative Eagle flies highest of all the birds.

5. **Positive** No one else is as honest as our principal.
Comparative Our principal is more honest than anybody else.
Superlative Our principal is the most honest of all.

6. **Superlative** She is the most successful teacher in our college.
Positive No other teacher in our college is as successful as she is.
Comparative She is more successful than any other teacher in our college.

7. **Superlative** She is one of the most successful business women in our country.
Comparative She is more successful than most of the business women in our country.
Positive Very few business women in our country are as successful as she is.

8. **Comparative** It is better to lend than borrow.
Positive Borrowing is not as good as lending.

9. **Superlative** The Ambanis are not the richest of all the Indian industrialists.
Comparative The Ambanis are not richer than some other Indian Industrialists.
Positive Some other Indian industrialists are at least as rich as the Ambanis.

10. **Positive** No other legendary hero was so valorous as Arjun.
Superlative Arjun was the most valorous of all the legendary heroes.

(b) Interchange of Affirmative and Negative Sentences

Study the following examples

1. **Affirmative** Only he is responsible for my failure in life.
Negative None but he is responsible for my failure in life.

2. **Negative** He could not climb up the tree.
Affirmative He failed to climb up the tree.

3. **Affirmative** As soon as she arrived, she went to bed.
Negative No sooner did she arrive than she went to bed.

4. **Negative** If you do not work hard, You will fail.
Affirmative Unless you work hard, you will fail.

5. **Affirmative** He is an honest person.
Negative He is not a dishonest person.

6. **Affirmative** I was doubtful of his success.
Negative I was not sure of his success.

7. **Affirmative** She is more intelligent than he.
Negative He is not so intelligent as she.

8.	**Affirmative**	Netaji was a greater freedom fighter than any other leader.
	Negative	No other leader was so great freedom fighter as Netaji.
9.	**Affirmative**	She is too clever to be cheated.
	Negative	She is so clever that she cannot be cheated.
10.	**Affirmative**	He is sometimes angry.
	Negative	He is not always angry.
11.	**Affirmative**	Everybody admits that he is very helpful.
	Negative	Nobody denies that he is very helpful.
12.	**Affirmative**	You must have given money to your poor friend.
	Negative	You must not have failed to give money to your friend.
13.	**Affirmative**	I will always remember you in my life.
	Negative	I will never forget you in my life.
14.	**Affirmative**	It is unlikely that he will give you money.
	Negative	It is not likely that he will give you money.
15.	**Affirmative**	Every body cried.
	Negative	(a) There was none who did not cry. (b) There was none but cried.
16.	**Affirmative**	I love my children.
	Negative	I am not without love for my children.
17.	**Affirmative**	He is bound to succeed.
	Negative	He cannot but succeed.
18.	**Affirmative**	It always pours when it rains.
	Negative	It never rains but pours.
19.	**Affirmative**	I saw her last when I visited Pune.
	Negative	I have not seen her since I visited Pune.
20.	**Affirmative**	I met him in 2009.
	Negative	I have not met him since 2009.
21.	**Affirmative**	The fort was burnt before it was surrendered.
	Negative	The fort was not surrendered until it was burnt.
22.	**Affirmative**	It is often difficult.
	Negative	It is not always easy.
23.	**Affirmative**	Look before you leap.
	Negative	Don't leap before you look.
24.	**Affirmative**	I met Malini five years ago.
	Negative	I have not met Malini for five years.
25.	**Affirmative**	Always speak the truth.
	Negative	Never tell a lie.
26.	**Affirmative**	Every one has feelings.
	Negative	There is no man who has no feelings.

27.	**Affirmative**	He always began a job which he completed.
	Negative	He never began a job which he did not complete.
28.	**Negative**	There is no smoke without fire.
	Affirmative	Fire causes smoke.
29.	**Negative**	There is no rose without a thorn.
	Affirmative	Every rose has a thorn.
30.	**Affirmative**	All those boys are intelligent.
	Negative	None of the boys is/are dull.
31.	**Affirmative**	We found a few students.
	Negative	We did not find many students.
32.	**Affirmative**	I am very tired.
	Negative	I am not a little tired.
33.	**Affirmative**	She accepted my offer.
	Negative	She did not refuse my offer.
34.	**Negative**	If you had not helped me I would have failed.
	Affirmative	But for your help I would have failed.
35.	**Affirmative**	Work or perish.
	Negative	If you do not work, you will perish.
36.	**Negative**	If you do not pay, you will be refused admission.
	Affirmative	Unless you pay, you will be refused admission.
37.	**Affirmative**	If Leena were at home, I would meet her.
	Negative	Leena is not at home otherwise I would meet her.
38.	**Affirmative**	She was forbidden to loiter in the gallery.
	Negative	She was asked not to loiter in the gallery.
39.	**Affirmative**	Sushma loves her father as much as she loves her mother.
	Negative	Sushma loves her father no less than her mother.
40.	**Affirmative**	Raghu has more wealth than common sense.
	Negative	Raghu does not have as much common sense as he has wealth.
41.	**Affirmative**	You know her nature as well as her husband does.
	Negative	Her husband does not know her nature better than you.
42.	**Affirmative**	He was more worthy of a praise than anyone else.
	Negative	None else was as worthy of praise as he was.

(c) Interchange of Assertive and Interrogative Sentences

Study the following sentences

1. **Assertive** I gave you money to buy a bike.
   Interrogative Did I not give you money to buy a bike?
2. **Interrogative** Was he not kind to help you?
   Assertive He was kind enough to help you.
3. **Interrogative** Who does not like to be praised?
   Assertive Everybody likes to be praised.
4. **Interrogative** Who can forget their sacrifice?
   Assertive Nobody can forget their sacrifice.
5. **Interrogative** Why waste money on luxuries?
   Assertive It is foolish to waste money on luxuries.
6. **Assertive** He could not have achieved success without your help.
   Interrogative Could he have achieved success without your help?
7. **Assertive** That is not the manner to do this work.
   Interrogative Is this the manner to do this work?
8. **Assertive** No one can be expected to do wrong to his parents.
   Interrogative Who can be expected to do wrong to his parents?
9. **Interrogative** What though I have lost a friend for your sake?
   Assertive It does not matter that I have lost a friend for your sake.
10. **Assertive** Their glory can never fade.
    Interrogative When can their glory fade?
11. **Interrogative** Have I ever refused to give you money?
    Assertive I have never refused to give you money.
12. **Interrogative** Why not stay here tonight?
    Assertive It is better we should stay here tonight.
13. **Interrogative** What is the use of going there?
    Assertive (a) It is no use going there.
    (b) There is no use of going there.
14. **Interrogative** If you stab him, will he not die?
    Assertive If you stab him, he will die.
15. **Interrogative** Why blame him?
    Assertive It is no use blaming him.
16. **Interrogative** What is that to me?
    Assertive It does not matter to me.

(d) Interchange of Exclamatory and Assertive

Study the following sentences

1. **Exclamatory** How smart she is!
   Assertive She is very smart.
2. **Exclamatory** What a pretty girl she is!
   Assertive She is a very pretty girl.
3. **Exclamatory** Oh that I were a doctor!
   Assertive I wish I were a doctor.
4. **Exclamatory** Alas! He died so young.
   Assertive It is sad (to think) that he died so young.
5. **Exclamatory** Would that she were here!
   Assertive I wish she were here.
6. **Exclamatory** Had you but completed your education!
   Assertive I wish you had completed your education.
7. **Assertive** It is very foolish of me to ask for money.
   Exclamatory How foolish of me to ask for money!
8. **Assertive** I wish I had come here last year.
   Exclamatory Would that I had come here last year!
9. **Exclamatory** Hurrah! we have won the match.
   Assertive It is a matter of joy that we have won the match.
10. **Exclamatory** To think of our living together!
    Assertive It is strange that we think of living together.
11. **Exclamatory** If only I could meet her now!
    Assertive I wish I could meet her now.
12. **Exclamatory** Alas! we have lost today!
    Assertive It is sad that we have lost today.
13. **Exclamatory** Bravo, well done!
    Assertive It is brave of you to have done well.
14. **Exclamatory** To think of our meeting here!
    Assertive I never thought of meeting you here.
15. **Exclamatory** What a piece of work is man!
    Assertive Man is a wonderful piece of work.
16. **Exclamatory** How wise of you!
    Assertive It is very wise of you.
17. **Exclamatory** Oh to be a queen!
    Assertive I wish I were a queen.
18. **Exclamatory** Oh to have been a prince!
    Assertive I wish I had been a prince!
19. **Exclamatory** Our Prime Minister and so weak!
    Assertive It is shocking that our Prime Minister is so weak.
20. **Exclamatory** Such a man and my husband.
    Assertive It is shocking that such a man is my husband.

21.	**Exclamatory**	What a pity! you have lost.
	Assertive	It is a great pity you have lost.
22.	**Exclamatory**	A child and so bold at this age!
	Assertive	It is wonderful that a child is so bold at this age.
23.	**Exclamatory**	O for a small house to live in Mumbai!
	Assertive	I ardently wish to have a small house to live in Mumbai.
24.	**Exclamatory**	Fie, Fie! you are a cheat.
	Assertive	It is contemptible that you are a cheat.
25.	**Exclamatory**	Alas! that ever a friend should be false.
	Assertive	It is sad that a friend should be false.

(e) Sentences Expressing Condition

1. If/In case you work hard, you will get through.
2. Unless you take medicine, you will not get well.
3. You will get well only if you take medicine.
4. Should you help me, I shall succeed.
5. Were I a doctor, I should treat you.
6. Had you gone there, you would have met her.
7. Supposing you win lottery, how will you spend money?
8. I shall go to the movie provided you allow me.
9. Do it and you will be awarded a prize.
10. Do not be late otherwise /or you will be punished.
11. Have you paid for this book? then take it.
12. One more game and we will play in the finals.
13. Without investing money you can't earn profit.
14. By going out you will catch cold.
15. But for examining me the doctor could not have diagnosed my illness.
16. I shall give you information in the event of your keeping it secret.
17. I shall give you information on the condition that you will not reveal it.

(f) Sentences Expressing Contrast

1. Although she is poor, she is honest.
2. Even though she came late, she was not punished.
3. Notwithstanding that she is wealthy, she is a miser.
4. Rich as she is, she is not honest.
5. Admitting that she is learned, she is not proud.
6. However hard you may try, you cannot compete with him.
7. However intelligent she may be, she cannot pass.
8. I shall do it whatever you may say.
9. She was tired, all the same, she did not go to bed.
10. He is very strict at the same time he is loving by nature.
11. For all that he may say nobody trusts him.

12. It was raining nevertheless she went away.
13. Even if you run fast, you will not get the train.
14. He was weak indeed, but he could walk.
15. She has married indeed, but she is not happy.
16. Come what may she will not desist from playing tricks.
17. Much as I would have liked to give her money, I had no means.
18. No matter what they said, he married a girl of his choice.
19. No matter where she is, she will call me up as usual.
20. I must go whether you come with me or not.

(g) Removal of Adverb too

Rewrite the following sentences removing the Adverb (too)

1. He is too tired to walk.
   He is so tired that he cannot walk.
2. She is too anxious for the safety of her husband.
   She is over anxious for the safety of her husband.
3. It is too cold to go on picnic.
   It is so cold that one cannot go on picnic.
4. The shirt is too loose for my body.
   The shirt is so loose that it does not fit my body.
5. It is too hot.
   It is excessively hot.
6. He is too eager for praise.
   He is over eager for praise.
7. The fort is too high for anyone to climb.
   The fort is so high that no one can climb it.
8. He was too selfish.
   He was selfish beyond limit.
9. My heart is too full for words.
   My heart is so full that I cannot utter a word.
10. He is too fast not to catch up with you any moment.
    He is so fast that he can catch up with you any moment.
11. She is too good for me.
    She is so good that I am no match for her.
12. This house is too small for me.
    This house is so small that it cannot serve my purpose.
13. This adversity is too much for anyone.
    This adversity is so harsh that no one can bear it.
14. My teacher is too fat.
    My teacher is fatter than she should be.
15. As a child Suhani was too active.
    As a child Suhani was more active than she should have been.

(h) Interchange of Parts of Speech

Following interchanges of one part of speech for another are made

1. **Noun**
   - (a) Noun into Verb
   - (b) Noun into Adjective
   - (c) Noun into Adverb
2. **Verb**
   - (a) Verb into Noun
   - (b) Verb into Adjective
   - (c) Verb into Adverb
3. **Adjective**
   - (a) Adjective into Noun
   - (b) Adjective into Verb
   - (c) Adjective into Adverb
4. **Adverb**
   - (a) Adverb into Noun
   - (b) Adverb into Verb
   - (c) Adverb into Adjective

Practice Exercise

1. (a) Nouns into Verbs

Replace the nouns in Italics in the following sentences by verbs

1. She got *success* in the examination.
2. Her *intention* was to harm me.
3. He gave me *advice*.
4. They can not get *admission* without documents.
5. I have a *disinclination* for work in office.
6. The *taste* of these mangoes is sour.
7. They have made an *agreement* to complete this work in time.
8. I have no *inclination* of going to the movie.
9. He is a *disgrace* on his family.
10. The *cost* of this refrigerator is very high.

(b) Nouns into Adjectives

Replace the nouns in Italics in the following sentences by Adjectives

1. She admitted her *guilt*.
2. The room was full of *dust*.
3. He is a man of great *courage*.
4. They do work with *skill*.
5. He is living in *peace* these days.
6. He was punished for his *negligence*.

(c) Nouns into Adverbs

Replace the nouns in Italics in the following sentences by Adverbs

1. She left the room in *anger*.
2. Please carry it with *care*.
3. She survived because of *luck*.
4. She is living in *peace* with her only son.
5. She listened to me with *patience*.
6. She listened to me with *attention*.
7. She left the room in a *hurry*.
8. He goes to Chandigarh *every* week.

Verbs

2. (a) Verbs into Nouns

Replace the Verbs in Italics in the following sentences by Nouns

1. My brother *promised* to help me.
2. This computer is *made* in India.
3. She accepted all that I *proposed*.
4. She was *bathing*.
5. She *signed* the documents.
6. I *need* money.
7. Please *help* me.
8. She was so intelligent that we *admired* her.

(b) Verbs into Adjectives

Replace the Verbs in Italics in the following sentences by Adjectives

1. She *differs* with me in her views.
2. She always *obeys* her brother.
3. He has *succeeded* in her work.
4. He *hoped* to succeed.
5. I *doubt* your honesty.
6. His success has *astonished* me.

(c) Verbs into Adverbs

Replace the Verbs in Italics in the following sentences by Adverb

1. She *hurried* to the bus stop.
2. I *forced* him to leave.
3. She *succeeded* in her task.
4. She *attended* to my advice.
5. They *helped* me in difficulties.
6. She *cares* for her duty.

Adjectives

3. (a) Adjectives into Nouns

Replace the Adjectives in Italics in the following sentences by Nouns

1. Exercise makes body *strong*.
2. Her actions are *careful*.
3. She is very *wise* in spending money.
4. Their expedition was *successful*.
5. He is a *courageous* man.
6. We are *proud* of our country.
7. The room is *dusty*.

(b) Adjectives into Verbs

Replace the Adjectives in Italics in the following sentences by Verbs

1. You have given me *pleasant* news.
2. Her favour was *intentional*.
3. She was *successful* in her job.
4. He *is careful* of his health.
5. Your behaviour was *annoying* to your wife.
6. We are *proud* of your success.

(c) Adjectives into Adverbs

Replace the Adjectives in Italics in the following sentences by Adverbs

1. She is leading a *peaceful* life with her daughter.
2. Be *careful* in your work.
3. She is *attentive* in learning computers.
4. His handwriting is *neat*.
5. I am *comfortable* in my seat.
6. He is a *slow* driver.
7. Her action is *intentional*.
8. I am *certain* that I will pass.

Adverbs

4. (a) Adverbs into Nouns

Replace the Adverbs in Italics in the following sentences by Nouns

1. Do not talk with children *angrily*.
2. Do you work *attentively*.
3. Enter the room *carefully*.
4. They did it *successfully*.
5. Stock taking is done *annually*.

(b) Adverbs into Verbs

Replace the Adverbs in Italics in the following sentences by Verbs

1. She went to the airport in a taxi *hurriedly*.
2. They always act *obediently*.
3. She does her duty *carefully*.
4. They served me *helpfully*.
5. She listened to my advice *attentively*.

(c) **Adverbs into Adjectives**

Replace the Adverbs in Italics in the following sentences by Adjectives

1. *Fortunately* they succeeded in the difficult task.
2. She is walking *gracefully*.
3. She behaved with me *disgracefully*.
4. She solved the problem *successfully*.
5. *Probably* she will succeed.
6. She was dressed *elegantly*.

Miscellaneous Exercise

Rewrite the following sentences as directed

1. His..............with the strangers astonished everybody. *(use noun of 'familiar)*
2. India is richer in heritage than most of the countries. *(use 'rich' in place of 'richer')*
3. A student of our school is a...............leader. *(use adjective of 'fame'.)*
4. We were disappointed when our tour was cancelled. *(make noun of 'cancel')*
5. He was happy to leave the house. *(use happily in the sentence)*
6. It is better to starve than beg. *(make gerund of 'to starve')*
7. There is possibility of his being late. *(use model 'may')*
8. She looks just as smart in saari as she does in jeans. *(use 'whether' in the sentence)*
9. None in their correct senses will ever do it. *(begin the sentence with 'none but')*
10. Our principal is the most honest of all in the college. *(make the sentence comparative)*
11. Suresh thought of a new plan. *(change voice)*
12. He could not complete the race as he had injured his foot. *(Rewrite by using verb prevent)*
13. Shivaji was one of the greatest warriors of India. *(Change into comparative degree)*
14. Sheena returned a month ago. *(begin the sentence with 'it is')*
15. For more information contact the Secretary. *(begin the sentence with 'should')*
16. You remembered to buy a pen for me. didn't you? *(begin the sentences with 'you did not')*
17. You have nothing to complain of. *(begin the sentence 'there is')*
18. Please read this letter. *(use phrasal verb beginning with 'go')*
19. He has refused to help me. *(begin the sentence with 'he said')*
20. It is better to lend than borrow. *(use gerunds for infinitives)*
21. The price of milk has risen steadily. *(make sentence using 'steady')*
22. The judge punished the guilty. *(make sentence using 'fail')*
23. If you do not come, I will not go to the movie. *(use 'unless' for 'if')*
24. His victory surprised me. *(make sentence using 'take')*
25. The driver lost the job for rash driving. *(begin the sentence with 'had')*
26. He gives me the same love as he gives her. *(rewrite the sentence using 'noless')*
27. Her failure in life disappointed her parents. *(make noun of 'disappoint')*
28. We did not have good time because it was too cold. *(begin the sentence with 'if')*

29. Of what use is this book to you? *(begin the sentence with 'This book')*
30. She is not such a wise lady as she is known *(make a comparative degree of 'wise')*
31. Put your tools away. People may fall over them. *(combine the sentences)*
32. I would rather die than flatter. *(rewrite the sentence using 'prefer')*
33. Nobody will deny that she is honest. *(use 'admit' in the sentence)*
34. It you cannot face the music, I will have to. *(make the sentence by using 'or')*
35. Although she was too young, the commission appointed her. *(use 'despite' for 'although')*
36. She is not so much wise as beautiful. *(make comparative of 'wise')*
37. This should be of the greatest value to mankind. *(make positive degree of 'great')*
38. The storm which had been a threat since Monday at last broke out with great fury. *(rewrite the sentence by using 'Threaten')*
39. Waste not, want not. *(begin the sentence with if)*
40. I accept your offer. *(use 'acceptable' in this sentence)*
41. Reena has more money than brain. *(write the sentence in 'positive degree')*
42. It is normal for a child to eat four times a day. *(make adverb of 'normal' in the sentence)*
43. I caught a train and went to Amravati. *(make a sentence with 'Perfect Participle')*
44. I was not sure that it was you. *(use 'doubtful' for 'not sure')*
45. I do not know her nature any better than you. *('use positive degree')*
46. She complained that the room was hot. *(make a simple sentence)*
47. Tanya is the most punctual of all the boys in her class. *('make a comparative degree')*
48. What long hair you have! *(end the sentence with 'is')*
49. Even if you try hard, you cannot earn much. *(use 'however' in the sentence)*
50. Do they believe in God? *(end the sentence with 'exists')*
51. Who replaced the player after he was injured? *(use 'substitute' for replace)*
52. She has not met me for years. *(make the sentence using 'ago')*
53. Only my friends are responsible for my adversity. *(make negative)*
54. All the atheletes complained that ameneties provided were far from satisfactory. *(make sentence with 'complain of')*
55. It is unlikely that he will help you. *(make the sentence using 'not')*
56. He attended the function. No one raised any objection. *(combine the sentence using 'gerund attending')*
57. The girls were not permitted to go on Picnic *(make sentence using 'let')*
58. I have not a map, I can't guide you. *(make the sentence using 'if')*
59. They found a little sugar in the kitchen. *(make a 'negative sentence')*
60. Sunil had visited Mohan only once before but he remembered the route. *(make the sentence using 'although')*
61. I met him last, when his father died. *(use 'since' for 'when')*
62. If only I could meet her again. *(begin the sentence with 'would that')*
63. The situation was filled with high drama. *(use 'dramatic' in the sentence)*
64. The sun rose and the fog disappeared. *(make the sentence with 'nominative' absolute)*
65. O, for a small place to live in the hills! *(begin the sentence with 'I wish')*

66. We worried about his attitude to the poor. *(begin the sentence with 'his attitude')*
67. It is sad that a friend should be false. *(make sentence using 'Alas')*
68. This is the last time you will ever sit in this room. *(begin with 'never' in the sentence)*
69. This sum is too difficult for me. *(make a complex sentence)*
70. It is wonderful that such a child is bold. *(begin the sentence with 'how')*
71. He refused to allow the late comers in and this annoyed them. *(begin the sentence with 'his refusal')*
72. Fie Fie! you are a cheat. *(change into 'assertive sentence')*
73. Fairies do not exist. *(make the sentence using 'out of the question')*
74. This plane flies direct from Srinagar to Delhi. *(rewrite the sentence using 'flight')*
75. What is that to you? *(make the sentence 'negative')*
76. This is the greatest discovery that the world has ever known. *(begin the sentence with 'never')*
77. Eat few rich dinners and you will need few medicines. *(rewrite the sentence with if)*
78. He will be angry if you come late. *(use 'and' in the sentence)*
79. The brilliant student surprised every one. *(use 'brilliance' in the sentence)*
80. It is no use blaming him. *(begin the sentence with 'there')*
81. I was so sure that I could depend on him. *(use 'dependence' in the sentence)*
82. You will have to write legibily. *(Write using prefix 'it' before legibily)*
83. Shall we ever forget these happy days. *(rewrite using 'never')*
84. This is not the manner to do this work. *('Write a clause after manner')*
85. His prompt reply will able us to take timely action. *(rewrite the correct sentence)*
86. As it was a recess time, the students were playing. *(being the sentence with 'it')*
87. Who does not like to be praised? *(change the sentence into assertive)*
88. That was not my meaning at all. *(rewrite using the verb 'mean')*
89. If you listen seriously, I will tell you all. *(rewrite the sentence using in the event of')*
90. I am glad that he has recovered from illness. *('rewrite the sentence using 'recovery')*
91. Do this to escape sufferings. *(make the sentence using 'last')*
92. It is likely that he will help you. *(rewrite the sentence beginning with 'he')*
93. Mr. Rahul is on leave, Mrs. Deepa .... English these days. *(Fill in the form of verb 'teach')*
94. Please sit down. *(change the voice)*
95. Gold jewellery is bought and sold here. *(change the voice)*
96. He is said to be a spy. *(begin the sentence with 'it')*
97. She denied to have visited the multiplex yesterday. *(begin the sentence with 'she desied that')*
98. This computer is made in India. *(use noun of 'made' in the sentence)*
99. Every one wept when he departed. *(use 'but wept' in the sentence)*
100. If you had not worked hard, you would have wasted this year. *(use 'hard work' in the sentence)*
101. Although she is glamorous, she is modest. *(use 'as' in the sentence)*

Answers

Part I

Practice Exercise 1 (a)

1. He confessed that he was guilty.
2. All depends on what his future is.
3. How old he is, is not known.
4. Speak what the truth is.
5. The fact that he was silent proved his complicity in the crime.
6. It appears that he is running temperature.
7. He denied that he had murdered.
8. It is believed that he is honest.
9. She informed me that she had arrived.
10. The news that he died is wrong.
11. It is belived that subhash Chandra Bose died in Japan.
12. I have already heard what he has said.
13. It is sure that he has been punished.
14. It is expected that he will give me money.
15. Mohit may do what he likes.
16. I wish that you may be successful in life.
17. He wishes that he should be a very rich person.
18. There is no truth in what he says.
19. (a) Where he is hiding is likely to be discovered very soon.
    (b) It is likely that his place of hiding will be discovered very soon.
20. We believe that the news is true.
21. That you are innocent is beyond any doubt.
22. I have long doubted if he is honest.
23. I have long suspected that he is guilty.
24. It is likely that his father will give him punishment.
25. (a) It is high time that I should leave India.
    (b) It is high time I left India.
26. That he will resign is out of the question.

Practice Exercise 1 (b)

1. I have long suspected that he is a thief.
2. The news that he has arrived has not been intimated.
3. Her remarks that I had failed were disgusting.
4. What is true is eternal.
5. It is expected that she will learn good manners.
6. Pay heed to what I have instructed.
7. She has a desire that she should learn swimming.
8. Her wish is that she should do social work in future.
9. It is reported that he has lost his reputation.
10. I kept on wondering if she would succeed.
11. Everybody is responsible for what he does.
12. That he will fall is certain.
13. She did not inform me what she was.
14. Nobody knows where he is.
15. She jumped at what I offered her.

Practice Exercise 2 (a)

1. Yesterday I bought a pen which is very cheap.
2. I saw a beggar who was begging from door to door.

3. This is the village where I was born.
4. Do you know the reason why he has failed?
5. The Value of exercise that we take is great.
6. The offence which he committed is not pardonabel.
7. They come across the students who were smoking by the roadside.
8. A man who is tired, cannot work well.
9. It is not the manner with which you use to please your boss.
10. He gave me money which I could spend.
11. The pen which is given by him is very cheap.
12. I have no friend whom I can talk to.
13. He was the last man who arrived at the party.
14. He gave me a news that was fake.
15. How can you believe a person who is dishonest.

Practice Exercise 2 (b)

1. We committed a mistake which was quite serious.
2. They found a piece of diamond which is rare.
3. We undertook a journey which was quite tiring.
4. The man who was tired could not do work well.
5. The dog felled the candle which was burning.
6. The murder which he committed ruined his life.
7. He invented a machine which is used for stitching.
8. He saw a candle which was burning brightly.
9. This is a classroom which is not the place to play.
10. He has a large family whom he has to educate.
11. He was the last man who attended the funeral.
12. Do you know the time when your father went.
13. Do you know the reason why she arrived earlier.
14. Nobody appreciated the way in which she behaved at the party.
15. I was informed of the place where he was living.
16. Kabir, who was a weaver, was a famous poet.
17. Everybody loves Mr. Verma who is our teacher.
18. The boys who live near my house are honest.
19. The place where the leader was cremated was thronged with people.
20. She told me the reason why she was late.
21. Shakespear, who was a great dramatist, wrote a number of plays.
22. The girl who has long hair is a cousin of my wife.
23. They live just near the bypass which is on the outskirts of the city.
24. The players whom the President awardeed cash prize were present at the function.
25. The offence which they committed intentionally is unpardonable.
26. I paid the debt which my father incurred.

Practice Exercise 3

1. Although he is experienced, he is not efficient.
2. Unless he works hard he cannot succeed.
3. When he was scolded, he left the room.
4. When the signal was given, the train started.

5. I shall be very glad if I help him.
6. He is so simple that he cannot win the game.
7. As he did mischief, he was punished.
8. The work was done, when I was present.
9. Though he is wealthy, he is not respected.
10. You must wait here till your father arrives.
11. Although he is poor yet he is honest.
12. Do it as best as you can.
13. Nobody must expect to become rich unless he works hard.
14. My heart is so full that I cannot utter a word.
15. He borrowed money from the bank so that he might continue his higher study.
16. She is undergoing slimming treatment because she is very fat.
17. The cat is swifter than the tiger.
18. I am thankful to you because you helped my brother.
19. If he had not got timely help, he would have died from burns.
20. She is so kind that she helps everybody.
21. He did not stop working until he got success.
22. They were afraid lest they should be caught in the shower.
23. You must act as the rules say.
24. He was promoted because he was very capable.
25. We shall leave for Shimla if weather permits.
26. Water is so hot that no one can drink it.
27. If all is well, I shall meet her parents today.
28. I shall be glad if I am invited.
29. I would be glad if I were there.
30. I would have been glad if I had been there.
31. Your behaviour was so bad that the guests could not bear it.
32. She is so good that I am no match for her.
33. He was so quick that he could overtake me.
34. As it was a junk food, we did not take it.
35. If we had not been poor, we would have been a happy family.

Part II

Practice Exercise 1 (a)

1. Her dishonesty is much regretted. **2.** He admitted his enemy's generosity.
3. I know the residence of your brother.
4. You must pay heed to the words of your officers.
5. Never say anything wrong. **6.** We believe in God's existence.
7. I expect him to pass. **8.** Unfortunately he died young.
9. He asked me the reason for giving money to his brother.
10. He confessed meeting her last night.
He confessed to have met her last night.
He confessed having met her last night.
11. I agreed to teach him. **12.** I informed him of her departure.
13. He appears to have been scolded by his father.
14. I ordered him to leave the room at once. **15.** People are certain of his honesty.

Practice Exercise 1 (b)

1. He confessed his guilt.
2. I do not care for his remarks.
3. Mohit may do any thing.
4. I have long doubted his honesty.
5. The rumour of his death is baseless.
6. His age is not known.
7. Her statement is disgusting.
8. His silence proved his complicity in the crime.
9. He denied to have murdered.
10. She appears to be absent today.
11. She was alleged to have abused him.
12. She wanted to know his name.
13. My hope is to earn a lot of money.
14. He is sure to have been punished.
15. He is expected to give me money.
16. All depends on his future.
17. I don't believe in his statement.
18. I agreed to his proposal.

Practice Exercise 2 (a)

1. (a) He is not a trustworthy man.
   (b) He is not a man to be trusted.
2. A careless student cannot succeed.
3. He is not a man to cheat anyone.
4. He has a large house to live in.
5. They made a false statement.
6. You can have anything of your choice.
7. Barking dogs seldom bite.
8. I know the reason of his failure.
9. Milton, a famous poet, wrote 'Paradise Lost'.
10. The train connecting New Delhi is late.
11. Childhood is a time to learn good habits.
12. The wounded man died last night.
13. Healthy people do not need a doctor.
14. Good deeds done by a man live after him.
15. The place of cremation of the leader was thronged with people.

Practice Exercise 2 (b)

1. Yesterday I bought a very cheap book.
2. You cannot believe a dishonest person.
3. The hard working persons succeed in life.
4. A wounded soldier was lying in the field.
5. The tired players could not perform well.
6. The monster proud of his power was defeated by Hercules.
7. In the street we saw a beggar begging from door to door.
8. The man wounded in the accident died last night.
9. The police discovered the weapon used to kill the victim.
10. The magic ball meant for the king was eaten by the jester.
11. Seema was the last person to leave for home.
12. My uncle was the first man to hear her name on the radio.
13. He has some bills to pay in cash.
14. I have no friend to talk to.
15. Childhood is a time to teach good habits to children.
16. The time of his arrival tomorrow is not certain.
17. All of us were told the reason of his becoming rich suddenly.
18. I remember very well the year of his retirement.
19. The residents of our colony were shouting for justice.
20. Rathore our captain, scored fifty runs.

21. Edison, a great scientist, invented electricity.
22. We visited the Taj, a unique building.
23. I shall travel by the Taj Express going to Agra direct.
24. The students hailing from Bihar are very hard-working.
25. Tomorrow I will board a train connecting Udaipur.
26. The news broadcast by the Voice of America is true.
27. I met a poet already known to me.
28. Mr. Gupta will buy the house built by me only last year.
29. The book lost by me yesterday has been found out.
30. Those living in glass houses should not throw stones at others.

Practice Exercise 3

1. He did in accordance with my wish.
2. We get up in the morning.
3. After having finished our work, we went home.
4. Seeing me, he ran away.
5. Walking in the garden she was addressed by a stranger.
6. He is kind enough to help everybody.
7. We went home after the arrival of the teacher.
8. He wrote fast to the best of his ability.
9. Without being threatened, he will not return money.
10. I succeeded beyond my expectations.
11. On being found out, the thief was arrested.
12. Despite being punished, she was not ashamed.
13. You can talk to your liking.
14. Inspite of being poor, he is honest.
15. Despite being honest, he is not hard working.
16. But for their help, I would not have gained success.
17. He ran fast to catch taxi.
18. On account of running fast, she was declared first by the teacher.
19. He being poor, we will help him.
20. God willing, you will succeed.
21. I make a promise to stick to it.
22. He was complimented because of his success.
23. He has come to Chandigarh to be treated by capable doctors.
24. It being fine we left for picnic.
25. While watching TV they were visited by their friends.
26. Crossing the road she was knocked down by a scooter.
27. Sania is too slow for a good tennis player.
28. She is so clever that she can see through your tricks.
29. Her sorrow is too deep for tears.
30. He will stick to his job so as to escape starvation.
31. The signal having been given the train started.
32. I have not had any rest since my arrival in Chennai.
33. No money having been given to me the project was not launched.
34. The house is too small for me.
35. The weather being very pleasant we went on a long drive.

Part III

Practice Exercise 1

1. You permit me and I shall leave the room.
2. He is a man of knowledge but he is a fool.
3. He committed a fault so he was punished.
4. He is wealthy but he is not respected.
5. He worked hard and secured high percentage of marks.
6. He returned and we asked him many questions.
7. He teaches Mathematics and Hindi also.
8. You sent me money so I am thankful to you.
9. He is not only rich but also learned.
10. He did not accept my request but left Jhansi.
11. He was sitting in the drawing room and watching T.V.
12. He had many contacts but never used unfair means.
13. He must admit his fault otherwise he will be punished.
14. He must work hard and will secure high percentage of marks.
15. He was dismissed for he embezzled money.
16. The weather was very fine so we left for swimming.
17. He will die and his son will inherit the property.
18. He was ignorant so he did not follow the rules.
19. He could not qualify examination and I was much surprised.
20. (a) This treatment is very costly so only the rich can afford it.
    (b) None but the rich can afford this treatment.
21. Do this or suffer.
22. He feared rain and went by car.
23. I am not invited and so I shall not go.
24. Neither this statement nor that statement is correct.
25. First desire and then deserve.

Practice Exercise 2

1. She is sick but she will come.
2. Come by car and we will take you to the temple.
3. It was cold so we did not go out.
4. The thief was found out and he was arrested.
5. She arrived and everybody welcomed her.
6. You must stop smoking otherwise you will suffer from lung disease.
7. I am not invited so I shall not go.
8. Listen seriously and I will tell you all.
9. He has recovered from illness so I am glad.
10. I had lost the pen but I have found it.
11. He had a dog and that was very faithful.
12. He is unlucky but he is never disappointed.
13. Do this otherwise you will suffer.
14. He is very intelligent but he cannot succeed.
15. He gave me money and I started business.
16. He is not at home otherwise I would meet him.

17. He may be at home and in that case I will give him money.
18. He will die and his son will inherit his property.
19. He must work hard and he will pass.
20. He spent more than he could afford.

Part IV

Practice Exercise

1. (a) **Nouns into verbs**

1. She succeeded in the examination.
2. She intended to harm me.
3. He advised me.
4. They cannot be admitted without documents.
5. I am disinclined to work in office.
6. These oranges taste sour.
7. They have agreed to complete this work in time.
8. I am not inclined to go to the movie.
9. He has disgraced his family.
10. This refrigerator costs a lot.

(b) **Noun into Adjective**

1. She admitted that she was guilty.
2. The room was dusty.
3. He is a courageous man.
4. They are skilful workers.
5. His life is peaceful these days.
6. He was punished for he was negligent.

(c) **Nouns into Adverbs**

1. She left room angrily.
2. Please carry it carefully.
3. She survived luckily.
4. She is living with her only son peacfully.
5. She listened to me patiently.
6. She listened to me attentively.
7. She left the room hurriedly.
8. He goes to Chandigarh weekly.

2. Verbs

(a) **Verb into Noun**

1. My brother made a *promise* to help me.
2. This computer is of Indian *make*.
3. She accepted all my *proposals*.
4. She was taking *bath*.
5. She put *signature* on the documents.
6. I am in *need* of money.
7. Please give me help.
8. Her *intelligence* won our *admiration*.

(b) **Verb into Adjective**

1. Her views are *different* from mine.
2. She is *obedient* to her brother.
3. He has been *successful* in her work.
4. He was *hopeful* of success.
5. I am *doubtful* of your honesty.
6. His success is *astonishing* to me.

(c) **Verb into Adverb**

1. She left for bus stop *hurriedly*.
2. I turned him out *forcibly*.
3. She did her task *successfully*.
4. She listened to my advice *attentively*.
5. They served me in difficulties *helpfully*.
6. She does her duty *carefully*.

3. Adjectives

(a) **Adjectives into Noun**

1. Exercise gives *strength* to our body.
2. She acts with *care*.
3. She spends money with *wisdom*.
4. They achieved *success* in their expedition.
5. He is a man of *courage*.
6. We take pride in our country.
7. The room is full of *dust*.

(b) **Adjectives into Verbs**

1. Your news has *pleased* me.
2. She *intended* to favour me.
3. She *succeeded* in her job.
4. He *cares* about his health.
5. Your wife was annoyed with your behaviour.
6. We *pride* ourselves in your success.

(c) **Adjectives into Adverbs**

1. She is liing with her daughter *peacefully*.
2. Do your work *carefully*.
3. She is learning computers *attentively*.
4. She writes *neatly*.
5. I am sitting *comfortably*.
6. He drives *slowly*.
7. She did it *intentionally*.
8. I will *certainly* pass.

Adverbs

(a) **Adverbs into Nouns**

1. Do not talk with children in *anger*.
2. Do your work with *attention*.
3. Enter the room with care.
4. They got success in doing this.
5. Stock-taking is done *every year*.

(b) **Adverbs into Verbs**

1. She *hurried* to the airport in a taxi.
2. They always *obey*.
3. She *cares* for her duty.
4. They *helped* me in difficulty.
5. She *attended* to my advice.

(c) **Adverbs into Adjectives**

1. It is *fortunate* that they succeeded in the difficult task.
2. Her gait was *graceful*.
3. Her behaviour was *disgraceful*.
4. She was *successful* in solving the problem.
5. It is *probable* she may succeed.
6. Her dress was *elegant*.

Miscellaneous Exercise

1. His familiarity with the strangers astonished everybody.
2. Very few countries are as rich in heritage as India.
3. A student of our school is a famous leader.
4. The cancellation of our tour disappointed us.
5. He left the house happily.
6. Starving is better than begging.
7. He may be late.
8. She looks smart whether she wears saari or jeans.
9. None but in their correct senses will ever do it.
10. Our principal is more honest than anybody else.
11. New plan was thought of by Suresh.
12. His injured foot prevented him from completing the race.
13. Shivaji was greater than most of the warriors in India.
14. It is a month since Sheena returned.
15. Should you require more information, contact the Secretary of the club.
16. You did not forget to buy a pen for me. did you?
17. There is nothing to complain of.

18. Please go through this letter.
19. He said that he would not help me.
20. Borrowing is not as good as lending.
21. There is a steady rise in the price of milk.
22. The judge did not fail to punish the guilty.
23. Unless you come, I will not go to the movie.
24. a) His victory took me by surprise
b) I was taken by surprise at his victory.
25. Had the driver not driven rashly, he would not have lost the job.
26. He loves me no less than he loves her.
27. Her failure in life caused disappointed to her parents.
28. If it had not been cold, we would have had good time.
29. This book is of no use to you.
30. She is not wiser lady than she is known to be.
31. Put your tools away lest people should fall over them.
32. I would prefer to die rather than flatter.
33. Everybody will admit that she is honest.
34. Face the music or I will have to.
35. Despite being young she was appointed by the Commission.
36. She is more wise than beautiful.
37. Nothing else is of as great value to mankind as this is.
38. The storm which had threatened since Monday at last broke out with great fury.
39. If you do not waste, you will not want.
40. Your offer is acceptable to me.
41. Reena has not as much brain as she has money.
42. Normally a child should eat four times a day.
43. Having caught a train I went to Amravati.
44. I was doubtful if it was you.
45. You know her nature as well as I.
46. She complained of the room being hot.
47. Tanya is more punctual than any boy in the class.
48. How long your hair is!
49. However hard you may try you cannot earn much.
50. Do they believe that God exists?
51. Who was substituted for the injured player?
52. She met me years ago.
53. None but my friends are responsible for my adversity.
54. All the athelets complained of unsatisfactory amenities.
55. It is not likely that he will help you.
56. No one raised any objection to his attending the function.
57. The girls were not let go on Picnic.
58. If I had a map, I could guide you.
59. They found little sugar in the kitchen.
60. Although Sunil had visited Mohan only once before, he remembered the route.
61. Have you ever visited Mumbai?

62. Would that I could meet her again.
63. The situation was highly dramatic.
64. The sun having risen the fog disappeared.
65. (a) I wish to have a small place in the hills to live in.
    (b) I wish I had a small place in the hills to live in.
66. His attitude to the poor worried us.
67. Alas! a friend should be false.
68. Never will you sit in this room again.
69. This sum is so difficult that I cannot solve.
70. How bold such a child is!
71. His refusal to allow the late comers annoyed them.
72. It is contemptible that you are a cheat.
73. Existence of fairies is out of the question.
74. The flight of the plane from Srinagar to Delhi is direct.
75. It does not matter to you.
76. Never has the world known such a great descovery.
77. If you eat few rich dinners, you will need few medicines.
78. He will be angry at your coming late.
79. The brilliance of the student surprised everyone.
80. There is no use of blaming him.
81. I was sure of my dependence on him.
82. You will not have to write illegibly.
83. We shall never forget these happy days.
84. This is not the manner how you should do this work.
85. His prompt reply will enable us to take timely action.
86. It was a recess time and the students were playing.
87. Everybody likes to be praised.
88. I did not mean it at all.
89. In the event of your listening seriously I will tell you all.
90. His recovery from illness has made me glad.
91. Do this lest you should suffer.
92. He is likely to help you.
93. Mr. Rahul is on leave. Mrs Deepa is teaching English these days.
94. You are requested to sit down.
95. We buy and sell gold jewellery.
96. It is said that he is a spy.
97. She denied that she had visited the multiplex yesterday.
98. This computer is of India make.
99. There was none but wept when he departed.
100. But for hard work you would have wasted this year.
101. Glamorous as she is, she is modest.

4

Punctuation

Punctuation is a system in which marks are used in writing to indicate pauses and division of sentences. The meaning of written communication is made clear to the readers by the use of these marks. In fact punctuation is the right use of putting in marks or stops in writing.

The following are the principal marks of punctuation.

1. Comma (,)
2. Apostrophe (')
3. Semi Colon (;)
4. Colon (:)
5. Dash and Parenthesis. (–)
6. Quotation marks (Inverted Commas) (" ")
7. Hyphen (-)
8. End marks
(a) Full stop (.)
(b) Question Marks (?)
(c) Exclamatory marks (!)

Besides punctuation marks, the students are required to know the use of .

(a) Capital letters
(b) How to write numerals?

Use of Comma (,)

(a) **The comma is used for a short or slight pause to separate words in a list but it is avoided before 'and'**

(i) Everything they will give me, food, clothes and salary.
(ii) We will need cake, candles, lights and all.

(b) **Used to separate Adverb Clause when it is followed by main clause**

(i) When the train arrives, we shall board it
(ii) Unless you take exercise, you will not lose weight.

(c) **Used to mark off non-restrictive adjective clause. In such cases Adjective clause acts as a co-ordinate clause**

(i) He ate contaminated food, which (and this) made him sick.
(ii) She went out with Arnav, who (and he) bought her a necklace.
(iii) She said that she would help me, which (but which) was not true.

NOTE Restrictive Adjective clause is restrictive in meaning.

Comma is not used to mark off restrictive clauses.

(i) My brother who is working hard is bound to succeed.

(ii) The boys who attended N.C.C. Camp will be awarded certificates.

(d) **Used to write Noun in Appositions**

(i) I would like to meet Mr. Kabir, your manager.

(ii) Mr. Kabir, the manager of our company, will call on you tomorrow.

(e) **Used for Parenthetical Expressions**

(i) We knew, of course, that he would not attend your marriage.

(ii) They are, however, intelligent.

(iii) Your friend, if I am correct, is dishonest.

(iv) They, as you know, will visit us next summer.

(v) Therefore, I like her.

(vi) Moreover, she is intelligent.

(vii) In fact, I like him.

(viii) Slowly, she entered the room.

NOTE Students should take note of the following phrases carefully. after all, to say the least, in several ways, I know, I am sure, however, of course, therefore, etc.

(f) **Used to separate nominative absolute**

The sun having risen, we left for the town.

The task having been done, They went to bed.

(g) **Used to separate initials and Titles**

Please call on Prof. Sharma, M.A., Ph.D.

(h) **Used while writing address**

Lt. General A.K. Chopra,
50, Arun Apartments,
Noida . (U.P.)

(i) **Used while writing dates**

July 10, 2008

10th July 2008 (No comma is required)

Thursday, July 10th, 2008

(j) **Used while expressing numerical expressions in group of there digits from right direction**

7, 297, 789

(k) **Used after solutions and complimentary close**

My dear son,
Dear son,
Yours sincerely,
Yours truly,

(l) **Used to separate a question tag from the sentence**
She is honest, isn't she?
It is a nice story, isn't it?

(m) **Used for omitted words**
She is dull, her sister, clever.
Reena is ten, Sheena, fourteen.

(n) **Used to write reported speech after/before**

(a) Reporting Verb:
"I am not going tomorrow, " said she.
She said, "I am not going tomorrow."
"I am not", she said, "going tomorrow."
"I am not going tomorrow," said she, "I am ill".

NOTE Comma is not used at the end when the reported speech is interrogative.
"Are you going tomorrow?" said she.
"Are you", said she, "going tomorrow?"

(o) **Used after words of address.**
Priya, bring me some fruit.
Bring me some fruit, Priya
I know, Shreya, time has come now.

(p) **Used for separation of words.**
Sleep, sleep peacefully.
Blow, blow fast
What she is, is well known.

(q) **Used to indicate the omission of a verb.**
Richa got house. Esha, cash
The bride was a Kaystha, the groom, a Brahmin.

2. Apostrophe (')

(a) **Used with 's' to indicate that a thing or a person belongs to somebody.**
Rohan's house
Children's school
Women's wardrobe
My sister's husband.

(b) **Apostrophe is not used in case of non-living things.**
The table's wood. *(incorrect)*
The wood of the table. *(correct)*
The book's price. *(incorrect)*
The price of the book. *(correct)*

(c) **In case of Plural Nouns and Proper Nouns ending with 's' Apostrophe without 's' is used at the end**

The Girls' hostel.
The Students' Club.
Kalidas' poems
Dickens' Novels

(d) **Pronouns do not required the use of apostrophe. Only 's' is used with pronouns**

Yours faithfully,
This house is hers
Ours is a large house.

(e) **The letters that are omitted are represented by an apostrophe while writing contracted form**

I'm, I've, Can't — It's
I'll, They'd — Won't

(f) **Apostrophe with 's' is used with figures and letters to make plural**

1. P's and Q's
2. 7's, 8's

But we say.
Fours, Sixes, Tens

(g) **Apostrophe with 's' is used to make abbreviations Plural. However, in some cases Apostrophe can be omitted too**

M.A.'s, in '89 (1989) — M.P's, Ph.D's
The 90s of the previous century. — *(Correct)*

3. Semicolon (;)

Semicolon is used almost as a period/full stop within a sentence. It is used at the end of a thought in place of 'and', 'but', because, etc to indicate that the thought continues into another thought.

1. Please do it; I shall give you money.
2. Krishna is dark-skinned; Radha is fair.
3. It is cloudy; it may rain.
4. Man proposes; God disposes.

4. Colon (:)

Colon is used when a list, quotation or a long speech is to follow after it. It is used to explain the words – Namely, as follows, following, for example, etc.

(i) Wordsworth wrote : Child is father of man.
(ii) The meaning can be explained thus : Honesty does not always pay.
(iii) They brought many charges against him namely : Murder, Rape and Theft.
(iv) Please send us the following items of furniture : Chairs, Tables, Benches and Stools.

5. Dash (–) and Parentheses

(a) Dash is used in a sentence to mark an abrupt end to indicate that the words within a dash do not belong there. They are treated as just afterthought. Sometimes they are parenthetical expressions. Double dashes are also known as parenthesis.

(i) They are – you know – crooks.
(ii) My friend – I am sure – is very sincere. (used for explanation)
(iii) The other players – Gambhir and Raina – are also part of the Indian team.
(iv) Please send me the detail such as – your age, your income, nature of the job.
(v) Antony lost for love all – kingdom, glory, friends and honour.

(b) **Used sometimes for colon**
We have received the following articles
(i) Photographs
(ii) Identity cards
(iii) Medical certificates

(c) **Used as a Pause**
(i) I wrote her a message......a message of peace and love.
(ii) He narrated a story......a story that amused everyone.

(d) **Used to indicate a missing word**
(i) Mrs...............is a very shrewd lady.
(ii) Please refer to page 20–25.

(e) **To resume a scattered subject. *For Example***
Honour, money, love......all were lost.
Friends, relative, partners......all are present.

6. Quotation Marks (' '), (" ") (Inverted Commas)

Quotation Marks are used to enclose words and punctuation in direct speech. They are also termed inverted commas when written as such (" ").

(a) She shouted, "We have to win."
(b) Used to enclose the names of books, poems, essays.
(i) I have bought, "Tales from Shakespeare."
(ii) Have you studied, "Ode to a Nightingale."

(c) Used to enclose exact words spoken, written or quoted with a view to highlighting them.
(i) 'Beware of Dogs' was written on the gate.
(ii) Political parties use 'secularism' as a 'catch vote slogan'.

7. Hyphen (–)

Hyphen is used to indicate words or parts of words that belong together.

(a) **Used to make compound adjective qualifying a noun**

10 year-old-boy
well-known actress
A 5-day week
A hundred-rupee note
Mother-in-law

(b) **Used after prefixes to separate two vowels and three consonants**

Co-ordinate
Co-operation

(c) **Used to make compound numbers:** (21 to 99)

Twenty–Six
Seventy–One

(d) **Used to separate constituents of compound words**

Door-to-door campaign
Double-storey apartments
Man-to-man relations

(e) **Used to write prefixes.**

Ex-husband
Vice-president
Non-violence

8. The End Marks

(a) The Full Stop (.) (b) The Question Mark (?)
(c) The Exclamation Mark (!)

(a) Full Stop (.)

(a) Also known as the longest period, a full-stop is used to end a sentence.

(i) They have arrived.
(ii) She will join our club.
(iii) Pay now and get out.

(b) Used after abbreviations and initials of the names. They may be omitted in current English

A.B. Vajpayee		A.K. Chopra
Feb.	U.S.A.	U.K.
Dr.	Prof.	Mr./Mrs.
e.g.	etc.	
U.N.O. (UNO)		M.L.A. (MLA)

(c) **Used after fractions, amount, time and date**

Fractions	Amount	Date
9.15 a.m.	50.75	5.9.05

(d) **Used at the end of the address**

10, Rama Kutir, Chandigarh.

(b) **Question Mark (?)**

Used after interrogative questions

(i) Are you staying there?
(ii) Could you please help me?
(iii) When did you meet her last?
(iv) How have you done?
(v) I asked her how she had done it.

NOTE In sentence (v) full stop instead of question mark is used because it is a question in Indirect speech.

Question Tag

They can do it, can't they?
She will come, won't she?
Asking a question or expressing a doubt in a statement.
She was married in 1992?
She is an honest (?) lady.

(c) **The Exclamation Mark (!)**

Used after interjections, the words and sentences expressing emotions such as joy, sorrow, surprise, pity, prayer, curse, etc.

(i) What a pretty child!
(ii) How good of you!
(iii) Ah! we are ruined.
(iv) O! What you have done.
(v) Oh God! I have sent the email to someone else.

Capital

(a) **Capital letters are used**

(i) To write God and Man in the widest sense.
God loves all.
Man is mortal.

(ii) Pronouns used for God also begin with a Capital letter
(i) God is great.
(ii) We worship Him.
But gods and goddesses used as deities do not begin with a capital letter.

(b) To write proper nouns.
Pearl, Arnav, Suhani, Shaurya.

(c) To write 'First person of the pronoun.
She likes me but I don't like her.

(d) To write Interjection O, Oh
Oh! We are ruined.

(e) To write a reported speech.
She said, "I am a queen."
They said, "We have won the match."

Numerals

How to write Numerals?

1. When a sentence contains one series of numbers, all numbers of the series should be written in figures. She has bought 4 chairs, 2 tables and 8 stools.
2. When a sentence contains two series of numbers, the number in one series should be written in words and the number in second series should be written in figures.

Five students have secured 90 marks and two have secured 85 marks.

3. Write Compound Numbers between 21 and 99 in words
   Twenty-one — Thirty-seven
   Seventy-four — Sixty-Four
4. Numerical expressions are set off in groups of three digits starting from right.
   7, 897, 684
   97, 684
5. When one number follows another number immediately, first number should be written in figures and the second, in words.
   Four 5- feet long pipes
   Two 15 by 12 feet rooms.
6. When a sentence begins with a number, the number should be written in words.
   Forty persons died in the accident and twelve were wounded.

Practice Exercise

Punctuate the following sentences.

1. reena said to the servant what have you been doing since morning the servant said madam i have been walking the dog reena said go at once to the kitchen what have i to do there the servant asked.
2. alas child said her mother you have eaten all that i had mother do not worry i can manage without food but what about you said shaurya you have not eaten too.
3. great god i would rather be a pagan than such a christian wrote wordsworth.
4. by god I have not done it.
5. good heavens I have lost my purse.
6. good morning suhani have you slept well said her mom you do not appear to have slept well asked suhani in turn you were awake when I got up to turn off the air conditioner.
7. i cannot go she said because rain has not stopped so far.
8. they are well now arnav said they can go but it is drizzling how can they go said my daughter pearl.
9. do not desire O my young friend to get what you cannot get said the fisherman.
10. the king said to the jester how dare you touch the magic thing meant for me be ready to face the consequences shedding tears the jester said I am sorry no use crying said the king I am crying for you my lord replied the jester why asked the king.
11. you expect every body the slave said to the master, to flatter you all the time why is it so.
12. the queen cried help help.
13. advise me deep said how can i solve this problem.
14. no said malini i have not heard this news.
15. young and old good and bad all must die.
16. the names of the students are rohit, meenakshi, rahul, sona and ankur.
17. oh dear i am tired today.
18. o yes i like singing you like dancing.
19. some are born great some achieve greatness.
20. you fools how dare you enter my room without permission.
21. she wouldnt go there my son.
22. for god's sake please help me.
23. ah i am undone my friends have ruined me.
24. alas what a fool i am he has after all cheated me.
25. the words the prohibited area were written on the wall.

Answers

Practice Exercise

1. Reena said to the servant "What have you been doing since morning?' The servant said, "Madam, I have been walking the dog." Reema said. "Go at once to the kitchen." "What have I to do there"? the servant asked.
2. "Alas Child", said her mother. "You have eaten all that I had." "Mother, do not worry. I can manage without food. But what about you?" said Shaurya. "You have not eaten too."
3. "Great God! I would rather be a Pagan than such a Christian." wrote Wordsworth.
4. By God! I have not done it.
5. Good Heavens! I have lost my purse.
6. "Good morning, Suhani. Have you slept well?" said her Mom. "You do not appear to have slept well," asked Suhani in turn. "You were awake when I got up to turn off the air conditioner."
7. "I can not go," she said, "because rain has not stopped so far."
8. "They are well now", Arnav said. "They can go." "But it is drizzling. How can they go?" said my daughter, Pearl.
9. "Do not desire O my young friend to get what you cannot get", said the fisherman.
10. The king said to the jester, "How dare you touch the magic thing meant for me? Be ready to face the consequences." Shedding tears the Jester said, "I am sorry. No use crying," said the King. "I am crying for you, my lord", said the Jester "Why?" asked the King.
11. "You expect everybody," the slave said to the master, "to flatter you all the time. Why is it so?"
12. The queen cried, "Help! Help!"
13. "Advise me," Deep said, "How can i solve this problem?"
14. "No," said Malini, "I have not heard this news."
15. Young and old, good and bad—All must die.
16. The names of the students are—Rohit, Meenakshi, Rahul, Sona and Ankur.
17. Oh dear! I am tired today.
18. 'O yes i like singing; you like dancing.
19. Some are born great; some achieve greatness.
20. You fools! How dare you enter my room without permission.
21. She wouldn't go there, my son.
22. For God's sake, please help me.
23. Ah! I am undone my friends have ruined me.
24. Alas! what a fool I am. He has, after all, cheated me.
25. The words, 'The prohibited Area', were written on the wall.

5

Spelling Rules

Introduction

English spelling is an intriguing part of learning English. **Max Miiller** (a scholar of comparative religion) went one step further and summed up the dilemma of those learning English. "English spelling is a national misfortune to England and international misfortune to the rest of the world.

Various scholars and linguists have suggested a number of ways to learn spellings such as the Dictionary method, the Dictation method, the Playway method, the Old drill method and so on.

Without going into the merits and demerits of any methods we may agree to the sound advice of U.S. Tomkinson that 'Caught rather than taught' is the best way to learn spellings.

In other words a student can solve the problem just by reading constantly and preparing a list of words that spell a danger.

There are many reasons for poor spellings. A few among them are poor memory, weak retention power and less of reading activity, therefore, correct spellings need constant writing practice, usage and power of recollection.

The more a student recollects a word, the more capability he acquires to avoid errors in spelling words.

Some Important Rules on Spellings

1. The end consonant is usually doubled when there is one vowel letter before it

(a) While adding 'ed, ing' *For example*

Stop + ed + ing	Stopped	Stopping
Spot + ed + ing	Spotted	Spotting
Admit + ed + ing	Admitted	Admitting
Regret + ed + ing	Regretted	Regretting
Recur + ed + ing	Recurred	Recurring
Plan + ed + ing	Planned	Planning

Exceptions

Suffered	Suffering
Benefited	Benefitting
Offered	Offering
Differed	Differing
Focus	Focusing

(b) While adding 'er' ,'est' to make comparative and superlative degree
For example

Thin	Thinner	Thinnest
Big	Bigger	Biggest
Sad	Sadder	Saddest
Fat	Fatter	Fattest
Mad	Madder	Maddest

(c) While making a noun of a verb by adding 'er'

Cut	Cutter
Swim	Swimmer
Run	Runner
Sin	Sinner
Rub	Rubber

(d) While adding Y to make an adjective of a noun.

Mud	Muddy
Fun	Funny

(e) If the stress is on the first syllable of a word that ends in "at, el, il, op, ip."

Equal + ed + ing	Equalled, Equalling
Travel + ed, ing	Travelled, Travelling
Level + ed + ing	Levelled, Levelling
Worship + ed + ing	Worshipped, Worshipping
Slap + ed + ing	Slapped, Slapping
Equip + ed, ing	Equipped, Equipping
Handicap + ed + ing	Handicapped, Handicapping
Signal + ed + ing	Signalled, Signalling
Model + ed + ing	Modelled, Modelling

2. The end consonant is not doubled

(a) When there is dipthong before it.

Reap + ed + ing	Reaped, Reaping
Heap + ed + ing	Heaped, Heaping
Team + ed + ing	Teamed, Teaming
Shout + ed + ing	Shouted, Shouting
Cool + ed + ing	Cooled, Cooling

(b) When there is a suffix with a consonant.

Sin + ful	Sinful
Woman + hood	Womanhood
Sad + ness	Sadness
Equip + ment	Equipment

(c) When the stress is on the second syllable.

Listen + ed + ing	Listened, Listening
Offer + ed + ing	Offered, Offering
Answer + ed + ing	Answered, Answering
Murmur + ed + ing	Murmured, Murmuring

3. Words Ending in 'y'.

(a) Verbs ending in 'y' change into 'i' while they are conjugated (Making form of verbs) but 'y' remains unchanged when suffix 'ing' is added.

Rely	Relied	Relying
Marry	Married	Marrying
Try	Tried	Trying
Carry	Carried	Carrying

(b) Words ending in 'y' with a vowel before it do not change.

Obey	Obeyed	Obeying
Pray	Prayed	Praying
Enjoy	Enjoyed	Enjoying

Exceptions

Say	Said	Saying
Pay	Paid	Paying
Lay	Laid	Laying

(c) When suffix 'ing' is added to verbs ending in 'ie', then change in to 'y'.

lie	lying
die	dying
tie	tying

(d) Nouns and adjectives ending in 'y' with a vowel before them, change into 'i' when suffixes er, est, ly, full, ness are added.

Happy	Happier	Happily
Fly	Flier	
Plenty	Plentiful	
Tidy	Tidier	Tidiest
Pity	Pitiful	
Sunny	Sunnier	Sunniest

4. When words ending in 'll' are compounded with double 'll', both words become single 'l'.

Will + full	Wilful
Full+fill	Fulfil

Exceptions

Well-being Farewell

5. Use of suffix 'ly' with adjectives to make adverbs

(a) Adjectives ending in 'l' are written with 'll' while adding suffix 'ly'.

Final + ly	Finally
Real + ly	Really
Useful + ly	Usefully
Playful + ly	Playfully

(b) Adjectives ending in 'le' are written without 'le' while adding suffix 'ly'.

Sensible + ly	Sensibly
Forcible +ly	Forcibly
Gentle + ly	Gently
Subtle +ly	Subtly

6. In words ending in 'n' retain 'n' when 'ness' is added

Keen	Keenness
Clean	Cleanliness
Mean	Meanness

7. The letter 'c' is followed by letter (ei) **and other letters by** (ie).

Receive	niece
Perceive	Siege
Deceive	Belief
Conceive	Achieve
Ceiling	Brief

Exceptions

Leisure, Counterfeit, freight, feign, their, height, heir, reign.

8. Words ending in 'll' are used with single 'l' when compounded with full, all, well, un, in dis

All + together	Altogether
All + most	Almost
Well + come	Welcome
All + ready	Already
Un + till	Until
In + still	Instil
Dis + till	Distil

9. The silent 'e' is not dropped when

(a) Suffix 'ly' is added

False + ly	Falsely
Safe + ly	Safely
Sure + ly	Surely

Exceptions

Whole + ly	Wholly
True + ly	Truly
Due + ly	Duly

(b) 'e' is not dropped after 'c' or 'g' while adding suffixes 'able', 'ous' beginning with vowel.

Peace + able	Peaceable
Trace + able	Traceable
Service + able	Serviceable
Courage + ous	Courageous
Advantage + ous	Advantageous
Manage + able	Manageable
Marriage + able	Marriageable
Charge + able	Chargeable

(c) 'e' is not dropped when suffixes beginning with consonant are added such as **ful, less, hood, ly, ment, ness.**

hate + ful = hateful	use + less = useless
care + ful = careful	improve +ment = improvement
like + ness = likeness	state + hood = statehood
Extreme + ly = extremely	achieve + ment = achievement

Exception (1)

Argue + ment = argument
Awe + ful = awful

Exception (2)

Final 'e' in the following words can be retained or removed.

like	likeable, likable
mile	mileage, milage
judge	judgement, judgment
abridge	abridgement, abridgment
acknowledge	acknowledgement, acknowledgment

10. The silent 'e' is dropped while adding

(a) suffixes such as 'ing, able, ary, ous'.

rove + ing = roving
care + ing = caring
age + ing = aging
value + able = valuable
note + able = notable
stare + ing = staring
advise + able = advisable
imagine + ary = imaginary
desire + ous = desirous
pore + ous = porous

fame + ous = famous
imagine + able = imaginable
love + able = lovable
move + able = movable

Exceptions like + able = likeable

(b) silent 'e' is dropped while adding 'y' to a noun

Stone + y = stony
Noise + y = noisy
Taste + y = tasty
Ice + y = icy

(c) The silent 'e' after consonant 't' is dropped when suffix 'tion' is added.

Pollute + tion = pollution
Frustrate + tion = frustration
Delete + tion = deletion
Deplete + tion =depletion

(d) 'e' is changed to 'i' in words ending in 'ce' when 'ous' as suffix is added.

Vice + ous = vicious
Malice + ous = malicious
Space + ous = spacious
Grace + ous + gracious

(e) 'ee' or 'oo' are not dropped with suffixes 'able, ing, full'.

agree	agreeable	agreeing
foresee	foreseeable	foreseeing
woo		wooing
glee	gleeful	—

(f) Final 'c' is changed to 'ck' before ed, ing, er

Panic	panicked
Picnic	picnickers

11. Making plurals – Some pitfalls.

(a) The plural of a noun is usually made by adding 's' to it

homes, arms, boys, flames

Exceptions

(b) Nouns ending in, 'o', 'kch', 'ch', 'ss' end in 'es' when changed in plural forms

wishes, switches, axes, asses, potatoes, tomatoes.

But add 's' only in abbreviated words ending in 'o' **photos, Pianos, dynamos.**

(c) When singular Nouns ending in 'f' or 'fe' are changed into plural add 'ves' in place 'of', 'f' or 'fe'.

Wife	Wives
Wolf	Wolves
Loaf	loaves
Thief	Thieves

Exception

handkerchief	handkerchiefs
chief	chiefs
cliff	cliffs
belief	beliefs

(d) When singular nouns ending in 'y' with a consonant before them are changed into plural 'y' changes into 'ies'.

Country	Countries
Lady	Ladies.

(e) Nouns ending in 'y' with a vowel word before them retain 'y' when 's' is added.

Joy	Joys
Day	Days
Play	Plays
Monkey	Monkeys

12. As a part of spellings a student is supposed to be aware of the mute (silent) **consonants *For example***

(i) 'b' is silent in
subtle, debt, debtor, doubt.

(ii) 'd' is silent in
grudge, hedge, sledge.

(iii) 'g' is silent in
malign, benign, assign, sign.

(iv) 'h' is silent in
honour, hour, honest, honorary, exhaust.

(v) 'k' is silent in
knife, know, knee, knight.

(vi) 'l' is silent in
balm, talk, folk, alms, palm, calm, chalk.

(vii) 'n' is silent in
Solemn, autumn, hymn, column.

(viii) 'p' is silent in
pseudonym, Psychology, Corps, receipt.

(ix) 't' is silent in
often, whistle, hustle, debut, depot, hasten, fasten.

(x) 'w' is silent in
write, wrath, wring, wrong, wrap.

(xi) 'h' is silent in
daughter, draught, sight, right.

Some Most Likely Pitfalls for Spelling Learners

A

Aggregate
Adjacent
Autumn
Accumulate
Accrue
Absence
Ascetic
Agree, Agreeable, Agreement
Address
Achieve
Already
Assassin
Annihilate
Acquire
Apparatus
Admissible
Acreage
Abridgeable, Abridgement,
Allot, Allotment, Allotted, Allotting
Accessible
Adversary
Assist, Assistant
Acquitted, Acquitting
Accommodate, Accommodation
Assess, Assessment
Awful
Aggravate
Athlete, Athletic
Accede
Accomplish, Accomplishment
Adolescent
Acquaint
Abstinence, Abstinent
Appearance
Assassin, Assassination
Advantageous
Arguable, Arguing, Argument
Acceptable
Accelerate, Accelerator
Annual
Admitting
Abbreviate
Allegiance
Allure
Aggrieved
Arrangement.
Advisable, Advise, Adviser, Advising
Appall
Acquise
Apostle
Amateur

B

Bouquet
Beggar
Balloon
Banquet
Bequeath
Battalion
Bidding
Business
Biscuit
Bureaucracy
Besiege
Beginner, Beginning
Busying
Beseech
Breakable
Bookkeeper
Believable, Believe
Blamable, Blameworthy
Betrayed
Besiege
Benefit, Beneficial, Benefited
Bony
Bureau
Beneficent

C

Ceiling
Coolly
Coercible
Caffeine
Colloquial
Commemorate
Challenge
Conscience, Conscientious
Cigarette
Credible
Collapsible
Celebrate
Canvass, Canvassing
Coming
Corroborate
Compatible
Contemptible
Commitment, Committed
Cancelled, Cancelling, Cancellation
Chagrined, Chagrining
Controlled
Conceit, Conceited
Conferred
Colossal
Cagey
Confectionery
Corruptible
Conscious
Convertible
Counterfeit
Counsel, Counselled
Collaborate
Conqueror
Changeable
Chauffeur
Concede
Commendable
Connoisseur
Collectible
Courageous
Contractible
Concurred, Concurrence, Concurrent
Colonel
Committee

D

Discernible
Dispelling
Dissimilar
Dysentery
Deficient
Defendant
Deterred, Deterrence, Deterrent
Dependable, Dependance, Dependent
Despicable
Desperate
Descendant
Dissipate, Dissipation
Distil
Dictionary
Diffidence, Diffident
Drunkenness
Dispensable
Dungeon (Subterranean cell to keep Prisoners)
Demagogue (Political Agitator)
Deference, Deferment
Deceit, Deceitful, Deceive, Deceiver, Deceiving
Difference, Different
Digestible
Discernible
Dishevelled (Unkempt, Untidy)
Dismissible

Enmity
Etiquette
Expungeable
Erosion
Extravagance
Ecclesiastic

Embarrass
Exceed
Equilibrium
Exchangeable
Exhaustible
Enforceable
Erroneous
Elementary
Exaggerate
Echoes
Eligible
Existence, Existent
Efficient
Exhilarate, Exhilarating
Excusable
Ecstasy
Eighth

Fulfil
Fahrenheit
Fascinate
Fierce
Feign (Pretend)
Freight
Forcible

Glamour
Grammar
Goddess
Grotesque
Guarantee
Gaiety, Gaily
Gauge
Grief, Grieve, Grievous
Glamorous
Gorgeous

Hierarchy
Harass, Harassment
Hypocrisy
Hygiene
Heinous
Haemorrage

Inoculate
Inadmissible
Inference
Impeccable
Illiterate
Immaculate
Inventor
Incurring
Irrefutable
Innocuous
Install
Impressible
Interchangeable
Imposter/Impostor
Infallible
Incorrigible
Insistence, Insistent
Impregnable
Idiosyncrasy
Irrevocable
Incredible
Intermittence, Intermittent
Innumerable
Irreparable, Irresistible
Incompatible
Irrelevant
Inadvertence, Inadvertent
Inedible

K

Kaleidoscopic

L

Likable (likeable)
Lodgment
Licentious
Livable
Luscious
Lovable
Lascivious
Legible
Licence
Languor
Leisure
Lieutenant

M

Miscellaneous
Munificent
Moustache
Martyr
Movable
Mischievous
Manoeuvre
Millionaire
Mosquitoes
Motto, Mottoes
Mimicked, Mimicking.
Millennium
Maintain, Maintenance
Manageable
Magnificient

Noticeable
Niece
Neigh
Newsstand
Ninth
Negligible

O

Omitted
Ostensible
Obsession, Obsessive
Opulence, Opulent
Omniscience, Omniscient
Oscillate, Oscillation, Oscillating
Occur, Occurred, Occurrence, Occurring
Obeisance
Offence

Pronunciation
Perishable
Permissible
Possible
Peaceable
Provable
Panicked, Panicking, Panicky
Profession
Perceivable, Perceive
Privilege
Potatoes
Professor
Prefer, Preference, Preferred
Perseverance, Persistence, Persistent
Prohibited
Procedure
Portable
Precede, Preceding, Predecessor
Producible
Playwright
Possess, Possession
Plebeian
Proficient
Parallel
Phenomena
Pursue, Pursuit
Patrolling
Pretence
Proceed

R

Renaissance
Reversible
Recede
Repellent
Resuscitate
Regretted, Regretting
Relevance, Relevant
Relief, Relieve
Repentance, Repentant
Replaceable
Refer, Reference
Referred
Receipt, Receive, Receiver
Reparable
Reconnaissance

Sponsor
Secretary
Sufficient
Splendour
Spontaneity
Succumb
Shield
Sergeant
Stationary
Skill, Skilful
Satellite
Siege (beleaguer)
Salable
Severity
Secede
Souvenir
Seismic
Serviceable
Suppress, Suppressible
Stationery
Supersede
Shriek
Sustenance
Stubborn, Stubborness
Sovereign, Sovereignty
Secondary
Seize, Seizure
Succeed
Subsistence
Sizeable
Suddenness
Superintendence, Superintendent
Scintillate, Scintillation, Scintillating
Salvageable
Susceptible
Sacrilege, Sacrilegious
Surfeit
Sleight
Strength

Travelled
Titillate
Tariff
Traffic, Trafficked, Trafficker
Traceable
Tangible
Threshold
Truly
Transmissible
Tranquillity
Trespass, Trespasser
Tyrannical, Tyrannize, Tyranny
Twelfth

Undiscernibly
Utterance
Until
Unmistakable, Unmistakably
Unparalleled
Usable, Using

Vacuous
Vicissitude
Vaccination
Verandha
Vigor, Vigorous
Vacuum
Value, Valuable
Vacillate, Vacillation, Vace, Vicious

W

Wintry
Wield
Weigh, Weight
Woollen, Woolly
Welfare
Weird
Wholly
Welcome

Work Book Exercise

Directions *Four words are given in each question, out of which only one word is correctly spelt. Find the correctly spelt word.*

1.	(a) Dansuese	(b) Danseuse	(c) Danseus	(d) Densuace
2.	(a) Restorent	(b) Restaurent	(c) Restarent	(d) Restaurant
3.	(a) Duration	(b) Dustur	(c) Electrisity	(d) Economicel
4.	(a) Poresistance	(b) Thesaurus	(c) Conspicous	(d) Renaisance
5.	(a) Impetous	(b) Ignoable	(c) Ignominious	(d) Idiosyncresy
6.	(a) Inconsistant	(b) Repentant	(c) Exponant	(d) Excultent
7.	(a) Acoustic	(b) Norcoctic	(c) Pesimist	(d) Permentant
8.	(a) Demagogue	(b) Deliverence	(c) Delinquancy	(d) Delibarative
9.	(a) Harrassment	(b) Embarrasment	(c) Fulfilment	(d) Denoument
10.	(a) Ebulient	(b) Jubilant	(c) Iminent	(d) Tolerent
11.	(a) Agnostik	(b) Accomplice	(c) Advercity	(d) Acrimonous
12.	(a) Malaign	(b) Arraign	(c) Asigne	(d) Degine
13.	(a) Cortege	(b) Damege	(c) Milege	(d) Plumege
14.	(a) Convinience	(b) Initative	(c) Concesional	(d) Exaggerate
15.	(a) Asiduous	(b) Nefarious	(c) Macaber	(d) Loqacious
16.	(a) Malignant	(b) Impertinant	(c) Independant	(d) Neglegent
17.	(a) Qstalt	(b) Imbrolios	(c) Ampasse	(d) Recondite

Revision Exercise

Direction (Q. Nos. 1-16) *Select the correctly spelt word from the following*

1. (a) Persue (b) Persoue (c) Pursue (d) Purseue
2. (a) Oppartunity (b) Oppertunity (c) Opportunity (d) Oppurtunity
3. (a) Achievement (b) Acknoledgement (c) Accreditted (d) Accoustomed
4. (a) Reciept (b) Reeciet (c) Reiceit (d) Receipt
5. (a) Execption (b) Ecseption (c) Ecxeption (d) Exception
6. (a) Turbulance (b) Turbulense (c) Turbulence (d) Terbulence
7. (a) Thresomical (b) Numerasy (c) Nepoteism (d) Tolerate
8. (a) Exacerbate (b) Exacarbate (c) Exacerbat (d) Exacarbat
9. (a) Preferred (b) Prefered (c) Prrefored (d) Prefearred
10. (a) Aggrression (b) Aggrresion (c) Aggression (d) Agrresson
11. (a) Forcsable (b) Foreseeable (c) Fourseeable (d) Foreseable
12. (a) Imunize (b) Immunaize (c) Imunaize (d) Immunize
13. (a) Dementia (b) Quaterain (c) Necrosis (d) Freneteic
14. (a) Glucose (b) Hermetec (c) Wigling (d) Derogaite
15. (a) Bordeux (b) Ambienc (c) Macakues (d) Culinary
16. (a) Metaled (b) Lonsome (c) Piquancy (d) Shufled

Directions (Q.Nos. 17-30) *Select the wrongly spelt word from the following*

17. (a) Extract (b) Eligible (c) Explaination (d) Extension
18. (a) Barrier (b) Barrel (c) Berry (d) Barren
19. (a) Assure (b) Assuredly (c) Assurable (d) Assurence
20. (a) Acheive (b) Receive (c) Contuneim (d) Continueiam
21. (a) Emphasis (b) Emolument (c) Stratagy (d) Strategy
22. (a) Booty (b) Brood (c) Blosom (d) Boast
23. (a) Curry (b) Curious (c) Cursore (d) Curse
24. (a) Satallite (b) Session (c) Satiate (d) Settle
25. (a) Professioinal (b) Preferential (c) Proverbial (d) Presidential
26. (a) Earn (b) Eerie (c) Early (d) Eagel
27. (a) Nerve (b) Neglect (c) Negative (d) Nerveous
28. (a) Board (b) Bliss (c) Behaive (d) Better
29. (a) Celebrity (b) Celebrate (c) Celeberation (d) Celebrant
30. (a) Require (b) Resembel (c) Reproduce (d) Reverse

Exam Practice

Direction (Q. Nos. 1 and 2) *Four words are given in each question, out of which only one word is correctly spelt. Find the correctly spelt word* **SSC CGL (Pre) 2015**

1. (a) Merth (b) Connoisseur (c) Gruesom (d) Appretiate
2. (a) Resurgense (b) Hephazzard (c) Comissioned (d) Fortuitous

Direction (Q. Nos. 3 and 4) *In the following question, four words are given in each question, out of which only one word is correctly spelt. Find the correctly spelt word* **SSC CGL 2015**

3. (a) Aquarim (b) Aquarium (c) Acquerium (d) Acquariam
4. (a) Facsimile (b) Fasimile (c) Fasimmile (d) Facsimilee

Direction (Q. Nos. 5-12) *In which following questions, four words are given out of which one word is correctly spelt, select the correct spelt word* **SSC CGL 2017**

5. (a) Jukstapose (b) Jaxtapuse (c) Juxtapose (d) Jaxtapose
6. (a) Amusemant (b) Ammusement (c) Ammusemant (d) Amusement
7. (a) Fourtyeth (b) Fourtieth (c) Fortieth (d) Fortyth **SSC CGL 2018**
8. (a) Tuition (b) Tution (c) Tuetion (d) Tuttion **SSC CGL 2018**
9. (a) Previledge (b) Pervailege (c) Privilege (d) Previllage **SSC CGL 2018**
10. (a) Taelant (b) Cleaver (c) Centiment (d) Serenity **SSC CGL 2018**
11. Select the wrongly spelt word **SSC CGL 2020**
    (a) Ostentasion (b) Persuasion (c) Mansion (d) Extension
12. Select the wrongly spelt word **SSC CGL 2020**
    (a) Flashy (b) Practicle (c) Elegant (d) Flexible

Direction (Q. Nos. 13-19) *In this section, a word is spelled in four different ways. You are to identify the one which is correct. Choose the alternative bearing the correct spelling from (a), (b), (c) and (d)* **CDS 2019**

13. (a) Accommodate (b) Acommodate (c) Accomdate (d) Acomodait
14. (a) Recommand (b) Reccommed (c) Recommend (d) Reccomand
15. (a) Argyument (b) Argument (c) Arguement (d) Argyooment
16. (a) Decisive (b) Desisive (c) Descisive (d) Desicive
17. (a) Aggressive (b) Agresive (c) Agressive (d) Aggresive
18. (a) Assassination (b) Asassination (c) Asasination (d) Assasination
19. (a) Embarassment (b) Embbarasment (c) Embrasement (d) Embarrassment

Directions (Q. Nos. 20-29) *In this section a word is spelt in four different ways. Identify the one which is correct. Choose the correct response (a), (b), (c) or (d) and indicate on the Answer Sheet accordingly.* **CDS 2020**

20. (a) Continuum (b) Continuem (c) Contuneim (d) Continueiam
21. (a) Stretegy (b) Stretagy (c) Stratagy (d) Strategy
22. (a) Commisionor (b) Commisioner (c) Commissioner (d) Comissioner
23. (a) Vacum (b) Vacuum (c) Vacuem (d) Vacam

24. (a) Psephology (b) Psefoloagy (c) Sephology (d) Psyphology
25. (a) Neuphrology (b) Nephrology (c) Neprology (d) Neaprology
26. (a) Psudonym (b) Pseudonym (c) Pseudanym (d) Seeudonym
27. (a) Pnumonia (b) Neumonia (c) Pneumonia (d) Numania
28. (a) Resilient (b) Resilint (c) Risilient (d) Realisent
29. (a) Suplementary (b) Supplementary (c) Supplimentary (d) Supplemantory

Directions (Q. Nos 30-34) *In each of the following questions a sentence with four bold words are given. One of these four words may be either wrongly spelt or inappropriate in the context of the sentence. Find out the word which is wrongly spelt or inappropriate, if any. That word will be your answer. If all the words given in bold are correctly spelt and also appropriate in the context of the sentence, then mark all correct as your answer.* **SBI Clerk 2015**

30. According to the **management** the bank is **likely** to **perform** better in the next **quarter**.
(a) Management (b) Likely (c) Perform (d) Quarter
(e) All correct

31. It is **difficult** to **gain access** to the hospital because there is no **permanent** road.
(a) Difficult (b) Gain (c) Access (d) Permanent
(e) All correct

32. One of the **most** important **tasks** of the **morden** government is to run an **efficient** welfare system.
(a) Most (b) Tasks (c) Morden (d) Efficient
(e) All correct

33. **Even experienced** bankers were **surprised** by RDFs decision to cut rates **prior** to the budget.
(a) Even (b) Experienced (c) Surprised (d) Prior
(e) All correct

34. The new **generation** is confident, tech savvy and is not **fearful** of **trying** new **things**.
(a) Generation (b) Fearful (c) Trying (d) Things
(e) All correct

Directions (Q. Nos 35-39) *In each of the following questions, a sentence with four bold words are given. One of these four words may be either wrongly spelt or inappropriate in the context of the sentence. Find out the word which is wrongly spelt or inappropriate, if any. That word will be your answer. If all the words given in bold are correctly spelt and also appropriate in the context of the sentence, then mark 'All correct' as your answer.* **SBI Clerk 2016**

35. All the **competitors** (a)/**completed** (b)/ the **race** (c)/ with just one **excepsion**. (d)/ All correct (e) **SBI Clerk 2015**

36. Poor **posture** (a)/ can **lead** (b)/ to **muscular** (c)/ **problems** (d) in later life. All correct (e)

37. The **pump** (a)/shut **off** (b)/ as a **result** (c)/ of a **mechanikal** (d)/ failure. All correct (e)

38. The **Principal** (a) gave a very **pompous** (b)/**speach** (c)/about the **portals** of learning. (d)/All correct (e)

39. **Copeing** (a)/with her mother's long **illness** (b)/ was a heavy **load** (c)/ to **bear**. (d)/All correct (e)

Directions (Q. Nos. 40-47) *The following questions consist of a sentence. Four of the words of the sentences are marked in **bold**, which may or may not be correctly spelled. Option corresponding to misspelt. It word is your answer. If there is no misspelled word in the sentence then choose (5), i.e., All are correct as your answer.* **IBPS Clerk 2019**

40. **During** the **course** of the day many meeting were **held** but the **agenda** was not shared with us.
(a) During (b) Course (c) Held (d) Agenda
(e) All correct

41. **Meazures** to increase both financial **inclusion** and **investment** in infrastructure will result in **gains** for the country.
(a) Meazures (b) inclusion (c) investment (d) gains
(e) All correct

42. **Education**, for most of us, is a necessary public good central to the task of nation **building** and, like fresh air, is **neceessary** to make our **communities** come alive.
(a) Education (b) building (c) neceessary (d) communities
(e) All are correct

43. The Budget's **provisons** for collecting more in taxes from the **incomes** of the super rich were aimed at **redistributing** wealth to bring about more **equitable** development.
(a) provisons (b) incomes (c) redistributing (d) equitable
(e) All are correct

44. Ideas **rejected** more than two **decades** ago during the **liberalisation** phase are back in **circulation**.
(a) rejected (b) decades (c) liberalisation (d) circulation
(e) All are correct

45. the proposal to **establish** a National Research Foundation, with an **overarching** goal to enable a culture of research to **permeate** through our universities needs to be **applauded** and widely supported.
(a) establish (b) overarching (c) permeate (d) applauded
(e) All are correct

46. **Policymaking** has three **essenteal** ingredients : technical elements, **administrative** inputs and political goals and **packaging**.
(a) Policymaking (b) essenteal (c) administrative (d) packaging
(e) All are correct

47. The Central **Bureou** of Investigation has set-up an Online Child Sexual **Abuse** and **Exploitation** Prevention **Investigation** Unit.
(a) Bureou (b) Abuse (c) Exploitation (d) Investigation
(e) All are correct

Answers

Work Book Exercise

1. (b)	**2.** (d)	**3.** (a)	**4.** (b)	**5.** (c)	**6.** (b)	**7.** (a)
8. (a)	**9.** (c)	**10.** (b)	**11.** (b)	**12.** (b)	**13.** (a)	**14.** (d)
15. (b)	**16.** (a)	**17.** (d)				

Revision Exercise

1. (c)	**2.** (c)	**3.** (a)	**4.** (d)	**5.** (d)	**6.** (c)	**7.** (d)
8. (a)	**9.** (a)	**10.** (c)	**11.** (b)	**12.** (d)	**13.** (a)	**14.** (a)
15. (d)	**16.** (c)	**17.** (c)	**18.** (b)	**19.** (d)	**20.** (a)	**21.** (d)
22. (c)	**23.** (c)	**24.** (a)	**25.** (a)	**26.** (d)	**27.** (d)	**28.** (c)
29. (c)	**30.** (b)					

Exam Practice

1. (b)	**2.** (d)	**3.** (b)	**4.** (a)	**5.** (c)	**6.** (d)	**7.** (c)
8. (a)	**9.** (c)	**10.** (d)	**11.** (a)	**12.** (b)	**13.** (a)	**14.** (c)
15. (b)	**16.** (a)	**17.** (a)	**18.** (a)	**19.** (d)	**20.** (a)	**21.** (d)
22. (c)	**23.** (b)	**24.** (a)	**25.** (b)	**26.** (b)	**27.** (c)	**28.** (a)
29. (b)	**30.** (e)	**31.** (e)	**32.** (c)	**33.** (e)	**34.** (e)	**35.** (d)
36. (e)	**37.** (d)	**38.** (c)	**39.** (a)	**40.** (e)	**41.** (a)	**42.** (c)
43. (a)	**44.** (c)	**45.** (e)	**46.** (b)	**47.** (a)		

6

Contractions

What is a Contraction?

Contraction is the short form of a word. It is formed by combining two words into one.

Forms of Contractions

The two words are usually contracted as follows

(i) Subject + auxiliary verb

(ii) Auxiliary verb + not

1. **Subject** (Noun and Pronoun) **and Auxiliary verb**

   Auxiliary Verbs are

   (a) To be – is, am, are, was, were

   (b) To do – do, did

   (c) To have –have, had

   (d) Modal auxiliaries

   Will, shall, can, could, may, might, should, must

   The contraction of subject + Auxiliary is made by dropping the beginning of the auxiliary verb. The dropped letter is shown by an apostraphe.

I am	I'm
I have	I've
I will/shall	I'll
Moni has	Moni's
Moni is	Moni's

2. **Auxiliary verb + not**

   This type of contraction is formed by dropping 'O' the dropped letter is shown by an apostrophe.

are not	aren't
was not	wasn't
am not	arent't

NOTE Since 'amn't' is wrong, use 'aren't for 'am not'.

NOTE In negative verb phrases with "be, have, will, shall, would and should." contractions may be used in two forms.
She's not or she isn't
He'll not or he won't

3. The common contractions are as follows

Singular Pronoun + Auxiliary verb

I am	I'm
I have	I've
I will/shall	I'll
I would, should, had	I'd
You are	You're
You have	You've
You will	You'll
You would, you had	You'd
She, He is/has	She's /He's
She, He will	She'll/He'll
It is, has	It's
It will	It'll

Plural Pronoun + Auxiliary verb

We are	We're
We have	We've
We will	We'll
We would, should, had	We'd
They are	They're
They have	They've
They will	They'll
They would/should, had	They'd

4. Noun + Auxiliary verbs

(i) Mohan is	Mohan's
(ii) Mohan has	Mohan's

The following contractions are not used with **nouns**

Kim should, would, had	Kim'd
Kim will	Kim'll

5. Auxiliary verbs + Not

am + not (amn't is not used as contraction form)

Is not	Isn't
Are not	aren't
Was not	Wasn't
Were not	Weren't
Do not	Don't
Does not	Doesn't
Did not	Didn't
Have not	Haven't
Has not	Hasn't
Had not	Hadn't
Will not	won't
Shall not	shan't
Might not	Mightn't
Must not	musn't
Ought not	oughtn't
Need not	needn't
Would not	Wouldn't
Should not	Shouldn't
Cannot	Can't
Could not	Couldn't

6. Some of the common contractions

Here is	Here's
There is	There's
That is	That's
That will	That'll
How is	How's
What is	What's
Who is	Who's
What will	What'll
Who will	Who 'll
Who would	Who'd

Work Book Exercise

Direction Fill in the blanks by choosing the correct option

1. Clouds .... blue. They are white.
(a) amn't (b) hasn't
(c) aren't (d) wasn't

2. Amir and Shweta ....wear masks.
(a) doesn't (b) don't
(c) isn't (d) hasn't

3. .... done many practice exercises today.
(a) I'd (b) I'm
(c) I'll (d) I've

4. .... meet us today at around 2 pm.
(a) They'l (b) They'll
(c) They'd (d) They'ld

5. Her name is Palak. .... 10 years old.
(a) He's (b) She'd
(c) She's (d) He'd

6. .... go to the railway station today.
(a) Tarun'd (b) Tarun will
(c) Tarun'll (d) Tarun've

7. You have been my best friend for years. .... you?
(a) Have'd (b) Haven't
(c) Hasn't (d) Hadn't

8. Amit and Kovid are thankful for your invitation. .... love to come to your party.
(a) They'll (b) They've
(c) They'd (d) Theyd'nt

9. .... going to the concert tonight as our father is unwell.
(a) We're (b) We'll
(c) We'd (d) We aren't

10. Yikes! .... a cockroach in my bed.
(a) There're (b) There'd
(c) There'll (d) There's

Answers

1. (c) **2.** (b) **3.** (d) **4.** (b) **5.** (c) **6.** (b) **7.** (b)
8. (c) **9.** (d) **10.** (d)